WITHDRAWN

MAHLER

MAHLER

A DOCUMENTARY STUDY

compiled and edited by

Kurt Blaukopf

with contributions by

Zoltan Roman

362 illustrations, 37 in colour

NEW YORK AND TORONTO
OXFORD UNIVERSITY PRESS · 1976

Translated from the German by PAUL BAKER, SUSANNE
FLATAUER, P. R. J. FORD, DAISY LOMAN and GEOFFREY
WATKINS

First published in German under the title *Mahler: Sein Leben,
sein Werk und seine Welt in zeitgenössischen Bildern und Texten*

Library of Congress Catalog Card No. 76-9218

Text filmset in Great Britain by Tradespools Ltd, Frome,
Somerset
Printed and bound in Italy by Amilcare Pizzi Spa, Milan

Contents

Preface

Years of research have brought to light an extraordinary wealth of material which makes possible a representation of Mahler's life and work from contemporary documents. Only a few years ago I was able to do no more than express the hope, in a biographical study (*Gustav Mahler*, Vienna 1969, London and New York 1973), that the documents necessary for an insight into Mahler's life might one day be made public.

The present volume contains contemporary pictures and written documents which illustrate various aspects of Mahler's world and reflect the diversity of his work. Mahler's relatively short life – he died in his fifty-first year – was rich in varied, although closely related, activities. The documentation must do justice to this abundance. It has to throw light on the nascent artist who, almost from the beginning, was not only an interpreter but also a creator; on the composer and his development; on the conductor of his own and others' works; on the innovator in matters of performance; on the adapter of other composers' works; on the theatre conductor who was also frequently the unacknowledged producer of his presentations and gave a new scenic impetus to opera under the impress of new tendencies in art; and finally on the opera director who had to deal with administrative problems. Needless to say, his private life must also be adequately documented: his parents' home; his education; the ideas current in his circle of friends; his wife and children; all the elements which made up Mahler's view of the world and of human existence.

A number of pictures and numerous texts are here published for the first time. This applies, for example, to extracts from letters which Mahler addressed to Anna von Mildenburg, and which are included by the kind consent of Frau Anna Mahler and Herr Heinrich Bauer. Many texts relevant to his biography and to the history of his work have had to be left out. This is inevitable in view of the quantity of Mahler's published and unpublished letters and the inexhaustible profusion of reports, interviews and reviews which appeared in the music periodicals and newspapers of Europe and the United States. The selection of documents assembled here, supplemented by brief notes, should help to clarify the picture of Mahler's activity by illustrating the response to it.

Since the 1960s world-wide interest in Gustav Mahler has been growing. This Mahler renaissance has been accompanied by numerous publications, including biographical essays; the vast majority of these are based on information which had long been available, and on published documents, and do not incorporate the material, in public collections and in private archives, which still awaits sorting and evaluation.

Knowledge of Mahler's life, and of the history of his works, has remained fragmentary, in spite of the increased interest in his music. Distinguished musicologists such as Ludwig Schiedermair (1901) and Guido Adler (1914) had at an early stage produced short monographs, the product of direct experience and personal knowledge rather than of systematic study of the sources. Nor did the apologias and analyses of Mahler's work by Paul Stefan and Richard Specht remedy this shortcoming. An early high-point of interest in Mahler's works was marked by the Amsterdam Mahler Festival in 1920. In the same year appeared Paul Bekker's invaluable book *Gustav*

Mahlers Sinfonien. Not until 1924 did Alma Mahler publish her edition of Mahler's letters – a selection which, despite its merits, gives an incomplete picture; for it contains, to give just one of many examples, none of the letters Mahler wrote to Richard Strauss.

The concert programmes of the 1930s indicate a falling-off of interest in Mahler's music. Although short Mahler monographs appeared in the United States (Gabriel Engel, 1932) and in the Soviet Union (Ivan Sollertinsky, 1932), in Germany the works of the 'Jewish' composer Mahler began to be eliminated from musical life under Nazi pressure. It was still possible for Bruno Walter to publish his book on Mahler in Austria in 1936; but Alma Mahler wrote the foreword to her reminiscences of Mahler, to which she added a further selection of Mahler letters, at Sanary on the Mediterranean coast of France after fleeing from Austria when it was annexed by Germany. The book finally appeared in German in Amsterdam (1940). In Greater Germany itself, all memory of Mahler was suppressed.

The end of the Second World War (1945) did not lead to Mahler's immediate reinstatement to his previous position. The modest beginnings of Mahler research had been interrupted; there was a lack of those studies of detail, research projects and dissertations that supply the essential groundwork for a reliable and complete portrayal of the life and work of a composer.

Such studies faced a specific obstacle: the fact that Mahler's life can be understood only through a sufficient knowledge of the political, social and cultural character of his surroundings. The Habsburg multi-national State and its peculiar cultural conditions set a decisive stamp on Mahler's life and work. Yet that State ceased to exist in 1918, and since then its life and culture have become increasingly remote. To give an outline of Mahler's spiritual physiognomy presupposes a reconstruction of this historical background; the documentation must include pictures and texts which make that vanished world recognizable.

This has been attempted here. Factual material has been given precedence over rhetorical pronouncements, whether for or against the *status quo*, which in themselves could fill many a volume. Reliable evidence, even where it serves only indirectly to assess the course of Mahler's life, has been preferred to conjecture. Such a treatment required the evaluation of evidence on politics, cultural history and musical performance. Hence arose the need to consult many archives and experts in Austria, Hungary, Czechoslovakia, the Federal Republic of Germany, the German Democratic Republic, the USA, France, the Netherlands and other countries.

A particular problem was posed by the study of Mahler's activity in Budapest and in the United States. His stay in Budapest (1888–91) could not have been adequately documented without careful study of numerous texts in Hungarian; and his work in New York has not, as this study goes to press, been the subject of any basic scholarly research. It is therefore fortunate that Dr Zoltan Roman, Associate Professor of Music at the University of Calgary, has been willing to contribute to the project his wealth of knowledge of Hungarian musical history, and the results of his own work as a Mahler scholar ('Mahler's Songs and their Influence on his Symphonic Thought', dissertation, Toronto 1970). The majority of the illustrations and textual documents which refer to Mahler's time in Budapest and New York have been collected and selected by him; and the editorial plan of these two sections of the book is his.

A problem of standardization is posed by the lack of concern, formerly common, over the spelling of proper names. For example, Gustav Mahler's father's first name is sometimes spelt Bernhard, then again Bernard; and Gustav Mahler himself persistently spelt the surname of the American Mary Sheldon as Scheldon. Errors of this kind have been corrected throughout, so as to make clear the identity of the person concerned. The titles of literary and musical works, normally quoted in the documents in German, have been given in the original language except for a few works better known to English-speaking readers by English titles.

This documentary study could never have been produced without much kind assistance, support, and sometimes sacrifice, on the part of many institutions and individuals. Particular mention is due to Frau Eleonore Vondenhoff, whose Gustav Mahler collection has enriched the material in this volume, and to a Mahler scholar who has recently died, Arnošt Mahler of Prague. They, and all the other people and institutions to whom we are indebted, are named on the following pages.

Publisher's note
There has been some difficulty, in the preparation of the English-language edition, over certain specialist terms of theatrical and musical life which have no convenient English equivalents. To avoid confusion the following admittedly inadequate system has been adopted: for (*General-*) *Intendant*, the head of the whole organization, 'General Manager'; for *Direktor*, 'Director'; for *Kapellmeister*, 'Conductor'; for *Musikdirektor*, 'Assistant Conductor'; for *Chordirektor*, 'Chorus Master'; for *Regisseur*, Stage Manager (an archaic usage; now called a producer or director).

The extracts from the source referred to as AM (see list on p. 13) have been translated from the German edition; there is, however, an existing English version of most of this material, published by John Murray (Publishers) Ltd: Alma Mahler, *Gustav Mahler, Memories and Letters*, enlarged edition, revised and edited and with an Introduction by Donald Mitchell, translated by Basil Creighton, London 1968.

Sources of Documents and Illustrations

Leningrad
Leningrad Philharmonic Orchestra
Mr Yulyan Y. Vaynkop

Moscow
Mrs Inna Barsova
Professor David Rabinovich

SWEDEN

Stockholm
Drottningholms Teatermuseum
Kungl. Musikaliska Akademiens
  Bibliothek
Musikhistoriska Museet
Stiftelsen Musikkulturens främjande

SWITZERLAND

Alchenflüh
Herr Samuel Schweizer

Basle
Universitätsbibliothek

Zürich
Professor Willi Reich

UNITED STATES OF AMERICA

Athens, Ga.
University of Georgia Libraries

Boston, Mass.
Boston Public Library

Bryn Mawr, Pa.
Theodore Presser Company

New Haven, Conn.
Osborn Collection, Yale University
  Library

New York, N.Y.
Dr Nicholas P. Christy
Library and Museum of the
  Performing Arts
Metropolitan Opera Archives
The New-York Historical Society

The New York Public Library
The Pierpont Morgan Library
Mrs Ula Pommer

Poughkeepsie, N.Y.
Professor Edward R. Reilly

Sherman, Conn.
Mr Eric Simon

Syracuse, N.Y.
Professor Frederick Marvin
Syracuse Public Library

Utica, N.Y.
Utica Public Library

YUGOSLAVIA

Ljubljana
Professor Dr Dragotin Cvetko
Mrs Alena Keršovan
Slovenska Akademija Znanosti in
  Umenosti.

A Note on the Illustrations

The editors have set out to present Gustav Mahler's life and work not only in contemporary written documents, but also in pictures; to show the towns and cities in which he lived, the means of transport by which he travelled, the houses in which he lived and composed, the theatres and concert halls in which he conducted, the people with whom he associated, the paper on which he set down his music. These pictures – covering, as Mahler's life did, a period of fifty years – demonstrate forcefully the changes that affected his surroundings, his art and his tastes.

7 Mahler grew up at Iglau (now Jihlava), in Moravia, still essentially a medieval town. He was already at secondary school when the railway reached Iglau. His studies at the Conservatoire transferred him from this small-town idyll to 26, 27 the Imperial capital city of Vienna, at the time when the Ringstrasse, with its massive and eclectically backward-looking architecture, was under construction. With elements of the classical and Gothic styles, with pastiches of Renaissance and Baroque, the upper bourgeoisie was creating a suitably impressive back-drop for its newly won social and political status. Even the painters of the period, the most celebrated of whom was Hans Makart, revelled in historical costumes and attitudes: and poetry, likewise backward-looking, echoed folksong.

We do not know in what ways this great, expanding and changing city affected the young Gustav Mahler. It may be that he paid no conscious attention to the architecture, painting and decorative art of the Ringstrasse era. His entire perceptive faculty was oriented towards music and literature, above all towards the still-controversial work of Richard Wagner, which he certainly first saw performed in sets designed in the style of Makart. We do know, however, that the literary tastes of his youth were partly formed by the fashionable inclination towards folk-song, fairy-tale and legend, as attested by his own verses and his choice of texts to set to music.

In Mahler's early adulthood the young artists – architects, painters, craftsmen and writers – began to rebel against this established art. They created a new art which corresponded to the various tendencies known elsewhere as Symbolism, Art Nouveau and Jugendstil, and which in Vienna was known as 211 the 'Secession'. It may be that Mahler would have paid no attention to this movement if he had not married into the very heart of the Vienna Secession, the Klimt group, through his union with Alma Maria Schindler. In Gustav Klimt himself, in Koloman Moser, Alfred Roller and Carl Moll, he gained friends and instructors who taught him to see and understand. The art of the Secession encompassed the whole environment, houses, furniture, clothes; it even gave a new appearance to the printed editions of Mahler's work. In Alfred Roller, Mahler found in addition a future stage designer, who was to create, with light and colour, a new style at the Vienna Court Opera. With his aid Mahler was able to realize his reforms in music drama and to liberate Wagner's work from its traditional décor and the example of Bayreuth. Even his literary taste changed, although he was seldom receptive to the latest developments (the romantic Orientalist Rückert was more to his taste than the modernist Dehmel). It is at least noteworthy that, from the time of his close association with the Secessionists, Mahler never again set a folk-song text to music.

The skyscrapers of Manhattan were the setting of Mahler's last years. However strange the skyline of New York may have seemed to a man who had grown up at Iglau and matured in Vienna, now that he had learned to see his eyes were open to the attractions of Broadway, Fifth Avenue and Brooklyn 278 Bridge.

Among the illustrations in this book, portraits of Mahler naturally occupy a prominent place. These in their turn reflect the changes that took place in his world. Daguerre had taken the first photographic portraits, daguerreotypes, in 1839. Technical advances followed, and by the middle of the century the first portrait studios were being established – primarily in big cities, but soon, too, in smaller towns. The décor of these studios, and the style of the photographs, corresponded to the taste of the time: people in their Sunday best in the luxurious surroundings of the studio. We see Mahler's mother in a 16 crinoline, her right hand leaning on the studio's little rococo table over which is draped a heavy cloth. His father faced the 15 camera in a similar pose, top hat in hand; and little Gustav, 17 for whom the table was clearly too high to serve as a support, was given a curvilinear chair on which his left hand rests while his right hand holds his little round hat.

The later photographs from Mahler's childhood and youth 36, 40 manage without props, yet remain within the limits of convention. This decreed that for an oblique view, the foreshortened side of the face had to lie in shadow yet was to be illuminated by reflective screens to such an extent that the features remained clearly visible. Yet it is not this stereotyped, stiff attitude, nor the various styles of beard and moustache which cover part of his face, that makes all portrait photographs of Mahler up to the 1890s appear uncharacteristic as compared with the later portraits. Most of the early photographs look as if they have been adapted in the manner of the time, that is by heavy retouching of the negative, to suit the individual photographer's ideal of beauty.

How radically the concept of the function of portrait photography changed within a few years is shown by the series of pictures, taken in 1907 in the rehearsal room of the Vienna 241–48 Opera House, which most vividly record the expressions, stances and gestures of the mature Mahler.

With the invention of the celluloid film in 1887, and the development and spread of the lighter and more manageable roll-film camera, photography, hitherto the domain of professionals and a very few amateurs, became accessible to wide circles. It is to the new technology that we owe the snapshots of Mahler in his circle of friends, on his summer holidays and with his children. The many technical deficiencies of such 237, 256 pictures are far outweighed by the documentary value of, for example, the photos of Mahler in the company of Max 232–35 Reinhardt, Josef Hoffmann, Gustav Klimt, Hans Pfitzner and Carl Moll, or indeed the pleasant holiday snapshots from 236 Maiernigg and Toblach.

In 1922, at the suggestion of Alma Mahler, Mahler's friend and collaborator Alfred Roller published a little book under the title *Die Bildnisse von Gustav Mahler* which reproduces eighty photographs and a series of portraits by artists. The dates and commentaries which Roller provided for these photographs form the basis of every iconography of Mahler. It has not been possible to trace the originals of all the photographs reproduced by Roller; many of them seem to have been lost. On the other hand many photographs have been preserved, in public and private collections, which do not appear in Roller's book. In dating these today, when so few witnesses of the Mahler era are still alive, it is often possible to give only an approximation.

As for portraits by artists, Roller's selection reproduces only Rodin's sculptures, the well-known illustrations by Fritz Erler, the etching by Emil Orlik (in profile) and the death mask by Carl Moll. This book contains in addition the portrait painted in 1907 by Akseli Gallen, further illustrations by Orlik, and a sketch by Kolo Moser. Portraits which can safely be assumed to have been painted, not from life but from photos or other sources, have not been included. One picture, showing Mahler taking a walk not far from Göding, is available only in photographic reproduction, and the original has not been traced. It has been included in this book for the sake of some characteristic traits which cannot otherwise be documented. An important additional source, excluded by Roller, lies in the contemporary caricatures of Mahler. Here particular mention must be made of the studies in movement by Schliessmann, which portray Mahler as conductor and in their way give a cinematic effect.

In the introduction to his book, Roller makes a wise remark, *à propos* of Mahler's appearance, which testifies to the artist's keen gift of observation: 'That gaunt face was a true mirror of its owner's every inner emotion, for which reason it is diversely portrayed by many people, according to the diversity of their relationship with Mahler.' If one compares the various reminiscences and memoirs which contain descriptions of Mahler's outward appearance, it is sometimes hard to believe that the person described is really one and the same. Many of his contemporaries considered him ugly, others handsome; some considered him daemonic, even satanic, others human and kind; some haughty, withdrawn, unapproachable, others accessible and likeable; some highly strung and jumpy, others calm and remote; many thought him amusing and many merely comic. Probably all these varied impressions are accurate. The later pictures make them all appear comprehensible. For whereas, in the case of many important artists whose works we know, we do not know what they looked like, in Mahler's case this is not so. Portraits, caricatures and photographs not only show how their creators saw and interpreted Mahler, but provide in their totality an eloquent picture of his outward appearance as it was formed by his inner life.

12

Abbreviations

AM	Alma Mahler, *Gustav Mahler, Erinnerungen und Briefe*, Vienna 1949.
ANBR	'Sonderheft Gustav Mahler', *Musikblätter des Anbruch*, vol. II. no. 7/8, 1920.
ARB	Alfred Roller, *Die Bildnisse von Gustav Mahler*, Leipzig and Vienna 1922.
BST	Bayerische Staatsbibliothek, Munich.
BWTV	Bruno Walter, *Thema und Variationen*, Frankfurt 1960.
CAS	Intendantur des Königlichen Theaters zu Cassel, Personal file on Gustav Mahler.
EV	Gustav Mahler-Sammlung Eleonore Vondenhoff, Frankfurt am Main.
JBFPP	Joseph Bohuslav Foerster, 'Gustav Mahler in Hamburg', *Prager Presse*, April–July 1922.
GA	Guido Adler, *Gustav Mahler*, Vienna 1916. (First publication in book form of a work which first appeared in 1914.)
GDM	Gesellschaft der Musikfreunde, Archiv, Vienna.
GMB	*Gustav Mahler Briefe. 1879–1911*, ed. Alma Maria Mahler, Vienna 1924.
HAM	Staats- und Universitätsbibliothek Hamburg, Literatur-Archiv.
HH1	Hans Holländer, 'Unbekannte Jugendbriefe Gustav Mahlers', *Die Musik*, vol. 20, no. 11, August 1928.
HH2	Hans Holländer, 'Gustav Mahler vollendete eine Oper von Carl Maria von Weber'; 'Vier unbekannte Briefe Mahlers', *Neue Zeitschrift für Musik*, vol. CXVI, December 1955.
HHSTA	Haus-, Hof- und Staatsarchiv Wien, Akten der General-Intendanz der Hoftheater, Akten der Hofoper.
HLG	Henry-Louis de la Grange, *Mahler*, vol. I, New York 1973 and London 1974.
LFZ	Liszt Ferenc Zeneakadémia, Budapest.
LKB	Ludwig Karpath, *Begegnung mit dem Genius*, 2nd edn, Vienna 1934.
LMPA	Library and Museum of the Performing Arts, New York, Music Research Library.
MVJ	Muzeum Vysočiny, Jihlava, Iglaviensia.
NBL	Natalie Bauer-Lechner, *Erinnerungen an Gustav Mahler*, Vienna 1923.
OAJ-F	Okresní archiv Jihlava, Drobné pozůstalosti, Fischer.
OAJ-G	Okresní archiv Jihlava, Latinské a německé gymnasium.
OAJ-PR	Okresní archiv Jihlava, Městská správa Jihlava od r. 1849, Politická registratura 1850–65.
ÖNB-BA	Österreichische Nationalbibliothek, Vienna, Bildarchiv.
ÖNB-HS	Österreichische Nationalbibliothek, Vienna, Handschriftensammlung.
ÖNB-MS	Österreichische Nationalbibliothek, Vienna, Musiksammlung.
ÖNB-TS	Österreichische Nationalbibliothek, Vienna, Theatersammlung.
ÖUM	*Die österreichisch-ungarische Monarchie in Wort und Bild*, Vienna 1886–1902.
PST1	Paul Stefan, *Gustav Mahler. Eine Studie über Persönlichkeit und Werk*, 2nd edn, Munich 1912.
PST2	*Gustav Mahler. Ein Bild seiner Persönlichkeit in Widmungen*, ed. Paul Stefan, Munich 1910.
RSP1	Richard Specht, *Gustav Mahler*, Berlin (1905).
RSP2	Richard Specht, *Gustav Mahler*, Berlin and Leipzig 1913.
WSTB	Wiener Stadtbibliothek, Handschriftensammlung.

The Plates

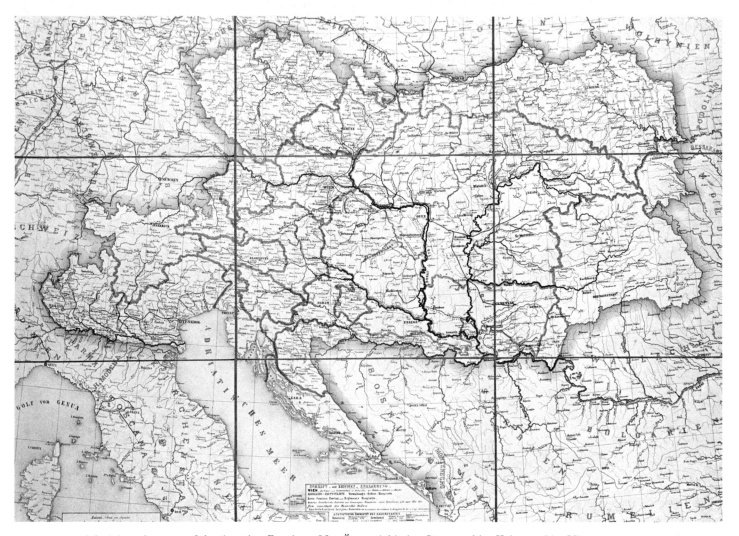

1. Administrative map of the Austrian Empire, 1860. Österreichisches Staatsarchiv, Kriegsarchiv, Vienna.
Mahler's birthplace lay in the Kingdom of Bohemia, which was part of the Austrian Empire. Even in 1860, the year of Mahler's birth, when this map was first published, it was in need of revision, for in the preceding autumn Austria had lost Lombardy, the territory surrounding Milan. By 1866, the Empire also had to cede the greater part of Veneto to the Kingdom of Italy.

2. Austrian military band. Colour print, Verlag Trentsensky, Vienna.
This contemporary print shows in diagram form the line-up of an Austrian regimental band. From his early childhood days Mahler came to know the trumpet calls and military music which still echo in his works.

Druck v. E. Sieger   Verlag v. M. Trentsensky, Wien.   14.

Aufstellung einer k. k. oestr. Armee-Division
Musikbande

1	2	3					4		5			6				
	Datum und Zahl des laufenden zur Beschneidungsvornahme oder den Mädchen zur Namensbeilegung ausgestellten Meldzettels	Der Geburt					Todtgeborene Kinder		Die Beschneidung oder Namensbeilegung			Des Kindes				
													Geschlecht		eheliche oder uneheliche Geburt	
Fortlaufende Zahl		Tag	Monat	Jahr	Haus-Nro	Ort	Stadt, Herrschaft, Gut	Kreis	männlich	weiblich	Tag	Monat	Jahr	Ort und Haus-Nro	mit genauer Angabe der Geburtstelle	männlich	weiblich	ehelich	unehelich
16	Vorlag nach franc. Phillipps vom 23t. Juli 1860 N. 27.	7	Juli	1860	9	Kallischt Pfarrbezirk zu Heinzendorf Eywanau					14	Juli	1860	Kallischt N. 9		Knabe	1	ehelich	

3. The house in Kalischt (Kališt) in Bohemia, where Mahler was born. Photograph. Archiv der Wiener Philharmoniker, Vienna.

4, 6. Entry in the register of births of the Jewish Community in Unter-Kralowitz (Dolní Kralovice), 1860, III, 44. Narodní vybor (National Committee), Prague.

The entry records that on 7 July 1860, at house no. 9, Kalischt, Administrative District of Humpoletz, a son by the name of Gustav was born in lawful wedlock to Bernard (Bernhard) Mahler, merchant of Kalischt, and Maria (Marie), daughter of Abraham Hermann and Theresie, née Hermann, of Ledetsch (Ledeč).

5. Imperial manifesto. *Wiener Zeitung*, 21 October 1860.

This proclamation ushered in the decline of absolute power in the countries ruled by Emperor Franz Joseph. As a result Jews were granted the right of domicile in places which previously had either been closed to them altogether or permitted only a limited number of Jewish settlers.

Wiener Zeitung.

№ 249. Sonntag den 21. Oktober 1860.

Kaiserliches Manifest.

An Meine Völker!

Als Ich den Thron Meiner Ahnen bestieg, war die Monarchie gewaltsamen Erschütterungen preisgegeben.

Nach einem Meinen landesväterlichen Gefühlen tief schmerzlichen Kampfe trat in Meinen Ländern, wie fast überall in den gewaltsam erschütterten Gebieten des Europäischen Festlandes, vor Allem das Bedürfniß einer strengeren Konzentrirung der Regierungsgewalt ein. Das öffentliche Wohl und die Sicherheit der Mehrzahl der ruhigen Bewohner der Monarchie erheischten dieselbe, — die aufgeregten Leidenschaften und die schmerzlichen Erinnerungen der jüngsten Vergangenheit machten eine freie Bewegung der noch vor Kurzem feindlich kämpfenden Elemente unmöglich.

Ich habe von den Wünschen und Bedürfnissen der verschiedenen Länder der Monarchie Kenntniß nehmen wollen und demzufolge mittelst Meines Patentes vom 5. März l. J. Meinen verstärkten Reichsrath gegründet und einberufen.

In Erwägung der Mir von demselben überreichten Vorlagen habe Ich Mich bewogen gefunden, in Betreff der staatsrechtlichen Gestaltung der Monarchie, der Rechte und der Stellung der einzelnen Königreiche und Länder ebensowohl, wie der erneuten Sicherung, Feststellung und Vertretung des staatsrechtlichen Verbandes der Gesammt-Monarchie am heutigen Tage ein Diplom zu erlassen und zu verkünden.

Ich erfülle Meine Regentenpflicht, indem Ich in dieser Weise die Erinnerungen, Rechtsanschauungen und Rechtsansprüche Meiner Länder und Völker mit den thatsächlichen Bedürfnissen Meiner Monarchie ausgleichend verbinde und die gedeibliche Entwicklung und Kräftigung der von Mir gegebenen oder wieder erweckten Institutionen mit voller Beruhigung der gereiften Einsicht und dem patriotischen Eifer Meiner Völker anvertraue. Ich erhoffe ihr segensreiches Erblühen von dem Schutze und der Gnade des Allmächtigen, in dessen Hand die Geschicke der Fürsten und Völker ruhen, und der dem tiefen und gewissenhaften Ernste Meiner landesväterlichen Sorgfalt seinen Segen nicht versagen wird.

Wien, am 20. Oktober 1860.

Franz Joseph m. p.

7	8	9	10	11	12	13
Namen des Vaters mit Angabe des Standes …	Name der Mutter mit Angabe des Standes, Wohnhaus-Nro und Namen ihrer Eltern, besonders bei ledigen Personen, deren Schupdominium genau anzugeben ist, wenn sie nicht hierher gehören	Eigenhändige Fertigung mit Angabe des Wohnortes, Haus-Nr., Schupdominium und Kreises — der Pathen oder Zeugen des Sandels oder Schames	des oder mehrerer Beschneider mit Wohnungsangabe	der Hebamme oder Geburtshelfers	Das Kind sammt seinen Eltern … ist fremd, und gehört nach	Anmerkung

7.   Iglau (Jihlava). Original engraving after a photograph. Friedrich Umlauft, *Die österreichisch-ungarische
Monarchie*, Vienna 1883, 825.
Soon after Mahler's birth the family moved to the
nearest sizeable town, Iglau in Moravia.

8.   The Heulos valley near Iglau. Book illustration by
Hugo Charlemont. öUM, *Mähren und Schlesien*, Vienna
1897, 29.
A steep slope behind the Church of St James links the
town with the romantic valley.

9.   The Stadtring in Iglau. Book illustration by Hugo
Charlemont. öUM, *Mähren und Schlesien*, Vienna 1897,
27.
The picture shows the top half of the great main square,
which was called the Stadtring.

10. Iglau, part of the Stadtring with Neptune fountain. Photograph. MVJ.

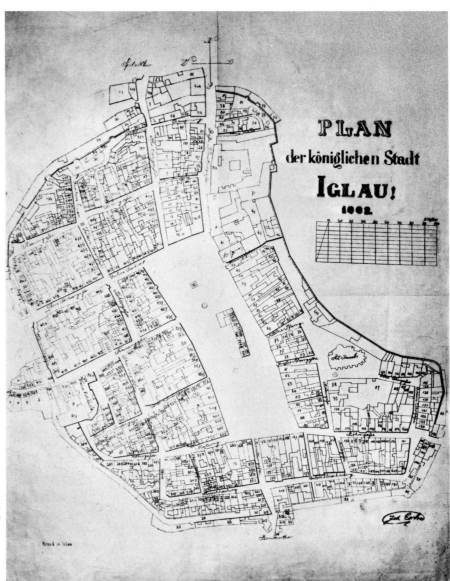

11. Plan of the city of Iglau, 1862. MVJ.
The plan shows the unusually large Stadtring; Pirnitzergasse, the street where the Mahler family lived, leads into its lower end.

12. Pirnitzergasse, Iglau. Photograph. MVJ.
The short lane (now Malinovského) rises towards the Stadtring. On the right of the photograph are the two houses where Gustav Mahler grew up.

14. Staircase at house no. 265 (Pirnitzergasse 4). Photograph. OAJ-F.
The Mahler family lived on the second storey of this house until 1872, when they moved next door.

13. The synagogue at Iglau. Photograph. MVJ.
A Jewish religious community had been founded in Iglau as early as 1861, and the synagogue was consecrated in 1863. In later years Bernhard Mahler's name is mentioned as a committee member of the religious community.

15. Gustav Mahler's father, Bernhard Mahler (1827–89). Photograph. IGMG, Nederlandse Afdeling, Wassenaar, Holland.

16. Gustav Mahler's mother, Marie Mahler, née Hermann (1837–89). Photograph. ÖNB-BA.

17. Gustav Mahler. Photograph, 1865–66. ÖNB-BA.

18.   A meeting of the Mastersingers of Iglau, 1612. Reproduction in ÖUM, *Mähren und Schlesien*, Vienna 1897, 285.
Meistergesang was one of Iglau's musical traditions. In 1571 a singing school was founded. The picture, rich in allegorical allusion, shows a singer on the Singer's Chair in the centre.

19.   A page from the handwritten music register of the Iglau Music Society. MVJ, 874.
The Iglau Music Society existed from 1819 to 1862. Also included in its register of written music are several symphonies: to begin with, three works by Haydn, two by Pleyel, the Haffner Serenade by Mozart (K. 250), and one each of the works of Peter von Winter (1754–1825) and Franz Vinzenz Krommer (1759–1831). Ultimately the Music Society's orchestra consisted of approximately equal numbers of professional musicians and amateurs.

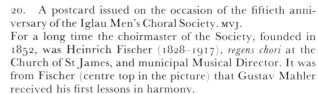

20. A postcard issued on the occasion of the fiftieth anniversary of the Iglau Men's Choral Society. MVJ.
For a long time the choirmaster of the Society, founded in 1852, was Heinrich Fischer (1828–1917), *regens chori* at the Church of St James, and municipal Musical Director. It was from Fischer (centre top in the picture) that Gustav Mahler received his first lessons in harmony.

21. The Hatscho. Painting by Karl Hruby. MVJ.
The Hatscho, a folk dance which originated in Iglau, is in two parts (a solemn three-four, followed by a galop in two-four time) and was played by four fiddles. There are traces of this dance in Mahler's music.

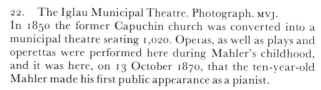

22. The Iglau Municipal Theatre. Photograph. MVJ.
In 1850 the former Capuchin church was converted into a municipal theatre seating 1,020. Operas, as well as plays and operettas were performed here during Mahler's childhood, and it was here, on 13 October 1870, that the ten-year-old Mahler made his first public appearance as a pianist.

23. Gustav Mahler. Photograph, c. 1871. OAJ-F.

24. A postcard showing a locomotive and a view of the railway station of Iglau. MVJ.
In 1870 Iglau became part of the Austrian railway network. In the autumn of 1871 Mahler travelled to Prague, where he attended the Neustadt High School (Neustädter Gymnasium) for a term.

25. The courtyard at no. 264 (Pirnitzergasse 6), in Iglau. Photograph. OAJ-F.
Bernhard Mahler acquired this house in 1872, having until then lived in the house next door with his family. The picture, which comes from Heinrich Fischer's unpublished papers, bears on the reverse the handwritten note: 'First floor and second floor still in the original tenure.'

26, 27.   Openring and Karlsplatz, Vienna. Chromolithographs after Franz Alt. Historisches Museum der Stadt Wien. Mahler went to Vienna in 1875. The Court Opera House, inaugurated in 1869, already stood in the Opernring, while on the Karlsplatz was the new building, opened in 1870, of the Society of the Friends of Music (in the background, left). As a pupil at the Conservatoire of the Society, Mahler studied here from the autumn of 1875 to the summer of 1878.

28. The Great Hall of the new Conservatoire. Drawing by Johann
Schönberg. *Über Land und Meer*, 1870, sheet 24.
Known as the Grosser Musikvereinssaal, this auditorium became the
centre of Vienna's concert life. It was here, where he had gained prizes
as a pupil, that Mahler later (1898–1901) conducted the Philharmonic
Concerts.

29. Theophil Hansen. Copperplate engraving by Gustav Frank.
Kupferstichkabinett, Akademie der bildenden Künste, Vienna.
This very active architect (1813–91) constructed the building of the
Society of the Friends of Music. Hansen's portrait is by Gustav
Mahler's cousin, Gustav Frank (b. 1859 at Wlaschim [Vlašim],
Bohemia). During Mahler's student days, he and Frank were close
friends. Twice, in 1902 and 1907, they met again in St Petersburg,
where Frank, who worked for the Imperial Russian Executive Depart-
ment for the Preparation of State Papers, rose to high rank.

31. Julius Epstein. Anonymous pencil drawing.
The pianist Julius Epstein (1832–1926), a professor at the Conservatoire, was not only Mahler's teacher, but also a fatherly friend.

30. The announcement of Mahler's concert at Iglau, 12 September 1876. MVJ.
After his first year as a music student Mahler gave a concert in his home town, during which he acquitted himself brilliantly both as pianist and composer.

32. Admissions register of the Conservatoire. GDM. The entry records the fact that on 10 September 1875 Mahler was accepted as a pupil to study the piano as his main subject; and that he left the Conservatoire with a diploma in Composition (studied under Professor Franz Krenn, 1816–97) at the end of the academic year 1877–78.

Buchstabe *M.* Conservatorium für Musik und darstellende Kunst
der Gesellschaft der Musikfreunde in Wien.

MATRIKEL.

Des Schülers Name und Vorname: Mahler Gustav

Geburtsort und Land: Iglau ; *Geburtsjahr und Monat:* 1860

Name und Stand des Vaters (Obsorgers): B. Mahler

Hauptfach *für welches der Schüler sich aufnehmen liess:* Clavier

Eingetreten am 10 September 1875 *mit welcher Schulbildung?* _____

War Stiftling de _____ *im Schuljahre 18* _____

War ~~Schul-~~ *befreit im Schuljahre 18* 75/76 – 77/78 *Revers Nr.* 218

Genoss an Unterstützung im Schuljahre 18 _____

Ausgetreten am 18 *wegen* _____

Entlassen am 18 *wegen* _____

Erhielt das ~~Abgangszeugniss,~~ *Diplom* ~~und die Gesellschaftsmedaille~~ als Absolvent für Composition pro 77/78

33. Anton Bruckner. Oil painting by Ferry Beraton. Historisches Museum der Stadt Wien.

Mahler called himself a pupil of Bruckner 'with more right than others', although he had actually never received instruction from him. Bruckner (1824–96) liked the young Mahler, who made the piano duet arrangement for Bruckner's Third Symphony, dedicated to Richard Wagner.

34. Joseph Hellmesberger. Oil painting by Wilhelm Vita. GDM.

Since 1851 Joseph Hellmesberger (1828–93) had been the director of the Conservatoire. He was leader of the well-known string quartet named after him, and coached a generation of violinists.

35. Richard Wagner. Oil painting by Franz von Lenbach, December 1871. Winifred Wagner, Bayreuth.
Wagner was the idol of Vienna's musical young people, who formed a Wagner Society. Mahler is mentioned in 1877 as a member of this society, from which he resigned in 1879.

36. Gustav Mahler. Photograph, 1878. ÖNB-BA.
The picture was taken during the year in which Mahler completed his studies at the Conservatoire.

37. The title-page of the piano score of Anton Bruckner's Third Symphony.
This, the first musical work which bears Mahler's name in print, was published in 1880.

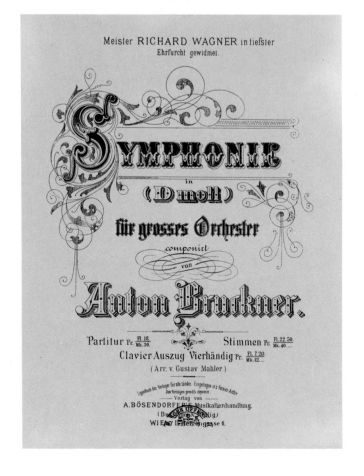

Meister RICHARD WAGNER in tiefster Ehrfurcht gewidmet.

Symphonie in (D moll) für grosses Orchester componirt von Anton Bruckner.

Partitur Pr. Fl. 18. Mk. 30.   Stimmen Pr. Fl. 22.50. Mk. 40.

Clavier Auszug Vierhändig Pr. Fl. 7.20. Mk. 12.
(Arr. v. Gustav Mahler.)

Eigenthum der Verleger für alle Länder. Eingetragen in's Vereins-Archiv.
Das Vortrags-gemäß deponirt.
Verlag von
A. BÖSENDORFER'S Musikalienhandlung.
(Bussjäger & König.)
WIEN, I. Herrengasse 6.

38. The form on which Mahler registered at the Faculty of Philosophy of the University of Vienna for the Winter Semester of 1877–78. Archiv der Universität Wien.

After passing his matriculation (or university entrance examination) at Iglau, Mahler registered as a student at the University of Vienna. He chose lectures on literature and the history of art. The subject *Allgemeine Geschichte* (general history) has been crossed out in ink, and the subject *Harmonielehre* (harmony) in blue crayon. University lectures on harmony were given by Anton Bruckner.

39. The programme of the Gala Concert at the Municipal Theatre, Iglau, on 24 April 1879. MVJ.

One of the performers at the concert, on the occasion of the 25th wedding anniversary of the Emperor and Empress, was Gustav Mahler who played a piano sonata by Schubert.

41. *Der Spielmann* ('The Minstrel'). Last page of the draft score. WSTB.

In March 1878 Mahler completed a poem in three parts which he was to set to music as *Das klagende Lied* ('The Lament'). In March 1880 he completed the short score of the second part, entitled *Der Spielmann*. The last page of music carries the note: 'End of the Spielmann! Sunday, 21 March 1880, as spring makes its appearance!' Mahler was occupied with the preparation of the full score until October 1880.

40. Gustav Mahler. Photograph, 1881. ÖNB-BA.
This picture was taken at Iglau.

42. The spa of Hall. Title-page of a brochure by H. Schuber, Vienna, 1873.
In the summer of 1880 Mahler who, up till then, had sought to earn his living as a piano teacher, accepted a brief engagement as conductor at the theatre of Hall in Upper Austria.

DER
KURORT HALL
IN
OBER-ÖSTERREICH
MIT SEINEN
JOD- UND BROM-HALTIGEN QUELLEN
VON
H. SCHUBER,
DOCTOR DER MEDICIN UND CHIRURGIE, MAGISTER DER GEBURTSHILFE UND DER
AUGEN-HEILKUNDE, BADEARZT ZU HALL IN OBER-ÖSTERREICH UND CHEF-ARZT
DES K. K. MILITÄR-ZÖGLINGS-SPITALES DASELBST.

WIEN, 1873.
IM SELBSTVERLAGE DES VERFASSERS. — IN COMMISSION BEI CARL CZERMAK.

43. A view of Laibach (Ljubljana). Colour engraving. Österreichisches Staatsarchiv, Kriegsarchiv, Vienna.
It was in Laibach, capital of the Duchy of Carniola, that Mahler spent the season of 1881–82 as conductor at the theatre. In this town, where Anton Krisper, a friend from his Conservatoire days in Vienna, lived with his family, Mahler gained valuable conducting experience.

44. The vegetable market in Laibach. Book illustration by Adolf Wagner. ÖUM, *Kärnten und Krain*, Vienna 1891, 483.

Landschaftliches Theater in Laibach.

Direktion: Alexander Mondheim-Schreiner.

Gerader Tag.

Sonntag den 2. April 1882.

Zum Vortheile des hies. Chorpersonals.

Aussergewöhnliche

Künstler-Akademie

unter gefälliger Mitwirkung der hiesigen Opern- und Schauspiel-Mitglieder, sowie der
Hrn. Concertmeister H. Gerstner und Capellmeister A. Mahler und der Regimentscapelle
des k. k. 26. Lin.-Inf.-Reg. unter persönlicher Leitung des Hrn. Capellmeisters Czerny.

Erste Abtheilung:

1. Adolf Müller: Ouverture zu Mädchen von der Spule, vorgetragen von der k. k. Regimentscapelle.
2. v. Hölzl: } Hab in der Brust ein Vögelein, Lied, } gesungen von Herrn Erl.
3. } In den Augen liegt das Herz, Lied, }
4. v. Mozart: Recit. und Arie aus der Oper Don Juan, gesungen von Fräulein Fischer.
5. v. Truhn: Herr Schmied, Lied für Baß, gesungen von Herrn Unger.

Zweite Abtheilung:

6. Richard v. Wagner: Erstes Finale aus der Oper Lohengrin, vorgetragen von der k. k. Regimentscapelle.

Eine Vorlesung bei der Hausmeisterin.

Posse in einem Akt nach dem Französischen von Alexander Bergen. — (Regie: Herr Linori.)

Personen:

Frau Marti, Hausmeisterin	Dr. Laari.	Cappelberg	Hr. Paur.
Anna Lambhof, Heiligste Tochter	Fr. v. Balgetta.	Sensel, Schustferjunge	Hr. Baur.
Manderl Theater, Wirthschaftsrin	Hr. Baßig.	Ein Herr	Hr. Krainel.
Georgette, Tochter der Frau Marti	Frl. Paulet.	Eine Dame	Hr. Paur.

Dritte Abtheilung:

7. Ch. v. Gounod: Meditation über Sebastian Bach's erstes Präludium, vorgetragen von der k. k. Regimentscapelle.
8. H. Vieuxtemps: Ballade und Polonaise, für Violin und Clavierbegleitung, vorgetragen von den Herren H. Gerstner und G. Mahler.
9. v. Suppé: Vergißmeinnicht, Lied, gesungen von Herrn Anwenth.
10. v. Mayerbeer: Bettler-Arie aus der Oper Prosel, gesungen von Fräulein Bruck.
11. v. Mattai: Es is nicht wahr, Lied, gesungen von Herrn Luzzatto.

Zu dieser Vorstellung macht die ergebenste Einladung   **Das Chorpersonale.**

Preise der Plätze: Eine Loge im Parterre und 1. Range sammt Entrée 5 fl. — Eine Loge im 2. Range sammt Entrée 4 fl. — Fauteuil
80 kr. — Sperrsitz im Parterre 70 kr. — Gallerie-Sperrsitz 50 kr. — Parterre oder Logen-Entrée 50 kr. —
Gallerie 20 kr. — Garnisonsbillet und für Studirende 30 kr.

Kassa-Eröffnung halb 7 Uhr. — Anfang 7 Uhr.

Druck von Klein & Kovač in Laibach.

45. Provincial Theatre, Laibach. Photograph. Institute of
Art History, Slovenska Akademija Znanosti in Umenosti,
Ljubljana.
In this house Mahler conducted operettas and operas, among
them Mozart's *Magic Flute,* which was favourably received.

46. Programme of a concert at the Provincial Theatre,
Laibach, dated 2 April 1882. GMG, Vienna, formerly the
property of Dr Hans Gerstner.
Mahler also performed in Laibach as a pianist. In this concert
Hans Gerstner and he played the Ballade and Polonaise for
violin and piano by Vieuxtemps.

Fr: Universität u. Convict Kaſſerne.

Hl. Dreifaltigkeits-Sæule.

Rathhaus.

OLMÜTZ
von Norden.

Astron: Uhr am Oberringe.

Hl. Marien-Sæule.

Biſchofs-Platz.

48. The Royal Municipal Theatre, Olmütz. ÖNB-BA.
Upon arrival, Mahler found the condition of the theatre, as well as the orchestra and the resident company, so inadequate that he felt like one 'whom the punishment of heaven awaits'. Nevertheless this engagement was to prove useful for Mahler's future career.

Königl. städt. Theater in Olmütz.

111. Vorstellung im Abonnoment.   Ungerader Tag.
Direction Em. Raul.
Dienstag den 23. Jänner 1883.

Die Stumme von Portici.

Große heroisch-romantische Oper in 5 Aufzügen
von Auber. — Capellmeister G. Mahler.

Personen:

Masaniello, neapolitanischer Fischer   Herr Krüger a G.
Fenella, seine Schwester   .   .   .   Frln. Delia.
Alfonso, Sohn des Vice-Königs . .   Herr Rust.
Elvira, seine Verlobte .   ,   .   .   Frln. Miles.
Lorenzo, Alfonso's Vertrauter   .   Herr Adam.
Selva, Anführer der Leibwache . .   Herr Manheit.
Eine Hofdame .   .   .   .   Frln. Mayer.

Morgen Mittwoch:

Zum Benefice des Schauspielers Herrn
Rudolf Retsch.

Der Narr des Glückes.

Königl städt. Theater in Olmütz.

8. Vorstell.   Abonn. susp.   Gerader Tag
Direction Em. Raul.
Samstag den 10. März 1883.
☛ Bei erhöhten Preisen. ☚
Zum ersten Male:
CARMEN.

Oper in 4 Acten von Georges Bizet. — Dirigent Herr Capellmeister Gustav Mahler.

Personen:

Carmen   .   .   .   .   .   .   Frln. Hild.
Don José, Sergeant .   .   Herr Krüger a. G.
Escamillo, Stierfechter .   Herr Manheit.
Zuniga, Lieutenant   .   .   Herr Fuchs.
Dancairo,) Schmuggler   Herr Martini.
Remendado,)   Herr Rust.
Micaela, ein Bauernmädchen   Frln. Miles.
Frasquita,) Zigeuner- .   Frln. Zimmermann
Mercédés,) mädchen .   Frln. Mayer.

Morgen Sonntag:

Der lustige Krieg.

49. A newspaper advertisement for the theatre at Olmütz.
Mährisches Tageblatt, 23 January 1883.

50. A newspaper advertisement for the theatre at Olmütz.
Mährisches Tageblatt, 10 March 1883.

< 47.   Olmütz (Olomouc), Moravia. Lithograph. ÖNB-Kartensammlung.
From January to March 1883 Mahler conducted operas at Olmütz.

Königl. Theater und obere Königsstrasse — Cassel

51.   The Royal Theatre, Kassel. Photograph. ÖNB-BA.
In the spring of 1883 Mahler was engaged as assistant conductor and choirmaster at this theatre, where he worked up to the end of the 1884–85 season. The theatre, built in 1769, and rebuilt in 1828, was originally the Court Theatre of the Duchy of Hesse. After Prussia's victory in the war of 1866 the Ducal Court Theatre became the Royal Theatre controlled from Berlin.

52.   Gustav Mahler. Photograph, 1883. ÖNB-BA.
This picture shows Mahler with a luxuriant full beard. He was still in Kassel when he shaved it off.

53.   Adolph Freiherr von und zu Gilsa. Photograph. ÖNB-BA.
From 1875 to 1906, Gilsa, originally a Prussian officer, was manager of the theatre in Kassel. It was from him that Mahler learnt, to use his own words, 'to obey in order to command'.

54. The Kassel steam tram. Photograph. Archive of *Hessische Allgemeine*, Kassel.
Since 1877 Kassel, which, with its approximately 60,000 inhabitants, was only a small town, had boasted a steam tram which travelled from the Königsplatz to Schloss Wilhelmshöhe, a distance of five kilometres.

55. The Register of Fines, kept by the Royal Theatre, Kassel. CAS 2661.
Mahler's name turns up twice in the register for the period from 1 to 30 September 1883. His first offence was 'the most annoying habit of walking very noisily on the heels of his boots during rehearsals and performances'. The second entry records that during conversation with several female members of the choir he was the cause of 'peals of laughter'.

56. A programme of the Municipal Theatre, Iglau, 11 August 1883. MVJ.
During the summer vacation which Mahler spent with his parents, he took part in a concert of music and recitation. He played two pieces by Chopin and accompanied the violin virtuoso Mila von Ott in Beethoven's Kreutzer Sonata. Displeased by poor artistic performances during rehearsals, Mahler shelved plans to play the accompaniment to the one-act operetta *Kaffeekränzchen* ('The Coffee Party').

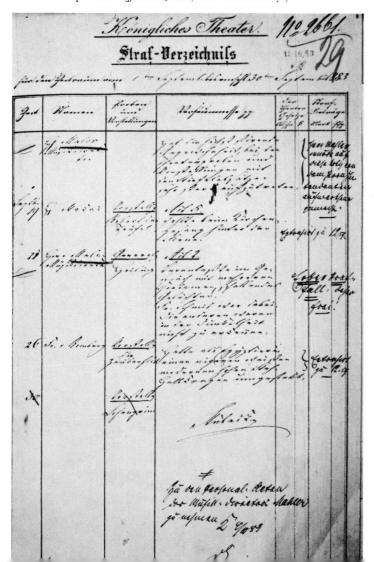

57. *Der Trompeter von Säkkingen* ('The Trumpeter of Säkkin-gen') by J. V. Scheffel. Title vignette, Stuttgart 1894.
This narrative poem by Josef Victor Scheffel was one of the most popular books of the nineteenth century. The 1894 edition was the 214th! In June 1884 Mahler composed the incidental music to accompany a series of tableaux based on *Der Trompeter von Säkkingen* which were performed during a charity performance in the Kassel theatre. Mahler's composition has not survived. A trumpet melody was incorporated into the second movement of his First Symphony, but this movement was later taken out by Mahler.

58. Gustav Mahler. Photograph, 1884. OAJ-F.

59. Gustav Mahler. Photograph, 1884, ÖNB-BA.

60. *Lieder eines fahrenden Gesellen* ('Songs of a Wayfarer'). A page from the score in Mahler's own hand. Professor Willem Mengelberg Stichting, Amsterdam.

At Christmastime 1884, profoundly affected by an experience of unrequited love, Mahler planned a song cycle. 'The songs have been imagined as though a wayfaring craftsman, who has had a fateful experience, sets out into the world . . .', he wrote to his friend Friedrich Löhr (GMB, 34). Both versions of the composition – one with piano, the other with orchestra – were published in 1897. The orchestral version, presumably, was not made until the 1890s. The beginning of the second song, shown here, was incorporated into the first movement of Mahler's First Symphony.

61. The Royal German Theatre in Prague (now the Tyl Theatre). Book illustration by Friedrich Ohmann. öUM, *Böhmen*, pt 2, Vienna 1896, 171.

In this house, rich in tradition, where in 1787 Mozart had first performed *Don Giovanni*, Mahler conducted the orchestra in the season of 1885–86. It was here that he was entrusted for the first time with tasks of great artistic significance.

62. Angelo Neumann. Photograph.

Angelo Neumann (1838–1910) was Director of the German Theatre in Prague. Having started his career as a singer, he became Director of the Municipal Theatre in Leipzig in 1876 jointly with August Förster, and in 1885 took over the direction of the theatre in Prague, which he held up to the time of his death. He was regarded as a 'conductor-spotter': it was he who had summoned Arthur Nikisch to Leipzig; it was he who first assigned to Mahler a repertoire suited to his talents, and he who in later years engaged, among others, Carl Muck, Franz Schalk and Otto Klemperer.

63. Neustadt Theatre, Prague, Photograph. ÖNB-BA.
During the summer season the Royal German Theatre used to organize performances at the Neustadt Theatre. Here Mahler conducted Mozart's *Don Giovanni* on 6 September 1885. This was the first important task that Neumann had entrusted to him.

64.   A programme of the Royal German Theatre, Prague, for 19 and 20 December 1885. Narodní Muzeum, Prague.
Mahler, whose name is not mentioned in the programme, conducted the first performances of *The Rhinegold* and *The Valkyrie* at Prague.

65.   Gustav Mahler. Photograph, 1886. ÖNB–BA.
The first thing Mahler's Viennese friend Friedrich Löhr noticed when he visited the composer in Prague was that his former full beard had been reduced to a neat moustache.

66. Laura Hilgermann. Photograph. ÖNB-BA.

This young singer with an unusual vocal range arrived in Prague during Mahler's time there and later followed him to Budapest and Vienna.

68. Johannes Elmblad. Photograph. Musikhistoriska Museet, Stockholm.

The Swedish bass (1853–1910) sang under Mahler in Prague, where for some time both men lived in the same house, at Lange Gasse 18.

Königl. Deutsches Landestheater.

Sonntag, den 21. Februar 1886
um 12 Uhr Mittags:
Zum Besten des deutschen Schulpfennig-Vereines.

Grosse Musik-Aufführung.

Orchester-Aufstellung auf der Bühne.

Das Orchester ist auf 85 Mann verstärkt durch die Mitwirkung hervorragender Künstler, Kunstfreunde und Schüler des Conservatoriums.

I. Abtheilung.

1. Duett. „Götterdämmerung".
(Brünnhilde und Siegfried) . . . Richard Wagner.
Brünnhilde . . . . Marie Rochelle.
Siegfried . . . . Adolph Wallnöfer.
Das Orchester des kön. deutschen Landestheaters.
Dirigent: Ludwig Slansky.

2. Verwandlungsmusik, große Chor- und Schluß-scene des I. Actes
„Parsifal" . . . . Richard Wagner.
Chorpart: Deutscher Männergesangverein. — Gesang-verein Sct. Veit.
Chordirigent: Musikdirector Friedrich Hessler.
Das Orchester des königl. deutschen Landestheaters.
Dirigent: **Gustav Mahler.**

II. Abtheilung.

Neunte Symphonie

für Soli, Chor und großes Orchester . . Ludwig van Beethoven.
Chorpart: Deutscher Männergesangverein. — Gesang-verein Sct. Veit.
Chordirigent: Musikdirector Friedrich Hessler.
Das Orchester des königl. deutschen Landestheaters.
Dirigent: **Gustav Mahler.**

Die Soli gesungen von Betty Frank, Laura Hilger-mann, Adolph Wallnöfer, Johannes Elmblad.

Der Chor besteht aus 200 Mitwirkenden (100 Damen und 100 Herren).

☞ Zwischen der ersten und zweiten Abtheilung findet eine längere Pause statt. ☜

Anfang um 12 Uhr.   Ende um halb 3 Uhr.

67. Concert announcement. *Bohemia*, 21 February 1886.

Among those taking the solo parts in the Ninth Symphony were Laura Hilgermann and Johannes Elmblad. Guido Adler reports that the powerful impression created by the concert gave rise to an address of thanks which Mahler received from German academic circles in Prague.

69. The Czech National Theatre in Prague (Narodní divadlo). Book illustration by Friedrich Ohmann. ÖUM, *Böhmen*, pt. 2, Vienna 1896, 183.

Mahler often visited this theatre. It was here that he came to know Slav operas and above all the works of Smetana, still little known outside Bohemia, to which he gave his support, first as a conductor and later as an opera director.

70. The New Theatre (Municipal Theatre), Leipzig.
Engraving by Adolf Eltzner. *Leipziger Illustrierte Zeitung*, 1869.
Museum für Geschichte der Stadt Leipzig.
This wood-engraving shows the inaugural performance on 28
January 1868. The auditorium could seat approximately
2,000 people. Mahler worked here as conductor during the
seasons of 1886–87 and 1887–88.

71. The New Theatre (Municipal Theatre), Leipzig. Out-
side view. Engraving by Adolf Eltzner. *Gartenlaube*, 1866.
Museum für Geschichte der Stadt Leipzig.
The theatre was situated in the centre of the city, facing the
Augustusplatz. At the rear, with its semicircular terrace, was
a pond with swans and a fountain.

72. Max Staegemann. After a photograph. Museum für Geschichte der Stadt Leipzig.

Max Staegemann (1843–1905) was Director of the Leipzig Municipal Theatre from 1882 to 1905. In August 1886 Mahler wrote: 'The Director has introduced me into his family, where I have already spent many delightful hours.' (GMB, 50.)

73. Arthur Nikisch. Photograph. ÖNB-BA.

Nikisch (1855–1922) was principal conductor in Leipzig. At first Mahler's relationship with him was clouded by jealousy. When Nikisch fell ill in February 1887, Mahler took over his entire repertoire, which included Wagner's *The Ring of the Nibelung*. It was ten years before their relationship became a friendly one; afterwards Nikisch became a supporter of Mahler's compositions.

DIE
drei Pintos.

Komische Oper in drei Aufzügen
von
C. M. von WEBER.

Unter Zugrundelegung des gleichnamigen Textbuches von Th. Hell,
der hinterlassenen Entwürfe und ausgewählter Manuscripte des Componisten ausgeführt:

der dramatische Theil
von
C. von WEBER,
der musikalische
von
G. MAHLER.

Klavier-Auszug mit Text M 8,...n.   Partitur M   Klavier-Auszug ohne Text M

Alle Rechte vorbehalten.

Verlag von C.F. KAHNT NACHFOLGER, Leipzig.

Eigenthum für
Russland,   Niederlande,
Mellin & Neldner, Riga.   H. Rahr, Utrecht.
                    Amerika,
            Edw. Schuberth & C?, NewYork.

74. Title-page of the piano score of *Die drei Pintos* ('The Three Pintos'). Leipzig 1888.

In Leipzig Mahler was encouraged to arrange and complete Carl Maria von Weber's operatic fragment *Die drei Pintos*. The first performance took place in Leipzig on 20 January 1888. Afterwards the work was taken up by many opera houses.

75. Café Français, Leipzig. *Illustrierter Führer durch Leipzig und Umgebung* (Woerls Reisehandbücher), Leipzig, n.d., XX. Mahler was a devotee of coffee houses. His 'local' in Leipzig was the Café Français on the Augustusplatz. 'There he would be almost every afternoon, surrounded by his fellow countrymen', reported Max Steinitzer, 'and there I spoke to him for the first time, in summertime, beneath the balcony, out of doors.'

76. Richard Strauss. Photograph, 1888. ÖNB-BA.
Richard Strauss came to Leipzig in October 1887. Mahler showed him his arrangement of the opera *Die drei Pintos*, about which Strauss made enthusiastic comments. This was the beginning of a friendly and mutually helpful relationship which lasted until Mahler's death.

< 77. 'How the animals buried the hunter'. Woodcut after a drawing by Moritz von Schwind. *Münchner Bilderbogen No. 44, Die guten Freunde*, Munich 1850.

< 78. The First Symphony. The beginning of the fourth movement of the original version which had five movements. Osborn Collection, Yale University, New Haven, Connecticut.

Mahler completed the First Symphony in Leipzig in March 1888. Schwind's picture suggested the mood of the fourth (now third) movement. At the first performance in 1889 the movement was headed *A la pompes funèbres*; at the performance in Hamburg in 1893, it was entitled, as in the autograph version, *Todtenmarsch 'in Callots Manier'* ('Funeral March "in the Manner of Callot"'). This title was inspired by E. T. A. Hoffmann's *Phantasiestücke nach Callots Manier*; the reference is to Jacques Callot (1592/3–1635).

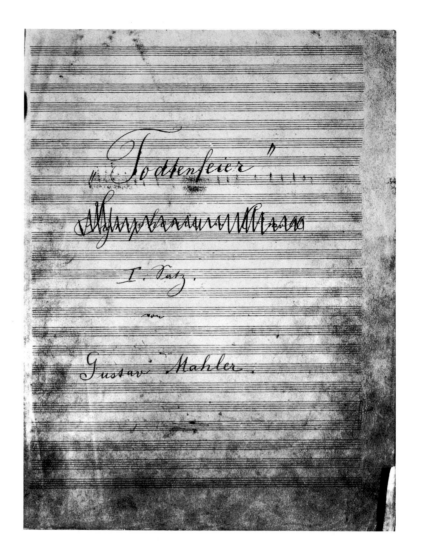

79. Jenny Perrin, née Feld, with her children. Photograph. Madame John Perrin, Brussels.

Jenny Feld was the owner of the autograph score of the First Symphony which, after her death, went to her son, John C. Perrin, and finally landed in the Osborn Collection. Jenny Feld, who was born in Budapest, came to Vienna in 1878, when she was twelve years old, for her musical education. Gustav Mahler was her teacher. According to family recollections Mahler is said to have given her the score as a token of gratitude for the family's kindness to him.

80, 81. *Todtenfeier* ('Obsequies'). Title-page and last page of Mahler's score in his own hand. Professor Willem Mengelberg Stichting, Amsterdam.

Mahler worked on this first written record of the first movement of the Second Symphony while staying in Prague in the summer of 1888. This had been preceded by sketches which have survived and on which the date is 8 August 1888. On the title page of *Todtenfeier* the line *Symphonie in C-moll* has been crossed out. The last page of the autograph bears the note *Prag 10. September 1888*. Mahler had come to Prague to conduct *Die drei Pintos* at the German Theatre.

82. The Royal Hungarian Opera House. Book illustration
by Theodor Dörre. öUM, *Ungarn*, Vienna 1893, III, 407.
The Budapest Opera House was opened in 1884. At the age
of twenty-eight Mahler was appointed Director. He took up
his post in October 1888 and held it until March 1891.

84. Gustav Mahler. Photograph, 1888. ÖNB-BA.

83. Ferenc von Beniczky. Wood engraving by Szigmond
Pollak. ÖNB-BA.
As Government Commissioner for the Royal Hungarian
Court Opera, Ferenc (Franz) von Beniczky engaged Gustav
Mahler, who had been recommended to him from several
quarters.

85, 86. Theatre Programme of the Royal Hungarian Opera House, 26 and 27 January 1889. Országos Széchényi Könyvtár, Budapest.

Mahler's first important achievement as Director of the Opera, and the first thing he did as a conductor in Budapest, was to start rehearsing Wagner's musical dramas *The Rhinegold (A Rajna kincse)* and *The Valkyrie (A Walkür)* in the Hungarian language. Following the tradition of those days, Mahler's name does not appear in the programmes.

87. Bianca Bianchi. ÖNB-BA.

Among the darlings of Budapest opera-goers was the German coloratura soprano Bianca Bianchi (1855–1947), whose real name was Bertha Schwarz. On 13 November 1889 she sang three songs by Mahler at a concert in Budapest.

88. The Danube at Budapest. Watercolour by Rudolf von Alt. Szépmüvészeti Múzeum, Budapest.

The Alt family of painters in Vienna, whose most important member was Rudolf von Alt (1812–1905), specialized in architectural and landscape watercolours. This view of the Danube, painted in the 1880s, conveys something of Budapest's delightful surroundings, which Mahler enjoyed on his long walks.

89. Ödön von Mihalovich. Drawing by Ferenc Márton. Magyar Nemzeti Múzeum, Budapest.

The composer Ödön (Edmund) von Mihalovich (1842–1929), from 1887 to 1919 director of the Royal Academy of Music in Budapest, was a passionate Wagnerian; hence he belonged to those musical circles who favoured the appointment of Mahler because he conducted Wagner's works. During the years Mahler worked in Budapest, and for a long time afterwards, Mihalovich proved to be a dependable friend.

90. Count Albert Apponyi. Oil painting by Ede Balló.
Magyar Nemzeti Múzeum, Budapest.
Mahler's most influential admirer in Budapest was Count
Albert Apponyi (1846–1933), one of the most brilliant
orators of the Hungarian Parliament, and in later years
Hungarian Minister of Religious and Cultural Affairs and
Hungary's representative at the League of Nations. Apponyi,
who had been on friendly terms with Franz Liszt and Richard
Wagner, was one of the co-founders of the Budapest Academy
of Music.

91. Lilli Lehmann as Donna Anna. Oil painting by Hans
Volkmer. Internationale Stiftung Mozarteum, Salzburg.
One of the outstanding singers of her time, Lilli Lehmann
(1848–1929) was a guest performer in Budapest in December
1890. Brahms was present at a performance of Mozart's *Don
Giovanni*, in which she sang the part of Donna Anna. He was so
delighted by Mahler's production that from then on he
informed everybody in Vienna that one had to go to Budapest
in order to see a really good performance of this work.

92. The tomb of Mahler's parents, Iglau. Photograph. OAJ-F.

Bernhard Mahler died in February 1889, and Marie Mahler in October of that same year. After the death of his parents Gustav Mahler took on the responsibility of caring for his younger brothers and sisters.

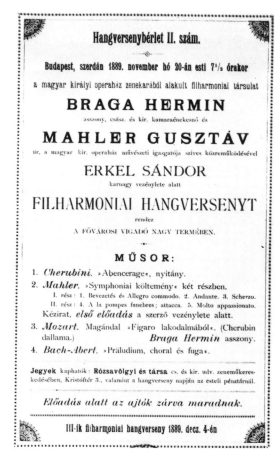

93. Programme of the Philharmonic Concert of 20 November 1889. Országos Széchényi Könyvtár, Budapest.

During a concert under the direction of Sándor Erkel, Mahler conducted his First Symphony which, at the first performance, bore the title of *Symphonische Dichtung* (Symphonic Poem) and consisted of five movements in two sections. The work had an unfavourable reception.

94. Friedrich Löhr. Photograph. Album des Archäologisch-Epigraphischen Seminars der Universität Wien.

During the 1880s and 1890s the archaeologist Friedrich Löhr (1859–1924) was Mahler's most intimate friend. After the death of Mahler's mother, Löhr took charge of the education of Otto and Emma Mahler. On the occasion of the first performance of the First Symphony he travelled from Vienna to Budapest.

A MALÉR-SZYFÓNIA.

(A Filharmóniai konczerten.)

Hatás !

95. Caricature referring to the first performance of the First Symphony, in the magazine *Bolond Istók*, 24 November 1889.
Mahler's friend, Hans Koessler, Professor at the Academy of Music, is beating the publicity drum; Ödön von Mihalovich is tweaking a cat's tail; Mahler is blowing into a gigantic musical instrument while conducting. The title of the caricature uses a play on words: Malheur-Syphon instead of Mahler's Symphony. *Hatás* means 'effect' in Hungarian.

96. Exit from the Opera House. Caricature in the magazine *Bolond Istók*, 2 November 1890.
On the back of Ferenc von Beniczky, shown here as a pachyderm, rides Mahler, his head adorned with the loyal newspaper *Pester Lloyd*, led by Ödön von Mihalovich, who is shedding tears over his never-performed opera *Toldis Liebe* ('The Love of Toldi'). Mahler's superior, Beniczky, had been appointed district governor *(Obergespan)* of the County of Pest in 1890. The caricaturist illustrates his exit from the Opera to the official residence of the *Obergespan*. Mahler is called Beniczky's '*Untergespan*'.

97. Count Géza Zichy. Photograph. Országos Széchényi Könyvtár, Budapest.
At the beginning of 1891 the pianist and composer Count Géza Zichy (1849–1924) was appointed administrator of the Opera House to succeed Beniczky. His first act was to restrict Mahler's rights as Operatic Director. It was on account of him that Mahler cancelled his contract prematurely and left Budapest in March 1891.

98. Jungfernstieg, Hamburg. Oil painting by Adolf Behrens, 1885. Museum für Hamburgische Geschichte, Hamburg.

99. Jungfernstieg, Hamburg. Pastel painting by Ernst Eitner, 1894. Museum für Hamburgische Geschichte, Hamburg.

100. 'The Concert'. Oil painting by Titian. Galleria Palatina, Florence.
A reproduction of this painting adorned Mahler's study in Hamburg. 'I could go on composing this picture for ever', he said. The young Bruno Walter noticed an odd resemblance between the music-making monk and Mahler. Originally the painting was held to be the work of Giorgione, but nowadays it is attributed to Titian.

Stadt-Theater.

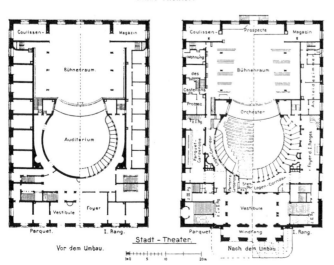

Vor dem Umbau.   Stadt - Theater.   Nach dem Umbau.

101. The Municipal Theatre, Hamburg, with ground-plan before and after the reconstruction completed in 1874. *Hamburg und seine Bauten*, Hamburg 1890, 140.
Mahler worked in this theatre as principal conductor from March 1891 to April 1897.

102. Bernhard Pollini. *Mitglieder des Hamburger und Altonaer Stadt-Theaters, Saison 1892–1893*, Hamburg 1893. ÖNB-BA.
Pollini (1838–97) was Director of the municipal theatres in Hamburg and Altona from 1874, in addition to which he also acted as a commercial impresario.

THERE IS NO CHARGE FOR THIS PROGRAMME.

Royal Opera — Covent Garden
THEATRE.
Under the Sole Direction of Sir AUGUSTUS HARRIS.
Supported by the following Unprecedented Combination of the First Musical Talent of Europe.

ITALIAN & FRENCH OPERA.

Tenors:—
Mons. JEAN DE RESZKE
Mons. VAN DYCK
Signor MONTARIOL
Signor MORELLO
Signor DIMITRESCO
Signor RINALDINI
Signor CORSI
AND
Signor DE LUCIA

Baritones:—
Mons. LASSALLE
Mons. DUFRICHE
Mr. ALEC MARSH
Mons. CESTE
Mons. ZOLTAN DOME
Signor TSCHERNOFF
AND
Mons. MAUREL

Basses:—
Mons. EDOUARD DE RESZKE
Signor ABRAMOFF
Mons. CASTELMARY
Mons. MIRANDA
Signor DE VASCHETTI
Signor CARACCIOLO
Mr. H. BISPHAM
Mr. MANNERS
Mr. FFRANGCON-DAVIES
AND
Mons. PLANÇON

Soprani:—
Madame MELBA
Madame NORDICA
Madame MRAVINA
Madame DOTTI
Miss FANNY MOODY
Mlle. BAUERMEISTER
AND
Madame EMMA EAMES

Madame CALVÉ
Mlle. TELEKI
Mlle. MINNIE TRACEY
Mlle. NINA BURT
AND
Mlle. ZÉLIE DE LUSSAN

Mlle. SIGRID ARNOLDSON
Mlle. SOFIA RAVOGLI
Mlle. FAURE
Mlle. FLORENZA
AND
Miss MARGARET MACINTYRE

Contralti:—
Mlle. GIULIA RAVOGLI
Mlle. PASSAMA
Mlle. JANSON
Mlle. MARIE BREMA
AND
Madame DESCHAMPS-JEHIN

Conductors:—
Signor MANCINELLI
Signor BEVIGNANI
Signor RANDEGGER
AND
Mons. LÉON JEHIN

Assistant Conductors:—
Messrs. SAAR and ROGER

GERMAN OPERA.

Tenors:—
Herr ALVARY
Dr. SIEDEL
Herr SIMON
Herr LIEBAN
AND
Herr LANDAU

Baritones and Basses:—
Herr GRENGG
Herr KNAPP
Herr REICHMANN
Herr LORENT
Herr LITTER

Herr LISSMANN
AND
Herr WIEGAND

Sopranos and Contraltos:—
Fräulein KLAFSKY
Frau ENDE-ANDRIESSEN
Fräulein BETTAQUE
Fräulein TRAUBMANN
Fräulein KOLLAR
Fräulein MEISSLINGER
Fräulein RALPH
Fräulein LIEBAN
Fräulein UPLEGER
Fräulein SIMON
Fräulein HEINK
AND
Fräulein FROEHLICH

Conductor:—
Herr MAHLER

Assistant Conductor:—
Herr FELD.

REPERTOIRE:—
*ROMEO ET JULIETTE, Gounod
*FAUST, Gounod
*PHILEMON ET BAUCIS, Gounod
*ORFEO, Gluck
*LOHENGRIN, Wagner
*DIE MEISTERSINGER, Wagner
*DER FLIEGENDE HOLLANDER, Wagner
*OTELLO, Verdi
*AIDA, Verdi
*LES HUGUENOTS, Meyerbeer
*LE PROPHETE, Meyerbeer
*THE FLIGHT OF ASIA, De Lara
*CAVALLERIA RUSTICANA, Mascagni
*L'AMICO FRITZ, Mascagni
*DON GIOVANNI, Mozart
*NOZZE DI FIGARO, Mozart
*ELAINE, Bemberg
*CARMEN, Bizet
*MANON, Massenet
Operas to be Performed in German.
*TRISTAN UND ISOLDE, Wagner
*RHEINGOLD, Wagner
*DIE WALKURE, Wagner
*SIEGFRIED, Wagner
DIE GOTTERDAMMERUNG, Wagner
*FIDELIO, Beethoven
*TROMPETER OF SAKKINGEN, Nessler

The Operas marked thus * have already been produced.

AT COVENT GARDEN THEATRE.

FORTIETH SUBSCRIPTION NIGHT.

SATURDAY, JULY 9th, at 8.30
Mascagni's Opera, in Three Acts,

L'AMICO FRITZ.
Fritz	Signor DE LUCIA
Rabbino	Mons. DUFRICHE
Hanezo	Signor DE VASCHETTI
Federico	Signor CORSI
Beppe	Mlle. GIULIA RAVOGLI
Caterina	Mlle. BAUERMEISTER
Suzel	Madame CALVÉ
Solo Violin	Mr. J. T. CARRODUS.
Conductor	Signor BEVIGNANI

FORTY-FIRST SUBSCRIPTION NIGHT.

MONDAY, JULY 11th, 1892, at 8,
Mozart's Opera,

DON GIOVANNI
Don Giovanni	Mons. MAUREL
Leporello	Mons. EDOUARD DE RESZKE
Masetto	Signor CARACCIOLO
Il Commendatore	Signor ABRAMOFF
Don Ottavio	Signor DIMITRESCO
Donna Elvira	Madame NORDICA
Donna Anna	Madame GIULIA VALDA
Zerlina	Mlle. SIGRID ARNOLDSON
Première Danseuse	Mlle. GIURI
Conductor	Signor RANDEGGER.

FORTY-SECOND SUBSCRIPTION NIGHT

TUESDAY, JULY 12th, at 8
Gounod's Opera, in Two Acts,

PHILEMON ET BAUCIS
Philemon	Mons. MONTARIOL
Jupiter	Mons. PLANÇON
Vulcan	Mons. CASTELMARY
Baucis	Mlle. SIGRID ARNOLDSON
Conductor	Mons. LÉON JEHIN

To be followed, at 10 o'clock, by Mascagni's Opera,

CAVALLERIA RUSTICANA
Turiddu	Signor DE LUCIA
Alfio	Mons. DUFRICHE
Lola	Signora GIULIA RAVOGLI
Lucia	Mlle. BAUERMEISTER
Santuzza	Madame CALVÉ
Conductor	Signor MANCINELLI

WEDNESDAY, JULY 13th, 1892, at 7,
Wagner's Opera,

DIE GOTTERDAMMERUNG
Siegfried	Herr ALVARY
Gunther	Herr KNAPP
Hagen	Herr WIEGAND
Alberich	Herr LISSMANN
Brünhilde	Frau KLAFSKY
Gutrune	Fräulein BETTAQUE
Waltraute	Fräulein HEINK
Woglinde	Fräulein TRAUBMANN
Wellgunde	Fräulein RALPH
Flosshilde	Fräulein FROEHLICH
Manen	Herr LORENT
Conductor	Herr MAHLER

AT COVENT GARDEN THEATRE.

FORTY-THIRD SUBSCRIPTION NIGHT.

THURSDAY, JULY 14th, 1892, at 8
Bemberg's Opera,

ELAINE
(FOR THE SECOND TIME.)
Lancelot	Mons. MONTARIOL
Astolat	Mons. PLANÇON
Lavaine	Mons. TRIESTE
Gauvain	Mons. DUFRICHE
King Arthur	Mons. CESTE
L'Ermite	Mons. EDOUARD DE RESZKE
Reine Genièvre	Madame DESCHAMPS JEHIN
Torre	Mlle. FAURE
Un Ménestrel	Madame COLLARD
Elaine	Madame MELBA

Mr. Stedman's Choir of Boys.
Conductor … Mons. LÉON-JEHIN

FORTY-FOURTH SUBSCRIPTION NIGHT.

FRIDAY, JULY 15th, 1892, at 8,
Mozart's Opera,

NOZZE DI FIGARO
Contessa	Madame EMMA EAMES
Susanna	Mlle. TELEKI
Marcellina	Mlle. BAUERMEISTER
Cherubino	Mlle. SIGRID ARNOLDSON
Il Conte	Mons. EDOUARD DE RESZKE
Basilio	Signor RINALDINI
Bartolo	Signor CARACCIOLO
Curzio	Signor IGINIO CORSI
Antonio	Signor DE VASCHETTI
Figaro	Mons. MAUREL
Conductor	Signor BEVIGNANI.

FORTY-FIFTH SUBSCRIPTION NIGHT.

SATURDAY, JULY 16th, 1892, at 8.
Wagner's Opera,

TANNHAUSER
(IN GERMAN.)

Doors Open Half-an-Hour before the Performance commences

Pit and Grand Tier Boxes, Six Guineas.
First Tier Boxes, 3½ Guineas. Second Tier Boxes 1½ Guineas.
Orchestra Stalls, One Guinea. Balcony Stalls, 15s.
Amphitheatre Stalls (First Two Rows), 10s. 6d.; Other Rows, 5s.
Amphitheatre, 2s. 6d.
Tickets to be obtained of
Mr. EDWARD HALL, at the Box Office, under the Portico of the Theatre, where applications for Boxes and Stalls are to be made.

SPECIAL NOTICE.
When Tickets cannot be obtained at the Libraries, application should be made direct to the Box-Office of the Opera House, Covent Garden where some of the Best Seats are reserved for Sale to the Public.

Box-Office open from 10 a.m. to 5 p.m. for Future Booking, and all day long for the Sale of Seats for the same evening.

Any Complaints should be addressed to Sir AUGUSTUS HARRIS.

The Pianofortes supplied by Bechstein;
Wenham Gas Lamps are in use in the Portico of the Theatre.

(vertical text between columns:) Applications for ARTISTS connected with the ROYAL ITALIAN and GERMAN OPERAS, for PRIVATE CONCERTS, and "AT HOMES," to be Addressed to the Concert Direction, DANIEL MAYER, 130, New Bond Street, W.

DRURY LANE THEATRE ROYAL
Under the Sole Direction of Sir Augustus Harris.

In consequence of the enormous success of the Opera Season, Overflow Performances will be given with the same Company of Artistes, Orchestra, and Mise-en-scène as at Covent Garden Theatre.

THIS EVENING
SATURDAY, 9th JULY, 1892, at 7.30,
AT DRURY LANE THEATRE
Wagner's Opera,

TRISTAN UND ISOLDE
(BY GENERAL DESIRE).
Tristan	Herr MAX ALVARY
Marke	Herr WIEGAND
Kurvenal	Herr KNAPP
Melos	Herr SIMON
Steuermann	Herr LORENT
Hirt	Herr LANDAU
Tange Seemann	Herr LIEBAN
Braugane	Fräulein RALPH
Isolde	Frau KLAFSKY
Conductor	Herr MAHLER.

MONDAY, JULY 11th, 1892, at 7.30
AT DRURY LANE THEATRE
Wagner's Opera, in Three Acts,

SIEGFRIED
Siegfried	Herr MAX ALVARY
Mime	Herr LIEBAN
Der Wanderer	Herr REICHMANN
Alberich	Herr LORENT
Fafner	Herr WIEGAND
Erda	Fräulein HEINK
Stimme des Waldvogels	Fräulein TRAUBMANN
Brünnhilde	Fräulein BETTAQUE
Conductor	Herr MAHLER.

THURSDAY, JULY 14th, 1892, at 8
AT DRURY LANE THEATRE
Nessler's Opera (in German),

DER TROMPETER VON SAKKINGEN
With the best Cast ever given.
Werner	Herr REICHMANN
Der Freiherr	Herr WIEGAND
Maria	Fräulein BETTAQUE
Conradin	Herr LORENT
Graf von Wildenstein	Herr LITTER
Damian	Herr LANDAU
Rector Magnificus	Herr MAAS
Haushofmeister	Herr SIMON
Gräfin	Frau HEINK

Studenten, Soldaten, Matrosen, Bauern.

In the Incidental Ballet in Act IV.:—
König Wein	Miss EVANS.
Prinz Waldmeister	Madame PHASEY.
Prinzessin Maiblüme	Mlle. A. GIURI.

Die Rheinweine, Rüdesheimer, Scharlachberger, Niersteiner, Marcobrunner, Steinberger, Hockheimer Domdechant, Johannisberger, Liebfraumilch, Blumen, Schmetterlinge Frösche.
Conductor, … Herr FELD.

Private Boxes from 2 to 7 Guineas. Stalls, 1 Guinea.
Grand Circle (First Row) 12s. Other Rows, 12s. 6d.
First Circle, (First Two Rows) 10s. 6d. Other Rows, 5s.
Balcony (Unreserved), 4s. Gallery, 2s. 6d.
Box-Office open from 10 a.m. all day. No Fees for Booking.
Evening dress indispensable in the grand and pit tier boxes, stalls, and dress circle — in all other parts of the house morning dress will be admitted.

THE WAGNER SOCIETY.
Annual Subscription, One Guinea.
Secretary, W. H. Edwards, 66, St. Mark's Road, North Kensington, W.
"RICHARD WAGNER'S PROSE WORKS,"
Translated by W. Ashton Ellis, Editor of
"THE MEISTER" (The Society's Quarterly).

THE BUGLE BRAND.

M. B. FOSTER & SONS
LIMITED (Established 1829),
ALE AND BEER MERCHANTS,
Offices—27 & 29, BROOK STREET, BOND STREET, W.
Stores—242 & 244, MARYLEBONE ROAD, N.W.
BASS' ALE & GUINNESS' STOUT.
The above Bottling supplied to this Theatre.

Printed by J. Miles & Co. 195, Wardour Street, Oxford Street, W.

---

108. Programme of the Royal Opera House, Covent Garden, 9 to 16 July 1892. Museum für Hamburgische Geschichte, Hamburg.

Up to 1892 even German operas were sung in Italian at Covent Garden. It was the performances in German under Mahler in June and July 1892 which heralded the change: *Fidelio*, *Tristan and Isolde*, and *The Ring of the Nibelung*. In addition to those at Covent Garden there were additional performances in the Theatre Royal, Drury Lane.

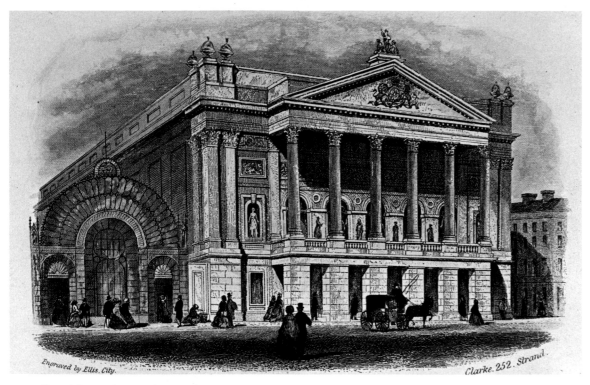

109. Royal Opera House, Covent Garden, London. Colour engraving. Covent Garden Opera House Archives, London.
The first complete performance of Wagner's *The Ring of the Nibelung* in London was conducted in this theatre by Mahler, who was giving guest performances with a German company.

110. Sir Augustus Harris. Coloured drawing by Spy. Covent Garden Opera House Archives, London.
The successful English impresario (1852–96) was Director of Covent Garden from 1888.

111. George Bernard Shaw. Watercolour by Bernard Partridge, 1894. Copyright *Punch* magazine. National Portrait Gallery, London.
When Mahler conducted in London, Shaw (1856–1950) was music critic of the weekly paper *The World,* and wrote a review of the guest performances by the German company.

112. Hamburg conductors. *Mitglieder des Hamburger und Altonaer Stadt-Theaters, Saison 1892–1893*, Hamburg 1893.
ÖNB-BA.
United on one page: choirmaster William Sichel, conductor Theodor Hentschel, and conductor Gustav Mahler.

113. Ernestine Heink-Rössler. *Mitglieder des Hamburger und Altonaer Stadt-Theaters, Saison 1892–1893*, Hamburg 1893. ÖNB-BA.
This contralto (1861–1936), later known by the name of Schumann-Heink, was a member of the Hamburg company. She sang Mahler's songs 'more beautifully than anyone else', wrote Anna Bahr-Mildenburg in 1915.

114. Max Alvary. *Mitglieder des Hamburger und Altonaer Stadt-Theaters, Saison 1892–1893*, Hamburg 1893. ÖNB-BA. Alvary (1856–98) was the celebrated heroic tenor of the Hamburg theatre. His 'sometimes positively grotesque manner of singing' (Bruno Walter) offended Mahler's ears, but his artistic conscientiousness made up for it.

115.   Programme of a concert on Good Friday, 31 March
1893. Theatersammlung der Universität Hamburg.

Since neither operatic nor theatrical performances were
permitted on Good Friday, concerts were performed
instead. This offered Mahler, who had had hardly any
opportunities of conducting concerts, the chance to
support the works of Anton Bruckner. Already in 1892 he
had performed Bruckner's *Te Deum*. In 1893 he repeated
this work and preceded it with the first concert performance of Bruckner's *Mass in D minor*.

116, 117.   Gustav Mahler. Photographs, 1892. ÖNB-BA.

118. Hans von Bülow. Oil painting by Franz von Lenbach. Bayerische Staatsoper, Munich.
Ever since his Kassel period, Mahler had revered the great conductor Hans von Bülow (1830–94). Bülow, who dominated Hamburg's concert life, thought highly of Mahler as an opera conductor and sent him a laurel wreath with the dedication 'To the Pygmalion of the Hamburg Opera'. He could not, however, bring himself to like Mahler's compositions.

119. Hans von Bülow as a pianist. Silhouette by Hans Schliessmann. *Wiener Schattenbilder*, Vienna, n.d.

120. Natalie Bauer-Lechner. Photograph. Property of Arthur Spiegler, Vienna.

Natalie Bauer-Lechner (1858–1921) had known Mahler since their days together at the Conservatoire. She played the viola in the Soldat-Roeger String Quartet. Her friendship with Mahler, particularly close during the 1890s, found expression in diary-like notes which, after her death, were published in edited form under the title *Erinnerungen an Gustav Mahler*, Leipzig 1923.

121. Inn at Steinbach am Attersee. Photograph. Samuel Schweizer Collection, Alchenflüh, Switzerland.

Here, in the Salzkammergut in Austria, Mahler spent the summer holidays of the years 1893 to 1896 with his brothers and sisters. Natalie Bauer-Lechner's notes report on his composing activities during this holiday period.

122. Mahler's summerhouse, Steinbach am Attersee. Photograph, ÖNB-BA.

Mahler had this summerhouse built to work in in 1894. It was there that he worked on his Second and Third Symphonies.

Titan

von

Jean Paul.

Erster Band.

Berlin, 1800.
In der Buchhandlung des Commerzien-Raths Matzdorff.

Blumen-
Frucht- und Dornenstücke;

oder

Ehestand, Tod und Hochzeit

des

Armenadvokaten

F. St. Siebenkäs

von

Jean Paul.

Erstes Bändchen.
Zweite, verbesserte und vermehrte Auflage.

Berlin,
in der Realschulbuchhandlung.
1818.

123. *Titan.* Novel by Jean Paul. Title-page of the first edition, Berlin 1800.
The novels of Jean Paul (1763–1825) were among Mahler's favourite reading matter. In 1893 Mahler gave his First Symphony the title of *Titan*, but later rejected this. The name of *Blumine* for the second (afterwards eliminated) movement also comes from Jean Paul's vocabulary.

124. *Blumen-, Frucht- und Dornenstücke* ('Flower, Fruit and Thorn Pieces'). Novel by Jean Paul. Title-page of the second edition, Berlin 1818.
During the revision of his First Symphony in 1893, Mahler gave to the first three movements the collective title of *Aus den Tagen der Jugend* ['From The Days of Youth'], *Blumen-, Frucht- und Dornenstücke.*

125. The Ludwig Concert Hall, Hamburg. *Hamburg und seine Bauten,* Hamburg 1890, 671.
Here, on 27 October 1893, Mahler conducted the revised version of his First Symphony. Klementine Schuch-Proska and Paul Bulss sang some of the *Wunderhorn* songs. The picture shows the tables set up for concerts with popular programmes, at which audiences could drink beer and smoke.

126.   Berta Foerster-Lauterer and Joseph Bohuslav Foerster.
Photograph. Narodní Muzeum, Prague.
The couple belonged to the circle of Mahler's Hamburg
friends. J. B. Foerster (1859–1951), composer and music critic,
published his memories of Mahler in many newspaper
articles as well as in his own memoirs, *Der Pilger* ('The
Pilgrim'), Prague 1955.

127.   Programme of the Hamburg première of Smetana's
opera *The Bartered Bride*. Theatersammlung der Universität
Hamburg.

128.   Berta Foerster-Lauterer as Marie (Mařenka). Photograph. ÖNB–BA.
The Prague-born soprano (1869–1936) came to Hamburg in
1893 where, under Mahler's direction, she sang the title role
in the opera *The Bartered Bride*. In 1901 she accepted Mahler's
invitation to the Vienna Court Opera.

129. Niederhafen (lower harbour), Hamburg. Photograph G. Koppmann & Co., *c.* 1888. Staatliche Landesbildstelle Hamburg. An enthusiastic walker all his life, Mahler had a predilection for roaming the dock areas of Hamburg.

130. Schaarmarkt, Hohler Weg and Church of St Michael, Hamburg. Photograph G. Koppmann & Co., Staatliche Landesbildstelle Hamburg.
It was at the Church of St Michael that, on 29 March 1894, the memorial service was held for Hans von Bülow who had died in Cairo on 12 February. A boys' choir sang the hymn *Auferstehn wirst du, mein Staub, nach kurzer Ruh* ('Arise, arise, my dust, after your brief repose'), which gave Mahler the inspiration for the finale of his Second Symphony.

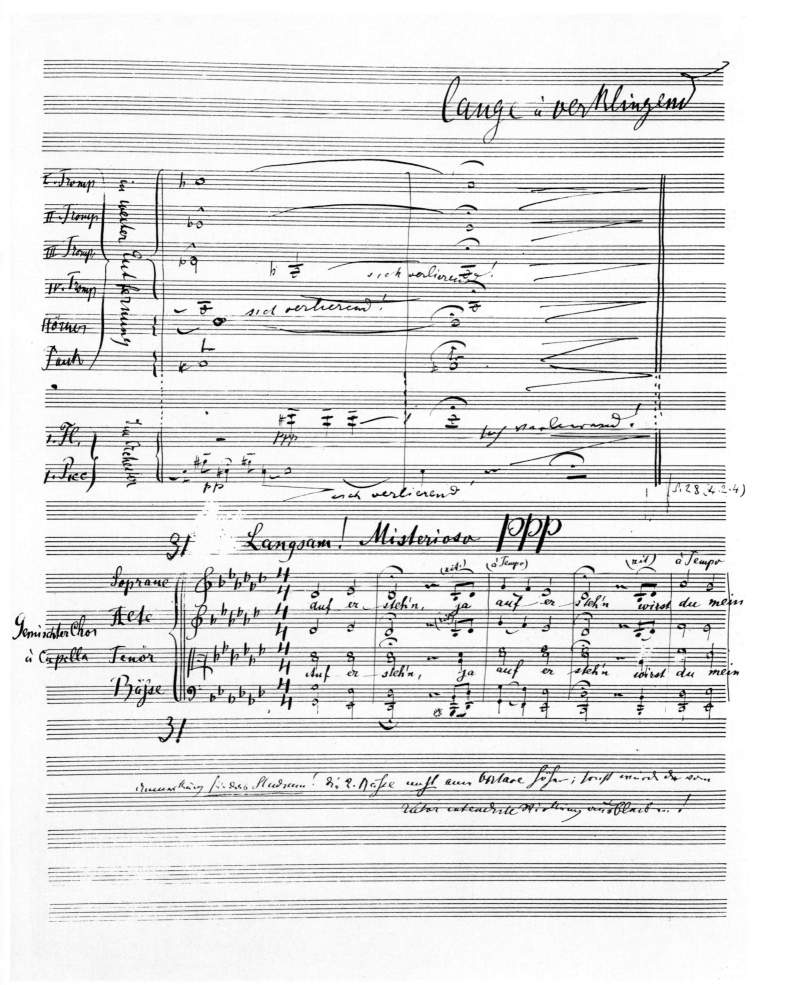

131. A page from the fifth movement of the Second Symphony, from the score in Mahler's own hand. Professor Willem Mengelberg Stichting, Amsterdam.
The page shows the beginning of the chorus *Aufersteh'n, ja aufersteh'n . . .* after a text by Klopstock which Mahler altered and supplemented with lines of his own.

132. Hermann Behn. Photograph. ÖNB-BA.
Among Mahler's patrons during his Hamburg period was
Hermann Behn (1859–1927). A lawyer by profession,
Behn was also a pupil of Anton Bruckner. He made a
two-piano arrangement of Mahler's Second Symphony
and had it printed at his own expense.

133. Justine and Emma Mahler. Photograph. ÖNB-BA.
After the death of his parents, Mahler took care of his
brothers and sisters. In 1894 he arranged for Justine
(1868–1938) and Emma (1875–1933) to come from
Vienna to Hamburg. In 1898 Emma married the cellist
Eduard Rosé, and in 1902 Justine married his brother, the
famous violinist Arnold Rosé.

134. Felix von Weingartner. Photograph. ÖNB-BA.
The performance of his Second Symphony in Berlin in
1895 earned Mahler the good-will of the conductor and
composer Felix von Weingartner (1863–1942). Weingartner conducted performances of movements from Mahler's
Third Symphony on 7 December 1896 in Hamburg, and
on 9 March 1897 in Berlin, in addition to supporting
Mahler in his lectures.

Mama bebe trugen fieber by Cost
in erfahren Murth um so angestellt.
Ich bin ganz ausgenstalt daruber,
weil ich bis geto dem Machal in der
Methode furt, dem übel zu steuern
das Titel der Schymd.

I -   ? [...] Sommer marschelustre

II Was mir die Blumen auf d. Wiese
                        erzählen.

III Was mir die Thiere im Walde erz.

IV Was mir die Nacht erzählt (der Mensch)

V Was mir die Morgenglocken erz. (die Engel)

VI Was mir die Liebe erzählt
Motto: Vater, sieh an die Wunden mein!
       Kein Wesen lass verloren sein!

VII Was mir das Kind erzählt
grüsse Herrn Schlesinger oder einer
angeht nicht den Wolff
            Schlussb. dem

                    Gustav

II. Sept. 95
Am heutigen Sedantag, der erst
geschossen, getrillt, gesoffen, geknallt
u. geraucht wird.

135. A letter from Mahler to Natalie Bauer-Lechner
dated 2 September 1895. Original, WSTB.
This letter contains the proposed titles for the original
seven movements of the Third Symphony. Mahler
changed these titles several times and finally omitted them
altogether.

136. Anna von Mildenburg as Brünnhilde in Wagner's
The Valkyrie. Photograph. ÖNB-BA.
At the start of the 1895–96 season, Anna von Mildenburg
began her engagement in Hamburg. She made her debut
on 11 September 1895, singing the role of Brünnhilde in
which Mahler had coached her. The young singer, for
whom Mahler soon conceived a violent passion, came to
be an interpreter of musical drama wholly commensurate
with his conceptions of the theatre.

137. Berlin Station, Hamburg. Photograph by G. Koppmann & Co., *c.* 1888. Staatliche Landesbildstelle Hamburg.
On several occasions Mahler travelled to Berlin from this station. On 4 March 1895, he conducted parts of his Second Symphony in Berlin; on 13 December 1895 the Second Symphony; and on 16 March 1896, among other works, the First Symphony.

138. Friedrichstrasse, Berlin. Contemporary photograph. L. L. Roger-Viollet, Paris.

139. The spa Bad Ischl, view from the Stephanieplatz. Indian ink drawing by Emil Jakob Schindler, 1886. ÖNB-BA.
During his holidays, Mahler made several trips from Steinbach am Attersee to Bad Ischl in order to visit Brahms. This
drawing is by one of the most important Austrian landscape painters. Schindler (1842–92) was the father of Alma
Maria Schindler, who became Mahler's wife in 1902.

141. Gustav Mahler. Photograph, 1896.
ÖNB-BA.
This picture was taken in Hamburg.

140. Johannes Brahms. Photograph. GDM.
The picture bears the note *Letzte Aufnahme* ('last photo'), as well as the
date of 15 June 1896. Shortly afterwards Mahler went to Ischl. 'This
time Brahms was particularly cordial,' he wrote to Anna von
Mildenburg.

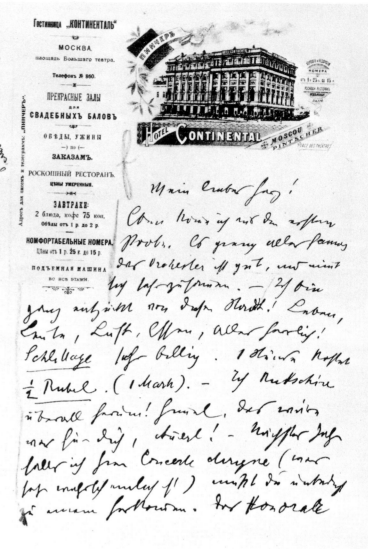

142.   A letter from Mahler to Anna von Mildenburg. From
Moscow, undated. ÖNB-TS.
On 15 March 1897, Mahler conducted a concert of the
Moscow Philharmonic Society. From Moscow he wrote
almost daily to Anna von Mildenburg. This undated letter
was written on the day of the first rehearsal. In it Mahler
writes, among other things: 'Everything went splendidly, the
orchestra is good, and on their toes. – I am enchanted by this
city! Its life, people, air, food, everything is grand!'

143.   Rudolf Kržyžanowski. Detail of a group portrait of the
Hamburg Municipal Theatre, 1897–98. ÖNB-BA.
Mahler and Kržyžanowski were fellow students at the
Vienna Conservatoire, and good friends. Later Mahler tried
to get him engagements as a conductor. Kržyžanowski came
to Hamburg in the autumn of 1896, without Mahler's
assistance. The Theatre Director, Pollini, actually managed
to play the two former friends off against each other.

144. Rosa Papier, photograph. ÖNB-BA.
Rosa Papier (1858–1932), who had been a celebrated young contralto, worked as a singing
teacher after she lost her voice. Together with
Wlassack she helped to bring Mahler to Vienna.

146. The funeral of Johannes Brahms. Photograph. ÖNB-BA.
Brahms, who for years had endeavoured to win
good-will for Mahler among Vienna's musical
circles, died on 3 April 1897, a few days prior to the
signing of Mahler's contract as Conductor of the
Court Opera. The picture shows the cortège after it
had left the house in the Karlsgasse where Brahms
died. In the background is the building of the
Society of the Friends of Music.

145. Eduard Wlassack with his family in a box at the Vienna Court Opera House.
Photograph. ÖNB-BA.
As Administrative Director of the General Management, *Hofrat* Wlassack (1841–
1905) exercised a powerful influence on personnel policies at the Court Opera.

147. Opening of the first exhibition of the Viennese artists' society, Wiener Secession. Pencil drawing by Rudolf Bacher. Historisches Museum der Stadt Wien.
Founded in 1897, the Secession later assumed great significance for Mahler's work. The drawing, made in 1898, shows, from left to right: the Emperor's adjutant, Emperor Franz Joseph, Gustav Klimt (president), Rudolf von Alt (honorary president), Josef Engelhart, Otto Friedrich, Carl Moll, Adolf Hölzel, Hans Tichy, Koloman Moser, Joseph Maria Olbrich, Rudolf Jettmar.

148. The Court Opera House in Vienna. Photograph. ÖNB-BA.
The picture shows the horse-tram on the Ringstrasse. Electric trams were gradually introduced in Vienna a year after Mahler took up his post.

Dinstag den 11. Mai 1897.

119. Vorstellung im Jahres-Abonnement.

Lohengrin.

Romantische Oper in 3 Akten von Richard Wagner.

Heinrich der Vogler, deutscher König	Hr. Grengg.
Lohengrin	Hr. Winkelmann.
Elsa von Brabant	Fr. Ehrenstein.
Herzog Gottfried, ihr Bruder	Frl. Berger.
Friedrich von Telramund, brabantischer Graf	Hr. Reichmann.
Ortrud, seine Gemalin	Fr. Kaulich.
Der Heerrufer des Königs	Hr. Felix.
	Hr. Schmitt.
Vier brabantische Eble	Hr. Schittenhelm.
	Hr. Frei.
	Hr. Marian.

Sächsische und thüringische Grafen und Eble.
Brabantische Grafen und Eble, Edelfrauen, Edelknaben.
Mannen, Frauen, Knechte.

Ort der Handlung: Antwerpen. — Zeit: Die erste Hälfte des zehnten Jahrhunderts.

Die neue Dekoration im 2. Akt von Anton Brioschi jun., k. k. Hoftheatermaler.

Kostüme nach Zeichnungen von Fr. Gaul.

Kassa-Eröffnung gegen halb 7 Uhr. Anfang 7 Uhr. Ende gegen halb 11 Uhr.

Mittwoch den 12. Die Jüdin.	Samstag den 15. Hans Heiling.
Donnerstag den 13. Das Heimchen am Herd.	Sonntag den 16. Die Afrikanerin.
Freitag den 14. Die lustigen Weiber von Windsor.	

Falls eine angekündigte Vorstellung abgeändert werden sollte, kann von den für dieselbe gelösten Karten auch zur Ersatz-vorstellung Gebrauch gemacht, oder der dafür entrichtete Betrag, jedoch spätestens am Tage der Vorstellung bis halb 7 Uhr Abends (resp. eine halbe Stunde vor dem für Beginn der Vorstellung angesetzten Zeitpunkt) bei sonstigem Verlust des Anspruches an der Kassa zurückverlangt werden.

Preise der Plätze:

Eine Loge Parterre oder I. Galerie	fl. 25.—	Ein Sitz Parterre 2.—4. Reihe	fl. 3.—
Eine Loge II. Galerie	fl. 15.—	Ein Sitz III. Galerie 1. Reihe	fl. 2.75
Eine Loge III. Galerie	fl. 10.—	Ein Sitz III. Galerie 2. Reihe	fl. 2.25
Ein Logensitz Parterre oder I. Galerie	fl. 6.—	Ein Sitz III. Galerie 3.—4. Reihe	fl. 1.25
Ein Logensitz II. Galerie	fl. 4.—	Ein Sitz IV. Galerie 1. Reihe, Mitte	fl. 2.—
Ein Logensitz III. Galerie	fl. 3.—	Ein Sitz IV. Galerie 1. Reihe, Seite	fl. 1.50
Ein Sitz Parquet 4. Reihe	fl. 6.—	Ein Sitz IV. Galerie 2. und 3. Reihe	fl. 1.50
Ein Sitz Parquet 2.—5. Reihe	fl. 4.50	Ein Sitz IV. Galerie 4.—6. Reihe	fl. 1.25
Ein Sitz Parquet 6.—9. Reihe	fl. 4.—	Eintritt in das Parterre (nur Herren gestattet)	fl. 1.—
Ein Sitz Parquet 10.—13. Reihe	fl. 3.50	Eintritt in die III. Galerie	fl. —.80
Ein Sitz Parterre 1. Reihe	fl. 3.50	Eintritt in die IV. Galerie	fl. —.60

Zu jeder im Repertoire angekündigten Vorstellung erfolgt Tags vorher bis 1 Uhr Nach-mittags die Ausgabe der Stammsitze; um 2 Uhr Nachmittags (Tags vorher) beginnt der allgemeine Verkauf von Logen und Sitzen.

149. Programme of the Court Opera House, 11 May 1897. ÖNB-BA.
During this repertory performance Mahler stood on the conductor's podium of the Court Opera for the first time.

150. Wilhelm Jahn. Silhouette by Hans Schliessmann. *Wiener Schattenbilder*, Vienna, n.d.
Jahn was director of the Court Opera from 1881 to 1897.

151. Hans Richter. Silhouette by Hans Schliessmann. *Wiener Schattenbilder*, Vienna, n.d.
Richter was principal conductor at the Court Opera House from 1875.

152. Gustav Mahler. Silhouette by Hans Schliessmann. ÖNB-BA.
Following Mahler's first appearance in Vienna, the critic Ludwig Speidel wrote in the *Fremdenblatt*: 'He belongs to the school of younger conductors who, in contrast to the rigid conducting style of older conductors, have evolved a more lively technique of expressing themselves. These younger men speak with their arms and hands, with turns of their whole body, if necessary . . .'.

153. Hugo Wolf. Etching by William Unger, Kupferstichkabinett, Akademie der bildenden Künste, Vienna.
Hugo Wolf (1860–1903) and Mahler were friends during their period at the Conservatoire. In spite of their later estrangement, Wolf was convinced that his opera *Der Corregidor* would be performed by Mahler at the Court Opera House. In the early autumn of 1897 he lapsed into a state of mental derangement; a quarrel with Mahler was said to have triggered this off.

Operndirigent Mahler.

154. Record of Mahler's appointment as Opera Director. HHSTA. The document, signed by the Emperor at the bottom left, contains the passage: '. . . I authorize the appointment of the Conductor Gustav Mahler as Artistic Director of the Court Opera House, according to the arrangements proposed. Mürzsteg, 8 October 1897.'

155. Gustav Mahler, opera conductor. Caricature by Theo Zasche. ÖNB-BA.
Wilhelm Jahn, the departing Director of the Court Opera House, is lying on the floor, holding in his hand the notice of his retirement. Mahler is perched on his stomach, receiving the incense of the press.

156. The Rosé Quartet. *Das Streichquartett in Wort und Bild,* ed. A. Ehrlich, Vienna 1898, 19.
From left to right: Arnold Rosé (first violin), August Siebert (second violin), Hugo von Steiner (viola), Reinhold Hummer (violoncello). From 1881 Rosé (1863–1946) was leader of the Court Opera Orchestra, while for decades, and despite several changes in membership, he led the string quartet named after him. From 1897 he and Mahler were intimate friends: he was later to become Mahler's brother-in-law. It was Siebert who in Iglau in September 1876 had publicly performed Mahler's violin sonata (now lost), accompanied by the young composer.

FAÇADE GEGEN DIE S.T VEITHKIRCHE.

OTTO WAGNER
ARCHITECT, K.K. BAURAT

157. The apartment house belonging to Herr Otto Wagner, in the District III, Rennweg 5 (= Auenbruggergasse 2). Drawing of the elevation by Otto Wagner. Plan- und Schriftenkammer der Stadt Wien.

During the years 1890–91 Otto Wagner, Vienna's leading architect, built a house whose entrance was opposite the Church of St Vitus in what was later to be called the Auenbruggergasse. It was one of the most modern and comfortable houses of the period. Early in 1898 Mahler rented a flat in this house where he lived, first with his sisters, and later with his wife. The police record registering this address as Mahler's is dated 19 February 1898; he is recorded as leaving on 7 October 1909.

158. *Lieder eines fahrenden Gesellen.* Title-page of the first edition. ÖNB-MS.

Towards the end of 1897, the publishing firm of Weinberger (Leipzig and Vienna) published this song cycle which Mahler had begun in Kassel in 1884 and revised later.

159. Gustav Mahler. Photograph, *c.* 1898. ÖNB-BA.

162. Siegfried Lipiner. Photograph. IGMG, Vienna.
As a result of early recognition by Richard Wagner and
Friedrich Nietzsche, the writer Siegfried Lipiner (1856–1911)
gained strong influence over Vienna's academic youth.
Contact with Lipiner and his philosophical writings formed
Mahler's thinking. From 1881 Lipiner was librarian of the
Austrian Parliament; among his writings was the libretto
for Carl Goldmark's opera *Merlin*.

160. Gustav Mahler with his sister Justine. Photograph, 1899. ÖNB-BA.

161. Gustav Mahler. Photograph, *c.* 1898. ÖNB-BA.

163. Curtain for Tragic Opera at the Vienna Court Opera House. Oil painting after Carl Rahl. ÖNB-TS.
The curtain, whose centrepiece depicts a scene from the Orpheus legend, was used for all serious operas. Like the curtain for comic opera, it was destroyed by fire in 1945.

164. Gustav Mahler. Silhouettes by Otto Böhler. ÖNB-BA.
Böhler's pictures illustrate Mahler's lively gestures when conducting; these grew more restrained in later years. The sheet of silhouettes was sold by the bookseller R. Lechner, who also offered postcards depicting three silhouettes each.

Opposite page:

165. Stage design for the opera *Eugene Onegin*: a ballroom. Design by Anton Brioschi. ÖNB–BA.
Mahler had already rehearsed and conducted this opera in Hamburg in the presence of the composer, Tchaikowsky. He presented it for the first time in Vienna on 19 November 1897.

166. Stage design for the opera *Dalibor*: a prison yard. Design by Anton Brioschi. ÖNB–BA.
Smetana's was the first new opera which Mahler put on in Vienna. The première took place on 4 October 1897.

176. Marie Gutheil-Schoder as Frau Flut. Photograph.
ÖNB-BA.
This singer, who was also a talented actress, came to Vienna
in 1900 and became one of the main supporters of Mahler's
style of music drama. The picture shows her in one of her star
parts, in Nicolai's opera *The Merry Wives of Windsor*.

175. Selma Kurz. Oil painting by John Quincy Adams.
Staatsoper, Vienna.
In the spring of 1899 Mahler discovered the young singer
Selma Kurz (1874–1933) in Frankfurt and engaged her for
Vienna. A famous coloratura soprano in later years, she sang
songs by Mahler at the Philharmonic Concert on 14 January
1900.

177. Anna von Mildenburg. Coloured charcoal drawing.
Unsigned, undated. ÖNB-BA.
After her work in Hamburg, Anna von Mildenburg joined the
company of the Vienna Court Opera in 1898, where she made
a significant contribution towards the realization of Mahler's
musical and stage ideas.

178. Laura Hilgermann as Carmen. Photograph.
ÖNB-BA.
This singer, who had already worked with Mahler in
Prague and Budapest, was engaged for Vienna in 1900.

179. Leo Slezak. Photograph. ÖNB-BA.
Slezak (1873–1946), who was one of the most popular
tenors of his time, was engaged for Vienna in 1901. In
his book *Meine sämtlichen Werke*, Berlin 1922, he good-
humouredly described his relationship with Mahler.

180. Hans Richter. Oil painting by Friedrich Georg
Papperitz. Richard-Wagner-Gedenkstätte, Bayreuth.
The portrait shows Richter (1843–1916) wearing the
cap and gown of an honorary doctorate at the University of Oxford. The great Wagner conductor bade farewell to Vienna in February 1900. Many people blamed
Mahler for his departure.

181. Alois Przistaupinsky. Photograph. ÖNB-BA.
Mahler's indefatigable secretary and assistant.

182. Colonel Picquart. Engraving by Ferrand Desmoulin, c. 1901. Bibliothèque Nationale, Paris.
Georges Picquart (1854–1914) formed the centre of a group of Mahler's French friends. The world had come to know his name through his creditable behaviour in the Dreyfus affair.

183. Paul Clemenceau. Drawing by Gertrud Zuckerkandl-Stekel, Paris. Owned by the artist.
Paul Clemenceau, brother of the statesman Georges Clemenceau, was a member of Picquart's circle. He was related by marriage to the Viennese art critic Berta Zuckerkandl. The drawing was made by Paul Clemenceau's niece.

184. Programme of a concert at the Trocadéro, Paris, on 21 June 1900. During the Paris World Exhibition the Vienna Philharmonic Orchestra gave a series of concerts under Mahler's baton. The first concert took place in the Théâtre du Châtelet; two further concerts were given at the Trocadéro, about whose faulty acoustics Mahler complained in an interview.

Salle des Fêtes du Trocadéro

JEUDI 21 JUIN 1900, à 2 h. 3/4

SOUS LE HAUT PATRONAGE DE

Madame la Princesse de METTERNICH SÁNDOR

3me Concert Philharmonique

DONNÉ PAR LA

Société Philharmonique
DE VIENNE

(WIENER PHILHARMONIKER)

Dont tous les Artistes sont Membres de l'Opéra
I. et R. de la Cour

SOUS LA DIRECTION DE

M. Gustav MAHLER

Directeur de l'Opéra I. et R. de la Cour

185.   Paris World Exhibition, 1900. Champ de Mars, with Eiffel Tower and Trocadéro in the background. Photograph. N. D. Roger-Viollet, Paris.

186.   Concert hall at the Trocadéro. Photograph. L. L. Roger-Viollet, Paris.

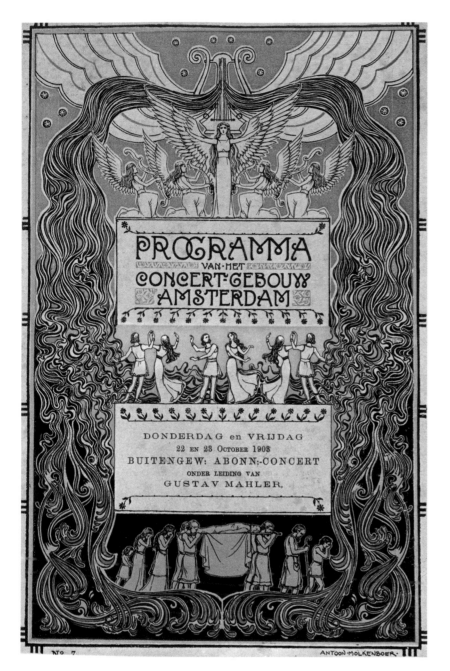

187. Cover of concert programme, Concertgebouw, Amsterdam, 22 and 23 October 1903. IGMG, Vienna.
In Holland, where Mahler first appeared as an interpreter of his own work in 1903, he immediately felt himself to be understood. The devoted advocacy of the conductor Willem Mengelberg, and the musical comprehension shown by audiences and performers alike, created for him the 'musical homeland' that he had elsewhere sought in vain.

188. First Symphony. Title-page of the printed edition. ÖNB-MS.
It was more than ten years after its composition that the First Symphony appeared in print. The title-page of the edition bears the note: 'with the support of the Society for the Advancement of German Science, Art and Literature in Bohemia'.

189. Concert programme of 17 February 1901. Archiv der Wiener Philharmoniker, Vienna.
The first performance of *Das klagende Lied* took place more than twenty years after its composition, at a non-subscription concert of the Vienna Choral Society under Mahler's direction.

190, 191. Stage designs for the opera *The Tales of Hoffmann*: Tavern and Great Hall (Giulietta scene). Designs by Anton Brioschi. ÖNB–BA.

In November 1901 Mahler produced Offenbach's opera, which had never before been performed at the Vienna Court Opera. Within a few days there were three first nights with the parts taken by different singers on each night.

192. Villa Mahler, Maiernigg. Photograph.
Ida Wagner Collection, Vienna.
Mahler bought a piece of land at Maiernigg on
the Wörthersee and built a country house there,
as well as a summerhouse to compose in. From
1900 to 1907 he spent his summer holidays there,
working on his Fourth, Fifth, Sixth, Seventh and
Eighth Symphonies.

193. Fourth Symphony. Page 157 of the autograph. GDM.
During the summers of 1899 and 1900 Mahler
was composing his Fourth Symphony, the score
of which was worked out in detail in the winter of
1900–01. The second movement is dated 9
January 1901. In the fourth movement Mahler
used the *Wunderhorn* song *Das himmlische Leben*
('Heavenly Life') which he had composed in
1892.

194. 'A hyper-modern conductor'. Mahler caricature by Hans Schliessmann. *Fliegende Blätter*, March 1901.
In these action studies Mahler is called 'Conductor Kappelmann'. The caricature was published at a time when Mahler was about to retire from the Philharmonic Concerts.

195. Franz Schalk. Silhouette by Hans Schliessmann, 1900. ÖNB-BA.
Franz Schalk (1863–1931) was made principal conductor at the Vienna Court Opera after Hans Richter's departure.

196. Bruno Walter. Caricature by Hans Böhler. ÖNB-BA.
Bruno Walter (1876–1962), whom Mahler knew from Hamburg, made his début at the Vienna Court Opera in the autumn of 1901.

197. Mahler on the conductor's podium. Silhouette, unsigned. ÖNB-BA.

199. Alfred Roller. Oil painting by Walter Hempel. Historisches Museum der Stadt Wien.
It was in the circles of the Vienna Secession that Mahler met the painter and graphic artist Alfred Roller (1864–1935), who introduced him to his ideas for revitalizing the stage. Mahler commissioned Roller to design a production of Wagner's *Tristan and Isolde*, and procured his appointment as director of set and costume design at the Opera House.

198. Anna von Mildenburg as Isolde. Oil painting by Franz Matsch. ÖNB-TS.
The Art Nouveau style which, in Vienna, was known as Secession, penetrated every sphere of life. Through Mahler's connection with Alfred Roller the style also invaded the stage of the Court Opera House. The painting depicts Anna von Mildenburg in a costume designed by Alfred Roller.

200. Carl Moll in his studio. Self-portrait, oil, *c.* 1905. Gemäldegalerie der Akademie der Bildenden Künste, Vienna. The painter Carl Moll (1861–1945), pupil of Emil Jakob Schindler and stepfather of Alma Schindler, who later became Mahler's wife, was a founder member of the Vienna Secession. 'It reminds one of a Schubert song,' was how Hermann Bahr characterized his style of painting. Moll owed his standing not only to his landscapes, townscapes and interiors, but also to his organizational achievements in the service of galleries and private collectors. His bond with Mahler was one of affectionate friendship.

201. Anna Moll. Oil painting by Carl Moll. Historisches Museum der Stadt Wien.

In this picture Moll set down the features of his wife Anna, mother of Alma Schindler. Anna Moll came from Hamburg, studied singing in Vienna, married the painter Emil Jakob Schindler in 1878, and, after his death, Carl Moll. Mahler loved and revered his mother-in-law: '. . . stay what you are to me now, a friend and mother (since that's the way fate curiously seems to want it)', he wrote to her (GMB, 400).

202. Berta Zuckerkandl and Sophie Clemenceau. Photograph. Owned by Dr Frédéric Zuckerkandl, Paris.
Mahler had met Sophie Clemenceau at the Paris World Exhibition in 1900. Sophie's sister Berta, who lived in Vienna and was married to the anatomist Emil Zuckerkandl, invited Mahler to her salon when Sophie came to Vienna on a visit.

203. Alma Schindler-Mahler. Photograph. Ida Wagner Collection, Vienna.
At Berta Zuckerkandl's house Mahler met Alma Maria Schindler (1879–1964) for the first time. She immediately aroused his interest.

204. The Hohe Warte in winter. Woodcut by Carl Moll. Historisches Museum der Stadt Wien.
During a walk on the Hohe Warte, 'through the crunching snow' (AM, 29), Gustav Mahler and Alma Schindler became engaged. Shortly before, Alma had moved into the villa on the Hohe Warte which the architect Josef Hoffmann had built for Carl Moll.

205. Gustav Mahler. Mezzotint engraving by Emil Orlik. ÖNB-BA.
Orlik (1870–1932), a painter and graphic artist born in Prague who was a member of the Vienna Secession, painted several portraits of Mahler. The mezzotint was done in 1902.

206. Gustav Mahler. Charcoal drawing by Emil Orlik, 6 March 1902. *95 köpfe von Orlik*, Berlin 1920. ÖNB–BA.

207. Mahler 1903. Sketches by Emil Orlik. *Mahler-Dopisy*, Prague 1962.

208. Marriage register of the Parish of St Charles Borromeo (Karlskirche), Vienna. ÖNB-BA.
Gustav Mahler and Alma Schindler were married on 9 March 1902. The marriage register records the date as 9 February, but this is obviously an error.

209. The Assembly Hall of the Nobility, St Petersburg (now the Hall of the Leningrad Philharmonic). Photograph. Leningrad Philharmonic.
Shortly after their wedding Mahler and his wife travelled to Petersburg, where Mahler conducted three concerts in this auditorium.

210. View of the Church of St Isaac, St Petersburg. Lithograph by Louis Philippe Bichebois and Victor Adam. Photo Harlingue-Viollet, Paris.
St Petersburg in the winter, and the bustling activity on the frozen Neva, made a deep impression on Mahler.

211. Members of the Vienna Secession preparing for their 14th exhibition. Photograph, April 1902. ÖNB-BA.
During this exhibition, whose focal point was a statue of Beethoven by Max Klinger, Mahler conducted the chorus from Beethoven's Ninth Symphony, 'Ihr stürzt nieder, Millionen?' 'Do you bow down, all ye millions?' set for wind instruments. In the picture, from left to right: Anton Stark, Gustav Klimt (in the armchair), Kolo Moser (in front of Klimt, wearing a hat), Adolf Böhm, Maximilian Lenz (reclining), Ernst Stöhr (with hat), Wilhelm List, Emil Orlik (sitting), Maximilian Kurzweil (with cap), Leopold Stolba, Carl Moll (reclining), Rudolf Bacher.

212. The building of the Vienna Secession. Photograph. ÖNB-BA.
Designed by Joseph Maria Olbrich, the exhibition building was opened in 1898. The Secession formed the centre of Austrian Art Nouveau until the walk-out of the group associated with Gustav Klimt in 1905.

214.   Title-page of the printed edition of the Third Symphony. ÖNB-MS.
The score was published in 1902.

213.   *Sehnsucht nach dem Glück* ('Longing for Happiness'). A section from the Beethoven frieze by Gustav Klimt. Österreichische Galerie, Vienna.
Among the most important works of art in the Secession's exhibition in April 1902 was the 24-metre-long Beethoven frieze. The figure of the knight, whose features recall Mahler, also appeared as Klimt's contribution to the volume of tributes to Mahler which Paul Stefan published in 1910 (PST 2).

215.   Programme of the first performance of the Third Symphony. IGMG, Vienna.
The symphony, only individual movements of which had been performed previously, was given complete for the first time at the fourth concert of the German Composers' Congress.

Tonkünstler-Versammlung zu Krefeld.

IV. Konzert
Montag, den 9. Juni, Abends 8 Uhr,
in der Stadthalle.

Programm:

Symphonie No. 3
in 2 Abtheilungen
für grosses Orchester, Alt-Solo, Frauen- und Knabenchor
von

Gustav Mahler.

Unter Leitung des Komponisten.

I. Abtheilung.
No. 1.   Einleitung und I. Satz.

II. Abtheilung.
No. 2.   Tempo di Menuetto.
No. 3.   Rondo.
No. 4.   Altsolo.
attacca   No. 5.   Frauen- und Knabenchor mit Alt-Solo.
attacca   No. 6.   Adagio.

Nach der I. Abtheilung findet eine Pause statt.

Alt-Solo: Frau L. Geller-Wolter.

216. Programme of the Court Opera House, 21 February 1903. ÖNB-BA.
With this première a new era began for the Vienna Opera. Roller's ideas for décor and lighting were met in some quarters with enthusiasm, in others with hostility.

217. Richard Mayr as King Mark. Photograph. ÖNB-BA.
Engaged by Mahler to come to Vienna in 1902, the bass singer Richard Mayr (1877–1935) appeared in the new production of *Tristan and Isolde*.

218. Erik Schmedes as Tristan. Bust by Gustav Herrmann. Dagmar Schmedes Collection, Vienna.
Called to the Vienna Opera in 1898, the tenor Erik Schmedes (1868–1931) developed, under Mahler's guidance, into an outstanding interpreter of Wagnerian heroic roles.

220. Gustav and Alma Mahler. Photograph. Archiv der Wiener Philharmoniker, Vienna.
Alfred Roller dated a very similar picture as having been taken at Basle in 1903. Presumably this photo was taken at the same time, when Mahler conducted his Second Symphony at Basle Cathedral.

219. Alma Mahler and daughter. Photograph. Ida Wagner Collection, Vienna.
The picture, presumably taken in Maiernigg in the summer of 1903, shows Alma Mahler with her first-born daughter Maria Anna (1902–07).

221. Rack railway up the Kahlenberg. Photograph. Historisches Museum der Stadt Wien.
In August 1903, while the family were still living in Maiernigg, Mahler stayed in the hotel on the Kahlenberg and travelled up there from the Opera every night. 'From the window a breathtakingly beautiful view on to the lights of Vienna', he wrote to his wife (AM, 387).

222. Gustav Mahler. Photograph. önb-ba.
According to Alfred Roller this picture, taken in 1904, shows Mahler on his way home from the Administrative Offices.

223. Gustav Mahler. Photograph. önb-ba.
The photo taken in 1904 shows Mahler, as Roller asserts, 'about to leave the Opera' with a characteristic facial expression 'when he was preoccupied with disagreeable thoughts'.

224. Concertgebouw, Amsterdam. Photograph. Professor Willem Mengelberg Stichting, Amsterdam.
Towards the end of October 1903, Mahler conducted the Concertgebouw Orchestra for the first time.

225. Gustav Mahler. Etching by Fritz Erler.
ÖNB-BA.
The artist Fritz Erler was a friend of Mahler's
friend Arnold Berliner. About the portrait
Mahler wrote in October 1906 to Berliner:
'Have received reproduction from Erler. After
my departure he seems to have made improve-
ments from memory. A pity!' (GMB, 304).

226. Gerhart Hauptmann. Drawing by Emil
Orlik. 95 Köpfe von Orlik, Berlin 1920. ÖNB-BA.
The German dramatist Gerhart Hauptmann
(1862–1946) met Mahler in Vienna and conceived 'a tender love for him which Mahler did
not altogether reciprocate' (AM, 107).

227. Hermann Bahr. Drypoint engraving by
Emil Orlik. Albertina, Vienna.
The Viennese writer Hermann Bahr (1863–
1934) was a doughty admirer of Mahler both as
conductor and composer. In 1909 Bahr married
the singer Anna von Mildenburg.

228. Oskar Fried. Drawing by Emil Orlik.
95 Köpfe von Orlik. Berlin 1920. ÖNB-BA.
A bond of sincere affection linked Mahler to the
German composer and conductor Oskar Fried
(1871–1942). Fried performed Mahler's Second
Symphony in Berlin and St Petersburg.

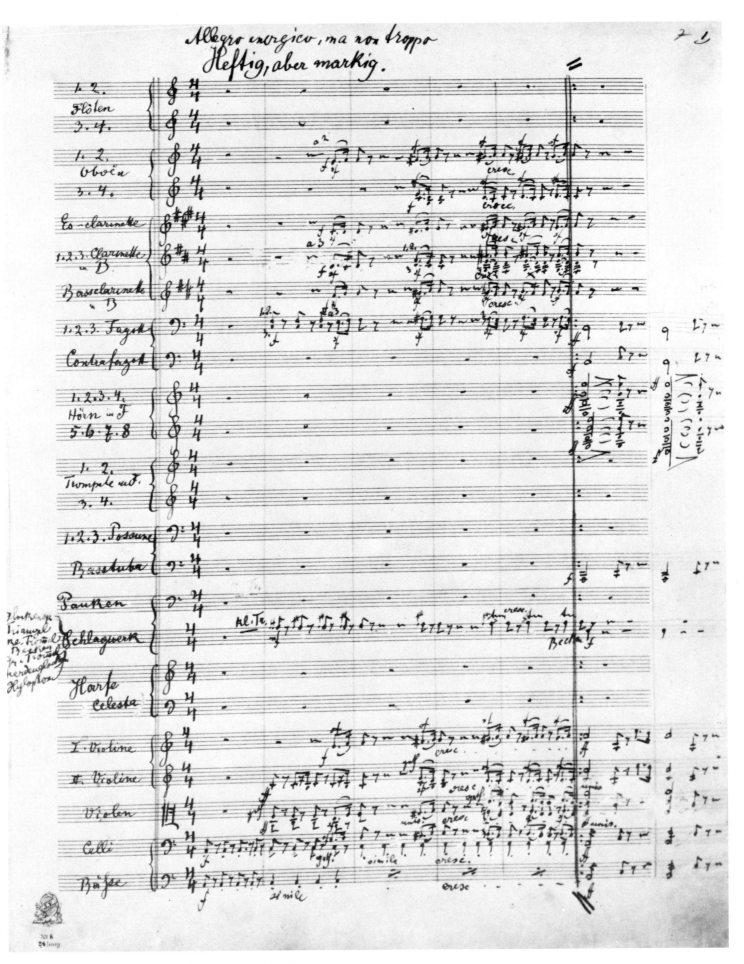

229. Sixth Symphony: first page of Mahler's autograph. GDM.
Mahler composed his Sixth Symphony during the summer holidays of 1903 and 1904, finishing the instrumentation on 1 May 1905 in Vienna. The instrumentation of the percussion (glockenspiel, triangle, snare drum, cymbals, bass drum, cowbells, and xylophone), which was somewhat unusual for those days, brought Mahler much ridicule.

GVSTAV MAHLER

LIEDER

FÜR EINE SINGSTIMME
MIT KLAVIER ODER ORCHESTER

———————— ✳ ————————

	KLAV.-AUSG.	ORCH.-AUSG. PART. STIÑ.	
REVELGE	M 2,—	M 4,50.	M 9,— n.
DER TAMBOURSG'SELL	„ 1,80.	„ 3,— .	„ 3,—.
BLICKE MIR NICHT ○ ○ ○ ○ ○ ○ ○ ○		○ ○ ○ ○	
○ ○ IN DIE LIEDER	„ 1,20.	„ 2,40.	„ 3,—.
ICH ATMET' EINEN ○ ○ ○ ○ ○ ○ ○ ○		○ ○ ○ ○	
○ ○ LINDEN DUFT	„ 1,20.	„ 1,80.	„ 1,80.
ICH BIN DER WELT { F DUR HOCH	„ 1,50.	„ 2,40.	„ 3,—.
ABHANDEN GEKOMMEN { ES DUR MITTEL	„ 1,50.	„ ABSCHRIFT	
UM MITTERNACHT { H MOLL HOCH	„ 1,50.	„ 2,40.	„ 6,—.
{ A MOLL MITTEL	„ 1,50.	„ 2,40.	„ 6,—.

AUFFÜHRUNGSRECHT   AUSGABE MIT
VORBEHALTEN.   KLAVIERBEGLEITUNG.

EIGENTUM DES VERLEGERS FÜR ALLE LÄNDER.
ALLE RECHTE VORBEHALTEN.
C. F. KAHNT NACHFOLGER, LEIPZIG.
COPYRIGHT 1905 BY C.F. KAHNT NACHFOLGER, LEIPZIG.

230. Showroom of the Wiener Werkstätte (Vienna Workshop). Photograph. Österreichisches Museum für angewandte Kunst, Vienna.
In 1903 the painter Kolo Moser and the architect Josef Hoffmann set up the Wiener Werkstätte, which gave new impetus to Viennese arts and crafts. Mahler, whose wife used to wear the special dresses designed by Moser to allow freedom of movement, and also the jewellery designed by Hoffmann, viewed the movement with interest.

231. Songs by Gustav Mahler. Title-page of the printed edition, ÖNB-MS.
Published in 1905, this small volume contained the songs *Revelge* ('Reveille') and *Der Tamboursg'sell* ('The Drummer Boy'), both settings of *Wunderhorn* texts (and composed in 1891 and 1901), as well as four songs set to words by Friedrich Rückert during the summer of 1901. The first edition shows that the typefaces designed under the influence of the Secession style had also begun to influence the printing of music.

232–235. A party in the garden of the Moll villa. Four photographs. ÖNB-BA.
232. Gustav Mahler, Max Reinhardt, Carl Moll, Hans Pfitzner.
233. Max Reinhardt, Gustav Mahler, Carl Moll, Hans Pfitzner and (presumably) Josef Hoffmann.
234. (presumably) Alfred Roller (standing), Alma Mahler (presumably), Carl Moll (in the foreground with his back to the camera), Gustav Klimt, Anna Moll, Max Reinhardt and Josef Hoffmann.
235. Max Reinhardt, Carl Moll, Gustav Mahler (half hidden) and (presumably) Alfred Roller (standing).
It is possible that these photographs were taken in May 1905 when the producer Max Reinhardt (1873–1943) took his Berliner Theater to Vienna for a series of guest performances.

236. Gustav Mahler at Maiernigg. Photograph. Ida Wagner Collection, Vienna.
According to Alfred Roller this photo was taken in the summer of 1905 when Mahler was working on his Seventh Symphony.

237. Gustav Mahler with his daughter Maria Anna. Photograph. Ida Wagner Collection, Vienna.
The picture shows Mahler on the stone terrace of his villa at Maiernigg. In the background is the Wörthersee.

238. Alphons Diepenbrock, Gustav Mahler, Willem Mengelberg and ladies. Photograph, March 1906. Willem Mengelberg Stichting, Amsterdam.
The photo was taken on the Zuidersee, in Holland. The composer Alphons Diepenbrock (1862–1921), a friend of Mengelberg, was very fond of Mahler.

239, 240.   The Moll villa. Built by Josef Hoffmann. Photographs. Österreichisches Museum für angewandte Kunst, Vienna.
In 1906 the architect Josef Hoffmann (1870–1956) built a new house on the Hohe Warte (Wollergasse 10, Vienna XIX). Here Mahler stayed during his last few visits to Vienna. The death certificate of 1911 also bears this address.

241–248.   Gustav Mahler. Eight photographs, 1907, by Moriz Nähr. ÖNB–BA.

The photographs were taken in the loggia of the Court Opera House.

250. Caricature on the occasion of a performance of the Sixth Symphony. *Die Muskete*, 19 January 1907.
On 4 January 1907, Mahler performed his Sixth Symphony in Vienna. The caricaturist pokes fun at the unusual percussion instruments used in the Symphony and puts the following words into Mahler's mouth: 'Good gracious! Fancy leaving out the motor horn! Ah well, now I have an excuse for writing another symphony.'

249. General Georges Picquart. Caricature from the series *Les hommes du jour* ('Men of the Day'). Bibliothèque Nationale, Paris.
During a visit by the French Mahlerians, led by Picquart, in the autumn of 1906, Mahler made a special effort to produce opera performances of exceptional brilliance. Picquart is supposed to have received word of his appointment as French Minister of War during a performance of *Tristan*. The caricaturist alludes to Picquart's enthusiasm for music.

Wozu wir noch die großen Gagen bezahlen?! —

C. Janauschek & Cie.
Wien, I., Kärntnerstraße
liefert uns viel billiger die schönsten Stimmen ohne Nebengeräusch.

251. Advertisement put out by a Viennese record shop. Drawing by Theo Zasche. *Aus dem Reich der Schminke und Tinte*, Vienna 1907, 41.
The singers' voices can be heard issuing from the horn of the gramophone. The opera director is made to demand why, in view of this, it is still necessary to pay singers' fees.

252.   Richard Strauss. Engraving by Géza Faragó,
1905. Graphische Sammlung Albertina, Vienna.

253.   Salome. Painting by Gustav Klimt, 1909.
Galleria internazionale d'Arte Moderna, Venice.
Oscar Wilde's play *Salomé* was published in 1893. In
1902 Max Reinhardt produced the work in
German, and the première of Richard Strauss'
opera *Salome* took place in Dresden in 1905.
Mahler fought in vain against the censor's decision
not to allow the work to be included in the repertoire
of the Vienna Opera.

254. The Comptroller of the Imperial Household, Prince Montenuovo, in the study of Emperor Franz Joseph at Schönbrunn. Oil painting by Karl Friedrich Gsur. ÖNB-BA. The Court Theatres were under the authority of the Comptroller. It was after a venomous campaign in the press during the spring of 1907 that Mahler asked him for his discharge.

255. Gustav Mahler in the Dolomites. Photograph. ÖNB-HS. According to Alfred Roller this picture was taken in 1909. However, the original photograph bears the handwritten remark: *Fischleinboden bei Sexten, 10. August 1907. Alfred Liebig fecit*. In August 1907 Mahler stayed at Schluderbach, in South Tyrol, not far from Sexten (Sesto).

256. Gustav Mahler with his daughters. Photograph. Ida Wagner Collection, Vienna. Mahler dearly loved both his daughters, Maria Anna (b. 1902) and Anna Justine (b. 1904). After the death of the elder daughter in July 1907, Mahler was found to have heart trouble.

257, 258. Hvitträsk. The studio and residence of the architects Herman Gesellius, Armas Lindgren and Eliel Saarinen. Photographs. Finnish Museum of Architecture, Helsinki.

In October 1907, Mahler went on a concert tour to St Petersburg and Helsinki. By motorboat and horse carriage, the Finnish painter Akseli Gallen took him to Hvitträsk, the country house, 30 km from Helsinki, which Finland's famous team of architects had built for themselves; 'quite *à la* Hohewarte, translated into Finnish', Mahler wrote (AM,400), alluding to the style of the artists who lived on the Hohe Warte in Vienna.

259. Arnold Schönberg. Painting by Richard Gerstl. Historisches Museum der Stadt Wien. Mahler publicly supported Schönberg (1874–1951), although he could not always go along with the younger man's music; he also gave Schönberg practical help when he was in need. After initial misgivings Schönberg became an apostle of Mahler's music, as did his pupils Alban Berg and Anton von Webern.

260. Entrance to the Bösendorfer Hall. Watercolour by Marie Arnsberg. Historisches Museum der Stadt Wien.
In this hall (situated in the Herrengasse in Vienna) Mahler listened to the first performance of Schönberg's Quartet in D minor on 5 February 1907. When some members of the audience protested, Mahler defended the work and almost became involved in a riot. In a letter to Richard Strauss, Mahler was enthusiastic about the Quartet.

261. *Symposion*. Oil painting by Akseli Gallen-Kallela, 1894, Sääksmäki-Helsinki, Finland. Owned by Aivi Gallen-Kallela-Sirén, Kallela Studio Home, Ruovesi, Finland. The reproduction of pictures by Akseli Gallen-Kallela takes place with kind permission of the copyright holders, Pirkko and Aivi Gallen-Kallela, Helsinki, Finland.
From left to right: Gallen-Kallela (1865–1931), who painted a portrait of Mahler in 1907; the composer Oskar Merikanto (1868–1924); the conductor Robert Kajanus (1865–1933), founder of the first Finnish concert orchestra; and Jean Sibelius (1865–1957). Sibelius has left us an account of his meeting with Mahler.

262.   Gustav Mahler. Oil painting by Akseli Gallen-Kallela, 1907, Hvitträsk, Finland. Owned by The Serlachius Art Foundation, Mänttä, Finland. The reproduction of paintings by Akseli Gallen-Kallela takes place with kind permission of the copyright holders Pirrko and Aivi Gallen-Kallela, Helsinki, Finland.

Mahler wrote to his wife about how this picture came to be painted: 'In the evening, when it was getting quite dark, we went, in the dusk, to sit by the fire, where huge logs were sizzling and glowing just as in a blacksmith's shop. Gallen, who had been staring at me strangely all through the journey (as a hunter will at a hare), suddenly set up an easel and began to paint me. Quite *à la* Rembrandt, illumined only by the open fire . . . Splendid as a painting and, at the same time, a strong likeness. You would be amazed!' (AM, 400).

1907 1907

Большой залъ Консерваторіи.

ВОСЕМЬ СИМФОНИЧЕСКИХЪ КОНЦЕРТОВЪ
(ШРЕДЕРА)

Въ Субботу, 27-го Октября,

Второй Концертъ

ПРИ УЧАСТІИ:

РАУЛЯ ПЮНЬО
(изъ Парижа)

и большого симфоническаго оркестра
ИМПЕРАТОРСКОЙ Русской Оперы
подъ управленіемъ

ГУСТАВА МАЛЕРЪ
(изъ Вѣны).

Начало въ 8¼ часовъ вечера.

Весь чистый сборъ поступаетъ въ пользу Общества вспомоще-
ствованія недостаточн. учащимся въ СПБ. Консерваторіи.

GESELLSCHAFT MUSIKFREUNDE
IN WIEN

Sonntag, den 24. November 1907, mittags halb 1 Uhr
== im großen Musikvereins-Saale ==

I. AUSSERORDENTL. GESELLSCHAFTS-KONZERT.

○ ○ ○ ○ ○

Zur Aufführung gelangt:

GUSTAV MAHLER ==
ZWEITE·SINFONIE (C-MOLL)
== für Soli, Chor, Orchester und Orgel. ==

1. Satz: ALLEGRO MAESTOSO. (Mit durchaus ernstem und feierlichem Ausdruck.)
2. Satz: ANDANTE CON MOTO.
3. Satz: SCHERZO. (In ruhig fließender Bewegung.)
4. Satz: „URLICHT" aus: „Des Knaben Wunderhorn".
5. Satz: FINALE.

MITWIRKENDE: ==

Frau ELISE ELIZZA, k. k. Hof-Opernsängerin.
Fräulein GERTRUD FÖRSTEL, k. k. Hof-Opernsängerin.
Fräulein HERMINE KITTEL, k. k. Hof-Opernsängerin.
Fräulein BELLA PAALEN, k. k. Hof-Opernsängerin.
Herr RUDOLF DITTRICH, k. k. Hoforganist.
Der SINGVEREIN DER GESELLSCHAFT DER MUSIK-
FREUNDE.
Das K. K. HOF - OPERNORCHESTER.

DIRIGENT: DER KOMPONIST.

Preis dieses Programmes 20 Heller.

Buchdruckerei: Wien, I., Dorotheergasse 7.

263. Programme of the second Schröder Symphony
Concert on 27 October (9 November) 1907.
Mahler conducted his Fifth Symphony in the Great Hall of
the St Petersburg Conservatoire.

264. Programme of the Society of the Friends of Music,
24 November 1907. GDM.
Mahler bade farewell to his Viennese audiences with a
performance of his Second Symphony.

265. Guido Adler. Photograph. Guido Adler Papers,
University of Georgia Libraries, Athens, Ga., USA.
The musicologist Guido Adler (1855–1941), university
professor in Prague and, from 1898, in Vienna, had been a
friend of Mahler since his early youth, and on several
occasions intervened to help Mahler with his career. After
Mahler's resignation as Director of the Vienna Opera, Adler
tried in vain to secure him the post of Director of the Vienna
Conservatoire.

266.   The liner *Kaiserin Augusta Victoria*. Photograph by G. Koppman & Co. Staatliche Landesbildstelle Hamburg.
It was on this ship that Mahler and his wife crossed the Atlantic for the first time in December 1907.

267.   Cherbourg. Quai Alexandre III and swing bridge. Photograph, *c*. 1900. Roger-Viollet, Paris.
This was the port where Mahler embarked for America.

268. Title-page of the announcement of the 1907–08 season. Metropolitan Opera, New York.

269. Heinrich Conried. Photograph. The New-York Historical Society.
Since 1903, the Metropolitan Opera had been directed by the Conried Metropolitan Opera Company, at the head of which stood the Austrian-born impresario Heinrich Conried (1848–1909). He engaged Mahler for New York. At the end of the 1907–08 season Conried resigned.

270. Metropolitan Opera House, New York. Photograph, c. 1894. The New-York Historical Society.
This theatre was inaugurated in 1883. Mahler worked there as conductor during the seasons of 1907–08 and 1908–09, and finally in March 1910.

271. New York, from Governor's Island.
Oil painting by Carlton T. Chapman,
1904. The New-York Historical Society.
Mahler and his wife arrived in New York on
21 December 1907. 'We were so excited',
reported Alma Mahler (AM, 162), 'that we
forgot our cares. They were to return.'

272. Hotel Majestic, New York. Photograph. The New-York Historical Society.
During his first stay in New York, Mahler
occupied a suite on the eleventh floor of this
hotel on Central Park.

273. Olive Fremstad as Isolde. Photograph. Metropolitan Opera, New York.
Olive Fremstad (1871–1951) was the Isolde in the first performance of *Tristan and Isolde* that Mahler conducted in New York.

274, 275. Programme of the Metropolitan Opera, 1 January 1908. Metropolitan Opera, New York.
The fact that this was Mahler's début has been emphasized by the words 'his first appearance'. The copy preserved in the archives of the Metropolitan Opera bears the 'o.k.' and signature of the stage manager, Anton Schertel.

Metropolitan Opera House.

Lessee CONRIED METROPOLITAN OPERA CO.

GRAND OPERA

SEASON 1907-1908

Under the Direction of MR. HEINRICH CONRIED.

WEDNESDAY EVENING, JANUARY 1, 1908,

at 7.45 o'clock

Tristan und Isolde

MUSIC-DRAMA IN THREE ACTS

BOOK and **MUSIC** by **RICHARD WAGNER**

(IN GERMAN.)

ISOLDE . . . . MMES. FREMSTAD
BRANGAENE . . . . HOMER

TRISTAN . . . . MM. KNOTE
KURWENAL . . . . VAN ROOY
KÖNIG MARKE . . . . BLASS
MELOT . . . . MÜHLMANN

CONTINUED ON NEXT PAGE.

PROGRAMME—CONTINUED.

EIN HIRT . . . . } . . . MM. REISS
STIMME DES SEEMANNS . }

EIN STEUERMANN . . . . BAYER

CONDUCTOR . . . . MR. GUSTAV MAHLER
(His first appearance.)

STAGE MANAGER . . . . . . MR. ANTON SCHERTEL

SYNOPSIS OF SCENERY.

ACT I.—The Deck of a Ship.

ACT II.—The Garden outside the Dwelling of Isolde (Cornwall).

ACT III.—The Castle Garden of Tristan (Brittany).

CHIEFS OF DEPARTMENTS.

E. CASTEL-BERT . . . . Technical Director
EDWARD SIEDLE . . . . Inspector of Stage
FRANK RIGO . . . . Stage Manager
ROMEO FRANCIOLI . . . . . } . . . Masters of Ballet
GIUSEPPE BONFIGLIO . . . . }
PIETRO NEPOTI . . . . Chorus Master
JAMES FOX . . . . Scenic Artist
FRED HOSLI . . . . Master Machinist
W. E. WARREN . . . . Master Carpenter
MME. LOUISE MUSEUS . . . . Costumer
WILLIAM PUNZEL . . . . Wig Maker
F. G. GAUS . . . . Electrician
W. G. SCATTERGOOD . . . . Engineer
ANDREW BOYD . . . . Superintendent of Building

Weber Pianos used exclusively.

Patrons would oblige the management by reporting any incivility on the part of the employees.

TELEPHONE BOOTHS in the Foyer of the Grand Tier for the convenience of the patrons.

Correct Librettos for sale in the Lobby.

CONTINUED ON NEXT PAGE.

276, 277. *Fidelio*: stage designs for act 1, scenes 1 and 2. Photographs. Metropolitan Opera, New York.
On 20 March 1908, Mahler directed a new production of this work. For this *Fidelio*, according to Alma Mahler, Mahler had arranged for the sets designed by Roller for the Vienna production to be sent to America (AM, 183). The *New York Daily Tribune* of 21 March 1908 noted that the Viennese décor had been most painstakingly copied by the Metropolitan.

278. Fifth Avenue, New York. Oil painting by Colin Campbell, 1907. The New-York Historical Society.

Mahler had a keen eye for the beauties of New York and loved to observe the crowds on Fifth Avenue.

279. Gustav Mahler. Caricature by Enrico Caruso. OAJ-F.

In April 1908 the tenor Caruso (1873–1921) drew this caricature which was published in New York. It was sent to Mahler's former teacher, Heinrich Fischer, at Iglau, stuck on a postcard.

280. Boston Theatre. Woodcut. *Boston Illustrated*, 1875. Boston Public Library.

Early in 1908 the Metropolitan Opera Company gave guest performances in Boston. Mahler conducted *The Valkyrie, Don Giovanni* and *Tristan and Isolde*.

281. Mahler's house at Toblach (Dobbiaco).
Photograph. ÖNB–BA.
Mahler and his family lived on the second storey
of this South Tyrolean farmhouse during the
summer months of the years 1908, 1909, and 1910.
They had sold their villa at Maiernigg because it
reminded them of their elder daughter's premature
death.

282. Mahler's summerhouse at Toblach. Draw-
ing by Carl Moll. *Der Merker*, vol. 3, no. 5.
Here, during the last three summers of his life,
Mahler worked on *Das Lied von der Erde* ('Song of the
Earth'), the Ninth Symphony, and the unfinished
Tenth Symphony.

283. Arnold Berliner. Painting by Eugen Spiro.
Die Naturwissenschaften, vol. xx, 1932, no. 51.
Ever since his Hamburg days Mahler had been on
friendly terms with the physicist Arnold Berliner
(1862–1942), who kept him informed of the latest
scientific discoveries. In the summer of 1908
Berliner sent a whole case of scientific literature to
Toblach.

284. *Das Lied von der Erde*. Third movement. A page from the draft score. GDM.
Mahler worked on this composition during the summer of 1908. Originally the third movement was entitled *Der Pavillon aus Porzellan* ('The Porcelain Pavilion'); it was later renamed *Von der Jugend* ('Of Youth').

285. Bruno Walter. Photograph. ÖNB-BA.
'I believe it is just about the most personal thing I have done so far,' wrote Mahler to Bruno Walter in the summer of 1908 about *Das Lied von der Erde* (GMB, 413). Mahler did not live to hear this work performed. Bruno Walter conducted the first performance in Munich in November 1911.

286, 287.   Imperial Jubilee Stamps, 1908. Design by Koloman Moser. ÖNB-BA.
In 1908 the monarchy of Austria–Hungary celebrated the sixtieth anniversary of the reign of Emperor
Franz Joseph. Mahler's friend Koloman Moser designed a series of postage stamps to commemorate
the occasion.

288, 289.   Programme of the Tenth Philharmonic Concert on 19 September 1908. Archives of the
Czech Philharmonic Orchestra, Prague.
In the course of the Prague Jubilee Exhibition, held to celebrate the sixtieth anniversary of the reign of
Emperor Franz Joseph, ten Philharmonic Concerts took place, with Mahler conducting the first and
last concerts. At the last one he conducted the first performance of his Seventh Symphony. The
programmes were published in German and in Czech.

10 helléřů.

JUBILEJNÍ VÝSTAVA V PRAZE R. 1908.
KONCERTNÍ SÍŇ

V sobotu dne 19. září o 7. hod. večer.

X. (POSLEDNÍ)
FILHARMONICKÝ KONCERT

GUSTAV MAHLER·

Symfonie č. 7. (E-moll.)

Prvni provedení vůbec.

Řídí skladatel·

I. Úvod a první věta.

II. Hudba noci. (Andante sempre sostenuto.)

III. Scherzo.

IV. Hudba noci. (Andante amoroso.)

V. Rondo — Finale.

JUBILÄUMS-AUSSTELLUNG PRAG, 1908.
KONZERTHALLE·

Samstag den 19. September um 7 Uhr abends.

X. (LETZTES)
PHILHARMONISCHES KONZERT

GUSTAV MAHLER:

Symphonie No. 7. (E-moll.)

Uraufführung.

Unter Leitung des Komponisten.

I. Einleitung und erster Satz.

II. Nachtmusik (Andante sempre sostenuto).

III. Scherzo.

IV. Nachtmusik (Andante amoroso.)

V. Rondo — Finale.

290. Kolo Moser. Self-portrait. Historisches Museum der Stadt Wien.

Koloman Moser (1868–1918), painter, graphic artist and craftsman, belonged to the circle of Mahler's friends from 1902 onwards. His two portrait sketches of Mahler show him in profile.

291. Emil Hertzka. Oil painting by T. von Dreger. Universal Edition, Vienna.

Through the initiative of Emil Hertzka (1869–1932), director of Universal Edition, this publishing firm took over the major part of Mahler's works, which had originally been published by others. In the summer of 1908 Mahler signed a contract for his as yet unpublished Eighth Symphony.

292. Gustav Mahler. Portrait sketch by Kolo Moser. Reproduced from a catalogue, Library and Museum of the Performing Arts, New York.

293. Prospectus of the Hamburg–America Line. Museum für Hamburgische Geschichte, Hamburg. In November 1908 Mahler, accompanied by his wife and daughter, left Hamburg on board a steamship of the Hamburg–America line on his second crossing to New York.

294. New York, from Jersey City. Photograph, 1908. Local History and Genealogy Division, The New York Public Library, Astor, Lenox and Tilden Foundations.
At the beginning of his second stay in New York, Mahler conducted three concerts of the New York Symphony Society.

295. Hotel Savoy, New York. Photograph, about 1910. Quinn Collection, The New-York Historical Society.
In the winter of 1908–09, and in the two winters following, Mahler lived at the Hotel Savoy, where most of the outstanding artists of the Metropolitan Opera stayed.

296. Otto H. Kahn. Photograph. The Bettmann Archive, Inc., New York.
The Metropolitan Grand Opera Company was founded after Heinrich Conried's resignation at the end of the 1907–08 season. Its president was Otto H. Kahn (1867–1935), the influential banker. Mahler was an occasional guest of Kahn's, but did not hold him in very high esteem.

297. Giulio Gatti-Casazza. Photograph, 1908. Local History and Genealogy Division, The New York Public Library, Astor, Lenox and Tilden Foundations.
The Italian Gatti-Casazza (1869–1940), who had directed La Scala in Milan since 1898, was appointed director of the Metropolitan Opera House in 1908.

298. Marcella Sembrich. Photograph, 6 February 1909. Metropolitan Opera, New York.
The picture shows the outstanding coloratura soprano (1858–1935) at her farewell concert, when she sang some of Rosina's arias from *The Barber of Seville*. At the end of the gala performance, Mahler appeared on the podium.

299. Auguste Rodin. Photograph. Roger-Viollet, Paris.
On his return from New York, Mahler stayed in Paris for some time during the spring of 1909. On this occasion Rodin (1840–1917) made a bust of Mahler, commissioned by Carl Moll (AM, 187).

300. Gustav Mahler. Bronze bust by Auguste Rodin. ÖNB-BA.
'Rodin fell in love with his model', reported Alma Mahler (AM, 187), 'and he was quite desolate when we had to leave; he wanted to continue working on Mahler.'

301. Mozart. Marble bust by Auguste Rodin. Musée Rodin, Paris.
Rodin said that Mahler's head was 'a synthesis of Franklin, Frederick the Great of Prussia, and Mozart' (AM, 188). This marble sculpture may bear Mozart's name, but it has Mahler's features.

302.   Gustav Mahler. Photograph. ÖNB-BA.
This snapshot was presumably taken near Toblach; it shows
Mahler in his walking outfit.

303.   Gustav and Alma Mahler. Photograph, 1909. ÖNB-BA.
The photograph shows the Mahlers on their way from
Toblach to Altschluderbach.

304.   Gustav Mahler with his daughter Anna. Photograph, Toblach, 1909. ÖNB-BA.

309. Theodore Spiering, Anna and Gustav
Mahler. Photograph, October 1909. EV.
Mahler made the crossing to the USA in the
company of the violinist Theodore Spiering
(1871–1925), whom he had engaged for New
York as concertmaster or leader.

311. Carnegie Hall, New York. Photograph. New York Public Library.
In the winter of 1909–10 Mahler worked predominantly as a concert conductor. He
conducted the orchestra of the Philharmonic Society, which had been restructured not
long before. Most of the concerts took place in Carnegie Hall, which was inaugurated
in 1891.

310. Louis Comfort Tiffany. Photograph. The
New-York Historical Society.
The American painter, architect and craftsman,
Louis Comfort Tiffany (1848–1933) was among
Mahler's admirers. He asked Mahler for per-
mission to attend orchestra rehearsals hidden
away in a corner, because he was shy (AM, 201).

312. Ferruccio Busoni. Silhouette by Hans
Schliessmann. ÖNB-BA.
Mahler knew the pianist and composer
Ferruccio Busoni (1866–1924) from his Leipzig
days. In the USA they became friends.

313. Théâtre du Châtelet, Paris. Photograph, 1905. Roger Viollet, Paris.

In this theatre Mahler conducted the first performance in France of his Second Symphony on 17 April 1910. The composer Claude Debussy, who was at the concert, is said to have left halfway through the second movement (AM, 213).

314. Comtesse Greffulhe. Photograph. Bibliothèque Nationale, Paris.

The Countess was president of the Société des Grandes Auditions Musicales, which arranged the concert on 17 April 1910. The figure of the Princesse de Guermantes in Marcel Proust's *A la recherche du temps perdu* is based on this elegant patroness.

322. Hall I at the Munich exhibition of 1908. *Die Ausstellung München 1908*, Munich 1908, 5.
The six exhibition halls had been built in 1907 from designs by Wilhelm Bertsch. It was in Hall I that the first performance of the Eighth Symphony took place in September 1910.

323. Poster of the first performance of the Eighth Symphony. IGMG, Vienna.

324. Mahler in conversation with Bruno Walter, Munich, September 1910. Photograph. EV.
Bruno Walter had conducted the preliminary rehearsals in Vienna of the Eighth Symphony.

325. Mahler conducting a rehearsal prior to the performance of his Eighth Symphony in the Exhibition Hall. Photograph. *Bild-Band der Stadtchronik München 1910/I*, no. 15, Munich 1910. Stadtarchiv Munich.

326. Gustav Mahler. Photograph. ÖNB-BA.
It is uncertain when this photograph was taken. According to the picture archive of the Austrian National Library it was in 1911.

The Philharmonic Society
of New York

1910... SIXTY-NINTH SEASON ...1911

Gustav Mahler . . . Conductor

MANAGEMENT LOUDON CHARLTON

Carnegie Hall

TUESDAY NIGHT, JANUARY 17
AT EIGHT-FIFTEEN

FRIDAY AFTERNOON, JANUARY 20
AT TWO-THIRTY

Soloist
MME. BELLA ALTEN
(of the Metropolitan Opera House)

All-Modern Programme

1. OVERTURE "Das Kätchen von Heilbronn" . . . . *Pfitzner*
2. SYMPHONY No. 4, in G major . . . . *Mahler*
    I Recht gemächlich
    II In gemächlicher Bewegung
    III Ruhevoll
    IV Sehr behaglich
        Solo Part: MME. ALTEN
3. "EIN HELDENLEBEN" Opus 40 . . . . *Richard Strauss*

The Steinway Piano is the Official Piano of the Philharmonic Society

---

The Philharmonic Society
of New York

1910... SIXTY-NINTH SEASON ...1911

Gustav Mahler . . . Conductor

MANAGEMENT LOUDON CHARLTON

Carnegie Hall

TUESDAY NIGHT, FEBRUARY 21
AT EIGHT-FIFTEEN

FRIDAY AFTERNOON, FEBRUARY 24
AT TWO-THIRTY

Soloist
ERNESTO CONSOLO
Pianist

Programme

1. SINIGAGLIA - Overture, "Le baruffe Chiozzotte, op. 32
2. MENDELSSOHN - Symphony No. 4, "Italian", op. 90
    I Allegro vivace
    II Andante con moto
    III Con moto moderato
    IV Saltarello: Presto
        INTERMISSION
3. MARTUCCI - Concerto in B-flat minor, op. 66
    I Allegro giusto
    II Larghetto
    III Allegro con spirito
4. BUSONI - - - - - "Berceuse élégiaque"
5. BOSSI "Intermezzi Goldoniani", for string orchestra, op. 127
    I Preludio e Minuetto: Preludio, Allegro con fuoco; Minuetto.
        Con grazia; with Trio, Poco più mosso
    II Gagliardo: Vivace
    III Coprifuoco: Blandamente
    IV Minuetto e Musetta: Minuetto, con moto; Musetta, alquanto
        meno mosso
    V Serenatina: Allegretto tranquillo
    VI Burlesca: Con molto brio

The Steinway Piano is the Official Piano of the Philharmonic Society

327, 328. Programmes of the Philharmonic Society, 17 and 20 January and 21 and 24 February 1911.
Mahler was weak and feverish when he made his last appearance as a conductor on 21 February. The concert of 24 February was conducted by Spiering; Ferruccio Busoni himself conducted his *Berceuse élégiaque*.

329. Gustav Mahler, last picture. Photograph. Anna Mahler Collection, Spoleto.
Fatally ill, and pronounced incurable by his doctors, Mahler was brought on board ship in the spring of 1911 for his last crossing to Europe. On board he got up almost every day, and we led him, or rather carried him, on to the sun deck. . . .'
(AM, 243).

330–332.   Gustav Mahler's death mask, taken by Carl
Moll. IGMG, Vienna (330–31), ÖNB–BA (332).

Mahler died on 18 May 1911 in Vienna. 'When on the
morning after the night of Mahler's death I took my
farewell of his mortal remains', Alfred Roller reported,
'his features still bore traces of the suffering of his final
death struggle. Klimt who saw him several hours later
told me how solemnly serene and majestically beautiful
they had subsequently become, and that is precisely how
Moll's wonderful death mask has preserved them for us.'

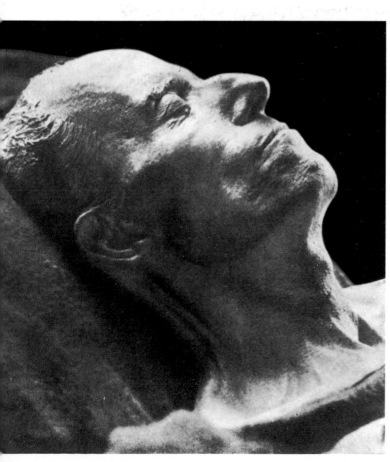

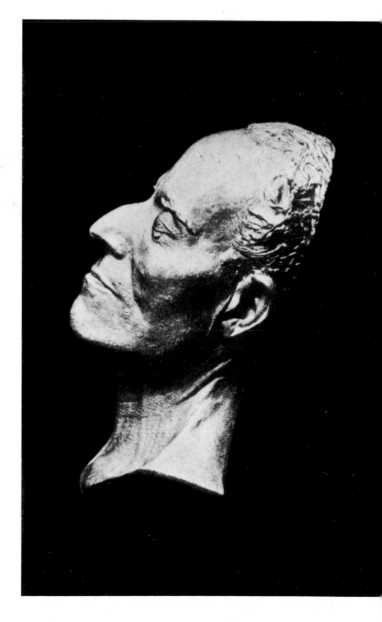

333. Entry in the register of births and deaths. ÖNB-BA.
The last line of the entry notes Mahler's profession as *'emer. Director d.k.k.Hofoper* (Director emeritus of the Imperial and Royal Court Opera); his place of residence as 'XIX. Wollergasse 10' (Carl Moll's villa); and the cause of death as septic endocarditis; it goes on to state that a cardiac probe had been carried out after death.

334. Mahler's grave. Photograph. ÖNB-BA.
Josef Hoffmann designed the gravestone in the Grinzing cemetery, inscribed only with the dead man's name.

Documents

On a bare plateau between meadows and forests lies the little Bohemian village of Kalischt (Kališt), where Gustav Mahler was born on 7 July 1860. His childhood and school years were spent about forty kilometres from the village of his birth, at Iglau (Jihlava), the second largest town of the margravate of Moravia. His musical studies took place in Vienna, the capital city of the Habsburg State. His first appointment as conductor took him to Hall in the arch-duchy of Austria-above-the-Enns, his second to Laibach (Ljubljana) in the duchy of Carniola, and the others to Olmütz (Olomouc) in Moravia, to Prague, capital of the kingdom of Bohemia, and to Budapest, capital of the king-dom of Hungary. All these countries and several more had been ruled since 1848 by the Emperor Franz Joseph I. In 1911, when Mahler died, Franz Joseph I was still on the throne. When Mahler journeyed from Iglau to Prague, Vienna, Laibach or Budapest, he remained within the territories ruled by the Emperor.

The Idea of the Austrian State

That nations of such diverse origins should have joined to-gether, more than three centuries ago, by voluntary treaty into a political whole within the Austrian State, I consider to be the act of a benevolent Providence. Let us assume that this had not happened, and that every one of these nations had retained its full sovereignty: how many and how bloody would have been the conflicts between them in the intervening time! Per-haps some of them would have disappeared by now as a result. The union restrained ambition and lust for power among the individual members of these nations; but did it also remove the opportunity for honourable activity as citizens of the State? The honour which is derived from doing violence to others is distinguished from the honour, or rather shame, of the robber not by its nature but only by its degree. But if it is asserted that this union has not always operated to the benefit of the individual parts which make up the whole, then I shall be the last to deny that much has happened that ought not to have happened, and that many things could have been better done.

Franz Palacky, *Österreichs Staatsidee*, Prague 1866, 23. (Franz [František] Palacky, 1798–1876, was a Czech historian and politician and a member of the Austrian parliament.)

Mahler's memories of Kalischt and his parents' home

We went past a few shabby peasant huts. At one of them Mahler said:

3   'You see, I was born in a miserable little house like that; we didn't even have glass in the windows. In front of the house was a pond. The little village of Kalischt and a few scattered huts were the only things near.

15   'My father (whose mother had maintained the family by peddling drapery) had already tried every possible way of earning a living, and with his exceptional energy he had worked his way further and further up. At first he had been a

carter, and had read and studied, while driving his horse and cart, all kinds of books – he had even learned a little French, which earned him the nickname of "coach-box scholar". Later he worked as a clerk in various factories, and then he became a private tutor. Eventually he moved to the little farm at Kalischt on marrying my mother – the daughter of a soap-boiler from Ledetsch – who did not love him, hardly knew him before the wedding, and would sooner have married another to whom her affection belonged. But her parents and my father were able to bend her will and make his prevail. They were as ill-suited as fire and water. He was rigidity, she was gentleness itself.'

NBL, 52–53. (Mahler's statement to Natalie Bauer-Lechner dates from 1896.)

His mother as martyr   16

His father, a strong, impulsive and sensual man (with no inhibitions), married a girl from a better Jewish family, named Frank, who – because she had had a limp since birth – was considered blemished and had no claim to a good 'match'. She loved another man, who took no notice of her, and so she married Bernhard Mahler without love and with total resig-nation. The marriage was decidedly unhappy from the very first. Children arrived, many children: twelve, in a row. This martyr suffered from a congenital heart condition which worsened rapidly through her successive confinements and the heavy housework.

The Mahlers had started off in a small way at Kalischt, a Moravian village. He owned a distillery which the family jokingly called a 'factory'. When freedom of movement for Jews was declared, Bernhard Mahler immediately moved to the nearest town, Iglau, where he set up his small business again.

AM, 13. (The maiden name of Mahler's mother was not Frank, but Hermann; Kalischt is not in Moravia, but in Bohemia near the Moravian border; GA, 95–96, names Gustav as the second of twelve children, HLG, 11–12, gives fourteen children in all.)

The town of Iglau around mid-century

Iglau consists of the town itself, surrounded by a double ring   7, 11 wall, and the 3 suburbs of Spital, Frauen and Pirnitzer. At a time when siegecraft had not reached its present standard, Iglau could be counted upon as a fortified place, although it is dominated on three sides by superior heights.

A remarkable embellishment at Iglau is the very regular, large square, the Stadtplatz, which is enclosed by pretty houses of two to three storeys, and decorated with three stone fountains and a large statue of the Virgin Mary; it is 1,038 feet long, 318 (on the south side) to 390 feet wide (on the north), and has an area of 361,440 square feet. There are few towns which can compare with Iglau in this respect.

Christian d'Elvert, *Geschichte und Beschreibung der (königlichen Kreis- und) Bergstadt Iglau in Mähren*, Brünn (Brno) 1850, 447, 450–51. (The Stadtplatz or Stadtring covered an area of more than 38,000 square metres.)

The language at Iglau is predominantly German, but the servants mainly speak Bohemian and Moravian. For a few years now the aspects peculiar to the *costume* at Iglau – the long, light blue cloth cloaks and black crape or gold caps of the women and girls of the middle classes – have been all but lost; the general German costume, and habits of luxury in clothing, have triumphed, here as elsewhere.

The Jews, who in the past have been tolerated here only as occasional visitors, have no synagogue. For a long time now a cookshop has existed in the Frauen suburb near the Tauben-kobel inn, recognized in 1809 as an established concern; a second one, paying rent to the town, was set up in the same year in the Spital suburb.

Christian d'Elvert, *Geschichte und Beschreibung* . . ., Brünn 1850, 459.

5 An Imperial decree of October 1860, published as a rider to the Imperial Proclamation *An Meine Völker* ('To my peoples'), formed the first step on the road to a parliamentary system, confirmed the equality of citizens before the law, and guaranteed freedom of worship to all. As a consequence of this, Jews could move into towns such as Iglau unhindered. In 1861 the Jews resident at Iglau set up their own religious community, among whose committee members Bernhard Mahler was numbered in later years. In 1863 the synagogue or temple was consecrated.

Announcement by the District Office

Announcement by the District Office (see transcription in following column).

The application from Bernard [*sic*] Mahler from Kalischt concerning his intention of producing sweetened alcoholic liquids by a cold process, and then of selling them retail as defined by the Court Decree of 6 December 1841, in sealed bottles containing at least one pint at Iglau, is noted and granted.

The request for a licence to sell these sweetened alcoholic liquids by the glass cannot be granted, taking into account the many already existing brandy and rosolio drinking-houses.

Notice of the foregoing is hereby given to Bernard Mahler, with the return of his appended application, to the Royal Imperial Tax Office, and to the town council at Iglau, the latter in fulfilment of the report of 5 October 1860, z.3451. Iglau, 28 February 1861.

OAJ-PR.

Mahler to Richard Specht on his father's position

The 'pothouse' (which you ascribe to my parents) seems to me a rather mean-sounding specification. I think it would be fair to describe my father's position as that of a tradesman.

GMB, 261. (From a letter of Gustav Mahler to Richard Specht from 1904. The objection refers to a study written by Specht which was shown to Mahler before publication. Specht took account of Mahler's objection; his pamphlet [RSP 1, 14] states: 'Mahler's parents were tradespeople of small means . . .'.)

The neighbours' son Theodor Fischer talks about Mahler

In the house numbered c. 265/0. 4 in the Pirnitzergasse, now   12, 14
the Znaimergasse, his father had a business in the 1860s and early 1870s, producing and selling liquor. On the first floor of this house the family also had a flat consisting of a large kitchen, a hall and two rooms. The large room was furnished as a sitting-room in the sober style of the time, with the standard rep coverings; there in a frame under glass hung his father's certificate as a freeman of Iglau, there stood a glass case with porcelain and glass and all kinds of unusual objects, a bookcase filled with the works of classical and contemporary authors which Gustav Mahler read at an early age, and there too stood the Vopaterny grand piano on which Gustav Mahler practised and studied as soon as he had piano lessons.

The settings for little Gustav's boyish games, which he played there with his brothers and sisters and the neighbours' children, were the Pirnitzergasse, the courtyard of the house next door, in which lived the future conductor Fischer with his family, the disused workshops in the same house, with their many corners, and the attics above them, with their secretive darkness where one could have adventures and make one's flesh creep.

Eagerly he used to listen to the fairy-tales that a nursemaid in the house next door used to tell the boys on gloomy Sunday afternoons, to keep them from making a noise, including the fairy tale, *Vom Klagenden Lied* ['Tale of the Lamenting Song'] which may have given rise to one of Mahler's compositions. As he grew older he and his schoolfellows were keen attenders at the municipal swimming classes.

His musical talent developed early on. Even in his earliest boyhood he played all kinds of tunes and songs on a concertina, by ear, with astonishing skill, and received his first piano lesson from the theatrical conductor Viktorin at the age of six, and later from the piano teacher Brosch.

He had many opportunities to hear good music performed, at oratorios in St James's Church (Mozart's *Requiem*) and at concerts of the town orchestra, as well as in the theatre, at operatic productions by amateurs and by an opera company which was good by the standards prevailing at the time. He received much encouragement in musical matters at the house of the conductor Fischer.

Theodor Fischer, 'Festrede bei der Mahler-Feier am 21. März 1931 im Stadt-theater Iglau', MVJ, no. 975. (Typescript, with handwritten additions, of a speech delivered by the retired Chief Magistrate *Hofrat* Theodor Fischer, a schoolfellow and boyhood friend of Gustav Mahler's. The Viktorin mentioned is Franz Viktorin, whom the *Deutsche Bühnenalmanach* of 1865, 1866 and 1868 names as conductor at the Municipal Theatre, Iglau.)

Discovery of a piano

Little Gustav showed musical talent early on. On the occasion of a visit to his mother's parents, who were mockingly called the 'duke and duchess' because of their airs of refinement, Gustav went missing, and was found much later, after a long search, in the attic of the house strumming on an old piano. From then on Father Mahler had made up his mind: Gustav would be a musician. At the time he was four years old.

AM, 14.

Guido Adler on music at Iglau

The boy grew up at Iglau, a German-speaking island in a turbulent sea of nationalism; he found rich musical nourish-ment in the folk-songs of both the nationalities among whom he spent his youth. His imagination was aroused by the wooded country, wreathed in legend, and the lively toing and froing of the garrison, whose trumpet-calls acquired a symbolic meaning for him. Reveille, Last Post and all the rest were transformed within him into sound images which crystallized about the figure of the old German man-at-arms. They appear with lively freshness again and again, even in songs and instrumental works of the later period, as in *Reveglie* ['Reveille'], *Tambour-Geselle* ['Drummer Boy'], *Der Schildwache Nachtlied* ['Night song of the sentinel'], *Der Gefangene im Turm* ['The Prisoner in the tower'], *Wo die schönen Trompeten blasen* ['Where the shining trumpets blow'], in the first and third movements of the Third Symphony, in the variations in the Fourth, etc. This also helps to explain Mahler's predilection for march rhythms of every kind, which are to be found time and again in his works, in joy and in sadness – finding the most beautiful transfiguration in the first movement of the Fifth Symphony, the passionate funeral march in C sharp minor, an intensifica-tion, as it were, of the mood in the corresponding movement of Beethoven's *Eroica*.

Impressions of his youth run like a scarlet thread throughout his work.

GA, 9–10. (Guido Adler, 1855–1941, Austrian musicologist, had like Mahler grown up in Iglau, attended the Conservatoire of the Society of the Friends of Music in Vienna, and was later a university professor in Prague and Vienna. Adler was a friend of Mahler's from early boyhood on.)

Musical life at Iglau was, until 1862, dominated by the performances of the Musical Society (Musikverein), founded in 1819. The stocks of scores listed, each with its opening theme, in the inventory of the Musical Society (MJV no. 874) form a rich repertoire in which the Viennese classics (particularly Haydn and Mozart) occupy a promi-nent place.

The orchestra of the Musical Society at Iglau

Practising members who participate in the orchestra of the Society are: 12 violin players, 4 viola, 2 violoncello and 2 double bass; 2 flautists, 2 oboists, 2 clarinettists, 2 bassoonists, 2 horn players, 2 trumpeters, 1 trombone player and 1 timpanist; hence

in total 34.

Among these are 15 who are professional musicians and thus receive a fee for their participation.

Johann Ferdinand Pokorny, 'Geschichtliche Skizze des Musikvereines in der k. Stadt Iglau in Mähren. Von dessen Entstehung im Jahre 1819 zu dessen Sistierung im Jahre 1862', MS.MVI, no. 1128.

Heinrich Fischer and the Iglau male voice choir

Fischer, Heinrich August, the pivot and the focus of Iglau's efforts and activities in the musical field for two decades, was born on 28 June 1828 at Iglau as the son of a householder and former head of the Protestant community there. At the age of 12, having in his earliest boyhood displayed a pronounced inclination towards music, he entered the Prague Con-servatoire as a pupil, where he devoted himself with great zeal for a period of six years to, in the first instance, his training as an oboist, and also to lessons in harmony and composition. . . .

Although a co-founder of the choir he nevertheless remained fairly remote from it until 1858 when he was elected Choir-master, which office he accepted and continues to perform to this day with great distinction.

In this new function, he naturally cultivated the male voices but created in addition a sizeable ladies' choir which made it possible for the choir on various occasions to give performances of major works: oratorios and, in 1867 and 1869, even two operas, of which the first was *Stradella*, the second *Trovatore*. In respect of the latter it must be mentioned that of all the operas performed of every kind it ranks in first place and received the entirely deserved acclaim of the public. . . .

Fischer is now a highly esteemed successor to the revered Choirmaster Pokorny, and, as the town's musical director, the founder and conductor of the *town band* which has an annual budget of 1,200 florins, and which plays, under his inspiration, even strictly classical music with precision.

Christian Ritter d'Elvert, *Geschichte der Musik in Mähren und Österr.-Schlesien*, Brünn 1873, addenda, 93–94. (In the list of the 'contributing members' in the *Bericht über die Tätigkeit des Iglauer Männergesang-Vereines im 25. Vereinsjahre 1876–77* ['Report on the activities of the Iglau Male Voice Choir in the 25th year of the association, 1876–77'], the name Bernhard Mahler appears. Heinrich Fischer died in 1917.)

First lesson in harmony

In [Heinrich Fischer's] house, Gustav Mahler, later a famous conductor and composer, used to come and go in his boyhood, which he spent at Iglau, where he received his first musical education. He [Fischer] instructed Mahler in harmony, and the latter remained attached to him as a result, even when he had already trodden the path of fame.

Theodor Fischer, 'Biographie von Heinrich A. Fischer', MSV, January 1931, MVJ, no. 712. (In 1908 Mahler sent 'to his old teacher and friend and to his worthy comrades in song' a congratulatory telegram on Fischer's golden jubilee as choirmaster: MVJ, no. 888.)

Guido Adler on tolerance and education at Iglau

Catholic priests and the rabbi, Dr J.J. Unger, uniformly supported religious education in family life, and tolerance was the highest principle of the humanistic education which was taught in secondary schools by estimable teachers and pre-pared by excellent primary school teachers. Even today I see them in my mind's eye as divine emissaries.

Guido Adler, *Wollen und Wirken*, Vienna 1935, 3.

	1st semester	2nd semester
Religion	excellent	excellent
Latin	satisfactory	satisfactory
German	satisfactory	very good
Geography and History	adequate	adequate
Mathematics	adequate, rather uncertain	adequate
Science	adequate, hesitant in descriptions	adequate
Handwriting	satisfactory	adequate
Physical training	very good	very good

Outward appearance: rather careless. General conduct: fair. Diligence: satisfactory.

From the catalogue of Class 1, academic year 1869/70, of the Imperial-Royal State High School [k. k. Staatsgymnasium], Iglau, OAJ-G.

Operatic productions at the Iglau Municipal Theatre in the performing season 1870–71

7.I.1871 *Norma*, 11.I. *Lucretia Borgia*, 14.I. *Martha*, 23.I. *Norma*, 30.I. *Robert le Diable*, 3.II. *Robert le Diable*, 17.II. *Martha*, 24.II. *Fra Diavolo*, 27.II. *Robert le Diable*, 2.III. *Fra Diavolo*, 4.III. *La Dame blanche*, 8.III. *Don Giovanni*, 13.III. *Don Giovanni*, 20.III. *Zampa*, 23.III. *Don Giovanni*, 27.III. *Zampa*, 30.III. *Fra Diavolo*, 1.IV. *Joseph*.

Anton Ph. Borzutzky, *Almanach des Stadttheaters Iglau*, Iglau, 1871, MVJ, no. 1004. (The season lasted from 15 December 1870 to 1 April 1871. The greater part of the programme was taken up by plays.)

First public appearance

22 On 13 October, as an exceptional circumstance, there was a non-subscription concert, in which a nine-year-old boy, the son of a Jewish businessman here, by the name of Maler [*sic*], gave his first public performance on the piano before a large audience. The success which the future piano virtuoso achieved among his hearers was a great one, and is much to his credit; but it could have been wished that he had had at his disposal for his charming playing just as good an instrument. If the budding artist's former teacher, the conductor Viktorin, hears of his success yesterday, he can certainly feel very pleased with his pupil.

Der Vermittler (Iglau), 16 October 1870. (The little piano virtuoso was already more than ten years old. The concert took place at the Iglau Municipal Theatre.)

Bernhard Mahler becomes a freeholder

25 At the end of 1872 the Mahler family moved to the house next door, c. 264/0. 6, in the Pirnitzergasse, now Znaimergasse, which his father had purchased. On the first floor of this house Gustav Mahler lived until he left Iglau.

Theodor Fischer, 'Festrede' . . ., MVJ, no. 975.

A term in Prague

His father's daily rages over the mess in Gustav's drawer (the only thing he had to keep tidy) were always forgotten by the next day, when a further noisy storm descended on him. He seemed strangely incapable of keeping this one little rule in mind. Nor were words all that descended on him; but whatever happened the boy went on dreaming. He had a rude awakening when he first came into contact with the ugliness of life at the home of the famous musician Grünfeld, in Prague,

where his father had sent him to study. It was not only that others wore his clothes, and his shoes, while he went hungry and barefoot; this he hardly noticed, and when he told me about it, he added, 'I took it for granted.' But once, sitting in a dark room, he was the unwilling witness of a brutal love scene between the maid and the son of the house which remained with him as a most unpleasant memory. Little Gustav sprang out to help the girl. But he was roundly abused, both by the youth Alfred and by the girl whom he had wanted to help, and sworn to silence.

This little episode made a remarkably strong impression on Mahler. As one can often be ill-tempered all day towards people who have crossed one in a dream, so Gustav never forgave the young pianist for this shock. Finally, someone told his father what neglect the boy was suffering. He found Gustav in a miserable state, took him to the inn, let him eat his fill, and then fetched what remained of Gustav's belongings from Herr Grünfeld's singular establishment. Meanwhile the lad sat in the inn, without moving an inch, until his father arrived, blazing with anger, and took him straight to the station and thence to Iglau.

AM, 14–15. (The school catalogue for 1871–72 records the Prague episode with the following comment: 'Arrived in the second semester, came from the Neustadt High School in Prague and brought a report from class 3, 64th out of 64', OAJ-G.)

Celebration concert at the Iglau Municipal Theatre

On the occasion of the marriage of the Archduchess Gisela a celebratory service was held on Saturday in the synagogue here, at which the national anthem was sung. Dr Unger gave a festival sermon. The Imperial-Royal District Administrator and the Mayor attended this celebration. In the evening of the same day the Imperial-Royal Regimental Band beat Retreat in full dress and played through the streets. On Sunday the poor people of the district, the inmates of the municipal workhouse and those receiving outdoor relief, joined in the celebrations. The guardians are to be congratulated on the trouble they took to ensure that the neediest and most deserving of the out-pensioners were able to attend the festivities. On Sunday evening the gala concert was held in the brilliantly illuminated Municipal Theatre. The house was full, and the audience splendidly dressed. The concert opened with Westmeyer's Kaiser Overture, performed by the Imperial-Royal Military Band, which played it with admirable precision; it was greeted with loud applause.

[Here follows a report on the performance of various other pieces and their reception by the audience.]

Then followed the Fantasia on Themes from the Opera *Norma*, for the pianoforte, by Sigmund Thalberg, played by the young virtuoso Mahler, who fully deserves the praise that we have often lavished on him in the past. He played this evening with as much brilliance as on previous occasions, and his performance was rewarded with a veritable ovation.

Mährischer Grenzbote (Iglau), 24 April 1873.

Death of Mahler's brother Ernst

Ernst's death was the first cruel experience in Gustav Mahler's childhood. He had loved his brother, and followed every stage of his illness with profound distress. It seems that he did not stir from his brother's bedside throughout the many months of his illness, and passed the time by telling him stories.

AM, 14. (Ernst Mahler, only one year younger than Gustav, died of hydropericardium in April 1874 [GA, 95]. This, Mahler's first conscious experience of death, lastingly affected him. In 1879 he wrote to Josef Steiner, who had written for him the libretto for his youthful opera *Ernst von Schwaben*, a letter that contained the following lines: 'And now we are again strolling together in a familiar landscape, and there is the organ-grinder holding out his hat in his skinny hand. And he is singing out of tune, but I can recognize Ernst von Schwaben's Greeting, and Ernst himself approaches and stretches out his arms to me, and as I look at him I see that it's my poor brother. . . .' (GMB, 7–8).

Mahler spent part of his summer holiday in 1875 staying with friends who lived in the neighbourhood of Časlau. He still retained pleasant memories of the farms of Ronow and Morawan four years later, as he showed in a letter to his friend Josef Steiner (GMB, 8). Gustav Schwarz, the local estate administrator, was told about the young pianist who could play difficult music at sight by a certain Herr Steiner, presumably a relation of Mahler's friend, and invited the schoolboy Mahler to visit him. On hearing him play the piano, he advised him to study music. Mahler admitted that he had wanted to do so for a long time, but said that he did not think he would be able to obtain his father's consent. Schwarz appealed to Gustav's father to allow his son to pursue his musical studies.

Mahler writes to Gustav Schwarz, estate administrator at Morawan

Iglau, 28 August 1875

Dear Sir,

Further to my father's letter, I also want to thank you, Sir, for your kind welcome and hospitality. I can only add that it will still be something of a struggle to induce my father to agree to our plan. He is showing signs of coming over to our side, but he is still not quite won over. As in Bürger's [ballad] *Wilde Jagd*, two knights are standing beside him, one on his right hand and the other on his left, and both of them pull him, first to one side and then to the other. I hope that the knight on the right will get the upper hand.

    'For that, O Werner, I need your help.'

My dear father has two fears: one, that I might neglect or interrupt my studies, and the other, that I might be ruined by getting into bad company in Vienna; and even when he seems to be inclining to our side, you must remember that I am entirely alone and have only myself to rely on in my struggle against the superior power of so many 'reasonable and mature people'. That is why I beg you to be kind enough to call on us on Saturday, 4 September, for you are the only person who can really win my father over.

Please give my kind regards to Frau Schwarz and to everyone at Ronow.

        Yours truly,
        Gustav Mahler.

Neues Wiener Journal, 6 August 1905.

Mahler's first call in Vienna in the company of Gustav Schwarz

Herr Schwarz met young Mahler as agreed, and they made the journey to Vienna, where they immediately called on Professor Epstein. But the Professor was then living out at Baden, so Herr Schwarz took his protégé there in order to get an expert opinion on him without delay. 'I recognized Mahler's outstanding gifts at once,' said Herr Schwarz; 'but when I came to Professor Epstein, I found him anything but delighted, for Mahler's piano playing did not impress him at all. It was only when Mahler played him some of his own compositions that Epstein showed any enthusiasm and said over and over again that they were in direct descent from Wagner, and asked me why I had not sent him a telegram asking him to come to Vienna.'

Neues Wiener Journal, 6 August 1905. (This account is based on an interview with Schwarz at the offices of the paper.)

Julius Epstein on his first meeting with his pupil

31 'I very well remember the day,' said Professor Epstein, 'when Gustav Mahler's father came to see me at the Conservatoire, introduced himself as Herr Mahler from Iglau, and asked me to examine his son; he wanted to know whether the boy had

enough talent to make music his career. I asked the father if the young man – Gustav Mahler was then barely fifteen – had shown enough enthusiasm for music. "He certainly has," Herr Mahler replied. "But I would rather he went to the Commercial School in Vienna so that he can take over my distillery later on." "That is as much as to say that you want me to decide his future," I said, "and that is a matter of conscience, and not as easy as you seem to think. Well, I'll do what I can." I asked Mahler to sit down at the piano and play me something. He had already composed several things, so he said, without any previous training, and I asked him to play me one of his own compositions. I let him play for only a few minutes; the composition was immature, and later on he destroyed it himself. But I realized immediately that I was in the presence of a born musician. I told his father so and added, "That young man will never take over your distillery." Mahler became a pupil at the Vienna Conservatoire soon afterwards, where he was taught the piano by myself and theory by Professor Krenn . . .'

Neues Wiener Journal, 19 May 1911. (The pianist Julius Epstein, 1832–1926; taught at the Conservatoire of the Vienna Society of the Friends of Music [Gesellschaft der Musikfreunde] from 1867 to 1901. His account, published on the day after Mahler's death, differs in a few points from that of Gustav Schwarz.)

The population of Vienna and the influx from the provinces

The result of the last census, held in accordance with the Imperial Law of 29 March 1869, showed the civilian population of the City of Vienna to be 607,615. . . .

Since under this law an official census is to be held only once every ten years, no more recent official statistics are available. In the intervening years, however, the Headquarters of the Imperial-Royal Police in Vienna have had two unofficial censuses made by the Security Services for their own purposes; these showed that the population of the city had risen to 628,053 by 1872, and to 673,865 by 1875. . . .

The more the city has become the centre of the political and industrial life of the Monarchy, however, the more people have left the provinces to settle there, and by 1869 these outsiders were already in the majority. Immigration from abroad, on the other hand, has remained almost unchanged; only in the last ten years has it shown a relatively small increase. At the end of 1869 the numbers of immigrants from the provinces of the Austro-Hungarian Monarchy were as follows:

Bohemia	101,542	Lower Austria	76,171
Bukovina	408	Upper Austria	5,437
Dalmatia	212	Salzburg	812
Galicia	7,564	Silesia	10,668
Carinthia	1,221	Transylvania	893
Carniola	1,454	Styria	5,405
Coastal Provinces	1,009	Tyrol	2,075
Moravia	57,167	Hungary	35,714
Military Frontier	518		

Carl Weiss, *Topographie der Stadt Wien*, Vienna 1876, 37, 38, 39.

Vienna in the second half of the nineteenth century

The expansion of Vienna was decreed in 1858 and energetically carried out from 1860 onwards; in the course of a decade an entirely new city was created. The transformation, during which the powerful bastions crumbled away and the lawns and avenues of the *glacis* became a dusty, shadeless desert, was a sad time for all the Viennese, but it was succeeded by the really splendid, magnificent quarter that rose from the rubble in the shortest possible time. In 1863 the old subdivision into suburbs was abolished and replaced by an Inner City and eight new suburban districts. The city limits were now marked by the Danube Canal, the River Wien and the new Lastenstrasse [road for heavy traffic] which skirts the city. The most important streets radiating from the centre became the boundaries between the suburbs.

Friedrich Umlauft, *Die Österreichisch-Ungarische Monarchie*, Vienna 1883, 663, 665.

The Conservatoire of the Society of the Friends of Music, which Mahler now entered, was a magnificent building only a few years old. By order of the Emperor in 1863, the Society was allotted a considerable plot of land, on which a building designed to hold the Conservatoire and the Society's concert hall was erected by the architect Theophil Hansen between 1867 and 1870.

27, 28   *The new home of the Society of the Friends of Music*

Hitherto the Society of the Friends of Music has been obliged to make the best of a small number of unsuitable classrooms. From now on, thanks to the gracious munificence of His Majesty the Emperor, and the generous support of donors and the First Austrian Savings Bank, the new building will comprise an adequate number of roomy, light and well-situated lecture halls. The fact that they are concentrated in one wing of the building and fitted out with every comfort, will make it possible to unify the whole of the instructional programme.

Jahres-Bericht des Konservatoriums der Gesellschaft der Musikfreunde in Wien, Schuljahr 1868–69, Vienna 1869, 58.

Guido Adler on the training at the Conservatoire

When Mahler came to the Conservatoire in Vienna at the age of fifteen, he was more gifted than he was proficient. Although he found good teachers there for harmony and the piano, the courses in the higher theoretical reaches (counterpoint and composition) were anything but thorough and effective. His talent had to rise above the handicap of this inadequate training, and Mahler was able to overcome these deficiencies many years later only by iron diligence and dedicated private study. As a young man he was so quick to learn that he covered the course by leaps and bounds. What profited him most was the inspiring activity of the Director, who taught by practical

34   example, playing chamber music. The Hellmesberger Quartet influenced us more than any course of lectures. Performances of the quartets of Beethoven's last period made a deeper impression than anything else that Vienna could offer, and had a stylistic influence on all the students of composition.

GA, 10–11. (Guido Adler had himself been a student at the Conservatoire from 1868 to 1874.)

In the autumn of 1875 Richard Wagner came to Vienna, and sent the musically-minded young people into ecstasies. Hugo Wolf, who, like Mahler, was studying harmony under Robert Fuchs, has given eloquent expression to this enthusiasm for Wagner.

Hugo Wolf on Wagner's visit to Vienna

35   Richard Wagner has been since 5 November in Vienna. He occupies, with his wife, seven rooms in the Imperial Hotel. Although he has already been so long in Vienna, I did not have the good fortune and joy to see him until 17 November, at a quarter to eleven, outside the stage door of the opera house, from where I went up on the stage and heard the rehearsal, at which Wagner was present.

    With a truly religious awe I gazed upon this great Master of Tone, for he is, according to present opinion, the greatest

opera composer of all. I went several paces towards him and greeted him very respectfully, whereupon he thanked me in a friendly manner. From that moment forward I conceived an irresistible inclination towards Richard Wagner, without having yet formed any conception of his music. At length, on Monday 22 November, I was initiated into his wonderful music. It was *Tannhäuser*, performed in the presence of the great Richard Wagner himself. I took up my place at a half past two, although the opera, exceptionally, only began at half past six (usually at seven o'clock). There was such a frightful scrimmage that I was worried about myself. I wanted to back out, but it was already impossible, for no one near me would make way. So nothing remained for me to do except to stay in my place. At last the door was opened, the whole crowd pushed their way inside, and it was fortunate that I was drawn into the middle, for if I had got to the side I should have been crushed against the wall. But I was richly compensated for my mortal anxiety. I got my good old place in the gallery. The overture was wonderful, and then the opera! – I can find no words to describe it. I can only tell you that I am a madman. After each act Wagner was tempestuously called for and I applauded until my hands were sore. I cried continually 'Bravo Wagner! Bravissimo Wagner!' and so on, so that I became nearly hoarse and people looked at me more than at Richard Wagner.

Letter to his father, 23 November 1875, quoted from Frank Walker, *Hugo Wolf*, London 1951, 27.

Mahler quickly made friends among his fellow-students at the Conservatoire, and kept in touch with them after he had left. Among these were Hugo Wolf, the same age as himself, Hans Rott, about two years older, Anton Krisper, about three years older, and Rudolf Kržyžanowski. One of the pupils was the eleven-year-old Arnold Rosenblum from Jassy, who, under the name of Arnold Rosé, later became leader of the Vienna Philharmonic Orchestra and Mahler's brother-in-law.

Friedrich Löhr on Mahler's friendship with Kržyžanowski

Rudolf Kržyžanowski was about one year older than Mahler and died four weeks after him. They were fellow-students at the Vienna Conservatoire, to which Kržyžanowski had been admitted several years before Mahler. He studied violin and piano, and later organ and composition. He had brilliant musical gifts and immense personal charm. During this time Mahler developed a profound affection for him, and they shared all the experiences and all the phases of human and artistic adolescence; for years they saw each other every day. Mahler maintained this affection in later life, remained undeviatingly faithful when things were going well for him and badly for his friend, and went out of his way to help him to get on; his affection remained unshakable, although it certainly was not always returned in like manner.

GMB, 473. (According to Friedrich Löhr, who quotes as his authority the dates in the reports of the Conservatoire, Rudolf Kržyžanowski was born in 1859. He later held posts as conductor at Halle an der Saale, Elberfeld, Munich, Prague and Hamburg – where he and Mahler were employed at the same time for one year – and from 1898 to 1907 at Weimar. He died in 1911.)

Extracts from the report on the competitions held at the Conservatoire, 1876

Piano Competition held on 23 June
First Year
. . .

* First Prize: Herr Simon Engel (Class of Professor Dachs) – Chopin: Bolero

* First Prize: Herr Gustav Mahler (Class of Professor Epstein) –
Schubert: Sonata in A minor, first movement
. . .

Competition in Composition held on 1 July (Class of Professor
Krenn)
First Year
* First Prize: Herr Gustav Mahler – First movement of a
Quintet.

* The symbol * indicates that the prize was awarded by unani-
mous vote.

*Bericht über das Conservatorium und die Schauspielschule der Gesellschaft der Musikfreunde
in Wien. Für das Schuljahr 1875–1876*, Vienna 1876, 83, 87.

Paul Stefan on Mahler's youthful compositions

Mahler composed a great deal in his student years. Apart from
the work he composed for the prize competition, which incidentally must have been written literally overnight, there was
a violin sonata that brought him a certain celebrity among his
friends; there is said to have been a 'Nordic Symphony', and
some of the earlier songs go back to this time. He wrote the
libretto for an opera, *Die Argonauten* ['The Argonauts'], in
alliterative verse, and composed some of the music. Furthermore *Das klagende Lied* ['The Lament'], the only work of his
youth that he still acknowledges, admittedly in a revised form,
was originally intended to be an opera.

PST, I, 14.

30   On the printed programme of the concert held at Iglau on
12 September 1876, both Kržyžanowski's and Mahler's
compositions are designated 'Quartet for Piano, two Violins
and Viola'. Although there can be no doubt that this programme was seen by the music critic of the newspaper
Mährischer Grenzbote, he writes of both works as piano
quintets. He is able to state that Mahler's quintet won the
first prize at the Vienna Conservatoire. Kržyžanowski's
composition seems to be identical with the work which,
according to the annual report of the Conservatoire, was
performed at a student concert on 22 December 1875
and described as 'Piano Quintet (C minor, first movement)'.

Concert in support of the Iglau High School

A Gustav Mahler Concert. A select audience attended the
concert on Tuesday evening given by Herr Gustav Mahler,
whom we have to thank for bringing Messrs Siebert, Grünberg
and Kržyžanowski to Iglau. Apart from the visit of Walter and
Door, it was one of the best of our concerts, and it was certainly
one of the most unusual, since it gave us the chance to make the
acquaintance of two composers, Herr Gustav Mahler and Herr
Rudolf Kržyžanowski.

The first piece on the programme was Rudolf Kržyžanowski's Piano Quintet, of which we heard only the first movement.
The merit of this work is that not only the themes, but also the
development, are very carefully worked out. The first subject
is tragic and the second passionate but restrained. The development begins with a double fugue, unfolds with passionate
momentum, and gradually sinks down to the point of repose,
an ingenious adaptation of the central theme (*Adagio*). The
first movement ends with a repeat of the main theme, which
now appears as a funeral march. We can justifiably maintain
that the composer of this quintet has created a beautiful work,
and that the time will come when we can number him among
the great. . . .

Herr Mahler, the organizer of the concert, first appeared as
a pianist, and his playing of Franz Schubert's *Wanderer*

Fantasia gave us the chance to admire his entirely original
interpretation and technique. It is only rarely that musicians
come before the public who know how to re-create music from
their own inner resources; it is this ability that is the ideal of
an executant artist.

The next two works, numbers 4 and 5, Sonata for Violin and
Piano and Piano Quintet, were both composed by Herr
Mahler. It is difficult for us to decide which of these two works
is the better. Both of them show an impressive wealth of ideas
and a great skill in execution which reveal him as a composer
of genius. Herr Siebert played the very difficult part in the
Violin Sonata beautifully, both in technique and interpretation. The piano part was played by the composer. All we
need say about the Piano Quintet is that it was awarded the
first prize at the Conservatoire in Vienna. We were struck, in
this as in the Violin Sonata, by a decided vein of drama.

The sixth piece (a Ballade by Chopin) was played by the
indefatigable concert organizer, who once again performed
superbly, and showed himself to be a worthy pupil of Epstein's.
The final piece of the concert was a Double Concerto for two
Violins by Alard, which was brilliantly played, with beautiful
shades of expression, by Herr Siebert and Herr Grünberg. The
performance of the two quintets was exemplary, and the
audience's enthusiastic applause after each item was well
deserved.

Mährischer Grenzbote, 17 September 1876.

Mahler to the Governing Body of the Conservatoire

I trust that the Worshipful Governing Body will forgive me for
having the temerity to renew my request, which has already
been refused once, to be exempted from tuition fees.

The fact is that my father is not in a position to support me,
let alone pay my tuition fees for me.

I am in no position to pay them myself, since so few people
want me to give them lessons; for this reason it is very question-
able whether I can remain in Vienna. My teacher, Professor
Epstein, has promised that he will arrange some lessons for
me shortly.

For the present I am again taking the liberty of requesting
exemption from paying the fees because I am not in a position
to do so for the reasons I have stated above, and so, to my great
sorrow, should be obliged to forgo the instruction at the
Conservatoire that is of such value to me.

Later, if my circumstances permit, I shall have the greatest
pleasure in meeting my commitments.

    Your obedient servant,

        Gustav Mahler.

I am taking the liberty of supporting this request, and am
prepared to guarantee the punctual payment of *half* the tuition
fees.

        Julius Epstein.

Ms., undated, GDM. (The letter bears a file number of the year 1876, which does
not, however, necessarily indicate the academic year to which Mahler refers.
The Register of the Conservatoire shows that for 1876–77 Mahler had to pay
half the tuition fees, that is '60 florins in 10 instalments'.)

Richard Specht on Mahler's financial position

Mahler's parents were tradespeople who were not well off, but
who never had to let their children go hungry. When he was a
young man in Vienna, he often came to the end of his monthly
allowance too quickly, and at such times stilled his hunger
with buttered rolls and coarse bread. This diet had no adverse
effect on his high spirits, for that was exactly the time, by his
own testimony, when he was at his happiest and most
thoroughly enjoying life.

RSP, I, 14.

Mahler apologizes to Hellmesberger, the Director of the Conservatoire

Since I regret my over-hasty decision, I am taking the liberty of begging you to regard my ill-considered action as not having happened, and to allow me to return to the Conservatoire. I shall make a point of showing myself worthy of this favour by unremitting hard work and by giving satisfaction to you, Sir, as well as to my Professors.

Ms, GDM. (This undated letter bears an old file number, H 83/C 1876. Hugo Wolf left the Conservatoire in the academic year 1876–77 'following a breach of discipline'.)

Mahler's results in his second year at the Conservatoire

Second Year. Half fees.			Academic Year 1876–77.
Piano (Epstein)	compulsory	1	First Prize in Competition
Choir training	compulsory		Did not attend
Chamber music	compulsory		
Orchestral training	compulsory		
Counterpoint (Krenn)	optional	3	Supplementary exam., 14 July. 1st exercise handed in late, 2nd exercise not ready, 3rd no year's assignment produced, and a 1st part of a fictitious work handed in; therefore not permitted to compete for the Prize for Composition.
II. Composition (Krenn) optional		3	

GDM, Matrikel des Konservatoriums.

Final Examinations at the High School, Iglau

Report drawn up on 14 July 1877 on the examination results of the private pupil Gustav Mahler after his second semester in the eighth class.

Written examination:

German: What motives led Wallenstein's various followers to desert him. After Schiller.

Mathematics: The candidate was excused the written examination, having done enough work to pass the leaving examination. Oral examination: setting out of equations and solution of the same. Equation of a straight line that passes through a given point and is parallel to another straight line. Tangents.

Just satisfactory

Physics: What determines pitch? Chromatic aberration. Light is not diffracted on passing through a medium defined by two parallel planes. Coefficient of cubic expansion.

Not satisfactory

Latin: Written, not satisfactory
Oral, Horace, Satires Book I/3 hardly satisfactory

Greek: Written (from Schenkl's Exercises, No. 26, 'The Docile Slave'), not satisfactory
Oral, Protagoras Chapter I less than satisfactory. According to his own admission the examinee has not studied either Crito or Homer

Not satisfactory

Psychology: 1) Attentiveness 2) Reproduction 3) Dreams 4) Doubts

Satisfactory

154

Oral examination:

German: Questions on the main concepts of aesthetics – the beautiful, the sublime, etc.; plot; the drama. The candidate admits that he has not even seen the set book.

Wholly unsatisfactory

Geography and Government of Austria: The Alps – the cities of Carniola – German linguistic enclaves – the language groups of Austria – sources of metals – the Compromise with Hungary – Austrian ministries.

Not satisfactory

OAJ-G.

From a school exercise in 1877

The Motives that led Wallenstein to Decline:
When a man is alone and only has his own fantasy for company, he often makes plans without ever thinking of how to put them into practice; they are little more than phantoms born of his poetic fantaisy [sic]; he dreams of future greatness and of glory and power, and gradually comes to think that he is actually living in his high-flown ideas and bold plans, which would only appear laughable to him if he considered them in the cold light of reason. Thus there generally arises a web of thoughts that makes him entirely oblivious of the world around him. If some incident or other shakes him out of this frame of mind, he will go quietly about his business, and it may be that an hour later he will have entirely forgotten what he had felt and thought in the confusion of his mind a short time before. Woe to the man, however, who takes such pleasure in these ideas of his that constant repetition makes him forget all the absurdity and incoherence contained in them! For the mere fact that a certain concept is gradually formed out of all this chaos makes him the slave of his imagination, and although he still gives no thought to the realization of his plans, he has gradually made them seem so real to himself that a certain obscure hope creeps into his heart. . . .

OAJ-G. (An essay question by Mahler, clipped into the 'Gustav Mahler' folder in the catalogue of the eighth class. The subject set was worded as follows: 'What motives led Wallenstein's various followers to desert him. After Schiller.' The German word *Abfall* can mean 'desertion' or 'decline'. Beside Mahler's title there is a comment, obviously in his teacher's handwriting: 'Subject deliberately altered. Not satisfactory.')

Mahler to Julius Epstein

Your 'Well-Tempered Highness' will excuse me if I modulate from the gentle *adagio* of my feelings through the dissonance of my anger to a wild *finale*, which is to be played *moltissimo rubato*. The fact is that I made my entry into the Matriculation Concerto a few bars too late, or rather I arrived here at Iglau a few days too late, so that I have not been able to take the examination and have had to put it off for two months. None the less I hope to complete the holiday task you set me to your complete satisfaction.

GMB, 11.

From a letter written by Mahler to Gustav Schwarz at Morawan

Iglau, 6 September 1877

. . . Thanks to your good offices I later managed to make a very good friend in Vienna, who has always treated me with the greatest sympathy and the warmest good will. It was you who opened the doors of the temple of the Muses for me, bade me enter, and led me to the Promised Land. As for my progress, I can say that I was not mistaken when I decided on my career, and that I am fulfilling the requirements of my teachers to their greatest satisfaction; perhaps, if fate permits, you will hear more of me this year. . . .

In order to tell you all this in person, I might perhaps have ventured to spend a day or two with you at Morawan, if I had not been prevented by the Matriculation examination which I have to take on the 12th of this month. . . .

Neues Wiener Journal, 6 August 1905.

Mahler sums up the course of his education

Here are the facts: 1860 born in Bohemia. – Spent my youth at the High School – learned nothing, but made music and composed continually from my fourth year onwards, even before I was able to play scales. – In my seventeenth year went to the University of Vienna, and rather than attend lectures (Faculty of Philosophy) was regular in my attendance at the Vienna Woods.

38

GMB, 201. (Undated letter to Max Marschalk, Hamburg, December 1896.)

33   Theodor Rättig on a performance of Bruckner's Third Symphony

As a member of the Choral Society, I attended almost all the orchestral rehearsals. To me it was a dramatic experience, pitiful and scandalous at the same time, to see how the young players in the orchestra laughed at the old man's incompetent conducting, for he had no idea of how to conduct and was reduced to giving the tempo, looking rather like a marionette. The composition itself struck me as being all the more impressive, and awoke in me the conviction that one of the most powerful musical geniuses of all time was about to tread the thorny path that is the normal and, one might say, preordained fate of such great men. The performance completely confirmed me in my opinion. There was at best a small group of ten to twenty young folk of both sexes who applauded; they were opposed by the hissing and laughing gang, and the oracles of the musical élite were sniggering: a marvellous joke to laugh about over the dinners that were awaiting them at home. When the audience had left the hall and the players had left the platform, the sorrowing master was surrounded by the small group of his pupils and admirers, but he only cried out, 'Oh, let me go, people don't want anything of mine.' At that I joined the circle; I expressed my admiration to the Master in the warmest terms, and offered to have the work, which had just been hissed off the platform, performed under the best possible circumstances at my own expense (about 3,000 florins). And, to the astonishment of the musical world, the work was so performed, and this event certainly gave the first positive impulse to the wider appreciation of its creator.

August Göllerich, *Anton Bruckner, ein Lebens- und Schaffensbild*, ed. and completed by Max Auer, Regensburg 1936, vol. IV, pt 1, 477–78. (Theodor Rättig was the proprietor of the Bösendorfer piano firm's publishing house, Büssjager & Rättig.)

The piano transcription of Bruckner's Third Symphony

I have it on the authority of his publisher, Theodor Rättig, among others, that Bruckner always spoke of Mahler with the greatest respect, and that he saw a great deal of him and often played his own recent compositions, new and old, to him. Whenever Mahler called on him, he always insisted on escorting the younger man down the four flights of stairs, with his hat in his hand.

And Mahler? It is certainly a remarkable fact, and not a well-known one, that he was one of the first to transcribe a Bruckner symphony as a piano duet. This transcription of the Third Symphony in D minor – the one with the trumpet theme, dedicated to Wagner – was published, probably in 1878, by Bösendorfer and Rättig. . . .

37

PST, I, 13. (According to an advertisement in the *Neue Wiener Zeitschrift*, vol. 1, no. 17, 10 March 1880, the piano transcription seems to have been published only at the beginning of 1880, at the price of 7.20 florins. According to August Göllerich (*Anton Bruckner*, Regensburg 1936, vol. IV, pt 1, 541); Mahler and Křžžanowski worked on it together; but that is not confirmed by the printed edition, which shows only the name of Gustav Mahler.)

Concert programme of the Society of the Friends of Music, Vienna, 16 December 1877. GDM.

Anton Bruckner. Silhouette. Hans Schliessmann, *Wiener Schattenbilder*, Vienna n.d.

155

Concert given by the Academic Wagner Society

On the 12th inst., the Vienna Academic Wagner Society gave its first evening reception of the season at the Bösendorfer Hall in the Herrengasse. It was attended by a large number of members and their guests, including two Ministers, Herr von Hofmann and Herr Stremayr, and Professors Gänsbacher, Epstein, Bruckner, Door and many others. . . .

The evening opened with Liszt's symphonic poem *Die Ideale*, played on two pianos by Herr Paumgartner and Herr Mottl. . . . The difference in personality between the two performers made it necessary for Herr Mottl to play the *secondo* part and Herr Paumgartner the *primo* in any duet that was to be played on *one* piano, and this was how the two pianists played the Adagio (second movement) and Scherzo (third movement) of Bruckner's Symphony in D minor later in the evening. Herr Bruckner is such a simple, modest man that he hardly dared to come forward to acknowledge the ovation that lasted for several minutes; in the end he did make a very shy appearance, and anyone who heard the enthusiastic applause must have realized quite clearly that this was no artificially organized reception. . . .

Neue Wiener Zeitschrift für Musik, vol. I, no. 6, 20 November 1879. (Felix Mottl, 1856–1911, studied at the Vienna Conservatoire, was a founder member of the Academic Wagner Society, and later became a respected conductor. Hans Paumgartner, 1843–96, pianist and music critic, married the singer Rosa Papier in 1881.)

Guido Adler on the Academic Wagner Society

Only a few teachers showed any liking for the 'new German' art, or even for the art of Wagner. But the young people felt an overpowering enthusiasm for Wagner which carried all before it, and which I shared. Mottl, a young doctor called Karl Wolf (not Hugo Wolf, as one reads in so many books), and I used to meet in order to play and sing Wagner's works. As others joined us, our singing parties were not always held in the house of one of us but in other places as well; thus I was able to persuade the principal of the Academy High School to allow us to hold meetings on school premises, and we founded the Academic Wagner Society, privately at first, and later, when I went to the University, publicly and by statute. My family was unsympathetic, and some laughed at me or pitied me – exactly as the public at large did.

Guido Adler, *Wollen und Wirken*, Vienna 1935, 10. (The *Fünftes Jahresbericht des Wiener akademischen Wagner-Vereins*, Vienna 1877, the Wagner Society's fifth annual report, includes Gustav Mahler and his friends in the list of members. According to the seventh annual report, Vienna 1880, Gustav Mahler, Rudolf Krżyżanowski, Fritz Löwy [Löhr] and Hans Rott resigned from the Society in 1879.)

Mahler on his relationship with Bruckner

I was never a pupil of Bruckner's; this rumour must have arisen from the fact that I was continually seen about with him in my earlier days in Vienna, and that I was certainly one of his most enthusiastic admirers and publicists. Indeed, I believe that at that time I was the only one there was, except for my friend Krżyżanowski, who is now working in Weimar. This, I think, was between 1875 and 1881. The letters he wrote to me date from all sorts of years, and hardly any of them contains anything of importance. I do not believe that one can do a man like him any good by publishing such documents. In any case, he who has eyes and ears can see and hear. My friendship with him lasted for seven whole years. To this day it still pleases me to remember how, one fine morning, he called me out of the hall during a lecture at the University (to the astonishment of those present) and played the wonderful theme of the Adagio to me on a piano that was thick with dust. At that time he was still remarkable for his youthful, almost childish gaiety and his inherent serene trustfulness; these qualities made friendship with him possible in spite of the great difference in our ages. In view of his character, which is equally well known to you, I was naturally bound to acquire a knowledge and understanding of his life and ambitions which, in return, cannot have been without influence on my own development as an artist and a man. And so it is true that I have more right than most others to call myself his 'pupil', and shall always do so in grateful honour of his memory.

August Göllerich, *Anton Bruckner*, Regensburg 1936, vol. IV, pt 1, 448–49. (Göllerich's continuer and editor, Max Auer, gives 1902 as the year in which this letter was written: 'Bruckner und Mahler', *Bruckner-Blätter* (Vienna), vol. III, no. 2/3, 1931, 24. Bruckner completed the score of his Seventh Symphony in September 1883.)

In the academic year 1877–78, Mahler, who had hitherto studied the piano as his main subject at the Conservatoire, began to specialize in composition. In his third year in Krenn's composition class, he competed for the Composition Prize on July 1878, and shared the first prize with Mathilde von Kralik, Rudolf Krżyżanowski and Rudolf Pichler. His prize composition was performed at the end-of-term concert on 11 July. That was the end of Mahler's training at the Conservatoire. The official Report for the academic year 1877–78 shows his name in the list of students who qualified in their main subjects that year, and in the list of those who received diplomas. The diploma was awarded only to students who had passed the prescribed examination in their main subjects with distinction, in their subsidiary subjects at least satisfactorily, and who had won a prize in the last competition held during their time at the Conservatoire.

Emma Adler remembers Mahler's friendship with Victor Adler

Meeting Gustav Mahler is one of my most pleasant memories. When my husband and I were engaged, we went to the end-of-term concert given by the students who had completed their courses at the Conservatoire and were about to leave. One of them was Gustav Mahler, who played one of his own compositions.

Year [?] later we came to know him personally. He was a friend of Lipiner's, who brought him to our house in the Berggasse. We liked Mahler's open, modest manner. One evening Victor asked him to play something to us, but Mahler laughed and said it was quite out of the question.

We were surprised by this curious behaviour. Victor asked him why he had refused, whereupon Mahler said that it got on his nerves to play on an upright piano, and that he simply could not understand how musically sensitive people could stand having such instruments of torture in their houses.

Soon after, Victor went with Mahler to buy a grand piano, which Mahler tested and passed fit for use.

At that time Mahler lived in very straitened circumstances and gave piano lessons. Victor had even tried to find some for him. Overexertion and undernourishment had made him highly strung; he knew it and laughed at himself for it. He told us that he talked loudly to himself in the streets and gesticulated with his arms, so that messenger boys used to rush up to him and offer their services.

Emma Adler, 'Biographie Victor Adlers', typescript, 107–08, Verein für Geschichte der Arbeiterbewegung, Vienna. (Emma Adler, 1858–1935, married Victor Adler, a doctor, in September 1878. Mahler was also friendly with her brother, Heinrich Braun.)

Siegfried Lipiner and his circle at the University

At a meeting of the Reading Society of German Students, during the discussion a very young, insignificant-looking man [Lipiner] rose to speak, and immediately gripped the attention of the audience by the power of his words. A few days later, at a smaller gathering, he read aloud to us a completed, full-length drama entitled *Arnold von Brescia*. That was the occasion on which he made his entry into a students' society that had existed for a long time; its nucleus was a group of old school friends, to which other members were admitted. A whole succession of young people, whose names are known or who have become famous today, joined this group sooner or later, either permanently or temporarily. At a time when the name of Nietzsche was not generally known, this group was studying his *Unzeitgemässe Betrachtungen* ['Thoughts out of Season'], then newly published. Indeed, it may be said that this group was a centre of vigorous intellectual life unique among the Vienna students of that time.

We were all aware of young Lipiner's quite unusual intellectual gifts and his undeniable intellectual superiority. We all believed in a great future for him, and, after the publication of his *Prometheus*, thought that this future would be in the realm of poetry. I admit for my part that I have met a great many very gifted and very clever people in the course of a long life, but that Siegfried Lipiner had the finest intellect that I have ever come across. He not only had the acuteness that is so often to be observed among Jews, but also that profundity of mind that penetrates to the very heart of things. Furthermore the extent of his knowledge was astonishing, and it was continually growing.

Engelbert Pernerstorfer, 'Nekrolog Siegfried Lipiner', *Zeitschrift des österreichischen Vereins für Bibliothekswesen*, vol. III, no. 2, 1912, 122–23. (Engelbert Pernerstorfer, 1850–1918, journalist and later Social Democratic member of parliament. Since his school days he had been a friend of Victor Adler, 1852–1918, who became leader of the Austrian Social Democrats. Pernerstorfer, Adler and many others belonged to the group that collected round Siegfried Lipiner, 1856–1911, among them Gustav Mahler, on whom Lipiner exercised an enduring philosophical influence.)

Lipiner on the subject of himself and his early works

Siegfried Lipiner, born on 24 October 1856 at Jaroslaw. Childhood spent in Galicia; at high school, first in Galicia, later in Vienna. Universities of Vienna and Leipzig. Original works: *Der Entfesselte Prometheus* ['Prometheus Unbound'] (Leipzig, Breitkopf und Härtel, 1876), *Renatus* (1878), *Buch der Freude* ['Book of Joy'] (1882) (still published by the same firm), *Über die Erneuerung religiöser Ideen in der Gegenwart* ['On the Renewal of Religious Ideas at the Present Day'] (a short work, 1878); translations – brief ones – from Polish in *Die Dioskuren*, articles in the *Deutsche Zeitung*. About to appear: *Herr Thaddäus* (the masterpiece of Adam Mickiewicz) translated by L. and *Bruder Rausch*. . . .

Handwritten *curriculum vitae* as postscript to a letter to Karl Emil Franzos, ms., WSTB. (Lipiner, whose epic poem *Der Entfesselte Prometheus* was admired by Nietzsche and Wagner, published little more in later years. He planned a trilogy on the subject of Christ, but it remained unfinished. One of his last works was a poem in honour of Mahler's fiftieth birthday. Lipiner died in 1911.)

Mahler's twofold talent for music and literature

It is a strange and little-known fact that for a long time this born musician gave up any idea of a musical career, and thought of becoming a poet. This occurred during that indeterminate process of fermentation that is typical of the young artist who is struggling to establish his ego, and groping uncertainly for the right way to do it.

RSPI, 17.

From the yearbook of the Conservatoire. *Bericht über das Conservatorium der Gesellschaft der Musikfreunde in Wien. Für das Schuljahr 1877–1878*, Vienna 1878, 590.

The competition for the Beethoven Scholarship Fund award was announced for the first time on 1 September 1876, but it turned out to be impossible to make an award. The somewhat unsuitable title was altered to the 'Beethoven Grant for Composition', and at the same time the period within which a student might compete for it was extended from six to ten years after completing his studies. It was again impossible to make an award in 1878. There were three applicants, among them Gustav Mahler, who had graduated from the Conservatoire that same year, and who submitted an Overture, *The Argonauts* (copy of opening theme preserved in the files).

Richard von Perger and Robert Hirschfeld, *Geschichte der k.k. Gesellschaft der Musikfreunde in Wien*, Vienna 1912, 166–67. (The file for the year 1878, which Hirschfeld quotes as his authority, can no longer be found in the Society's archives. On the other hand the prize committee minutes for 1879 have been preserved, with the opening themes of the competitors' compositions attached. In 1879 the Beethoven Grant for Composition was awarded to Hugo Reinhold; Mahler's friends Hans Rott and Rudolf Pichler were unsuccessful.)

Mahler, Wolf and Kržyžanowski

Mahler and Wolf had been friends ever since they were both young. Their poverty drove them to rent a room together, and to share it with a third by name of Kržyžanowski; they all lived there for a couple of months. As all three were musicians, they were all very sensitive to noise. When one of the three was busy composing, the other two had to spend the whole night walking round the town. In this way Mahler once composed a quartet movement for a competition in one night, while the others were banished to the streets. They slept on benches in the Ringstrasse.

Mahler gave lessons; Wolf could find few or none. When their money gave out, one of them always cancelled all his outstanding lessons. He did this in the following way: he rang the doorbell, said he was obliged to leave the city, and asked to be paid for the lessons he had already given. So one of them always got more money immediately, and that meant a couple of lunches for them all. Of course it also meant that a pupil was lost for ever.

The three friends discovered *The Twilight of the Gods* together. In their passionate enthusiasm they screamed the trio between Gunther, Brünnhilde and Hagen so horribly, that the landlady appeared in the doorway, trembling with rage, and gave them all notice to quit on the spot. She stayed in the room until the young gentlemen had packed their scanty possessions, and locked the door behind them scolding all the time.

AM, 82–83. (*The Twilight of the Gods* was first produced in Vienna on 14 February 1879, and the complete *Ring of the Nibelung* on 26, 27, 28 and 30 May 1879.)

Teaching the piano on the Puszta

Puszta-Batta, 18 June 1879

I am living here on a Hungarian Puszta [steppe], with a family that has engaged me for the summer; I have to give piano lessons to the boys, and now and then to elevate the family to a plane of musical inspiration. I sit and wriggle like a gnat in a spider's web. But the Moor does his duty.

Yet when I go out for a walk on the heath in the evening, I climb a friendly linden tree that stands there in solitude, and I look out upon the world from its topmost branches; the Danube goes on its age-old way before my eyes, and the glow of the setting sun flickers in its ripples; behind me in the village the evening bells all sound the Angelus together, and the sound is brought to me by a friendly breeze; and the branches of the tree swing to and fro in the wind and rock me to sleep, like the Erl King's daughters, and the leaves and blossoms of my beloved tree press tenderly against my cheeks. Everywhere there is peace, holy peace! Only from far away there comes to me the melancholy croaking of a toad, sitting sadly in the rushes.

From a letter to Josef Steiner, GMB, 7.

[Batta, June 1879]

Your letter has found me in a state of the most fearful homesickness. I simply cannot stand it any longer.

I am delighted to be able to tell you that the family is going to the seaside at Nordeney on 12 August, and that I shall soon be as free as a bird. I hope to join you soon at Seelau. . . .

From a letter to Emil Freund, GMB, 13. (Emil Freund, 1859–1928, was in the same class as Mahler at school at Iglau in 1873, and had been studying law at the University of Vienna since the autumn of 1877. He later became Mahler's lawyer.)

Batta, 16 July 1879

. . . I will be silent about my sufferings. How could I describe them to you, you who have not yet endured the pain of loneliness, the grief that heartless people inflict, the repulsiveness of this awful communal life, where we live like ants in an anthill!

On 10 August (I shall certainly write to you again before then) I am going to Vienna, from where I shall go on to Iglau. I hope to be *sure* of seeing you there.

You simply can't think, my dear Albert, how I am looking forward to seeing human people again, and how I am longing to hear the sound of the organ and the pealing of the bells once more. I seem to hear the beating of angels' wings when I see people dressed up for church; they kneel before the altar and pray, and add their songs of praise to the sound of drums and trumpets.

Alas, there has been no altar for me for a long time; the vast heavens, which are God's temple, rise above me, lofty and silent. I cannot reach up to them, and yet I should so like to pray. Instead of chorales and hymns, the thunder roars, and instead of candles the lightning flickers.

Away, away, you elements! I do not understand your language, and when you sing praises to God it sounds like fury to my human ears!

From a letter to Albert Spiegler, ms., The Pierpont Morgan Library, New York, and The Mary Flagler Cary Charitable Trust.

Two young Viennese, who were studying at the University at the same time as Mahler, were later among his most intimate friends: Friedrich Löhr and Albert Spiegler. In the winter semester of 1877, Friedrich Löhr (born Löwi; 1859–1924) entered his name for two courses of lectures which were also attended by Mahler; he later worked at the Austrian Institute of Archaeology. Albert Spiegler was a student of medicine; he never practised, but did private research on dietetics.

94

Friedrich Löhr on Mahler's friendship with Albert Spiegler

Dr Albert Spiegler was one of Mahler's oldest and most intimate friends in Vienna; he was also Lipiner's closest friend. Before Mahler left Vienna to go abroad, he was a frequent guest of Spiegler's family; and later, during summer holidays and while he was living in Vienna before his marriage, he spent much of his spare time – what little leisure his extraordinary volume of work allowed him – in Lipiner's and Spiegler's homes. Frau Nina Spiegler always remained Mahler's dearest woman friend.

GMB, notes, 478.

Mahler to Anton Krisper

Why is it that I have not had a single line from you, so that I have no idea where you are to be found?

My way of life for the last two months can be told in few words: I have

*　　*　　*

I am starting again, after having to break off for half an hour, as that brute of a housemaid has forgotten to fill my lamp, so that I have been obliged to go and call on all the tradesmen in the Cottage Quarter who are likely to sell paraffin; at last a kind-hearted one opened his shop for me; it's now half-past ten.

Well, to return to my way of life. My dear friend, I have got myself quite badly entangled in the silken chains of the darling of the gods. The hero 'now sighs, now wrings his hands, now groans, now entreats', etc., etc. I have really spent most of the time indulging in every kind of bitter-sweet daydream; I have said 'Ah' when I got up and 'Oh' when I went to bed; I have lived in my dreams and have dreamt while I was awake, and now the two months have sped by and the Christ Child is with us – and ought to bring me something really lovely. I shall be at Iglau in a week and shall awake from my rosy dreams to a yet more rosy day.

Yet another shadow now looms in the background of my visions, but I must await the arrival of the man who casts it. When he shows himself, I will tell you more about him – I can only hazard a guess that it is some sort of age-old Nordic king, who wants to frighten me out of my peace of mind with his heroes and his drinking-bouts. I have also sipped a drop of hippocrene – well, when the heart is full the lips cannot remain sealed.

Enough of this odious simpering – I have forced myself into a facetious pastoral style so as not to fall into the old, trite lamentations. I don't want to sigh, but I don't want to smile either. Several squadrons of imprecations and curses are quartered in my φρήν [mind]; I don't want to let them march out. The Devil take this beggarly life! My eyes are like a couple of squeezed-out lemons, and there is not a single tear left in them. I must taste all the sorrows of this world; I shall not be spared a single one.

All this is going to puzzle you. I am afraid I shall soon be in a position to give you a fearsome explanation of it. Till then, a fond good-bye; write soon. I shall now go to bed, for I need rest.

Goodnight, dear Anton! Goodnight!
Your faithful friend,
Gustav Mahler.

Karl Ludwigstrasse 24, Cottageverein, Vienna.

If you can, lend me a fiver, but only if you have it to spare.

Vienna, 14 December. I have been carrying this letter around in my pocket for two weeks. Answer by return! I go home on Friday.

HHI, 812–13. (The allusion to 'rosy dreams' is a reference to Josephine Poisl, the daughter of the postmaster at Iglau; he dedicated three songs composed in February and March 1880 to her: *Im Lenz* ['In Spring'], *Winterlied* ['Winter Song'] and *Maitanz im Grünen* ['May Day Dance in the Meadows'].)

Hugo Wolf to his father, 17 December 1879

I must have 40 florins – it is a confounded nuisance that I can't get them here. I am moving to the Cottage Quarter near Vienna tomorrow so that I can live more cheaply, and also pay more attention to my work and studies.

So write to Karl Ludwigstrasse 24, Cottage-Verein, Währing. I do not need the money immediately; however I must have 20 florins by 5 January. If you could send me 10 florins in advance, my position would be very much easier.

The reason why I have no lessons again is quite simple. Krżyżanowski went on tour with Wilt and Christoff as their accompanist, and wanted to be away for two months, so he handed his lessons over to me. But then Frau Wilt fell very ill at Brünn, which meant that the tour came to an end and K. came back after a week and took the lessons back from me. So that is clear. And now, dearest Father, how are you? I should love to be told that you are in better spirits. One more thing:

if you are thinking of coming to Vienna, you will be very comfortable if you stay with me. I have a lease for a year, bedroom, study, entrance hall, kitchen, loft and cellar, for the reasonable rent of 45 florins a quarter, or 15 florins a month – furnished of course. I also have a good piano, for which I shall not have to pay rent yet because my friend Mahler, who is vacating my future house tomorrow, has paid it up to January. The instrument is excellent.

Hugo Wolf, Eine Persönlichkeit in Briefen, Leipzig 1912, 45.

Mahler to Anton Krisper

Why haven't you written? Haven't you had my letters? My life goes on in the same old way. Spring has come overnight, and with it the old yearning and melancholy. I have just written a few verses which I am sending to you, because they can show you my state of mind better than anything else.

FORGOTTEN LOVE
How drear is my heart! How vain is everything!
How great is my longing!
O, how the distance stretches endlessly
from vale to vale!
My sweet love! For the last time!
Alas, must this pain for all eternity
burn in my heart!

How faithful and bright in days gone by
were the rays from her eyes!
I gave up wandering altogether
in spite of winter's perfidy!
And when the spring had passed away
My love adorned her fair hair
with wreaths of myrtle!

My wanderer's staff! again to-day
come out from the corner!
You slept for long! So now make ready!
For I am come to wake you!
I bore the pain of love for long
And however wide the world may be –
Then come, my true companion!

How sweetly smile both hill and dale
in waves of blossom!
For spring with his ever sweet song
has come already!
And flowers are blooming everywhere
And little crosses stand everywhere –
they have not lied!

Before anything else, I want to tell you about a plan for a walking tour that I mean to go on in July with Heinrich and Krżyżanowski; we are definitely counting on your coming with us. We shall go through the Bohemian Forest first (the only primeval forest in Europe, inhabited by a strange and individual race with wonderful women), then on through the Fichtel Mountains. Eger – Bayreuth – Nuremberg – and finally to Oberammergau for the Passion Play – it will all take only three weeks, and then we all go straight home, only if possible I want you to spend a few days with me at Iglau. Don't you like this idea? It would be quite wonderful; this is what we discussed last summer.

Undated letter, postmark Vienna, 3 March 1880, HHI 18–82.

Hugo Wolf and the idea of an opera on the subject of 'Rübezahl'

In the course of conversation it occurred to Wolf to write a fairy-tale opera. This was long before Humperdinck, and certainly an entirely new idea. They considered many subjects and decided on *Rübezahl*. Mahler was young and impetuous, and the whole idea attracted him so greatly that he began to

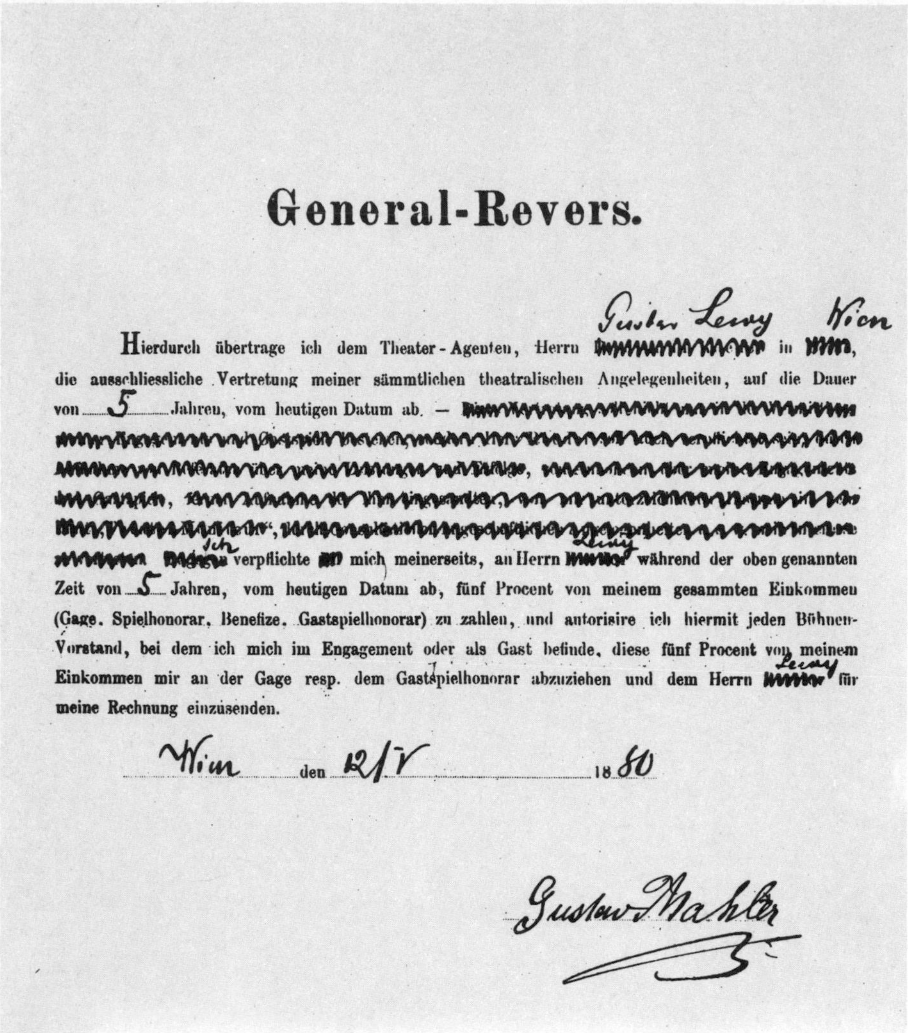

Mahler's contract with his agent. WSTB.
On 12 May 1880 Mahler appointed the
Vienna agent Gustav Lewy as exclusive
representative for 'all his theatrical affairs'
for a period of five years and undertook
to pay him 5 per cent of his gross income.

write the libretto that very night, finished it in one day and
innocently brought it to Wolf as soon as it was ready. But
Wolf had also begun, and he was so angry at being forestalled
that he immediately gave up all thought of composing such an
opera; he never forgave Mahler. Outwardly they remained
good friends for a time, but they never again sought each
other's company.

AM, 83. (Rübezahl is a mountain sprite in German folklore.)

Julius Epstein on Mahler's appointment at Hall

One day my pupil asked my advice. He had been offered the
post of Conductor at Hall. His parents and friends were against
his accepting a post with what they called a backwoods
theatre. But I decided for him: 'Take it at once! You'll very
soon work your way up. You'll be offered a better job in no
time.'

Mahler accepted my advice.

Illustriertes Wiener Extrablatt, 19 May 1911.

Drama and music at Hall

Of the two *pianos* that stand in the Pump Room, one is for
general use and the other, a magnificent Bösendorfer grand, is
reserved for professional players. Just outside the Pump Room
is the *Park*; it is very suitably laid out and beautifully kept. Its
numerous shady paths and arbours provide pleasant walks
and secluded resting places, and there are also landscaped
hills with delightful views. *The Pump Room Orchestra* plays in

the Park twice a day, from seven to half-past eight in the morning and from six to half-past seven in the evening, and delights
the strollers by the precision and warmth of its playing of a
varied and attractive repertoire of classical and dance music.

To the left of the Park, from which it is separated by a single
villa, is the entrance to an Esplanade, thirty feet wide, with
three strips of greenery, which curves like a horseshoe for four
hundred yards towards the so-called Hadring Copse, and
then back to the Park. It runs past the theatre, which is small,
but pretty and very well equipped, and in which a company
adequate for modest requirements performs plays three or
four times a week. Concerts are held there from time to time.

H. Schuber, *Der Kurort Hall in Ober-Österreich mit seinen Jod- und Brom-haltigen
Quellen*, Vienna 1873, 27–28.

A curious conducting appointment

Mahler was eighteen when he went to Bad Hall, where the
father of the operetta singer, Fräulein Zwerenz, gave him a very
unusual appointment as conductor at the summer theatre.
His duties included putting the music sheets on the players'
desks before the performance, dusting the piano, and collecting
the music after the performance. In the intervals he had to
push a pram round the theatre with the baby Mizzi Zwerenz
in it. One thing he would not agree to do was to play small
parts on stage. He often said later what a pity it was that his
pride prevented it, as he would have learnt a lot of things that
would never come his way again.

He was so out of place there that a group of well-dressed
aristocrats, who had gathered round the painter Angeli, invited

42

him to join them. Mahler felt very flattered at being noticed by the first cultured people he had met there. He blossomed. They went for long expeditions together, which naturally took him away from his duties more and more, until on one occasion he came back long after the beginning of a performance, and so lost his job. They all saw him off at the station, and he went away with the assurance that he was to visit them all in Vienna, and very happy to have made friends with such splendid people. As soon as he knew that they were back in Vienna he set off on his round of calls, and found all their doors closed against him. He immediately felt that he had been snubbed because he was a Jew; he avoided meeting new people, and from then on fell back on the friends of his youth. (It may well not have been because he was a Jew at all, but because he was a holiday acquaintance.)

AM, 138–39. (The impresario Karl Ludwig Zwerenz ran the theatre at Iglau for the 1880–81 season. Hall was not Bad Hall until later; Mahler was nearly twenty.)

Mahler writes from Hall to Albert Spiegler

Where is Lipiner? It is really very inconsiderate of him to be trailing round the world with *Rübezahl* in his luggage and not to write a single line to me, when I am crying out for it. I do not even know whether it is still extant – for it is the only copy that I possess – and I should very much like to work at it again, although I am so angry about it that it hardly gives me any pleasure any more. Please send me his address, and do what you can to see that I get my manuscript back. . . .

From an undated letter, postmark 21 June 1880, ms., The Pierpont Morgan Library, New York, and the Mary Flagler Cary Charitable Trust.

Vegetarians, Wagnerians and Socialists

Our obscure vegetarian restaurant was situated in the very middle of the best part of Vienna, among old aristocratic palaces and magnificent government offices, on the corner of the silent, dreamy Wallnerstrasse and the Fahnengasse which was dark and scarcely two metres wide.

A small glass door led from the street down some stone steps into the semi-darkness of the vaults, which received very little of the light of day, through little barred windows set flush against the plaster, so that the reddish butterfly flames of the wretched gas lights had to burn from dawn till dusk. . . .

One customer in particular dined there fairly frequently: Dr Victor Adler, who was not yet thirty years old. He was very soon to give up the practice of medicine in order to devote all his energy and his very considerable ability to furthering the cause of Socialism. It is well known that he was the real founder of the Austrian Social Democratic Party, and that he later played the most important part in launching the Vienna *Arbeiter-Zeitung* [Workers' News]. He was the first Foreign Minister of the Austrian Republic, but he died in the autumn of 1918, only a few days after being appointed.

Although he was not strictly speaking a vegetarian, he had acquired an interest in this way of life from a relation of his by marriage, Dr Heinrich Braun; Braun and his brother Adolf came to our restaurant every day and were dedicated advocates of a purely vegetable diet. Dr Heinrich Braun later became very well known for his sociological work and his marriage to Lilly von Gizicky . . .

Dr Victor Adler was already a widely read and deeply cultivated scholar, and the conversations I had with him have been of outstanding value to me in later life. We discussed current affairs, historical theories, Richard Wagner, Ibsen, and Shelley as a revolutionary poet and vegetarian, as well as neurology, psychiatry, and other scientific subjects. He was on very friendly terms with people of all classes and professions. He was daily in the company of the historian Dr Heinrich Friedjung, young Hermann Bahr, and Dr Michael Hainisch

and Dr Thomas Masaryk, who were both destined to become Presidents of their respective countries. One of his best friends, however, was that shy, melancholy, sensitive poet Siegfried Lipiner. He was about twenty-four years old then and a frequent visitor to our restaurant; he soon became one of our closest friends. A short time before he had been engaged in an active correspondence with Friedrich Nietzsche, to whom he had sent his *Der entfesselte Prometheus*. . . .

Together with Braun and Lipiner, Dr Emanuel Sax also belonged to Victor Adler's circle. Sax was another vegetarian; he was a man of medium height, thin and high-shouldered, with a sharp, hollow-cheeked face and flushed, somewhat prominent cheekbones. He too was a man of great intelligence, and was profoundly interested in sociological problems; at that time he had just begun to write a comprehensive work on cottage industries in Thuringia. The book appeared in three volumes in the course of the following year, and made a great sensation with its extremely forceful, vivid descriptions of the misery of the Thuringian workers; its author soon became very well known, and indeed has influenced subsequent German legislation. . . .

The autumn of 1880 brought a quite unexpected event that was of importance to us. The October number of the *Bayreuther Blätter*, the magazine that for some years had spread Richard Wagner's ideas far and wide, printed a great discourse by the Master on the subject of 'Religion and Art'. In this article, which owed its inspiration to the same emotion as the recently completed *Parsifal*, Wagner wrote in the most passionate terms in favour of vegetarianism, which he described as the one hope of salvation that remained to the profoundly degenerate human race.

'There are strong inherent reasons,' we read, 'that make it possible even to regard modern Socialism as significant from the point of view of the social structure of our country, as soon as it sincerely makes common cause with the threefold union of vegetarians, animal lovers and advocates of temperance.'

Such a close alliance, Wagner continued, would seem to justify the hope of recovering a real religion, and of a thorough-going regeneration of the human race. The result of these portentous utterances on Wagner's part was that our vegetarian-minded circle expanded rapidly and attracted new members, particularly young musicians who, inspired by 'Religion and Art', joined us in our demand for a diet that did not require the slaughter of animals.

One day a slim young man, with fair hair, a little down on his chin and upper lip, a pale face and a rather piercing pair of eyes, came into the restaurant. He hardly spoke a word, and what he did say amounted to an occasional wary growl. His name, as I later discovered, was Hugo Wolf, and I was told that he had already composed some beautiful songs some years before.

Another new habitué of our vegetarian restaurant, also obviously brought to us by Richard Wagner, was the pianist August Göllerich, a favourite pupil of Franz Liszt's. At that time he was also very friendly with Anton Bruckner, whose near neighbour he was. He began a large-scale biography of Bruckner but never finished it. He died many years ago as Conductor at Linz.

And then a few more young men arrived, close friends of Heinrich and Otto Braun's, and of Lipiner's. One of them was on the short side; an unusual irritability was already noticeable in his curiously seesawing gait; his small face, intellectually tense and exceptionally mobile, was framed by a brown beard. His talk was always witty; he spoke with a strong Austrian accent. He always carried a bundle of books or music under his arm, and conversation with him was generally sporadic. His name was Gustav Mahler.

We were more than usually aware of him because he was the first man to make a piano transcription of a Bruckner symphony. In later years I often talked about Mahler to Bruckner, from whom I have never heard anything but praise of the younger man's great talent.

Gustav Mahler and Hugo Wolf had known each other since their Conservatoire days, and their relationship was that of old school friends. Many years later Hugh Wolf told me how, when they were still very young, he once met Mahler in the Herrengasse with a roll of music under his arm. On being asked what he was carrying, Mahler replied that it was some songs he had only just composed, and he asked Wolf to have a look at them. Wolf read the manuscript through in the street very attentively and said, grinning with pleasure, 'Very fine! Tiptop! I like them immensely!' Mahler, delighted by this opinion, dropped his eyes, hesitated self-consciously and said, 'Well, I think we've got Mendelssohn beat!'

On one occasion, I forget what, we organized a vegetarian dinner, with speeches and music, in the dining-room of an old hotel that has long since disappeared. All those who attended it were vegetarians. Cyrill Hynais, a pupil of Bruckner's, played his 'Ocean Symphony' on the piano, the young opera singer Josef Reiff-Heissiger sang some of Loewe's Ballads, and I contributed [Mozart's] *In diesen heiligen Hallen*. At the piano was Herr Gustav Mahler, then twenty-one years old.

Friedrich Eckstein, *Alte unnennbare Tage!*, Vienna 1936, 105 sqq.

Mahler to Emil Freund

Vienna, 1 November 1880

I have had to endure so many shocks recently that I cannot bring myself to speak to anybody who knew me in my happier days.

I can only reply to what you tell me by telling you something equally heart-breaking: my friend Hans Rott has *gone mad*! I cannot help fearing that the same thing will happen to Krisper.

The news came to me at the same time as your letter, and at a time when I badly need to hear something more comforting. Wherever you look you see misery, which assumes the oddest disguises in order to harass the children of men . . . I have been a total vegetarian for a month. The moral effect of this way of life, resulting from the voluntary subjugation of my body and my consequent freedom from craving, is immense. You can imagine how greatly I am inspired by it when I tell you that I expect it to lead to a *regeneration* of the human race. . . .

My *fairy-tale* is finished at last – a real child of much toil, on which I have already been working for a whole year. But something good has come of it. My next task is to leave no stone unturned to get it performed.

GMB, 14–15.

Mahler on his 'fairy-tale'

The first work in which I really found myself as *Mahler* is a *fairy-tale* for chorus, soloists and orchestra: *Das klagende Lied*! I describe this work as my Opus 1.

GMB, 204. (From a letter to the composer Max Marschalk, written in December 1896.)

Second unsuccessful application for the Beethoven Prize

Since the endowment of the Beethoven Prize for Composition the adjudicators have found themselves able to make an award this year for the second time.

The following were adjudicators: Herr Josef Hellmesberger, Court Conductor, Herr W. Gericke, Court Opera Conductor, Herr J. N. Fuchs, Herr Hans Richter, Professor Krenn and the two composers Herr Joh. Brahms and Herr Goldmark. They awarded the Prize to Robert Fuchs, formerly a student,

Robert Fuchs. Woodcut after a drawing by M. Ledeli. GDM. Fuchs (1847–1927) was Mahler's professor of harmony at the Vienna Conservatoire.

and now a teacher, at the Conservatoire, for a Piano Concerto in B flat minor. They were also in the pleasant position of being able to commend the works submitted by two other competitors, namely an Overture, and a setting of the Dervish's Song, for Grillparzer's *Der Traum ein Leben*, composed by Victor R. von Herzfeld, and an Overture in F by H. Fink, as being worthy of an award.

Rechenschaftsbericht der Direktion der Gesellschaft der Musikfreunde in Wien für das Verwaltungsjahr 1881–82, Vienna 1883, 8.

. . . Gustav Mahler again competed for the Prize with *Das klagende Lied* for soloists, chorus and orchestra, and was again unsuccessful. Perhaps it was this that moved Goldmark, who was an adjudicator, to insert a very remarkable comment into the report: 'Herr Goldmark considers it desirable that, in assessing the works that have been submitted, the awarding committee should agree on certain principles with regard to the priority to be given either to the dexterity and skill shown in the construction of the works, or to talent; even if it shows less technical proficiency.'

Richard von Perger and Robert Hirschfeld, *Geschichte der k.k. Gesellschaft der Musikfreunde in Wien*, Vienna 1912, 167.

In September 1881 Mahler went as musical director to the Provincial Theatre (Landschaftliches Theater) at Laibach (today Ljubljana in Yugoslavia), where he conducted all the operas and most of the operettas during the 1881–82 season. The repertory included the following operas: *Il Trovatore* by Verdi, *The Magic Flute* by Mozart, *The Barber of Seville* by Rossini, *Faust* by Gounod, *Der Freischütz* by Weber, *Alessandro Stradella* by Flotow and *The Merry Wives*

41

of *Windsor* by Nicolai, and the following operettas: *Giroflé-Giroflà* by Lecocq, *Boccaccio* by Suppé, and *Der Lustige Krieg* by Johann Strauss.

Anton Krisper, Mahler's friend from Conservatoire days, had settled at Laibach with his family, and Mahler lived with them. (See Hans Holländer, 'Gustav Mahler', *The Musical Quarterly*, October 1931, 455.)

The Duchy of Carniola and its capital, Laibach

43, 44 Laibach, Ljubljana in Slovenian and Labacum or Aemona in Latin, is 303 metres above sea level. It extends along both banks of the clear, deep, sea-green River Laibach (Ljubljanca), and lies in a crescent round the steep Castle Hill. It is in a level valley formed by two mountain spurs which divide the Laibach peat bog from the sandy Plain of the Save. The Laibach, which was canalized in 1826, runs into the River Save an hour's walk below the town, part of which is surrounded by the waters of the Gruber Canal, which was dug in 1780 when the marshes were drained. Laibach formerly had nine suburbs, . . . but is now subdivided into five municipal districts. The population amounts to 26,284 inhabitants, of whom 1,666 are military personnel; of the rest, 59% are German and 40·5% are Slovene. In accordance with the warm climate, the streets in the centre of the town are narrow, irregular, and overhung by tall houses, the main street being the only exception; the outlying districts, on the other hand, have a number of beautiful streets, squares and private houses, especially the new quarter near the large and well-situated railway station.

Friedrich Umlauft, *Die Österreichisch-Ungarische Monarchie*, Vienna 1883, 748.

The employees of the Laibach Theatre for the 1881–82 Season

45 According to the information given us by the Director, Herr Alexander Mondheim-Schreiner, the staff of our Provincial Theatre for the 1881–82 season, which opens on the 24th of this month, consists of the following: Technical-artistic staff: Herr Alexander Mondheim-Schreiner, the Director, is in charge of staging and is directly responsible for the stage management of operettas and farces; Herr Adolf Wallhof is Stage Manager for dramas and comedies; Herr Louis Linori Stage Manager for opera; Herr Gustav Mahler, Conductor; Georg Mayer, Orchestra Director; Frau Marie Schreiner is Box Office Manageress; Herr Emil Zeigenhofer, Technical Manager; Herr Josef Schild, Prompter; and Herr Johann Hamberger, Chief Wardrobe Master, with assistants.

The following performers are listed for *opera* and *operetta*: Fräulein Caroline Fischer, dramatic soprano; Fräulein Leopoldine Ranek, principal soprano in operetta and juvenile roles in opera; Fräulein Hedwig von Wagner, principal soprano in operetta and popular comedy; Fräulein Emma von Sonnleithner, mezzo-soprano roles in opera and operetta; Frau Rosine Wallhof-Bomm, maternal roles in opera and operetta; Fräulein Anna Giersig, secondary singing roles; Herr Leopold Tellé, first operatic tenor; Herr Julius Klein, first tenor in operetta and lyric tenor in opera; Herr Ottokar Payer, first baritone; Herr Wenzel Petro, baritone; Herr Ernst Unger, serious bass roles; Herr Louis Linori (stage manager), *buffo* bass parts in opera and operetta.

The *chorus* consists of seven ladies and seven gentlemen; the *orchestra* of eighteen full-time players.

Laibacher Zeitung, 8 September 1881.

Conducting début with the Egmont Overture

Provincial Theatre. – The opening of the Diet of the Duchy of Carniola was celebrated on Saturday by the first performance of the season at our Theatre, the exterior of which was brilliantly illuminated for the occasion. This gala performance was attended by the Imperial-Royal Provincial President with his family, and by several members of the Diet, as well as by a large audience. Bauernfeld's comedy *Bürgerlich und Romantisch* was performed, and it gives us great pleasure to report that this opening evening was a great success. . . .

The gala evening was introduced by Beethoven's *Egmont* Overture, played with precision by the orchestra under the Conductor, G. Mahler.

Laibacher Zeitung, 26 September 1881.

Mahler's first opera at Laibach

Provincial Theatre. – Yesterday Herr Mondheim's management made its début with its first operatic production, and we are glad to be able to state that the evening was a success; the house seemed to be sold out, and our public showed once again that Laibach's long-standing reputation as a genuinely music-loving city is still fully justified. Verdi's *Il Trovatore* went without any significant mishap, and the ladies, Fräulein Caroline Fischer (Leonora) and Fräulein Bruck (Azucena) were rewarded with enthusiastic and well-deserved applause in the middle as well as at the end of the acts. Messrs Tellé (Manrico), Payer (Count Luna) and Unger (Ferrando) gave of their best, although the baritone did not win as much approval from the audience as the tenor and bass. The orchestra, conducted by Herr Mahler, played strongly.

Laibacher Zeitung, 4 October 1881.

From the reviews of Mozart's 'Magic Flute'

The repeat of *The Magic Flute* yesterday went as well as the first performance, and we hope to be able to enjoy this opera several more times this year, for our leading singers, Chorus and Orchestra work together very successfully to do justice to the imperishable masterpiece. . . .

The Magic Flute has been rehearsed with great care, enthusiasm and application under the Conductor, Herr Mahler.

Laibacher Zeitung, 29 and 31 October 1881.

The Laibach Philharmonic Society

Music found a new home in Laibach in the year 1702, when the Philharmonic Society was founded. It has continued to exist as evidence of the town's long-established cultural life. It is the oldest musical society in Austria-Hungary, 110 years older than the Society of the Friends of Music in Vienna, and 91 years older than the Conservatoire in Paris. The explanation of this striking phenomenon can be found by a glance at the life of that time in general, and at the intellectual life of Laibach in particular. In those days the sons of the citizens of Laibach used to go to Italian universities to equip themselves for their future professions at home, and especially to Bologna. With the background of useful knowledge which they had acquired there, they also brought the refined manners of the centres of Italian culture back to their homes, and founded the sort of scientific and cultural societies that they had come to know in Italy.

ÖUM, *Kärnten und Krain*, Vienna 1891, 404–05.

Mahler at a Philharmonic Society concert

[The fourth concert] of the Philharmonic Society, conducted by its Chief Conductor, Herr Anton Nedvĕd, with the kind co-operation of the Conductor of the Provincial Theatre, Herr Gustav Mahler, was held yesterday. Like all the previous concerts of the Society it was enjoyed by a large audience which listened attentively to all the numbers in the programme, which we published on Saturday, and did not spare its applause. The first piece, Suite in canonic form by Grimm, was

VIERTES CONCERT

der

philharmon. Gesellschaft in Laibach

unter der Leitung ihres Musik-Directors Herrn

Anton Nedvĕd

und freundlicher Mitwirkung des Herrn

Gustav Mahler,

Kapellmeister des landschaftl. Theaters in Laibach.

Sonntag, den 5. März 1882

im landschaftlichen Redoutensaale.

Anfang um halb 5 Uhr nachmittags.

PROGRAMM.

1.) J. O. Grimm: Suite in Canonform für Streichorchester :
    a) Allegro con brio ;
    b) Andante lento ;
    c) Tempo di Menuetto ;
    d) Allegro risoluto.

2.) F. Mendelssohn-Bartholdy: Capriccio brillant, op. 22. H-moll, für das Pianoforte mit Begleitung eines Streichquartettes; Herr G. Mahler.

3. a) J. Brahms: Liebestreue, ⎫ Lieder mit Pianofortebegl..
   b) A. Dorn: Schneeglöckchen, ⎬ ges. v. Frl. Carol. Witschl.

4.) L. Boccherini: Menuett für Streichorchester.

5. a) R. Schumann: Waldscenen, *a) Jagdlied,*
    b) Vogel als Prophet, ⎫ Herr
   b) F. Chopin: Polonaise, op. 53. As-dur. ⎭ G. Mahler.

6.) Ant. Dvořák: Serenade, E-dur. für Streichorchester :
    a) Moderato ;
    b) Tempo di Valse ;
    c) Scherzo ;
    d) Larghetto ;
    e) Finale.

Der Saal wird um halb 4 Uhr geöffnet.

Der Eintritt ist nur den Vereinsmitgliedern gegen Abgabe der auf Namen lautenden Eintrittskarten gestattet. Da nach § 16 der Statuten Familien das Recht zum Eintritte für drei in gemeinschaftlicher Haushaltung lebende nicht selbständige Angehörige zusteht, so wolle für jedes weitere, an den statutenmässigen musikalischen Aufführungen theilnehmende Familienmitglied eine separate Eintrittskarte beim Herrn Vereinskassier Carl Karinger gegen Entrichtung des statutenmässigen Jahresbeitrages von 1 fl. gelöst werden.

Anmeldungen zum Eintritte in die philharm. Gesellschaft werden in der Handlung des Herrn Carl Karinger, Rathhausplatz. entgegengenommen.

Programme of the fourth concert of the Philharmonic Society, Laibach, 1882.

played by the orchestra with great tenderness and restraint, the Andante lento receiving the most applause. This composition, so rich in musical beauty, was followed by Mendelssohn's *Capriccio brillant* for pianoforte accompanied by a string quartet, which gave Herr Mahler the best possible opportunity to introduce himself to the Laibach audience as a fine pianist with a brilliant technique that he knows how to put to the best possible use. Herr Mahler won the first prize for composition at the Vienna Conservatoire, where he was a piano pupil of Professor Epstein's. His performance yesterday, especially his brilliant solo playing of pieces by Schumann and Chopin, was greeted with lively applause. . . .

Laibacher Zeitung, 6 March 1882.

From the memoirs of the Laibach Conductor Hans Gerstner

As a pianist he did not impress us, but his performance of Mozart's *The Magic Flute,* for which he had only operetta resources at his disposal, made us realize that he was a very gifted conductor of opera. Laibach, where he worked from 1881 to 1882, had the honour of being the starting point of his great career. I was very friendly with Mahler. He was a vegetarian, and he often came to join us at the Rose Inn and drank two glasses of Pilsner beer after leaving the theatre at night.

Hans Gerstner, 'Lebenserinnerungen', ms., Dr Hans Gerstner, Vienna. (During Mahler's time at Laibach, Hans Gerstner was orchestral leader, and later Conductor, of the Philharmonic Society. On 2 April 1882 Mahler played the piano for Gerstner at a concert.)

Mahler's Laibach performances are relayed by telephone

Dramatic Performance by Telephone – at Laibach. On Sunday and Tuesday *Der lustige Krieg* and *The Barber of Seville* were performed at our Provincial Theatre. During these performances tests were made in the presence of invited guests with telephone lines set up in the Director's office by Herr Geba. Not only was the musical part superbly audible, but the spoken word was also plainly heard. Two Siemens telephones with acoustic horns, and two microphonic transmitters (supplied by E. Berliner of Boston) were installed in the two lowest boxes on either side of the stage, and Siemens, Dr Böttcher and Bell telephones served as receivers.

Laibacher Zeitung, 16 March 1882.

Theater.

Heute (ungerader Tag) zum Vortheile des Herrn Kapellmeisters Gustav Mahler: Stradella. Oper in 3 Acten von Friedrich v. Flotow. Uebertragung per Telephon in der Theater-Directionskanzlei. Extra-Entrée für Theaterbesucher à Person 50 kr.

Theatre advertisement, *Laibacher Zeitung,* 23 March 1882.

Benefit performance

Provincial Theatre. – Yesterday we heard Flotow's charming opera *Alessandro Stradella* for the first time this season; our indefatigably active and energetic Conductor, Herr Gustav Mahler, had chosen it for his benefit; it had been carefully rehearsed and went very well. When Herr Mahler appeared, he was greeted with loud applause by the fairly large audience and with a flourish by the orchestra. He was also presented with a large laurel wreath decorated with broad loops of ribbon, a sign of appreciation that was well earned by this excellently trained musician who really takes his difficult task seriously, and who has had a great many troubles and worries throughout the season.

Laibacher Zeitung, 24 March 1882. (It was the custom to give the receipts of a benefit performance in full or in part to the beneficiary. Shortly after this benefit performance the season, and Mahler's engagement at Laibach, came to an end.)

Friedrich Löhr on his walks with Mahler in the Vienna Woods

We went for an awful lot of walks at that time when we were living together, and thoroughly enjoyed them. Our favourite places were the slopes up to the Leopoldsberg and the Kahlenberg and right on to the Hermannskogel; sometimes we went further off to the wooded hills and meadows round the Josephswarte, the watchtower on the Parapluieberg above Perchtoldsdorf, where my family and I spent the summer for several years from 1882 on. An orgiastic [*sic*] worship of nature, a tender love of the charms of an old Austrian village and all the memories it evoked, the conscious harmony of our souls – such was the essence of our sentimental wanderings, although we did not talk much on the road. Our first walk to Heiligenstadt, of which Mahler speaks, and which must surely have led us along the way trodden by Beethoven into Heiligenstadt and Nussdorf, must have been in the year 1882 after Mahler's return from Laibach, when I first became so friendly with him. . . .

GMB, notes 473. (Löhr's description of their walks together appears as a footnote to a letter of 10 October 1883, from Kassel, in which Mahler reminds his friend of their walks in 1882.)

Conductor gives guest performance at Iglau: 'Boccaccio' by Suppé

Fräulein Hassmann, who made her début as Fiametta, possesses many of the qualities necessary for making a success of juvenile parts, a really impressive voice, a lively delivery, and a charming appearance. . . .

The ensembles were performed with the precision that can only come from incisive conducting; the sceptre was wielded by our compatriot Gustav Mahler, who has embarked on his career as a conductor with so much success at Laibach.

Mährischer Grenzbote, 21 September 1882.

The years of Mahler's childhood and education had been a time of tolerance and liberal optimism. When he began his apprenticeship as a conductor, the political atmosphere had already changed radically. The so-called Compromise with Hungary in 1867 had divided the Monarchy into two equal sovereign states, Austria and Hungary, which were united by a common foreign policy and common dynasty. Both halves of the Monarchy contained Slavs, who fought for their political and cultural rights more energetically every year.

A French view of Austria-Hungary

As long as the Habsburgs were Emperors of Germany, they had no trouble in ruling the more or less German provinces of their realm; when Napoleon took their empty imperial title away from them, and Bismarck threw them out of Germany sixty years later, they at last remembered that they were Kings of Bohemia, Hungary and Croatia. They realized that it was perhaps high time to concern themselves with Austria, study her needs, and seek means of contenting her. Constitutions succeeded one another, as fruitless as they were numerous, and full of promises that were never put into effect. Franz Joseph, who was still filled with the old ideas of German imperialism, was afraid of the Slavs. Instead of relying on the support of this young and powerful race, he thoughtlessly and purposelessly loaded it with chains and delivered it to Hungary bound hand and foot. The Compromise of 1867, which created the Austro-Hungarian Dual Monarchy, is a thousand times more unjust than Prince Metternich's centralism. Without any consideration of the complaints of the Slav provinces, which are treated like defeated countries, the 1867 dualism divides the Empire into two large halves separated by the River Leitha, Austria (Cisleithania) and Hungary (Transleithania). The Czechs and Slovenes thereafter found themselves ruled by the Germans in Vienna, while the Slovaks, Romanians and Croats were obliged to obey the Magyars in Budapest. This constitution, very liberal in appearance, since Article 19 guaranteed absolute equality to each nationality, was in its application nothing but a trap. As in the past, the Germans continued to rule in Bohemia, and the Hungarians continued to oppress all their neighbours of foreign race.

Joseph Roy, *Le Kahlenberg, Etudes sur l'Autriche*, Lyon 1883, 305–06.

Natalie Bauer-Lechner describes her first meeting with Mahler

I first met Mahler at the Conservatoire; later I met him briefly at the house of the Pichlers, the family of a fellow student of his, who were very kind and hospitable; there we spent happy, carefree hours such as are possible only in early youth. I met him for longer at the Kraliks', where they asked him to play the Prelude to *The Mastersingers*, which he did so magnificently that he conjured forth all the thunder of an orchestra. As a rule Mahler behaved like an 'unlicked cub' in all 'refined' circles, and never seemed to feel at ease. When we came to sit together at supper, however, he thawed out completely and we became deeply involved in an absorbing conversation about *Wilhelm Meister*.

NBL, 1–2. (Richard von Kralik, 1852–1934, author and art historian, a friend of Lipiner's. Natalie Bauer-Lechner, 1858–1921, was to be one of Mahler's closest friends until his marriage.)

Mahler to Ludwig Bösendorfer, the Viennese piano manufacturer

As I am temporarily not in a position to provide myself with a piano, although it is essential for me to have one, I remember your generosity on which I have so often made demands; and [two words crossed out] I think of the friendly sympathy with which you used to treat me. I join the throng of petitioners and make so bold as to ask you if you happen by chance to have an old instrument that you could lend me for a few months. . . . I shall be at Bergstrasse 20, 4th Floor, Door 26, Vienna IX until 5 December, and then at Wipplingerstrasse 12, 2nd Staircase, 4th Floor, right-hand door. . . .

Ms., GDM. (Undated letter, probably written in late autumn 1882.)

Mahler to Anton Krisper

Please accept my somewhat belated good wishes for the New Year. Let this be the first thing I say to you after a long silence. I received your last letter some time ago at Iglau, and you may be interested to hear that while I was there I conducted a performance in which the leading soprano was a certain Fräulein Hassmann who is the most superficial woman I have met for a long time. Anyway I didn't stay there long, but embarked on a very jolly nomadic life in Vienna, that is to say I move into another district every fortnight. I have already been in Vienna for three months and am now in my fifth home, not counting various hotels. You will easily be able to understand that my work has not been progressing very fast; now, even if I were in the best frame of mind, I am continually disturbed by the crying of a small child – and so I am driven from one annoyance to another. None the less, I hope to finish the first act of *Rübezahl*. By the way, the libretto has taken on an entirely new look since you saw it. Quite a lot of it has really not turned out badly.

HHI, 813. (The New Year greeting is for 1883.)

Sudden summons to Olmütz

Theatre News. – Herr Raul, the Director of the Theatre, following a number of disagreements occasioned by the Conductor, Herr Kaiser, has dispensed with his services. For the rest of the season, the running of the opera company will be entrusted to the young conductor Herr Gustav Mahler, who has been summoned from Vienna by telegram. The forthcoming opera productions will show whether he succeeds in performing his task with complete adequacy.

Mährisches Tagblatt, 12 January 1883. (Olmütz is now Olomouc.)

Mahler to Richard Kralik

I am sorry I was prevented from coming to the *Musica sacra*, but at the moment I am Conductor of the Olmütz Opera, and the distance is too great. However I hope that I shall have the

48

pleasure again soon. Best wishes and kind regards to everybody. A friend of mine is bringing you Palästrina [*sic*]. Will you be kind enough to deliver the *Commer Volume* to Dr Adler. His address is Belvederegasse 12, Vienna IV.

Undated postcard, Vienna postmark, ms., WSTB. (The Commer volume to which Mahler refers – the name is barely legible – could be volume 9 of the Collected Works of Palestrina, edited by Franz Commer. The Dr Adler referred to is probably Guido Adler.)

Description of the town of Olmütz in Moravia

47 Olmütz (Olomouc) is the second city in Moravia, but the ecclesiastical metropolis and the principal fortress that guards the extensive Moravian Lowlands. It lies in a flat, marshy district on the River March and in time of war the whole neighbourhood can be flooded. . . . Olmütz has three suburban districts and 20,176 inhabitants (65% German), including a garrison of 4,656 men. The town is well built, and like all Slav towns, has large squares. The most impressive buildings are the Archbishop's Palace, the Gothic cathedral, containing the tomb of King Wenceslas III who was murdered here in 1306, the churches of St Maurice and St Michael, the Town Hall, the fine Arsenal and the New Barracks. Olmütz formerly had a university, reformed in 1827, which in 1855 was closed with the exception of the Imperial-Royal Theological College which is still in existence. There are also two high schools, a secondary school, a teachers' training college and a public reference library of 60,000 volumes. Olmütz has an important textile industry and a rosolio distillery. The town has a flourishing trade, which is much benefited by the three railway lines that intersect here.

Friedrich Umlauft, *Die Österreichisch-Ungarische Monarchie*, Vienna 1883, 827.

In January 1883 Mahler was appointed Conductor of operas at the Municipal Theatre at Olmütz, through the intermediary of the agent Gustav Lewy. A quarter of a century later, the baritone Jacques Manheit recounted his memories of Mahler's work at Olmütz to the Viennese journalist Ludwig Karpath. In the introduction to this article, Karpath writes: 'I have cut all unnecessary side issues out of an article by Mahler's former colleague, which is well worth reading, and given it a form suitable for publication in a magazine. The essence of it remains untouched.'

Jacques Manheit on Mahler at Olmütz

It happened at Olmütz on 10 January 1883, the evening on which the popular resident Conductor, Emil Kaiser, was to conduct *L'Africaine*. Everything went perfectly well until the fourth act, but then an action of Kaiser's, which I do not wish to mention here, caused such a scandal that he was not allowed to finish the performance. Our Director, Herr Emanuel Raul, was in the utmost despair; we simply no longer had a Conductor. He sent telegrams everywhere, but it seemed almost impossible to find a suitable Conductor in the middle of the season. At last, on 13 January, the Director surprised us with the news that he had found a young Conductor who was reputed to be a genius, but who was also considered to be a very unusual person. The Director asked us to treat him with great forbearance. The following day, at nine o'clock in the morning, the new Conductor, whose name was Gustav Mahler, held a rehearsal for the chorus. When we went to a full vocal rehearsal an hour later, the chorus singers came to us in absolute despair and maintained that they were completely hoarse and could not work with the new Conductor any more. We soloists, full of curiosity, went into the rehearsal room, where Mahler was already sitting at the piano warming his hands in his coat-tails. His head was covered with long, dishevelled hair,

52 he had the beginnings of a black beard, and he wore a large

horn-rimmed pince-nez on his very prominent nose. He started the rehearsal without bothering to introduce himself to anybody. All his colleagues, men and women alike, regarded the new Conductor with unconcealed hostility, which they expressed loudly and without reserve. Mahler, however, did not react to any of the interruptions, but harshly demanded compliance with his instructions. No one dared to contradict the young man.

Two days later we saw him on the podium for the first time. We were performing *Les Huguenots*. After the first act the bass who was singing Marcel stormed breathlessly into the dressing-room shouting, 'I can't sing with this man. He holds his baton in his right hand, then in his left, and keeps on passing his free hand over his face, so that I can't see any of his cues.' When Mahler heard this serious complaint he replied quite equably, 'Yes, my dear friend, conducting makes me very hot and I perspire too much, so my pince-nez keeps slipping off and I have to catch it with my free hand. But I'll put it right straight away.' So he went to the wardrobe master for a broad piece of ribbon, fastened his pince-nez to it, and hooked it round his ears. But now he looked so comic that when the singers looked down on him from the stage, they were convulsed with laughter. Somehow we got to the end of the performance.

Then we all hurried to our favourite bar, the Goliath Restaurant, where the members of the company and a lot of theatregoers, journalists and officers gathered every evening. I was the only one who was on friendly terms with Mahler, and they looked daggers at me when I came into the bar with him. I introduced the new Conductor individually to everybody, for it never occurred to Mahler to introduce himself to anybody. Caring nothing for the contempt of the beer and wine drinkers at our table, he began by ordering a bottle of water, and then told the waiter at great length to bring him two helpings of spinach cooked in plain water, and a few apples. Being a convinced Wagnerian, he thought he was obliged to be a vegetarian. (As is known, Wagner preached vegetarianism for a time, without ever practising it himself. [L.K.]) At that time Mahler was also keen on Professor Jaeger's theories about wool. He spoke passionately about all these things, and picked a violent quarrel with a schoolmaster, who called me aside and told me plainly that I must get the newcomer out of there as quickly as possible or there would be an almighty row. Under some pretext or other, I persuaded Mahler to accompany me to the coffee house next door. We played billiards. While I was playing my first break, Mahler danced round the table holding a cue which he swung to right and left, describing great circles in the air. Being absorbed in my play, I noticed only later that a number of officers had come up to the table, one of whom whispered in my ear, 'Who in the world is this extraordinary man?' I did not like seeing the gentlemen of the garrison laughing at my opponent, so I asked him, 'Whatever exercises are you doing, my dear Conductor?' 'You go on quietly with your game,' he answered; 'I have just been conducting through the first act of *Les Huguenots*. Your colleagues are very hard on me, so I am practising signalling their entries for them.' (This ironic remark might have been made by the Mahler of today. [L.K.])

Gradually the inhabitants of the little town got used to the peculiarities of the young conductor, whom his colleagues had certainly not come to like but had learnt to fear. His way of demanding and commanding was so decisive that nobody dared to oppose him, particularly because the standard of performance had greatly improved under his management. It must not be forgotten that Mahler hardly knew a single opera, and had learnt each one during rehearsal. It was a matter of no concern to him that nobody sought his company; all that he insisted upon was that we should all do our duty. I regarded myself as all the more fortunate in being able to see him often. I was able to learn something of his inner life, and knew even then whose spiritual offspring he was.

The following episode is extremely characteristic. One day I met Mahler in the coffee house, entirely engrossed in himself. I asked him sympathetically why he was so sad, and he replied that he had had bad news from home and that his father was ill. I tried to comfort him and went on my way. On the next morning, just as I was going from my home to the theatre, I saw a man running through the streets; he was quite distraught, sobbed loudly, and pressed his handkerchief against his eyes; I recognized Mahler with difficulty. I naturally remembered the incident of the day before, so I went up to him anxiously and asked him quietly, 'In heaven's name, has something happened to your father?' 'Worse, worse, much worse,' he howled at the top of his voice: 'the worst, the worst has happened, the Master has died.' It was 13 February 1883, and Richard Wagner had died. After that it was impossible to talk to Mahler for days. He came to the theatre for rehearsals and performances, but was inaccessible to everybody for a long time.

Mahler had his benefit towards the end of the season. He wanted to perform *Joseph* by Méhul. The whole of our company consisted of twelve soloists and a chorus of ten men and twelve women. The work requires fourteen solo singers and a chorus as well. I shook my head incredulously and explained to Mahler that it was impossible to carry out his plan. But he did carry it out, and in a way that showed genius. By that time Olmütz knew that Mahler was a great artist. How the little man managed to do it I don't know, I just remember the rehearsals, which I shall never forget. Mahler jumped from the podium, across the double-bass players, on to the stage, produced, stage-managed and conducted. The performance was attended by Herr Ueberhorst, the senior Stage Manager of the Dresden Court Opera. He had come to hear me sing. As we sat together in a restaurant after the performance, Ueberhorst said to me, 'You can only gasp at the man who manages to bring off a performance like that.' I pointed to Mahler, who was sitting at another table, and remarked to Ueberhorst that Mahler would be very willing to go to Dresden. Ueberhorst looked Mahler up and down and then burst out laughing: 'No, no, that figure, that appearance, it would be quite impossible at Dresden!'

Some years later, Mahler became Director of the Royal Opera in Budapest. He gave me an engagement. I couldn't believe my eyes when I saw him again. Well dressed like all other civilized men, clean-shaven, and his hair very carefully done. We had lunch together. And then I really had to laugh; the man whose devotion to Richard Wagner had once made him a vegetarian now ate knucklebone and horse-radish sauce with the greatest enjoyment. He displayed his enthusiasm for Wagner in another way.

Ludwig Karpath, 'Aus Gustav Mahlers Wanderjahren', *Montags-Revue*, Vienna, 18 May 1908.

Mahler to the theatrical agent Gustav Lewy

Olmütz, 6 January 1883

I am making so bold as to send you a review of the performance the day before yesterday of *Un ballo in maschera*, the first opera that has been rehearsed *by me*; perhaps this is all the more significant because this paper was obviously influenced from the very beginning, and even before I had appeared before the public, by a conductor who lives here, 'stewed in the cabbage'.

Furthermore the newspaper does not report the fact, I do not know why, that I received an enthusiastic curtain call from the public after the *third act*.

Ms., WSTB. (Many of Gustav Mahler's letters are undated, and so raise serious problems for editors and biographers, especially when there are no postmarked envelopes. The foregoing letter to Lewy is for once dated, and even so the month is wrong. The first performance of *Un ballo in maschera* took place on 4 February; the letter must therefore have been written on 6 February and not on 6 January. As Mahler wrote to Max Marschalk in 1896: 'The reason why I seldom date my letters is that I generally don't know what the date is!' GMB, 205. *Im Kraut gedünstet*, 'stewed in the cabbage', is a Viennese spoonerization of *Im Dienst ergraut*, 'grown old in the service'.)

From the review of 'Un ballo in maschera'

Chorus and orchestra performed very well. The Conductor, Herr Mahler, therefore deserves an honourable mention.
Die Neue Zeit, 5 February 1883.

Mahler on his position at Olmütz

I am crippled, like a man who has fallen from heaven. From the moment I crossed the threshold of the Olmütz Theatre, I felt like a man who is awaiting the judgment of God.

If you harness the finest horse to a cart with oxen, all it can do is to sweat away and drag along at an ox's pace. I feel so besmirched that I hardly dare to appear before you . . .

So far, thank God, I have hardly conducted anything but Meyerbeer and Verdi. I have managed to intrigue enough to get Wagner and Mozart firmly removed from the repertory, for I could not bear to conduct anything like *Lohengrin* – or *Don Giovanni* – down to this low level. Tomorrow we have *Joseph*, an uncommonly likeable work, which has something of Mozart's charm. I thoroughly enjoyed rehearsing it. And I must say, in spite of the unspeakable insensitivity of my people, they do a good deal for my sake, and went about it this time rather more seriously. Admittedly it was only their way of showing pity for me as an 'idealist', which is their highly contemptuous description of me; for they cannot grasp the fact that an artist can become wholly absorbed in a work of art. Often, when I am on fire like that and want to take them with me to higher flights, I notice their astonished faces and see them exchanging sympathetic smiles; then my enthusiasm dies for a while and I want to run away for ever. I only recover my courage when I feel that I am suffering for the sake of my Masters, and that I may perhaps be able to set a spark of my fire alight in the souls of these poor people; then, in many a better moment, I vow that I will hold out for their sakes, even in the face of their derision.

From a letter to Friedrich Löhr of 12 February 1883, GMB, 19–20.

From the review of 'Carmen'

It is regrettable that a succession of misfortunes has prevented a really proper performance of Bizet's *Carmen* on our stage. The approaching end of the season made the management decide not to do anything about the scenery, and it would be pointless to rebuke them for this today. It would be equally impossible to make the management responsible for a dereliction of duty on the part of a number of chorus singers, whose failure to attend considerably detracted from the success of the opera. There was yet another misfortune: immediately before the dress rehearsal, the management was forbidden to have schoolchildren in the choruses for which they had already been rehearsed. If, after all that, the opera still had some success on our stage, it was wholly thanks to the Conductor, Herr Mahler, who so skilfully brought out its merits and beauties that the shortcomings of the performance, and especially of the staging, were at least partially concealed. Except for some rather feeble flute playing in the second act, the orchestra performed magnificently for him, and deserves every praise. The chorus, or rather what was left of it, did as well as could be expected.

Mährisches Tagblatt, 13 March 1893. (Mahler was still to conduct *Rigoletto* at Olmütz – for his own benefit performance – and *Il Trovatore*. The *Mährisches Tagblatt* announced his departure on 19 March.)

Königl. städt. Theater in Olmütz.

157. Vorstellung im Abonnement.   Ungerader Tag.

Direction Em. Raul.

Donnerstag den 15. März 1883.

Debüt des Fräulein Ida Rott.

Der Troubadour.

Oper in 4 Abtheilungen von Giuseppe Verdi.

Dirigent Herr Capellmeister **Gustav Mahler.**

Personen:

Der Graf von Luna . . . Herr Manheit.
Leonore . . . . Frln. Hild.
Azucena, eine Zigeunerin   Fräulein Rott.
Manrico . . . . . . Herr Krüger a. G.
Fernando, Lunas Vertrauter Herr Fuchs.
Ruiz, Manricos Begleiterin Herr Martini.

Morgen Freitag:

Benefic- und Abschieds-Vorstellung des Ober-Regisseurs Herrn Dominik Klang.

Nihilisten der Liebe.

Theatre advertisement, *Mährisches Tagblatt*, 15 March 1883.

The agent Gustav Lewy recommends Mahler for a post at Kassel

Vienna, 12 May 1883

I hear that you are looking for an Assistant Conductor, and take the liberty of recommending Herr Gustav Mahler as strongly as possible. Herr Mahler is a graduate of the Vienna Conservatoire, and has so far been employed by the Provincial Theatre at Laibach and the Municipal Theatre at Olmütz, where he was chief Conductor. He is a thoroughly cultured and conscientious young man, so much so that I do not think that you are likely to find a better one for the vacant post. Herr Ueberhorst, the Stage Manager at Dresden, whom Mahler met while working at Olmütz, is the best person to tell you about him.

Ms., CAS.

Ueberhorst, the Stage Manager at Dresden, recommends the appointment

Dresden, 14 May 1883

On an official visit to Olmütz recently I met Herr Gustav Mahler, the young Conductor there, who is quite outstanding. He had only very moderate resources for opera, but he had rehearsed those that I attended with refined taste and great precision; furthermore, when conducting in the theatre, where I was able to watch him very closely, he showed that he had the energy and tact necessary for welding his rather weak forces into an harmonious whole.

He is an accomplished score-reader and pianist.

If you have not yet made a definite decision about filling this post, Sir, I should like to take the liberty of directing your attention to this highly cultured and genuinely musical young man. He would be an energetic addition to your staff.

Ms., CAS.

Will you consider appointment Royal Assistant Conductor and Chorus Master here starting October? If so request *curriculum vitae* by return. Further details by post.

Von Gilsa.

CAS.

In May 1883 Mahler went to Kassel to present himself to the General Manager, Baron von Gilsa. Kassel, the capital of the Electorate of Hesse until a few years earlier, had been the capital of the Prussian Province of Hesse-Nassau since 1868, and the former Electoral Court Theatre had become a Royal (Prussian) Theatre, with a management indirectly responsible to Berlin. Baron Adolf von und zu Gilsa, a captain in the Field Artillery Guards, had been awarded the Iron Cross, First and Second Class, in the Franco-Prussian War of 1870–71. He managed the theatre at Kassel on military lines.

Probationary period and conclusion of an agreement

On 22 May 1883 Mahler presented himself in person, and agreed to a probationary period from then until 30 June inclusive, during which time he would perform the following tasks:

(a)   Conduct the Overture to *William Tell*;
(b)   Direct various chorus rehearsals;
(c)   Direct various solo rehearsals;
(d)   Conduct the dress rehearsal of *Hans Heiling*.

All his probationary activities gave satisfaction to the General Manager. The attached contract of employment with Mahler was signed on 31 May 1883.

CAS.

The contract signed on 31 May was valid for three years, from 1 October 1883 to 30 September 1886. In return for an annual salary of 2,100 marks, Mahler undertook to perform punctually and conscientiously all the functions and duties of Assistant Conductor and Chorus Master. This contract, which, among other things, forbade Mahler to give any public performances at Kassel outside the theatre, was accompanied by a Schedule of Duties that ran to twenty paragraphs.

From the Schedule of Duties of the Assistant Conductor and Chorus Master of the Royal Theatre:

1.   The Assistant Conductor and Chorus Master of the Royal Theatre will be loyal and obedient to His Majesty the Emperor and King, and regard it as his first duty to protect and further His Majesty's interests, to the best of his ability, and to do nothing to His Majesty's disadvantage.

2.   He will concentrate on his official duties as trainer of the Theatre Chorus which will be under his control, and make adequate preparations for the production of such operas as he shall be instructed to rehearse or conduct by the Management of the Royal Theatre, as well as other musical works, such as farces, musical comedies, ballets, dances, etc., making the most practical use of the available performers and installations with a view to achieving a good ensemble performance. . . .

4.   In the exercise of his official duties he is always subordinate to the Conductor and, in the case of the employment of the Chorus in operas that he is not instructed to produce, to the Chief Stage Manager of the Royal Theatre. . . .

7.   The omission or shortening of vocal passages at the request of the singers may not be permitted without the previous consent of the Management of the Royal Theatre, even during

the performance, unless as a matter of urgent necessity. . . .

9. The Assistant Conductor and Chorus Master is obliged:

(a) To arrange such musical works as were originally written for larger forces than those of the Royal Theatre, in order to make them suitable for performance on the stage, if the Management has a special interest in presenting them here.

(b) To orchestrate incidental songs and other musical arrangements.

(c) To provide such compositions as the Management deems desirable for special occasions. . . .

CAS.

Mahler to Friedrich Löhr

As soon as I got back from Bayreuth, I received your present at a moment when it fell like a ray of light from heaven into my utmost gloom.

I cannot tell you what you and your letter mean to me. Your unshakable love has enabled you to see through the desolate veil of the present and to look deep into my heart; you have faith in me, who have lost all faith in myself. I should find it difficult to explain to you what is the matter with me now. When I left the Festival Theatre, incapable of speech, I knew that the greatest, most painful thing had happened to me, and that I should have it with me in all its sanctity for the rest of my life. And so I came home again and found those whom I love so poor, so heavy-hearted. . . . My parents, with their poor, tormented hearts, shackled by poverty and worries, myself, so hard and cruel to them – and yet I cannot do otherwise although I hurt them to the quick. And now I must be away again in three weeks to take up my new duties!

I ran into Heinrich at Eger; we did some walking in the Fichtel Mountains and went to Wunsiedel. . . .

Undated letter from Iglau, July 1883, GMB, 22–23. (*Parsifal* was the only work performed at the Bayreuth Festival in 1883. Mahler's summer visit was a pilgrimage not only to the shrine of Wagner but to that of his own literary idol, Jean Paul, who was born at Wunsiedel and died at Bayreuth.)

Jean Paul (Jean Paul Richter, 1763–1825) was the favourite writer of the young Mahler and his circle. Those who read Mahler's letters to the friends of his youth are reminded of Jean Paul more than once. Mahler seems to have found a kindred soul in this man who was born almost a hundred years before him. In Jean Paul's novels he found the same all-embracing love of nature as he felt himself, the same cult of friendship, the rapid changes of mood to which he was liable, and his constant preoccupation with the meaning of life and of suffering. Mahler's exaltation, his sensibility, and even his choice of words, were influenced by Jean Paul.

Jean Paul's poetic description of an arrival at Bayeuth

He climbed the edifice of joy – and the glowing curtain of mist hung over Bayreuth – the sun stood on the mountains like a king on the stage and watched the bright veil burning as it floated downwards, and its fluttering, glimmering flakes of ash which were wafted and strewn over gardens and flowers by the morning breezes. At last nothing was shining but the sun alone in the sky. Beneath this glory he entered the favourite abode of his Beloved, and all the buildings seemed to be shimmering in the air, like mighty, magic castles which had floated down from ethereal heights.

Each new street excited his throbbing heart; a slight deviation from the path pleased him like a postponement or increase of his rapture. At last he reached the Sun Inn, the point at which he was nearest to the sun, the metallic sun of

the inn sign which, like the real sun, drew this wandering star into its orbit. . . .

Jean Paul, *Blumen-, Frucht- und Dornenstücke oder Ehestand, Tod und Hochzeit des Armenadvokaten F. St. Siebenkäs, Werke*, vol. 2, Munich 1959, 360–61.

A charity concert at Iglau

Although I was younger than Mahler, I had a very friendly relationship with him which found particular expression in our playing duets on the piano with vigour, perseverance and enthusiasm for hours together. This did not please our fathers, who were quite incapable of recognizing the beauties of a Beethoven symphony, and whose only feeling was pity for 'the nice piano'. Later when Mahler, the young Assistant Conductor from Kassel, came back to Iglau for his holidays, the Red Cross asked him to take part in a charity concert in the Municipal Theatre. Among other things, there was to be a performance of a ballad opera, *Das Kaffeekränzchen* ['The Coffee Party'], which Mahler was to accompany on the piano. Things began to go wrong during the rehearsals. The utterly trivial music, with its little scraps of humour which was entirely lost on Mahler, did not interest him in the least; he played absent-mindedly, made ironic remarks about the music and the singing of the ladies in the cast, and did not keep time, so that he soon made himself very unpopular.

The grand piano stood in the middle of the orchestra pit in front of the stage. At the public dress rehearsal Mahler sat at the keyboard and I sat beside him, as I had to turn over. Mahler was in a bad temper. They were scarcely half-way through the ballad opera when he jumped up with his usual vehemence, knocked his chair over, slammed down the lid of the piano, cast a furious look at the ladies who were performing rather amateurishly on the stage, then, turning to me, he said, so loudly that he was heard at least in the first few rows of the stalls, 'Look here, Bruckmüller, you accompany this damned nonsense yourself, it's too much for me.' With those words he stamped out of the orchestra pit. I saved the situation by taking up the accompaniment as quickly as I could where Mahler had left off, and played to the end of the piece.

At the concert itself Mahler played Beethoven's Kreutzer Sonata with the virtuoso violinist Fräulein Ott von Ottenfeld, and I again turned pages for him. In his impatience he could never wait for the right moment to turn the page, but kicked me several times, long before he got there, obviously to remind me of my duty. I put up with it once or twice and then I started to get my own kick in first.

Then he played really brilliantly, I turned over blamelessly, and the audience had no idea that there had been any footwork under the piano.

Hans Bruckmüller, 'Aus Gustav Mahlers Jugendzeit', in *Igel-Land, Mitteilungen für Heimatkunde in der Iglauer Sprachinsel*, no. 33 (bk 2), December 1932. (The charity concert was held in the Municipal Theatre at Iglau on 11 August 1883. Fräulein Ott von Ottenfeld, whose professional name was Mila von Ott, was a well known violinist in the 1880s; Mahler was still corresponding with her in 1897. 'Perhaps we'll play together again one day, as we did in the past,' he wrote; 'and I promise to plague you, just as I did then.' GMB, 233.)

Mahler to Friedrich Löhr

c/o Mittlere Karlstrasse 17,
Second Floor,
Kassel, 19 September 1883

I am conducting *Robert le diable* this evening; His Lordship the Court Conductor keeps all the classics for himself; he is the jolliest 4/4-beater I have ever come across. Naturally I am the 'pigheaded young man' who refuses to receive initiation from him into the mysteries of art. . . .

GMB, 24. (Mahler had arrived at Kassel on 21 August 1883; clearly he was very soon at loggerheads with Wilhelm Treiber, the Graz-born Court Conductor.)

I am sending you a few more reviews of my conducting of *Das Glöckchen des Eremiten*. I must tell you that these two critics are very hard to please, and never miss the chance of praising me as opposed to Treiber, the Chief Conductor. Circumstances have altered to such an extent that *Management*, orchestra and singers, as well as the *critics* and the *public*, think *more highly* of me than they do of Treiber, and the critics never fail to say so. Admittedly Herr Treiber's contract cannot be set aside *for the present*, so he naturally gets more conducting than I do. But it is not entirely impossible that something unpleasant might happen to the above mentioned gentleman. I don't want to speak more plainly.

Ms., WSTB. (This undated letter from Kassel was presumably written at the end of October 1883.)

118, 119   An unusual musical event took place at Kassel on 24 and 25 January; Hans von Bülow, who was the most famous conductor of his time, and a world-famous pianist, gave a concert at Kassel with the Meiningen Court Orchestra of which he was the creator and conductor. Before the first concert which Bülow conducted, Mahler tried to call on him, but the hall porter of the Schirmer Hotel, where Bülow was staying, refused to let him in.

Mahler to Hans von Bülow

Most honoured Master!
Forgive me for approaching you, at the risk of appearing impertinent, in spite of having been turned away by the hall porter of your hotel. When I asked you for an interview, I did not yet know what a flame your incomparable art would kindle in my soul. In plain terms, I am a musician who is wandering without a guiding light in the dreary night of present-day musical life, and who is a prey to all the dangers of doubt and confusion.

At the concert yesterday, when I beheld the fulfilment of my utmost intimations and hopes of beauty, it became clear to me that I had found my spiritual home and my master, and that my wanderings would come to an end now or never.

And now I am here to beg you to take me along in any capacity you like – let me become your *pupil*, even if I had to pay my tuition fees with my blood. What I can do – or what I might do – I do not know; but you will soon find out. I am twenty-three and was a student at Vienna University and studied the piano and composition at the Conservatoire; now, after the most wretched wanderings, I am employed as Assistant Conductor at the Theatre. You will know only too well whether this hollow activity can satisfy one who believes in art with all his heart and soul and sees it travestied everywhere in every conceivable way. I give myself to you heart and soul, and if you will accept the gift, I cannot think of anything that could make me happier. If you will be kind enough to reply, I am ready for anything you have in mind.

At least send me a reply. Yours in eager expectation,
Gustav Mahler.

Ms., CAS. (Bülow handed this effusion to the Kassel Conductor, Wilhelm Treiber, for transmission to the management of the Royal Theatre, where it was incorporated into Mahler's personal file.)

Almost at the same time another young composer, whose name was not even known to Mahler, wrote a letter of thanks to Hans von Bülow. This was the nineteen-year-old
76   Richard Strauss, whose Serenade for Wind Instruments

Bülow had performed at Meiningen. The amount of support and encouragement this performance gave to young Strauss must be gauged in relation to Bülow's position in the musical life of Germany, which made him the idol, and the spiritual father-figure, of all young musicians.

Richard Strauss to Hans von Bülow

Berlin, 8 January 1884

Once again I feel the need to express my most profound and grateful thanks to you, not only for performing my Wind Serenade at Meiningen, of which I unfortunately heard only yesterday, but especially because you are going to be so kind and generous as to perform my little work in three other towns during your tour. I discovered all this yesterday at Wolff's Agency, and do not know how my work has deserved to be so honoured by you, and how I can thank you enough for taking such a kindly interest in me and my work.

'Hans von Bülow/Richard Strauss, Briefwechsel', in *Richard Strauss-Jahrbuch 1954*, Bonn 1953, 8. (Hermann Wolff, concert agent in Berlin, was founder of the Philharmonic Concerts in Berlin and later of the Bülow Concerts at Hamburg.)

Alma Mahler on Mahler's unhappy love affairs, and love poetry, of the Kassel period

He fell in love with two singers at the same time, and they made fun of him. He suffered pain and anguish, and wrote poems to both of them, not knowing that they were friends, and that they showed their trophies to each other; in the end they exposed him to gossip and unpleasantness. He fled from Kassel towards the end of the season and was able to breathe freely again only in the train. He had, as I have said, constantly written poems to them both; if he completed a poem in the middle of the night, the lateness of the hour did not prevent him from sending it off immediately by messenger. He was not in the least worried by their fury at being disturbed.

AM, 140. (When Alma Mahler talks of a double love affair, she is presumably following the account that Mahler himself gave her some twenty years after the event. His letters from the years 1884–85, on the other hand, mention only one passion, unrequited, for the coloratura soprano Johanna Richter, who joined the Kassel company at the same time as himself.)

Der Trompeter von Säkkingen. Ein Sang vom Oberrhein ('The   57 Trumpeter of Säkkingen. A Lay of the Upper Rhine') was the title of a narrative poem by Joseph Victor von Scheffel which was one of the best-sellers of the nineteenth century. The first edition appeared in 1854, and by 1883 it had been reprinted 110 times.

The lyric theatre soon got hold of this humorous-sentimental tale of 'love and trumpet-blowing'. In 1882 it inspired Emil Kaiser, Mahler's predecessor at Olmütz, to compose a lyric opera. Two years later the Conductor at Leipzig, Victor E. Nessler, composed another opera with the same title, which was given its world première at the Leipzig Municipal Theatre under Arthur Nikisch on 4 May 1884, and which was later performed at almost all opera houses where German was sung. Mahler had to conduct it dozens of times during his year in Prague. When a concert in aid of the General Pensions Institute of the Fellowship of German Stage Personnel was organized at the Kassel theatre, it was decided to include *tableaux vivants* based on the poem *Der Trompeter von Säkkingen*. Mahler, who was on the managing committee of the 'Support Fund for Retired Members of the Royal Theatre Orchestra, their Widows and Orphans', composed the music for these *tableaux vivants*. It was played only once at Kassel, but later revived at Mannheim and in other places. The score has not been preserved.

Victor von Scheffel to the Members of the Fellowship of German Stage Personnel

I am very glad to give my consent to a performance of *Der Trompeter von Säkkingen* in the form of *tableaux vivants* at the Royal Theatre at Kassel. This was successfully done by the Mining Association during the Carnival at Stuttgart a few years ago, and the linking narration, decorations costumes and the final festive procession of all the participants were highly effective.

Deutsche Bühnenzeitung, 23 June 1884.

Mahler to Friedrich Löhr on his music for 'Der Trompeter von Säkkingen'

Kassel, 22 June 1884

In the last few days I have had to compose music for *Der Trompeter von Säkkingen* at breakneck speed; it is going to be staged as a series of *tableaux vivants* in the theatre tomorrow. The opus was finished in two days, and I must confess that I am very happy with it. As you can imagine, it has not much in common with Scheffel's affectations; it goes far beyond the poet's reach. . . .

GMB, 27–28.

From the programme of the charity concert held at Kassel on 23 June

Der Trompeter von Säkkingen

performed in seven *tableaux vivants* with linking narration. Based on the poem by Victor von Scheffel. Music composed by the Assistant Conductor, Herr Mahler.
First Tableau: Serenade on the Rhine. Second Tableau: First Meeting. Third Tableau: May Day on the Mountain Lake. Fourth Tableau: Trumpet Lesson in the Honeysuckle Arbour. Fifth Tableau: Attack in the Castle Garden. Sixth Tableau: Successful Love. Seventh Tableau: Meeting in Rome.
The narration is recited by Herr Thiess.

Deutsche Bühnenzeitung, 23 June 1884, 311. (There was a variety of music and recitations in the programme, including the fourth act of Meyerbeer's *Les Huguenots* and the fourth act of Verdi's *Il Trovatore*. *Der Trompeter von Säkkingen* was the last item.)

Max Steinitzer on Mahler's later opinion of his 'Trompeter' music

Mahler wrote the incidental music for a series of *tableaux vivants*, based on *Der Trompeter von Säkkingen*, which were staged at the Court Theatre at Kassel (for the benefit of the orchestra pension fund, I think); he regarded it as absolutely worthless. I have never heard of it since, but it is just possible that some part of it might still be found at Kassel. He brought with him to Leipzig only the score of a small extract, which expressed its subject very well, I thought: Werner is playing a serenade across the Rhine to the castle where Margareta lives. Mahler found it too sentimental and was annoyed that he had written it; and I had to give him my word to destroy the piano arrangement that I had made of it. As far as I can remember, the trumpet solo began like this:

Friedrich Löhr on the summer of 1884 at Perchtoldsdorf near Vienna

Mahler came to us at Perchtoldsdorf on 1 July, and stayed until after 7 July, which is his birthday. Shortly afterwards I stayed with him at Iglau, and this was the climax of an association that had lasted for two years; our different careers meant it could never be so close again, but it was the basis of a lifelong friendship that was to be indissoluble. The two important things in our life at Perchtoldsdorf in those days were our walks and our many long hours of music. The windows of my room on the first floor of the Eders' house in the marketplace were closed in spite of the summer heat, but more and more people collected beneath them, and listened in astonishment. How few people are left today who know what it meant to hear Mahler playing the piano in those days. (He used to say that five or six years before then was the time when he had really been able to play.) I have never known such a total disembodiment of a human physical skill. . . . But what is there to say, in words, about the effect of his playing? When I look back, a shiver runs down my spine at the thought of the sublime happiness that was given to me, as Mahler's only listener, including all Beethoven's Sonatas, Bach's *Well-Tempered Clavier*, and other works by the most beloved Masters. . . .

GMB, notes, 473–74.

Josef Stransky on a memorial anthem for the death of Empress Maria Anna

When I was eight, I spent my summer holidays with relations in the small Bohemian town of Ledetsch, where an aunt of Mahler's lived. She was his mother's sister, and her house was the most important in the place; the local dignitaries of Ledetsch regarded it as an honour to be invited by Frau Freischberger. My relations made that quite plain to me, and so I was full of awe as I entered the house, when we were invited for afternoon coffee. She was a thin woman with serious grey eyes and a smiling mouth; as soon as we arrived she proudly told us that her young nephew Gustav, who was already the admired idol of the family, had come to see her with a friend, and that they would soon be back from their walk. They came in at that moment. I can still see them; they both had fine heads with black hair and sparkling eyes, and they both gesticulated violently. They took hardly any notice of the other visitors at first, but went on with their discussion without any sense of embarrassment. At last they consented to sit with us at the coffee table. Mahler stroked my hair and asked my name; when I told him, he said, 'You have the same name as the village schoolmaster, for whom I have composed the memorial anthem for the Empress Maria Anna. Are you a relation of his?' And as I could say that I was, I felt that a sort of connection had been established between this admired man and my insignificant self.

Josef Stransky, 'Begegnungen mit Gustav Mahler', *Signale für die musikalische Welt* (Berlin), 19 July 1911. (The Empress Maria Anna, Ferdinand I's widow, died in Prague on 14 May 1884. Stransky's meeting with Mahler, therefore, cannot have happened before the summer of 1884. Josef Stransky, 1872–1936, was then twelve years old, not eight. He later became a conductor, and worked at the German National Theatre at Prague and the Hamburg Municipal Theatre. In 1911 he followed Mahler as Conductor to the New York Philharmonic Society.)

Max Steinitzer, 'Erinnerungen an Gustav Mahler', ANBR. (As Steinitzer's quotation shows, the same trumpet melody was inserted into the slow movement, known as *Blumine*, of the First Symphony. Mahler disowned his *Trompeter* music, even in symphonic form; and this movement was omitted when the Symphony was printed. It was first published in 1968.)

Mahler to Friedrich Löhr, on his return to Kassel

I arrived here yesterday and have already taken my first rehearsal. I had hardly set foot in the streets of Kassel before I was gripped by the old powerful inhibition, and I don't know how I am to recover my equilibrium. I have met her again and she is as enigmatic as ever! All I can say is, God help me! You probably noticed at our last meeting that I was rather gloomy – it was the old fear of the inevitable. I am going to see her, to pay my 'courtesy call', this afternoon, and then I shall know how I stand.

GMB, 31–32.

Mahler requests permission to run a choral society

Herr Franke has called on me on behalf of the Committee of the Münden Mixed Choral Society, to invite me to become the Society's artistic director. I should have to undertake to spend one evening a week at Münden, if possible. In view of the fact that my predecessor, Herr Hempel, directed the Society for years under the same conditions, and of my assurance that my service at the Royal Theatre will not suffer in any way, I request a favourable reply to this application.

Ms., CAS.

Mahler as conductor of the Münden Choral Society

It is little known that Gustav Mahler was a chorus master in our province for a year. . . . In 1884–85 he conducted the Münden Choral Society. The commemorative publication of 1910, which prints a picture of Mahler, reads as follows: 'All those who then belonged to the Society will remember with real pleasure his unique way of inspiring and carrying with him the oldest and the youngest members alike. On two occasions, when we expected him at a rehearsal, he did not appear. We found out later that he had boarded the train at Kassel and had immediately plunged into a study of the vocal score. When – some time later – he returned from the world of music to this one, and looked out of the window to see if he had arrived at Münden, he realized that he was still at Kassel sitting in an uncoupled carriage.'

His absent-mindedness could also take the oddest forms, as when we sat with him for a short time after the rehearsal, smoking cigarettes and drinking tea; it happened more than once that he thought he had drawn on his cigarette when he had actually taken a mouthful of tea, and when he exhaled, tea sprayed out instead of smoke. He laughed at that more than anybody.

Hannoverscher Courier, 25 May 1911, EV.

Mahler applies to Angelo Neumann for a change of employment

Kassel, 3 December 1884

I take the liberty of introducing myself to you and putting myself forward for possible employment. I am Assistant Conductor at the Court Theatre here, and conduct *Robert le diable*, *Hans Heiling*, *Der Freischütz*, *Rättenfänger*, etc. You will have no difficulty in obtaining information about my capabilities either from here, or from Herr Ueberhorst, the Chief Stage Manager in Dresden, who knows me very well. I am very anxious to give up my position here as soon as possible, chiefly because I want more demanding work and as Assistant Conductor here I can find nothing worthy of my powers. Will you sooner or later need an energetic young conductor who – and now I am obliged to praise myself – has knowledge and experience, and is not incapable of breathing life and inspiration into a work of art and into those who are collaborating with him?

Prager Tagblatt, 5 March 1898. (Angelo Neumann, 1838–1910, originally a

singer, had been Director of the Municipal Theatre in Leipzig. He won international fame as the founder of the 'Flying Richard Wagner Theatre' which performed Wagner's major works in various cities in Germany, Austria, Italy, Holland and Belgium. When Mahler wrote to him, he was Director of the Bremen Opera. In his reply he asked Mahler to write again 'as soon as you read of my changed circumstances'. A few months later Neumann became Director of the German Theatre in Prague.)

The genesis of 'Lieder eines fahrenden Gesellen'

Kassel, 1 January 1885

I spent the first minutes of this year in a rather strange way. I sat alone with her yesterday evening, and we awaited the coming of the New Year almost in silence. Her thoughts were not about the present, and when midnight struck and tears flooded from her eyes, I was so overcome that I did not dare dry them. She went into the next room and for a while stood silently at the window, and when she came back, crying quietly, the nameless grief stood between us like an eternal wall, and I could only press her hand and go. When I came out of the door, the bells were ringing, and the solemn chorale rang out from the tower. Ah, dear Fritz, it was just as if the great world stage manager had wanted to make it all artistically perfect. I wept all through the night in my dreams.

And now about my activities. I have composed a song cycle, six songs at present, all dedicated to her. She hasn't seen them. What can they tell her beyond what she knows. I will enclose the last song, although the inadequate words cannot even tell a small part. The songs are a sequence in which a wayfaring craftsman, who has had a great sorrow, goes out into the world and wanders aimlessly. . . .

Dear Fritz! Everything you know about her is a misunderstanding. I have begged her forgiveness for everything, and sacrificed my pride and self-respect. She is all that is lovable in this world. I would willingly give my last drop of blood for her. But I know that I have to go away. I have done all I can, but still I can see no way out.

From a letter from Mahler to Friedrich Löhr, GMB, 33–34. (The song cycle, in its published version, comprises only four songs, not six.)

Mahler announces his Leipzig appointment to Albert Spiegler

Kassel, 23 January 1885

You must know that I have been appointed (First) Conductor at the Leipzig Municipal Theatre, most probably starting next summer. I shall be on an absolutely equal footing with Nikisch. . . . As you see, I am a very lucky man, but, believe me, without being a bit happier.

I live like a Hottentot, and cannot speak a sensible word to anybody. The Kassel people are so stuck up that I would rather talk to a Viennese cab driver.

I have worked at a lot of things, even if only 'for the drawer'. I might now have the influence and the opportunity to perform my own compositions, but the climate of ineptitude here makes every performance a matter of such absolute indifference to me that I do not move a finger to obtain one.

My grateful thanks to all of you, the Adlers, Pernerstorfer, and Bondi for your New Year greetings. *Perhaps you could possibly get Friedjung to publicize my promotion in the Viennese papers,* if possible with a *'short obituary'* as well. That could be very useful to me in the future, although there are not many rungs of the ladder left for me to climb now. But my final goal is and always will be Vienna – I can never feel at home anywhere else. . . .

Ms., The Pierpont Morgan Library, New York, and the Mary Flagler Cary Charitable Trust. (The historian Heinrich Friedjung, 1851–1920, a friend of Victor Adler's, was then a contributor to the liberal nationalist *Deutsche Zeitung*, which was published in Vienna, and of which he later became Editor.)

Mahler informs Gustav Lewy of his appointment to Leipzig

Kassel, 16 March 1885

The first thing I have to tell you is that I have been engaged as Conductor at the Leipzig Municipal Theatre as from July 1886, and shall work my probationary period there in July and August this year. My private concerns make it supremely important to me not to spend next season *at Kassel*. I have unendurably *little* to do here – only *one opera* each week, and often only every other week. You can quite understand that in the end that becomes insufferable to a young man who wants to *learn*.

I am now asking you to find me a *suitable* engagement for *next Winter*. The General Manager knows everything and approves of what I am doing. He will not refuse to release me. . . .

Ms., WSTB.

Mahler to Friedrich Löhr, on love and money troubles

Kassel, 28 May 1885

When I wrote some time ago to tell you that my relationship with 'her' had entered a new final phase, that was only a theatrical trick, like announcing a final performance, in order to announce a 'positively final' one the next day. The final phase has become a positively final phase, and as there are only three weeks left before I leave here for ever, it is not very likely that there will be a 'positively final phase of all' in response to public demand. But I guarantee nothing.

How are my prospects in Vienna? Shall I get a few lessons? I am rather anxious to, for I have saved nothing here, as you can imagine. I shall have great difficulty in avoiding a debtors' prison. . . .

Send me the number of the *Deutsche Worte* in which your essay is printed.

GMB, 39–40.

Friedrich Löhr's criticism of the architecture of the Ringstrasse in Vienna

Who'll buy Classical – Gothic – German or Italian Renaissance? And all of it – what more could you ask – neatly displayed; for this is the architectural old-clothes market of the Imperial capital city of Vienna. Now, in an old-clothes market everybody grabs what he particularly wants. So I stand in front of a building. I know quite well that it is the Imperial Parliament. Anyone who does not know this already is certainly not going to guess it; it is a house built in the style of a Greek temple. Imposing columns soar upwards; it is surrounded by friezes above which there are pediments. I go in, and a guide attaches himself to me; not without need, for I immediately fall into serious intellectual difficulties, not to say confusion. . . .

Hanns Maria (Friedrich Löhr), 'Über einige Einflüsse der Antike auf unsere Kultur', *Deutsche Worte*, vol. v, no. 1, 184–85. (This essay, for which Mahler asked his friend in his letter of 28 May 1885, expresses the mood of the younger generation, which already disliked the style of the Ringstrasse, even before it was completed.)

During his last months at Kassel, Mahler divided his time between his work at the theatre and the preparations for a musical festival in which choirs from Münden, Kassel, Marburg and Nordhausen were to take part. The great project immediately encountered difficulties. Treiber, the senior Conductor, who had undertaken to rehearse the orchestra for the festival, withdrew, whereupon the Kassel theatre orchestra refused to cooperate. It then became necessary to put together a scratch orchestra consisting of the band of an infantry regiment and members of the Weimar, Meiningen and Brunswick Court Orchestras. The planned performance of Beethoven's Ninth Symphony had to be abandoned, and Mahler's task was reduced to rehearsing and conducting Mendelssohn's oratorio *St Paul*, with a chorus of four hundred and the soloists Rosa Papier, Paul Bulss and Heinrich Gudehus. The festival was held from 29 June to 1 July 1885 in the Infantry Drill Hall at Kassel, temporarily converted into a concert hall.

Mahler on the Kassel musical festival

When two or three choral societies join forces in the name of art, do you think that any good can come of it? The fashion at present is to be musical – patriotic – festive. The choice of me has provoked dreadful party strife which very nearly wrecked the whole project. They cannot forgive me my youth here, particularly the people in the profession. Our orchestra is on strike because the Lord Chief Conductor sees he has made a fool of himself, and the General Manager himself has even had the brazen cheek to appeal to my magnanimity to give the whole thing up. Naturally I told him where he got off, so I am now a dead man in the Theatre.

From a letter to Friedrich Löhr, April 1885, GMB, 36–37.

. . . So far everything has gone as well for me as it possibly could. I have reaped honour and glory in full measure.

I have been given a large diamond ring, a gold watch, a commemorative album and so on. On the other hand my old watch is in pawn and I shall almost certainly have to pawn most of the valuables I have just been given to pay for my journey to Iglau, where I go tomorrow.

From a letter to Friedrich Löhr, 5 July 1885, GMB, 42–43.

Angelo Neumann's recollections of Mahler's début in Prague

When the newspapers printed the news that I had been appointed to manage the Royal German Theatre in Prague at the beginning of 1885, one of the very first applications I received came from a man whose name was quite unknown to me. He was the chorus master at Kassel, who applied for the post of Conductor in Prague, confessing that he was not getting on very well at Kassel; he was allowed to conduct only things like *Der Waffenschmied* and *Zar und Zimmermann*. . . . I engaged the young musician after talking things over with him. Even before he conducted, I had evidence of his passionate love of music at a dress rehearsal of *Lohengrin* conducted by Anton Seidl. I was stage-managing it myself, as it was to be the first production of my directorship; during the wedding procession in the second act, I suddenly heard a voice in the pit saying loudly, 'Good God, I should never have thought it possible to rehearse like that; it's wonderful!' On the day after the performance of *Lohengrin* Seidl and I decided to allow the young hothead to conduct Cherubini's *Les Deux Journées*, the performance in honour of the Emperor's birthday. The new conductor, who put all his available energy into this task, seemed to us to move about too much when he was conducting, and in this way reminded us strongly of Bülow. Even when a lot of people questioned the wisdom of letting him conduct the gala performance, we stuck to our decision. His début was a success, and resulted in the young man being given a contract at the German Theatre for a year. When I came to consider the cast and allotment of parts for the programme I was planning for the season, I entrusted the young conductor with *Rhinegold* and *Valkyrie* which were to be in the repertory for the first time.

Angelo Neumann, 'Mahler in Prag', in PST2, 7–8. (Anton Seidl, 1850–98, a Wagner conductor and assistant to Angelo Neumann for many years, was offered a post in New York and left Prague very soon after the beginning of the 1885–86 season.)

The capital of Bohemia is rightly famous for its wonderful situation. Alexander von Humboldt considers that there is none finer in Europe, except Constantinople, Naples and Lisbon. The broad Vltava, with its many islands, divides the city into two main areas. The Hradčany, with its slopes covered with houses, and the even higher, partly wooded, Laurenzi Hill, rise steeply almost out of the water. The Hradčany is crowned by the enormous castle and the magnificent cathedral. The larger quarter, east of the river, slopes gently up to the surrounding hills, and only the steep slopes of the Višehrad fortress at the southern end stand directly on the river bank. In the town itself a walk along the Francis Embankment offers the most impressive view of the river, islands and quarters on the left bank, while the best view of the extensive city, its many towers and its magnificent position can be had from the Hradčany or the Laurenzi Hill. The river is crossed by four bridges in addition to the old stone Charles Bridge and two railway bridges. The impressive Francis Suspension Bridge soars above the beautiful Schützeninsel or Archers' Island, which, with the nearby Sophia and Dyers' Islands, is Prague's chief entertainment centre. Campa Island, opposite the Lesser Town, and Hetz Island, the largest of them, are also worth a visit. Prague is divided into five main quarters . . . [Including the suburbs] it has about 280,000 inhabitants, of whom three-fifths are of Czech nationality, two-fifths of German. In Prague itself 79.2 per cent use Czech and 26.6 per cent German as their everyday language.

Friedrich Umlauft, *Die Österreichisch-Ungarische Monarchie*, Vienna 1883, 799.

The German and Czech Theatres in Prague

61, 63, 69 Plays used to be performed in Czech in the German Theatre on two or three afternoons a week for the lower classes, until the Czechs built a small temporary theatre. After twenty years of economy and hard work it was replaced by the magnificent National Theatre, which is their pride and joy. In earlier times the German theatre was largely attended by Czechs and by 'Utraquists', that nearly extinct variety of Bohemians who spoke German and Czech equally badly; little by little there was a gradual process of separation which came to an end with the opening of the Czech National Theatre, after which the Czechs went exclusively to the Czech Theatre and the Germans exclusively to the German. In the meantime Prague had become a Czech city, with the result that the Czech Theatre caters for the public of a great city while the German Theatre attracts only the public of a provincial town. . . .

Unfortunately the Czech National Theatre was opened at a time when the German Theatre was managed by Kreibig, one of those managers who can distinguish themselves by a good season in small Austrian towns, but who have not the commercial acumen, enterprise, comprehensive literary culture or basic knowledge of art necessary for running a large one. The Czech Theatre began to batten on the lifeblood of the German; the German public lost the habit of going to its own theatre, which avoided collapse, but in appearance only.
62 However Angelo Neumann was called in to save it from disaster, and at a stroke the German public was back. He engaged an entirely new company and embarked on a period of great activity. Drama and opera filled the house every evening, and the performance of Wagner's *Ring* acted as a magnet to the whole theatre-going public of Prague. . . .

Heinrich Tewele, 'Die nationale Bedeutung des Deutschen Theaters in Prag', *Dramaturgische Blätter und Bühnen-Rundschau* (Berlin), XVII, 15 January 1888.

Prague, 6 September 1885

This is the first time I have had time to write you a line; dear Toni will have told you how I am getting on here; I can add that so far everything exceeds my expectations. Orchestra, chorus, soloists and manager treat me with the greatest respect and, as long as nothing goes wrong in the meantime, I can say that I have taken a big step forward this year, more significant than all the rest put together. I am going to conduct *Don Giovanni* this evening; it is a sure sign of Neumann's special confidence in me that he trusts me with this opera, because it has great significance for Prague; it was for Prague that Mozart composed, rehearsed and conducted it himself. It is in this work that the Prague people demand the *highest* standard. It is a foregone conclusion that the papers, and especially the *Tageblatt*, will pounce on me, for I can tell you in advance that they will all cry, 'Woe, woe, "Tradition" has gone to the devil.' By 'tradition' they mean the time-honoured (i.e. slovenly) way of staging a work. I have not let it bother me in the least, and shall quietly go my *own* way this evening. This is the time when you can share my happiness, if you visit me. I am expecting you here *as soon as possible*!

Liebste Mutter, ed. Paul Elbogen, Berlin 1929, 243–44. (A collection of 'Letters of Famous Germans to their Mothers'.)

Neustädter Theater.

Sonntag, den 6. September 1885.

216. Abonnements-Vorstellung.

Don Juan.

Große Oper in zwei Acten. Musik von W. A. Mozart.
Die Original-Recitative in der Einrichtung des k. k. Hofopernheaters in Wien.

Personen:

Don Juan	. . . .	Joseph Beck
Leporello sein Diener	. . . .	Wenzel Dobsch
Don Pedro, Gouverneur	. . . .	Johannes Elmblad
Dona Anna, seine Tochter	. . . .	Marie v. Moser
Don Octavio	. . . .	Adolf Wallnöfer
Donna Elvira	. . . .	Katharina Rosen
Masetto, ein Bauer	. . . .	Felix Ehrl
Zerline, seine Braut	. . . .	Sarolta Le Pirk

Bauern und Bäuerinnen. Musikanten. Diener.

Im 1. Act Menuett, arrangirt von der Balletmeisterin Bertha Milde, ausgeführt von Stefanie Weiger, Anna Güttich, Luigi Mazzantini und dem Corps de Ballet.

Anfang um 7 Uhr.   **Ende gegen 10 Uhr.**

Unpäßlich Ludwig Röbe.

Preise der Plätze:

Loge 1. Rang und Parquet	. . . . 8 fl. — kr.	1 Sperrsitz (3 Rang)	. . . — fl. 50 kr.
1 Loge im 2. Rang	. . . . 6 fl. — kr.	1 Stehplatz im Parquet	. . . 1 fl. — kr.
1 Sperrsitz im Parquet in den ersten 3 Reihen	. 2 fl. 50 kr.	1 Stehplatz (Parterre, Tribune und 1. Rang)	. — fl. 80 kr.
1 Sperrsitz im Parquet von der vierten Reihe angefangen	1 fl. 50 kr.	1 Stehplatz (2. Rang)	. . . — fl. 50 kr.
1 Sperrsitz (Tribune, 1. Rang)	. . 1 fl. 80 kr.	1 Stehplatz (3. Rang)	. . . — fl. 20 kr.
1 Sperrsitz (2 Rang)	. . . . . 1 fl. — kr.	1 Studenten-, Garnison- und Kinderbillet	. — fl. 40 kr.

Neustädter Theater.

Montag, den 7. September 1885.   217. Abonnements-Vorstellung.

Der Troubadour.

Oper in 4 Acten nach dem Französischen des S. Camerano von H. Proch. Musik von Verdi.

Der Billetverkauf für den laufenden Tag findet an der Tageskasse des königl. Deutschen Landestheaters von 9 Uhr Vormittags bis 2 Uhr Nachmittags, der Vorverkauf für den nächstfolgenden Tag (gegen die übliche Vorverkaufsgebühr) von 12 bis 2 Uhr Nachmittags statt.

Buchdruckerei von Gottlieb Schmelzer, Prag. — Verlag der Direction des kgl. Deutschen Landestheaters.

Programme of the first performance of *Don Giovanni* to be conducted by Mahler; it took place at the Neustadt Theatre, the summer venue of the German Theatre in Prague. Narodní Muzeum, Prague.

Mahler to Friedrich Löhr

Rittergasse 24, Prague, 28 November 1885

It is difficult to tell you what I am doing. I should like to begin my letter with sighs, for that is the custom! I have some good news for you! I have already conducted *The Mastersingers* three times, and I am going to conduct *Rhinegold* and *Valkyrie*, which are to be put on soon. Such tasks absorb all a musician's energies, as nothing else could – particularly if he is like me and has to enter the lists to fight for the sanctity of art.

Yet in spite of everything time is as empty and dull for me as it ever was, and I long for a really serious talk with you.

GMB, 44.

From a review of the première of 'Rhinegold', conducted by Mahler

Yesterday's performance of *Rhinegold*, the preliminary evening of Wagner's Nibelung Trilogy, was brilliant. The audience entered the entirely new world, revealed by the subject, language and music of this remarkable work, in a most receptive mood. . . . Presenting this work is a task of gigantic difficulty; settings in the original Bayreuth style helped as much as the thorough, painstaking preparation to which the performance of the orchestra and singers bore witness. . . . The mood of the audience was most enthusiastic; at the end of both acts there were endless curtain calls in which the conductor of this excellent performance, Herr Mahler, joined the singers on the stage.

Prager Tagblatt, 20 December 1885.

Mahler to Baron von Gilsa, the General Manager at Kassel

What a lot of trouble the unruly schoolboy made for you; you must often have needed all your forbearance not to lose patience with me. I hope to be able to show you from now on that I shall not put my master to shame and that your well-intended admonitions have fallen on fertile ground.

I am getting on very well here. So far I have conducted *new productions* of *Don Giovanni*, *Les Deux Journées*, *Fidelio*, *Tannhäuser* and *Mastersingers*; *the first performances here* of *Trompeter*, *Rhinegold*, and *Valkyrie*, and am busy preparing a new *Tristan* and a Mozart cycle. So I have plenty to do for five months. I would love to have given up my contract at Leipzig to stay here, but the Director, Herr Staegemann, refused to allow it. And so I have to take the dreary road to Leipzig next August, where I am bound to get involved in the most painful rivalry with Nikisch.

From a letter of 29 December 1885, ms., CAS.

Quarrel with the Director, Angelo Neumann

Every opera conducted by Mahler seemed to take on a new lease of life. The inevitable result was Angelo Neumann's fear that the young man might get beyond his control. His remedy on such an occasion was to 'cut him down to size' as he put it. He did this in the time-honoured way by ordering Mahler out of the orchestra pit.

Bowed down with shame and anger after this tender dismissal, Mahler locked himself in his room and would not see anybody. He would not even open the door to Elmblad, his room-mate, who came to me and told me what had happened. When I spoke to Angelo Neumann about it, however, he said, 'The director of a theatre must have principles, and it was my duty to demonstrate the correctness of mine in the sight of everybody. Nobody can say that I have not paid suitable tribute to Mahler's outstanding talent. *If he writes* and tells me

that he is sorry he flouted my authority I will again allow him to continue his practical training here. My Ballet Mistress has more practical experience than he has, and he has got to accept *what she says*, with a good grace, *and act accordingly*. He did not, *so I sent him off*. That is my right as his employer. When you are conducting *Faust* it's a lot of *stuff and nonsense* to quote the composer, or refer to a prescribed tempo, as he did.'

This was what I had to put to Mahler. He flatly refused to apologize to Neumann in writing. All the same his daemonic urge to do creative work, and a desire to be rehabilitated in the eyes of the stage staff, led him to offer to work until the end of the season, if Neumann would offer satisfaction *to him*. . . .

Julius Steinberg, 'Aus Mahlers Prager Kapellmeisterzeit', *Fremdenblatt* (Vienna), 25 May 1911. (This article by Steinberg, a Prague journalist, did not remain uncontradicted. On 27 May 1911, in the same newspaper, a Dr Richard Batka called on 'all artists who knew Neumann well to testify whether it even seemed possible for him to behave like that'. Even Julius Steinberg's daughter, Gisela Wien-Steinberg, published a report differing from her father's account of the incident in the *Neues Wiener Journal* of 29 June 1921. All that seems certain is that there was a serious quarrel between the Director and his Conductor over the ballet scene in Gounod's *Faust*, that the Director finally gave in, and that they became life-long friends.)

Mahler conducts Beethoven's Ninth Symphony

. . . Herr Mahler conducted both the long extract from *Parsifal* and the symphony from memory, a magnificent testimony to his exact knowledge of the two works. He shaped every nuance in the air with his hands, recalling the tradition of the peculiar manner of conducting the religious choral music of the Middle Ages, which included the shaping of the melody by movements and gestures of the hand. It was universally recognized that Herr Mahler's conducting showed every part of the work to its best advantage. He subtly and artistically brought out the colouring of the first movement by stressing certain notes by *crescendi* and *diminuendi*, and by a careful use of light and shade; by the choice of a moderate tempo for the passages in 3/4 time he introduced a brilliant contrast into the second movement and made a clear-cut distinction between the *adagio* and the yearning of the D major episode. As regards the chorus in the last movement, the poem inspired Beethoven with visions that led him beyond the abilities of the human voice, and sometimes even tempted him to do violence to it. . . . The result of this is the difficulty of obtaining flowing, unforced singing of the choruses, and for this reason the excellent performance given by the ladies and gentlemen of the chorus, whose superior musical education had largely to compensate for their lack of the professional singer's practised technique, is all the more praiseworthy.

Bohemia, 23 February 1886. (This concert, which Mahler conducted on 21 February, was a repeat of one conducted on the anniversary of Wagner's death by Carl Muck. Carl Muck, 1859–1940, worked at the German Theatre in Prague from 1886 to 1892.)

Angelo Neumann to Mahler

Herr Angelo Neumann, Director [of the German Theatre], has written the following letter to the Conductor, Herr Gustav Mahler: 'Now that I have returned, I must write and congratulate you on your outstanding success in conducting Beethoven's Ninth Symphony. As we shall soon no longer be working together, and you are going to join one of the most distinguished institutions in Germany, for which I was once privileged to work for three years, the best I can wish is that you will be as successful in finding a position corresponding to your musical abilities in your new sphere as you have been here. Yours very sincerely, Angelo Neumann.' It appears from this letter that the differences that once arose between Herr Neumann and Herr Mahler over different interpretations of an artistic matter have now been settled.

Bohemia, 1 March 1886.

From Friedrich Löhr's account of his three-week visit to Prague

Mahler has absolutely no social life, that is to say he is generally at home when he is not at the theatre, but he is very well known, as often happens in small towns, so we often saw a lot of people willy-nilly. . . . I went to the theatre a lot, and saw *Der Trompeter* twice, as well as *Lumpazivagabundus* by Nestroy, *Rhinegold, Valkyrie* and *Tannhäuser*, went to both performances of the Wagner Memorial Concert, and to *Carmen* at the Czech Theatre. Now I must say that Mahler's conducting gave me enormous pleasure. You will not believe how great and mature and enthralling his conducting is; there is no longer any trace of fidgetiness, and he combines overwhelming energy with youthful fire. . . . Just one example: when the concert was repeated, he conducted the Ninth Symphony, eight days after the first performance. During that week he had a serious row with the Director, Angelo Neumann, which looked like leading to a permanent quarrel at the risk of a breach of contract. I was very glad to be here at the time, and I did my best to persuade him to stand by his rights and firmly make his point *vis-à-vis* the Director; the affair ended, however, with a flattering apology from the Director, who had not expected such an outcome. So it was that Mahler did not know that he was to conduct the symphony until two days before; and indeed, except for a single rehearsal with a small section of the strings (mainly concerned with the recitative of the basses), he was obliged to conduct without a rehearsal, because no time had been allotted to him. In spite of this, his incomparably energetic, emphatic style of conducting, and the vigour and inexorable firmness with which he imposed his will on his performers, enabled him to give a performance that was entirely different from the one under Muck. . . .

From a letter from Friedrich Löhr to an unknown correspondent, about March 1886, ANBR, 305.

Mahler's songs and Bruckner's Third Symphony at a concert in Prague

A concert was held on Sunday afternoon in the Winter Garden of the Grand Hotel in aid of the Benevolent Fund for Indigent German Law Students. It was a monster concert, for in two and a half hours twenty-eight items were performed, counting separate movements and encores. Fräulein Betty Frank sang an aria from Peter von Winter's opera *Das unterbrochene Opferfest*, a very suitable choice for showing off the outstanding agility of her voice. She also sang three original songs by Mahler, of which the last, *Hans und Grete*, was encored. . . . The instrumental numbers of the concert were played by the augmented orchestra of the German Theatre conducted from memory by Herr Mahler. We first heard Mozart's G minor Symphony. . . . A second, very interesting orchestral piece was the Scherzo from Anton Bruckner's Third Symphony, dedicated to Richard Wagner; Bruckner, who lives in Vienna, had to wait till he was over sixty before music lovers suddenly took notice of him and his Seventh Symphony, which, even then, provoked widely differing judgments. . . . This performance of the Scherzo of the Third, composed as long ago as 1873, which Herr Mahler has also arranged as a piano duet, allowed us a glimpse of Bruckner's genius and his masterly command of orchestration. . . .

Bohemia, 20 April 1886. (The song *Hans und Grete*, composed in 1880, originally bore the title *Maitanz im Grünen*.)

Mahler to Max Staegemann, now Theatre Director in Leipzig

Prague, 7 June 1886

72 I shall be able to arrive at Leipzig on 24 or 25 July, having obtained Herr Neumann's consent today, and shall make the best possible use of the time that remains to me before the date you have chosen for my preliminary tests. . . .

GMB, 66. (Max Staegemann, 1843–1905, had been Director of the Leipzig Municipal Theatre since 1882.)

176

Leipzig and its surroundings

Although situated in a plain not remarkable for natural beauty, watered by three rivers, the White Elster, the Pleisse and the Parthe, Leipzig's surroundings are not lacking in charm. The visitor who chooses to direct his steps further afield will be able to enjoy the deciduous woods to the south and west, the so-called Rosental [Rose Valley] to the north, and the fertile regions of the north-east. The Ring Walk is also regarded as one of the city's special attractions, and the fine new buildings not infrequently induce architects to make a longer stay. . . .

Leipzig is the capital of the German book trade, which has an importance here not exceeded by any other town. Many firms, some of them world-famous, distribute works of literature through the publishing, retail, antiquarian and distributive branches of the trade. The head offices of 853 firms engaged in the book trade, including art and music publishers, are situated in Leipzig.

Leipzig und Umgebung, Leipzig 1899, 1–2. (Mahler used to choose the Rosental, which is mentioned above, for his long walks.)

Tchaikowsky's opinion of the young Arthur Nikisch

The Leipzig Opera is proud of its brilliant conductor, a young man who specializes in the music dramas of Wagner's last creative period. I heard him conduct *The Rhinegold* and *The Mastersingers*. The orchestra at the opera is the same as at the Gewandhaus, that is to say, absolutely first class. However faultless its concerts may be when conducted by Karl Reinecke, it is only possible to appreciate the excellence of its achievements by hearing it play Wagner's difficult and complicated scores, and then only when it is conducted by such an admirable master of his art as Herr Nikisch. His conducting has nothing in common with the famous and, in its own way, inimitable style of Hans von Bülow.

Bülow is flexible, restless, and sometimes makes an effect by a gesture that is meant to catch the eye; Arthur Nikisch is wonderfully restful, avoiding every superfluous movement, and at the same time astonishingly powerful, energetic and controlled. He does not conduct; it seems as if he were surrendering to some secret magic. He is hardly noticed, he takes absolutely no trouble to attract the attention of his audience, and yet one feels that the huge orchestra, like a single instrument in the hands of a wonderful master, submits completely and willingly to the commands of its chief.

This chief is a very pale young man of about thirty; he is of medium height, with splendid flashing eyes, and he really must have some sort of magic power that enables him to force the orchestra to thunder like the thousand trumpets of Jericho at one moment, to coo like a dove the next, and then to die away on a breath-taking, mysterious note. And that all happens in such a way that the listeners do not even notice the little conductor who quietly dominates his slavishly devoted orchestra.

Peter Ilyich Tchaikowsky, *Musikalische Erinnerungen und Feuilletons*, ed. Heinrich Stümcke, Berlin, n.d., 52–53.

. Mahler on his relationship with Nikisch

. . . You will want to know how I stand with Nikisch! He often 73 gives me great pleasure, and I can watch a performance under him as restfully as if I were conducting it myself – although all that is highest and most profound is a closed book to him. But how rarely I manage to bring it to light myself – I generally have to be satisfied with preventing real crudeness, and have to let things slide right and left.

I never have anything to do with him personally; he is cold and keeps me at arm's length – either from self-love or mistrust – how can I tell! In short, we pass each other without speaking!

From an undated letter to Friedrich Löhr, presumably written in October 1866, GMB, 53.

Mahler asks Baron von Gilsa to arrange a new appointment for him

. . . As I had foreseen, I am walking on hot bricks here; after the dominant position I had in Prague, I can no longer submit to being a pale moon circling round the star of Nikisch, as I must here.

Of course everybody says, 'Patience, you have to make your way!' But you must know, my dear Baron, that patience has never been my strong suit.

My former chief has made a wonderful offer to re-engage me, but I know quite well that the Director, Herr Staegemann, would never let me go at this price. It would certainly be quite different if your intervention enabled me to find a position of the first rank at a leading theatre.

From an undated letter, received at Kassel 25 October 1886, ms., CAS.

Mahler to Director Staegemann, on conducting the 'Ring'

Leipzig, 6 November 1886

You know that it was tacitly agreed between us until a certain point in time that, if the *Nibelung* came up, I was to share the conducting of these works with my colleague. I have documentary evidence of this.

You also know that my abilities and my nature make it impossible for me to remain in a situation in which I am excluded from projects of that sort.

I beg you to reflect also that there are even commercial reasons why I ought not to be denied this exceptional opportunity of winning the confidence of the public.

GMB, 68.

Leipzig, 27 November 1886

After mature consideration of the present conditions, I am convinced that it would be very incorrect of me to ascribe to you any of the blame for the situation that has become so painful for me.

On the contrary, it is quite clear to me that you are absolutely right from your own point of view, and that you cannot act otherwise.

I refer to my letter of December last, in which I foretold what has now come about, and I wish to express to you personally my genuine regret for all the measures which I am obliged to take from now on. I now ask you to release me.

GMB, 69–70. (No letter from Mahler to Staegemann of December 1885 has been published, but Mahler mentions to Baron von Gilsa in a letter of 29 December 1885 (p. 175) that he would gladly have given up his contract at Leipzig, but that Staegemann would not agree.)

Offers from Hamburg and Karlsruhe

Herr Mahler has received a brilliant offer from Herr Pollini of the Municipal Theatre, Hamburg. He has received another from Karlsruhe to succeed Herr Mottl, who has accepted an appointment in Berlin.

Leipziger Tageblatt und Anzeiger, 4 January 1887. (In letters to Friedrich Löhr [GMB, 55 and 60], Mahler also refers to an offer from Angelo Neumann to go to Prague and to one to go to New York in place of Anton Seidl.)

At the beginning of February Arthur Nikisch succumbed to a severe inflammation of the lungs, which prevented him from conducting for many months. Mahler took over the entire repertory, including Wagner's *Ring*, for which he had fought in vain a few weeks before. The junior Conductor was now able to convince the critics of his ability.

Mahler conducts the new 'Valkyrie' in place of Nikisch

. . . If the orchestra did not reach the same high standard of performance as it did in *Rhinegold*, this is probably due to the last-minute change of conductor. The brilliant Herr Nikisch is confined to his sick bed, and it is very fortunate that Herr Mahler knows the work in such detail that he could readily take over the conducting. This performance does great credit to his talent. The orchestra played the preludes to the three acts quite beautifully, and many other marvellous details deserve special reference. The staging did the greatest credit to our theatre, and was a brilliant example of the perspicacity of the stage manager, who is also the theatre Director; our public owes him a hearty vote of thanks for the exemplary rehearsing of this work. . . .

Leipziger Tageblatt und Anzeiger, 11 February 1887.

What the Orchestra said about Mahler

'It's as if we'd been plain daft before Herr Mahler came along, as if it had needed him to come from Prague to show us what *piano* means, as if we could never get on without new flashy tricks all the time – if Nikisch doesn't get better soon, the whole orchestra's going to be off sick.'

Sikkus (Max Steinitzer), 'Porträtskizzen und Momentbilder: Gustav Mahler', *Rheinische Musik- und Theaterzeitung*, 31 July 1903. (The author, a Tyrolese, has attempted in the original German to reproduce the Saxon dialect.)

The Orchestra complains to the Leipzig Town Council

The undersigned members of the Committee of the Municipal Orchestra are regretfully obliged to ask, in the name of the members of the Orchestra, for your protection and support owing to the unworthy way in which it is treated by the Conductor, Herr Mahler.

No impartial observer will deny that the members of the Municipal Orchestra do their duty with faithful devotion, no matter who is conducting them. We rely upon the opinion of the critics and of our other Conductors (Nikisch, Reinecke and Rust).

The above-named gentlemen are content with what we are able to achieve, but it is an entirely different matter with Herr Mahler, who has hardly been satisfied with a single member of the Orchestra during rehearsals, and who not infrequently demands what is absolutely impossible. When this cannot be done, the member of the Orchestra involved is accused of malice and stubbornness.

If the artistic standards of the Orchestra are not to be impaired, the self-respect of individual members must not be trifled with in this way in the future.

Gunter Hempel, 'Gustav Mahler in Leipzig', *Musik und Gesellschaft*, vol. XVII, November 1967, 784–85. (The same orchestra had refused, nine years before, to play *Tannhäuser* under the youthful Nikisch, as Angelo Neumann tells us in his *Erinnerungen an Richard Wagner*, Leipzig 1907, 69.)

The Theatre Director, Staegemann, rejects the complaints of the Orchestra

In January the signatories complained about the 'incompetence' of Herr Mahler, but a few days later (after Herr Mahler had taken over *Valkyrie*), Herr Barge said that he felt impelled to tell me that he had made a mistake. There was also some mention of Herr Mahler's hot temper, which I was obliged to reject categorically; Herr Mahler is very strongly opposed to the abuses which are current here, but as he is always objective, his zeal can be insulting only to those who are disposed to be insulted.

Letter from Staegemann to the Leipzig City Council, Gunter Hempel, 'Mahler in Leipzig', *Musik und Gesellschaft*, vol. XVII, November 1967, 785.

As a young man, Mahler was the incarnation of Man as Expression, among so many for whom only Man as Form exists. He had the best intentions of being polite, but whenever anybody made some shallow or commonplace remark (which may have been exactly what the moment required), his glance became far too piercing. Before he could control himself and compose his features as conventional good manners demanded, his feelings had already shown in his face. Being warmly appreciative of every kind of serious endeavour, he was a close friend of Karl Perron's, an interested patron of Paul Knüpfer's and an admirer of the intuitive talents of such a woman as Josephine von Artner. But pretensions, imperfections, and dilettante dabbling with the arts were so abhorrent to him that his feelings were immediately evident, however good his manners remained.

A musician of considerable eminence meant it politely when he asked him, at an evening party, for his opinion on a question of interpretation about which he, the speaker, did not agree with Richard Wagner. Before Mahler could produce the necessary polite smile, he had let slip what he really thought: 'When Wagner has spoken, other people hold their tongues.' At the same party, which was attended almost entirely by musicians, a young man sat down at the piano and played a composition entitled 'In the Quiet Valley', written in a drawing-room style so unthinkable in such company that everybody was struck dumb with embarrassment. In order to end the painful silence, Mahler went up to the offender and said with an irresistible smile, 'Absolutely true to life. I recognize that valley, at least I think so. Styria. Thank you very much.' Then he shook hands with the young man who blushed with pleasure. . . .

On such occasions Mahler could be so like Hoffmann's description of 'Kapellmeister Kreisler' in *Kater Murr* that it was quite uncanny. . . .

Sikkus (Max Steinitzer), 'Porträtskizzen und Momentbilder: Gustav Mahler', *Rheinische Musik- und Theaterzeitung,* 31 July 1903. (The author of this portrait, Max Steinitzer, was an intimate friend of Mahler's during his Leipzig days.)

Mahler completes Weber's opera fragment 'Die drei Pintos'

After the death of Max Maria von Weber in 1881, the precious heritage passed to his son, Captain Carl von Weber, together with a collection of expert opinions to the effect that it was impossible to complete the work, and a persistent desire to do it nevertheless. At Captain von Weber's request, several of the leading musicians of our time made attempts, but all were unsuccessful. It was not until Captain von Weber had been writing plays for some years that he thought he could venture to make another attempt, starting out from an entirely different standpoint. Meyerbeer had recognized the weaknesses of the existing libretto, and had planned an entirely new one; Captain von Weber envisaged retaining the original text and the words of the songs for which the music had already been sketched; he also proposed to develop the ending, as economically as possible, from the existing, completed exposition. He adopted Meyerbeer's idea of using music from other works by Weber; among his unprinted compositions there was a plentiful supply of music full of humour and gaiety, which fitted quite naturally into the style of such *Pinto* music as existed. This disposed of many of the difficulties that stood in the way of completing *Die drei Pintos*, but one of the chief ones, the state of Weber's sketches, remained unsolved. This is not the place to describe what they were like in any great detail; suffice it to say that all the distinguished musicians who had held the intricate scrawls in their hands had quailed at the undertaking. . . . It was pure coincidence, and a very happy one, that brought such a capable man to this difficult task. In the early summer of 1887, Captain von Weber handed the *Pinto* sketches to Herr Gustav Mahler, then Conductor here, and after he had spent the quiet, peaceful hours of his summer

Programme of the German Theatre, Prague, 18 August 1888. Narodní Muzeum, Prague.
The Prague playbill mentions Mahler's entr'acte under the title 'Pinto's Dream: Symphonic Interlude'.

holiday listening to the ghost that still lived in Weber's gentle manuscript, he expressed himself willing to attempt to give them a final shape worthy of their creator. The two editors worked together in perfect harmony, and in six months gave final form to the fragmentary opera *Die drei Pintos*.

Leipziger Tageblatt und Anzeiger, 19 January 1888.

Meyerbeer on Weber's sketches for 'Die drei Pintos'

. . . Studied the *Pinto* sketches in order to become really familiar with them again before I work at them. . . . These sketches have to be not only orchestrated but figured and harmonized as well. To a large extent Weber has composed only the vocal parts, very seldom written the bass, even more seldom indicated an instrumental figuration. A terrifying task; so little to go on, and yet such work as exists, the singing parts, must be treated in the most conscientious way possible, and I would not leave a note out or change one for any money.

Giacomo Meyerbeer, diary entry for 30 April 1846, quoted from Hans Becker, 'Meyerbeers Ergänzungsarbeit an Webers nachgelassener Oper *Die drei Pintos*', *Die Musikforschung*, vol. VII, 1954, 308–09. (Meyerbeer first planned to complete the opera from the existing sketches soon after Weber's death in 1826, and finally abandoned the idea many years later.)

Everything went really well for me; in Leipzig a fortnight ago I scored a really great success with my symphony, which only had the edge taken off it by the venom of a few scribblers. But that doesn't matter! The public and the orchestra were very agreeable, especially the orchestra, which I was very pleased with; it mastered the symphony quite excellently after two short rehearsals and showed itself to be a very intelligent body; the woodwind was not quite to my liking, but the string quartet was outstanding. The new concert hall really delighted me. I made a new, very charming friend in Herr Mahler, who struck me as being an exceptionally intelligent musician and conductor, one of the few modern conductors who know anything about modifying tempo, and he displayed admirable views, especially about Wagner's tempi, as opposed to those of the accredited Wagner conductors of today.

Mahler's adaptation of Weber's *Drei Pintos* strikes me as being a masterpiece; I am quite enchanted with the first act which Mahler played to me; it is quite a different kettle of fish from *Silvana*: genuine and delightful Weber, and a work of genius! I think you will be pleased with it too! It has all Weber's technical mastery; there is no trace of the amateurishness that shows up here and there in the other operas.

Letter of 29 October 1887, 'Hans von Bülow/Richard Strauss, Briefwechsel', in *Richard Strauss Jahrbuch 1954*, Bonn 1953, 53.

Mahler to his parents, on the forthcoming première

Today I shall just briefly wish you a happy New Year, and good health in particular; for I have a certain hope of being now able to provide for the rest myself. The director of German opera in New York, Mr Stanton, has just sent me word; he is coming over for the performance and wishes to acquire the opera for America. Well, he can bring a fair-sized bag of dollars with him, then.

On Christmas Eve I was first at the Webers' and then went with them to the Staegemanns'. I have received so many presents from all quarters that I simply cannot enumerate everything to you. . . .

At the theatre *Pintos* is being studied diligently. Everyone has gone at it with a will, which they have not done here before. Now I have written one more new entr'acte which is one of the best that can be found in opera. Beforehand, though, no one will be allowed to know what is by me and what is by Weber, or else the critics would have an easy time of it. The money I have not yet received, but should you suddenly need any I can now lend 1,000 marks with ease and will send it to you forthwith. So let me know.

Undated letter, written at the end of 1887, HHZ, 131.

Distinguished guests at the première of 'Die drei Pintos'

The first performance, which takes place on Friday of next week, of the posthumous comic opera by Carl Maria von Weber, *Die drei Pintos*, should give rise to an élite theatrical evening. A large number of distinguished visitors will be present at the première of *Die drei Pintos*. Those expected are: His Excellency Count Platen, General Manager of the Dresden Court Theatre; Count Hochberg, General Manager of the Berlin Court Theatres; General Managers von Perfall (Munich), von Bronsart (Weimar), von Puttlitz (Karlsruhe); Directors von Gilsa (Kassel) and von Ledebur (Schwerin); Royal Conductors Schuch (Dresden) and Levi (Munich); Prof. Wüllner (Cologne); Directors Pollini (Hamburg) and Hofmann (Cologne); the writers on music Messrs Hanslick and Speidel from Vienna, G. Davidsohn and Prof. Ehrlich from Berlin, Ludwig Hartmann from Dresden, Ernst Pasqué from Darmstadt. The *Norddeutsche Allgemeine Zeitung, Vossische Zeitung, National-Zeitung, Kölnische Zeitung, Frankfurter Zeitung, Bohemia* of Prague, the big Hamburg and other newspapers are sending their permanent opera reviewers to Leipzig. Even from America there is a visitor in the shape of a deputy of Major Stanton, Director of the Metropolitan Grand Opera House in New York, specially sent over for the première.

Leipziger Tageblatt und Anzeiger, 15 January 1888.

Mahler to his teacher at Iglau, Heinrich Fischer

Thank you for thinking of me! It has been a wonderful time, the last half year!

At present I am finding it magnificent fun, how the critics have fallen in with me and are giving the praise to *my* pieces. For 'business reasons' I must keep quiet about it all for the time being; when all is revealed the critics may well tear their hair somewhat at their own hastiness and lack of thought – the world may be astonished – and my friends have a little pleasure in me.

Undated letter, postmark 23 January 1888, ms., OAJ-F.

Mahler to his parents, on the success of 'Die drei Pintos'

. . . Today the house is sold out again. Do not be surprised if my achievement is belittled in the newspapers. For 'business reasons' it must be kept secret for the time being what is by me and what is by Weber. This much I can now tell you: two popular numbers which are now mentioned in newspapers everywhere (students' chorus and the Ballad of Tomcat Mansor), are by me, as are many more. All this must unfortunately be kept secret until the opera has been produced everywhere. For the time being, the less honour, the more money! That will come later when all is revealed.

74

ENTRE-AKT.

Entr'acte from *Die drei Pintos*. Piano score. Leipzig 1888.
This was the first original composition by Mahler to appear in print.

At all events I am from today a 'famous' man. Conductor Levi from Bayreuth was also here and frightfully enthusiastic about me. He told me, too, that Cosima Wagner had written him a four-page letter about me. . . .

The 10,000 marks from the publisher have already been deposited for me in the Reichsbank. Just think, Weber and his wife did not want to put the money into my hands at all, but took it to the bank themselves and gave me only the deposit receipt for fear that I might squander the money. Now come the royalties, the value of which one cannot yet calculate absolutely, because it just depends on how many theatres perform the opera, and how many times. At present, then, I have at my disposal the above-mentioned sum, or rather do not have it at my disposal but have the deposit receipt for it. Now I am going to conduct *Pintos* again. When it is produced in Vienna you must come and hear it.

Undated letter, written at the end of January 1888, HHZ, 131–32. (The publisher of *Die drei Pintos* was C. F. Kahnt Nachfolger, Leipzig.)

Bülow is annoyed at Richard Strauss's enthusiasm

Indeed – I must confess this to you with absolute candour – I had a *grudge* against you for several weeks. Really! I could only assume on the one hand that you were pulling my leg, or on the other that, even worse, you had suffered an acute lapse of judgment – where *Die drei Pintos* is concerned. On your recommendation I ordered the vocal score (which, incidentally, is a monster of orthographical and 'syntactical' impurity) and with the best will in the world I found it impossible to dredge up anything praiseworthy. What is Weber's, what is Mahler's – it makes no difference – the whole thing is through and through a piece of infamous, outdated trash.

Letter of 27 March 1888, 'Hans von Bülow/Richard Strauss, Briefwechsel', in *Richard Strauss Jahrbuch 1954*, Bonn 1953, 59.

From Max Steinitzer's reminiscences of Mahler in Leipzig

Sometimes when I went with him as far as the garden gate of that house (Gustav-Adolf-Strasse 12), he would afterwards say with a half-expectant, half-worried look, 'Sdeinidhä' – a Czech had once pronounced his name thus, to his great amusement, and Mahler repeated it time without number – 'Perhaps today the *devil* will come!' This was the name he gave to the mood from which the first motif of the Finale of the First Symphony and the first movement of the Second originated, and which gave to his features at that time their almost constant expression.

ANBR, 297.

Mahler on the funeral march and Finale of the First Symphony

77, 78 For the third movement (*marcia funebre*) the fact is that the external stimulus for it came to me from a famous children's picture, 'The Huntsman's Burial'. Yet at this point it is irrelevant what is portrayed – it is just a question of the *mood* which is to be expressed, and from which the fourth movement then suddenly springs, like lightning from a dark cloud. It is the cry of a heart wounded to its very depths, from which the uncannily and ironically brooding sultriness of the funeral march takes its origin. Ironically in the sense of Aristotle's *eironeia*. . . .

From a letter to Max Marschalk, 20 March 1896, GMB, 185–86. (The funeral march was originally the fourth movement of the symphony. Mahler wrote these lines when he had already deleted the Andante.)

Work on the First Symphony

Mahler composed the whole symphony in Leipzig in the space of six weeks in addition to conducting and rehearsing constantly; he worked in the morning from the time he got up

until 10 o'clock and in the evenings whenever he was free. Meanwhile – in a magnificent March and April – he constantly went walking in the Rosental. The public holidays on the death of Kaiser Wilhelm were like a gift to him: ten days which he used most thoroughly.

'But what was more to me than anything else', Mahler once said to me, speaking of that time, 'the world then had a refuge for me. It was my relationship with the Weber family. I had come into contact with him, the composer's grandson, through the *Pintos* for which he completed the text for me, and the musical, radiant presence of his wife, her mind constantly turned to the highest things, gave new substance to my life. Their charming children, too, were very deeply and warmly attached to me, as I to them, so that we were happily devoted to one another.

'When I had completed the first movement – it was towards midnight – I ran to the Webers' and played it to them both, whereupon they, to fill in the first A harmonic on the violins, had to help me out in treble and bass on the piano. All three of us were so enthusiastic and happy that I had no finer hour with my First Symphony. Then we went strolling happily together in the Rosental for a long while.'

NBL, 150 (Kaiser Wilhelm I died on 9 March 1888.)

Mahler to his parents after completing the work

Well, today my work was completed and I can say, thank the Lord, that it has turned out well. I hope to take another large step forward with it. Tomorrow the Staegemann and Weber families will be here for coffee (I have a wonderful apartment), and then I will play the Symphony for them a second time. The first time it created a downright sensation with them, and they wanted to hear it again immediately.

With the performance, of course, I shall have no difficulty as I am already a 'famous' man. You ask, dear Mother, how many there are in the Weber family? It consists of husband and wife, two daughters and one son. One daughter is nine and the other six; the son is seven. They are all enormously fond of me and often visit me and bring me flowers. The wife sends me all kinds of things. Chickens, cakes, apples, figs, linen, tea, coffee, etc., in which she anticipates my needs. I often lunch there, too, and have dinner, and the same at the Staegemanns'. Sunday is the first performance of the *Pintos* in Hamburg, the Wednesday after is the same in Munich, and during May the opera will go to Dresden and Kassel! The other theatres, including Vienna, are not producing the opera until next winter. . . .

Undated letter from Mahler, written at the end of March 1888, HH2, 132.

Ethel Smyth on Mahler's feelings for Marion von Weber

All this time [1888] I had been seeing a great deal of the von Webers, people I had met off and on in Leipzig society for many years, but who though cultivated and musical, were not in the sacred Herzogenberg set. Weber, a captain in the Leipzig regiment, was either grandson or nephew of the composer, and his wife a Jewess, niece of old Madame Schwabe's. . . . The poor Webers' subsequent history was tragic. Gustav Mahler, who was then one of the conductors at the Leipzig Opera, fell in love with her and his passion was reciprocated – as well it might be, for in spite of his ugliness he had demoniacal charm. A scandal would mean leaving the Army, and Weber shut his eyes as long as was possible, but Mahler, a tyrannical lover, never hesitated to compromise his mistresses. Things were getting critical, when one day, traveling to Dresden in the company of strangers, Weber suddenly burst out laughing, drew a revolver, and began taking William Tell-like shots at the head-rests between the seats. He was overpowered, the train brought to a standstill, and they took him to the police station raving mad – thence to the asylum. Always considered rather queer in the Army, the Mahler business had broken down his brain. . . .

Mahler's life was full of incidents of this sort, and knowing him even as slightly as I did I can well believe it, not being able to conceive that any woman who loved and was beloved by him could resist him. I felt this even when I saw him last (it was at Vienna in 1907) . . . and it is one of the small tragedies of my life that just when he was considering the question of producing *The Wreckers* at Vienna they drove him from office. . . . At the time I am speaking of in Leipzig I saw but little of him, and we didn't get on; I was too young and raw then to appreciate this grim personality, intercourse with whom was like handling a bomb cased in razor-edges.

Ethel Smyth, *Impressions That Remained*, London 1919, II, 164–66. (Ethel Mary Smyth, 1858–1944, came from London in 1877 to the Leipzig Conservatoire, and became a student of Heinrich von Herzogenberg. Her opera *The Wreckers* was performed in Leipzig in 1906, under the German title of *Strandrecht*.)

Friedrich Löhr on Mahler's last months in Leipzig

It was a time of emotional turmoil, unsurpassed in the whole of his life; and he always kept its most intense moments to himself in solemn secrecy.

GMB, notes, 480.

The yearbook of the Leipzig Municipal Theatres (*Almanach der vereinigten Stadt-Theater in Leipzig*, Leipzig 1888) gives a clear picture of the theatrical hierarchy which was operative at that time. At the top stands the Theatre Committee of the City Council with the Mayor at its head; then follows the management, in this case Max Staegemann as Director and lessee of the United Municipal Theatres, immediately below him the senior production staff (*Oberregie*). Under this title one finds the chief dramatic Stage Manager, Herr Gettke, and the chief operatic Stage Manager, Herr A. Goldberg. Only after this come the other Stage Managers, the Conductors (*Kapellmeister*) and Assistant Conductors. Goldberg, as Chief Stage Manager for opera, was thus senior to Mahler. A fierce conflict with him was the immediate cause of Mahler's request to be removed from his position.

Mahler presses Staegemann for release from his contract

Leipzig, 16 May 1888

In the well-known standing difference between myself and Herr Goldberg, I must again return to the request I made to you for my discharge.

Firstly I consider it totally irreconcilable with the authority due to me as Conductor and necessary for my office, that I should be made to lose face in front of the staff, as Herr Goldberg's conduct did to me, without vindication. I therefore believe that after that occurrence I can no longer carry out my duties with the authority which is as necessary in my own interest as it is in yours and in that of the cultural institution to which I belong. . . .

GMB, 72–3.

Mahler's departure from Leipzig

The extremely talented musician, the Conductor Gustav Mahler, whose musical revival of *Die drei Pintos* by C. M. von Weber deserves and has found the highest recognition, has been discharged from his association with the Leipzig Municipal Theatre *at his own request*.

Leipziger Tageblatt und Anzeiger, 24 May 1888.

Mahler to Max Steinitzer (*from Iglau, summer 1888*)

How kind it is of you to be so good to me! Please keep giving me news about Leipzig – and *everything*! About the symphony I don't know what to do! I don't want it to be first performed at a beer concert. . . . At present I am quite incapable of telling you about myself. Only to the extent that there is no prospect of finding another appointment quickly, and I honestly confess to you that this causes me great concern. For now I need a demanding occupation to avoid going under.

ANBR, 297.

While Mahler was worrying because he had no prospect of an appointment, his friend Guido Adler, professor of the history of music in Prague, had taken a decisive step on his behalf. He had drawn Mahler to the attention of the Prague cellist David Popper (1843–1913), who since 1886 had been employed as professor at the Royal Academy of Music in Budapest. From Popper's letters to Guido Adler, it is clear that the initiative came from Adler. On his recommendation Popper, who did not know Mahler, approached Ödön von Mihalovich (1842–1929), who had been Director of the Royal Academy of Music in Budapest since 1887. Mihalovich, a pupil of Hans von Bülow, was an admirer of Franz Liszt and Richard Wagner.

From David Popper's letters to Guido Adler

Königswart, 4 July 1888

In immediate reply to your letter I can tell you that I shall forward its main content, on the subject of Herr G. Mahler, to the place where the decision on the final occupation of the long-vacant position in Pest, itself an ancient mare's nest, will finally be taken. Let us hope for success; I wish it as you do. Fourteen days ago I left the matter at the stage where serious discussions were apparently flourishing with a very famous foreign conductor. Things may have changed overnight since then, as has already occurred so often in this case. . . .

Königswart, 11 July 1888

Herewith the reply of the Director, Herr von Mihalovich, to my letter on the Mahler affair. Of course the matter will not rest there, and, as stated expressly in the letter, Herr Mahler will be the subject of the most thorough enquiries in the near future provided Mottl's appointment is not confirmed meanwhile.

I was very eloquent on Mahler's behalf, but as you can see from the enclosed letter the appointment of an opera and concert conductor, whose genius is taken for granted, is a secondary consideration; the prime concern of these gentlemen is the organizational talent and activity of the future Opera Director, to whose lot will fall the cleaning out of an artistic Augean stable.

Now the thing to do is wait patiently! The decision cannot be long delayed: when the leaves fall in autumn, then the scales will fall from the eyes of the new Opera Director in Pest, who is in no way to be envied. The position is extremely well-paid (10,000 florins), and that at any rate is some consolation!

Königswart, 17 July 1888

. . . I was extraordinarily touched by your complete support of Mahler 'the man'. This important passage in your letter will be of grave moment for the full appreciation of the prospective Director in Budapest, and, as you yourself gave me permission to do, I am also sending the entire contents of your last letter to Herr von Mihalovich.

Mss., Guido Adler papers, University of Georgia Libraries, Athens, Ga.

'Die drei Pintos' at the German Theatre in Prague

Yet not only the composer, but also the conductor Mahler came through a magnificent dress-rehearsal yesterday when he roused the Prague orchestra to an achievement which stands at a rare artistic peak. It was as if the spirit of Weber, who used to conduct the Prague orchestra seventy years ago, had possessed the musicians, so nobly, so delicately did they play, so graciously did they form the delightful melodies.

Prager Tagblatt, 18 August 1888. (Mahler conducted the première of his composition, which took place on the Emperor's birthday on 18 August, and four more performances in the same month.)

During his stay in Prague in August and September 1888, Mahler was working on the first movement of his Second Symphony, which he had begun immediately after the completion of the First Symphony (D major). The first draft of the score of the first movement bears the date 'Prague, 10 September 1888'. The heading 'Symphony in C minor' is crossed out and replaced by the title *Totenfeier* ('Obsequies').

Mahler on the 'Totenfeier'

80, 81   I have called the first movement *Totenfeier*, and if you wish to know, it is the hero of my Symphony in D major whom I am bearing to his grave and whose life I, from a higher vantage point, am reflecting in a pure mirror. At the same time it is the great question: *Why have you lived?* Why have you suffered? Is it all just a huge, frightful joke?

From a letter to Max Marschalk, 26 March 1896, GMB, 188–89. (The archaic spelling *Todtenfeier*, used in the caption, was Mahler's own.)

Maurus Jókai on the rise of the city of Budapest

Even in the year 1848 a great Hungarian statesman said, 'Budapest is not Hungary in the way that Paris is France.' Yet, since then, things have progressed to such an extent that today everyone says, 'Budapest is the heart of Hungary'. . . .

Thirty years ago the city of Pest was still shrouded in the dust-clouds of a sandy desert, the Rákos; today this sand has been stabilized by streets and trees. And in the Buda mountains, where previously there was hardly any life, the rack-railway runs past rows of magnificent country houses, and an excellent water system sprays streams of water over fresh gardens. Thirty years ago all that seemed just a dream. The
88   stranger seeing Budapest for the first time is astounded at the beautiful situation of this twin city. There on a proud height rises the royal palace of Buda, the Blocksberg looks out over the limitless plain of the Alföld, between two rows of palaces the mighty Danube surges beneath three solid bridges, the middle one of which is the suspension bridge, a masterpiece of bridge-building, and in the midst of the river sleeps the romantic Margaret Island while a swarm of steamboats bustle about. Smoking chimneys announce far and wide that the capital has a well-developed manufacturing industry, and the teeming throngs of workers on the river embankments indicate a booming trade. The view of Budapest in the evening from the suspension bridge is especially magical, when the twin rows of lamps along both banks mingle in the distance with the lights of the other bridges and call forth in the dark mirror of the Danube the redoubled illusion of a seaside bay. The most picturesque panorama, though, is to be seen from the eastern slopes of the Schwabenberg: at the foot of the mountain, divided by the blue Danube, lies the twin city with its

high-domed cathedral, its belt of green woods, and the varied outline of the Buda mountains.

In thirty years Budapest has become a rich city and a Hungarian city. Both assertions may be powerfully reinforced by quoting some figures. The Hungarian capital has spent during this time nearly 30 million florins on the chief source of national culture, its schools. And while the city has been developing its national character it has also striven to keep in step with European culture.

ÖUM, *Ungarn*, Vienna 1893, III, 3–5. (Maurus [Móric] Jókai, 1825–1904, was a fellow revolutionary of Petőfi's in 1848, and later became a parliamentarian and author. One of his short stories was the source of *The Gipsy Baron* by Johann Strauss, 1885.)

In the year 1884 the Royal Hungarian Court Opera had moved into the magnificent new building in Andrássy Street; the expected cultural revival, however, had not occurred. The position of Artistic Director and Chief Conductor was held by Sándor (Alexander) Erkel (1846–1900), a son of the composer Ferenc (Franz) Erkel (1810–93), who through his operatic works ranks as founder of the Hungarian national opera. General dissatisfaction with Sándor Erkel's conduct in office brought with it a management crisis which lasted for years. At the beginning of 1888 the General Manager of the Court Theatres was dismissed.
83   Secretary of State Ferenc (Franz) von Beniczky, a cultivated man but a politician inexperienced in the problems of the theatre, received the task as 'Government Commissioner' of finding a remedy. Initially he tried to obtain Felix Mottl as Artistic Director of the Opera House, before he engaged Mahler.

Ludwig Karpath on his first meeting with the new Director

It was on the afternoon of 30 September 1888. On a Sunday. I had come back from a fairly long walk – and went past the
82   Royal Hungarian Opera House. Like all aspiring performers I was always hanging around the building, and so as usual I stopped at the stage-doorkeeper's office to request some piece of information from him. Then I saw a clean-shaven little man who, without taking any notice of anyone, came through the office with rapid step and dashed up the stairs to the Director's office. 'That's the new Director!' observed the lanky porter.

'What? There's a new Director, and nobody knows about it? Surely the opera has a long-standing Director, Alexander Erkel, isn't he in office any more?'

'More than that I don't know,' replied the porter. 'I was just told that I should let this gentleman into the building – he came here this morning too – because he's the new Director.'

'What is his name?' I enquired further.

'Gustav Mahler,' replied the porter.

It was the first time in my life I had heard the name, and I was rather unwilling to credit the appointment as Director of the Royal Opera House of this man who looked so young. Nevertheless I hurried to the editorial offices of a newspaper where I had friends, and reported what had happened.

The news of this appointment came as a bombshell throughout the city, all the more so as Mahler's name was completely unknown. The appointment had been prepared with the greatest of care, and so secretively that literally no one had any idea of it. Let it not be forgotten that Mahler was at that time still a Jew – he was baptized only later, in Hamburg – and this fact alone was such as to cause a sensation. Just as great a commotion was raised over the salary, by the standards of the time exorbitantly high, of ten thousand florins per annum for a period of ten years. The Royal Opera House was deeply in debt for various reasons; Alexander Erkel was ill and had his own problems; the budget had swollen; something decisive had to happen. Into the shoes of the General Manager, who had reduced the institution to financial ruin, had stepped a Government Commissioner with, of course, all the powers of a General Manager, an uncommonly clever, conciliatory and distinguished official . . . Franz von Beniczky.

LKB, 11–12. (Ludwig Karpath, 1886–1936, born in Budapest, was later a music critic in Vienna.)

Hungarian newspaper comment on the appointment of a non-Hungarian

The question of the directorship of the Royal Hungarian Opera has still not been solved. The Government Commission has renewed the contract with Sándor Erkel, which links this excellent conductor to our opera house for a further three years; yet the Directorship will be carried on by Erkel only until another suitable person is found for this position. After unsuccessful negotiations with Arthur Nikisch and Felix Mottl, discussions have lately been in progress with the former Leipzig Conductor Mahler, concerning the position of Director. Mahler has been staying in Budapest for several days already and has been in frequent touch with the Government Commissioner, but from what we hear no agreement has yet been reached between them. At the same time the Government Commission is working on the final appointment of a Chief Stage Manager. Recently – according to a rumour – an outstanding member of our opera has been considered in this connection, one who has already given proof of his talent as a stage manager on several occasions. . . . We regard it as essential in any case that the Chief Stage Manager be a Hungarian – even if the Director is to be a foreigner.

Pesti Hirlap, 1 October 1888.

Policy statement by the new Director of the Opera

I will work body and soul, with zeal and enthusiasm. For three months I have been studying the situation in Budapest, and I have discovered a whole flood of startling facts. The most startling, though, is that Hungary, richer than any other European nation in magnificent singing voices, has not made any serious effort to create a national opera company. Art needs pure methods above all else in order to produce an artistic effect; experiments exact a cruel price. It must not be forgotten, even for a moment, that the text of an opera is an artistic factor equal in value to the music. I cannot get over the fact that in Hungary no serious concern has been shown about the language in which the text is sung. Quite apart from the national aspect, I know of nothing more inappropriate in an opera, from the point of view of artistic effect, than singing it in two languages. This has a damaging effect on the music itself.

In a bilingual performance, in which the musical dialogue is carried on in Italian by the lady and by her admirer in Hungarian, I consider it impossible for the composer's intentions to be truly fulfilled. It would be more natural, that is, more acceptable artistically, if the opera were sung completely without the text; at least the beauties of the music are not ruined. Equally it seems to me to be artistically senseless for the singer to learn the Hungarian text mechanically, so that his foreign pronunciation is audible with every syllable; this sort of constraint makes the healthy development of an artistic institution impossible, and therefore I shall consider it my first and foremost duty to exert all my energy in making the opera into a truly Hungarian national institution.

Budapesti Hirlap, 7 October 1888. (The newspaper reporter emphasizes that he is reporting Mahler's statements verbatim, by which clearly is meant an exact translation of an interview carried out in German.)

In the early months of his appointment at Budapest Mahler made no appearances as conductor. He concentrated on rehearsing the first performances of Wagner's *Rhinegold* and *Valkyrie* in Hungarian. Both works were performed exclusively with Hungarian singers. To avoid bilingual performances Mahler put a stop to guest engagements, turning away even prominent artists if they were unable to cope with Hungarian.

A Hungarian Stage Manager and a Hungarian Chief of Production

The Chief of Production at the Opera House, Ede Ujházy, and the new operatic Stage Manager, Kálmán Alszeghy, were officially introduced to the personnel of the Opera House at twelve midday today by the Government Commissioner, Ferenc von Beniczky. The Commissioner expressed to the artists present his pleasure at the theatre's success in securing the services of Ujházy as Chief of Production. In his speech he emphasized at some length that by this appointment he wishes to attain the point where all performers at the Royal Hungarian Opera can not only sing but also portray dramatic character and are capable of pronouncing and accenting the Hungarian language correctly; further, that the choruses and movements *en masse* on the stage should come to life and the performances thereby be more finished in every respect; he asks the members of staff to do their best to support the three pillars of the Royal Hungarian Opera House – the Director, the Stage Manager and the Chief of Production – in their important task. (Cheers.) . . .

Nemzet, 15 November 1888, morning edn. (Ede Ujházy, 1844–1915, an outstanding character actor, had been a member of the National Theatre since 1870. Kálmán Alszeghy, 1852–1927, began his career as production assistant at the National Theatre.)

Count Albert Apponyi on Mahler as an operatic producer

Mahler is not merely an orchestral musician – as are other famous conductors I could easily name – but in the works which he conducts he governs with sovereign authority the stage, the action, the movements of the soloists and the chorus; so that a performance rehearsed and produced by him is in every way artistically complete. His eye extends over the entire production, the scenery, the machinery, the lights. I have never met such a harmoniously rounded artistic character.

Ms., HHSTA. (This is one of the few pieces of evidence that Mahler also worked as a producer at the Opera in Budapest. The extract quoted is to be found in the letter of recommendation which Count Apponyi sent to the board of the Vienna Court Theatres on 10 January 1897, when Mahler's appointment in Vienna came under discussion. Apponyi, 1846–1933, was one of the most brilliant orators of the Hungarian Parliament and was the Hungarian Minister of Culture, Education and Religious Affairs, 1906–10.)

Orchestral rehearsal for 'The Valkyrie' in enlarged orchestra pit

Yesterday, in the orchestra pit made deeper for this purpose, the first orchestral rehearsal of Wagner's *Valkyrie* took place, personally conducted by the Director, Herr Mahler.

Pester Lloyd, 19 December 1888.

Mahler to Staegemann in Leipzig

I shall probably spend Christmas Eve this year completely alone – as there is no performance – and I still have absolutely no private social life. Now I am firmly into the *Ring* rehearsals, but I have a definite lack of tenors and the most absurd difficulties at every turn and every step. But I shall stand firm!

Please give your family my warmest regards. I assume, too, that this greeting will also reach friend Perron, and wish you all a peaceful and happy time.

GMB, 75.

Mahler to his parents

Both public dress rehearsals were a *glorious* success – all Pest is aroused. Enclosed are extracts from the many countless articles and letters I have already received. The [Government Commissioner] is very happy. Soon I shall write and tell you more.

It was another enormous success! How are you? Do write more often.

Undated letter, probably of 25 or 26 January 1889, ms., The Pierpont Morgan Library, New York, and The Mary Flagler Cary Charitable Trust.

85 *An anti-Wagnerian praises Mahler's 'Rhinegold'*

There is in the history of the world no artistic development whose course is surrounded by so many barefaced lies, so many deceitful tricks, so much hypocrisy, as Wagnerism. No one in the world has had such an understanding of the technical aspect of composition as Wagner, and none of the leading personalities of music has been so miserably poor, so desperately unproductive, in respect of the basic pre-requisites of composition, which are feeling and imagination, as he.

Today's success is the splendid result of the tireless application, the conscientious labour, and the great enthusiasm, which Herr Mahler has devoted to the preparation of the performance.

Nemzet, 27 January, morning edn. (The author of this review was probably József Keszler, 1846–1927, a prominent critic, educated in Paris.)

The Government Commissioner thanks the Director of the Opera for the Wagner premières

86 With the production of *Rhinegold* and *Valkyrie* you, Sir, have brilliantly achieved two points of your artistic programme, for on the one hand you have shown what one is capable of achieving through sheer hard work, while on the other hand you have also proved that with our national resources, so often and so unjustifiably disparaged, even the most difficult artistic tasks may be carried out; you have shown that it is possible to produce the greatest artistic creations of the present day, without the addition of people from outside, and in the Hungarian language. This circumstance will certainly fill every patriot with real joy and contentment.

Open letter from Ferenc von Beniczky to Mahler, *Pester Lloyd,* 29 January 1889. (The premières of *Rhinegold* and *Valkyrie* had taken place on 26 and 27 January.)

Mahler's father died at Iglau on 18 February 1889. This notice, with the thanks of the bereaved for messages of sympathy, appeared in the *Mährischer Grenzbote* on 24 February.

184

Friedrich Löhr on his visit to Mahler in Budapest

On 17 April 1889 I travelled to Pest and spent Easter from Maundy Thursday to the evening of Easter Monday at Mahler's. We spent a lot of time in the open air again, in the city, in the area round Buda, on the Margaret Island; and at home he would once more sit down at the piano, and play me parts of the Second Symphony which was taking shape within him. At the opera there was at the time under his direction only *The Barber of Seville* and *Das Glöckchen des Eremiten.* Among the people of whom he saw a great deal, I have pleasant memories of Herr von Mihalovich, that outstanding and serious musician Professor Kössler, of the Pest Conservatoire, whom I met again later at Mahler's in Salzburg and Berchtesgaden, the singer Bianchi, the actor Ujházy, and Dr Ebner and his family. How absolutely resolutely Mahler prepared the ground for his plans in a foreign country may be attested by the fact that on Easter Saturday he gave a most sumptuous dinner for a small circle of performers and others which was totally suited to Magyar taste, passed off with great animation, was enthusiastically praised, and yet also bore fruit for his serious plans.

GMB, notes, 479–80. (The German composer Hans Kössler, 1853–1926, taught composition at the Budapest Academy of Music; among his pupils were Ernst von Dohnányi, Béla Bartók and Zoltán Kodály. Bianca Bianchi, 1855–1947, a German coloratura soprano, married the Hamburg Theatre Director, Bernhard Pollini, in 1897.)

Wilhelm Kienzl hears Mahler confess his longing for German singing

So I came, too, to beautiful Budapest, where I made the acquaintance of Gustav Mahler, at that time Director of the Royal Opera, who invited me to a rehearsal of *Figaro* conducted by him in his own peculiar way. When we then dined together he expressed most eloquently his unutterable longing for German singing, a longing which – as he said – was growing stronger day by day, regardless of the magnificent and completely independent position he had in Budapest.

Wilhelm Kienzl, *Meine Lebenswanderung,* Stuttgart 1926, 135. (Wilhelm Kienzl, 1857–1941, was an Austrian composer. Mahler's new production of *The Marriage of Figaro* had its first performance on 27 April 1889.)

Mahler to Friedrich Löhr's wife

I am in the midst of work – *Lohengrin* on Sunday! Very bad news from home – the end is expected hourly. Under no circumstances can I leave here before Monday....

No improvement has occurred in my condition – to make the rehearsals possible I am taking morphine.

GMB, 82–83. (This undated letter was written in the week before 15 September 1889. The bad news refers to Mahler's mother. In addition Mahler's eldest sister Leopoldine, married name Quittner, was seriously ill. She died on 27 September 1889.)

Friedrich Löhr on the illness and death of Mahler's mother

It was the time when, after long suffering, Mahler's mother died. His sister Justine could no longer cope with the exertion of nursing and all the worry, and showed signs of an impending collapse; the question arose as to whether she could be allowed to stay with her dying mother. Thereupon Mahler, who at that time was feverishly busy in Pest, hastened to Iglau, visited his mother, looked after her and took his sister for a few days to Vienna to recuperate; there he sought a doctor's opinion on her condition. His mind set at rest by the doctor's advice, he was able to let her go back to Iglau. For a short time his mother's condition improved; but she died on 11 October 1889. A woman richly endowed with the feminine virtues, the gentleness and tenderness of her presence, her kind heart and warm sensitivity must remain, for those who knew her well, unforgettable.

GMB, notes, 480–81.

Mahler to Friedrich Löhr

I have just received the post from Iglau. Please send me directly all the details you can – particularly on the way things are now organized. From what I hear Justi[ne] will go to you for a while; where can we put Emma? Any expenses, of course, need not be spared; I am now entirely concerned to make the interim period, until the time when I can accommodate both my sisters, bearable for them to some extent.

At the moment I cannot leave.

Undated letter, mid-October 1889, GMB, 83–84.

Friedrich Löhr on the housing of Mahler's brothers and sisters

92   After the death of Mahler's mother the household at Iglau was split up (his father had died on 18 February 1889). His brother and sister, Otto and Emma, the latter fourteen years old at the time, lived for a year in our household, in the same house as the one we were living in; his sister Justine soon went to live with Mahler in Pest, where he had taken an apartment at number 3 on the Theresienring.

GMB, notes, 481. (Mahler's brother Otto was then sixteen years old and was studying at the Vienna Conservatoire; Justine was twenty. In addition Mahler was supporting his twenty-two year old brother Alois.)

Worry over his sister Justine

Justine had nursed their mother until her death, and Mahler loved his sister as his beloved mother's legacy to him. He had her come to Budapest, and there Justine, without any experience, took over the housekeeping. He was so concerned about her that he carried her in his arms every day up the four storeys to his apartment, as she had been greatly weakened by nursing her mother.

AM, 18–19.

Bianca Bianchi sings three Lieder by Mahler

Chamber music evening. The Krancsevics quartet was appearing today with a programme which was sound in its instrumental part and interesting for the additional songs, three *Lieder* by Herr Gustav Mahler, performed by Fräulein

87   Bianchi, accompanied on the piano by the composer. . . . In his songs Herr Mahler reveals himself as a subtle, genuinely musical talent which is going its own way, aloof from well-known and well-loved musicians. His melodic line is unusual, the piano part rich in harmonic subtleties, its expression noble. He is less fortunate in grasping and retaining the mood which the poem exudes. Through Leander's poem *Es klopft an das Fenster der Lindenbaum* ['On the window the lime tree knocks'] runs a fresh, bright draught of air; it is a waggish joke at the expense of a late sleeper. . . . One expects a teasing, country melody with a lively beat, instead of the gentle, sweet, much too refined tones in which this simple text was musically presented. Similarly, the second Leander text, *Es wecket meine Liebe die Lieder immer wieder* ['My love for ever brings forth songs'], an ideal choice for a composer by virtue of its unified, dreamy mood, is not quite matched by the melancholy, if deeply felt, melody. The right tone is struck in the third song, *Scheiden und Meiden* ['Parting'], which is kept genuinely within the folk-song style; only at the end does the artistically handled singing voice disturb, as it flutters up almost *alla concertante* to the upper octave.

August Beer, *Pester Lloyd*, 14 November 1889.

Gustav Mahler also received his share of the acclaim; he accompanied the singer on the piano and showed himself to be just as great a performer as his songs reveal him to be an accomplished musician.

Kornél Ábrányi, *Pesti Hirlap*, 14 November 1889.

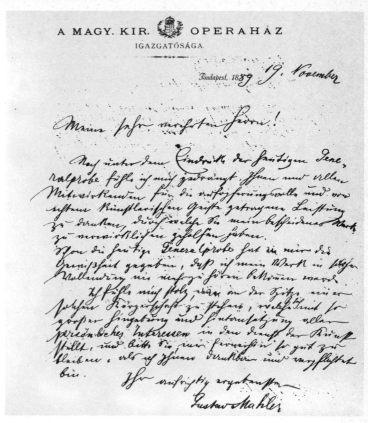

Mahler's letter of thanks and congratulations to the Budapest Philharmonic Orchestra, after the final rehearsal for the first performance of the First Symphony.

Friedrich Löhr on the performance of the First Symphony in Budapest

'. . . Now, just after hearing the symphony for the first time, and hearing it with very deep emotion, I am very glad to be hearing it again tomorrow . . .', I wrote to my wife. This time the occasion of my visit to Pest was the first performance of Mahler's First Symphony; it took place on 20 November 1889, 93 and I had in fact arrived there early on Tuesday 19 November, in order to attend the final rehearsal at midday. I presume that Otto came with me, but I have no real recollection of it. That our meeting was entirely overshadowed by this performance goes without saying. Indeed, Mahler himself had heard his work for the first time during rehearsal; perhaps this was the main thing for him, and a landmark in his progress. But the reception, too, that the work received had to be inwardly digested. The circle in Pest close to Mahler was deeply moved, but a substantial part of the public there was unfeeling and uncomprehending, as they were towards anything that was new in form; in particular, the dynamic forcefulness of the work's expression of tragic emotion came as an unpleasant shock, startling them out of their mindless routine. The *attacca* leading into the last movement so alarmed an elegant lady sitting next to me that she dropped everything she was holding on to the floor.

GMB, notes, 481–82.

Extracts from the reviews of the first performance of the First Symphony 95

It is only a short time since we came to know and value the young Director of our Opera House as a composer of songs. . . . The truth of the saying, *le style c'est l'homme*, was completely vindicated by the piece of music we heard today. This symphonic composition is the work of a young, unbridled and untameable talent, which must forcibly stem the flood of melodic motifs pressing forth from it, which knows no limits or boundaries, which breaks through the framework of all conventional forms and seeks to create something new. . . . The Director of the Opera can feel content with his success. Not only was he applauded on his appearance at the podium – as praise in advance and as recognition of his activity hitherto in the theatre – but a storm of applause broke out at the end of every movement of his work.

József Keszler, *Nemzet*, 21 November 1889, morning edn.

[The second part] begins with a kind of funeral march, yet we do not know whether we should take this 'funeral march' seriously or interpret it as a parody. We are inclined to assume rather the latter, as the main motif of the funeral march is a well-known German student song, *Bruder Martin, steh' schon auf*, which we ourselves have frequently sung, albeit not at funerals but while happily drinking. When the notes of the funeral march have died away a long pause follows. Then suddenly the cymbals clash, the clarinets and violins strike up shrilly, the drum thunders out, the trombones bellow; in a word, all the instruments run riot in a mad witches' dance. Then gradually some of the themes and motifs of the first part return, only to be drowned once again in a wild Bacchanal. . . .

The [second part] is an enormous aberration on the part of a mind of genius. Yet the first part deserves to be spared from the wreck. Were the composer to write a fitting finale to the first three movements of his work – his gift for this was proven particularly by the beautiful thematic composition and brilliant instrumentation – then he could produce a symphony which would tower far above the everyday mass-produced pieces.

Kórnel Ábrányi, *Pesti Hirlap*, 21 November 1889.

It is natural for a modern conductor, like Mahler, to be conversant with all orchestral effects, all too conversant; hardly a movement which does not appear before us decked out in all the panoply of brass, triangle, cymbal and big drum; and yet alongside all this there are delicate combinations such as only a fine ear can discover. If we gather all this into an overall impression, then we can only say that Mahler not only deservedly ranks, as far as his outstanding capabilities as conductor are concerned, among the first exponents of the art, but resembles them also by the fact that he is no symphonist. All our great conductors, Richter, Bülow, Mottl, Levi, Wüllner and others, have either themselves recognized in good time, or given public proof of, the fact that they are not composers, without damaging their position and their dignity in other respects. The same is true of Mahler; we shall recognize his efforts as Opera Director no less thankfully, and always be pleased to see him on the podium, so long as he is not conducting his own compositions.

Victor von Herzfeld, *Neues Pester Journal*, 21 November 1889. (Victor von Herzfeld, 1856–1920, previously Mahler's successful rival in the Beethoven composition competition, was employed as Professor of Theory at the Budapest Conservatoire; he was music critic of the *Neues Pester Journal* from 1888 to 1890, and was in addition a member of the Hubay Quartet, to which David Popper also belonged.)

Mahler's memory of the performance

. . . I remember with deep emotion the time when you were almost the only one who, after that unhappy performance of my First, did not 'tactfully' avoid me. . . .

From an undated letter from Mahler to Ödön von Mihalovich, ms., LFZ.

How much effort Mahler put into finding good singers for the Budapest opera house who were prepared to sing their parts in Hungarian is shown by his extensive correspon-

dence with Laura Hilgermann and her husband. Laura Hilgermann (1867–1937), a contralto who also sang soprano parts, joined the German Theatre in Prague at the same time as Mahler and had taken part in the performance of Beethoven's Ninth Symphony which Mahler conducted in 1886. Her husband, the actor Siegfried Rosenberg, was also at the German Theatre in Prague. When Laura Hilgermann came to Budapest, after prolonged persuasion from Mahler, she rapidly became a favourite of the public. In 1900, when Mahler was director of the Court Opera, she joined him in Vienna.

From a letter to Laura Hilgermann and her husband

As far as the roles themselves are concerned, *Mignon* is quite all right with me as the first one.

We do not yet have *Orpheus* in the repertoire, however, so I would request you to leave it out and, as we intended in the first place, to choose Amneris instead.

For the third Cherubino is quite all right with me, and I hope to put on this opera in January.

Given the nature of our relationship, and given the tendency to add on forthwith to a guest appearance a permanent appointment or (if this is not possible because of a contractual obligation) a further *lasting* relationship which would make your wife one of us straight away, we have plenty of time to discuss everything in more detail when you arrive in Budapest. Should your wife not yet be ready with Amneris then we can perhaps repeat *Mignon* once or twice and in the meanwhile she can catch up with the parts she has not done. I am sending you the part of Mignon as it is sung here. *Of course* with recitatives.

If your wife wants to make a cut or some other change, she is entirely free to do as she wishes.

Likewise I am also sending you Amneris once more – although I vaguely remember having seen both parts in your possession already.

Letter of 27 November 1889, ms., HAM.

On 29 November 1889 a review was published in the German-language *Pester Lloyd* of a repertory production of Meyerbeer's *Les Huguenots* in which 'for artistic reasons' – as a communiqué put it – the entire fifth act was deleted. The music critic of the *Pester Lloyd* sharply attacked this innovation, on dramatic grounds, and provoked thereby a detailed rejoinder by the Opera Director which was published the very next day.

Mahler on 'Les Huguenots' and operatic drama in general

In the course of this article the view is expressed 'that an opera is not an arbitrary succession or jumble of arias, duets, etc., but a *drama* set to music, which follows the same rules as any drama that is spoken'.

So it *should* be, in my opinion, too, but it will hardly come as news to anyone if I say that in most 'operas' this is unfortunately not the case. Quite the contrary: nearly all operas which belong to the era before Richard Wagner are in fact, with very few exceptions, only an 'arbitrary jumble' of pieces of music which are tied together by the loose, external thread of a plot; and of all operas it is well known that those of Meyerbeer, and *Les Huguenots* in particular, suffer most from this deficiency.

Les Huguenots, performed uncut, lasts six hours; and in Paris, where they once wanted to give an unabridged performance, they had to resort to the expedient of giving it on two successive evenings.

An opera house which does not wish to imitate this Parisian experiment has to be prepared to cut at least three hours of music from this work in order to make it capable of performance, and thus in the course of time a fixed set of cuts has evolved out of practical experience and is now accepted in every theatre in the world. In this now customary arrangement, nothing of the last act remains except the part known in theatrical jargon as the shooting scene; and as the world has a high opinion of muskets and cannon, people have become accustomed to seeing Raoul and Valentine well and truly shot dead on stage, as a necessary conclusion to the opera.

Now the question arises: is it possible to spare the audience this painful moment without thereby harming the sense of the whole?

Let us now examine the conclusion of the fourth act: the two lovers have just broken through all the restraints of life and custom which have hitherto separated them from one another, and have pledged themselves to one another with all the unfettered emotion which accompanies the sense of imminent death. Raoul tears himself away from the burning embraces of his beloved and hastens, amid the distant thunder of the cannon, the din of the tocsins and the fiery glow of Paris as it burns, to join his brethren who are now going to their death for that which they hold most holy. We know that no Huguenot will survive this night; we are therefore free of all doubt as to Raoul's fate.

Valentine lies on the ground in a deep swoon, from which we sense that she will not awaken.

Is it now nice or necessary that we, moved to the core by this scene, the most beautiful and the only dramatically true one in the work, should see the curtain rise again after a pause of ten minutes for one brief moment – and for what? In order to see a sanguinary muddle in which these two lovers fall before the brutal crash of the assorted ballistic instruments, wordless and defenceless like hunted hares. And scarcely has this happened before the curtain falls on this truly circus-like pantomime.

In one of the most immortal masterpieces, namely Mozart's *Don Giovanni*, for many decades now – and this has been endorsed by the most eminent music critics – *the original closing scene has been omitted and the opera concluded quite simply 'for artistic reasons' by the penultimate scene!* – Would anyone now dare to demand a return to the original ending as great Mozart wished it to be?

Pester Lloyd, 30 November 1889.

Sharp attack by a Hungarian musical journal

In the last year and a half not a single Hungarian opera has been performed in the Royal Hungarian Opera House. Is this a proper state of affairs? We think not. . . . Or can it be the only aim of the Hungarian Opera House to produce foreign operas in the Hungarian language? And even if it is true [that the operas of Ferenc Erkel no longer draw the public], it is impermissible that in the Royal Hungarian Opera House a season should pass without the production of one Hungarian opera.

Herr Mahler, do not think the Hungarian public is so naive as to be dazzled by a few words of greeting in Hungarian which you have learned by heart and trot out in front of the General Manager whenever the opportunity arises! The Hungarian public knows that you do not yet speak Hungarian, and, although it wishes you to learn the Hungarian language – ultimately in your own interests – you should not think that you will be called to account over that. The Hungarian public will, however, call you to account in the light of your promise to further Hungarian music and art.

It appears that the Director has fallen into the hands of bad advisers. He must beware, lest his otherwise honest intentions founder on his antipathy for Hungarian music and Hungarian composers, and he himself be dragged down into the depths.

Zenelap, 30 January 1890. (The assertion that no Hungarian opera had been performed for a year and half does not accord with the facts.)

In May 1890 Mahler went on a journey through Italy, with his sister Justine, in which he visited Florence, Bologna, Milan and other places. They ended their journey in the Hinterbrühl, a summer resort near Vienna, where Mahler and Friedrich Löhr had rented a villa with a large garden. Here Mahler, his brothers and sisters, and the Löhr family, spent the summer months of 1890.

Friedrich Löhr on Mahler's journey to Italy

. . . A principal element of most visits to Italy, enthusiasm for the incomparable treasures of pictorial art there, was lacking in Mahler; one language of art, that of music, possessed him alone and entirely. Thus he avoided the collections, even the most famous, in Florence, just as he later did in Paris. Not that he was incapable of being impressed by visual works of art, if something really great was placed before him: later, when I gave him photographs of the reliefs of the Ludovisi Throne, including the *Birth of Aphrodite*, he was highly delighted and enthusiastic. But his own initiative impelled him, in places unknown to him, only towards the attractions of nature, which for him were never-failing, in the blooming countryside of Florence and Fiesole as in the environs of Paris.

GMB, notes, 482–83.

Friedrich Löhr on the summer in the Hinterbrühl

The duration of this richly eventful time was fortunately long enough for its benefits to take effect upon Mahler – such natural beauty, contentment and at every moment the longed-for freedom; the whole of life was arranged for his benefit here. There was fulfilment, whenever he needed it, of his often passionate longing to converse and communicate, and a charming sitting-room with the most beautiful view for him to be alone in. There was also a considerable amount of movement and coming and going in the house, on the part of numerous guests and also of the residents themselves. Until July, I was kept in the city by my teaching duties and joined those in the Hinterbrühl mainly on Sundays only. Otto remained behind with me on account of his studies. At this time Mahler often went into the city; once he even went briefly to Pest on professional business; or he spent the night with friends at nearby Kaltenleutgeben. Then in July, when I became free for long periods of time, and was now completely alone with Mahler for the greater part of the day, I did not hesitate to honour my obligations to other friends and went to spend a week with Sax at Aussee. Then we heard that Mahler's state of health, and his state of mind, had taken an ominous turn for the worse. Theatre officials were coming from Pest to report to him, and he was already working on the preparations for the coming season, reading through scores that were being considered for performance, including – with growing astonishment – that of Mascagni's *Cavalleria rusticana*, which had just arrived, and which he at once decided to perform. The new era of his greatest creative achievements had not begun; within him fermented all the new sensations of the summer life to which he abandoned himself with all the power of his passionate nature. He was a model of sociability and good humour – except when a sudden thought made him oblivious of all around him, or when, alone with me, in a state of unrestrained emotion but hardly capable of speech, he sensed within him echoes of past, painful ecstasies of the soul.

GMB, notes, 483.

Mozart's 'Don Giovanni' and the treatment of the recitatives

. . . Whatever we might object to in the soloists, the new interpretation of the opera ought indeed to grip the audience: we heard Mozart's music in its complete stylistic purity, with absolute choral discipline, with fresh tempos and with all its subtlety of nuance. Mahler knows how to clean layers of dust from such a masterpiece and restore it. On the conductor's podium this time stood an upright piano as well, because in the recitative passages, which our singers have hitherto spoken without musical accompaniment, *parlando*, Mahler has restored the original accompaniment and plays this himself on the piano while conducting. His idea was novel, and by no means a bad one; in the orchestral pauses the sound of the piano is pleasant, and it is the most appropriate accompanying instrument. The Stage Manager deserves recognition for the collective scenes and the ensemble playing, but most of all for the rapid changes of scene.

Budapesti Hirlap, 17 September 1890. (The première of the new production took place on 16 September.)

Among the voices of acclaim were mingled louder and louder critical comments. The dismissal of Ede Ujházy as Chief of Production in September 1890, for reasons of economy, indicated a divergence from the original conception. Further, dissension appeared, fomented by one section of the press, within the Opera itself.

Demand for resignation

The policy which he so proudly and confidently announced on his appointment has not been put into practice. He has not even come close to attaining it during his two years working here; so far from bringing order into the artistic arrangements of our Opera House, he has confused them even further. Under his leadership the artistic level of our opera has not risen but has been decisively lowered. . . . If Herr Mahler still possesses any self-respect – and we have no right to assume the opposite – then under these circumstances he can do nothing other than to renounce his position for which – as his two-year occupation of it has shown – he has not the necessary qualifications.

Pesti Hirlap, 5 November 1890.

Mahler to the Hamburg Theatre Director, Bernhard Pollini

Budapest, 7 November 1890

Having just returned from a journey I have found your favour of 2 November with contract enclosed. After perusal of this, I must return to a point of which you probably took no further notice in the light of the new direction of our negotiations, but by which, as you will see from the relevant letter, I set great store.

I would have accepted your offer of 12,000 marks salary per annum, provided that you undertook to pay the customary taxes, duty and pension contribution.

As I have by this time given proof in every way of my readiness to oblige you, I ask you to concede to me on this point and permit me to insert this additional stipulation into the contract which was sent to me.

There will then be nothing standing in the way of my entry into association with your institution.

GMB, 118–19. (Mahler already seems to have realized by the autumn of 1890 that he could not stay in Budapest, although his contract was supposed to run for a further eight years.)

91   Lilli Lehmann (1848–1929) was one of the most notable sopranos of her time. Her repertoire comprised 170 roles, ranging from Wagner at Bayreuth to Offenbach operettas. She was Geraldine Farrar's and Olive Fremstad's teacher,

and started the Mozart festival in Salzburg in 1901. In her autobiography, despite reservations, she expresses great admiration of Mahler. She had been working since 1886 at the New York Metropolitan Opera when she met Mahler for the first time in Budapest in 1890.

Lilli Lehmann on her guest appearance in Budapest

. . . Gustav Mahler entered my artistic life as Director of the National Opera in Budapest. A new man, with a strong will and understanding. He had told me in a letter that my fees were in excess of his budget, but that he considered my visit in a leading role to be entirely necessary in order to give the members of his company an artistic example towards which they should strive. We spent an enchanting time in a small select circle there. Mahler, in all his devout spontaneity, steering towards his goal; the marvellous Hungarian tragedienne, Marie Jassay, a kind of Ristori, and yet with an innate simplicity and naturalness, who was always studying; Count Albert Apponyi and Professor Mihalovich, our dear friends   89, 90 from Bayreuth, and my small niece. We went everywhere together. All my roles I sang in Italian, and only that of Recha (*La Juive*) – as the choice had been left to me – in French, without having any idea that Perrotti would sing the part of the Jew in Italian. Everyone else was singing in Hungarian, and one can just imagine the cosmopolitan confusion of languages in these operatic performances in which every foreigner, singing without a prompter, had to remain true to his own language. In *Don Giovanni*, Mahler, at that time still young and fiery, took the short trio for male voices in the first act at the fastest *allegro*, because *alla breve* is written over it – which does not in this case mean an increased but only a more tranquil tempo. Mahler made the same mistake in the mask trio without an *alla breve* signature, but here I immediately cast my veto, and never again – so I believe – did he relapse into his *allegro* folly in *that* passage. When I discussed it with Bülow, he was horrified, and said about the *alla breve* exactly what I have just written.

I can still picture Mahler kneeling in front of our stove, brewing up a medicine for Hedwig H. in a tin ladle according to his grandmother's recipe, for which he brought everything with him. At Frau Jassay's his missing coat buttons, lost heaven knows where, were usually sewn on for him. We often walked, leapt and dashed around with him, over bush, over briar, in the magnificent countryside round Budapest, and we had a marvellous time.

Lilli Lehmann, *Mein Weg*, Leipzig 1913, II, 157–58.

Celebrities in the audience at the Philharmonic Concert

The third Philharmonic Concert, which takes place tomorrow, Wednesday 17 December at 7.30 in the evening in the large Redoutensaal, conducted by Alexander Erkel, will be attended by Dr Johannes Brahms and Eugen d'Albert, who arrived in the Capital on Tuesday. In artistic circles this concert is arousing very active interest, which is heightened still further by the participation of Frau Lilli Kalisch-Lehmann. Frau Lehmann is singing Weber's great aria 'Ocean thou Mighty Monster' from *Oberon*, and Dr Brahms is conducting his Academic Festival Overture and his Second Piano Concerto in B flat major in person; the latter will be performed by Eugen d'Albert.

Pester Lloyd, 17 December 1890.

Brahms hears 'Don Giovanni' at the Budapest Opera

On the evening before a concert, for which Brahms had come, the opera *Don Giovanni* was being staged. Mahler's friends in the elite of the musical and other fields in Budapest had free access to a box. Hans Kössler and Victor von Herzfeld, two professors at the Academy of Music, had drawn Brahms's attention to Mahler's *Don Giovanni* and suggested going to the performance.

'I wouldn't dream of it,' the Master snapped at them. 'No one can do *Don Giovanni* right for me, I enjoy it much better from the score. I've never heard a good *Don Giovanni* yet. We'd be better off going to the beer-hall.'

There was no contradicting that. In the evening both gentlemen were so able to arrange it that they went past the Opera House towards 7 o'clock. 'It will probably be too early. The beer won't have been going long. Come in here for just half an hour.'

'All right then', growled the Master. 'Is there a sofa in the box?'

'Of course.'

'Then it's all right. I'll sleep through it.'

They took their seats, the friends at the balustrade of the box, Brahms on the sofa. After the overture they heard from the rear of the box a strange grunting sound. The unarticulated utterance of approbation was followed by many others in a paroxysm of admiration which made the hearts of the gentlemen at the balustrade beat faster.

'Quite excellent, tremendous – he's a deuce of a fellow!'

Brahms leapt from his sofa, and when the act was finished he hurried on to the stage with his friends and embraced the frail little man to whom he owed the finest *Don Giovanni* of his life.

When, seven years later, the question of a successor for Jahn was raised in Vienna, Brahms remembered the name of Gustav Mahler, and he and Hanslick gave an influential testimony in favour of this artist which may have been partly if not wholly decisive in his appointment in Vienna.

Neues Wiener Journal, 19 May 1911. (At the *Don Giovanni* performance of 16 December 1890, which Brahms attended, Lilli Lehmann was singing Donna Anna.)

171 *Mahler to Richard Heuberger*

I am tremendously pleased that you are giving us the pleasure of a visit. The ticket is ready for you, please have it fetched from the office – or let me know the name of the hotel where you are staying and then I will have it sent there. At all events, I do request that we should meet after the opera. Perhaps you will come up on to the stage? That Brahms was so appreciative makes me very happy – I consider this the greatest success that has yet fallen to my lot. . . .

Letter of 23 December 1890, *Anbruch*, vol. XVIII, no. 3, 65. (Richard Heuberger, 1850–1914, Viennese music critic, choral conductor, and composer of the operetta *Ein Opernball*. Heuberger's letter to Mahler in which he announces his arrival for the Budapest première of Mascagni's *Cavalleria rusticana*, and which must also have contained Brahms's judgment, has not yet come to light.)

From Richard Heuberger's review of the Budapest 'Cavalleria rusticana'

Gustav Mahler, the energetic and intelligent director of the Royal Opera in Budapest, has stolen a march on every theatre outside Italy by producing the most outstanding new opera from Italy by Mascagni, whose fame has spread rapidly. Soon we shall have the chance to hear this unusual work, and so a fairly precise report on the latest musical event in the Hungarian capital may be of particular interest. . . .

The production, conducted by the Opera Director, Herr Mahler, may be described – under the prevailing circumstances – as quite exceptional. Only a conductor and stage manager of Mahler's unusual talent and unparalleled enthusiasm for work can accomplish such a thing with beginners. Of the few principals two, Turridù (Herr Szirovatka) and Alfio (Herr Veres), were decidedly beginners, and only after the most detailed instruction was it possible to put them on the stage in these two important roles. However, Mahler's baton has limitless force, and Mahler has managed to instil into all his players his own insight. To watch this affords an unusual, unfortunately truly rare pleasure. We made the acquaintance of an excellent dramatic singer in Fräulein Szilágyi, who sang and acted Santuzza touchingly. . . . The orchestra did excellently. . . .

Wiener Tagblatt, 28 December 1890.

Even in October 1890 rumours were circulating in Budapest of an imminent replacement of the Commissioner, Ferenc von Beniczky. *Pesti Hirlap* announced on 29 October 1890 that Count Géza Zichy would take over the position of Commissioner at the beginning of the coming year. Géza (von) Zichy (1849–1924) came from a widely ramified Hungarian aristocratic family. Although he had lost his right arm in his early youth, he taught himself to be a pianist and made several successful concert tours. Zichy was also a composer of operas, orchestral and piano pieces. His official appointment took place on 22 January 1891 and was made public on 30 January. A few days earlier Ferenc von Beniczky took his leave of the Court Theatres in an open letter in which he surveyed the achievements of the Budapest Opera House in his era, which was at the same time the era of Gustav Mahler.

Beniczky sums up the Mahler era

. . . I took over the Theatres in the midst of a crisis which was all but a catastrophe, with reduced material means, with restrictive decisions and directions from the Parliament and the Government; I took them over at a moment when the most important question was whether it was possible, or advisable, to keep the Opera going at all – and I am handing over to my successor both institutions in a consolidated material and artistic condition. That I did not succeed in satisfying every ambition, in gratifying every wish; that here and there I wounded a personal interest, a personal vanity, sometimes because my duty bade me do so, sometimes perhaps unintentionally – that is more than probable; it is probable, too, that I could perhaps in one matter or another have achieved a greater success. . . .

When I took over the management of the Theatres I stated that I did not wish to control the artistic direction closely but to leave it, together with responsibility for it, to the Artistic Directors. To this programme I remained faithful right up to the end, and that this was right is attested by the results.

I do not think I have to mention the artistic direction of the National Theatre, because this has not been subject to attacks. The artistic direction of the Royal Hungarian Opera House, and in particular the new Director's policy, has, however, repeatedly been sharply attacked. These attacks can be traced to personal motives. The new Director was attacked because he kept to his programme: 'Work, work, work, and, where possible, use of indigenous resources.'

Despite the many difficulties against which the new Director has had to battle, there have come to the Royal Hungarian Opera House, since 1 October 1888, i.e. since he began work: I. The following operas and ballets which had never previously been performed in Budapest or had been removed from the repertoire of the National Theatre decades ago:
(a) Operas: (1) *The Pearl Fishers*, (2) *The Daughter of the Regiment*, (3) *Nachtlager in Granada*, (4) *Rhinegold*, (5) *The Valkyrie*, (6) *Georg Brankovics*, (7) *Das Glöckchen des Eremiten*, (8) *The Merry Wives of Windsor*, (9) *Des Teufels Anteil*, (10) *Templer und Jüdin*, (11) *Asraël*, (12) *Cavalleria rusticana*, (13) *Hochzeit bei Laternenschein*, and (14) *Der Waffenschmied*;
(b) Ballets: (15) *Puppenfee*, (16) *Der neue Romeo*, (17) *Sonne und Erde*, (18) *Csárdás*;

(19) The opera *Tales of Hoffmann* was rehearsed, costumed and the scenery prepared for the production; but as a result of Fräulein Bianca Bianchi's illness – which circumstance incidentally caused considerable disturbance in various directions – the production had to be temporarily postponed. . . .

II.   Newly rehearsed, with a new cast and in part with totally new scenery, the following operas were performed:
(20) *The Marriage of Figaro*, (21) *Lohengrin*, (22) *Merlin*, (23) *Mignon*, (24) *Aida*, (25) *Die Königin von Saba*, (26) *Die Nürnberger Puppe*, (27) *Don Giovanni*, (28) *Bánk bán*, (29) *Un ballo in maschera*, (30) *Fidelio*, (31) *Jeanettens Hochzeit*.

The rehearsal and production of thirty-one works in the twenty months of performing time from 1 October 1888 to the end of January this year is a testimony to the work of the management and the members of the company, in the face of which any attack appears only as ill-will.

In the Royal Hungarian Opera House the account closed with a saving on the budget of 2,993 florins 64 kreuzer in 1888, with a saving of 20,265 florins 93 kreuzer in 1889, with a saving of 24,618 florins 96 kreuzer in 1890. From these sums too I created a special fund; this fund, which is transferred to my successor, had increased by the end of 1890 to a total, including interest, of 48,784 florins 28 kreuzer.

These are the results I have achieved. It goes without saying, of course, that the responsibility for any deficiencies which may be discovered lies with me and I accept it also. On the other hand I must ascribe the credit for the successful results to the departmental heads in these institutions. . . .

Pester Lloyd, 25 January 1891. (In February and March, when Mahler was still Director in Budapest, the following works were given their first performance: *A vig cimborák* by Károly Huber, *Loreley* by Mendelssohn, and the ballet *Viora* by Károly Szabados.)

97   *From the inaugural speech of Commissioner Géza Zichy*

Ladies and Gentlemen, do not expect any programme from me. You know my past, which is certainly poor in achievements, yet in *its direction and its endeavours* was always consistently Hungarian. Here, too, I can only say: I wish to attain a Hungarian art on a European level, now still with the help of foreigners, later from our own capabilities.

Egyetértés, 3 February 1891.

The powers of the Opera Director are restricted

Now, as ever, the final decision in all important matters remains incumbent upon the Commissioner, yet much more latitude for his immediate intervention is opened up by the new statute. Thus in the new statute the section numbered 13 in the old one is deleted, under which the Commissioner did not intervene directly in the choice of the repertoire and the apportionment of roles; section 16 of the new statute lays down that at the weekly meetings under the chairmanship of the Commissioner the latter alone makes the decisions. A completely new provision, section 20, similarly lays down that the Commissioner has the right to terminate appointments on his own responsibility and without consulting the Artistic Director. In the Opera assessment committee the Commissioner replaces the Director as chairman, and the latter has only the right to make suggestions. The most important provision of the new statute appears to be, at all events, that of section 40, on the position of the Artistic Director, which states: 'Any or all of the . . . powers of the Artistic Director may be exercised by the Commissioner in person, on his own responsibility, for appropriate reasons and in cases of emergency to which such reasons apply, in so far as he obtains the consent of the Minister of the Interior, which consent with reference to individual powers may be sought after the event and with reference to all powers must be sought prior to the event.'

Neues Pester Journal, 19 February 1891.

The consequences of the new statute

The investment of the Commissioner with the plenary powers of an Artistic Director has of course not failed to make its repercussions felt in the personal relationship between Count Géza Zichy and Herr Mahler. . . . A relationship such as currently prevails between Commissioner and Director cannot persist without seriously damaging the institution's repute. . . . The arrival of the Commissioner means in fact the departure of the Director, which is impending but has not yet taken place. . . . Herr Mahler is now adopting a waiting posture. He now no longer possesses any influence on the management of the Opera. The appointment of Countess Vasquez was terminated without his knowledge, the opera [*Toldis Liebe*] by Mihalovich, which had already been accepted for production, was shelved without the Director being consulted. The Director learns of the repertoire from the newspaper, like any other mortal. . . .

Neues Politisches Volksblatt, 21 February 1891.

96

Gustav Mahler sets aside his contract

At midday today Herr Gustav Mahler ceased to be Director of the Royal Opera House. A few days ago he wrote a letter to the Commissioner, Count Géza Zichy, in which he stated his readiness to set aside the contract between himself and the Royal Opera House, which still had eight years to run, in return for a settlement of 25,000 florins. At midday today Count Zichy informed Herr Mahler of the acceptance of this proposition and paid to him forthwith the settlement sum of 25,000 florins, with which the relationship between Herr Mahler and the Royal Opera House appears to be at an end.

We are requested to publish the following statement:

'Sir, – From today I have resigned from the position of Artistic Director of the Royal Hungarian Opera House and have relinquished my office into the hands of my superiors. I was unfortunately not given the opportunity to take my leave, from the spot where I worked and strove for nearly three years, of the Budapest public which has so kindly honoured my efforts, of the personnel of the Royal Opera House which has faithfully and hard-workingly stood by me. I hereby do so by this means, and combine with it my heartfelt thanks to the press of the Capital for the manifold assistance and recognition that my activities have found here. I depart from my post in the consciousness of having faithfully and honestly fulfilled my duty, and with the sincere wish that the Royal Hungarian Opera House may blossom and flourish.

Budapest, 14 March 1891.   Gustav Mahler.'

Pester Lloyd, 15 March 1891.

The public calls for the departed Mahler

In the Pest Opera House, *Lohengrin* was performed on Tuesday evening with Frau Schroeder-Hanfstängl, from Frankfurt am Main, as Elsa. The audience used the performance as a tremendous demonstration in favour of Gustav Mahler, who has resigned as Director after being forced out of his position by the new Commissioner, Count Zichy, because he is a German. The first act was interrupted three times by stormy cries for Mahler. Detectives restored order in the gallery.

Hamburgischer Correspondent, 20 March 1891, evening edn.

Justine Mahler to Siegfried Rosenberg in Budapest

Vienna, 26 March [1891]

My brother has asked me to inform you that as he has to conduct *Tannhäuser* on Easter Sunday he cannot stop on his journey in either Dresden or Berlin. He left here yesterday evening and arrives in Hamburg this afternoon at 5.30. Then tomorrow he has his first rehearsal. Furthermore, he asks you to order from Kalmár, 29 Andrássy Street, 6 full-length pictures, as these are certainly the best, and to have them sent to him in Hamburg.

Ms., HAM.

Bruno Walter describes the Free Hanseatic City of Hamburg

Hamburg was considered to be Germany's second city after Berlin; in the minds of the people of Hamburg it was the first. A rivalry existed between the two great cities, which held each other in low esteem – in a comedy by Blumenthal a Hamburg senator, when a young man told him that he had been born in Berlin, said: 'Well, one's got to be born somewhere, after all.' Berliners found the big seaport boring; Hamburg saw the capital of the Reich as an upstart newcomer. At all events, Hamburg was a city with a personality formed by history, which one could not say of Berlin, and the magnificent vista of the quarters of the city which lay around the Inner and Outer Alster lakes, with the Jungfernstieg as the main thoroughfare, the mighty harbour, the maze of the sailors' entertainment quarter in St Pauli, the beautiful Elbe villages of Blankenese, the 'Luhe', and so forth – everything had character and told of the life of a Hanseatic city, which looked outwards to the sea and the world, while the majority of German cities were living in a state of introspection. Incidentally, Hamburg was not only a city, it was also a state, which set great store by its equality of status with the other German states, in particular with the mighty and unloved Prussia; its citizens had poise and dignity, and the artistic world enjoyed particular attention in official quarters because prestige value was placed upon Hamburg's importance as a cultural centre. But it was not only to civic pride, it was rather to a widespread, genuine enthusiasm for art, that the theatre owed its commanding role in the intellectual life of the city. Hamburg was what was then called a theatrical city, i.e., the theatre and its performers enjoyed especial popularity, and anything that the Municipal Theatres had to offer by way of opera and drama, anything that the other theatres achieved, particularly the excellent company of the Thalia Theatre (called by the locals 'Thaa-liatheater' with the accent on the first syllable), was dear to the hearts of the people of Hamburg and was discussed with interest by a wide section of the population.

The management [of the Hamburg Municipal Theatre] also produced a regular number of operatic and dramatic performances . . . in the little neighbouring town of Altona, which one reached via St Pauli.

BWTV, 103–4. (Bruno Walter, real name Schlesinger, 1876–1962, German conductor, born in Berlin, was at the Municipal Theatre, Hamburg, from 1894.)

J. B. Foerster on Hamburg's musical scene

Hamburg's musical circles at that time were led by a few older musicians; at their head stood the worthy, kindly but rather colourless von Bernuth, Director of the Conservatoire and retired Conductor of the Association of Hamburg Friends of Music; next to him ruled the old Director Mehrlens, a corpulent, easy-going gentleman who looked like the captain of a merchant ship, always amicably smiling and attentive, yet with little force of temperament, Director and Conductor of the Bach Society. Behind this first rank of conductors there worked, worthily and honestly, Julius Spengel, Director of the Cecilia Association, with childlike, faithful, astonished eyes and a melancholy expression, an enthusiastic musician but not a sufficiently energetic orchestral conductor; lastly the pianist and conductor Max Fiedler, a strong artistic temperament,

yet rather one-sidedly devoted to the Brahms cult which understandably was blooming in Hamburg; this devotion was shared by Spengel and the Director of the Hamburg Philharmonic, Professor Richard Barth, an excellent violinist, but a pedantically dry conductor.

New tendencies in music were served by only one man: the little-recognized but very worthy director of popular orchestral concerts, Julius Laube, the predecessor of that doughty champion of the art of the new era, José Eibenschütz. . . .

Hans von Bülow was attracted to Hamburg by the fact that he had friends there, by the magical beauty and peace of the suburb of Uhlenhorst, by the beckoning green of broad gardens, and by the azure-blue, idyllic Alster. When he appeared in the concert hall and theatre, he immediately began to 'clear out' certain traditions. His effervescent spirit could bear no easy-going approach, his pure artistry no half-measures. A short time before I had been present at a concert in the Sofieninselsaal in Prague, at which Bülow as conductor announced from the podium, in Czech, that he had made an alteration to the programme, namely that he would play Dvořák's overture Husitská as his final piece; I had seen Bülow interrupt the performance of Beethoven's F sharp major Sonata in the Konviktssaal, because one string of the piano was out of tune; I had been there when the master, whom the whole hall was awaiting – he was severely delayed as a result of a sudden storm – appeared on the podium in galoshes with an umbrella streaming with rainwater. Here in Hamburg I found the public excited and highly interested in countless little anecdotes which the members of the orchestra, as well as the audience, were all too willing to relate; how, for example, the great conductor, after glaring – baton in hand – at the audience in the gallery a few times, finally stated that he would only begin when 'the gentleman in the gallery had finished picking his teeth', or how after long and tumultuous applause – he had performed Beethoven's Ninth – giving his thanks from the rostrum for the acclaim which he was accepting 'on behalf of Beethoven who unfortunately cannot be here', he announced that for him, Bülow, applause was insufficient, just as he hated words, and therefore was to demand of the audience that they prove their expressed enthusiasm by their deeds: 'for we shall now take the liberty of repeating the Finale of the Symphony for you'. And he completed his address: 'Please don't rush for the exits; I have had all the doors closed.'

So I found myself in a psychological atmosphere which was fully charged with electricity. On the one side Bülow and, as I already knew, Mahler too, on the other the 'Brahmans' (this was the name given to the partisan admirers of the Hanseatic city's great son, Johannes Brahms). On one side the Municipal Theatre, with an incredibly rich programme which was supplemented every season by the latest works of contemporary literature; on the other concerts with, in many cases, outdated programmes, and conductors who, except for Laube, Fiedler and Spengel, were indifferent if not actively hostile to what their own day had to offer.

Both trends naturally found their representatives in criticism. Besides some indecisive and 'careful' critics there stood, in the progressive group: the witty German-Bohemian Ferdinand Pfohl, the pugnacious W. Zinne, later the deeply-searching Dr Arthur Seidl and the careful and judicious Heinrich Chevalley; among the conservatives were the good-natured old Emil Krause, a warm admirer of Anton Dvořák, and Josef Sittard, a dogged enemy of everything Slavonic.

JBFPP, 9 April 1922. (The composer and music critic Joseph Bohuslav Foerster, 1859–1951, husband of the soprano Berta Foerster-Lauterer, was a member of Mahler's circle of friends in Hamburg.)

Enthusiasm for the new conductor

In the Conductor Herr Gustav Mahler our Opera has gained a motive force of the first order. If the great reputation that preceded him made us expect a superb achievement, then Herr

191

Programme of the first performance conducted by Mahler in Hamburg.
Universität Hamburg, Theatersammlung.

Loss of status

Mahler, when he followed the honourable call to Hamburg,
had been Opera Director in Budapest, the leading personality
in the musical life of a capital city, in charge of a richly
equipped court theatre; the bearer of a public office in a highly
elevated social position, belonging as of right to the highest
social circles. 'When I was in Budapest', he once told me,
'Ministers made return visits to me. Here in Hamburg' – he
choked out his short, scornful laugh – 'none of the Senators
thinks of doing so. Senators, lawyers, businessmen . . . that's an
audience for you.' He, who was by no means a sociable person,
let alone a society musician or a salon virtuoso, was nevertheless put out, if not wounded in his pride, to see, after his first
experiences in Hamburg, that his official position and his
personal social standing had declined by comparison with his
rank in Budapest: a loss of status with which he had to come to
terms. Against that, however, his position as Conductor at the
Municipal Theatre offered him as rich a sphere of activity as
any musician could possibly wish for. . . .

*Ferdinand Pfohl, 'Mahler und Nikisch', in Jahrhundertfeier des Hamburger Stadt-
theaters, Hamburg 1927. (Ferdinand Pfohl, 1865–1949, born in Bohemia, lived
in Hamburg from 1892 onwards as a music critic.)*

Wagner cycle in May 1891

The performing season of 1890–91, now drawing into the last
of its nine months, will yet bring us a R. Wagner cycle (ten
evenings), as usual at this time of year, under the direction of
Gustav Mahler, a Lortzing cycle and a small cycle of classical
plays (six evenings). At the beginning of the holidays works
will begin in Hamburg which, apart from the introduction of
electric lighting, are to serve to beautify the theatre and improve the security of the uppermost seats. Unfortunately, even
in this rebuilding, the improvement, so desirable and so
urgently requested, of those features which no longer appear
worthy of an establishment of the standing of the Hamburg
Municipal Theatre, is excluded. These are the lack of space
on either side of the stage, the awkward access to the stage from
the street (particularly during rehearsals when changes of
scenery, etc., are taking place), the oppressive lowness of the
dressing-rooms, the lack of a green room. . . .

Deutsche Bühnengenossenschaft, vol. xx, no. 17, 26 April 1891, 155.

Mahler exceeded even these expectations and, a thing which
only happens in the rarest of cases, electrified the audience on
the very first evening by his brilliant conducting. The same
ovations were given to the new leading Artistic Director of our
Opera yesterday after the last act of Wagner's *Siegfried* as on
the previous Sunday at the opera *Tannhäuser*. Herr Mahler is
a conductor who has in his command not only the notes in
the score, but, what is more, the spirit of the artistic work;
and he also possesses the gift of transmitting this spirit to
the entire cast and carrying them along with him. There is no
entry that is not cued by him, no dynamic shading that remains unobserved; Herr Mahler holds the reins in his hand
with an energy which binds the individual firmly to him, draws
him, we might say, with magical force into his own world of
thought. The spiritual and artistic influence that such a conductor exerts on an orchestra was particularly easy to recognize yesterday; at times we thought we had before us a completely new instrumental ensemble. How clearly, rhythmically
defined, carefully nuanced and phrased everything seemed;
how the great climactic moments in the last two acts were en-
hanced! If Herr Mahler displays the same qualities in classical
opera as in Wagner's music dramas, then our Opera may
count itself fortunate to have such a brilliant conductor at its
head.

*Hamburgischer Correspondent, 1 April 1891. (The author of this review was Josef
Sittard, one of the leading conservative critics in Hamburg at that time.)*

Mahler had taken up his appointment in Hamburg two
months before the end of the season. Nevertheless he conducted thirty-five times before the season closed on 31 May
(Irmgard Scharberth, 'Gustav Mahlers Wirken am Hamburger Stadttheater', *Die Musikforschung*, vol. xxii, 1969,
447); i.e. on average every other day. Mahler spent part of
the summer of 1891 with Rudolf and Heinrich Krżyżanowski, part of it alone on an extensive tour of Scandinavia from
which he brought back enduring impressions of the landscape. During the three-month break the auditorium of the
Hamburg Municipal Theatre was renovated and fitted
with electric lighting, which functioned for the first time
at the opening performance of the 1891–92 season. The
opera on that occasion was *Fidelio*, conducted by Mahler.

From a review of 'Fidelio'

In his conducting of the entire performance Herr Mahler
proved his well-known energy and his artistic zeal down to the
finest detail. This zeal leads him just occasionally to the
border between what is true and what is artificial. In passing,
just one or two particular impressions: the conductor gives in
all too freely to his fondness for stretching out slow tempi, in
the very first *adagio* bars in the introduction to the overture in

E major; he does it again in the canonic quartet, and yet again in the prisoners' first chorus; while on the other hand in the first finale the *Leb wohl, du warmes Sonnenlicht* ['Farewell, you warm sunlight'] of the chorus alienates one by its hasty, over-cheerful performance; even the *sotto voce* and *sempre piano* specified by Beethoven in the canon and in the prisoners' first chorus was taken to its uttermost limits and hence seemed in its expression to be more affected than credible.

Hamburger Nachrichten, 3 September 1891.

Mahler to his sister Justine

. . . Incidentally I was recently in a great state of excitement. You see, Bülow's factotum suddenly comes to me and asks me on his behalf to conduct the next concert for him, as he is seriously ill. I – ready right away – draw up a lovely programme immediately; no sooner does Bülow see it than he declares himself well again, etc., etc. By the way, I must always be ready here to deputize for him any time. . . .

Alfred Rosé, 'Gustav Mahler and Hans von Bülow', *Neues Wiener Journal*, 23 September 1928, EV. (Alfred Rosé states that the letter quoted was written in 1891.)

Mahler plays his 'Totenfeier' to Bülow

118, 119   Mahler carried on talking. 'So I called on Bülow some time ago and asked him whether he would care to see the score that I have just played for you. He said, "You play the thing for me, the score is rather complicated, and at least I shall be hearing the authentic interpretation . . .".

'I sat down at the piano and played. After a while it occurred to me to look at Bülow, and I saw that he was covering both ears with his hands. I stopped playing. Bülow noticed at once and told me to continue.

'I played. After a few bars I looked up at Bülow again. He was sitting at the table again, with his hands pressed over his ears, and the same business was repeated. I stopped. Bülow immediately told me to go on playing. Perhaps he – the celebrated pianist – did not like my style of playing, or my touch; or maybe my *forte* was too loud for him, too vehement, too rough; and then I remembered his extreme nervous sensitivity, how often he complained about violent headaches. All this passed through my mind semi-consciously, for I carried on playing without any further interruption, having made up my mind not to look at Bülow any more, and in the heat of the performance I even forgot he was there.

'When I had finished I remained silent, as you will understand, and waited to hear what Bülow would say. But my sole auditor remained mute for a long time; then he made a vigorous movement and, turning to me with a gesture of rejection, said : "Well, if that's music, then I know nothing about music!"

'We parted in a friendly manner, but I had the feeling that, while Bülow regarded me as a capable conductor, he nevertheless considered me a bad composer.'

JBFPP, 16 April 1922. (It is clear from a letter to Friedrich Löhr that Mahler's visit to Bülow must have taken place in November or December 1891.)

103   ### The first German performance of Tchaikowsky's 'Eugene Onegin'

Mahler had meticulously rehearsed the first German performance of *Onegin*, and Tchaikowsky had come in person to conduct his work. At the final rehearsal, however, with the composer in charge, there were frequent mishaps. Tchaikowsky was not cuing the entries. We begged Mahler to intervene. He did this by getting behind Tchaikowsky's podium and bringing us in at the right moments. Anxiously we awaited the performance; we expected a catastrophe. The curtain rose; and who was standing on the podium? Gustav Mahler! Our

astonished faces must have looked really comical, for even today I can still see Mahler's smirk. We sang with tremendous enthusiasm, and had a great success.

Mary Kraus-Weiner, 'Erinnerungen an Gustav Mahler'. *Teplitzer Zeitung*, 30 May 1911, EV. (The first German performance of *Eugene Onegin* was on 19 January 1892. Marie (or Mary) Weiner was the leading female singer of the Hamburg Opera company during the 1891–92 season.)

Richard Strauss to his parents, on Mahler's brother Otto

Weimar, 31 January 1892

. . . Do you happen to have read Hanslick's review of the performance of *Don Juan* in Vienna? It's supposed to be really excellent, I shall get hold of a copy right away. The Vienna success seems to have been shared; Mahler (Hamburg) yesterday sent me a letter from his nineteen-year-old brother, from Vienna, who writes very enthusiastically and exhaustively, with great understanding of the piece. The young people are certainly coming along!

Richard Strauss, *Briefe an die Eltern*, Zürich 1954, 148. (Otto Mahler evidently heard Richard Strauss's symphonic poem *Don Juan* at the Vienna Philharmonic concert on 10 January 1892.)

Mahler to Anton Bruckner

Hamburg, 16 April 1892

At last I am very happy to be able to write to you that I have performed one of your compositions. Yesterday (Good Friday) I conducted your glorious and powerful *Te Deum*. Both the *performers* and the *whole audience* were most deeply affected by the overwhelming form and truly sublime conception; and at the end of the performance I experienced what I consider to be the greatest triumph for any work – the audience remained sitting without a sound, without stirring; and not until the conductor and the performers had left their places did the storm of applause break out.

Anton Bruckner, *Gesammelte Briefe*, new series, Regensburg 1924, 329–30.

Mahler on his engagement as guest conductor in London

The engagements in London have all been settled – even before *I* had said anything. Between you and me, Harris would rather have had Hans Richter, who would of course have been a tremendous asset for the London enterprise, in view of his standing there. However, this seems to have fallen through – and so I have been engaged. . . .

I must tell you in confidence that, as far as *most of the singers* are concerned, the only thing they expect from the whole undertaking is 'prestige', and nearly all of them except Alvary and Klafsky – perhaps also your humble servant, will be happy to make their expenses. If we *have a success*, then perhaps it may even lead to the permanent establishment of German opera at Covent Garden – and perhaps drive the Italians right out.   109

I am telling you this under the seal of *strictest confidence*! . . .

If you write anything about me for the German papers, please keep it very *unpretentious*, and do *not* call me 'Director'; this always seems to annoy Pollini, because it makes him feel out of it. . . .

Undated letter to Siegfried Rosenberg, written in 1892, ms., HAM. (Sir Augustus Harris, 1852–96, English impresario, was manager of Covent Garden Opera House from 1888. Max Alvary and Katharina Klafsky were members of the Opera company of the Hamburg Municipal Theatre. The guest engagement in London was arranged by Pollini.)

Studying English with Dr Arnold Berliner

When the trip to London was fixed up, Mahler began to learn English. He built up his vocabulary in a notebook, in which he wrote down the words and expressions that he would need in the theatre. B[erliner] had to 'hear' him during his daily walk, and get him to form appropriate sentences. . . .

Note on Mahler's letters to Dr Arnold Berliner, GMB, 125.

Arnold Berliner (1862–1942), who taught Mahler the rudiments of the English language, had studied physics in Breslau, worked at the General Electric Company in the USA, and during Mahler's stay in Hamburg was employed at the bulb factory of the Allgemeine Elektrizitäts-Gesellschaft (AEG). Through Berliner, Mahler was introduced into the household of the distinguished dermatologist Albert Neisser (1855–1916), with whom he maintained contact, personally and by correspondence, until after becoming Director of the Vienna Opera. With Berliner himself Mahler developed a warm friendship which was interrupted only for a few years, and which lasted until Mahler's death. Under his guidance Mahler took up the study of natural science.

Arnold Berliner's feeling for the arts

His innate interest in art was intensified and cultivated by contact with the Neisser household, to whom he owed so much; thus he was able to become a friend of the musician Mahler and of the painter Erler. It is impossible to imagine his life lacking what music and painting have bestowed upon him. His artistic perceptions are, however, characteristically independent and original. He listens with his own ears and looks with his own eyes; that is how he likes to put it. . . .

Wolfgang Windelband, 'Dem Siebziger Arnold Berliner', *Die Naturwissenschaften*, vol. xx, 1932, 914. (One of the best-known portraits of Mahler was painted by Berliner's friend Fritz Erler.)

The 1891–92 season in Hamburg and Altona

. . . During the period from 1 September last year to 31 May this year, there were 278 performances at the Hamburg Municipal Theatre (including 7 matinees) and 270 in Altona. As regards the proportion of operas to plays, in Hamburg, with 201 performances, operas preponderated, while in Altona, with 203 performances (12 together with operas), plays were in the majority. New productions included 7 operas and 1 concert piece (*Te Deum*) as well as 34 in the sphere of drama (plays of all types). . . . In the sphere of opera, Richard Wagner again leads with 65 performances; moreover (in H. only) 10 pieces, including the new production of *Tannhäuser*, were put on 22 times. Mascagni's *Cavalleria rusticana* stood up well in its second year with 53 performances (34 in H., 19 in A.). Among the classics, Beethoven scored 7 performances (*Fidelio*, *Eroica*), Mozart 18, and Gluck 3 (*Orpheus*). The number of repeats of Bizet's *Carmen* (15) and Thomas's *Mignon* (12) again afford evidence of the popularity of these works.

Deutsche Bühnengenossenschaft, vol. xxi, no. 25, 19 June 1892, 239.

Mahler writes (in English) from London to Arnold Berliner

I shall only to give you the adresse of my residence, because I hope to hear by you upon your life and other circumstances in Hambourg.

I myself am too tired and excited and not able to write a letter.

Only, that I found the circumstances of orchestra here bader than thought and the cast better than hoped.

Next Wednesday is the performance of 'Siegfried' which God would bless.

Alvary: Siegfried, Grengg: Wotan, Sucher: Brünhilde, Lieban: Mime.

This is the most splendid cast I yet heard, and this is my only trust in these very careful time.

Please to narrate me about all and am

yours Mahler

I make greater progress in English as you can observe in this letter.

Undated letter, GMB, 125. (The first performance of *Siegfried* under Mahler was given in London on 8 June. The guest engagement was started with this part of Wagner's *Ring* because the tenor, Max Alvary, wished to make his début with a brilliant role. Karl Grengg and Rosa Sucher were guests from the Berlin Opera.)

Bernard Shaw at the London performance of 'Siegfried'

15 June 1892

Last Wednesday I was told that Siegfried was to be produced that evening at Covent Garden. I was incredulous, and asked my informant whether he did not mean Carmen, with Miss Zélie de Lussan in the title part. He said he thought not. I suggested Faust, Les Huguenots, even Die Meistersinger; but he stuck to his story: Siegfried, he said, was really and truly in the bills, and the house was sold out. Still doubting, I went to the box-office, where they confirmed the intelligence, except that they had just one stall left. I took it, and went away wondering and only half convinced. But when I reached the theatre in the evening a little late, fully expecting to find notices on the seats to the effect that Siegfried was unavoidably postponed, in consequence of the sudden indisposition of the dragon, and Philémon and Cavalleria substituted, I found the lights out and the belated stall-holders wandering like ghosts through the gloom in search of their numbers, helped only by the glimmer from the huge orchestra and some faint daylight from the ventilators. . . .

I think it will not be disputed that the Covent Garden orchestra, if it had half the opportunities of the German one, could handle the score of Siegfried not only with much greater distinction of tone and consequent variety of effect, but also with a more delicate and finished execution of the phrases which make up the mosaic of leading-motives, and with a wider range of gradation from *pianissimo* to *fortissimo* than Herr Mahler's band achieved, excellent in many respects as its performance certainly was. This is no mere conjecture: we have already heard the Siegfried blacksmith music and forest music played by our own orchestras in concert selections better than it was played on Wednesday last. . . .

The impression created by the performance was extraordinary, the gallery cheering wildly at the end of each act. Everybody was delighted with the change from the tailor-made operatic tenor in velvet and tights to the wild young hero who forges his own weapons and tans his own coat and buskins. We all breathed that vast orchestral atmosphere of fire, air, earth, and water, with unbounded relief and invigoration; and I doubt if half-a-dozen people in the house were troubled with the critical reflections which occurred to me whenever the orchestra took a particularly rough spin over exquisitely delicate ground, as in the scene between Wotan and Erda. It is not to be doubted that all the women found Brynhild an improvement on Carmen and Co.

I say nothing of the great drama of world-forces which the Nibelung story symbolizes, because I must not pretend that the Covent Garden performance was judged on that ground; but considering how very large a proportion of the audience was still seated when the curtain came down at half-past twelve, I think it is fair to assume that the people to whom Wotan is nothing but an unmitigated bore were in a minority.

Bernard Shaw, *Music in London 1890–94*, London 1931, ii, 118 sqq. (Shaw was under a misapprehension: Mahler was conducting an English orchestra which was evidently supplemented by a few German players.)

Paul Dukas recalls Mahler's performance of 'Fidelio' in London

. . . One of the most wonderful musical memories of my life is of a performance of *Fidelio* in London, in the course of which he [Mahler] conducted the *Leonora* Overture No. 3, interpreting Beethoven's genius so marvellously that I had the feeling of being present at the original creation of this sublime work.

PST 2, 81. (Paul Dukas, 1865–1935, French composer, was at that time also a music critic.)

Mahler to Friedrich Löhr, on the cholera epidemic

What a terrible calamity in Hamburg! It is frightful; how it will affect me I don't yet know! The theatre is to reopen on the 16th – I have not yet made up my mind! Shall I go or not? – Oh well, perhaps time (i.e. the 16th) will provide the answer!

Undated letter from Berchtesgaden, August 1892, GMB, 98.

The cholera epidemic is discussed by the Berlin Medical Association

. . .Professor Dr Virchow, Government Medical Officer, who opened and chaired the meeting . . . then commented that, as before, the cholera had been brought into Germany from outside. According to a statement prepared by the Imperial Health Department, the disease first appeared in Hamburg on 18 August, with 16 people affected and 2 deaths, and then increasingly took hold. The peak occurred on 27 August, on which day 684 cases were recorded.

Hamburgischer Correspondent, 8 September 1892, evening edn.

Beginning of Mahler's enmity with Pollini

Mahler, seized with fear of cholera – in such human matters he was by no means a hero! – had not returned to Hamburg from his summer vacation at the time required by his contract; his presence there was urgently needed for work at the theatre, scheduling and programme planning. Mahler was thus in breach of contract, and found himself in the position of having to pay a penalty of 12,000 marks to Pollini, which would have swallowed up the whole of his annual salary as resident Conductor. For Mahler, who had no resources of his own, such a sum would have been impossible at that time. In the event, the trouble was . . . settled by the mediation of a friend. But from that day on Mahler hated and detested his Director; and Pollini in turn became set in an attitude of spiteful hostility towards his Conductor; this antagonism assumed more and more distressing forms in the years that followed.

Ferdinand Pfohl, 'Mahler und Nikisch', in *Jahrhundertfeier des Hamburger Stadttheaters*, Hamburg 1927, 82.

Bülow excuses himself from conducting Mahler's songs

My many, and far from superficial, attempts to find my way, mentally and emotionally, into the very special style of the songs which you kindly sent me have been so unsuccessful that I find myself unable to take the responsibility, either to the composer or to the singer, for the performance of these songs at the concert on 7 November. In consequence of this conviction, I have begged Concert Director Wolff to approach you with the request that you should personally rehearse and conduct your compositions.

Marie von Bülow, *Hans von Bülow in Leben und Wort*, Stuttgart 1925, 176.

Mahler to his sister Justine in Vienna

. . . So [Amalie] Joachim stood up to Bülow and put my *Humoresken* on the programme for the second concert. Herr v. Bülow was again kind enough to refuse to accept them, on account of their 'very special style'. Just another really friendly encouragement to joyful creativeness? . . .

Alfred Rosé, 'Gustav Mahler und Hans von Bülow', *Neues Wiener Journal*, 23

September 1928, EV. (Amalie Joachim, contralto, primarily a concert singer. The *Humoresken* referred to were *Der Schildwache Nachtlied* ['The Sentry's Serenade'] and *Verlor'ne Müh* ['Wasted Endeavour'], based on texts from *Des Knaben Wunderhorn*. Amalie Joachim sang both songs at a Berlin Philharmonic Concert on 12 December 1892.)

Mahler takes on the fifth Bülow concert

In the 1892–93 season Bülow conducted for the last time. This was the tenth concert. The fifth had been conducted by Gustav Mahler, the sixth and seventh by Erdmannsdörfer, the eighth by Rubinstein, and the ninth by Muck. Continuing illness had prevented Bülow from taking the intervening concerts. His last concert, on 20 March 1893, was again devoted to the works of Beethoven and ended, as so often, with the *Eroica*. Sadly, the wish to be able to welcome Bülow back again at the head of the Subscription Concerts, introduced as a permanent feature of our artistic life as far back as 1 November 1886 by the Hermann Wolff Concert Management of Berlin, was not to be realized.

Emil Krause, 'Hamburg als Musikstadt', notes and reminiscences, typescript with ms. additions, 209–10, Staatsarchiv Hamburg. (The concert that Mahler conducted in place of Bülow took place on 12 December 1892, the same day on which Amalie Joachim sang Mahler's *Humoresken* in Berlin.)

Mahler describes his excessive work-load

. . . It's incredible, the amount I am conducting here. Just for fun I'll tell you my programme for the current two weeks:
Monday 16   *L'Amico Fritz* (first performance)
Tuesday (today)   *Siegfried*
Wednesday 18   *L'Amico Fritz*
Friday 20   *Tristan and Isolde*
Sunday 22   *L'Amico Fritz*
Monday 23   *Fidelio*
Tuesday 24   *Magic Flute*
Wednesday 25   *Lohengrin*
Thursday 26   *Yolanta* (opera by Tchaikowsky)
Friday 27   *Valkyrie*
Saturday 28   *L'Amico Fritz*
Monday 30   *Der Widerspenstigen Zähmung* (opera by Götz)
Tuesday   *L'Amico Fritz*!
So there are only *3 free evenings*, all told . . .
I conducted the Bülow concert here as substitute for the sick Master. Among other items I conducted the C minor! – Just imagine, I was reprimanded by some of the local critics in the most *indecent* manner, like a schoolboy, for my 'interpretation'. . . .

From an undated letter to Ödön von Mihalovich, 17 January 1893, ms., LFZ. (By 'the C minor' Mahler means Beethoven's Fifth Symphony.)

Revision of the First Symphony

When Gustav Mahler was working on his First Symphony, he often played me the gist of the preliminary sketches and movements just completed. He was frantically seeking a grand and striking title for this, his first symphony: 'I implore you, find me a name for the symphony!' I said to him, 'Just call it "Nature Symphony" or something of the sort, and for the third movement add the marking: "Funeral March in the Manner of Callot", because it is extremely strange: grotesque, bizarre, a fantastic spectacle. . . .' He hesitated, however, because he did not possess the *Fantasiestücke in Callots Manier* [by E. T. A. Hoffmann]. That very same day, by chance, I saw in the window of a bookshop a fine edition of these famous *Fantasies*; I bought it and took it to him.

A few days later Mahler told me he had at last found an appropriate title for his symphony: 'I shall call it *Titan*.'   123, 124

Ferdinand Pfohl, *Gustav Mahler*, Hamburg 1973, 17. (What Pfohl describes was a revision of the First Symphony. The finale carries the note, 'revised 19 January 1893' in Mahler's writing, and at the end of the Scherzo the indication 'Renovatum, 27 January 1893'; the second movement was revised in August 1893. At the performances in 1893 and 1894 Mahler used the title *Titan* for the First Symphony; and the fourth movement, following Pfohl's advice, he called 'Funeral March in the Manner of Callot'.)

Title-page of the First Symphony. Ms., Osborn Collection, Yale University, New Haven, Conn.

Visiting-card with ms. invitation. '*Kapellmeister* Gustav Mahler offers many thanks and would like to know whether Herr Zinne would care to join him, Dr Berliner and perhaps Sichel after the performance. If so he requests that he should await him after the performance at the stage door.' Ms., Hamburger Öffentliche Bücherhallen, Archiv der Musikbücherei.

Wilhelm Zinne made the following note in pencil on the card: 'Relates to the first performance of Bruckner's D minor Mass, for which he used my score. Z.' The undated invitation was written either on the day of the performance – 31 March 1893 – or shortly before.

Justine Mahler discovers a summer retreat, Steinbach am Attersee

In May of this year [1893], as always, Justine Mahler looked for a summer place for her brother that would be in a beautiful country setting, far from the turmoil of the crowds, and above all very peaceful; it was during the holidays that he worked hardest at his composing. They finally found Steinbach, which not only satisfied all these requirements as well as being cheap (which was also very important) but in addition was situated just over the lake from Nussdorf, where Mahler's friends Victor Adler with his family and Engelbert Pernerstorfer spent the summer. Five rooms were rented at the inn. Mahler, his sisters

Justine and Emma, and Natalie Bauer-Lechner, a long-standing friend of the family, distributed themselves among these very primitively furnished rooms. Any furniture that they needed was simply knocked up from rough wood and covered with cheap cretonne. A leather sofa, which was moved from one room to another as required, was the showpiece of the furnishings. The Bösendorfer company placed a baby-grand piano at his disposal. With their own kitchen and private dining-room, Gustav Mahler and his sisters, as well as their visitors, who often stayed for a considerable time, were able to feel at home. There were no other residents at the inn; at most there were occasional tourists.

The Mahlers moved in during June 1893, and the field, glowing with the full splendour of blossoming wild flowers, on which Mahler gazed through his window, gave him the idea of building a little summerhouse to work in at its lake end. This was done in the following summer, 1894.

Alfred Rosé, 'Intimes aus Gustav Mahlers Sturm- und Drangperiode', *Neues Wiener Journal*, 19 August 1928, EV. (Alfred Rosé visited the Attersee in the summer of 1928 with his mother, Mahler's sister Justine Rosé-Mahler, and in this article he relates her memories.)

Natalie Bauer-Lechner's memories of Steinbach in July and August 1893

The Andante of the Second Symphony:
'That's a marvellously beautiful couple of themes I picked up today from the sketch for the Andante of my Second Symphony; God willing, I hope to complete it here, as well as the Scherzo,' said Mahler, who, after a session of composing, was quite carried away for some time afterwards and confronted his own affairs like a stranger: 'The two little sheets I wrote them on, back in Leipzig, when I conducted the *Pintos* there, have been worrying me so, and not without justification, as I now see. For there is a great wide stream of melody gushing through them; the one intertwined with the other, and all the time putting out new branches with inexhaustible abundance and variety, culminating in a tremendously intricate pattern. And how delicately the lovely thing develops out of its own riches – if you could follow that it would give you a lot of pleasure!

'And that's the only way to create anything: wholeheartedly. It's no good playing around with a little scrap of theme, varying it and fuguing it and having to spin it out for God knows how long so as to get a movement out of it. I can't bear the economical method: it all has to be there, enough and to spare, and it has to keep pouring out all the time, if it's going to be worth anything.'

Mahler completed his Andante in seven days, and said himself that he had reason to be pleased with it.

The mystery of creation:
'Today', Mahler told me, 'I went through the Scherzo of my Second Symphony again; I haven't looked at it since I first wrote it, and it absolutely amazed me. It's a remarkable, fearful, great piece! I didn't realize this when I was composing it.

'Creative activity and the genesis of a work are mystical from start to finish, since one acts unconsciously, as if prompted from outside, and then one can hardly conceive how the result has come into being. In fact I often feel like the blind hen who finds a grain of corn.

'But, more rarely than with whole movements or works, this instinctive mysterious force appears with individual passages, and then it's the most difficult and the most significant ones. Generally it's those that I don't want to attack directly, those I'd like to dodge around, and which nevertheless hold me fast and finally force their way to the right expression.

'This is what has just happened to me in the Scherzo, with one passage which I had already given up and cut out, but then after all I included it on an inserted sheet. And now I can see that it is the most essential, the most powerful passage of the whole thing. . . .'

NBL, 7, 8–9.

Mahler invites the critic Davidsohn to Hamburg to hear the First Symphony

Hamburg, 18 October 1893

On the 27th of this month an orchestral concert is to be held here at which, in addition to the performance of a big orchestral work, six of my *Humoresken* – which you already know – will be sung (by Bulss together with Frau Schuch from Dresden).

Nothing would be more important for me than the presence at this concert of a representative of the Berlin press, and nothing would give me more heartfelt pleasure than to know that you, esteemed Sir, were among the auditors – and judges. . . .

Please do not be misled by the admitted fact that up to now all my works have been consistently turned down by the professional orchestral concert conductors on account of the 'very special character' of my compositions, and I had even given up the idea that I should ever (at least in my lifetime) be performed in public.

Now at last I have the opportunity; nevertheless I am aware that I shall encounter strong opposition (and especially among the press) which could, in unfavourable circumstances, easily have the effect of blocking my access to the public, perhaps for years ahead. . . .

Neues Wiener Journal, 21 June 1923, EV. (The orchestral work referred to was the revised version of the First Symphony, entitled *Titan*. Also at this concert, six of the *Wunderhorn* songs were performed.)

Ferdinand Pfohl on Mahler's rehearsal of the First Symphony

125   The Ludwig Concert Hall was situated at the St Pauli Gate, at the entrance to the Reeperbahn, the international street of amusements. The vast, rambling building contained a magnificent concert hall capable of holding an audience of at least 1,500, if not more. It was the home of the popular orchestral concerts. The resident orchestra there was the Laube Orchestra, a capable orchestral society directed by a former military band conductor, Julius Laube, and supported from his pocket. . . . The Hamburg Philharmonic Society employed his well-trained and technically capable orchestra for their Society concerts – they had no choice, since there was no other concert orchestra in Hamburg. . . .

To give a better idea of the popular character and pattern of the concerts in the Ludwig Concert Hall, it should be explained that there were regular Wednesday concerts at which classical programmes alternated with modern evenings, standard works of orchestral instrumental music with the works of Tchaikowsky and of contemporary composers. . . .

The rehearsal began. In the calm of his demeanour, in the total concentration of his energy on artistic effect and in the intensity of his purpose, Mahler, up at the conductor's stand, looked like a figure of bronze. It was extraordinarily gripping and at the same time instructive to be there and appreciate Mahler's tremendously meticulous preparation; through all the development sections of his work he brought out the lines with sculptural clarity while conveying every emotional nuance of the music. First he ran his symphony straight through, then he praised the orchestra for the high standard of their sight-reading, after which he started on the real, strict study rehearsal, going into the smallest details of performance. Now it was the turn of Mahler the inexorable, whose approbation no orchestra had yet found it easy to win. Dozens of times he rapped to stop them, elucidated one passage or another for the players, and kept them to the most precise execution, as if for one of Beethoven's symphonies. For him there was no such thing as an easy work, whether his own or

somebody else's. He regarded all music, whatever its origin, as equally difficult.

When, in the transition to the finale, where the instruments of the orchestra burst out into a great, terrible cry, the kettledrum did not manage to reach the full strength of the fortissimo needed for its part, Mahler had the passage repeated several times. However, as the result still fell far below Mahler's requirements, the conductor-composer was seized with a fury; he jumped down from the conductor's stand into the orchestra, rushed at the kettledrum, snatched the sticks from the player's hands and began to play the passage himself, in person, to the amazement of the orchestra. He performed this feat, of a kind wholly unfamiliar to him, with total sureness and with thunderous, elemental force. This scene reached its peak of tension when the sticks suddenly flew out of his hands, as he attacked the instrument with furious force; bouncing off the skin of the drum, they whizzed through the air in a wide arc and landed in the middle of the orchestra. This moment was so overwhelming that the orchestra, and the few friends who had turned up for the rehearsal of the Symphony, broke out into loud applause. . . .

Ferdinand Pfohl, *Gustav Mahler*, Hamburg 1973, 50–51. (The performance had a great public success; Paul Bulss had to repeat the song *Rheinlegendchen*. Except for Ferdinand Pfohl, the critics were neutral or negative.)

In 1892 the publishers Schott in Mainz had published the   104 fourteen *Lieder und Gesänge* for voice and piano. In 1893 Mahler wished to have the *Wunderhorn* songs (at that time entitled *Humoresken*) also published, with orchestral accompaniment. At the Hamburg concert on 27 October 1893 Klementine Schuch-Proská sang three of these songs: *Das himmlische Leben*, *Verlor'ne Müh'*, and *Wer hat dies Liedel*   105, 106 *erdacht?* At the same concert Paul Bulss sang three more songs: *Der Schildwache Nachtlied*, *Trost in Unglück*, *Rheinlegendchen*. On 13 November 1893 Bulss sang the same songs at a spa concert at Wiesbaden, with Mahler conducting. Shortly afterwards Mahler heard from Schott that they had decided not to publish the *Humoresken*. The following letter relates to this decision.

Mahler on Schott's rejection of the 'Humoresken'

The enclosed letter, which I have just received from Dr Strecker, seems to me sufficiently interesting to send you as it stands. It gives you the last word on this business for the present. *What now?* Perhaps you have an idea? (i.e. do you know a publisher who would be less excessively cautious than our friend Strecker?) Some parts of this letter which you may not be able to understand refer to a performance of the three *Humoresken* in Wiesbaden, at a spa concert. I myself conducted. The public was friendly (even called me back once). As I am not familiar with the public there, I have no yardstick for rating the applause. Just because *I Pagliacci*, a piece by now thoroughly familiar and often enough presented to the public, had to be *repeated*, Dr Strecker feels the voice of God has spoken. Now my conversation with him, as well as his present letter, is of the greatest interest as evidence of a new kind of criticism of the arts, not previously encountered by me: the *publisher's point of view*.

One thing, however, I have already seen! A public which does not know me personally, or anything about *my music*, will always in the first place simply be taken by surprise, and I know that the reason is to be found not in any '*excessive profundity*', but *only*, surely, in the *austerity* and *absence of ornamentation* in the style. . . .

Undated letter from Mahler to an unknown addressee, ms., Samuel Schweizer, Alchenflüh. (Ludwig Strecker, 1853–1943, was head of the publishing firm B. Schotts Söhne in Mainz. Leoncavallo's opera *I Pagliacci* acquired great popularity soon after its original performance in Milan on 21 May 1892.)

100
J.B. Foerster calls on Mahler in the Fröbelstrasse

After repeated knocking and waiting, I entered a poky room. Mahler was not there. I saw a bed, over which hung a faded laurel wreath. The withered laurel already had that delicate patina harmonizing beautifully with the olive green ribbon. I went closer and read on the ribbon, printed in dull gold, the inscription: 'To the Pygmalion of the Hamburg Opera – Hans von Bülow'. Back at home, I collected my new impressions, telling my wife everything. . . . I saw the narrow bedroom again, and the furniture in the study, where the grand piano, the bookcase and the writing-desk caught the eye. The piano stood in the middle of the room, and was almost covered with music. Against the wall at one side was an upright piano, which Mahler preferred to use, and on which the score of a cantata by J.S. Bach stood open. The choice of pictures was also interesting. I saw none of the usual family portraits, only a fine reproduction of Dürer's *Melancholy*; a photograph of a picture previously unknown to me, *St Antony of Padua Preaching to the Fish*; and lastly a copy of Giorgione's [*sic*] famous panel: a monk, just touching the keyboard of an instrument, and producing a sound of harmony. The expression on the face of the monk is wonderfully characterized, and I understood Mahler when he once said to me: 'This is a picture I could compose for ever'. . . .

Our first conversations naturally concerned the adored Lady Musica, and J.S. Bach was the hero. As I could see a Bach cantata was open on the piano, I must have made some remark about the great music director of the famous old St Thomas's Church in Leipzig, and Mahler spoke of his great admiration of Bach's genius, at the same time regretting that the cantatas in particular receive far too little attention, and have thus remained practically unknown. . . .

'Here in this Castalian fount I wash away all the grime of the theatre,' he once said. As I have said, he often had good reason to do so, for Pollini, although he knew the value of Mahler's judgment, accepted many scores for performance which had not passed through Mahler's hands before, and which those hands touched only with disgust. . . .

Even then, at the beginning of our friendly relations, I observed that Mahler saw R. Strauss as his only rival; he got hold of every one of his scores, which were just being brought out in rapid succession by J. Aibl in Munich. . . .

JBFPP, 9 and 16 April 1922.

Richard Strauss writes to his parents from Hamburg

Hamburg, Streich Hotel, Monday, 22 January 1894

. . . I am spending a lot of time with Mahler, who is very charming and has conducted a splendid performance of *The Bartered Bride*, and with a Dr Behn; they are spoiling me with
132
their hospitality. I have called on Bülow twice; the second time he made his appearance and sat with us for an hour. He is of course very sad and weak, but Egypt, where he is going in ten days' time, may restore his health. . . .

Richard Strauss, *Briefe an die Eltern*, Zürich 1954, 193–94. (Dr Hermann Behn, 1859–1927, lawyer and composer, a pupil of Bruckner's, was a friend of Mahler's and a promoter of his work. Bülow died in Cairo on 12 February 1894.)

110
Negotiations (in English) for a second guest appearance in London

Dear Sir Augustus!

I suppose, You prepare a German opera first rate. In this case I am with plaesure to your disposition. Please to communicate me exactly the circumstances of your enterprise – (the combination of the orchestra, of the company you dispose, and about the 'Repertoir' you intend) – and I hope, we shall soon agree together.

My terms are: 50£ for week and voyage and other expenses free. Excuse, please, my bad Englisch. It is a pitty – I have all

vergotten since my last sejourn in England. I hope, to see you soon again Yours sincerly Gustav Mahler.

Ms. draft of letter, Oswald Brod Collection. (The ms. carries the following note signed by Behn: 'Draft for a letter to Sir Augustus Harris in London, written by *Kapellm.* Gustav Mahler at my writing-desk on 4 March 1894.' The negotiations came to nothing.)

Mahler to his sister Justine, on the funeral ceremony for Bülow

29 March 1894

. . . At last the great day has come. The funeral ceremonies will last from 9 o'clock in the morning until about 5 o'clock (when the funeral reception will be held at B.'s). All I hope is that the mourning ladies do not set up a sort of Bülow Museum (and perhaps exhibit his overnight kit and laundry bills). The things people do with a sick or dead man like Bülow; the young ones and the living are left to struggle along. . . .

Alfred Rosé, 'Gustav Mahler und Hans von Bülow', *Neues Wiener Journal*, 23 September 1928, EV.

J.B. Foerster on the idea for the finale of the Second Symphony

It began to look as if the Symphony would remain a torso. Mahler wrapped himself in silence, and I felt it would be tactful to make no reference to his unfinished work.

Then, one day, the Hamburg papers carried the unexpected tidings of the death of Hans von Bülow. The news came from Cairo. . . .

I joined Mahler in mourning Bülow: the *Totenfeier* was played in his honour and in his memory, though only for the two of us and without other witnesses; but our hearts were full of gratitude for this great artist. . . .

Soon afterwards we received the information that Bülow's body was to be brought to Hamburg and buried at Ohlsdorf. After six weeks the ship arrived at Hamburg Free Port, and the Senate of the Free Hanseatic City invited all the intelligentsia to the 'Funeral Ceremony for Dr Hans von Bülow' in the venerable Church of St Michael.
130
It was ten o'clock in the morning on 29 March 1894 when the simple coffin in which Bülow found his last resting-place was borne into the church. . . . The programme of the funeral service was as follows: Organ Prelude by J.S. Bach, followed by Bach's Chorale from the *St Matthew Passion*, 'When I depart . . .', then readings from Holy Scripture and singing by the St Michael's Church boys' choir (Chorale from Klopstock's *Messias*: 'Arise, arise, my dust, after your brief repose'). Then Senior Pastor Behrmann spoke the memorial oration, and the church service concluded with Bach's Chorale from the *St John Passion*, 'Rest well, ye precious remains . . .'.

Rise up again, yea, thy dust shall rise up again after its brief repose; He who created thee shall grant thee eternal life. Hallelujah!

The children's voices! They rang out like the voices of angels, like a prayer holding within it a sweet sense of hope; and on their wings they bore wondrous power, solace, enchantment, and unspoken grief. . . .

The funeral procession started. Siegfried Wagner, Bülow's daughter Frau Thode, and her husband Professor Henry Thode, represented the family. When the funeral procession reached the Municipal Theatre, where the great master-conductor had so often excited the admiration of his audience, he was greeted by the mournful tones of Wagner's funeral march from *The Twilight of the Gods*. . . .

Even at the Municipal Theatre I did not see Mahler. However, by midday I could delay no longer; as if under the influence of a magic power, full of my own emotions and in a state of inexplicable excitement, I hastened to him. I open the door of the study and see him at the writing-desk, pen in hand, a little bent over the score. I remain standing in the doorway, Mahler suddenly turns round, sees me, and cried, 'Foerster, I've got it!'

And I, as if inspired, understand what he means, and reply: 'Rise up again, yea rise up again!' ...

Amazed and startled, Mahler stares at me: I had divined and uttered his inmost thoughts: Klopstock's poem would be the inspiration and the foundation of the final movement. This, then, was the origin of the last movement of the Second Symphony, begun on that memorable day of Hans von Bülow's funeral in Hamburg.

131

JBFPP, 7 May 1922.

Postcard to Arnold Berliner from Steinbach am Attersee

122 *I have got down to work!* That is the main thing! My summer-house (in the meadow), just built, an *ideal* place for me! Not a sound for miles around! Surrounded by flowers and birds (which I do not hear, but only see). I should be very glad to have Helmholtz's talk. Do you have any news of the Behns? Please give them my best regards! ...

Undated card, postmarked Weissenbach 15 January 1894, ms., BST. (Hermann von Helmholtz, 1821–94, German physicist. Mahler's daughter Anna remembers that her father's library contained many volumes of Helmholtz's works.)

Mahler tells his brother Otto of the completion of the Second Symphony

Dear O., This is to announce the happy arrival of a healthy, bouncing last movement. Father and infant doing as well as can be expected, the latter not yet out of danger. It has been christened with the name: *Lux lucet in tenebris*. Silent sympathy is requested. No flowers by request.

Other gifts will, however, be acceptable.

Yours, G.

Ms., ÖNB-HS. (The Latin motto means 'Light shines in the darkness.')

Bruno Walter on his first impressions of Mahler in 1894

... And now he was standing there in person in the theatre office as I emerged from my introductory call on Pollini: pale, thin, of small stature, with a long head, his high forehead framed in jet-black hair, keen eyes behind spectacles, with lines of suffering and humour in a face that exhibited, when he talked to someone, the most amazing changes of expression. ...

141

My next memory of him recalls him at the rehearsal of *Hänsel und Gretel*, the new production then in preparation at the Hamburg Opera. Never before had I encountered such an intense personality or dreamed how a sharp, pointed word, an imperious gesture, a concentration of will-power, could throw others into anxiety and terror and force them to blind obedience. A weak accompanist at the piano provoked Mahler to impatience: suddenly – oh what happiness! – he saw me, a forbidden spectator standing in the wings, and asked whether I had enough confidence to accompany the opera – till then unknown to me – at sight. He responded to my haughty 'Of course!' with an amused smile and the invitation to replace our unfortunate colleague, who was dismissed with a wave of the hand. In the forest scene, the gradation of the repeated echo as sung did not satisfy him; Mahler turned to me and said: 'I expect you know what it is like in the forest – just rehearse the echo for me.' Thus the first rehearsal gave me right away a complete impression of Mahler's style as a per-forming artist: guiding and commanding, absorbed in the work, sure of his objective, vehement and harsh when faced with poor execution, but kindly, open-hearted, sympathetic, where he scented talent and enthusiasm.

Bruno Walter, *Gustav Mahler*, Vienna 1936, 11–12.

The Hamburg concert season 1894–95

The 1894–95 season included eight concerts under Mahler, with the collaboration of top-class soloists, as before. The core of the instrumentalists was formed by thirty-one players from the Mohrbutter Orchestra, working together with the artists employed previously. Mahler inspired the players under his control in a most praiseworthy manner and achieved great success in all the concerts. The performance of Beethoven's Ninth on 11 March 1895 was particularly memorable, when the Bach Society provided the chorus. The soloists were Josefine von Artner, a member of the Theatre company, the concert singer Anna Bünz, Nicolo Doerter and Hermann Gausche. Mahler's interpretation was brilliant; in its sub-jective way, it brought out much that had gone unperceived before. It was an almost illustrative rendering, a 'painting' [*Mahlerei*] in the widest sense. That there were objections to the additions made by Mahler is understandable. These – the trombones and the introduction of instruments not used by Beethoven in the first movement, the trumpet parts in some passages of the Scherzo, the three bars omitted in the Scherzo, the elimination of an important repeat, the banal use of the piccolo in the Scherzo, many other additions for reinforcing, e.g. E flat clarinet etc., and then the illustrative band music (offstage) at the B flat tenor solo with men's chorus in the finale, and much besides – produced such an inartistic effect that everybody was forced to recognize the arbitrariness of this subjective interpretation. People were of course not un-prepared for such peculiarities, having in mind the improve-ments which Mahler had introduced in the score of the Seventh (22 October 1894) and which he considered to be right! But nobody would have thought it possible that his sub-jective post-creation would go as far as absolute musical 'illustration' in the Ninth. ...

Emil Krause, 'Hamburg als Musikstadt, Aufzeichnungen und Erinnerungen', typescript with ms. supplementary notes, Staatsarchiv Hamburg.

J. B. Foerster on Mahler's concert season

It was during the 1894–95 season in Hamburg that Mahler conducted the eight subscription concerts – a season which I was able to enjoy also. The programmes clearly demonstrated Mahler's preferences. Beethoven led the field with the Pastoral Symphony, the Ninth Symphony, and the overture *The Consecration of the House*; next came Schubert with his Great C major Symphony. Schumann was represented by the youth-fully gay B flat major Symphony, and Berlioz by the Fantastic Symphony and *Roman Carnival*. Nor was Richard Wagner neglected ... and Bruckner, Mahler's teacher, was of course in the programme; Mahler brought out the sweetly-oppressive yearning of his Romantic Symphony with intense emotion.

Although, as I have said, the effect of Mahler's inter-pretation on all discerning auditors was deep and decided, and in many cases unique and unforgettable, nevertheless his efforts did not receive the desired and hoped-for approbation of the critics, whose opinions were divided and who regarded Mahler simply as a theatre conductor of genius. Without the stage and the footlights, he was thought to be not in his proper element. And thus the unexpected again happened, and after a single season Mahler was replaced at the Hamburg Philhar-monic by Felix Weingartner.

I shall never forget those performances conducted by Mahler, especially those of the Beethoven, Berlioz and Bruckner symphonies; it was then that I encountered Bruckner's symphonic music for the second time. The idio-syncratic but always deliberate and positively motivated modi-fications of tempo, the slight re-scorings, and the shifting of part of the orchestra 'behind the scenes' in the finale of the Ninth, were all external changes decided on by Mahler after mature consideration and careful weighing-up of all the circumstances. ...

JBFPP, 30 April 1922.

Bruno Walter on Mahler, Dostoyevsky and other literature

'Who is right, Alyosha or Ivan?' was the question put to me by Emma, Mahler's younger sister, during one of my visits; and when I looked surprised, she explained that she was talking about the chapter in Dostoyevsky's *Brothers Karamazov* entitled 'The brothers become acquainted', with which her brother was so passionately involved that she had assumed he would have spoken to me about it. This conversation between Ivan and Alyosha does in fact indicate explicitly a state of mind similar to Mahler's in his psychic distress, his suffering for the suffering in the world, and his search for solace and exaltation; it encompasses everything that Mahler thought, said, read and composed on the questions of 'Whence? For what purpose? Whither?' He experienced moments of calm belief, and was fond of quoting Hans the Stonebreaker's words from Anzengruber's courageous play *Die Kreuzelschreiber*: 'Nothing can happen to you'. But the atmosphere of his being was stormy and incalculable, and his happy, childlike smile vanished without any visible cause before a wave of unrestrained, despairing sorrow. Through him I came to Dostoyevsky, who quickly took hold of my mind; Mahler also inspired me with an interest in Nietzsche, with whose *Also Sprach Zarathustra* he was just then much occupied; and when he learned of my liking for philosophy he gave me Schopenhauer's works, at Christmas 1894, thus opening for me the door to a world which I have never lost sight of since.

BWTV, 115–16. (The Zarathustra song *O Mensch! Gib acht!* found its way into Mahler's Third Symphony, which was strongly influenced by Nietzsche.)

Rehearsal of three movements of the Second Symphony

Yet the 'first performance' [Berlin, 4 March 1895] was, as regards the *Totenfeier*, Andante and Scherzo movements, not a true première, since this had taken place earlier, in 1894, at the little Konventgarten hall in Hamburg – and behind closed doors. An extremely narrow circle of intimate friends was invited one day to come and hear three movements of the new Symphony. The players of the Municipal Theatre Orchestra, who loved and admired the genius of their conductor, assembled at their desks in the morning. Mahler appeared, followed by the faithful Weidich, an elderly musician who was a member of the Municipal Theatre company. . . .

The rehearsal began. Mahler rapped for stops almost continuously and signalled to Weidich, who entered every change of the score in his note book, so as to be able to correct everything in the parts after the improvised concert. We heard only: 'Cellos in unison with bassoons – cut out oboes – double the flutes – harmony goes to the trombones', etc. Weidich soon had his note book full, some small changes were made immediately and were tried to see how they sounded; and then only followed a splendid performance of the three movements mentioned above, with no more interruptions by the conductor.

JBFPP, 14 May 1922.

Mahler on his prospects and wishes for the future

So: Up to now I am not included among the great stars of the universe. It is true that I have received some 'propositions' from agents to take on Richter's position – but this is just hot air. These gentlemen are just trying it on, they are not acting for anybody. I think you have hit the mark with your word *reservatio*. As things now stand in the world, my Jewishness blocks my entry into any Court Theatre. Neither Vienna, nor Berlin, nor Dresden, nor Munich is possible for me. That's how the wind blows everywhere at present. In my present peculiar (but not particularly miserable) mood, it doesn't worry me much. Believe me, I don't find our artistic way of

life at all alluring at this time. In the end, it is always and everywhere the same story of lying, thoroughly poisonous, dishonourable behaviour.

Suppose I came to Vienna. With my way of going about things, what would I find in Vienna? I would only need to have one try at instilling my interpretation of a Beethoven symphony into the illustrious, Richter-bred Philharmonic to come up against the bitterest opposition right away. After all, this has already happened to me *here*, where, thanks to the whole-hearted support of Brahms and Bülow, my position is uncontested.

What a storm I have to endure every time I try to escape from the perpetual routine and introduce something of my own for a change. There is just one thing I would like: to work in a small town where there is no 'tradition' and no guardians of the 'eternal laws of beauty', among ordinary simple people, for the satisfaction of myself and the very small circle of those capable of keeping up with me. If possible, no theatre and no 'repertoire'! But of course, as long as I have to pant after my dear brothers in their intrepid course, and until I have made some provision for my sisters, I have to keep on with my lucrative and profitable artistic activity. . . .

From an undated letter to Friedrich Löhr, Hamburg, end of 1894 or January 1895, GMB, 101 sqq. (Since the death of his parents in 1889, Mahler was not only looking after his two sisters, but was also taking care of the education and welfare of his brothers Otto and Alois. In this he was helped by his Vienna friends Friedrich Löhr, Emil Freund and Nina Hoffmann-Matscheko.)

Alma Mahler on the brothers Otto and Alois

Otto . . . a highly gifted musician, but lacking in seriousness and staying-power, was Mahler's firm favourite. He employed private tutors to make sure of getting him through his school career, and later obtained jobs for him as assistant répétiteur in small German towns, but these always turned out badly. Otto grumbled and was dissatisfied, always comparing himself with Mahler and Mahler's position, and finally committing suicide. . . .

Alois, the second, was sickly from birth (like all the children, including Gustav, he had inherited their mother's heart trouble), and must be considered as a fool rather than a dreamer. He had all sorts of ridiculous ideas. For example, he once hired an old horse and got a pair of riding-breeches made with one red and one blue leg: 'German man-at-arms'. Thus attired he rode all round the streets of Iglau, to the joy of the passers-by and the agonized shame of the family.

AM, 17.

Nina (Anna) Hoffmann, née Matscheko (1844–1914) was the author of the first monograph on Dostoyevsky in the German language. She did not simply base her work on the Russian literature already available, but visited Russia in 1897–98, and there made contact with Dostoyevsky's friends and his widow. Mahler's enthusiasm for Dostoyevsky, the 'poet of compassion', was greatly strengthened, if not actually initiated, through Nina Hoffmann's influence. In the social responsibility movement of the 1900 period Nina Hoffmann played an important part. She devoted the last years of her life to religious and theosophical studies. She was married to the painter Joseph Hoffmann (1831–1904), to whom Richard Wagner entrusted the design of the scenery for *The Ring* at the first Bayreuth Festival in 1876.

Friedrich Löhr on Nina Hoffmann and Otto Mahler

'Nina' was our dearest friend Frau Nina Hoffmann-Matscheko, the wife of the painter Joseph Hoffmann. Author of the book on Dostoyevsky (Berlin 1899) and of *Madame Guyon* (Jena 1911), she died on 10 October 1914. She became acquainted with Mahler through us, and she had for a time an extremely cordial and active association with him; she did a great deal to help him and his family. Mahler was not always disposed to treat her susceptible nature with due care – and the course of life tended to produce misunderstandings and entanglements; but when he was in the right mood they got on well together. Mahler told her a great deal about himself, and trusted her; thus she recalled with great agitation Mahler's visit to her one summer in the 1890s at Marienbad. . . .

[Otto Mahler], not yet twenty-two years old, put an end to his own unhappy young life. He had escaped from the fetters of compulsory study, but this sick mind, this no doubt pure, high-minded subjectiveness, totally shut in upon itself, had produced greater and greater alienation from the world, and even the musical talent so highly prized by his brother failed him when the time came to give an outlet to it. On 6 February 1895, at the home of his old friend Nina, he shot himself.

GMB, notes, 487.

Wilhelm Kienzl on Mahler's first concert in Berlin

At one of the Philharmonic symphony concerts directed by Richard Strauss, Gustav Mahler as a guest conducted the first three movements of his Second Symphony in C minor from the manuscript; it was, to the best of my knowledge, the first (partial) performance of this nowadays frequently played work. Mahler's achievements were at that time (he was still Conductor in Hamburg) far from generally recognized. The theme of the first movement, introduced with great weight in the basses and then broadening out, impressed me. In the course of the movement, all sorts of daring harmonic and instrumental strokes were noticeable, particularly one obstinately dissonant *fortissimo* passage in the brass. Richard Strauss, who was taking a rest from conducting during this number, had invited Muck and me to sit down in an unoccupied box and enjoy Mahler's work together. When this particular brass passage occurred Strauss, sitting on my left, turned to me wide-eyed with enthusiasm: *'Believe me, there are no limits to musical expression!'* At the same time Muck, on my right, twisted his face into an *unmistakable* expression of horror, and the single word *'Frightful!'* escaped through his clenched teeth. I, the 'man in the middle', thus had a good opportunity to observe the opposite effects of art on differently endowed natures, and the paramount subjectivity of all appreciation of art.

Wilhelm Kienzl, *Meine Lebenswanderung*, Stuttgart 1926, 143. (The concert took place in Berlin on 4 March 1895.)

Chamber-music evenings in the Parkallee

In the new apartment in the Parkallee a new life really began. Enclosed within the comfort of his four quiet walls, Mahler felt himself secure, and in this peaceful haven, after the day's efforts, he enjoyed having guests in the evenings. When his week's programme permitted, he invited a few special friends, and within this enthusiastic circle he forgot all the sombre and painful events which time had brought him.

Those moving and beautiful evenings in the Parkallee! The consecrating influence of music was naturally present. . . .

At the piano was Mahler. The programmes were always chosen from the works of the classical composers; the lion's share went to Beethoven, Mozart and Schubert, but Schumann's and Mendelssohn's chamber works were also often played. Now and then, when an opera was being performed at the Municipal Theatre with a small orchestra, the master of the house invited a few other musicians and there were performances of quintets and sextets, and even on one occasion Beethoven's E flat major Septet.

Mahler was a splendid pianist. There was no virtuosity about his playing; naturally, he did not devote to his technique either any special attention or the necessary time, yet his tone was faultlessly balanced, his touch vigorous and yet delicate, and the execution ravishing in expression and feeling.

JBFPP, 18 June 1922. (During the 1894–95 season Mahler moved to Parkallee 12, where he had a large third-floor apartment in which his sisters Justine and Emma also came to live.)

In the spring of 1895 Mahler took up cycling. Bicycles had been manufactured in Germany since 1881, and soon afterwards clubs had been established in Hamburg to popularize the new sport. In April and May 1895 Mahler had some correspondence with Wilhelm Zinne, the critic friend of Bruckner, in which he mentioned his attempts at cycling. This correspondence reveals something of Mahler's otherwise little documented humorous aspect.

Report to the critic Zinne on cycling

I start off tomorrow evening. In case I do not see you again, here's to a happy get-together after the holidays. There is universal admiration of me on my cycle. I seem to be absolutely born for the *Rad* [cycle], and I'm sure to be appointed to the *Geheimrad* [*Geheimrat*, Privy Council] some time.

I've already reached the stage that all the horses avoid me, but I'm still not good at *ringing my bell*; at this point I often alight (very rapidly). I can't bring myself to race past a cab just like that, though they do really deserve it, they always stay in the middle of the road without considering that for such a dynamic cyclist all roads are too narrow.

So, all (still just) hale!
Your most devoted
Gustav Mahler,
Fahr-Radius
and Road Diameter.

Undated letter to Wilhelm Zinne, Hamburg, end of May 1895, ms., Hamburger Öffentliche Büchereien, Archiv der Musikbücherei.

Natalie Bauer-Lechner on the joys of cycling

How wonderfully independent is the cyclist! He needs no stable or groom, has no worry about the temper or the fluctuating strength of a living creature, and he can even be a poor devil owning not a penny. Yes, cycling would be perfect, if it were not that rain and bad roads make things so frightfully, mercilessly difficult. But when heaven smiles on us there is nothing more rewarding and delightful than flying through enchanting places on the little iron horse with its giant strides, and cooling yourself on a hot day, as with thousands of fans, just by the rapid motion. But when the way lies through shady forest paths, or in the depth of a valley, by a cool river-bank under the mountainside, or along the shore of some sparkling lake inviting one to bathe – and to dive into the waves after a cycle run is the epitome of poetry and enchantment! – then the senses are often overwhelmed by bliss, it is all too marvellous, enough to excite the envy of the gods!

Natalie Bauer-Lechner, *Fragmente*, Vienna 1907, 187. (During the summer vacation at Steinbach, Natalie Bauer-Lechner was Mahler's cycling companion.)

The genesis of the Third Symphony, at Steinbach am Attersee

Almost before he had arrived, Mahler got to work on his Third Symphony. 'This one, I hope, will bring me applause and money,' he said to me jokingly on one of the early days, 'for *this* is humour and gaiety, an enormous laugh at the whole world.' But by the next day he had already changed his tune: 'You know, there's no money to be earned from the Third either! Its gaiety is not going to be understood or appreciated: it's the gaiety that soars *above* the world of the First and Second, with their conflict and pain, and it can exist only as the product of that world.

'It's not really appropriate to call it a symphony, for it doesn't stick to the traditional form at all. But "symphony" means to me building a world with all the resources of the available techniques. The content, continually new and changing, determines its own form. This being so, I must always first learn again to re-create my medium of expression even though I can, I believe, now consider myself completely master of the technique.'

Coming straight from his work, all emotional and excited, Mahler said to me while we were taking a walk: 'That was how I cut the Gordian knot, by the idea of introducing language and human voices into my Second Symphony, where I needed them to make myself understood. A pity I didn't have this in my First! However, I shan't hesitate in the Third, I shall use two poems from *Des Knaben Wunderhorn* and a glorious poem by Nietzsche as the basis for the songs in the short movements.

'"Summer comes in" will be the prologue. For this I need a military band, to achieve the crude effect of the arrival of my martial hero. It will really be as if the garrison band were marching in. You get a rabble hanging around at such a time which you never catch sight of otherwise.

'Naturally, there has to be a struggle with the adversary, Winter; but he is easily vanquished, and Summer, in the fullness of power, gains the undisputed mastery. This movement, as introduction, will be kept humorous, even grotesque.

135 'The titles of the consecutive parts of the Third will be:
1. Summer marches in.
2. What the flowers in the meadow tell me.
3. What the creatures in the forest tell me.
4. What the night tells me (Mankind).
5. What the morning bells tell me (The Angels).
6. What love tells me.
7. What the Child tells me.

'And the whole thing I shall call 'My Joyous Science' – it is that, too!'

NBL, 19–20. (Contrary to this synopsis, the Third Symphony contains only six movements, and the titles have been much altered. In the summer of 1895, he told Friedrich Löhr on 29 August, Mahler completed the score except for No. 1. About no other work was Mahler so communicative as about his 'Joyous Science', a title borrowed from Nietzsche.)

Mahler to Friedrich Löhr, on Hamburg, Vienna and the Third Symphony

Hamburg, Bismarckstrasse 86, 29 August 1895

143 Krżyżanowski is really going to be engaged here from 96. It is years since I heard from him directly. Pollini is saying nothing about it either, but that is his usual way. It has no bearing whatever on my position at the theatre here – at the most, it can only be the pleasure of having such a colleague.

About Vienna, I have heard nothing since my conversation with Bezecny.

My new Symphony will take about 1½ hours to play – it is all in large-scale symphonic form. . . .

It is my most individual and most powerful work. . . .

GMB, 106–07. (Mahler had for years promoted the interests of his youthful friend Rudolf Krżyżanowski by his recommendations. Krżyżanowski, who had previously been Conductor for Angelo Neumann in Prague, came to Hamburg in 1896. Mahler had been negotiating with Count Josef von Bezecny, General Manager of the Vienna Court Theatres, at the beginning of June 1895. On returning to Hamburg, Mahler, together with his sisters, moved to a new apartment, Bismarckstrasse 86.)

A sensation at the Hamburg Municipal Theatre

Frau Katharina Klafsky-Lohse has been declared by the governing body of the Theatrical Managements Association to be in breach of contract, as has also her husband, the con-

ductor Otto Lohse, in the following terms: 'Herr Otto Lohse on account of non-fulfilment of engagement; Frau Katharina Klafsky-Greve, now Frau Katharina Lohse-Klafsky, also on account of non-fulfilment of engagement in aggravated circumstances; the latter has left unrepaid an advance of 10,000 marks made to her.' Both have gone to America and have accepted engagements with the Damrosch Opera Company.

Deutsche Bühnengenossenschaft, vol. XXIV, no. 37, 13 September 1895. (The Damrosch Opera Company, founded by Walter Damrosch in 1895, organized performances of operas in New York, at the Academy of Music and the Metropolitan Opera, as well as tours of other cities.)

This breach of contract, on the part of the conductor Lohse and the dramatic soprano Katharina Klafsky, gave unique chances to two young artists. Mahler's young friend Bruno Walter was promoted from Chorus Master to Assistant Conductor; the untried twenty-three-year-old singer Anna von Mildenburg took over Klafsky's parts at very short notice. Anna von Mildenburg (1872–1947), Viennese born and a pupil of Rosa Papier, took up her engagement at the beginning of the 1895–96 season. The magazine *Deutsche Bühnengenossenschaft* had already announced this engagement in the issue dated 22 June 1895.

Anna von Mildenburg on her first rehearsals with Mahler

I was asked to come to the first piano rehearsal at the theatre. My répétiteur had before him the piano arrangement of *The Valkyrie*, and I must have studied my Brünnhilde really well, 136 for my accompanist found nothing wrong. When we reached: 'Father, father, say, what ails you?', the door was pushed open violently. A small man, wearing a grey summer suit, entered; he had a dark felt hat in his hand and squeezed under his arm a badly rolled umbrella. His face was burnt absolutely black by the sun. He looked at us out of his bright grey-blue eyes with marked aversion. When the répétiteur tried to greet him, the newcomer cut him short. 'Carry on,' he said irritably, slamming the door, but without coming nearer. He stood as if ready for flight, the door-handle in his hand, and the accompanist went on playing but pressed his lips together slightly, and I understood what he meant: M. So it was Mahler. I closed my eyes; my hands twisted together convulsively; all my fervent hopes and longings flooded into my singing, and the passage 'See, Brünnhilde pleads' became a supplication, a child-like timid prayer for patience and forbearance, a cry for help in the miserable state to which all my bright young hopes had been reduced by my few days at the theatre. At this point the man at the door frightened me by stamping violently. His hat flew on to the piano, his umbrella after it, the répétiteur was pushed from his stool with a 'Thanks, I don't need you any more'. . . .

The first thing I gained from Gustav Mahler's method was a confidence that liberated me from all doubts and apprehensions. A feeling of infinite security enveloped me straight away in our first year together. . . .

He made me sing my 'Hojotoho' once more, and remained silent; then the couple of passages after Fricka's exit – still no word. Then came 'See, Brünnhilde pleads'; but by then I had lost my self-control. I laid my head on the piano and began to cry. For a few moments he sat there embarrassed, biting his lower lip. Then he suddenly gave a frightful shout at me. The terror in my face must have been very comical, for he now began to laugh unrestrainedly, shaking all over. With his two hands thrust into his trouser pockets, he rushed madly round the room. However, he then sat down quietly and cleaned his spectacles, and I understood from his first kind words that I had done splendidly and had no need to worry so far. But then he started to shout again: 'And you'll have to go on crying until you just sink in the general theatrical mire of mediocrity. Nobody cries then.' But I already understood that his glance was not always threatening. This knowledge made me communicative and reassured, and when I had talked out my troubles I no longer felt alone.

The fact that I had Mahler at my side in the early years of my stage career has been an enduring blessing; the more I developed, and the more mature I became, the greater also was my gratitude. . . .

'Precision is the heart and soul of any artistic achievement,' Mahler told me at that first rehearsal, and I know now that it was a benediction for my whole life. When Mahler explained to me his 'proscribed' note values I understood immediately that he was thus showing me a new way to achieve the correct emphasis and phrasing and the appropriate expression which were not yet ready to emerge spontaneously and naturally from my inner being. Through his guidance every smallest note became important, became a help in my difficult task, and in the same way he taught me to attach just as much significance to rests as to sung notes. At that time, of course, it was not yet possible for me to give a rest its necessary and proper duration by 'living' it mentally; but Mahler, who recognized and understood this, knew ways of guarding me, in my youthful immaturity, from falsification of the meaning of what I sang. Thus he never allowed one to prolong *fermate* – those acid tests of talent and style in musicianship and singing – to arbitrary lengths, but gave them a precise value. . . . In a few comprehensive and thorough piano rehearsals Mahler first worked through my part alone with me. On those occasions he told me a lot about Richard Wagner and advised me earnestly above all to make a thorough study of his writings. Before I even had an opportunity to get them for myself, he sent the books to my apartment with a kind message. . . .

Anna Bahr-Mildenburg, *Erinnerungen,* Vienna 1921, 12 sqq.

Interest in Hugo Wolf's opera

Above all: Let Wolf know that he should send *me* his opera if he cannot, or does not wish to, find a home for it elsewhere. If it is within my power, I will see that it is *performed*; that is, *if it seems to me worth performing.* You need not pass on that last remark, or else put it in a less doubtful form. . . .

From a letter to Natalie Bauer-Lechner, 2 September 1895, ms., wst. (It is not known whether Mahler thereupon received the score of Hugo Wolf's opera *Der Corregidor*; the work was not performed in Hamburg.)

Mahler asks Arnold Berliner for a loan

Can you lend me another 170 marks? If you can, please send it *by return.* When I have the opportunity I will tell you about a shabby trick of Pollini's which has left me temporarily very embarrassed.

Please let me know by return, in any case. . . .

Undated letter, postmarked Hamburg, 16 September 1895, GMB, 141. (The 'another' in the first sentence is evidence that Mahler was already in debt to Dr Berliner. In March 1896 Mahler enquired about the size of his 'account' with Berliner, so that he could repay his debts.)

The financing of the performance of the Second Symphony in Berlin

For the rest, this expensive concert was not all a business undertaking on Mahler's own part; it was two Hamburg friends, Dr Hermann Behn and Wilhelm Berkhan, who paid the considerable costs of the concert – 5,000 marks – out of their own pockets. Hermann Behn gave further proof of his devotion and passionate enthusiasm by having his own excellent two-piano arrangement of the work engraved at his own expense.

Ferdinand Pfohl, *Gustav Mahler,* Hamburg 1973, 39. (The concert on 13 December 1895 was organized by Wolff, whose management was, however, evidently not prepared to carry the financial risk.)

Mahler to Anna von Mildenburg

Berlin, 8 December 1895

My dearest Anna,

This is not going to be a 'long, long' letter. There is not enough quiet for that here (within and without!) The distances here are all so enormous, and I still have a lot to do to get my army into good shape. But yesterday morning was so special and beautiful that I must tell you about it. I was thinking about you all the time, and how you would have loved it too.

As you know, at the end of the last movement of my symphony I need *bell tones* which, however, cannot be produced by any musical instrument.

I had therefore thought of going to a bell-founder as the only person that could help me. I found one at last. To get to his workshop takes about half-an-hour by train. It is in the Grünewald neighbourhood. Well, I got up very early in the morning. Everything was gloriously covered with snow. The cold stimulated my somewhat depressed organism (for that night also I had had little sleep). When I reached Zehlendorf – that is the name of the place – and made my way between firs and pines quite covered with snow – all very countrified – a pretty church sparkling joyfully in the winter sunshine – my spirit *expanded*, and I saw how free and grand mankind can become when it turns back from the unnatural and restless bustle of the big city to the quiet house of nature. You grew up in a small town, too, and you must feel with me.

After a long search I discovered the foundry. I was received by an old gentleman with splendid white hair and beard – such a calm friendly gaze that I straight away felt myself back in the days of the old craft guilds. To me it was all so good and so beautiful. Then I conversed with him: he was, I admit, somewhat slow and diffuse for my impatience. He showed me splendid bells, including a massive one that he has cast on the Kaiser's orders for the new cathedral. The sound was mystic and powerful. I had thought of something similar for my work. But the time is still a long way off when even the costliest and best will be good enough to be useful in an important work of art.

In the meantime I found some bells that were more modest but still useful for my purposes, and parted from the dear old man after a stay of about two hours. The way back was again glorious. But then to the General Theatrical Management offices: and then the waiting started! Those faces in the ante-chamber – those skeleton people – every inch of their faces showed the signs of self-tormenting egoism – it makes everybody so *unhappy*! Always *I* and *I* – never *you, you, my brother*! Do you understand me, my Anna?

By chance Director Pierson, the man I was concerned with, came out of his office, and as soon as he saw me he settled my business; otherwise I might have had to wait for *hours longer*; just imagine! Even the half-hour had depressed me so much that I wanted to go away already.

But now, thank God, I've fixed up everything, and now the word is, 'into battle!' For me this is certainly preferable to skirmishing at the outposts.

From my account it must have seemed to you that I went on my journey *alone*. In fact Behn came with me, but he is truly discreet and never disturbs such moments. At 1 o'clock I lunched at a restaurant, and must have eaten *something fatty*. That was the end of me. Of course you know I can digest anything – anything except fatty or spicy things! You must already have noticed how careful my sisters are in this respect. I suffered with my migraine for two hours, a really *agonizing* state. You were once with me when I had an attack, do you remember? It was the Werther rehearsal! – after which you sent me your 'Dear Sir – A. Mildenburg' letter.

I did not receive your yesterday's letter until I got home in the evening; the headache was already a bit better, so I was able to enjoy your dear words untroubled. How happy I am that you are so *straightforward* and *natural*; there is nothing I find more horrible than a person who makes himself out to be other and better than he really is.

Young people are often like this, even high-minded ones; I can remember myself well, how careful I used to be about the style of my letters, how anxious I was to write so-called 'good letters'.

But really it was all because I had not yet found *myself*, and the person I was writing to was just an opportunity to set out my own thoughts. My dear, sweet (I don't really like that word, but it just came into my head, so it may as well stand – and that is what you are to me) Anna! I beg you, never take up a pose – *no cosmetics*, either *inside* or *outside*!

My sisters have become so poor! I feel like a criminal! I can't get it out of my mind. You are right – we must leave it to *time*, the all-powerful master. Only stay steadfast and *fond* of me – and have compassion for the good people; then you and I will surely find the right way.

From tomorrow, please write (if you write, but you must *never make yourself* do so, however much I long to have a line from you) in a *disguised* hand, so that nobody will know it is from you. Only your last letter, in which you tell me when you are *arriving*, can be written in your own hand (and with your beautiful little arm).

How kind, my darling girl, that you are writing smaller for my sake. A thousand good wishes and *kisses* (if permitted), Your

Gustav

Well, I see this letter has got a bit longer than I thought at first.

Ms., ÖNB-TS, A29 093 BAMM. (Parts of this letter quoted GMB, 157–58.)

134 *Felix Weingartner on his impressions of Berlin and Hamburg*

During the period of my Hamburg concerts I often met Gustav Mahler. I had heard his Second Symphony in Berlin and had told him that I found more genuine musicality in that work than in the symphonic poems of R. Strauss. In Hamburg he showed me sketches for a Third Symphony, planned on an even larger scale, which confirmed my previous opinion. I appreciated his enthusiasm for art and the fact that he felt as unhappy under Pollini's direction as I had done previously. The coincidence of many of our views and feelings brought us closer together. They are really making things hard for him. While others have been covered with fulsome praise, a Mahler performance has always been the signal for silly abuse. This was another thing I sympathized about; I have had plenty of experience myself in this respect. . . . I often spent several

133 hours at his flat, which was looked after by his sisters, and Anna von Mildenburg, a lovely girl with a lovely voice, was a frequent guest. Just as in his compositions there is valuable material mixed with banalities that are hard to bear, so also in his interpretations his intellectual enthusiasm seemed to kindle with incomprehensible extravagances. He talked about his version of Schubert's D major Symphony in which he had reinforced the glorious melody of the trio in the scherzo with three trumpets. He alarmed me with the information that he wanted to have the march section in the finale of Beethoven's Ninth Symphony played by an orchestra outside the hall, to resemble an approaching military band. Once he had set his mind on something, he would not listen to any objections.

Felix Weingartner, *Lebenserinnerungen*, Zürich 1929, II, 84–85. (Felix [von] Weingartner, 1863–1942, conducted the 1895–96 season of 'Bülow Concerts' in Hamburg, which had been conducted by Mahler in the previous year.)

On the conception of the Second Symphony

Hamburg, 17 December 1895

For me, the conception of the work never involved laying down the details of a *process*, but at the most of a *feeling*. The basic *idea* of the work is clearly expressed in the words of the final chorus, and an illuminating light is thrown on the first movements by the sudden appearance of the contralto solo. That I afterwards often see, in various individual parts, actual events – so to speak – occurring dramatically before my eyes can easily be comprehended from the nature of the music. The parallelism between life and music may be deeper and wider than we are yet in a position to understand.

From a letter to Max Marschalk, GMB, 179–80. (Max Marschalk, 1863–1940, originally a painter and photographer, was from 1895 onward critic of the *Vossische Zeitung* and a contributor to other papers. He became known as a composer through his music for plays by Gerhart Hauptmann, who later became Marschalk's brother-in-law. Mahler's many letters to Marschalk between December 1895 and April 1897 are among the most informative of Mahler documents.)

During 1896 Natalie Bauer-Lechner came to Hamburg a number of times. Mahler's holiday companion now saw something of his everyday life, and she recorded many details and conversations in her memoirs. She came to Hamburg on tour with the Soldat–Roeger Quartet, in which she played the viola.

Natalie Bauer-Lechner visits Hamburg in January 1896

Mahler has a capital life here with his sisters – in so far as one can live in Hamburg; the appealing name of the district, Hohe Luft [High Air], is at the same time symbolic of Mahler's creative activity. A little house standing in a garden with a view over meadows and fruit trees, just for the three of them and the two maids. Mahler has taken possession of the whole of the upper floor: a room for the piano, a study and a bedroom.

When I arrived I found Mahler busy on the orchestration of his *Lieder eines fahrenden Gesellen*. . . .   158

For my sake one evening Mahler organized a performance by him and Walter, at Behn's place, of the latter's piano arrangement of Mahler's Second, just for me and a few very close friends. . . . .

NBL, 21, 22.

Mahler on his interpretation of the concept of 'Nature'

It always strikes me as strange that most people, when they talk about 'Nature', think only of flowers, birds, forest breezes, etc. Nobody knows the god Dionysus, Great Pan. So! there you already have a sort of programme – that is, a sample of how I make music. It is always and everywhere just natural sound! This seems to be what Bülow once described to me with the significant words 'symphonic problem'. There is no other kind of programme that I recognize, at least for my works. If I have given them titles, off and on, this is because I have wanted to set up a few signposts to show emotion where to transform itself into imagination. If words are necessary for this purpose, then we have the articulated human voice, which can enable the boldest intentions to be realized – just by combination with the explanatory word! But now it is the world, Nature as a whole, that is aroused, so to speak, from unfathomable silence to sound and resonance. . . .

From a letter to Richard Batka, dated 18 February 1896, GMB, 214–15.

One person who did not agree with the general enthusiasm for the musically magnificent opera performances under Mahler was – Mahler himself. He suffered under the weaknesses of the staging, which neither the considerable acting talents of many singers, nor the dramatic realism of his music-making, could conceal. He did not talk to me at that time about the theoretical obstacles in the path of the operatic producer – perhaps he did not recognize them as such until the period of his reforming activity in Vienna – but he certainly did complain often, and over the whole dynamic range of nuances, from humorous head-shaking to blank despair, at the personal deficiencies and stupidities of the Chief Stage Manager, B., who perforce worked with (and often against) him during the whole of his time at the Hamburg Opera.

BWTV, 108–09. (The Chief Stage Manager of the Hamburg Municipal Theatre was Franz Bittong.)

Mahler replies to a letter from a member of the public

Hamburg, 2 March 1896

Dear Madam, Please believe a composer who has usually felt only the thorns in his crown, that you have given me very great, heartfelt pleasure by your few words, which prove to me that my 'experience' has been comprehended by a fellow-being and has drawn her into a 'common experience' with it.

You will scarcely believe that this is the *first intimation* that somebody unconnected with my life has responded with a joyful 'Yes' to my earnest question – for this is indeed above all the work of a new artist: a new formulation of a content which is both old and new. I could not understand how such a dead silence could suddenly succeed those vehemently loud tones. My thanks to you! I am coming back on 16 March. You would like to have some facts about my life? The following will probably be useful as long as you do not have a set of my works available – only they can in reality speak of my life.

Born 7 July 1860 in Bohemia. Came to Vienna at the age of 15. Conservatoire and university. The need to take up some outside activity and to earn a living led me to the theatre, where I have been working without interruption since my twentieth year. At first came the little miseries of provincial conditions, and later the *very big* ones of the famous 'arts centres'. The first work with which I came before the public was the editing of Weber's *Pinto* sketches, and the completion of the whole work, in 1888. This is moreover the one thing I have done for the theatre. My whole trend is in the direction of the symphony. The one in D major, which I shall present in Berlin on 16 March, was composed before the C minor, in 1888. In addition, I have a third one in my desk. There are also a number of choral works, large and small – songs, ballads, etc. . . . .

I am now 35 years old – very uncelebrated and very *unperformed*. But I keep trying and don't let things get me down. I have patience, and I wait!

Letter to Annie Mincieux, *Basler Nachrichten*, 13 July 1923. (Annie Mincieux was a writer and portrait painter, at that time living in Berlin. At the concert referred to, on 16 March 1896, Mahler performed his First Symphony, without the titles added in 1893; the first movement of the Second Symphony; and the *Lieder eines fahrenden Gesellen*, in the orchestral version, sung by Anton Sistermans.)

16 March 1896: Concert of Mahler's works in Berlin

The number of tickets sold for the concert was extremely small; only 48 marks, I believe, was taken for tickets, while on the other hand the performance cost Mahler thousands.

Mahler was not excited before the concert. Everything went splendidly, apart from a false entry in the horns which he quickly got under control. The reception from the audience, half-filling the Philharmonic Hall, was fairly warm and positive, apart from scarcely noticeable hissing after the first move-

ment of the Second Symphony and the *Bruder Martin* movement of the First. There were even calls for an encore of one of the songs, but Mahler did not allow this. He was hurt by the cool reaction of the audience, and no matter what people said to him, he only replied very sadly, shaking his head, 'No, they didn't understand it.'

Fortunately there was one person there – apart from us close friends – who did understand Mahler, and who grasped what it was all about. This was Arthur Nikisch, who, on his way home from Moscow, had stayed overnight in Berlin expressly to hear the concert; he appeared to be enormously and sincerely impressed by Mahler's work, and even promised to perform at least three movements of his Second during the coming winter.

NBL, 31.

Natalie Bauer-Lechner on the summer of 1896 at Steinbach

Mahler had left his sketches for the first movement of the Third Symphony in Hamburg, and was in despair because he could do nothing without them. Fortunately Dr Behn was staying not very far from Hamburg, on the Baltic; Mahler requested him, by express letter, to go to Hamburg and find the papers and send them on immediately. However, there were still five or six days to go before the papers could arrive, and it is impossible to describe the impatience and anguish suffered by Mahler (and all of us with him) during this time. On top of all this, the piano had not yet arrived from Vienna, so Mahler sat in his summerhouse like an eagle with fettered pinions, unable to fly. . . .

Although still without his sketches, Mahler was able to make some use of his first few days in the summerhouse: he set to music a song from *Des Knaben Wunderhorn* entitled *Lob des hohen Verstandes* ['Praise of Lofty Intellect'], a delightful slap at the critics. 'In this case', he told me, 'it was only necessary to be careful not to spoil the thing in any way, and to render exactly what is there, whereas in other cases you can often put a lot in and give greater depth and breadth to the text by means of the music.'

NBL, 36, 40.

Mahler to Anna von Mildenburg, on the Third Symphony

Although it is thundering out there, a long way off, I'm going to pack a bag and cycle over to Ischl. My work *is completed*, and I must get away to have a little rest. I am fairly exhausted. I shall stay away for four or five days; I don't know yet where I shall stay, but I think I shall do a bit of climbing. But when I get back there will be a sizeable piece of work awaiting me – to score the work from the sketch. I hope to be able to send you a card now and then during the trip, as the opportunity arises.

You can go for lots of nice walks, and bathe. Enjoy it all! I am absolutely infinitely happy that my great work is completed, but quite fidgety from writing down all those notes! So you must be content with just these few lines. Thousands of kisses and hugs from Your

Gustl.

Steinbach, 11 July 1896.

Autograph, ÖNB, TS, A29138 BAMM. (Mahler had composed the missing first movement of the Third Symphony.)

To Anna von Mildenburg on returning from Ischl

Dearest Annerl, I returned from my trip today. Just imagine, I had hardly left Hallstatt when I felt unwell, and in the end (at Salzburg) this turned into a full-size migraine. This is something that happens to me several times a year. I have never described it to you; it is one of the most horrible things you can imagine. This time it lasted two days. At Ischl it was

139

splendid. Brahms was particularly cordial on this occasion and – something he never did before – invited me to send him the symphony that was printed this year; I shall do this tomorrow. Now I have to put the finishing touches to my work, which I should like to get done before I go to Bayreuth. . . .

Schlesinger is due to arrive tomorrow. I have invited the poor chap to spend a couple of weeks with us, so that he can recover a bit. Up to now he has been with his parents in Berlin, and seems to be in very poor health.

Undated letter, probably 17 July 1896, ms., ÖNB, TS, A29125 BAMM. (In the summer of 1896 only Behn's piano arrangement of the Second Symphony was available in print. Schlesinger is better known as Bruno Walter.)

140 The last visit to Brahms

He was gravely ill and could not move away from Ischl. Mahler visited him there and afterwards described his sombre mood of disgust with life, the mood Brahms himself had expressed in the first of the *Four Serious Songs*, whose words run thus:

> As with beasts, so it is with the sons of men;
> As dieth the one, so dieth the other,
> One breath have both.
> Yea, beast and man have one breath only,
> And man is not better than the beast.
> For all, indeed, is vanity.

Mahler told how he took his leave of Brahms in the evening, and as he went along a dark corridor to the door he turned round and saw the sick man go to an iron stove and take out of its interior a piece of sausage and some bread. And he described the grotesque impression made by this 'student supper' of the composer facing death, the black helplessness and loneliness manifested in that last glimpse, and he murmured over and over again when he thought about it, with deep emotion: 'for all is vanity'.

BWTV, 122.

Brahms on Mahler's Second Symphony

It is interesting to note the opinion formed by Brahms on the C minor Symphony, of which he saw the score in manuscript: 'Up to now I thought Richard Strauss was the chief of the iconoclasts, but now I see that Mahler is the king of the revolutionaries.' Kössler, who passed this dictum on to me soon afterwards, also added that Mahler seemed to be somewhat put out by Brahms's words.

Ludwig Karpath, 'Persönliches von Gustav Mahler', *Der Merker*, 1 April 1913, 251.

The critic Chevalley on Mahler's relations with Pollini

When, in 1896, I moved to Hamburg and took up my duties as opera critic, the battles between Mahler and Pollini, which had hitherto been hidden and had been fought out behind the scenes, had exploded into the open and become public knowledge. Mahler had 'compromised' himself in the eyes and ears of Hamburg's conservative musical circles, then still very influential, by the first of his published works, and even more by a number of concerts that he had conducted. He had risked programmes which gave recognition to what were then modern works , and he had lost credit, and caused shock and terror in worthy old maids of both sexes, by performances of Beethoven saturated with his own fiery spirit, and in particular by a performance of the Ninth Symphony in which he imparted heightened dramatic tension to the last movement by the placing of the orchestra and dared to cut a few bars from the Scherzo. . . . All this gave a boost to Pollini's courage; from then on he ceased to be afraid of Mahler, and briskly and with

206

complete lack of consideration set about making Mahler's position untenable. With this in view, at the beginning of the 1896 season he invited Krżyżanowski – certainly quite a capable conductor, but insignificant in comparison with Mahler – to Hamburg and, by reducing the privileges and authority of Mahler's post, made room for a second position at his theatre. Pollini transferred to Krżyżanowski works which he knew Mahler was particularly fond of, including *Tristan* and *The Mastersingers,* and set out to annoy Mahler especially by giving him the job of conducting *Norma.* In this, however, he made a mistake, for Gustav Mahler thought extremely highly of *Norma,* as had Wagner. 'Tears come into my eyes every time I come to "See, O Norma, see"', Mahler said to me himself once when I took him to the theatre to hear a performance of *Norma* in which Mildenburg sang Norma and Foerster-Lauterer Adalgisa. Again, on the business of accepting new operas, about which Pollini's knowledge was absolutely nil, and which were liable to be foisted on him by publishers and other contacts, Mahler's influence had vanished. And not only that; Mahler was even forced to rehearse and conduct works whose acceptance he had never recommended, such as a one-acter entitled *Runenzauber* by the Danish composer Hartmann and a highly padded opera entitled *Gloria* by Ignaz Brüll, the amiable composer of *Das Goldene Kreuz.* The man with the money gave the orders, and Mahler, who was then extremely busy with his own works, obeyed, more snappish than sulky. . . .

Heinrich Chevalley, 'Mahler und Hamburg', concert programme, Concertgebouw, Amsterdam, 11 January 1923.

Mahler on Anna von Mildenburg

Her voice is a soprano, even in tone in every register, and of rare beauty and power; she is unusually tall; her face is capable of great expressiveness, from the gaily childlike to the daemonically agitated. When I add that her acting talent, her enthusiasm and her application are equal to her other advantages, then I have said enough to explain the high hopes I have of this still very young and *unspoiled* artist, whose great possibilities are at present recognized only by a few. She has been on the stage for only a year, and in this short time she has made such incredible progress that even the ill-disposed have been amazed.

From a letter from Mahler to Cosima Wagner, dated 24 October 1896, ms., Richard Wagner Archiv, Bayreuth. (In this letter Mahler recommended Mildenburg for Bayreuth. She sang Kundry in *Parsifal* at Bayreuth in the summer of 1897.)

Mahler's daily routine in the autumn of 1896

He rises at 7 a.m. – in spite of going late to bed – and while he is getting on with his cold shower in the bathroom he is already ringing impatiently for breakfast, which he takes alone in his room just as soon as he has dressed. When he is feeling well, these morning hours are his heaven, the only time that belongs, even in winter, just to him and his work. With his coffee and a cigarette he first reads for a while (*Des Knaben Wunderhorn*, Goethe and Nietzsche at present – but he absolutely avoids all the newspapers). After that he gets down to work as fast as possible, and during the few hours when things go well, before 10.30 when he has to go into town for rehearsal every day, he makes such good use of his time that while I was there he managed to complete and make a fair copy of the enormously long first movement of the Third. Then he dashes into town on foot – a three-quarter-hour walk – and at midday comes home the same way.

The rest of the time is occupied with orchestra, chorus and solo rehearsals, at which he directs and exercises his people to such effect that their performances reach heights never touched before. . . .

Mahler arrives home very hungry and impatient at 2.30, heralded as he comes along the road by his signal:

which calls everybody to the table and the soup.

Great importance is attached to the arrival of the mail every day; for Mahler never tires of expecting 'the summons to the God of the southern zones', as he calls it jokingly, meaning actually an offer of an engagement from anywhere to go anywhere – only to get away from Hamburg! This – is a sad sign of his great unhappiness in his present position.

After the meal, and after a short nap, usually again disturbed by musical visitors – opera composers, librettists, singers, etc. – Mahler nearly every day strolls round to see the copyist Weidik [Weidich]. These visits, on which I usually accompany him, are combined with our own walks; in the environs of Hamburg, if Mahler is not conducting in the evening, otherwise just a half-hour round about the neighbourhood. . . .

At 6 o'clock, either to the Opera, from which Mahler usually returns in a very bad temper – where, in his opinion, nobody does anything and nobody can do anything: 'An Augean stable that even Hercules would not be able to clean up!' – or if he is free the evening is spent at home chatting or making music, bewailing sorrows or rejoicing.

NBL, 57–58.

Natalie Bauer-Lechner on the printing of the Second Symphony

One of the chief results of my stay in Hamburg this time was that I managed, by my efforts with some of Mahler's Hamburg wellwishers and admirers, to get the score of his Second Symphony printed. One day when we were invited to lunch at Berkhan's (Mahler had been unable to come because of a migraine), the champagne gave me a little extra inspiration to describe to Berkhan, in clear and heartrending terms, Mahler's trouble and distress over his unprinted works: how he always dragged the heavy music portmanteau around with him on his summer trips and would not risk leaving it for an instant; how he could not go away anywhere without trembling for the danger to his manuscripts from fire or water or robbery; and above all how much more difficult it was to get his works widely known and performed, because he could not send the scores of his symphonies to different people. Berkhan saw this all so clearly that not only did he most nobly promise at once to bear most of the cost of the printing, but he also undertook to find a benefactor to provide the rest of the money.

NBL, 60–61. (The Second Symphony was published in February 1897 by Verlag Hofmeister of Leipzig. The cost of the printing was borne by the Hamburg merchant Wilhelm Berkhan and the lawyer Dr Hermann Behn.)

Mahler to Weingartner, on the performance of the Third Symphony

. . . Yesterday Dr Behn told me the gist of his conversation with you, and this has given such joy as I have only rarely experienced in my life before. I could not think of anybody to whom I would entrust my work more confidently and cheerfully than to you. . . . I admit candidly that in my wildest dreams I have often thought that the Berlin Court Orchestra, which under your direction has become the leading orchestra in Germany, might bring this work to life under your baton. But I hesitated lest my approach to you – probably the busiest conductor in Europe – might come at an inopportune time; and perhaps also to some extent on account of the feeling that a refusal from you would hurt me more than from anyone else. If you should find it worthy of taking under your protection, this would make me very happy. In fact I know nobody other than yourself who would have the courage, or the strength, to tackle it. . . .

Letter to Felix Weingartner, dated 14 November 1896, Carmen Weingartner-Studer, 'Gustav Mahler und Felix Weingartner', Österreichische Musikzeitschrift, vol. xv, June 1960, 308. (Weingartner conducted the second, third and sixth movements of Mahler's Third Symphony in Berlin on 9 March 1897.)

In the summer of 1895 Mahler was already negotiating with Baron von Bezecny, General Manager of the Imperial-Royal Court Theatres in Vienna. In late autumn he began his real fight for an appointment as Conductor at the Vienna Court Opera. The moment was favourable, as Wilhelm Jahn, the Director of the Court Opera, was suffering with eye trouble, urgently needed to have his work-load reduced, and was indeed likely to retire within a foreseeable time. A month before Mahler's official written application, Siegfried Lipiner, Librarian of the Austrian Parliament, had already visited the Theatre Directorate with the object of dispelling doubts regarding the appointment of Mahler. As well as his Jewish origin, his reputation for 'craziness' seems to have been the main obstacle to the invitation to Vienna.

Siegfried Lipiner on Mahler's temperament

Please permit me a few remarks, further to the interview regarding Mahler which you were kind enough to grant me recently; it has been pointed out to me that M.'s temperament, his way of dealing with opposition, is not always well spoken of. Nothing can be more unjust. Mahler has the nature of a genius, a passionate nature, that is true; but his passion has absolutely nothing in common with that purely momentary *violence* that is allied with superficiality. To accomplish as much as possible, and to get others to accomplish as much as possible – that is what he wants, and he pursues this aim with the greatest constancy and lively energy. . . . However, he also combines with this energy the greatest self-control and an often unbelievable *patience*. . . .

Letter from Siegfried Lipiner, dated 21 November 1896, to the General Management of the Court Theatres, ms., HHSTA.

The hierarchy in the Vienna Court Theatres

Supreme Court Theatre Directorate. His Imperial and Royal Austrian Apostolic Majesty's Principal Comptroller, His Serene Highness Rudolph Prinz von und zu Liechtenstein. . . . Imperial and Royal General Management of the Imperial-Royal Court Theatres. His Excellency Joseph Freiherr von Bezecny, Imperial and Royal Privy Councillor and Departmental Chief, General Manager of the Imperial-Royal Court Theatres. . . .
Bureau of the Imperial and Royal General Management of the Imperial-Royal Court Theatres. Administrative Director Dr Eduard Wlassack. . . .

Neuer Theater-Almanach für das Jahr 1897, Berlin 1897, 532.

Mahler's letter of application to Vienna

I hear from various sources that the matter of the post of Conductor at the Vienna Court Opera will become urgent in the very near future. The kind reception which Your Excellency has extended to me on a number of occasions encourages me to take this opportunity of drawing Your Excellency's attention to myself.

It is of course scarcely necessary for me to say that, if the choice among the candidates for this post should fall on me, I should do everything possible within my power to show myself worthy of this honour and to prove my gratitude to Your Excellency through loyal and devoted service.

From Mahler's letter to the General Manager of the Vienna Court Theatres, Baron von Bezecny, ms., HHSTA.

Mahler asks his Budapest friends for their sponsorship

This is to request you to do me a favour on which the whole pattern of my future life depends. The matter of the Conductor or Director post in Vienna is now acute. *My name* is among those receiving 'serious consideration'.

Two circumstances are against me. First, I am told, is my 'craziness', which my enemies drag up over and over again whenever they see a chance of blocking my way. Second, the fact that I am Jewish by birth. As regards this latter point, I should not fail to inform you (in case you are not already aware of the fact) that I completed my conversion to the Catholic faith soon after my departure from Pest. . . .

I have also written to Count Apponyi in similar terms. As you know, I have absolutely no connections!

My entire hope is that you and Count Apponyi will exert your influence in my favour. Only one last effort is needed, since my appointment in Vienna, as I have just heard officially, is under serious consideration. . . .

From a letter to Ödön von Mihalovich, 21 December 1896, ms., LFZ. (Mahler's statement is untrue: he was not baptized until 23 February 1897.)

Mahler to the singer Rosa Papier

Hamburg, 22 December 1896

Yesterday I received a letter from Frau Bauer, setting out in detail the substance and outcome of your conversation. I had already expected something of the kind. In now writing to thank you for your great kindness and sympathy, I would emphasize that, however this matter turns out for me, it was an enormous pleasure to learn that you, dear Madam, were prepared to give me your trust and sympathy. And permit me to add also that I have for a long time now reciprocated these sentiments most cordially. Such a pronounced feeling can indeed only exist on a mutual basis, and I am convinced that if we were living near one another we should become sincere friends.

I already had this feeling when we met twelve years ago at Kassel; but you, of course, were already a great and celebrated artist while I myself was an unknown musician; and you probably scarcely remember the occasion.

LKB, 34–35. (It was not only Natalie Bauer-Lechner who drew Rosa Papier's attention to Mahler, but also her pupil Anna von Mildenburg.)

Mahler asks Carl Goldmark to intercede

23 December 1896

. . . What it would mean to me to settle thus into such a well-ordered artistic organization and to escape for ever from this enervating 'commercial theatre' – you can no doubt yourself imagine. – *Now can you do anything for me?* . . .

LKB, 36.

Mahler mobilized his whole circle of friends and acquaintances in order to obtain the post of Conductor at the Court Opera, which he had from the beginning seen as a stepping-stone to becoming Director. Mahler's Budapest admirers, Count Albert Apponyi and Ödön von Mihalovich, wrote enthusiastic letters of recommendation to Vienna; *Obergespan* Ferenc von Beniczky, one-time Government Commissioner for the Budapest Opera, joined them, although slightly more cautiously.

Obergespan von Beniczky to His Excellency the General Manager of the Court Theatres

I must confess that I know Mahler as a highly strung man in some ways, which is caused by his profession; but I am able to recommend him most warmly to Your Excellency since I know him to be not only highly gifted as a musician, conductor and director, but also possessed of sound judgment in respect of the

administrative sides of an artistic institution; and above all he is an honourable man through and through, so that I may assert with complete conviction that his advantages more than compensate for this weakness.

Letter of 15 January 1897, ms., HHSTA.

The influence of Rosa Papier on the all-powerful Hofrat Wlassack

Let us make it clear at once: Mahler's appointment to Vienna was due to Rosa Papier-Paumgartner. She was one of the best and most popular singers of the Vienna Court Opera, but after a bare ten years on the stage she was forced to retire by a throat complaint. But she maintained her connection with Viennese musical life by becoming an outstanding singing teacher. . . . At that period she had great influence, for she was very friendly with *Hofrat* Dr Eduard Wlassack, Administrative Director of the General Management of the Court Theatres, who died in 1904. Wlassack was all-powerful. . . .

LKB, 28, 29.

Doubts about the appointment to Vienna

25 January 1897

Everything is still undecided in Vienna. How long they will ramble on in the usual fashion is quite unpredictable. My informants tell me there would be no doubt at all about my appointment – if I were not a Jew. But this is what will probably settle it, and so Mottl . . . will win. Still, a remark of Liechtenstein's – made in response to a plea on my behalf by one of my protectors who was not named (but I can well imagine it was an emissary of yourself or of Count Apponyi) – does leave me some ground for hope. For when the question of my origins was touched upon, he said: 'Things are not as bad as that yet in Austria, for anti-semitism to decide matters of this kind.' He himself is said to be well informed about me and to have a very favourable opinion of me!

From a letter from Mahler to Ödön von Mihalovich, ms., LFZ.

Mahler to Rosa Papier, on a meeting with the Court Opera Director, Jahn

. . . I met Jahn in Dresden and took the opportunity of a frank discussion with him. As far as I could gather from his very cautious and circumspect comments, I shall not have to contend with opposition from this quarter. The upshot of his remarks to me was that he has not the slightest intention of resigning, but will await the result of his eye-operation and then take on a conductor, which he regards as necessary under the present circumstances. He will, as he put it, 'bear me in mind' when the time comes.

From a letter of 5 February 1897, LKB, 41.

The Vienna Court Opera under Wilhelm Jahn

. . . He was a musician of almost Gallic brilliance and bravura, a conductor of sublime elegance, grace and charm, a stage manager of exquisite taste combined with vibrant self-assurance. He had come from Wiesbaden (which is after all one of the most French, most cosmopolitan cities in Germany), where he had attracted Wagner's attention as a conductor of *The Mastersingers*, which he had given with a sense of humour, a lightness of touch and a serene seriousness hitherto unknown – and played it without cuts, too – and now brought the Vienna Court Opera to its peak as a place of aristocratic luxury and highly civilized entertainment. Had he not had Hans Richter to assist him, the Jahn era, which lasted seventeen years, would merely have been one of the finest and most exuberant periods of great theatrical entertainment; but as it was there were not only all those evenings of delight in fine playing and fascinating adventures in word and sound, but uplifting ones, too, when Richter was at the podium and brought Wagner's works to life   and Mozart, Beethoven, Gluck as well. . . .

Richard Specht, *Das Wiener Operntheater, Erinnerung aus 50 Jahren*, Vienna 1919, 27–28.

From the Baptismal Register of the Parish of St Ansgar, Hamburg

PLACE OF BIRTH: Kalischt in Bohemia
SEX: male
FULL NAME: Gustav Mahler
DAY AND HOUR OF BIRTH: 7 July 1860
PARENTS' NAMES: Bernhard Mahler, born at Deutsch–Brod
      Marie Mahler, née Herrmann, born at Ledetsch, Bohemia
DAY OF BAPTISM: 23 February 1897
GODPARENTS' NAMES: Theodor Meynberg
OFFICIATING PRIEST: Swider, Curate

Baptismal Register of the (Catholic) Parish of St Ansgar, Little St Michael's Church, Hamburg, 1897, no. 29.

From a lecture by Felix Weingartner

An important contemporary figure who is insufficiently recognized as a composer is Gustav Mahler. His works are of colossal length and require unusually large forces. This makes them difficult to perform and to understand. But if we disregard this problem – and it really is of secondary importance – and direct our attention to the composer himself, we encounter a deep and powerful sensibility, which will and can find its own expression and says what it has to say without regard for the possibilities of performance or of success. A characteristic trait is Mahler's preference for broad and weighty themes. I think for example that those who described the first movement of his Second Symphony as a monstrosity when it was performed in Berlin quite simply failed to grasp the massive structure of the principal theme; in which case it would of course be difficult for them to follow its development. Another typical feature, and one of his greatest assets, is the utterly *musical* character of his compositions, even when he is working to a programme. Mahler is a musician through and through, similar in many ways to his teacher Bruckner; only he is better at working out his material and constructing a movement than the latter. One may sometimes encounter bizarre elements in his works, or difficulties for which there is no obvious reason, or one may speak of excessive diffuseness and perhaps of insufficient self-criticism in the choice of themes; still, everything Mahler writes bears the stamp of a fertile imagination and of a passionate, even fanatical enthusiasm. These are characteristics on which great hopes may be founded. . . .

Felix Weingartner, *Die Symphonie nach Beethoven, ein Vortrag*, Berlin 1898, pp. 97–98. (The printed edition bears the following note: 'This lecture was given in a shortened form in Berlin on 11 February, in Bremen on 15 March, in Munich on 26 March and in Hamburg on 9 April 1897.')

Mahler to Max Marschalk

Moscow, 13 March 1897

What a frantic rush! Tuesday evening there was my failure in Berlin, and today I am already here – and all seems to me just a dream. I have not yet read any of the Berlin papers, since I left immediately the following day. Just the *Börsenkurier* [the Stock Exchange Courier]! But that was enough for me to see that this time I really shall be so battered and thrashed that no tailor will ever 'patch me up'! But I should like to know whether I got through to *you*! That evening I had to listen to so much nonsense from friend and foe alike that I was left quite stupefied by it all. Please send what you wrote to me in Munich,

c/o Dr Heinrich Kržyžanowski, Schellingstrasse 70. I shall get there on Thursday the 18th. There is a concert *here* on Monday – I am quite *enchanted* with the city! Everything is so peculiar and exotically beautiful! In the end it will all be just a dream, and when I wake I shall find I am living on Mars.

GMB, 211. (Weingartner had conducted three movements from Mahler's Third Symphony in Berlin on 9 March.)

A Moscow critic on Mahler as conductor

Eighth Symphonic Meeting of the Moscow Philharmonic Society: The Fifth Symphony of Beethoven, *Siegfried Idyll* and *Rienzi* Overture by Wagner.

This was the orchestral programme of the Philharmonic Society on 3 March [15 March by the Gregorian calendar]. This time Moscow had its first chance to see the Hamburg conductor Herr Mahler at the head of the orchestra. . . . The most characteristic trait of his conducting is his clarity: he allows nothing to be lost, nothing is smudged over. But may we call his artistic temperament great? To judge by his Wagner Herr Mahler is a passionate man, but to judge by his Beethoven he is phlegmatic. In truth, probably neither view is correct: he is rather a first-rate technician with the skill to get from the orchestra whatever he wants; but what the orchestra, thus subservient, does in response to his artistic demands is not so much the result of the spiritual fire of the conductor but rather the inevitable consequence of his carefully thought-out reading of the score and a certain penchant for originality. It is this element which I think best explains Mahler's interpretation of the Fifth Symphony. I have never before heard it performed so slowly. Mahler really did perform it 'in his own manner'. And at first one may be inclined to see this 'manner' as coldness, but if you listen carefully and sympathetically you will come to a different conclusion, for you will grasp the logic of the structure of this new conception, a structure which is perhaps less satisfying than the traditional, objective one we have long known, but which nonetheless, perhaps as a consequence of the conductor's deep thinking, is unquestionably founded on something solid and not on anything fortuitous. . . .

Novosti Dnya, 9 (21) March 1897.

Natalie Bauer-Lechner on the concert in Munich

The two concerts which Mahler gave with the Kaim Orchestra shortly after his Moscow successes gave him even greater pleasure. For here was a group of young musicians who were at once completely won over to him, and who stood by him through thick and thin. They carried out all his intentions, and after a few (albeit very intensive) rehearsals found themselves able to execute his wishes in performance.

'The awful bad habits,' Mahler said to me, 'or rather the imperfections which I have encountered with every orchestra, such as failing to observe the markings and thus flouting the sacred rules of dynamics and of the hidden innermost pulse of a work – I was not spared any of this, here any more than elsewhere. As soon as they see a *crescendo* they immediately play *forte* and speed up the tempo, while a *diminuendo* makes them drop at once to *piano* and slow down. Subtle gradations like *mezzo-forte*, *forte*, *fortissimo* or *piano*, *pianissimo* and *pianississimo* you will seek in vain. Even more difficult to achieve are *sforzando*, *fortepiano* and *rubato*. And if you ask them to play what is not actually written down – as is necessary a hundred times when accompanying singers in opera, where they need to be able to respond to every slightest inflexion of the finger – well, then you are lost with any orchestra.

'But the Munich band caught on remarkably quickly, so that it was a joy to make music with them.'

NBL, 62. (The Kaim Orchestra was founded in 1893 by a private patron, Franz Kaim. The Kaim Concerts continued until 1908 and were then taken over by the Munich Concert Society.)

Constituent Meeting of the Secession

The Society of Artists in Austria [Vereinigung bildender Künstler Österreichs], which is the official title of the Vienna 'Secession', held its constituent meeting on Saturday [3 April 1897]. At present it numbers 40 ordinary members, who were invited to join by the steering committee and who have accepted the invitation in writing. The painter Gustav Klimt was unanimously elected President of the Society, and the following painters were co-opted on to the Executive Committee: Rudolph Bacher, Wilhelm Bernatzik, Joseph Engelhart, Johann B. Kraemer, Carl Moll and Koloman Moser. The first business of the Society of Artists in Austria was an act of homage to the doyen of Austrian art, Rudolph [von] Alt, who was elected by acclamation Honorary President of the Association. . . .

Neues Wiener Tagblatt, 6 April 1897.

147 *Hermann Bahr on the objectives of the Vienna Secession*

In Paris and Munich the purpose of the 'Secession' [from academic institutions] was to give a new art its rightful place, from which, according to the young artists, it was being excluded by the 'elders'. In other words an argument among artists about artistic form. Depending on one's aesthetic viewpoint, one could call it a struggle of modern art against tradition; or, more modestly, a struggle for new techniques; or even, if one did not approve of innovations, an attempt to set up today's fashion against eternal laws. In any case, it remained a dispute within art. Both sides had the same end in view: the service of beauty. It was only about the means that they disagreed. Both were invoking art, only in different words. Artists stood opposed to artists. It was a battle between schools, doctrines, temperaments or whatever you may call it. Here in Vienna this is not what it is all about. Here we are not arguing for or against tradition. We have no tradition. It is not a struggle between the old art and the new, nor about some change in artistic outlook. It is art itself for which we are struggling. The Society does not reproach the [established] 'Association' [Genossenschaft] with being too 'old-fashioned', or call upon it to become 'modern'. The accusation is simply: 'You are manufacturers, we want to be painters!' That is the issue in a nutshell. Money or art, that is the question behind the Vienna Secession. Are Viennese painters to remain industrialists, or are they to be allowed to become artists? He who believes paintings are goods, like trousers or cigars, should remain in the 'Association'. But those who seek to manifest the forms of the soul in paintings and drawings will join the 'Society'. It is not a dispute about aesthetics, but about two attitudes of mind: between the commercial mind and the artistic. . . .

Hermann Bahr, *Secession*, Vienna 1900, 6–7. (Hermann Bahr, 1863–1934, the Austrian critic, essayist, dramatist and novelist, was a leading champion of the Vienna Secession and also an admirer of Gustav Mahler. In 1908 Bahr married Anna von Mildenburg.)

Mahler to the General Management of the Court Theatres

148 I confirm that I am willing to accept an engagement as Conductor at the Vienna Court Opera Theatre for one year from 1 June at an annual salary of 5,000 (five thousand) florins, and that this declaration holds good until 15 April this year. Vienna, 4 April 1897.

Ms., HHSTA.

172 *Mahler to the critic Ludwig Karpath*

7 April 1897

Dear friend, the decision will be made *tomorrow*; the chances are still said to be good.

210

Unfortunately I must rush back because of instructions received! Please send everything of interest to me in Hamburg, Bismarckstrasse 86. I hope to see you soon!

Many thanks for your friendship. . . .

Transcript from Ludwig Karpath's posthumous papers. (Karpath was partly privy to Mahler's and Rosa Papier's efforts.)

A new Conductor at the Vienna Court Opera   151, 180

Vienna, 8 April

An unprepossessing notice of two lines in today's *Wiener Abendpost* announces that Herr Heinrich [*sic*] Mahler, former Director of the Budapest Opera, has been engaged as a Conductor at the Vienna Court Opera House. This appointment seems to have been treated as a State Secret until its semi-official revelation at the Court Opera itself. . . . The laconic brevity of the announcement in the *Abendpost* makes one wonder what position Herr Gustav Mahler will occupy alongside the three Conductors who have been with the Court Opera for years – Hans Richter (since 1875), Johann Fuchs (since 1879) and Joseph Hellmesberger (since 1886). Or might Herr Mahler be destined for some other function at the Court Opera? . . .

Neue Freie Presse, 9 April 1897.

Mahler to Wlassack

It is now all-important for me to introduce myself artistically in Vienna as advantageously as possible, and to that end the period of Richter's absence seems to me the most propitious. I think the best would be a Wagner opera and *Fidelio*, which would represent both the main directions and should satisfy both the Wagnerians and the classicists. The main thing after that would be to sketch out a plan of campaign for next season and to prepare *new* productions and *new works* in such a manner that, with careful planning and full use of personnel and time, one new production and one new work could both be brought out together. This way we should already be able to make a start on widening this wretchedly restricted repertoire in the course of the coming season. And I know from experience that the public is very easy to win over as soon as it senses *things are looking up.*

Ms., HHSTA. (The letter is dated Hamburg, 9 April 1879, which is clearly a slip of the pen. It should be 1897.)

The foundation of the Secession inaugurated in Vienna a new era for the visual arts; the appointment of Mahler a new era of musical theatre. April 1897 was important for Vienna on the political front, too: Dr Karl Lueger, the most popular politician of the Christian Socialist Party, became Mayor. The Christian Socialist movement, which drew its support in the main from peasants and small businesses, combined ideas of social reform with anti-semitic agitation.

Reception in the anti-semitic press

In our edition of 10 April we printed a note on the person of the newly appointed Opera Conductor, Mahler. At the time we already had an inkling of the origin of this celebrity and we therefore avoided publishing anything other than the bare facts about this unadulterated – Jew. The fact that he was acclaimed by the press in Budapest of course confirms our suspicion. We shall refrain completely from any over-hasty judgment. The Jews' press will see whether the panegyrics with which they plaster their idol at present do not become washed away by the rain of reality as soon as Herr Mahler starts his Jew-boy antics at the podium.

Reichspost, 14 April 1897.

Hans Richter congratulates his new colleague

Vienna, 19 April 1897

Many thanks for your kind note. Forgive me if I do not proffer a detailed written reply; but I can tell you straight away that you will not find in me a hostile colleague; indeed you will find me to be a benevolent and accommodating comrade in the cause of art once I have gained the conviction that your work is an asset to the imperial institution and a gain for our noble art.

LKB, 67.

The Vienna Court Opera and its acoustics

It is the most ideal opera house in the world, built in the style of an age which had not yet learned – or had already forgotten – the beauty of the functional and the emphasis thereon carried to its utmost conclusion: an age of luxury, of magnificence for its own sake and of extravagant comfort. But the elements which are unbearable in many a palace of that era: the showiness, the gaudy pomp, the plain dishonesty – when the opulent façade of a palace on the Ringstrasse was the mask for the apartment of a stock exchange jobber – these elements are marvellously genuine and noble. . . .

These walls resonate in sympathy; the sound of a particular voice at a particular spot is strangely coloured and strengthened as if the silent caryatids were suddenly singing too (and they really do); in the vaulted ceiling live sleeping harmonies, which are suddenly called to life by the resonance below. The whole auditorium is impregnated with music, every spot is sensitive to some particular tone-colour or reverberation, and so mysterious is this resonance that – absurd as it may sound – it would be a criminal experiment to switch the layout of instruments in the pit by putting, say, the heavy brass with the percussion on the left, and the woodwinds on the right side of the house; the whole highly peculiar, subtle and sensitive acoustic would be thrown into confusion and danger.

To begin with, these acoustics – it is a fact which is scarcely to be credited – were so fiercely impugned and the whole building, which no other court theatre anywhere can equal, was so heaped with scorn and denigration, that one of its architects committed suicide and the other followed him to the grave very soon after. It was one of those fine Viennese witch-hunts such as are stirred up every five years against someone or other who has dared to produce something unconventional, great and new, without previously shyly asking if he may take the liberty. . . . . .

Richard Specht, *Das Wiener Operntheater, Erinnerung aus 50 Jahren*, Vienna 1919, 8–10.

Natalie Bauer-Lechner on Mahler's first rehearsal with the Opera orchestra

Lohengrin was the work it fell to Mahler to conduct for his debut, and for this he was allotted no more than a single rehearsal. For this rehearsal there was one thing which filled him with anxiety: the speech which he was told he must make to the musicians. Although he was a most vivid and lively impromptu talker, he had a blind fear of 'speech-making', which he would never do at any price unless it was absolutely indispensable. Now he went around for days cursing this speech and at his wits' end as to what to say. In the end, as he told us, it went off quite well in spite of his embarrassment. But as soon as he started on the *Lohengrin* prelude his agitation vanished at once. He played it through with them once, then explained to them how *he* saw it, went over every detail and turned everything inside out from A to Z.

In fact, he said he had never encountered an orchestra so capable of learning and carrying out his musical intentions. 'I was more advanced with them after one rehearsal than with

others after years. Of course, the Vienna house idealizes the tone to a quite incredible degree, whereas elsewhere poor acoustics can blunt and coarsen everything. But the greatest contribution comes from the Austrians' sheer musicality: the enthusiasm, the warmth and the great natural talent which they all possess.'

NBL, 73–74.

From a letter to Anna von Mildenburg

Vienna, 17 May 1897

Yesterday and the day before I did not even have a chance to say a word to you. It was a crazy succession of congratulations, visitors etc.! Thank God! the whole crisis is now over! The whole of Vienna has greeted me with absolute enthusiasm! Now next week we have *The Valkyrie, Siegfried, The Marriage of Figaro* and *The Magic Flute*. There is hardly any doubt now that I shall be Director in the foreseeable future. . . . Tell me how things are with you in the theatre (in the penitentiary)! . . . It's terrific! The whole staff are absolutely magnificent.

GMB, 167.

Karl Kraus on the new Court Opera Conductor

A new conductor has entered the Opera House recently with the panache of a Siegfried, and you can see in his eyes that he will soon have done with the bad old ways. Herr Mahler has conducted his first *Lohengrin* with a success which was unanimously acknowledged by the whole press. There is a rumour that he is soon to be made Director. Then, presumably, the repertoire of our Court Opera will no longer consist exclusively of *Cavalleria rusticana*; native Austrian composers will no longer have their manuscripts returned to them unread (they will be returned read); and singers of merit will no longer be shown the door without reason. The new conductor is said to have given such effective proof of his energy that intrigues are afoot against him already.

Breslauer Zeitung, 16 May 1897. (Karl Kraus, 1874–1936, satirist and critic.)

Arnold Rosé. Silhouette. Hans Schliessmann, *Wiener Schattenbilder*, Vienna n.d., 23.

Ludwig Karpath on Mahler's friendship with Arnold Rosé

To start with, Mahler looked for a furnished flat, and found one in the Universitätsstrasse, where however he stayed only for the first few weeks, for in the meantime he had found a suitable flat on a twelve-months' lease at Bartensteingasse, no. 13, and it was to this address that he moved with his sisters Justine and Emma in the following autumn. Since both the ladies were still in Hamburg I joined Mahler on his walks through the streets of Vienna. He had immediately taken up with Arnold Rosé, the leader of the orchestra at the Court Opera, whom he had previously known and whose company he enjoyed more than anyone's.

LKB, 62 (Arnold Rosé, 1863–1946, studied at the Vienna Conservatoire at the same time as Mahler, became the leader of the Court Opera Orchestra at the age of eighteen, and in 1883 founded the Rosé String Quartet, of which he was to be the leader (with changes in the other parts) for decades. The number of the house in the Bartensteingasse was actually 3, as can be seen from Mahler's letter of 16 November 1898 to the General Manager.)

Hugo Wolf to his mother, on the performance of his opera

Vienna, 4 June 1897

. . . It is now certain that *Der Corregidor* will be performed in the coming season. I today received a definite promise to this effect from the new Conductor, Mahler (an old friend of mine). Mahler is now all-powerful at the Vienna Opera. He himself will rehearse and conduct my work, which is all to the good, since Mahler is the man who can realize my intentions as no one else could.

Ernst Decsey, 'Aus Hugo Wolfs letzten Jahren', *Die Musik*, October 1901 (2), 141–42.

A throat abscess following tonsillitis led Mahler to start his holiday in the Tyrol early, in the middle of June. He was accompanied by his sisters Justine and Emma and by Natalie Bauer-Lechner. From Kitzbühel Mahler soon went on to Steinach and Gries am Brenner, and from there to Vahrn in the South Tyrol. During the summer holiday Mahler received the news of his appointment as Vice-Director of the Court Opera, a promotion which had obviously been planned from the beginning.

Mahler to Rosa Papier, from Kitzbühel

. . . The splendid air and refreshing peace have already turned me into half a Hercules (unfortunately I am most decidedly lacking the other half!). – We all stroll around in the hills and woods – and swim a bit in the Schwarzsee, which is quite near; when it gets too hot we sleep or read. That is a true picture of a life I do not remember ever having led before. If my conscience sometimes pricks me, I quickly remind myself that I am con-valescing – which is a dignity I have experienced only in the past two weeks – and carry on with *dolce far niente*.

I feel sorry for my good friends in Vienna – especially you and Dr Wlassack, left behind to breathe in the dust of the city.

It is particularly sad for Wlassack to be prevented by the present situation from doing anything to improve his health. It makes me feel like a real sybarite. Sometimes I dream with my eyes open – especially in the afternoon when I am lying on my sofa, and the blue sky and green meadows look in through the windows of my room, with the birds making music in the background. And then the last few weeks pass in review before me as though they were images in a dream. Just think how it has all come about! You can imagine, dearest friend, with what heartfelt emotion I arrive in the Frankenberggasse on this

tour of memories and experiences – and stay there, the true starting point of all these events, and the home of the real stage-manager of this comedy – which may yet turn into a genuine drama, if not for the gods, at least for men. And if you are the stage-manager, Wlassack is the conductor, who set the tempo and brought on the *stringendo* and *allegro energico* happily just at the right moment. . . .

Undated transcript in the posthumous papers of Ludwig Karpath.

Natalie Bauer-Lechner to Rosa Papier, on Mahler's relationship with Anna von Mildenburg

Your intimation of the imminent offer to Mildenburg of a contract in Vienna came yesterday evening like a bombshell in our Tyrolean haven of peace: you cannot imagine the terrible effect it had, not only on us women but even more on Mahler himself. . . .

Your kind and well-intentioned advice and 'revelations' to Gustav about M., however willingly – especially as it comes from *you* – he accepts and is guided by it, can and *will* not make one iota of difference to his relations with her, or rather to her boundless power over him and his *total* inability to overcome his unresisting weakness for her. This has from the beginning been the danger for him, that in her presence he has always consciously, and with open eyes, simply allowed himself to be irretrievably enmeshed in her net, so much so that other people (however close to him they may be, and however much he may otherwise like them) – and above all *he himself*, what-ever effort he makes, can do nothing about it. And because he felt this, and painfully learned the truth of it for himself and for others during the most frightful period of his life (from the moment that M. came to Hamburg till the moment that he had to leave because of her – only because of her), there has been and still is for him, and for everyone associated with her, only *one* salvation and that is *separation* from her. So it is the most dreadful misfortune that can befall G. if M. really does come to Vienna (and, my dear, do not imagine that I am exaggerating: you would only have needed a single day with them in Hamburg to understand our worst anxieties, and more than that, with your dear, lively sensitivity, to share our deepest concern). And so, if there is still time for anything to be done, I implore you to try to avert this disaster which threatens us all!

From a letter from Natalie Bauer-Lechner dated 24 June 1897, transcript in the posthumous papers of Ludwig Karpath.

Mahler to Rosa Papier on the offer to Anna von Mildenburg

Gries am Brenner, 2 July 1897

. . . Above all I openly confess to you that I cannot say our friend Wl. [Wlassack] is wrong. It would really be asking a lot to abandon the engagement of an artist of M.'s importance for purely personal reasons.

I must say I had to smile too, at the way our friend put it, for it reminded me too much of my own way of thinking; it is these small things that most clearly illuminate the elective affinities of two natures. I think, dear friend, we must let this one go. Anyway it is still a whole year yet; and this will give me time to overcome the difficulties between M. and myself, which at present stand in the way of successful co-operation. By the way, I must ask you for absolution for not having shown your kind letter to our mutual friend Frau Bauer as you wanted me to. (If I understood you correctly.) On this question she seems to me excessively worked up, which is quite unlike her. I do not know what she wrote to you but I am sure she will have completely overshot the mark. . . .

Transcript in the posthumous papers of Ludwig Karpath. (Anna von Milden-burg appeared in guest performances at the Vienna Court Opera in December 1897 and began her contract there in September 1898.)

Mahler to Anna von Mildenburg

Dearest Anna,

I must burst in upon you with an important question which I can now postpone no longer, although I should have liked to spare you it, now that you have such a great prospect before you. I have smoothed the path for you in Vienna to the extent that you will shortly be receiving an offer of a contract there, *with Pollini's agreement*. But if you accept it is *absolutely essential* (now that I have a clear view of the whole situation) that we should then restrict our personal intercourse to the minimum, or we shall once again make each other's life a misery. The whole staff are already on their guard as a result of scandal-mongering from Hamburg and the news of your engagement would burst upon them like a bomb. If we were then to provide the slightest grounds for suspicion etc., *my own position* would become *impossible* within no time and I should have to pack my bags again as I did in Hamburg. You too would suffer in the same way again, even if in your case it might not be a life-or-death matter. And so I ask you, dearest Anna: have you the strength to work with me in Vienna and – at least for the first year – to renounce any private relationship and any form of favour from myself? I hope you realize it will be *no less difficult for me* than for you and it is only the direst necessity which forces me to ask the question. But it is too crucial, and neither of us may have any illusions on the subject. I beg you, my dear Anna, however busy you may still be with your work, write me a few lines in reply – but be completely *frank* and *honest*! The offer will be sent to you shortly. The difficulties with Pollini will be overcome without need of any effort on your part. But now that everything is more or less arranged my heart trembles and I ask both myself and you, *what* we shall both be taking on.

Please reply at once. Your answer will make a great deal of difference to me. I almost think we shall be taking on an *intolerable* ordeal. And if you share my opinion I beg you simply to refuse the offer and accept one from Berlin, which you will also receive shortly.

Whatever happens it is of course *desirable* that you should receive the offer of a Vienna contract; and that is why I have taken the matter so far there without first asking you. Please, answer me at once, *without the slightest reserve*, even if it's only a few lines. Further explanations after I get your letter!

Fondest greetings, my dearest Anna, from your

Gustav.

Best wishes to your mother, too.

Undated letter, ms., ÖNB-TS, A29195 BAMM. (Written across the top of the letter, in another hand, presumably Anna von Mildenburg's: 'To Bayreuth *before my first Kundry*!!')

Baron von Bezecny to the Director of the Opera, Wilhelm Jahn

Vienna, 13 July 1897

... I have decided, for the period of your sick-leave, or rather for as long as you are prevented from directing the Opera in person, to entrust your functions to the Conductor, Herr Mahler, as your deputy. . . .

HHSTA.

Mahler cables the tenor Andreas Dippel

21 August 1897

Siegfried will be given uncut this time. Please come prepared. Should much welcome rehearsal with you.

Draft of a telegram, HHSTA. (Andreas Dippel, 1866–1932, heroic tenor, worked in Vienna 1893–98 and in New York 1898–1908. From 1908 Co-Director of the Metropolitan Opera.)

Hugo Wolf on 'The Ring'

Right from the first act [of *The Valkyrie*] there were such overwhelming and magnificent moments that Hugo Wolf, who attended every performance, said: 'We have heard here – as in the whole of this *Ring* – what we had never heard before, and what indeed we had given up all hope of ever encountering other than in the score itself.'

NBL., 85.

Bruno Walter visits Vienna in September 1897

To say that I got to know Vienna or tried to find my way through its unknown streets would not convey the dreamy feeling of already being acquainted with its streets and squares, its monuments and buildings, which overcame me as I walked, or rather floated, along. Of course: that was the Prater that I had so often read about, and these were the cabbies driving along its central avenue – straight from the Viennese *Fiakerlied* ['Cabbies' song'] into the driving seats of their rubber-tyred four-wheelers; there stood the Court Theatre, the Burg-theater, whose proud history I knew so well, and St Stephen's Cathedral, whose lofty form I had been taught to know, love and venerate by countless illustrations, the splendid St Charles' Church, the Karlskirche, at the back of which Brahms had lived for years, then the Schwarzspanierstrasse, where Beethoven had died; here was the noble, mighty Hofburg, where Emperor Franz Joseph reigned, the Ringstrasse, the museums and here the Musikvereinssaal, the concert hall where all music's greatest glories had been heard, and – above all – here was the Imperial and Royal Court Opera, the sumptuous edifice of Van der Nuell and Siccardsburg, and in it the greatest living musician as its guiding light. . . .

It was splendid to be able to have lunch with Mahler and his sisters in their comfortable flat in the Bartensteingasse nearby; it took your breath away to enter the noble and magnificent interior of the Court Opera, and to see Mahler's elegant rooms, his management office and the rehearsal room, which some forty years later, from 1936 to 1938, were to be my own. I got to know Mahler's friends, of whom I had heard so much and who then became my friends and remained so for decades, to the end of their lives. . . .

BWTV., 134–5.

Hugo Wolf's catastrophe

It was some weeks ago that friends and associates of Hugo Wolf began to notice an unusual nervous excitement in him. His speech became very hasty and was accompanied by excited gesticulation. A few days later it became evident that Wolf was mentally disturbed, the first conclusive evidence occurring during a visit to the Court Opera singer Winkelmann. As he entered the singer's salon Wolf said: 'Have you heard, I am the Director of the Vienna Court Opera.' Winkelmann thought his visitor was joking, and replied that of course Herr Mahler was manager of the Court Opera. Wolf then approached him mysteriously and whispered in his ear: 'I have already disposed of Mahler, and I have already arranged things with the Comptroller, Prince Liechtenstein. Your contract, my dear Winkelmann, will be renewed immediately. . . .' The catastrophe followed the next day. Wolf suffered in his flat a delirious fit of such violence that force was necessary to restrain him. He struck out violently, threatened all who approached him, and shouted incessantly that he was the Director of the Court Opera. Friends were quickly summoned and arranged for him to be taken to a private institution.

Neues Wiener Tagblatt, 9 October 1897. (It was said that the crisis was brought on by an argument with Mahler about the performance of *Der Corregidor*. Hermann Winkelmann, 1849–1912, heroic tenor, the first Parsifal at Bayreuth, had been at the Vienna Court Opera Theatre since 1883.)

Police charge against demonstrators, Vienna, 26 November 1897. Wood engraving from the *Leipziger Illustrierte Zeitung* after a drawing by Franz Schlegel. ÖNB-BA.

In the autumn of 1897 the Austrian Prime Minister, Badeni, put forward a 'Linguistic Ordinance' the effect of which would have been to give the Czech language equal status with German in the Crown Lands of Bohemia and Moravia. This government move sparked off violent anti-Czech riots in Vienna. In this atmosphere of communal hostility Mahler's staging of the Bohemian national opera, Smetana's *Dalibor*, was regarded by the Czechs and anti-Czechs alike as a political act. Mahler often said: 'I am rootless three times over: as a Bohemian among Austrians, as an Austrian among Germans, and as a Jew everywhere in the world.'

On Smetana's 'Dalibor', the first new work under Mahler

166   . . . In *Dalibor*, too, we feel the all-pervading presence of musical genius: there is scarcely a page of the score which does not bear the characteristic stamp of an original mind. Where the work becomes weak – it reaches its climax with the magnificent finale of the second act and then falls off rather sharply – it is not Smetana's fault but that of Joseph Wenzig, the librettist. The last act is dramatically quite inadequate; the performance took account of this and tried to save it, musically at least, by reprieving the hero and ending with the apotheosis of the heroine. Whatever one may think of this violation of the original, which converts *Dalibor* into *Milada*, the magnificence of the performance itself does not suffer one bit by it. This is largely the achievement of Herr Mahler, the new miracle-worker of the Court Opera. It needed a miracle to preserve that institution, which was sick to the core, from impending ruin; let us be glad the man has been found who is capable of carrying out the miracle. A performance like this means the beginning of a new era for the Vienna Court Opera; it combined the highest imaginable individual freedom of expression with the strictest and most conscientious objectiveness and accuracy, and enabled every performer without exception to achieve a personal success. . . .

The opinion was expressed in some quarters that last night's première in the Court Opera might be used for political purposes, and in the interests of completeness we must take note of the fact. . . . In view of the subject of the work, and its composer, it came as no surprise that the Slav element was strongly represented in all parts of the House, and one certainly saw people who would not normally come to the first performance of a new opera. Thus, for example, very many Czech members of the Imperial Parliament were there. . . .

Max Kalbeck, *Neues Wiener Tagblatt*, 5 October 1897.

Anonymous letter to the Director of the Opera

So *Dalibor* is in the repertoire again!! You just cannot stop fraternizing with this anti-dynastic, second-rate Czech nation who are good for nothing but acts of violence against the German and Austrian State.

How anyone can stoop so low is incomprehensible. . . .

Letter from 'A German Austrian', dated 7 November 1898, HHSTA.

The roots of German nationalism in Austria

Hitherto the conflict has not at all been one of principle. The bone of contention was initially [a village like] Cilli or Weckelsdorf, or an appointment at *Hofrat* level, or a school, or an office; ultimately it came to be all the public offices in Bohemia, Moravia and Silesia. The Czech civil service entered upon a struggle for the more or less exclusive right to hold office. The German middle classes in Austria, which only a few generations ago had provided the civil administration for all the Habsburg domains and for the Holy Roman Empire of the German Nation, found themselves squeezed out of the German Empire, out of Hungary, out of Galicia and finally even out of the lands of the Crown of Wenceslas and the Slavonic parts of the Alps, and restricted to the small area of the old heartland. The material effect of this explains the violence of the resistance on the part of the Germans.

Synopticus (Karl Renner), *Staat und Nation*, Vienna 1899, I. (Karl Renner, 1870–1950, was Chancellor from 1918 to 1920 of the first Austrian Republic, and first President of the Second Republic.)

Natalie Bauer-Lechner on Mahler's appointment as Director of the Court Opera

On the evening of 9 October I collected Mahler from the opera after the performance of *Zar und Zimmermann*. As I met him under the arcades he called out to me, 'I've been appointed!'...

The salary which Mahler received under various titles for this appointment (which was not a contract but a Civil Service post for life) amounted to 12,000 florins along with a further remuneration of 1,000 florins. But of even more value to him than this high salary was a guaranteed pension of 3,000 florins which was due to him the moment he left this post....

Meanwhile his joy and satisfaction with what he had achieved, and what still remained to be done within the given framework, alternated with resentment and pain over the stresses of the life he was forced to lead.

NBL, 88–89. (Mahler's appointment is dated 8 October 1897.)

Hermann Bahr on the Court Opera as Festival Theatre

Only the naive innocence of a man so utterly blind to the world could succeed in the wantonly reckless enterprise of turning a Court Opera House into a Festival Theatre.... To carry out this idea, the idea which created Bayreuth, in a Court Theatre, of all places, could only be undertaken by a man living in a fantasy world, a man with not even an inkling of reality, a man so carried away by his sacred mission that in the end the whole city became seized and intoxicated by it – for a while.

Neue Freie Presse, 22 March 1914.

Mahler compared with Richter

The appointment of Gustav Mahler as Director of the Court Opera is an event which on the strength of his work as Acting Director can only be greeted with joy and happy expectation. What we have experienced so far by way of artistic achievement may be expressed in the four names Wagner, Mozart, Lortzing and Smetana, which is to say that under the new management we shall be able to count on careful and sympathetic attention to every branch of musico-dramatic art.

Even the many friends and admirers of Hans Richter, who regard the appointment of Mahler as a snub for the conductor of genius they so rightly acclaim, will have to admit, if they consider the matter dispassionately, that this degree of equal involvement with works of very unequal merit could not have been expected from Richter.

J. S. (Josef Scheu), 'Feuilleton: Gustav Mahler und Hans Richter', *Arbeiter-Zeitung*, 16 October 1897.

Max Graf on Mahler as an operatic conductor

Perhaps even greater than his energy is the flexibility and adaptability of his mind, which permits him to transform himself from work to work and from composer to composer to such a degree that he is able to reproduce works and composers with the subtlest differentiations of period and style. This gift of getting under the skin of each work and becoming completely imbued with its spirit, of reacting to old works with wit and historical awareness as well as superiority, while

bringing to modern works the inner passions of a man of the nineteenth century – this is above all the criterion of an eminently modern talent. And so at the two extremes of his gifts stand on the one hand Wagner's *Tristan and Isolde* and on the other Mozart's *Marriage of Figaro*.... The former Mahler conducts with an intense and impassioned exaltation which lashes all the fervour of the work from its utmost depths. But *Figaro* he infuses with a delicate and witty serenity, shaping the most intimate turns of phrase with the final gloss of perfection. These two works, which we have never yet heard so supremely well executed at the Vienna Opera, seem to me to embrace the depths and peaks of Mahler's nature. It is at these frontiers that his talent explodes at its most brilliant, most powerful and most astonishing. The middle register of his genius – say Beethoven symphonies, *The Mastersingers, Siegfried* – seems to me less striking, the way you often hear violins whose E- and G-strings have a magnificent tone, while the middle strings are duller and less vibrant. Here Hans Richter, with more roast beef and less nerves in his body, is the stronger man. I see these two men not as opposites but as counterweights, who complement one another in an extraordinary and perfect manner. It is where Richter's limits end that Mahler's talent begins, and despite my extreme admiration for the former as a strong and manly artist I must say that he has never been capable either of the innermost depths of passion and excitement that the complete realization of *Tristan and Isolde* demands, nor of that subtlety and grace necessary in Mozart; on the other hand he has achieved great things in the middle sphere of spiritual power and energy.

Max Graf, *Wagner-Probleme und andere Studien*, Vienna (1900), 124–26. (Mahler conducted *The Marriage of Figaro* several times in August and September 1897 with increasing box-office success. *Tristan and Isolde* he directed for the first time on 24 October.)

Mahler on his post as Opera Director

... I have not a free second to write! So come and see, you'll not regret it! – Everything is going much better than I ever imagined! And much worse, for my job absorbs me completely and seizes me body and soul. Not a chance of '*working*'!

From Mahler's letter to Hermann Behn, 26 November 1897, ms., The Pierpont Morgan Library, New York, and the Mary Flagler Cary Charitable Trust.

The struggle against the claque and the star singers

At that time they put up with everything from him. Things that before him no one would have dared to do: the presumption of performing Wagner operas uncut, the elimination of the claque (sworn to on oath), the darkening of the auditorium to force the audience to concentrate and become involved with the pictorial reality of the stage setting; the exclusion of latecomers at performances of demanding works; in a word, the education of the public....

To be sure it was not terribly long before people became aware of the danger of this de-Viennization, and a chorus of revenge began to assemble. But, as I said, this did not come until later.

But something else began at once: resistance in the House itself. Mahler was rash enough to do without 'favourites' and would have no truck with any form of stardom. And not only that: he had taken it upon himself to show what is meant by ensemble; what it meant to feel a single will shaping the whole. Immediately there was uproar; spoilt singers like Van Dyck or Renard became openly hostile, though they were defeated in the end.

RSP, 2, 73–74. (Ernest van Dyck, tenor, and Marie Renard, soprano, were two of the most popular singers at the Court Opera.)

An audience with the Emperor and with the Comptroller

. . . Even the Emperor said to him recently, when Mahler had an audience with him: 'I must say you have made yourself master of the situation in the Opera House in no time at all!' And Prince Liechtenstein is delighted with Mahler's energy and the success with which he tackles everything. 'You really are a winner!' he exclaimed not long ago as Mahler entered the room. 'The whole of Vienna is talking of you and is full of your achievements. Even the oldest and worst reactionaries say, "There's certainly always something happening in the Opera nowadays, whether you agree with it or not."'

NBL, 94.

265 *Guido Adler seeks a subsidy to print Mahler's symphonies*

. . . It is obvious from the foregoing that works like this can be performed only in major cities with large orchestras or at music festivals. And so it is difficult to find publishers for them. Only the Second Symphony has yet been published, in full score and in a piano duet arrangement, and then only because two patrons were so enthusiastic about the work in performance that they paid the costs. But further performances of even this work are hampered by the fact that the parts are not printed. Despite repeated enquiries from Belgium, France, Holland and even America the composer has been unable to supply the parts. Of the First and Third Symphonies not a note has been printed. . . .

188   The expense of printing the score, vocal score and parts of the First and Third Symphonies and the orchestral parts of the Second will amount to about 12,000 florins, according to the calculations of Eberle & Co. in Vienna, one of the best-equipped printers, who publish among other things the symphonies of Bruckner. On the recommendation of the undersigned as adviser they have agreed to take on Mahler's works, too, on the understanding, and with the wish, that part of the costs can be raised in the form of a subsidy. In accordance with the foregoing notes on the artistic value of these works it should be regarded as a duty and an honour for our Society to take urgent steps to ensure their publication. Therefore: to accomplish on the one hand the great task which it is our duty here to fulfil, and on the other hand to pay due respect to the apportionment of our finances, the proposal should be put that we vote 3,000 florins for the publication and propagation of the works of Gustav Mahler, payable in two instalments, the first payment at once, the second instalment in January 1899. We attach one condition to this grant, namely that the following note should appear on the orchestral and vocal scores of the First and Third symphonies and on the cover of the orchestral parts (or perhaps on the violin part) of the Second: 'with the support of the Society for the Advancement of German Science, Art and Literature in Bohemia'.

From Guido Adler, 'Zweites Referat über Gustav Mahler', dated Prague 24 January 1898, for the Gesellschaft zur Förderung deutscher Wissenschaft, Kunst und Literatur in Böhmen, transcript, Guido Adler Papers, University of Georgia Libraries, Athens, Ga.

Leoncavallo on his meeting with Mahler

Mahler too I valued very, very highly as a director, despite personal differences that I had with him; but he is full of idiosyncrasies, sometimes even a bit dotty. He conducted my *Bohème*; Renard, Dippel and Ritter sang the main parts. It was heavenly! But I said I should have preferred to see Van Dyck in Dippel's part. You should have seen, heard and read the consequences of this 'unjustified' wish – it was atrocious!

'Eine Unterredung mit Leoncavallo', *Neues Wiener Journal*, 7 June 1904. (The première took place on 23 February 1898. Mahler, who had no high opinion of the work, was obliged to perform it by a contract signed by his predecessor.)

216

Performance of the First Symphony in Prague

Angelo Neumann, the Director of the Royal German Theatre in Prague, who had once promoted Mahler as a conductor, now took the trouble to seek recognition for him as a composer. He put Gustav Mahler's First Symphony on the programme of one of the Philharmonic Concerts, and invited the composer to conduct the work himself. Franz Schalk, at that time the leading conductor in Prague, had gone to the trouble of rehearsing the Symphony with the utmost care, so that Mahler had relatively little work to do and was radiantly happy with the successful performance. Naturally the theatre was sold out for such an occasion, and the composer was greeted with tumultuous applause.

Josef Stransky, 'Begegnungen mit Gustav Mahler', *Signale für die Musikalische Welt* (Berlin), 19 July 1911. (The concert took place on 3 March 1898.)

Instructions for the rehearsals of the First Symphony

A *fifth trumpet* for the last movement would be marvellous if it could be obtained.

A second harp ditto.

When I mark *Dämpfer* the horns should use mutes. The marking *gestopft* means with the hands.

I beg of you, dear Schalk, *only* the fullest complement of *strings*. But no passengers! . . .

I am in a terrible hurry and look forward to making your closer acquaintance during my stay in Prague!

Please take care of the score; it is my *sole* copy! Perhaps you would drop me another line on the progress of rehearsals. Most important for you to arrange separate rehearsals of wind and strings!

In the *first movement* the *greatest* delicacy throughout (except in the big climax). In the last movement the greatest power. Very desirable to strengthen the *horn section* at the end! The *third movement* humoristically (in the macabre sense).

The trio in the scherzo quite gently and tenderly.

The introduction to the first movement *sounds of nature, not music!*

Undated letter from Mahler to Franz Schalk, ms., ÖNB-MS. (Franz Schalk, 1863–1931, pupil of Anton Bruckner, from 1900 Principal Conductor of the Vienna Court Opera, 1918–29 Director of the Vienna Opera, partly in conjunction with Richard Strauss.)

Letter of thanks to the Director of the Czech National Theatre

Vienna, 23 February 1898

Director Neumann has told me that you have been most kind and helpful in making a number of musicians available for my performance. I thank you most heartily for this great favour, which alone enables me to realize my artistic intentions.

From a letter to Director Šubert. Narodní Muzeum, Prague. (For the performance of the First Symphony the orchestra of the German Theatre was strengthened by musicians from the Czech National Theatre.)

Mahler declines an offer from the poet Richard Dehmel

Please accept my warmest thanks for your confidence, which both honours and pleases me greatly. I certainly feel touched by a mutual affinity which speaks from your verses; and I could imagine no higher task than to breathe new life into them by setting them to music. But: are you not aware that I am at present a Theatre Director? This is a sorry chapter in my life – but it must be carried through to the end. It will certainly be two years before I am able to gather enough strength to write music of my own. Indeed, it has come to the point where the very thought of such an enterprise would simply be a painful thorn in my side. . . .

From an undated letter, ms., Staats- und Universitätsbibliothek, Hamburg, Dehmel-Archiv. (Richard Dehmel, 1863–1920, German lyric poet, had presumably met Mahler in Hamburg.)

Mahler's reading in the summer of 1898 included the verse drama *Adam* by Siegfried Lipiner, which was conceived as the prelude to a trilogy on the life of Christ. This trilogy, which was to consist of the tragedies *Maria Magdalena*, *Judas Ischariot* and *Paulus in Rom*, occupied Lipiner for many years, but remained unfinished.

Mahler to Siegfried Lipiner

162

Just a line to confirm that your *Adam* has just arrived. What a joy! At last! I have just finished the first act! Outside a summer storm is raging! It was uncanny how it seemed to blow in upon your verses, always on cue! This is a truly Dionysian work! Believe me, I am the only man alive who understands this. I find a similar trait in the *Bacchae* of Euripides. Only Euripides is always talking about things and never gives you them. *What* actually is it, then, that puts all living things into the power of Dionysus? Wine intoxicates and elevates the drinker! But *what* is wine? Dramatic art has never yet succeeded in giving what comes automatically with every note of music. Your verse breathes *this* music. It is quite unique in the world. It does not tell of wine and portray its effects – it *is* wine, it *is* Dionysus!

Undated letter, June 1898, GMB, 279.

Mahler to Behn, on his sister Emma's engagement to Eduard Rosé

Vahrn, 30 July 1898

. . . My pains have still not yet eased up; it really does seem to be a long-drawn-out business. That I have not worked much in the circumstances is obvious. I have added a few more pieces from *Des Knaben Wunderhorn.* . . .

Meanwhile Emma has got engaged to the brother of the leader of our orchestra, Rosé; since she told your wife I assumed you would also be in the picture. But actually the whole affair is being kept quiet and before the end of August the pair will be sailing off to Boston, where the groom lives – he is a cellist in the symphony orchestra there.

Ms., The Pierpont Morgan Library, New York, and the Mary Flagler Cary Charitable Trust. (Eduard Rosé, cellist, 1859–1943, brother of Arnold Rosé.)

Hans Richter thanks Mahler for granting him leave

Vienna, 27 August 1898

Many thanks for so kindly and readily granting me this leave. But I need it; for the pains in my arm must be serious indeed to make me abandon *The Mastersingers*. I hope the rest will make me fit enough to take up my duties again.

Letter to Mahler from Hans Richter, transcript in the posthumous papers of Ludwig Karpath.

September 1898: Wagner's 'Ring' without cuts

That Mahler is one of the most enthusiastic admirers of Wagner as a *composer* he has recently demonstrated most brilliantly in his capacity as Director of the Opera. For he has at last succeeded, on 20, 21, 23 and 25 September, in carrying out triumphantly what none of his predecessors had ever dared to offer to the Viennese public: the gigantic undertaking of a totally uncut complete performance of the colossal *Nibelung* tetralogy.

Mahler achieved the realization of this cherished idea by a step-by-step approach. *The Rhinegold* had long since been performed here without cuts, but it was not until February of this year (on the occasion of the guest performance of Herr Friedrich as Alberich) that the last cuts were eliminated from *Siegfried*. And now the few remaining gaps in *The Valkyrie* have been restored, and above all the great Norn scene from *Twilight of the Gods*, which is omitted from almost all *Ring* performances outside Bayreuth, has been reinstated. There are things to be

said both for and against such uncut cycles of the *Ring*. The decisive question in practice is always simply whether it is possible to obtain in a normal opera house a big enough audience willing to make the physical and mental effort the whole cycle demands. Well, in this respect Director Mahler's approach was completely justified by its success: the house totally sold out night after night, a devoted, indeed a real festival atmosphere in the auditorium, enthusiastic applause at the end of each act, reaching a great climax after the sublime ending of the whole in the final chords of *The Twilight of the Gods*. The performances were all conducted by Director Mahler himself, and you could hear quite plainly that each one had been rehearsed anew completely from scratch. Many a fresh voice, new to Vienna, was used to good effect; and especially our most engaging new Siegfried, Herr Schmedes, and our imposing new Brünnhilde, Fräulein von Mildenburg, enjoyed an unimpaired triumph. Mahler repeated the whole *Nibelung* cycle only ten days later with essentially the same artistic as well as commercial success.

Theodor Helm, 'Feuilleton: Wiener Musikbrief', *Pester Lloyd*, 16 November 1898. (Erik Schmedes, 1868–1931, originally baritone, then heroic tenor, engaged by Mahler for Vienna in 1898.)

Erik Schmedes on his Director

218

This is a stage manager and a conductor in whom the singer can have absolute confidence. I do not look at him when he is conducting, but the feeling that he is conducting sustains the singer and protects him from all the pitfalls. Mahler is a strict critic . . . so you can be all the more pleased by his praise.

Neues Wiener Journal, 26 June 1904.

Conductor of the Vienna Philharmonic

Today [26 September 1898] a deputation of the Philharmonic called on Mahler, to his immense surprise, to ask him to take on the direction of the Philharmonic Concerts. Mahler could not resist the temptation to conduct concerts at long last (the dream of his life!), although it is scarcely conceivable how he is going to cope with all the Opera business as well. In fact in the evening, after he had agreed, he almost regretted it, because he feared he could not do justice to both tasks and that the Opera would suffer. But the next morning he regarded the matter with more confidence – as he said, he could well expect a bit of work from himself. It would be particularly valuable to him in respect of the orchestra, since he would now, with the concerts, have complete artistic control of it.

167

NBL, 106. (The Vienna Philharmonic, which was made up of the members of the Court Opera Orchestra, gave eight subscription concerts and one extra concert each season.)

Anti-semitic opposition before Mahler's first Philharmonic Concert

It cannot be denied that the present Director of the Court Opera has done some good as a new broom. We must give him due credit for securing the performance of Wagner's operas without cuts and doing his best to do these operas justice in performance. . . . Herr Mahler's manner of conducting is not above criticism. . . . It often happens that Herr Mahler's left hand does not know what the right is doing. . . .

Mahler's left hand often jerks convulsively, marking the Bohemian magic circle, digging for treasure, fluttering, snatching, strangling, thrashing the waves, throttling babes-in-arms, kneading, performing sleights of hand – in short it is often lost in *delirium tremens*, but it does not conduct.

How much better is the style of conducting of our own Hans Richter, who is certainly no less inspired by the Wagnerian muse than Mahler. The majestic calm, every movement to the point, not a single insignificant or unnecessary gesture. It is Richter's restraint that reveals the master. . . .

Herr Mahler has now reached the point of wanting to improve on Beethoven. In one of his Philharmonic Concerts he is to perform Beethoven's A minor Quartet, Op. 132 – with the prayer of thanksgiving on recovery from illness – as an orchestral work.

Does Herr Mahler really think Beethoven could not have done this himself, had he wanted to, and that Beethoven refrained from orchestrating the work simply because his guardian angel whispered in his ear that one day someone would come whose imagination would be better suited to orchestration, and that his name would be Mahler?

In fact Beethoven must have had a decidedly imperfect gift for orchestration, for he wrote the *Coriolan* Overture without an E flat clarinet, so Mahler has to write it in for him. . . .

If Herr Mahler wants to make corrections let him set about Mendelssohn or Rubinstein – that's something of course the Jews will never put up with – but let him just leave our Beethoven in peace. We like and admire him as he is, without the E flat clarinet and without Mahler. . . .

E. Th., 'Die Judenherrschaft in der Wiener Hofoper', *Deutsche Zeitung*, 4 November 1898. (On 6 November the *Deutsche Zeitung* proudly announced that Mahler had dropped the E flat clarinet as a result of this attack.)

168 *Eduard Hanslick on the first Philharmonic Concert of the 1898–99 season*

'In all and every time – Joy and pain combine.' This old verse, the motto of Schumann's *Davidsbündler* dances, ran through our minds as we entered the Musikvereinssaal yesterday, where Mahler was to direct the first Philharmonic Concert. The pain was over the loss of Herr Richter, who, after conducting these concerts for many illustrious years, has now with surprising suddenness relinquished his post. What made him do it? 'Officially' a chronic weakness of his right arm – a misfortune which has somehow not prevented him from going on to conduct a series of concerts in London, then more in Budapest and on the Rhine. So was it perhaps the much higher financial reward of these guest appearances abroad? This was a fairly understandable consideration. But the embarrassment and perplexity of his orchestra were no less understandable. However they found a friend in need in Gustav Mahler, who, in spite of his already excessive burden of work as Director of the Court Opera, agreed at once to accept the post abandoned by Richter. And that is the joy to follow the pain. Our Philharmonic could not wish for a better or more respected Director – a conviction which also took immediate possession of the public. As soon as the first provisional announcement named Mahler as the new conductor of the Philharmonic Concerts the whole series was sold out at once. We do not need to assure our readers that Director Mahler yesterday fully justified this remarkable expression of confidence. We heard Beethoven's *Coriolan* Overture and the *Eroica*. Sandwiched between them was Mozart's G minor Symphony – pieces which our excellent orchestra have for years had so securely in their heads and fingertips that they could perform them passably in their sleep. This did not stop Mahler from studying them with the orchestra from scratch in three long and painstaking rehearsals. What he wanted was a 'wide-awake' performance, inspired with living spirit and complete dedication. And in yesterday's concert the result was a quite new experience. This is not the place – nor have I the space – to go into all the new musical details which flashed out like diamonds, without however any loss of unity of form or style. Mahler's prime objective of bringing out the dominant character of every piece of music and strictly maintaining the work's individual style throughout came through most clearly in Mozart's G minor Symphony. Many might have preferred more energetic accents and more glowing colours; but Mahler concluded that it was only thus and no other way that he could preserve the individuality of this lucent, immaculate Grace between

218

Beethoven's two volcanoes. The effect of the *Coriolan* Overture and above all of the *Eroica* Symphony was indescribable. We have hardly ever heard these works so clear and vivid in the finest details of their fabric, and yet so overwhelmingly great and powerful in their overall effect. The audience of the Philharmonic – who are used to the best – gave free rein to their enthusiasm at the end of each piece and in the *Eroica* even at the end of each movement, and did not tire of calling the new-found captain of their crack battalion back again and again. All's well that begins well.

Neue Freie Presse, 7 November 1898.

Mahler moves to the Auenbruggergasse

To the Royal and Imperial General Management of the Royal-Imperial Court Opera:
The direct telephone link between the Court Opera Theatre and my private apartment at Bartensteingasse 3, Vienna I, which was established last year on my petition, no longer appears necessary. Instead I beg leave to have my new flat at Auenbruggerstrasse 2, Vienna III, connected to the public telephone network and for gracious approval of the sum of 100 florins per annum as rental. . . .

Submitted 16 November 1898, HHSTA.

157

On the printing of Bruckner's Sixth Symphony

I am most honoured to be able to reply to your valued letter by informing you that we shall complete the orchestral parts for Bruckner's Symphony No. 6 by the end of December, which means we shall be able to put them at your disposal by the beginning of January. The full score can unfortunately not be produced at the same time since we need it to check the orchestral parts, but this does not affect the performance since we imagine that you, Herr Direktor, can manage with the manuscript score for rehearsals. Nevertheless the score will be completed, along with the piano score, as early as the second half of January. . . .

Letter from the music printers Eberle & Co., Vienna, to Mahler, 6 December 1898, HHSTA. (Mahler conducted the first performance ever of the Sixth Symphony of Bruckner at the Philharmonic Concert of 26 February 1899.)

As early as his Hamburg concerts Mahler had performed a string quartet by Schubert in orchestral form. In the Vienna Philharmonic Concert of 15 January 1899 he put Beethoven's String Quartet in F minor, Op. 95, on the programme in an arrangement for string orchestra. Experiments of this kind not only offered Mahler's opponents a welcome opportunity for attack but upset even the critics who were well-disposed towards him. All these re-scorings for larger forces did not originate in a mere thirst for originality – which is what Mahler was accused of – but were the consequence of his view of the history of music, which he saw as a development from small to ever greater bodies of sound.

Mahler on the need for a large orchestra

. . . Music became more and more universal – the number both of performers and listeners constantly increased. The chamber gave way to the concert hall; and the church, with its new instrument the organ, gave way to the opera house. And so you see, if I sum up again: we moderns need such great forces to express our ideas, be they great or small. Firstly because we are obliged, in order to protect ourselves from misinterpretation, to spread the many colours of our rainbow over various palettes; secondly because our eyes have learnt to see ever more and more colours in the rainbow and ever finer and subtler modulations; thirdly because if we want thousands to hear us in the over-large auditoriums of our concert halls and opera houses we simply have to make a lot of noise. Now you will perhaps be like one of those women who can almost never be truly convinced – only persuaded – and ask, 'Does that mean that Bach is less great than Beethoven and Wagner greater than both?' But my answer to that is that you must ask someone who is able to survey the whole spiritual history of mankind at a single glance.... So away with the piano! away with the violin! They are good for the 'chamber', if you are alone or with a friend and wish to conjure up the works of the great masters – as a faint echo – rather the way a copper engraving recalls to your memory the richly coloured original by Raphael or by Böcklin....

Letter to Gisela Tolney-Witt, February 1893, published in *Neue Zürcher Zeitung*, 10 May 1958, out-of-town edn.

Mahler's Second Symphony at the Philharmonic Nicolai Concert

Here, too, the orchestra was at first uncomprehending and baffled, but then, with a few exceptions, became increasingly spellbound and did all it could to master its great and difficult task. Those opponents tried to prevent the performance of the Second even at the last moment. Once again an article appeared in an anti-semitic newspaper, inspired, as before, by the slanders of a few members of the orchestra. Just as on the day before the first Philharmonic Concert, they tried to bring Mahler down; their hope was that where they had failed with Mahler the conductor of the Philharmonic they might succeed with Mahler the composer. But the better part of the musicians supported him, and those who had protested against the performance of the Symphony as being a work 'which had failed and been hissed everywhere else' were obliged to hold their tongues....

The success which the Symphony had in Sunday's concert exceeded our expectations. The very fact that the great Musikvereinssaal was all but sold out demonstrated the interest people felt in Mahler. The first movement was greeted with vigorous and fairly general applause. The second, known to a part of the audience from the previous year (under Löwe), appealed, as always, to most people; even the philistines nodded their worthy heads and sanctioned its 'beautiful tunes'. ... The Scherzo, with its macabre humour, was perhaps the most difficult part for people to understand, and the end of it came so unexpectedly that for a while they were deathly silent, and then only a few people clapped. The *Urlicht* ['Primal Light'] made a very deep impression. It was applauded for so long that Mahler was even constrained to repeat it – but this was not because of the applause but because he wanted to have the third, fourth and fifth movements played without a break, and by repeating the *Urlicht* he was at least able to preserve the continuity of the last two.

The last movement, with its terrible din at the beginning and the cries of fear and terror of all the souls; the march to which the hosts swarm up to the Last Judgment from all sides; and the completely unexpected resolution and redemption in the most sublime, soaring Chorus of Resurrection (*Auferstehen*) – all this had a most powerful effect on the greatest part of the public. The remainder of the audience – unconverted, indeed perhaps outraged at the work, their disapproval written all over their faces – did not however dare, as in earlier times, to express themselves with hissing or catcalls.

So the concert concluded with a storm of applause and jubilation which called Mahler countless times back into the hall and followed him into the foyer, up the steps and even out into the street.

Mahler was really very pleased by the reception of his Symphony, and at dinner afterwards – as he had been in the days beforehand, after the rehearsals – he was in that sublime and passionate ecstasy which came upon him above all when he was able to live through his own music.

The notices which appeared in the papers next day about his Symphony brought him down to earth somewhat, for they showed hardly more comprehension than had those he had received before in Berlin....

NBL, 114–16. (The concert took place on 9 April 1899. The Andante from the Second Symphony had been performed in Vienna by the Kaim Orchestra of Munich under Ferdinand Löwe on 3 March 1898. Löwe, 1865–1925, a pupil of Bruckner, was a conductor at the Vienna Court Opera from 1 October 1898 to 30 September 1899.)

The General Manager of the Court Theatres, Baron Dr Joseph von Bezecny, who had invited Mahler to Vienna, was replaced in February 1898 by Baron August Plappart von Leenher. Fourteen months later, on 24 April 1899, Mahler wrote a forty-three-page memorandum to the Chief Comptroller. In this note Mahler complained about the attitude of the General Management which interfered with his rights as Director. The immediate cause was trivial – it was about certain singers who had obtained leave of absence from the General Management behind the back of the Opera Director – but the petition went far beyond this question into matters of principle concerning the relationship of the artist to bureaucracy.

Mahler on the responsibilities of the Opera Director

In fact it is one of the features of the peculiar position of a Director that generally speaking there cannot be any actual officially defined limits of authority; this is an inescapable consequence of the fact that he performs his essential duties not as the organ of an executive body but as an individual, with all an individual's feelings and ideas – which means also his own convictions in major matters and his own grasp of detail. Now this means that in any event *he* bears the *responsibility* for the achievements of his institution and that he is entitled to certain *rights*, not only because of his official position but also by virtue of the *decree* which appointed him. The consequences of this situation cannot always easily be followed down to the last detail in specific instances. If the Director in a given case holds the conviction or, in the true sense of the word, the *view*, that painted scenery is not adequate for this work, that it decisively weakens the effect of the décor, and if his well-motivated wish is not granted, what should he then do to bring home the validity of his point? If the General Management 'does not share the opinion of the Director and can by no means accept that our scenery, which has been perfectly good enough for years, should now suddenly be declared unusable', then, leaving aside the problem of the moment, the Director is faced with a problem of far-reaching significance. This is a question of judgment in artistic matters. The argument that something has been good enough up till now and is therefore still good enough can be used to prevent any improvement. And there were, and still are, many things in need of improvement which appeared good enough before, and this applies to questions of staging as well as to musical matters. In the theatre, unfortunately, purely musical successes are not successes *at all*. And if the attractiveness (or indeed the sheer *novelty*) of the stage setting – some detail that adds to the clarity, liveliness, harmoniousness of the décor or to that elusive correlation between stage and music – if its only consequence is that the performances are better attended, then the increased takings far outweigh the often quite insignificant cost of making the improvement. To block this expenditure may seem a small saving but in truth it often means a serious – but unfortunately not easily calculable – loss. ...

Agathe and Ännchen in *Der Freischütz* need new costumes. A verbal application is turned down. I try to manage without; but it cannot be done. The faded dress of the one, the far too aristocratic cut of the other (Ännchen!): it is impossible. I am obliged to have the costumes made without waiting for a reply

219

to the note justifying the request which had been sent off *at the same time*: the performance is to take place *next* day. I had not imagined that it would upset His Excellency the Head of the Imperial and Royal General Management that the Opera Director had given way to an urgent necessity in order to avoid putting something in utterly bad taste on the stage – especially when he clearly explained the need in writing at the same time. . . .

Let the purpose of these remarks not be misunderstood. I wish to make it clear that it is in the interest of the theatre that, if the Director is to be given overall responsibility, he must be free to make his own decisions on matters of detail. . . .

Submitted to the Chief Comptroller, 24 April 1899, copy to the General Management, 24–5, HHSTA.

Josef Stransky on Mahler's stay in Prague in June 1899

Gustav Mahler came from Vienna to conduct the Ninth; I had the honour of directing *Parsifal* excerpts. It is easy to imagine how every detail of such an event is firmly engraved on the youthful conductor's memory. Thus I remember how Gustav Mahler, who otherwise had no fear of the devil himself, became nervous as we went up the steps to Angelo Neumann's office. 'Isn't that strange,' he said. 'In Vienna I am the Director of the Imperial Opera and here I am trembling like I used to, when I was a little junior conductor and had to go in to see Angelo Neumann, the man with the grand manner.'

In the first orchestral rehearsal for the Ninth, Mahler sent all the other musicians home and kept back just the cellos and basses, devoting the whole rehearsal to the recitative passages of the last movement. The fruits of his careful preparation were appreciated later in a truly overwhelming performance which I shall never forget. . . .

During this visit to Prague Mahler took the opportunity of listening to new Bohemian operas at the Czech National Theatre – not surprising in view of his perennial lively interest in all new works. At the same time he was openly and sharply critical if something seriously displeased him. He was an utterly frank character. This, for example, the composer Fibich discovered to his cost when he came to our box in the Czech National Theatre during a performance of his opera *Šarka*, obviously expecting to hear a favourable opinion of his music. Instead Mahler tore him off such a strip that I felt really sorry for him.

After this performance we had a long session in the café, which was the occasion of another interesting event. In a quiet corner of the café sat Emil Orlik, now so famous as a painter and engraver. He observed us at length and then called me over and begged to be introduced to Mahler. The Master agreed, and during the lively conversation Orlik sketched Mahler's characteristic profile on a postcard. Mahler was delighted and sent the card straight off to his sister. He invited Orlik to come to Vienna, and so that evening was the real starting-point for the universally admired etching which Orlik was later to produce.

Josef Stransky, 'Begegnungen mit Gustav Mahler', *Signale für die musikalische Welt* (Berlin), 19 July 1911. (Emil Orlik, 1870–1932, did a series of Mahler portraits. From 1903 he was a member of the Vienna Secession.)

Busoni describes a meeting with Hans Richter

[London,] 22 June 1899

Yesterday evening I bumped into Richter in the street: he took me where all the Germans feel at ease, namely to the Gambrinus.

'Ah, sorry I wasn't in Vienna when you played, but I heard old Mahler gave you a lecture in the rehearsal. That really is the limit! He can't abide soloists because he's got no routine and won't conduct from the score, but a conductor has got to

be able to do that as much as a pianist, hasn't he?' And so he went on, straight from the heart. . . .

Ferruccio Busoni, *Briefe an seine Frau*, Erlenbach-Zürich 1935, 25. (Richter's remarks are reported by Busoni in an unreproducible Viennese brogue. Busoni had played Beethoven's 'Emperor' Concerto under Mahler in the Vienna Philharmonic concert of 19 March 1899.)

The 1898–99 Opera Season in retrospect

In the 1898–99 season this work was continued. Richard Wagner's great operas were performed without cuts in accordance with Wagner's instructions, and while for some years the composer of *Die Puppenfee*, Josef Bayer, had achieved the greatest number of performances, this year Wagner headed the list with fifty-seven performances. Gustav Mahler deserves particular thanks for the way in which he took up Weber's *Der Freischütz*; and he paid his respects to French opera with a charming performance of *La Dame blanche*, and to the Italian opera with a sparkling revival of *Rigoletto*.

Max Graf, 'Wien, Hofoperntheater', offprint from *Deutsche Thalia*, Vienna and Leipzig 1902, 2.

Birthday letter to Friedrich Löhr

A strange fate has brought us, at the beginning of this, our fourth decade, as physically close together as we were in our youth, and yet in fact we are farther apart and have less contact than when I was in the north and you in the south. But I hope you too will realize that this separation is merely one of space, or rather time; for that is how it is, believe me. You and I cannot treat each other like anyone else. Now that I am not free for myself I cannot be free for you. But I will tell you one thing: wait a little longer, and Directorship and all the other tomfoolery will be with the Shades in Tartarus, and we shall find each other again in the golden light.

Undated letter, 4 July 1899, GMB, 288–89.

Natalie Bauer-Lechner on the summer of 1899 at Bad Aussee

22 July

Today we went for a walk up the Pfeiferalm. Mahler was especially delighted because we did not meet a soul all the way. At the top we sat for a long time on the veranda of the chalet. Mahler was absorbed in the magnificent view and even more in the deep stillness of the place. . . .

Later he began to talk of the fatal interruptions and breaks in his production: 'With my composing these last three summers I have been like a swimmer who does a few strokes just to convince himself that he can still swim at all. Or perhaps it is a question of checking whether the spring has not perhaps run dry; mine is still trickling a little, but no more.'

So it is really his Fourth Symphony which has fallen into Mahler's lap at the eleventh hour! For though he had given up working after *Revelge* because of all the interruptions, we suddenly realized he was in the grip of another composition – and to judge by hints and appearances not a small one but a major work, which made him all the more conscious of the noisiness of the place and of the fact that the holiday was coming to an end. How much of it he has salvaged in these last ten days God only knows – even though we are used to miracles in his case. Despite all the obstacles he works wherever he can, even on his walks (on his own and often even with us, for he lets us go ahead), and he has not done that since the days of *Das klagende Lied*. But everywhere he turns he is disturbed by the holiday visitors, and he longs for 'home' and solitude as never before.

NBL, 119–21. (His companions that summer were Natalie Bauer-Lechner, Justine Mahler and Arnold Rosé.)

205–07

In August 1899 Natalie Bauer-Lechner and Justine Mahler undertook an exploratory visit to the Wörthersee, a lake in Carinthia, to try to rent a suitable place for Mahler to stay the following summer. A chance meeting with Anna von Mildenburg resulted in their making the acquaintance of an amateur architect by the name of Theuer, who advised them not to rent a house but to build one. Mahler was summoned by telegram from Vienna and with Theuer's assistance discovered a plot in the woods by the lake at Maiernigg.

Mahler on the building project at Maiernigg

22 August 1899

The plans returned enclosed with thanks. The reduced-scale Plan I seems to me the most suitable in every respect, and I think this would be the one to choose. I have just received Fräulein von Mildenburg's letter and request you to begin the excavations immediately if necessary, so that when I come to Maiernigg on 10 September this question will no longer be outstanding. Please act as you think fit in each and every respect. I declare myself in agreement with whatever you decide.

We have already so completely espoused our plan for the future that we should find it most painful if insuperable difficulties should finally arise. But we hope that our friend Theuer will have the answer to all the problems. . . .

Letter to the architect Theuer, ms., ÖNB-HS.

Enlargement of the Opera company

The number of singers employed has reached a level hitherto unknown in the Opera. Mahler has at last acquired his own mezzo-soprano in Hilgermann, who is excellent in ingénue and sentimental roles. And Kurz's success as Mignon was a veritable breakthrough: she is just the youthful lyric talent he needs.

NBL, 123–24. (Selma Kurz, 1874–1933, coloratura soprano, began her engagement in Vienna on 1 August 1899 and sang there for thirty years.)

Selma Kurz on her discoverer

It was in Frankfurt am Main that Gustav Mahler first heard me, not long after he had gone to Vienna. A few weeks later I received the invitation to an audition at the Vienna Court Opera. I sang various things to Mahler, first in the rehearsal room and then on the stage, and each time he asked me, 'Why on earth are you so excited?' When I didn't answer he finally burst out, 'You are engaged! How much do you want?' But I was so overwhelmed by my sudden good fortune, which had always fascinated me as a distant dream: coming to Vienna, to the Court Opera – that I burst into tears and stammered, 'Give me anything you like.' From the very first day Mahler had shown a quite particular personal and artistic interest in me. He was enraptured with my voice and pursued my development with that intensity which was typical of him. It was only through Mahler that I found my true speciality. For I had been trained as a contralto and it was he who first introduced me to coloratura singing. . . . Working with Mahler in rehearsals was marvellous. Through his will-power and his enthusiasm he compelled one to give of one's very best, and he too was completely exhausted and wrung dry after every rehearsal.

Selma Kurz, 'Mein Entdecker', *Moderne Welt* (Vienna), 1921, Gustav Mahler issue.

Selma Kurz sings Mahler songs at a Philharmonic Concert

What particularly excited the curiosity of the public was the five songs with orchestral accompaniment by G. Mahler, sung by Fräulein Selma Kurz. The poems are taken partly from *Des Knaben Wunderhorn*, partly from a song-cycle, *Lieder eines fahrenden Gesellen*, for which the composer himself is said to have written the verses. . . . These new 'songs' are hard to classify: they are neither *Lieder*, nor arias, nor dramatic scenes, but have something of all of these. In form they are nearest to Berlioz's orchestral songs.

Mahler, one of the most modern composers, has sought, as often happens, to escape into the extreme, into naiveté, into unsullied natural feeling, the simple, indeed inarticulate language of old folk-songs. But it was against his nature to treat these poems with the straightforward artlessness of earlier composers. While retaining a folk-like vocal line he underpinned it with a richly scored accompaniment, full of wit, agility and abrupt modulations, produced not on the piano but by the orchestra. For folk-songs an unusually large, indeed complex orchestration, with three flutes, piccolo, three clarinets, bass clarinet, cor anglais, four horns, two harps. The contradiction, the dichotomy between the concept of 'folksong' and this highly elaborate, sumptuous orchestral accompaniment cannot be denied. But Mahler has accomplished this hazardous enterprise with extraordinary subtlety and masterly technical skill. Now, at the beginning of a new century, it is worth saying, every time a new work by a member of the musical 'Secession' (Mahler, Richard Strauss, Hugo Wolf, etc.) is performed, that it is very possible that the future will be theirs. Fräulein Selma Kurz performed the really difficult Mahler songs from memory, with complete control of both words and music, with a full, round voice and a warm and thoroughly natural expressiveness.

Eduard Hanslick, *Aus neuer und neuester Zeit*, 2nd edn, Berlin 1900, 76–77. (The concert took place on 14 January 1900.)

Richard Heuberger on Mahler's 'touching-up' of Beethoven's Ninth

On the paintings of old masters the art-lover may discover – with horror – traces of over-painting from many different eras. One art-gallery director has overlaid the work of older and generally more important fellow-artists to suit the fashion of his day, and his successor has done so in the fashion of his. Efforts are now being made everywhere to remove the traces of such senseless conceits, to allow the masters to speak to us as *they* saw fit. But in music it is in our age that attempts are being made to introduce the entirely irresponsible idea of 'touching-up' the works of the classics. What we were given yesterday under the name of 'Beethoven's Ninth Symphony' is a regrettable example of this aberration, this barbarism. A whole multitude of passages had been completely re-orchestrated, which means changed in their sound and thus also in their meaning, changed against Beethoven's clearly expressed will. . . .

We are among the most genuine admirers of Director Mahler in respect of his remarkable efforts in the theatre, and believe ourselves to be completely free of any suspicion of malicious misrepresentation of this rare artist or his achievement; all the more reason why in this case we must loudly and clearly call a halt. . . .

Neue Freie Presse, 19 February 1900. (The concert was on 18 February; Beethoven's Ninth Symphony was repeated on 22 February.)

Mahler on 're-scoring' Beethoven

As a consequence of certain published statements it is possible that some members of the public might be led to conclude that the works of Beethoven, and in particular the Ninth Symphony, had been subjected to arbitrary alterations in matters of detail. It seems appropriate, therefore, to make an explanatory statement.

By the time his deafness became total, Beethoven had lost the intimate contact with reality, with the world of physical sound, which is indispensable to a composer. This happened at the very period in his creative life when the increasing power of his conceptions impelled him to seek new means of expression and a previously unheard-of forcefulness in the treatment of the orchestra. This is well known, as is the fact that the construction of the brass instruments of the period rendered unplayable certain sequences of notes which were necessary to complete the melodic line. It was this same deficiency which ultimately occasioned the improvement of these instruments; and to fail to take advantage of this, in order to achieve perfection in the performance of Beethoven's works, would be perverse.

Richard Wagner, who endeavoured all his life, in word and deed, to rescue Beethoven's works in performance from an intolerable state of decadence and neglect, has shown in his essay 'On the Performance of the Ninth Symphony of Beethoven' (*Works*, vol. 9) the way to achieve a performance of this symphony which is as close as possible to the intentions of its creator. All recent conductors have followed Wagner's lead; the director of today's concert has done the same, out of a firm conviction acquired and fortified through his own experience of the work, and without essentially going beyond the bounds set by Wagner.

There can of course be no question of re-scoring, altering, or 'emending' Beethoven's work. The long customary augmentation of the strings has long ago brought in its train an increase in the number of wind instruments, which are there purely to reinforce the sound, and *have not in any way been allotted a new orchestral role.* In this matter, as in every point concerning the interpretation of the work as a whole or in detail, it can be shown by reference to the score (the more detailed the better), that the conductor, far from imposing his own arbitrary intentions on the work – but also without allowing himself to be led astray by any 'tradition' – has been concerned to identify himself completely with Beethoven's wishes, down to the most apparently insignificant detail, and to avoid sacrificing in performance, or allowing to be submerged in a confusion of sound, the least particle of the Master's intentions.

Vienna, February 1900.   Gustav Mahler.

Mahler's defence of his changes to the instrumentation of Beethoven's Ninth Symphony. The leaflet was distributed at the concert of 22 February 1900.

Hans Richter asks to be released from his contract

14 February saw the end of the twenty-eighth year of my activity at the Imperial-Royal Court Opera and it is my right to claim a pension appropriate to my length of service. Although I have signed a new contract, which was to take effect on 1 April, I wish to beg the highly respected Management to release me from this contract and not to restrict or obstruct my right to be relieved of my duties or to draw my pension – especially as the new contract is expressly subject to the Pensions Statutes and no clause takes away my right to draw a pension after twenty-eight years' service. My request to be relieved of my post is the result of the fact that I can no longer carry out my duties fully; my health is no longer strong, and in particular my nervous energy is no longer adequate to meet the heavy demands of my work. For the last few years it has been only with the utmost exertion that I have been able to hold out to the end of a performance. . . .

LKB, 158–9. (As well as this official request for retirement, which was handed in on 28 February 1900, Mahler also received a private letter from Richter asking him to support his request 'in the name of humanity' [LKB, 160–61].)

Press commentary on Richter's departure

The way in which Richter's position in Vienna was made intolerable constitutes one of the ugliest chapters in the history of musical Vienna. It would be quite wrong to assume that Mahler openly opposed him; on the contrary he was careful

enough to ensure his praise was unending. Which left his henchmen and their organs, the Jewish newspapers, to work all the more systematically. . . .

Deutsche Zeitung, 3 March 1900.

Richter's criticism of Mahler

. . . What Mahler does in *Tannhäuser* is simply nonsense. I mean the end of the third act, the chorus of the younger pilgrims. It is nonsense because it proves that Herr Mahler is unaware of the characteristics of the instrumentation of *Tannhäuser,* or has not thought about them. Throughout the whole opera the religious, serious, and let us say, moral element is constantly represented by the wind band. If Wolfram or one of the other 'virtuous' singers rises to his feet his song is introduced and sometimes accompanied by violas and cellos, in a low register, and by the woodwind, as well as the principal accompaniment on the harp, of course. As soon as Tannhäuser speaks the sensuous violins immediately spring up. The intentional contrast between these two groups of instruments is obvious in the prelude to the second act: the chaste rejoicing of Elisabeth (oboe), interrupted by the scornful laughter of Venus (violins). . . .

Now Mahler has cut the woodwinds from the chorus of the younger pilgrims and they appear with the redeeming staff to the sound of the violin accompaniment which is characteristic of Venus. That is a bad example to the younger generation. Mahler's influence would be much more valuable if he would only drop his delusion of being able *to improve the great masters,* including Wagner, whose skill as an orchestrator was acknowledged even by the most hidebound newspaper hacks. . . . I maintain all this . . . but I must add that I nevertheless believe Mahler is the right man for the post of Director of the Court Opera. It is simply preposterous to underestimate his great abilities. I have always acknowledged this. Especially his eye for everything on the stage. But is there no one who has enough influence over him to overcome his arrogance?

Neues Wiener Tagblatt, 28 September 1902.

Franz Schalk engaged for the Vienna Opera

Vienna, 7 April 1900

The sooner you can make it the happier I shall be. So please do your utmost. You will however be certain to be able to begin here at any rate by 1 May at the latest. I believe you will then still have enough time for the rehearsals of *Fedora.* . . .
P.S. I should naturally very much prefer it, if you could perhaps come straight after Easter, after all.

Letter to Franz Schalk, written in an unknown hand but with Mahler's signature, ms., ÖNB-MS. (Schalk directed the first Vienna performance of Umberto Giordano's *Fedora* on 16 May as part of an Italian season.)

Marie Gutheil-Schoder begins her engagement as Carmen

Vienna, 26 May 1900

An important artist today joined the ranks of our Court Opera: Frau Gutheil-Schoder. A few months ago she appeared here in a few roles and aroused our deepest interest. It was a foregone conclusion that she would be engaged. Director Mahler, himself a great talent, a man of passion, has a fine nose for talent, and especially so for such passionate gifts as those of Frau Gutheil. He has secured the services of this remarkable artist, and has brought her to Vienna from her home in Weimar earlier than was originally envisaged. . . . Her Carmen, which she sang again today before a breathlessly attentive audience, and her Nedda, which we still remember as a great experience, form a programme. A quite remarkable and select, if not perhaps particularly long programme. . . . As from today

Carmen is a magnificent production which quite holds its own alongside *The Marriage of Figaro* and other operas which have been totally regenerated by Director Mahler....

From a review by Richard Heuberger, *Neue Freie Presse*, 27 May 1900. (Marie Gutheil-Schoder, 1874–1935, sang at the Vienna Opera until 1926.)

Paris International Exhibition, 1900

... It was here that the principal building of the first Paris International Exhibition was erected forty-five years ago (the foundation stone still exists), and now once again the path leads here to a similar, only much greater and more brilliant festival of all nations. The Parisians of those days would be amazed if they could see the magnificent splendour of the road which now stretches from the Champs-Elysées over the Pont Alexandre III right down to the Invalides.... But the most precious item on show is still the city itself, Paris, with all the contrasts which live peacefully side by side in her streets....

185
186 The Champ de Mars too is gleaming, shimmering white in white, and together with the Trocadéro it forms the second principal venue of the exhibition. The back-drop here is the great Machine Gallery of 1889, which however has been completely transformed and now bears the proud name of Palace of Electricity. In front of it, growing, indeed tumbling out of it, there rises the great 'Water-castle', the most gigantic ornamental fountain you ever saw, a magic play of water jets and tumbling cascades such as the overheated imagination of a demented stage designer could not make more enthralling. You have to imagine it all encrusted with the gleam of countless lamps, bejewelled with the colours of changing lights, and bespangled with artificial suns and stars....

'Feuilleton: Von der Pariser Weltausstellung', *Neue Freie Presse*, 27 May 1900.

The Vienna Philharmonic at the International Exhibition

The Vienna Philharmonic, who are leaving for Paris on 14 June to perform several Philharmonic Concerts there under the patronage of Princess Pauline Metternich, and in whom lively interest is being expressed in Paris, have already held many rehearsals under their Conductor, Director Mahler.

Neues Wiener Tagblatt, 10 June 1900.

Colonel Picquart at the first Paris concert of the Philharmonic

The first concert of the Philharmonic at half-past two this afternoon [18 June] drew a large audience to the Théâtre du Châtelet, despite the unusual hour and oppressive heat. In the boxes many members of the French aristocracy were to be seen, as well as distinguished foreigners.... The public
182 showed considerable interest also in Colonel Picquart, who has become known through the Dreyfus case; he appeared in civilian dress and followed the playing of the Viennese artists with close attention....

Neues Wiener Tagblatt, 19 June 1900.

Berta Zuckerkandl on Georges Clemenceau and Colonel Picquart

In August 1897 Georges Clemenceau came as always to stay with us in Vienna after his rest at Karlsbad. We spent the summer on the Kahlenberg.... It was not until we began driving through the delightful scenery up the slopes of the Kahlenberg that he began to talk – about the Dreyfus affair, but most especially about Colonel Picquart. He was the most idealistic figure among the noble group of men who fought to set Captain Dreyfus free. And if it was Scheurer-Kestner and Zola who spoke out for Dreyfus's innocence, it is Clemenceau who is to be thanked for the discovery of the second military plot, which was directed against Picquart, and for Picquart's release later from a long and dangerous imprisonment....

Berta Szeps-Zuckerkandl, *Ich erlebte fünfzig Jahre Weltgeschichte*, Stockholm 1939, 183–84.

Théâtre Municipal du Châtelet

LUNDI *18 JUIN 1900, à 2 heures 1/2*

SOUS LE HAUT PATRONAGE DE

Madame la Princesse de METTERNICH SÁNDOR

Ier Concert Philharmonique

DONNÉ PAR LA

Société Philharmonique

DE VIENNE

(WIENER PHILHARMONIKER)

Dont tous les Artistes sont Membres de l'Opéra I. et R. de la Cour

SOUS LA DIRECTION DE

M. Gustav MAHLER

Directeur de l'Opéra I. et R. de la Cour

Concert programme, Paris, 18 June 1900.

Berta Zuckerkandl was a daughter of the Viennese journalist Moritz Szeps, who managed the *Neues Wiener Tagblatt* until 1886 and afterwards the *Wiener Tagblatt*. Through his position of confidence with Crown Prince Rudolf, and his friendship with the French politician Georges Clemenceau (1841–1929), Szeps played a political role behind the scenes until the Crown Prince's suicide in 1889. In April 1886 Berta Szeps married the anatomist Emil Zuckerkandl, while in the same year her elder sister Sophie married the French mining engineer Paul Clemenceau, a brother of the statesman. Georges Clemenceau was one of the witnesses to the marriage, and this was the occasion of his first secret conversation with the Austrian Crown Prince. Paul Clemenceau and his wife Sophie gathered in their home in Paris a circle of artists and art-lovers. It was there that Berta Zuckerkandl met the sculptor Auguste Rodin and other French masters, whose works she promoted in Vienna through her influence as an art critic. The well-known critic Ludwig Hevesi reported that it was in Berta Zuckerkandl's salon in Vienna that the idea of the Vienna Secession was first expressed: 'It was there that the few modern men met who gave it substance and began the struggle for the rejuvenation of art in Vienna.' Gustav Mahler came into contact with Berta Zuckerkandl through his French admirers Paul and Sophie Clemenceau, and it was through her that he met his future wife.

The French Mahlerians

My sister Sophie had gathered a circle of music-lovers around her. Following the tradition established by her father, she continued the work of cultural *rapprochement* between Austria and her second home, France. Her friends General L'Allemand, Picquart and Paul Painlevé, the famous mathematician and later Prime Minister, were enthusiastic admirers of their common friend Gustav Mahler. From 1900 to 1908 they attended almost every concert that Mahler conducted outside Austria. They followed him everywhere.

Berta Szeps-Zuckerkandl, *Ich erlebte fünfzig Jahre Weltgeschichte*, Stockholm 1939, 184–85.

The critic Pierre Lalo on Mahler as a conductor

M. Mahler, like most German conductors of his generation, has faults which constitute the precise opposite of the faults of our French conductors. In France no one devotes any thought at all to the scores of the masters, whereas our neighbours devote too much. They see an intention in every note; everything is emphasized; and this leads to excessive complication of the structure, destroying the construction of the piece. . . . Regrettably M. Mahler, who is one of the most remarkable symphonists of the German school, decided not to take the opportunity of performing one of his own works, and played no more than an excerpt from a Bruckner symphony; the whole symphony would have been more worth while.

Pierre Lalo, *Le Temps*, 26 June 1900. (The critic was a son of the composer Edouard Lalo.)

Natalie Bauer-Lechner on the summer at Maiernigg

During the first week of his stay at Maiernigg, Mahler was unable to get down to work straight away, as he usually did (for example in the summerhouse at Steinbach, where his inspiration often took hold within the first twenty-four hours). He was quite upset, indeed in despair, said he would never do anything again, and already saw his superstitious fear, that he would have a house to compose in but be unable to write anything, as a cruel reality.

Of course the cause was the ill-health that had troubled him since Paris, but perhaps even more to blame was the nature of his creative effort this year, for he had to pick up the threads from the previous year's sketches of his plan for a Fourth Symphony. After the abrupt interruption at the end of the holiday at Aussee, to find his way back into the work, and re-establish the original flow, was probably the most difficult thing he had yet achieved.

When he then began to work (he kept completely silent on the subject, but I believe that it was on his birthday), he was in his summerhouse from seven in the morning till one o'clock – and later even for eight or ten hours – and thanks to the beautifully mild climate and the delicious air in the forest he was able to stand the strain better than previously.

NBL, 136. (In the summer of 1900 Mahler was already able to work in his summerhouse, but the living quarters were not yet finished.)

Mahler to Nina Spiegler, on the Fourth Symphony

Vienna, 18 August 1900

This summer has been so marvellous for me that I feel really equipped for this winter. . . .

I shall be putting the finishing touches to my work in the winter this year; and that will give my life a focal point amid the turmoil, which is something I have always especially missed in these last few years.

224

One feels so God-forsaken if one has to carry on living without the thing that one holds most sacred. I, especially, am miserable and am obliged to wear a mask which you probably sometimes see leering rather strangely at you. Last winter this was particularly so, for the work which I have this year completed had to be left off, just in the midst of the tenderest, truly embryonic beginnings, and *abandoned*.

I could not imagine how it might be possible to pick up such delicate threads again. However, it is strange. Once I find myself out in the country and alone with myself, everything mean and trivial is as if extinguished and disappears without trace. . . . I must say I now find it rather hard to get to grips with things here again; I still live half in, half out of the world of my Fourth. It is so utterly different from my other symphonies. But that *must be*; I could never repeat a state of mind, and as life progresses I follow new paths in each new work. That is why it is always so difficult at the beginning to get down to work. All the routine you have acquired is useless. You have to begin learning anew to do something new. So one remains forever a *beginner*! Earlier, that frightened me and filled me with doubts about myself. But now I understand it I see it as a guarantee of the genuineness and durability of my works.

So this year for the first time I look to the future without the worst of my anxious doubts – although I should still not dare to be confident. . . .

Ms., The Pierpont Morgan Library, New York, and The Mary Flagler Cary Charitable Trust.

Anna von Mildenburg as coach

Mahler is now having Miss Kurz rehearse the part of Sieglinde for the *Ring*, at the same time employing Miss Mildenburg – who not only sings and acts her own part incomparably but also has a masterly comprehension and command of the whole work – as a kind of demonstrator and singing teacher; she sings and demonstrates everything for her younger colleague, exactly as Mahler demands and suggests; for she understands him as no other artist has ever done.

NBL, 148.

Max Kalbeck on the salvaging of a neglected masterpiece

It was sown mortal and is risen immortal. The regeneration of Mozart's *Così fan tutte* is nothing short of the rescue and preservation of a much-maligned and underestimated masterpiece. The opera appeared to us yesterday for the first time in a form approaching the perfect image of an ecstatic lover of the music, and at the same time went a long way towards fulfilling the expectations of the cooler, critically minded public. Everyone was generally satisfied, and for the first time the work appealed as strongly as some new work which is impatiently awaited and whose success is assured; and the feeling of tedium in the course of the second half was not too noticeable. . . .

Neues Wiener Tagblatt, 5 October 1900. (The première of the new production took place on 4 October.)

Max Graf on Mahler's love of his new productions

Mahler was most touchingly attached to his new productions. The work upon which he had bestowed his spiritual energy he enveloped in tenderness and would have most preferred to put it under a glass cover. When he had to go to Munich after the performance of *Così fan tutte* and was obliged to leave the second performance to another conductor, he asked me to go to the theatre and to telegraph him a report on the performance the same night. He trembled at the thought that the new production might be compromised during his absence.

Max Graf, *Die Wiener Oper*, Vienna 1955, 85.

The Munich Hugo Wolf Society organized a concert on 20 October 1900, in which Mahler performed his Second Symphony. At a party which took place after the performance he made the acquaintance of the young musicologist Ludwig Schiedermair (1876–1957), who was then engaged on a Gustav Mahler study for the series *Moderne Musiker*. The remarks Mahler made that evening on the subject of programme music found their way into this essay.

Mahler on programme music and programme notes

After the concert an illustrious company gathered, consisting of leading artists, scholars and writers, to spend what was left of the evening with Mahler in an atmosphere of relaxation and merriment. Somebody introduced the subject of programme notes. It was as though lightning had struck in a bright and sunny landscape. Mahler's eyes lit up more than ever, he raised his forehead, jumped up from the table in his excitement and cried out impassionedly: 'Away with programmes, they arouse false impressions. Leave the public to their own thoughts about the work they are to hear, do not force them to read while they are listening and fill their minds with pre-conceived ideas! If a composer himself has forced on his listeners the feelings which overwhelmed him, then he has achieved his object. The language of music has then approached that of the word, but has communicated immeasurably more than the word is able to express.' And Mahler took up his glass and emptied it with a cry of 'Death to programmes!' And the rest of us looked at one another understandingly.

Ludwig Schiedermair, *Gustav Mahler*, Leipzig (1900), 13–14.

From two letters to Ludwig Schiedermair

Vienna, 2 November 1900

I prattled a great deal of what I think in that jovial company that got together after the concert – you must have heard; including what I said about 'programmes'. This is not the place for me to present a connected statement of what I think on the subject. Thanks to my profession I am in such a terrible *rush* that I literally do not have time even to eat or sleep properly. . . . In any case I hope I have expressed myself sufficiently clearly in my works and that you can absorb the emotion and the experience they embody without verbal explanations, if you approach them with your inner eyes and ears open. It would be a genuine release for me to find someone who was able to see and hear simply from the score and from his own self. One thing you will also already have noticed, that just as my physical life develops rather than simply progressing, so also that life expresses itself in the sequence of my works – and when I say that I begin a new symphony roughly where the previous one finished I do not mean simply tying a new thread on to the end of the old one that is already fully spun out. In a word – I hope that you will approach the tender creations of the artist (however intractable their content may make them) not as a botanist but as a poet. . . .

[no date]

Many thanks for your little book, which I have read with interest. I have the impression I come off quite well in it. If you really mean to do essays on the First and Third, then please be *careful*! You seem to be quite wide of the mark, as far as I can judge from your brief comments. The Third has nothing to do with the struggles of an individual. It would be more accurate to say: it is nature's path of development (from stiff materiality to the greatest articulation! but above all the *life of nature*!)
Dionysus – the driving, creative force. – The titles that I originally added to the work are indicative, but they are so

inadequate and have been so thoroughly misunderstood that I have dropped them again. They may perhaps help to lighten the darkness for you a little – but – careful how you use them and interpret them! Let me emphasize again what I have already said: just as they were in any case only added *afterwards* because the work was not understood, they have been dropped again because they were misunderstood. . . . The First has not yet been grasped by anyone who has not lived with me.

Mss., BST.

From the memories of a Viennese Promenader

Two or three years passed, and we had become striplings at the Conservatoire, young men and women, and Mahler was the director of the Philharmonic Concerts. And for us that meant two and a half hours of queuing before the locked door of the Musikvereinssaal in the biting cold and snow, followed – once we had purchased our precious ticket for the Promenade – by another two hours of indescribable intoxication . . . our first experience of the *Eroica* and all the other wealth of classical music. But much more fateful events were to come. In 1900 Mahler gave the first Vienna performance of his First Symphony, and the malicious haters of genius, and above all of pure and absolute genius, were on hand with all their weapons prepared for the offensive. There was a regular first-night riot, with hissing, whistling, enraged shouting and fisticuffs – a so-called flop. But even then it was already evident that this filthy torrent of hostility was directed not so much at what must at the time have been quite a difficult work, but rather at the personality which bore the name of Gustav Mahler. Only the youngest listeners stood amidst the thunderous noise, overwhelmed by the power of that serious, bespectacled figure, and clapped and cried themselves hoarse with applause. Not, of course, because they had grasped the full import of the work in all its strength and all its weakness, but because their impassioned and unshakable feelings told them: this is the pure confession of a great man. A handsome, dark-haired boy musician was my constant companion at the Philharmonic concerts. . . . We rushed to the rostrum with the others and called Mahler out again and again in wild ecstasy, while the Antis behind us roared their insults, and we can never forget the pain in the smile with which Mahler acknowledged our applause. . . .

Maria Komorn, 'Mahler und die Jugend', *Neues Wiener Journal*, 31 August 1930. (The first Vienna performance of Mahler's First Symphony took place at the Philharmonic Concert of 18 November 1900.)

Emma Adler on Mahler's politics

Mahler always kept his distance from political life and political parties. That his sympathies were Socialist ones, everyone knows who came into contact with him. At the elections in 1901, despite his post as Imperial-Royal Director of the State Opera [*sic*], he openly cast his vote for the Socialist candidate in his constituency.
The name of the candidate was Victor Adler.

Emma Adler, 'Biographie Victor Adlers', typescript, 108, Verein für Geschichte der Arbeiterbewegung, Vienna. (Victor Adler was the opponent of the sitting Christian Socialist member in the final ballot of 7 January 1901 of the parliamentary election for constituency II, ward 5. This constituency included the Vienna III district, in which Mahler lived. Dr Adler was not elected.)

In 1900 two popular singers who had been engaged during the Jahn era retired from the Court Opera: on 26 January Marie Renard gave her farewell performance as Carmen; and on 30 September the tenor Ernest van Dyck left. As in the case of Hans Richter, the anti-Mahlerian press blamed the Director for the loss of these two artists. Miss Renard's roles were taken on by Marie Gutheil-Schoder and Selma

Kurz. In place of Van Dyck a young tenor from Brünn (Brno) was engaged: Leo Slezak, 1873–1946. After a guest performance in January 1901 he began his contract in Vienna in September of that year.

179 *Leo Slezak's recollections of his Director*

I thank the Fates for the privilege I had of working under the direction of this man for seven whole years, in the Storm-and-Stress period of my artistic development.

To be sure, he was awkward as a Director; indeed, I should go so far as to say he was often intolerable. But as soon as he began working with us, in the rehearsal room or on the stage, every trace of crossness went with the wind, all the petty annoyances of everyday life were forgotten in a flash, and we were proud to be able to follow this genius through thick and thin. . . . Those Mozart cycles, *Entführung aus dem Serail, Così fan tutte, The Magic Flute, Fidelio, Huguenots, La Juive,* all the new productions: the rehearsals were a constant source of ideas. Every remark was a gift for life. None of us would ever dream of leaving the rehearsal room if Mahler was working on a scene in which we did not appear. . . . His way of working drew from the singer everything he had to give.

However rowdy Hesch, Demuth and I were at other times, when we were on the stage together in Mozart, with Mahler conducting, we kept quiet, concerned lest any flaw might tarnish the complete success of the performance.

But if it was perfect Mahler was scarcely recognizable, came on the stage to us, praising us and handing out 20-heller pieces. And those of course were the moments I took advantage of to wheedle out some leave of absence or other. In deep and moving tones I described to the Director the advanced stage of my misery, which could be relieved only by a guest appearance in Brünn or Prague.

He laughed: 'Be off with you then, in God's name, but when you come back at least behave yourself for a while.'

Leo Slezak, *Meine sämtlichen Werke*, Berlin 1922, 247–48.

Dedication to Anna von Mildenburg in 'Das klagende Lied'

The loftiest lament
Yesterday I heard.
Dear singer,
Take this gift from me,
As from 'my younger days!'

Printed vocal score of *Das klagende Lied* with dedication in Mahler's own hand, ÖNB-MS. (Anna von Mildenburg noted on the inside page of this volume: 'Gustav Mahler gave me this at Christmas after the *Twilight of the Gods.*')

189 In February 1901 Mahler rehearsed the first performance of his youthful work *Das klagende Lied* (completed in 1880). Before it was printed he had undertaken a major revision of the score. The première took place on 17 February 1901 in the great Musikvereinssaal as an extraordinary concert of a Vienna choral society (the Singakademie). The soloists were Anna von Mildenburg, Elise Elizza, Edith Walker and Fritz Schrödter. The orchestra was the Court Opera Orchestra with an additional wind band, the singers were the members of the Singakademie and of the Schubert Union. The concert agency that organized the event had announced 500 performers on their posters.

The Vienna critics on Mahler's youthful work

Today Mahler is performing his youthful follies; but he would not compose like that any more.

Robert Hirschfeld, *Wiener Abendpost*, 23 February 1901.

A harmonic effect that is a real stroke of genius is the seven-part choral entry in part one over the sixteen-bar-long pedal point on F (*O Spielmann*). Mahler's music never fails to make a significant impression when it succeeds in keeping itself within bounds. But when he composes 'a joyful noise', it's a corybantic hubbub. . . .

Gustav Schönaich, *Wiener Allgemeine Zeitung*, 20 February 1901.

This poem, for all its simplicity a moving piece, has spread out, in the course of composition, to monstrous proportions.

Richard Heuberger, *Neue Freie Presse*, 18 February 1901.

Das klagende Lied seems to us more a skilfully laid out assortment of more or less crude or subtle acoustic effects than an artistically moulded and inspired musical organism.

Max Kalbeck, *Neues Wiener Tagblatt*, 19 February 1901.

Just think what Karl Löwe produced from similar material! And all he needed was one voice and a piano. . . .

Josef Scheu, *Arbeiter-Zeitung*, 24 February 1901.

Herr Mahler has as a composer an advantage that only very few have ever enjoyed: the power to entrust his works to the best performers imaginable; his symphonies to the best orchestra in the world, the Philharmonic, his songs to the best singers, and the interpretation to one of the most adept of conductors: Gustav Mahler. . . .

In the concert hall *Das klagende Lied* soon found the majority of the audience on its side. Herr Mahler, conductor and composer, received tumultuous applause. Part of the audience, non-members of the Mahlerian community, remained cool. They were unfortunately unable to acclaim the conductor without receiving the thanks of the composer.

Hans Liebstöckl, *Die Reichswehr*, 18 February 1901.

Operation and convalescent leave

Director Mahler will undergo an operation in a sanatorium next week and after leaving hospital will go to the south. The première of the opera *Lobetanz*, which is scheduled for the middle of March, will be conducted by Court Conductor Schalk.

Neues Wiener Journal, 3 March 1901. (Since Mahler was away on sick leave the Philharmonic concert of 10 March was directed by Court Conductor Joseph Hellmesberger.)

Anti-Mahler feeling within the Philharmonic

In Philharmonic circles the opposition to Director Mahler continues to gain the upper hand. The conductor's over-agitated, highly strung temperament, his exaggerated zeal in ordering preliminary rehearsals, but above all his weakness in lending his ear to the whims of his 'trusted favourites', are robbing him of the sympathies of many players who until now have been members of his party, whether from conviction or opportunism. Eager efforts are being made to nominate a new candidate for this post of honour. The whole business is being handled in strict secrecy in order to avoid any possible confrontation. The re-appointment, as is known, will take place in September. Perhaps Director Mahler, who has now been apprised of the planned campaign against him, will succeed in calming the agitation by making new promises.

Die Reichswehr, 2 April 1901.

Justine Mahler to Ludwig Karpath

Thank you very much for your letter and the newspaper cuttings. Naturally I have not breathed a word to my brother; he does not read any newspapers here and so he will know nothing of the whole business, anyway it is immaterial what *Die Reichswehr* may write, the most important thing is that my brother will certainly no longer conduct the Philharmonic concerts because he simply cannot stand the strain. He will certainly not conduct any Wagner this season, he is conducting act one of *Die Königin von Saba* for the first time at a gala performance, but don't tell anyone! ! This way he will escape an ovation, which overstimulates his nerves, and anyway it has long been his intention to do *Die Königin von Saba* for Vienna. . . .

Ludwig Karpath. (Mahler revived Goldmark's *Die Königin von Saba* on 29 April 1901.)

Max Graf on the Opera Season 1900–01

There were only two new works. In the 1897–98 season there had been four operas and three ballets; in 1898–99 five operas and two ballets; in 1899–1900 four operas and two ballets. The first new work (13 November) was the opera *Der Bundschuh*, libretto by Max Morold, music by Josef Reiter. It portrays in powerful verse an event from the Upper Austrian peasants' revolt, in other words a piece of historical folk art. The music is characterized by a certain wild power, whose roughness indicates the originality of Reiter's musical talent. It has a powerful, earthy character of its own which comes out especially in the popular scenes at the beginning. The second half of the opera – the love scene – is weaker. The opera was performed five times. Second new work (18 March) was *Lobetanz*, libretto by Bierbaum, music by L. Thuille. Berlin had already put it on. The text is a 'tale of love' in olde worlde verse. The music is the work of a tasteful, accomplished musician, without strong originality but highly cultivated – the exact opposite of Reiter. What is interesting is the appearance of large, rounded musical structures and a mosaic of individual scenes treated melodramatically. This work too was unable to establish itself; there were six performances. Quite a large number of operas were brought into the repertoire in new productions. Namely (based on the detailed notes by A. J. Weltner in the *Abendpost* on 20 and 21 June 1901): eight operas and two ballets (the date in brackets is the year the work was last performed): *Così fan tutte* (1891), *Il Trovatore* (1897), *Romeo and Juliet* (1899), *La Traviata* (1899), *Rienzi* (1893), *William Tell* (1899), the ballets *Braut von Korea* (1899) and *Rouge et noir* (1898), *Hamlet* (1898), *Martha* (1895).

Così fan tutte was given a delightful performance on the revolving stage, which proved a suitably intimate setting for comic operas like this. *Rienzi* appeared with resplendent pomp, as did Goldmark's *Königin von Saba*. . . . This year Richard Wagner once again heads the list, and the number of performances of his work is still rising. 70 evenings were devoted to him this year (including the complete tetralogy six times) as against 58 performances in 1899–1900. After him comes Joseph Bayer with 48 performances of 6 ballets. In third place comes Verdi with 5 operas, 31 performances, including 13 sold-out performances of the new production of *Il Trovatore*. . . .

Max Graf, 'Wien, Hofoperntheater', offprint from *Deutsche Thalia*, Vienna and Leipzig 1902, 7–8.

Mahler engages Bruno Walter for the Vienna Opera

Splendid! I am leaving for the Wörthersee this evening but have arranged everything so that as soon as we have your final acceptance you will be sent a two-year contract from 1 July with 6,000 florins annual salary. (The shortness of the contract is so that your salary can be increased when it is renewed.) Everything else we can deal with by correspondence. . . .

One thing is absolutely vital. Your engagement must *not* be made public before you arrive in Vienna. I have the most cogent reasons for this. *Not even in Berlin!* The best will be for you to introduce yourself with a new work! I am planning to start with *The Tales of Hoffmann* and Puccini's *La Bohème*. Undated letter, June 1901, GMB, 273–74.

A couple of days after Justi and me, Mahler arrived in Maiernigg full of expectation and curiosity about his new house.

Within a few days Justi had sorted out the interior fittings and what was lacking on the exterior, so that, although plenty still remained unfinished, the whole did look lived-in. The situation of the house, between the woods and the lake, is so entrancing in itself that you are constantly being charmed anew by it. Two magnificent great stone terraces (an open one on the main floor, and the covered loggia beneath it) afford the most extensive views over the lake, which also beckons one from every window, just as the high tips of the pines and alders in the wood seem to be peeping in on all sides. But Mahler's balcony in front of his attic storey is like a high watch-tower. 'It is too beautiful', he said, 'it is more than a man deserves.'

NBL, 159.

Mahler to Richard Strauss

Maiernigg am Wörthersee, near Klagenfurt
6 July 1901

The Fourth is at the printers! But I shall scarcely have the material ready by then and in any case I should not like to set a new work – the first of mine which is perhaps more practically suited to current conditions and is therefore likely, given an unprejudiced and sympathetic reception, to earn me the sole reward that I ask for my works: to be heard and understood – I should not like to set this work before the Berlin public, to whom I am unknown and who will be alienated in advance by a narrow-minded press. I have promised the first performance to Munich; and since there is even a 'split' down there – Kaim and Odeon are both fighting for it – I already have enough to keep me occupied and, I therefore beg you, dear Strauss, not to include my Fourth in your own plans for the time being.

As far as the Third is concerned I must insist on having all my requirements fulfilled in performance. The six bells are not at all the most important thing – there's no need to insist on them; perhaps four would be available – that would be enough. But the *acoustics* of the Kroll Hall are said to be *bad*! Is that true? If it is, dear friend, do not do anything of mine there! The *orchestra* must be tip-top! The rehearsals must be very full – and – my work lasts for two hours – there is not room for anything else on the same programme. That applies equally to Berlin and Krefeld!

Please do not be upset by the fact that my initial response to your friendly sympathy consists of nothing but difficulties. I am well aware that if it is within your power you will sweep them all away and I shall be with you with a thousand joys. But I also have another reason to plead for the Third, and that is that for the present I know no one other than yourself who would *dare* to produce this monster. So the Third! the Third! I might add that if you have a good choral society at your disposal there is *Das klagende Lied*, which has made the strongest impression of all my works so far. It lasts for 40 minutes. You could perhaps couple it with some other vocal work. The chorus has a relatively small but very important and difficult part. I could provide the soloists ready-trained. Shall I send you the score, and if so where to?

Now, about your *Feuersnot*! I have heard through the grapevine that the censors will not pass the work. Whether it is a total ban or just difficulties I have not yet been able to discover. Unfortunately nothing can be done for the time being, until

227

September comes; then I shall call on the censor myself. At present he is on holiday! Might you in the end have the same problem in Dresden? What a disaster that would be. I at any rate will not give up.

Ms., Dr Franz Strauss Collection, Garmisch-Partenkirchen.

Natalie Bauer-Lechner on the compositions of the summer of 1901

Within the last few days Mahler has spoken to me for the first time about his work this summer, his Fifth Symphony, and in particular about the third movement: 'The movement is immensely difficult to work out because of the structure and the supreme artistic mastery which it demands in all its relationships and details. The apparent confusion must resolve itself into perfect order and harmony, as in a Gothic cathedral. . . .

'The human voice would be utterly out of place here. There is no call for words, everything is said in purely musical terms. It will be a straightforward symphony in four movements, too, with each movement independent and complete in itself and related to the others only by the common mood.' On 10 August, in his hut in the woods, Mahler played me the seven songs which he has done in fourteen days (each composed one day and orchestrated the next). Six are by Rückert and one, *Der Tambourgesell* [*Tamboursg'sell*, 'The Drummer Boy'], is from *Des Knaben Wunderhorn*. . . .

About the *Tambourgesell* and the *Kindertotenlieder* ['Songs on the Deaths of Children'] he said he felt sorry he had to write them and he pitied the world that would one day have to hear them, so terribly sad was their content. About the *Lindenzweig* [*Ich atmet' einen linden Duft*, 'I breathed a soft fragrance'] he said the very kind thing that it contains something of a contented, happy feeling such as one feels in the company of a dear person of whom one is completely sure without a single word needing to pass. The very text of *Blicke mir nicht in die Lieder* ['Don't look into my songs'] is so characteristic of Mahler that he might have written it himself. But he regards it as the least significant of them all and said that as a result it would probably be the first to find favour and have the widest appeal.

Mahler had already finished his holiday work for this year, and was planning to spend the last few days resting but was suddenly seized by the composition of Rückert's poem *Ich bin der Welt abhanden gekommen* ['I have left the world behind'], which had been planned right at the beginning but had been put aside in favour of the Symphony. He himself said of the uncommonly full and restrained character of this song that it was feeling from the heart right up into the lips but it never passed them! He also said this was himself!

NBL, 164–65. (Mahler composed the first three songs of the *Kindertotenlieder* in the summer of 1901, but the fourth and fifth were not written until 1904.)

196 *Bruno Walter's début in Vienna*

In the *Aida* performance of 28 September a new young conductor, Herr Bruno Walter (from Berlin) showed his paces. In his gestures he apes Gustav Mahler. The same agitated and sharply angular gestures, the same waving, the same entranced look, the same sharp cuing of the instruments, the same bustling nervousness: but it is not genuine, a copy, a pose. Beneath all these affected mannerisms lies buried a good kernel: command of the stage and of the orchestra.

Max Graf, *Die Musik*, November 1901 (1), p. 261.

Bruno Walter to his parents

Vienna, 29 September 1901

Aida was very excellent; Mahler and his whole circle congratulated me with great sincerity; Mahler said I was 'a big boy now'. The orchestra behaved splendidly; they followed me

with genuine fire and at the end of each act crowded round and said kind things. What the public thinks of me I could not assess: *Aida* has no overture, and the loud applause in the course of the opera may of course just as well have been for the benefit of the singers. I include a few reviews, they are all in this same vein, unpleasant, unobjective, petty, or rather ridiculous. Mahler says there is nothing more trivial than what the press here says; it is a company of idiots, barks like a dog at every new face, then growls for a while and after a few years one is 'our man Walter'. . . .

We went to the Mahlers' for supper recently. Lipiner, Frau Bauer and Dr Freund were present. Mahler's cordiality to me is quite touching, quite as he always was, only a little milder and quieter as he gets older; as an artist – we had heard him conduct *Tristan* – he is an unattainable ideal. Of antique stature and simplicity of manner. Else, too, is quite taken with him. Lipiner, who had come to Mahler's with the firm intention, as he said, of holding his tongue, was as captivating in his conversation as ever; he spoke with true wisdom and depth about Goethe and the fifth act of *Faust*, Part Two – I admired him once again as an exceptional, a spellbinding character. They have all welcomed us with great cordiality here. . . .

Bruno Walter, *Briefe*, Frankfurt 1969, 44–45. (Else was Bruno Walter's wife.)

Marie Gutheil-Schoder on Mahler's staging

The thing I found interesting about Mahler as a stage manager was his attention to detail, to the inner structure of a scene. He particularly liked pauses and silences. They were more important to him than anything. For it was through them that he created the inner life, the emotional content of the moment, the temperament, the humour. For example a scene from the *Merry Wives:* second tableau, Mistress Ford's chamber. 176 Mistress Ford pretends to be unhappy, weeps crocodile tears and laments the jealousy of her husband, who has just made a great scene. Then Ford approaches her submissively and says: 'I had a letter which told me Sir John Falstaff was with you.' At this revelation Mistress Ford normally springs up at once with cries of how and what and Heavens above. But Mahler made me stay quite motionless and count out a full bar quite slowly after Ford's confession – this created a big pause, and with it, of course, great suspense, both on stage and in the audience. And the outburst of the insulted lady after this rhythmic pause gained immensely in effect – and humour.

Marie Gutheil-Schoder, *Erlebtes und Erstrebtes*, Vienna 1937, 52–53. (The première of the new production of Nicolai's opera took place on 4 October 1901. Mistress Ford is known in the opera as Frau Flut; see ill.)

Alma Schindler on her origins and youth

I am the daughter of a sort of national monument. My father, Emil J. Schindler, the idol of my childhood, came from an old patrician family. He was the most important landscape painter of the Austrian Monarchy. . . .

My father was highly musical. He had a wonderful voice, a bright tenor, and sang Schumann *Lieder* and the like with great accomplishment. His conversation was fascinating and never ordinary. I spent hours with him and stood and stared at the revelatory hand that guided the paint-brush. I dreamt of wealth for the sole purpose of smoothing the path of creative men. . . .

One of my great experiences was a journey we undertook. My father was commissioned by Crown Prince Rudolf, for his 'The Monarchy in word and picture', to do ink-drawings of all the Adriatic coastal towns from Dalmatia down to Spizza. We are given a tramp steamer, which had to wait everywhere until my father had finished his work, and went first to Ragusa [Dubrovnik]. We stayed half the winter there and then carried on in the freighter to Corfu, where we spent the other half of the winter. . . .

We had had an upright piano sent from Corfu, and it was here, at the age of nine, that I began to compose and write music. Since I was the only musician in the house, I was able to make my own discoveries, without being pushed into them. . . .

Then my father died. It was in the summer of 1892; he was on his first pleasure trip, which he was able to afford after paying off all his debts. Though young at fifty he suddenly fell ill and at first no one could understand the virulence of his disease. . . .

Five years later my mother married my father's pupil, the painter Carl Moll. She married a pendulum, but my father had been a mainspring!

These youthful years completely separated my inner life from my environment. My surroundings became indifferent to me and music became my all.

The blind organist Josef Labor taught me counterpoint, I raced through the whole literature of music and screeched all the Wagner roles until my fine mezzo-soprano voice was in ruins. I lived in a musical paradise which I made for myself.

Following my father's wishes I sought the mentors of my youth in the older and wiser men of our artistic circle: Max Burckhard, who taught me to read in the serious sense, and later Gustav Klimt, the elegant Byzantine painter, who intensified and expanded the concept of 'Seeing-with-your-own-eyes', which he had learned from my father. . . . Gustav Klimt had entered my life as my first great love, but I had been a naïve child, drunk with music and untouched by life and the world. The more I suffered through this passion the more I sank into my own music, and so my unhappiness became the spring of blissful abandon. My wild composing was set on a more serious course by Alexander von Zemlinsky, who had recognized my talent at once. I composed page after page of sonata movements from one day to the next, lived only for my work and abruptly retired from all social intercourse. . . . It was almost a matter of course that I fell in love with Zemlinsky, who was an ugly creature.

I had first met Zemlinsky at a small party and we went through the people around us with malicious sarcasm. Suddenly we looked at each other. 'If we can think of someone about whom only good can be said, we'll drain a glass to him!' And with one voice we cried: 'Mahler!'

Alma Mahler-Werfel, *Mein Leben*, Frankfurt 1963, 11, 13, 14, 15, 16, 17, 24. (Emil Jakob Schindler, 1842–1892; Carl Moll, 1861–1945, a pupil of Schindler's, painter and art-director, co-founder of the Vienna Secession; Max Burckhard, 1854–1912, jurist and writer, from 1890 to 1898 Director of the Burgtheater, the Court Theatre, where he introduced the works of Ibsen, Hauptmann and Schnitzler; Gustav Klimt, 1867–1918, painter, first president of the Secession; Alexander von Zemlinsky, 1872–1942, composer and conductor, teacher of Arnold Schönberg and Erich Wolfgang Korngold. In January 1900 Mahler had performed Zemlinsky's opera *Es war einmal* at the Court Opera.)

202   On the occasion of a visit of Sophie Clemenceau to Vienna, her sister Berta Zuckerkandl gave a party in her house to which Mahler was invited. Among the guests was Alma Schindler.

Alma Schindler's first encounter with Mahler

203   Strangely enough Mahler took note of me immediately; not only because of my face, which could be called beautiful at the time, but also because of my sharp, tense manner. He looked at me through his glasses long and searchingly. The last guests arrived and we went in to dinner. Klimt and Burckhard sat either side of me, and we made a boisterous threesome and laughed a great deal. From the other end of the table Mahler watched and listened, unobtrusively at first, then more openly, and finally called out enviously, 'Can't we all share the joke?' He did not pay much attention to his poor neighbour at the table that evening. . . .

After we had left the table and gathered into little groups the conversation turned to the relativity of all beauty. 'Beauty!'

Gustav Klimt. Drawing by Emil Orlik. *95 Köpfe von Orlik*, Berlin 1920. ÖNB-BA.
Klimt (1867–1918), the leading Austrian painter of the turn of the century, was a friend of Mahler's. Alma Mahler tells us that Mahler started off with no feeling for visual art at all, but gradually, through his 'exceptional eagerness to learn', came to take pleasure in paintings. 'Moll, Klimt, Roller and Kolo Moser vied with one another to be his teacher' (AM, 201).

And Mahler said he found the head of Socrates beautiful. I agreed strongly with him and said for my part that the musician Alexander von Zemlinsky was beautiful. Mahler shrugged and said that was going rather far. Whereupon my blood was up and I turned the conversation into a particular discussion of Zemlinsky. . . .

We had long since left the group we were in, or the others had gone off. We had around us that vacuum which two people who have found one another immediately generate. I promised him then 'to come some time or other when I had something worthwhile'. He smiled mockingly as if to say 'I shall have a long wait,' and invited me and the two sisters Clemenceau and Zuckerkandl, who came in at that moment, to come to the Opera for the dress rehearsal of *The Tales of Hoffmann* the following morning. At first I hesitated – my composition exercise for Zemlinsky was not yet finished – but then the excitement got the better of me and I agreed to go.

190, 191

AM, 9–10.

Eduard Hanslick on 'The Tales of Hoffmann' at the Opera

The first act, the most light-hearted and musically the most pleasing, is notable for its exemplary ensemble. It may be mentioned in passing that it is characteristic of Director Mahler that even as late as the dress rehearsal he had the violins repeat the very simple opening bars of the G major waltz at least half a dozen times until the ebb and flow of the *rubato* was to his entire satisfaction. Mahler can hardly be an admirer of Offenbach's; but once he has undertaken to conduct a work it receives his complete attention and devotion.

Neue Freie Presse, 15 November 1901. (The première took place on 11 November 1901 and was repeated on 12 and 14 November, each time with a different cast.)

A critical voice at the Munich première of the Fourth Symphony

The fifth Kaim Concert came upon us with Gustav Mahler's latest Symphony, his Fourth. This took us rather by surprise; it was, moreover, the 'first performance anywhere' of the work.

229

Anyone who had hoped for a sign of progress on Mahler's part towards something healthier, a return to the original fountain-spring of all art, which is naturalness, was doomed to disappointment. No trace of spontaneity, not a single autonomous idea, no original feeling, indeed not even pure colours for the impure images – nothing but technical skill, calculation and inner deceit, a sickly, ill-tasting Supermusic. The weeds that germinated in the Third Symphony, in which Mahler still manages to show himself from his better side, have burgeoned in this work into a thorny mass of noxious vegetation. Here a major compositional talent seems to be dissipating energy purely for its own sake. Everywhere a display of the most extraordinary orchestral fireworks to dress up an amorphous stylistic monstrosity collapsing under the weight of its own surfeit of clever detail. No, I can never share the enthusiasm that some felt; the work's impression on me was highly disquieting.

Theodor Kroyer, *Die Musik*, December 1901, 548–49. (The concert took place on 25 November 1901. Theodor Kroyer was born in Munich in 1873 and after completing his studies worked as music critic of the *Allgemeine Zeitung*. He later became highly regarded for his musicological studies, especially on sixteenth-century music, carried out in the universities of Munich, Heidelberg, Leipzig and Cologne.)

Bruno Walter interprets the Fourth Symphony at Mahler's request

In order to characterize the difference between programme music, in which music becomes relegated to such a trivial existence, and Mahler's music (and all absolute music), I should like to describe briefly the birth of the Fourth Symphony (which is certainly similar to the genesis of the earlier works): Mahler, who had set to music the lyric *Das himmlische Leben* ['The Heavenly Life'] years ago, was stirred by this delightful, child-like representation of life in Heaven and felt himself transported into just such an utterly serene, strange and distant sphere; and the thematic material which came to him from this very personal world of feeling he worked into a symphony. Since this was of course a world of his own in which he lived . . . , so also its musical counterpart presented much that was new and surprising. Here as always Mahler had no intention of illustrating any particular events or ideas. The themes which originated in this sphere were developed along symphonic principles in accordance with their own unusual characteristics and naturally resulted in equally unusual combinations. No programme would ever help you understand this work, or any other symphony by Mahler. It is absolute music, unliterary from beginning to end, a four-movement symphony, organic in every movement and entirely accessible to anyone with a feeling for subtle humour.

From Bruno Walter's letter to Ludwig Schiedermair, 5 December 1901, ms., BST. (The recipient of this letter published parts of it at once, in the second January 1902 issue of the journal *Die Musik*, in the course of an article on Gustav Mahler as a symphonist.)

Mahler to Alma Schindler

28 November 1901

In all haste, dear Fräulein Alma, I have put together for you those of my vocal compositions which have so far been published and am sending them to you (what a pity for me that I cannot bring them over myself), and in the meantime I shall enjoy the warm feeling that you will now have to concern yourself with me a little and that you will be thinking of me. When I come on Monday (I am counting the hours until then like a young boy) I will play from them for you whatever you want or need. . . .

AM, 255.

Decisive walk in the snow

And we walked through the crunching snow, side by side, distant and close – down towards Döbling, from where he

230

wanted to telephone home to say he would not be in that evening. Every few minutes his shoelaces came undone and he chose the highest spots to put his foot up and tie up the lace. I found his childish helplessness touching. In Döbling then we went to the post-office – but he did not know his own telephone number. So he had to phone the Opera and have the message passed on, without explanation, that he would not be in, which had never happened before in the nine years he had been living with his sister. Then we climbed silently back up the hill.

Quite out of the blue, Mahler suddenly said: 'It is not so simple to marry a person like me. I am completely free, must be, cannot tie myself materially anywhere. My position at the Opera is from day to day.'

I felt very awkward. Without asking about my feelings, he was dictating his will to me, his commands for life. I was silent for a moment and then said: 'That goes without saying for me. Do not forget that I am an artist's child, have always lived with artists and indeed regard myself as an artist, too. I have never thought otherwise about these things.'

I still remember how the snow glittered at every lamp and we drew each other's attention to this fairy-tale beauty without saying a word. Nothing more was spoken on the rest of the way. Mahler seemed serene and calm. In tacit collusion we went straight up to my room. Upstairs Mahler kissed me. Then he began, as if it were a matter of course, to speak of being married as soon as possible. To him everything seemed arranged after these few words on the way home.

AM, 29–30.

204

Mahler to Alma Schindler

Palast Hotel, 12 December 1901
Berlin W.

In utmost haste!

In a frightful rush between arrival and first rehearsal hurried, fervent greetings and a cry from the heart for you! Your dear letter of last Sunday was my travelling companion. I have studied it like the New Testament. It taught me my past and my future. If I get round to it before the day is out I shall relate my whole life-story since I received your letter (which to me is a kind of 'Hegyra', the date from which the Mohammedans begin their calendar). That is the point where my new life began. From now on it is only with reference to you that I can live, breathe, be. In Berlin I shall be conducting my work myself. Oh, if only you could be here! But – however necessary it is for others to derive the key to my existence from my works, you, you, my Alma, will start with me, with the all-embracing present, and will learn everything, made clear-sighted through love, you will be I, I shall be you. . . .

AM, 261. (Mahler conducted his Fourth Symphony in Berlin in a concert directed by Richard Strauss on 16 December 1901; on 19 December there followed a performance of the Second Symphony in Dresden.)

The relations between Strauss and Mahler after the Berlin concert

Richard Strauss, who was more and more taken with the work with each rehearsal, was finally overwhelmed, especially by the third movement, of which he declared he could not write an Adagio like that. He also told Mahler afterwards, in the company of a large number of friends, that he had learned immensely from him! 'Your Second Symphony in particular I have looked at very closely and found it a source of great inspiration.' As a sign of his esteem Strauss afterwards sent him the scores of his complete works.

NBL, 178.

While I was in Berlin I talked very seriously to Strauss and tried to show him the cul-de-sac he is in. But I am afraid he could not follow me properly. He is a very nice fellow; and very touching in his relations with me. And yet I can be nothing to him – for although I can see over and beyond him, of me he can see only the pedestal.

From a letter from Mahler to Alma Schindler, 19 December 1901, AM, 275.

Mahler forbids his fiancée to compose

I wrote to him once that I could write no more for the present because I still had work to finish (I meant my compositions, which had meant everything to me until then). It angered him that anything in the world could mean more to me than writing to him. He sent me a long letter in which he forbade me to compose any more. But how that hurt me!

I cried the whole night. Early in the morning I went to my mother in a flood of tears. She was so horrified by this demand that she, who loved Mahler so dearly, seriously told me to break off my connection with him. This total devotion to me on her part brought me to my senses. I became calmer and steadier and finally wrote a letter in which I declared and promised to him what he wanted me to declare and promise – and I kept the promise.

AM, 33–34. (The letters that Alma Mahler published do not include the one forbidding her to compose.)

Bruno Walter informs his parents of Mahler's engagement

Vienna, 30 December 1901

Well, what do you say to Mahler's engagement? What a surprise, eh? Justi's engagement to our leader, Rosé, is past history; but they would both have given up their marriages if Mahler had not got engaged, too; Justi would not have left her brother alone otherwise. He has surprised everyone with his engagement; even the Lipiners and Spieglers heard about it through the newspapers; so did we, of course. Even Justi found out about it only by chance two days before, when she bumped into his future father-in-law with him in the street and, having expressed surprise at his intimacy with that gentleman, was answered by Mahler: 'Well, I'll tell you something, it's because I am engaged to his daughter.' His bride Alma Schindler . . . is twenty-two, tall and slim and a stunning beauty, the most beautiful girl in Vienna; from a very good family and very rich. But we, his friends, are very concerned by this; he is forty-one and she twenty-two, she a celebrated beauty, used to a brilliant social life, he so unworldly and solitary; and so on – one could cite quite a number of objections; he himself feels very embarrassed and uncomfortable at being engaged and becomes furious if people congratulate him. . . . But their love is said to be a great one. . . .

Bruno Walter, Briefe, Frankfurt 1969, 52–53.

Alma's view of Mahler's old friends

The few people that Mahler had dragged around with him like leg-irons from his early youth were completely alien to me and must always be so. An old lawyer, stupid and importunate, an old librarian, stupid and importunate, and, to cap it all, Siegfried Lipiner and his circle. Brahms once said of him: 'This deceitful Polish dog interests me.' He could not be better characterized. For Brahms it was easy and amusing to associate with him, but at that time the villain was more than I could cope with. All these 'friends' gathered round the famous man, the Director of the Opera, whose box they regarded as their own, and they were not willing to budge an inch from their position for my sake.

I was introduced to Lipiner at Mahler's house. Very condescending, called me 'girl', examined my mind and feelings, expected me to say that Guido Reni, who meant nothing to me, was a great painter; and I failed to pass muster. I was

reprimanded for reading the *Symposium*, which of course I could not understand, etc. . . .

AM, 37. (The result of this antipathy was that Mahler's old friends – Lipiner, Löhr, Albert and Nina Spiegler, Natalie Bauer-Lechner – disappeared from his life. An exception was his legal adviser, Dr Emil Freund.)

The Fourth Symphony at a Vienna Philharmonic Concert

The participation of the Court Opera Director Gustav Mahler lent the fifth Philharmonic Concert added attractiveness and a special character. The Musikvereinssaal, which has tended to show big gaps in the audience at recent concerts of the Court Opera Orchestra, was this time full to the last seat. Beethoven's overture to *König Stefan*, conducted with warmth by Herr Joseph Hellmesberger, was gratefully received. Thereupon Herr Mahler mounted the podium to present in person his *opus novissimum*, his Fourth Symphony in G major, and was greeted with a roar of applause. The noise persisted for a long time and the conductor again and again had to lower his baton to thank the public for the thunderous ovation. As to the new work, the most contradictory rumours were abroad. While some spoke with enthusiasm of a great new musical achievement, others asserted that no crazier piece had ever been heard. It was also related that everywhere the symphony had appeared in Germany it had been hissed down. The Viennese public could thus hardly approach the new work with an entirely open mind. Nevertheless, they were not led into taking fanatical sides either for or against the symphony, but listened to the strange work with great concentration. . . .

Neues Wiener Tagblatt, 13 January 1902. (The Vienna performance of the Fourth Symphony took place on 12 January. On 20 January Mahler directed a further performance of this Symphony and of *Das klagende Lied*.)

PHILHARMONISCHE CONCERTE.

Sonntag, den 12. Jänner 1902

mittags präcise ¹/₂1 Uhr

im grossen Saale der Gesellschaft der Musikfreunde

V. Abonnement-Concert

veranstaltet von den

Mitgliedern des k. k. Hof-Opernorchesters

unter der Leitung des Herrn

JOSEPH HELLMESBERGER

k. u. k. I. Hof-Capellmeister

PROGRAMM:

L. v. BEETHOVEN . . . . Ouverture zu »König Stephan«, op. 117.

GUSTAV MAHLER . . . . Symphonie in G-dur Nr. 4 (neu), unter der Leitung des Componisten. (Erste Aufführung in den philharmonischen Concerten.)

Gesang: Frl. M. Michalek, k. k. Hofopernsängerin.

Das Nicolai-Concert findet am 26. Jänner 1902 statt.

Bösendorfer Concertflügel

benützten in diesen Concerten: Eugen d'Albert, Maria Baumayer, Dr. Johannes Brahms, Dr. Hans von Bülow, B. F. Busoni, Teresa Carreno, Fanny Davies, Illona Eibenschütz, Annette Essipoff, Art. Friedheim, Alfred Grünfeld, Josef Hofmann, Sofie Menter, Adele a. d. Ohe, Max Pauer, Wladimir de Pachmann, Hugo Reinhold, Anton Rubinstein, Moriz Rosenthal, Camillo Saint-Saëns, Emil Sauer, F. X. Scharwenka, Ed. Schütt, Bernhard Stavenhagen etc.

Programme of the Philharmonic Concert, 12 January 1902. IGMG.

Vienna, Hotel Bristol. Tuesday

Here since Saturday! Yesterday Monday dress rehearsal of *Feuersnot* under Mahler's direction, which unfortunately, because of his terrible nerviness, did not go as well as I expected after Saturday's rehearsal, in which particularly the magnificent Vienna orchestra had delighted me in the highest degree. It is decidedly the best and finest-sounding orchestra in Europe. Décor is splendid, the costumes extremely original and unusual, everything superbly rehearsed, the gifted Demuth well cast as Kunrad, Fräulein Michalik equally so as Diemut. Today I had a final positioning rehearsal to liven up the chorus and a lighting rehearsal and so I hope that tomorrow everything will go for the best. . . . Mahler is very nice, the whole staff are making every possible effort. Theatre fully sold out.

Richard Strauss, *Briefe an die Eltern*, Zürich 1954, 251. (The letter was written on 28 January 1902. The première took place the next day.)

Mahler is forced to remove 'Feuersnot' from the repertoire

Vienna, 18 February

Dear friend, I am so disgusted with the attitude of the Viennese press, and above all that the public so tamely followed its lead, that I cannot get over it. How nice it would be to be able to cast the whole tawdry business in their faces! Here are the receipts of the performances: I 3100 fl., II 1600 fl., III 1300 fl., IV – on Carnival Monday, one of the best evenings of the year – 900 fl.! (In fact cancelled at the last minute!) Alas, alas, for the present I must withdraw the work. But I shall not give up the fight yet!

Letter from Mahler to Richard Strauss, Dr Franz Strauss Collection, Garmisch-Partenkirchen, quoted from *Gustav Mahler und seine Zeit*, catalogue, Vienna 1960, 34–35.

Request for leave from the General Management for a visit to St Petersburg

To follow up the verbal notification already given I hereby request in writing that note be taken that in the second half of the month of March, during which, owing to Easter week, several days occur on which the Opera is closed, I am to conduct three concerts in St Petersburg. I should at the same time like to take the opportunity of going to several ballet performances there, so that, provided the General Management raises no objection, I intend to leave for this purpose on 9 March. . . .

Vienna, 1 March 1902

HHSTA. (Mahler and Alma Schindler were married on 9 March 1902 in St Charles' Church [the Karlskirche], Vienna. Their journey to St Petersburg was thus their honeymoon.)

Alma Mahler's recollections of St Petersburg

Mahler arrived in Petersburg with frostbite, a temperature, cough and sore throat, and I too soon caught it from him. Even so these three weeks were unforgettably beautiful. He was reduced to a whisper at the rehearsals, but was so well understood that magnificent performances were produced. . . .

Mahler had a relative there by the name of Frank, who was a high government official. This cousin showed us around Petersburg, brilliant restaurants, wonderful streets; the Hermitage, palaces, a phenomenal, strangely alien life. The Neva was frozen over, and many tramlines were laid over the river. Towards evening they began skating; the whole length of the river was alive with people. . . .

AM, 46–47. (Mahler's cousin Gustav Frank, born 1859, had studied at the Academy of Fine Arts in Vienna from 1877 and had friendly relations with Mahler. In 1890 he accepted an invitation from the Imperial Russian Department for the Preparation of State Papers to work as a copper engraver. By 1902 he was already in charge of the art department.)

A Russian view of Mahler as a conductor

Mahler's external demeanour even exceeds Nikisch in lack of movement; for all their precision his gestures are extraordinarily restrained, almost imperceptible. The performances are directed with great concentration and application of intellectual power, which is maintained at a constant level of intensity. Only occasionally does it appear that this tension is relaxed; this is connected with the conductor's penchant for slow *tempi*. One cannot help remarking, moreover, that almost every *decrescendo* is also a *ritardando*. On the whole Mahler proved an interesting artist and had great success. The performance of the Third Symphony of Beethoven seemed to come from a single impulse. The clarity and definition of the parts is astonishing; not a single note of the score was lost. And on top of that there is the masterly distribution of light and shade in the working out of the details, the subordination of individual elements to the principles of lightness and homogeneity in the development of the whole, and the absence of all affectation. What noble simplicity there was in the funeral march, what absence of any seeking after superficial effect in the Scherzo! Our whole attention is seized by the inner content of the piece as it develops. . . .

Mahler transmits Mozart's enchanting G minor Symphony in a very life-like, bright, strong and energetic performance, without a trace of mannerism. . . . Mahler presented a Mozart out of costume, which gave him as it were a new character and once again confirmed Mahler's ability to concentrate our attention on the inner content and meaning of the music he is performing.

Russkaya muzykal'naya gazeta, no. 10, 1902, 302–03. (The review refers to the first St Petersburg concert, which took place on 5 (17) March in the Assembly Hall of the Nobility, now the Leningrad Philharmonic. The description of Mahler's restrained movements is one of the earliest pieces of evidence of the change in Mahler's style of conducting.)

Hans Pfitzner on Mahler's conducting gestures

Gustav Mahler, an exemplary conductor, and one of the most strong-willed men I have known, taught himself in the course of his life the greatest restraint at the rostrum. However, the 'little movements', which he made his own and which were the result of discipline in his case, have unfortunately been blindly taken as a model, and have inevitably led . . . to extremes of incomprehensibility.

Hans Pfitzner, *Werk und Wiedergabe*, Augsburg 1929, 139. (Hans Pfitzner, 1869–1949, German composer.)

Beethoven at the Secession

In May 1902 a private celebration for Max Klinger was prepared in the Secession. The painters of the Secession had selflessly painted frescoes on the walls. Of these only those by Gustav Klimt were saved; they were taken down from the wall at vast expense. All the walls were thus decorated with allegorical frescoes connected with Beethoven, and in the middle the Beethoven memorial by Max Klinger was to be erected and exhibited for the first time.

Then Moll came to Mahler to ask him to conduct at the opening, and he made the occasion a labour of love. He took the chorus from the Ninth:

> *Ihr stürzt nieder, Millionen?*
> ['Do you bow down, all ye millions?']
> *Ahnest Du den Schöpfer, Welt? . . .*
> ['Feelst thou thy creator, world?']

and set it for wind alone, rehearsed it with the winds of the Court Opera and performed the chorus, which in this instrumentation sounded as hard as granite. The shy Klinger entered the hall. When the music started from on high he stood as if rooted to the spot. He could not restrain his emotion and tears ran slowly down his face.

AM, 50. (Max Klinger, 1857–1920, German painter, etcher and sculptor. His *Beethoven* constitutes an attempt to emulate the polychrome sculpture of the ancient world.)

208

209, 210

211–13

In order to fulfil their function and provide a worthy setting for the centrepiece of the exhibition, Klinger's *Beethoven*, the exhibition rooms had to be given a monumental character. The limited means available, and the absolute necessity of using nothing but genuine materials and avoiding dishonesty and conceit at all costs, made it essential to keep to the greatest simplicity of both materials and expression. A rough coating of the walls, which also enlivens them at the same time, therefore appeared the most obvious thing to use. The alternation of this with smooth, clean surfaces set up the architectural articulation of the walls. The rooms were to be given distinction exclusively through the artistic value of the painted and sculptural decoration of the walls. Any part of this decision with any strong personality of its own had to be located in the two side galleries to preserve the tranquillity necessary for the enjoyment of the central work in the exhibition. The two side galleries open into the main hall, which in itself emphasizes the importance of the latter. Also the visitor is thus not confronted with the work without preparation; it first becomes visible from an elevated position and from a distance.

'Max Klinger, *Beethoven*', *XIV. Ausstellung der Vereinigung Bildender Künstler Österreichs, Secession*, catalogue, Vienna 1902, 23–24. (Josef Hoffmann, 1870–1956, architect, draughtsman and decorative artist.)

Alma Mahler hears the Third Symphony in Krefeld

The performance was breathlessly awaited, for even during the rehearsals everyone had realized more and more the greatness and richness of meaning that dwelt within the work. After the first movement tremendous cheering broke out. Richard Strauss went right up to the podium and applauded ostentatiously, so that the success of the movement was sealed. And after each movement the audience seemed more gripped, in fact after the last movement the public was seized by a wild frenzy and the audience sprang up from their seats *en masse* and pressed forward. Strauss became more and more passive, and at the end was not to be seen.

I sat somewhere among strangers, for I wanted to be alone and had refused to sit with my relations. My excitement was indescribable; I cried and laughed to myself and suddenly felt the movement of my first child. I was so utterly convinced of Mahler's greatness by this work that that night, amid tears of happiness, I swore to him my recognition of his genius, the love that wanted only to serve him, my eternal desire to live for him alone.

AM, 55–56. (The concert took place on 9 June 1902. Until then only individual movements of the Third Symphony had been performed. Among the audience was the Dutch conductor Willem Mengelberg, who that night became an admirer of Mahler. Mahler's first child, Maria Anna, was born on 3 November 1902.)

Alma Mahler on the genesis of the Fifth Symphony

From there [Krefeld] we went straight to Maiernigg, where we lived completely quiet and relaxed. Mahler had his sketches for the Fifth Symphony with him, of which two movements were completed, the others merely outlined. I tried to play the piano quietly, but when I asked him he had heard me, even though his work-house was a long way off in the wood. And so I changed my occupation and copied everything that he had finished of the Fifth Symphony, always straight away so that I finished my manuscript only a few days after he himself did. He began to get more and more used to not writing out the parts in full, only the first bars, and then I learnt to read and hear scores as I wrote them, so that I became more and more a genuine help to him.

AM, 57.

Mahler to Nina Spiegler, on his summer's work

You must forgive me! I am head over heels in *work* – really have scarcely time to breathe. . . . Of myself I can most happily report all the best: you know all my wishes and demands on life concentrate on whether my work is progressing well or not! And that it certainly is, to the highest degree, as well as ever before. So you may conclude everything is perfectly as it should be!

Undated postcard from Maiernigg, postmarked 31 July 1902. The Pierpont Morgan Library, New York, and The Mary Flagler Cary Charitable Trust.

In the circles of the Vienna Secession, which he frequented after his marriage, Mahler made the acquaintance of the painter Alfred Roller, at that time Director of the Vienna School of Arts and Crafts. This meeting was decisive for the second half-decade of Mahler's activity at the Vienna Court Opera. In Roller he found a stage designer ready to make a completely new start. Alfred Roller (1864–1935), who until 1902 had had no practical experience of the theatre, was by 1 June 1903 in charge of the stage design department of the Court Opera.

Mahler invites Alfred Roller home

My wife and I ask you to join us to eat tomorrow at one. Moser will be here, too. I personally should be very pleased if you can accept since we could then talk a little about *Tristan* before I go away (which will be on Saturday). Messrs Lefler and Brioschi I have put in the picture (without mentioning any names), and they are taking it with as good grace as they can muster.

Undated letter, summer or autumn of 1902, GMB, 319. (Heinrich Lefler was head of stage design at the Court Opera from the summer of 1900 to 31 May 1903. Anton Brioschi had been a scene-painter at the Court Opera Theatre since 1886, and until Roller's engagement designed the sets for most of the new works and new productions there.)

Roller's first operatic première: 'Tristan und Isolde'

There would of course be no point in insisting on eternally imitating the décor of the first *Tristan*. Sets and décor at the time the work was written were still a matter of craft, not art. It was not until 1876, for the décor of *The Ring*, that Wagner found in Joseph Hoffmann an artist whose imagination and great technical skill overcame these enormously difficult problems. The design for *Tristan* must aim for much more intimate and subtle effects, as befits the subject. Professor Roller, who knows Wagner's works intimately, has judged these effects and realized them with the finest artistic sense. The idea of having the ship come on to the stage diagonally proved to be entirely felicitous. It made possible a splendid play of light on the sea, which was now visible to the audience over the side of the ship. The raising and lowering of the curtain and the sail produced extremely felicitous colour-contrasts. The over-all coloration, determined by the richly nuanced orange of the dominant sail, satisfied the eye without distracting it from events on stage. The intentions which underlie the décor of the second act are extremely ingenious and derive from an intimate understanding of the mysterious interplay of allusions within the text: 'In darkness you – but I in light.' The poetic opposition of Day and Night which dominates this scene is reflected by the setting. The bare wall of the royal castle reflects white moonlight, while the bench on to which the two lovers sink is plunged in darkness. This has certain disadvantages. The darkness hides the expressions of the lovers, and the rostrum surrounded by bushes conceals Isolde's first entry: here she slips out of a little side gate instead of appearing as usual, very effectively, framed in a huge castle portal. The third act is a work of decorative art. The whole stage is bleak and desolate. The mighty lime-tree, among whose roots Tristan lies, the hill upon which Tristan dies, and against which the expiring Isolde so gloriously stands out, bear witness that a man with a true vocation has here put himself at the service of the work.

G.S. (Gustav Schönaich), *Wiener Allgemeine Zeitung*, 25 February 1903. (The première took place on 21 February; Mahler conducted; Anna von Mildenburg and Erik Schmedes sang the title roles. Schönaich, who had known Wagner personally, was considered to be the Wagner specialist among the Viennese music critics.)

We may betray to the curious who were unable to secure entry to the sold-out House that the first act is orange-yellow, the second mauve and the third dough-coloured. Friends of the Secession will be very pleased to see Tristan and Isolde wandering amid strangely Impressionistic landscapes. One thing should be made clear from the outset: of the spirit of Wagner – despite many artistic details, including for example Herr Schmedes's new nose – there was precious little to be seen. . . .

Hans Liebstöckl, *Reichswehr*, 22 February 1903.

Hugo Wolf's funeral

At three in the afternoon the funeral cortège moved off from the mean and lowly dwelling towards the Votive Church, Ferstel's magnificent Gothic building. It was a symbol of the triumphal procession on which the poor maligned composer had set out through the power of his art. All the pomp was laid on with which great men are carried to the grave. . . . As in Italian churches, the nave contains no pews, except for a very small number. Nevertheless the whole great space was packed full, for very many people wanted to be seen there in public who had never lifted a finger for Wolf, who had had not a word, not a look for him, at most perhaps a shrug. Now all of a sudden there they all were. The Imperial Capital and Royal Residence of Vienna, his home town of Windischgrätz, the Society of the Friends of Music, the Conservatoire, had sent wreaths and representatives, Court Opera Director Mahler, many Court Opera singers, even many music critics, appeared; and many, many more. There was no end to one's astonishment.

Max Vancs, 'Hugo Wolfs letzte Lebensjahre, Tod und Begräbnis', *Die Musik*, no. 12, 1903, 443. (Hugo Wolf died on 22 February 1903; the funeral took place on 24 February.)

A concert in Lemberg (*Lvov*)

27 March 1903

On 2 and 4 April performances of one of my compositions will take place in Lemberg, which I have been invited to conduct.

I take the liberty of enquiring of Your Excellency whether any obstacle stands in the way of my going to Lemberg for this purpose for five days from 31 [March] to 4 April.

Request from Mahler to the General Management, 27 March 1903, HHSTA.

Mahler reports to his wife on the rehearsals in Lemberg

. . . The rehearsal was at 10 o'clock. When I mounted the rostrum the orchestra greeted me with a fanfare of trumpets and drums – you can imagine the face I made: like a cat in a thunderstorm. Then I played *my First* with the orchestra, which behaved superbly and was obviously well prepared. Several times I broke into a cold sweat. For goodness' sake, where do people put their ears and their hearts, if they can't understand *this*! The second rehearsal is this afternoon at four, and in the evening I am going to the Italian Opera here – *Tosca* by Puccini. Feel very fresh and in a good mood today. Life here has such a funny face again. Most absurd of all are the Polish Jews, who run about here like the dogs in other places! It's

highly entertaining to watch them! My God, and these are the people I am supposed to be related to! How cretinous the racial theories seem to me, if this is the evidence, I can't tell you!

Undated letter, April 1903, AM, 285.

From 12 to 15 June 1903 the Thirty-Ninth Composers' Congress of the All-German Musical Society took place in Basle. As part of this musical occasion, at 7 p.m. on 15 June, Mahler conducted his Second Symphony in Basle cathedral. The work was rehearsed by the conductor Hermann Suter, to whom Mahler gave practical instructions in a letter.

Mahler's instructions for the Basle performance of the Second Symphony

Vienna, 27 May 1903

Most hearty thanks for your report, which greatly pleases and reassures me. Certainly I shall be satisfied with a short session of about an hour with the chorus at the piano. Since there will be an opportunity in the evenings of the last week to run through the last part of my symphony with the chorus accompanied by the orchestra, the final rehearsal should then go off more or less without a break.

With the strings I should be grateful if you would be so kind as to arrange the division so that where it is marked *Hälfte* just the front desks play, and later at the *Tutti* the others join in. At the marking *geteilt*, please arrange for the right- and left-hand players to take a part each – divided into several parts, from player to player – not from desk to desk.

For the 'Last Trump' it is usually difficult in the concert hall to have the wind instruments set up off-stage on different sides. How will this be in the church? I should think this sort of thing could be done very effectively there? At any rate I should like to have a little prior rehearsal sometime, at an odd moment, with the extra instruments in question so as to avoid *very* time-consuming hold-ups with the full orchestra. The passage is rhythmically very difficult to keep together, and the effect I am after can only be obtained after several attempts. If my rehearsals take place as originally proposed on 9, 10 and 11 June, I intend to arrive in Basle on the evening of 8 June.

Ms., Universitätsbibliothek Basel, Handschriftensammlung.

Telegrams from the Court Opera Management to the Director in Basle

8 June 1903

Yesterday *Carmen* 5300. Reviews Goritz in post. Unfavourable. Is he to go on as Telramund on Saturday? Hesch father dead. Two days leave.

9 June 1903

Yesterday *Siegfried* 6100. Letter Wondra posting today. Request decision Goritz. Otherwise all well.

10 June 1903

Yesterday *Aida* 3600. All well. Received telegram.

11 June 1903

Yesterday *Twilight* 6800. According report Selar Frau Engelin coming for audition nineteenth but requests travelling expenses. Is this to be promised? Harder recommends tenor Jörn, Berlin, who may become free there in 1904 owing engagement Naval.

13 June 1903

Yesterday *Louise* 2800. Goritz hoarse, has refused Telramund tomorrow. Demuth put on. Otherwise no news.

14 June 1903

Yesterday 5850. Lagen very temperamental as Santuzza, as a result very over-played, singing very uneven, much good but also much unsatisfactory, but noteworthy. Critics partly favourable, partly unfavourable. Shall I put her on as Amneris on Tuesday and in *Louise* on Thursday? If Goritz gets better shall I put him on in *Mastersingers* and *Louise*? Slezak feels voice so tired that he declares he cannot sing *Aida*, *Huguenots*, *Mastersingers*. Shall I engage Winkelmann, who is already on leave, for Stolzing and perhaps *Aida* for additional fee?

15 June 1903

Yesterday *Lohengrin* 4450. OK with Forst. Goritz singing *Louise* and *Mastersingers*, Langen Amneris and Louise mother. Slezak cancelled, Winkelmann singing.

Telegram drafts, HHSTA. (The figures at the beginning of each telegram refer to the day's takings, in Austrian crowns.)

The Basle 'National-Zeitung' on the performance

The performance of the work was an achievement for which no praise seems to us too high. From our – in this case considerably augmented – orchestra we have never heard anything like these dynamics, and Mahler's conducting was a brilliant illustration of what true genius can achieve. And at the same time the superb calm of the man, strictly avoiding any superfluous gesture. He performed with the chorus the same miracle as with the orchestra. Who has ever heard a *pianissimo* like that from our choral society?

National-Zeitung (Basle), 17 June 1903.

Maiernigg 1903: Work on the Sixth Symphony

In the summer two movements of the Sixth were finished and the ideas for the remaining movements were completed in his head.

Since I played a lot of Wagner, Mahler thought of a sweet joke. He had composed for me the only love-song he ever wrote, *Liebst Du um Schönheit*, and he put it between the title page and first page of *The Valkyrie*. Then he waited day after day for me to come across it, but for once I did not open this score at that time. Suddenly he said: 'Today I fancy having a look at *Valkyrie*.' He opened the book and the song fell out. I was happy beyond words and we played the song that day at least twenty times.

AM, 79.

In the summer of 1903 Mahler had the pit of the Court Opera Theatre lowered by 50 cm and at the same time extended from 47 to 59 square metres. Originally it had been his intention to have the pit deepened to 1·5 metres, but technical difficulties prevented this. Even this small change resulted in protests from the Viennese press, who were concerned for the acoustics of the house. In an interview Mahler explained his reasons for the alterations.

Mahler in an interview about the orchestra pit and the stage

'Even the small deepening of the pit will now make it possible to give the public an unobstructed view of the stage and to modulate the orchestral sound and make it less obtrusive than before, which is of particular importance in Wagner operas. I want to create the orchestra I need and consider right in the interests of art. Today's orchestra is no longer a unit which functions independently and need pay no attention to what is going on in the rest of the theatre. The orchestra must serve the theatre in the same way as other factors, such as the lighting, the full effect of which on the stage we still do not know. The way the musicians sit in the orchestra today, the music stands are lit far too brightly. This disturbs the audience, whose attention is inevitably distracted, and it thus introduces a false note into the stage atmosphere. If the orchestra is lowered the conductor is put nearer the *musicians*, who should be grouped round him in a *fan shape*, and this is what will now be done. Putting the orchestra lower is important for a discreet orchestral sound and important for the purposes of discreet lighting. I purposely avoid the words 'lighting effects'. We do not need crude effects, we want to make the *light* serve the theatre in *all* its grades, nuances and degrees of strength. To be always out for powerful effects is inartistic. But the matter does not end with the lighting; the whole of modern art has a part to play on the stage. Modern art, I say, not the Secession. What matters is the conjunction of all the arts. . . . The lowering of the orchestra is not meant to apply to all operas; there will be a movable podium which can be raised or lowered as the need arises. For Mozart's *Marriage of Figaro* – I choose this as an example – a sunken orchestra is not necessary.'

Illustriertes Extrablatt, 9 September 1903. (Mahler was only partially able to put these theories into practice.)

In October 1903 Mahler visited Amsterdam for the first time in order to conduct works of his own with the Concertgebouw Orchestra. On 22 and 23 October he directed his Third Symphony, which had been rehearsed by Willem Mengelberg, and on 25 October the First Symphony. Willem Mengelberg (1871–1951) gave Mahler a very hearty welcome and had him to stay in his own house.

Mahler to his wife from Holland

The final rehearsal yesterday was splendid. There were two hundred boys from the school, accompanied by their teachers (six of them), to roar the *Bim-bam*, and an extraordinary women's chorus of 330 voices! Orchestra *splendid*! Much better than in Krefeld. The violins just as beautiful as in Vienna. All the performers will not stop clapping and waving. If only you could be here! Now I am at table (a great appetite from walking and sailing). My hosts are charming and let me come and go as I please. . . : The musical culture in the country is stupendous! The way these people *listen*!

From a letter of 22 October 1903, AM, 323.

Mahler to Max Kalbeck, on his version of 'Euryanthe'

This time I have trespassed on your preserves, and must therefore beg absolution. I imagine that you would like to be put in the picture before Saturday's performance as to the changes I have made in the text and (in some cases – inevitably) in the music. I have marked the vocal score for you so that all the differences *vis-à-vis* normal performances are immediately noticeable, so you will find your way without any particular loss of time.

I should be happy if poor Euryanthe, whom I love immensely, were to be helped a little so that she could eke out on the stage if not a princely existence, then at least a middle-class one; she would deserve it, after all, simply for the sake of her very respectable progeny.

Undated letter, presumably January 1904, GMB, 297. (The première of Weber's *Euryanthe* as edited by Mahler took place on 19 January 1904. The critic Max Kalbeck was much in demand as a translator and adapter of opera libretti.)

At the beginning of February 1904 Mahler conducted his Third Symphony in Heidelberg and Mannheim. Between the two concerts, Mahler wrote a good-humoured letter to his wife in Vienna. When he was alone on a concert tour he used to write to her almost daily.

Mannheim, 2 February 1904

So Heidelberg was yesterday! Went off splendidly. Performance first class à la Krefeld. Wolfrum behaved toppingly and is, I think, completely won over. This morning came to Mannheim with Neisser (who does not leave my side and is very pleasant). Another rehearsal. Lunch with the General Manager. And tomorrow, thank God, off home again. I have now had more than enough of strange hotels and am already looking forward to you. This time I hope I have moved a step forwards again. . . .

This damnable wandering from place to place is a frightful fate, but it *has* to be! That I can see quite clearly.

The ineluctable Nodnagel has written a ghastly analysis and gushes like a girl. The only people I meet are conductors and professors (between you and me, a lot more agreeable to me than faceless women). That you have been a hit I am not surprised. You in your new dress are a similar number to my Third in a good performance.

AM, 301. (Philipp Wolfrum, 1854–1919, composer, organist and Professor of the History of Music at the University of Heidelberg, conducted the preliminary rehearsals for the Heidelberg performance. Professor Albert Neisser, dermatologist, friend of Arnold Berliner, combined his journey to the Mahler performances with a lecture of his own.)

A year after Hugo Wolf's death: 'Der Corregidor' at the Court Opera

. . . Well, Hugo Wolf has provided this text with music of which it is hard to convey adequately how many subtleties it contains, how delightful the melodic ideas are that sometimes surprise and sometimes entrance us, how remarkable its filigree work is, how many witty points captivate us in it – and how weak the whole thing manages to sound dramatically.

Everywhere one is reminded of the *Lieder* composer – admittedly no ordinary *Lieder* composer, but Hugo Wolf. . . . The style of *The Mastersingers* is his model. It is above all the dialogue that disappoints us. It is especially astonishing that Wolf, whose remarkable ability to evoke in his music the very spirit of language is quite undisputed, in the opera only rarely manages to set a phrase vividly and strikingly.

Gustav Schönaich, *Wiener Allgemeine Zeitung*, 20 February 1904. (The first performance took place on 18 February 1904.)

226 *Gerhart Hauptmann to Mahler*

Ospedaletti, 28 February 1904

Dear Mahler, it seems so unnatural to me to let a conventional barrier stand between us. Now that I once again believe in happiness I imagine we shall meet in the not-too-distant future as two healthy, active, age-old comrades who address one another as *Du*. Just because in our youth we had no contact with one another, why should our maturity pay the price when our inner paths are the same?

I have a genuine longing to hear your music and penetrate to the core of it!

AM, 333. (Gerhart Hauptmann, 1862–1946, German dramatist, had met Mahler and his wife in Vienna at the home of Max Burckhard. The writer and the composer had immediately become friends. Hauptmann wrote this letter after recovering from a serious illness.)

'Der Corregidor' in the original version

Director Mahler is a clever man, who in view of his well-grounded reputation as the most stubborn and unapproachable of all theatre directors can occasionally allow himself the luxury of an apparent yielding to public opinion. He had been accused of weakening the effect of Hugo Wolf's *Der Corregidor* through dramatic and musical alterations. In a flash, for yesterday's performance he restored the original score and suppressed the re-arrangement of the acts and the cuts at the

end – obviously with the objective of demonstrating that a *major* strengthening of the over-all impression could not thereby be achieved. And this of course proved to be absolutely right. . . .

Gustav Schönaich, *Wiener Allgemeine Zeitung*, 20 March 1904.

Foundation of an Association of Creative Musicians

The Association of Creative Musicians in Vienna held its constitutive General Assembly on 23rd of last month. Court Opera Director Gustav Mahler was unanimously elected Honorary President; he had already declared himself willing to be elected. Then the Committee was elected and the decision was taken to organize three orchestral and three chamber and *Lieder* concerts next season with programmes consisting exclusively of new works, to establish contact with the Vienna Concert Society over the provision of an orchestra and to engage soloists for the chamber music and *Lieder* recitals. An invitation is now being sent to all Austrian and German composers, as well as all foreign composers living in Austria and Germany, who would like to be heard at these concerts to send in works (manuscripts in fair copy) to the archivist . . . up to and including 31 May this year. Works received after this date can be given only secondary consideration.

Neues Wiener Journal, 5 May 1904. (The members of the Association included Arnold Schönberg, Alexander von Zemlinsky and Bruno Walter.)

General Manager Plappart on the financial successes of the Court Theatres

'We have every reason', says the General Manager of the Court Theatres, His Excellency Herr Plappart, 'to be satisfied with the state of the Court Theatres. In both the Burg [Court Theatre] and the Opera the receipts have risen considerably, and in both theatres our expectations were exceeded. A few figures will illustrate this. In the Opera in the period from 1 January to 17 May, our takings amounted to 715,809 crowns. We had budgeted for receipts of 666,900 crowns in this period. So that in these four-and-a-half months the Opera showed a surplus of 48,909 crowns. In every single month the target was exceeded in both the Burg and the Opera. And the target for the current year is always based on the receipts for the previous year. From 1 January 1904 to end of December the Opera's takings were 1,543,665 crowns. The target for this period was 1,485,900 crowns. In the month of December, for example, the target was exceeded by more than 20,000 crowns. Of course, even with all these brilliant returns from the Opera, there is no chance of making a profit: the daily costs in the Opera House run to 10,000 crowns. In this daily figure the proportion attributable to wages alone amounts to 6,656 crowns. . . . At the Burgtheater we were very lucky with several new works; at the Opera none of the recent new works has maintained its place (except *The Tales of Hoffmann*). But the public does come to the ordinary repertoire operas, and it is a fact that the attendance levels and the atmosphere in both the Court Theatres are better than in any previous year.'

Neue Freie Presse, 22 May 1904.

Mahler announces to Arnold Berliner the birth of his second daughter

I dare not give up any of my summer. On Wednesday I make off to Maiernigg. On 15th my wife had a baby girl and must remain here for at least three weeks. I shall leave her in the care of her mother and go off to the lake completely alone. You know why. It is an absolute duty, and the Neissers will realize this. The première of my Fifth takes place in Cologne on 15 October. Shall I perhaps see you there?

Undated letter, postmarked Vienna 19 June 1904, GMB, 302. (Mahler's younger daughter, Anna Justine, was born on 15 June 1904.)

Alfred Roller describes Mahler's daily round at Maiernigg

In Maiernigg am Wörthersee, which was his summer residence for seven years, he used to get up at half-past five, had his first swim alone, and then hurried quickly down secret paths to his summerhouse, hidden deep in the woods, where his breakfast was ready waiting for him. Then followed about seven hours of uninterrupted work. Before lunch he went for another swim and then usually made music with his wife Alma and played with his children. After lunch he had a short rest, which was something he never permitted himself in town, however tired he might be from the morning rehearsal. If you tried to persuade him on such occasions to rest a little he used to refuse with the remark 'it is just quite ordinary physical fatigue'. This short afternoon rest out in the country was then followed after about four o'clock by long daily walks, on which his wife usually accompanied him. It was often not easy for her. For he could walk at a brisk march tempo without feeling the pace. When walking slowly he would put one foot almost daintily in front of the other and stretch his legs out straight at the knee. . . . He was thus a narrow-gauge walker. But walking quickly, as he did on these long walks, he would lean forwards, his chin stretched out, and step firmly, almost stamping. This gait had something tempestuous, something quite triumphant about it. Mahler was quite incapable of strolling. His body always had bearing, if not always a conventional one. He went uphill far too quickly. I could scarcely keep up with him then. He usually began his swim with a high dive. Then he swam a long way under water and did not reappear until he was way out in the lake, rolling comfortably in the water like a seal. To row a boat with Mahler was no pleasure. His stroke was very powerful and far too rapid. But his strength enabled him to maintain the exertion for a long time.

The evenings in the country he regularly spent in the company of his wife. She often read aloud to him, he sometimes to her. She reports that in these summer months – the time of his real work – he was always more approachable, more human, more indulgent than in the town. He even overcame his shyness to the extent of playing half-finished works to her. At that time Mahler gave the impression of being completely healthy. He slept splendidly, liked his cigar, and enjoyed a glass of beer in the evening. Spirits he avoided completely. Wine he drank only on special occasions. His preferences were Moselle, Chianti or Asti. One or two glasses were enough to make him lively, and he then produced puns by which, as Frau Alma put it, he was himself fabulously entertained. But for all his enjoyment of sensual pleasures, including those of the table, he was a man of great moderation. You never saw him overdo anything; he abhorred drunkenness as he abhorred obscenity or indecency. The strict cleanliness which he maintained in his person was also preserved, without any prudishness, in his conversation and undoubtedly also in his thoughts.

ARB, 16 sqq.

Alma Mahler on the composition of the Sixth Symphony

In the summer we were visited by Zemlinsky, with whom I had again sometimes made music in the winter, who reverenced Mahler like a god, and whom Mahler liked more and more, and by Roller, whom he had liked from the beginning; and so things became quite lively around us. Mahler became more human and more communicative. He completed the Sixth Symphony and added three more songs to the two *Kindertotenlieder*, which I could not understand. . . . I said straight away at the time, 'For God's sake, you are tempting Providence!'

The summer was beautiful, free of quarrels, happy. At the end of the holidays Mahler played me the now finished Sixth Symphony. I had to keep myself free of everything in the house,

to have plenty of time for him. Once again we went arm in arm up to his forest hut where we could be completely undisturbed in the midst of the wood. All this always took place with great solemnity.

After he had sketched the first movement Mahler had come down out of the wood and had said, 'I have tried to capture you in one of the themes – whether I have succeeded I don't know. You'll just have to put up with it.'

It is the great soaring theme in the first movement of the Sixth Symphony. In the third movement he illustrates the unrhythmic play of the two little children as they toddle through the sand. Horrible – these children's voices become more and more tragic and at the end there is just the whimper of a little expiring voice. In the last movement he describes himself and his destruction, or, as he later said, the destruction of his hero: 'The hero who suffers three strokes of Fate, of which the third fells him like a tree.' These are Mahler's words. No work ever flowed so directly from his heart as this did. We both wept then. So deeply did we feel this music and what it told us of the future. 229

AM, 91–92.

Mahler on his Sixth Symphony

My Sixth will pose puzzles which can only be broached by a generation which has imbibed and digested my first five.

From an undated letter to Richard Specht, written in 1904 or 1905, GMB, 262.

Alfred Roller's recollections of the 'Fidelio' of October 1904

In the old production the chorus of prisoners, first act, prison courtyard, had gone as follows: the complete chorus made its entry from the cells on the right and left, formed a semi-circle on the brightly lit stage and then burst into song: '*Ha, welche Lust*, etc.' This preposterous entry of the chorus took place during the gripping orchestral prelude and thus struck me as all the more unfortunate. When I presented Mahler with my models for the new production I explained to him how I saw the scene: the prisoners struggling up from the depths one by one, slowly, in twos and threes, unused to walking, feeling their way along the wall, poor, earthen, suffering worms. Mahler agreed at once; 'However, you must not forget that I must cue the entry. This is a musical requirement, which you don't understand. But even so we could get a double quartet on to the stage your way, and that will be enough. I shan't need more than that.' The guardians of 'tradition' were very horrified. Professor Wondra said to me reproachfully: 'The Men's Choral Society sings this chorus two hundred strong!' Good old Stoll, who was producing, therefore made a final attempt to change Mahler's mind after the first rehearsal, and, as we came over the gangway on to the stage (after the first act), he came towards us at the front of the stage on the right and in a quite restrained tone reminded Mahler of the *tradition*, that this piece of music had always been regarded as a star turn, a sort of solo, for the chorus. . . .

Mahler put great emphasis on the *intimacy* of Rocco's parlour. Flowers in the window! These must be lit up by the sunbeam that appears at the beginning of the canon. The contrast to the prison courtyard had to be as great as possible. The latter was to look damp and mouldy. The designs for both these he accepted at once and approved them strongly. The first sketches for the dungeon he turned down: 'Too far gone, too much like Nibelheim.' The version we did afterwards satisfied him completely. . . . 276, 277

LKB, 126–27. (Hubert Wondra, Chorus Master at the Opera; August Stoll, Stage Manager. The première of the new production of *Fidelio* took place on 4 October 1904.)

237

Last page of the score of
the Sixth Symphony.
Ms., GDM.

Hermann Bahr on Roller's scenic art

Thus, what is called the atmosphere of a dramatic scene is the result of the scene; it does not exist until the scene creates it. And if, when the curtain rises, it is already evident in the setting before we have been prepared for it by the course of the drama, it cannot be effective. To begin with, Roller perhaps did not really grasp this, but he came to feel that the 'stylized' décor, the décor as an expression of the emotional atmosphere, must not appear until the feelings of the audience have been brought by the events on stage to the point where they actually demand to be reflected in the setting. This is the key to his designs, which fulfil a double function. At first they operate simply as a placard saying 'Imagine Tristan's ship, or Florestan's dungeon.' But then, when the stage atmosphere begins to affect the audience, when they lose their personal feelings and succumb to the dramatic transformation, they are no longer felt as just any old ship or any old prison but as an image of what has been heard: sounds become images. At its best for me always in *Fidelio*, when Leonore sets to against Pizarro, outside the horns [*sic*] announce the liberator, the fanfare is repeated in the interpolated overture [*Leonora* No. 3], and then at last, through this intense, light-hungry atmosphere, the bright day dawns.

Hermann Bahr, *Tagebuch*, Berlin 1909, 38.

Mahler to his wife, from Cologne

Final rehearsal yesterday went off *very well*! Performance excellent! Audience immensely interested and attentive – despite all their puzzlement in the early movements! After the Scherzo even a few hisses. Adagietto and Rondo seem to have won the day. A lot of musicians, conductors, etc., arrived from elsewhere. Hinrichsen is *enthusiastic* and has already secured my Sixth with the greatest excitement. He added jokingly: 'Only please don't hold me to ransom!' Which I shall certainly not, since he is such a nice fellow. Walter and Berliner, the two old faithfuls, have arrived. Walter came yesterday in time for the final rehearsal; he will tell you everything. Berliner not until this morning – sitting in there now and crying because you have not come. I think he only came here for your sake.

Concert this evening then. I'll telegraph tomorrow and then go straight to Amsterdam. To begin with write to: Amsterdam Concertgebouw. That's enough.

That you are not here, Almschi, has spoilt the thing for me and I almost don't give a damn about the whole business. You would love the work!

Kiss the little angels from me! And all get yourselves better, for Heaven's sake!

AM, 317–18. (Alma Mahler gives the date of this letter as 19 October 1904, but the first performance of the Fifth took place on 18 October.)

Bruno Walter on the première

I clearly remember the première of the Fifth in Cologne in 1904 for a particular reason: it was the first and, I think, the only time that a performance of a Mahler work under his own baton left me unsatisfied. The instrumentation did not succeed in bringing out clearly the complicated contrapuntal fabric of the parts, and Mahler complained to me afterwards that he never seemed to be able to master the handling of the orchestra: in fact he later subjected the orchestration to the most radical revision that he ever felt obliged to undertake.

Bruno Walter, *Gustav Mahler*, Vienna 1936, 38–39.

From a review of the Fifth Symphony

. . . It must be said that Mahler is considerably less original in invention than in execution, and this disparity, which becomes the more prominent as the dimensions of his works increase, renders unalloyed enjoyment quite impossible – not to speak of his predilection for dissonance and jarring harmonies. Mahler's art is the art of a great solitary. There is something wild and elemental about it. The often wilful nature of the development of his themes, which leads to sudden, sometimes crude outbursts; the almost unvaried massiveness of the orchestration, which often uses the individual groups of instruments in unison to produce a great intensification of expression, makes this quite apparent. . . .

Rheinische Musik- und Theater-Zeitung, vol. v, no. 25, 504, EV.

The new 'Rhinegold': 'magical lighting'

But the most beautiful tales in this new production are told by the lights. They swathe the gods in brilliance and serenity; they leave them wallowing in murky mists. The movement on stage is frozen, as it were, into a series of pictures which are then, however, invested with a truly inner movement by the magical changes of lighting. The pictorial effect is increased by the layout of the principal scene of action, the 'open area on the mountain heights'. Rising in a series of terraces, the stage, which is a mass of flowers, perfectly suits the various groupings of the gods; on the highest level the giants appear, thus towering above the others all the more ominously. The final subtle communion between stage and music is established by Mahler's art. It is he who gives light to the orchestra. The element of tone-painting, which in *Rhinegold* predominates over emotional expression, is completely fused with the paintings on the stage.

Julius Korngold, 'Feuilleton', *Neue Freie Presse*, 25 January 1905. (The première of *The Rhinegold* in Mahler's and Roller's new production took place on 23 January 1905. Julius Korngold, 1860–1945, was Hanslick's successor on the *Neue Freie Presse*.)

On 29 January 1905 the Association of Creative Musicians, of which Mahler was Honorary President, organized a concert at which the *Kindertotenlieder* and other songs to texts by Rückert (composed in 1901) had their first performance. *Wunderhorn* songs were also on the programme. The soloists were Anton Moser, Fritz Schrödter and Friedrich Weidemann. The concert was repeated on 3 February 1905. Among the audience at this second concert was Anton von Webern (1883–1945), who had been a composition pupil of Arnold Schönberg's since 1904 and was at the same time studying musicology under Guido Adler.

From Anton von Webern's diary, Friday 3 February 1905

Repeat of the Mahler evening – songs with orchestra – organized by the Association of Creative Musicians. Mahler's *Wunderhorn* songs are marvellous. The themes folk-like, and what lies between the lines grasped with genius and con-

Cartoon inspired by the first performance of the Fifth Symphony, in Vienna. Rudolf Effenberger, *Fünfundzwanzig Jahre dienstbarer Geist im Reiche der Frau Musika*, Vienna 1927.
The orchestral attendant at the concerts of the Society of the Friends of Music in Vienna, Rudolf Effenberger, was also a cartoonist. After the Vienna première of the Fifth Symphony on 7 December 1905 he did this impression of the tuba player taking his chance of a rest during the Adagietto.

vincingly expressed. His songs on texts by Rückert I found less satisfying. I found some parts sentimental, and I can only explain these occasional lapses into sentimentality on Mahler's part – which seem incomprehensible in view of his greatness and genuineness as a man – by the thought that his compositions are direct outpourings of emotion which here and there become tainted with sentimentality because of their intensity. . . . What I admired in all the songs is the tremendous expressiveness of the vocal line, which often possesses an overwhelming inner truth. I am thinking here particularly of the fourth of the *Kindertotenlieder*, or *Ich atmet' einen linden Duft!* The sound of his orchestration is true through and through.

After the concert there was a gathering of the members and guests of the association in the Anna-Hof. I had the opportunity of gaining a much closer personal acquaintance with Mahler. I shall always remember these hours spent in his presence as particularly happy; it was, after all, the first time I had found myself in direct contact with a great man. Almost everything I heard him say is fixed in my memory, and so I intend to note it down in this book which is so dear to me.

To begin with we spoke of Rückert's poetry. Mahler said: 'After *Des Knaben Wunderhorn* Rückert was the only thing I could do – this is poetry at first hand, all other poetry is second-hand.' He added that he did not understand everything in the *Wunderhorn* songs. The conversation turned to counterpoint, as Schönberg said only the Germans could write counterpoint. Mahler refers to the old French composers (Rameau, etc.) and will accept only Bach, Brahms and Wagner as great contrapuntalists among the Germans. 'Our model in this matter is nature. Just as the whole universe has developed from the original cell – through plants, animals, men, to God, the highest being – in music, too, a whole piece should be developed from a single motif, a single theme, which contains the germ of all that is to follow.' In Beethoven there is almost always a new motive in the development. But he should have been able to base the complete development section on one theme; and it is in this sense that Beethoven is not a great contrapuntalist. Variation is the most important element of musical work, he said. A theme has to be quite exceptionally beautiful – a few by Schubert for example – to make a repeat of it without alteration successful. For him Mozart's string quartets ended at the double bar. The task of the creative modern musician is to combine the counterpoint of Bach with the melody of Haydn and Mozart.

Österreichische Musikzeitschrift, vol. xv, no. 6, 303–04.

Revolution in Russia

This 22 January was the first day of the Revolution in Russia, more frightening than 13 and 18 March once were in Vienna and Berlin. It was solemnly proclaimed in a petition of almost Biblical grandeur and simplicity of language, which begged the Tsar to come to the Winter Palace at a specified hour to hear the demands of the people. 'We have only two paths: liberty and happiness or the grave!' The Tsar did not appear; he had the petition handed over to him the day before yesterday in Tsarskoye Selo by Prince Svyatopolk-Mirsky, who for a time had the confidence of the people, and the wall that separates him from his people has become greater instead of being demolished. Since yesterday it has been stained with blood, which will be hard to wipe away. . . .

Neue Freie Presse, 23 January 1905. (The unrest and strikes in Russia and Russian Poland lasted until March 1905.)

Mahler cancels a journey to Moscow

The unsettled conditions at present prevailing in Russia, as a result of which even personal safety cannot be completely assured, and in which artistic activity is quite impossible, have led me to abandon the visit to Moscow, and I must ask you to release me from the agreement made with you. Perhaps the engagement can be renewed later, once normal conditions have returned.

Undated draft of a letter, probably written in March 1905, to the Hermann Wolff concert agency, Berlin. HHSTA.

The composer Fried tells how he became a Mahler conductor

It was in 1904. Schalk, who was planning the first performance of my *Das trunkene Lied* ['The Drunken Song'] under the aegis of the concerts of the Society of the Friends of Music, had invited me to come from Berlin for the rehearsals. I consented, and in the course of the very first conversation, Schalk asked me whether I had already called on Director Mahler. I said no. . . . But straightaway next day – it was the final rehearsal of *Das trunkene Lied* – Schalk came up to me and informed me that Director Mahler had expressed the wish to make my acquaintance. . . . When I now thus saw him before me, this master in his own house, so unjustly feared and maligned, my first impression I can only call extraordinarily beautiful. Above all this impression was very strong on a human level. This man

looking at me, through stern and forbidding spectacles, and yet with a child-like curiosity and with that unadulterated frankness which is concerned only to fathom out and penetrate the essential humanity in other people – this man, with his child-like and yet utterly manly head, struck me as positively beautiful to look at. His gaze, which penetrated everything and laid bare the innermost being, the deep bell-like voice, his mouth whose fine cut spoke of unshakable energy, while its almost feminine line testified to kindness and inner warmth, and not least the intensity of his gestures and of his whole being – all this together made him irresistible. . . . I had just succeeded Professor Gernsheim as director of the famous Stern Choral Union in Berlin, and was firmly determined to break with the centuries-old tradition of this more than conservative Society. . . . Now, Mahler was planning a performance of *St Elizabeth*, as I was; and his interest in my project was all the stronger in that he was proposing a staged performance in the Opera Theatre. The manner in which I intended to interpret *St Elizabeth*, and which I explained to Mahler with all my characteristic vehemence and concern for the innermost spiritual recesses of a work of art, seems to have met with such wholehearted approval on his part that he immediately said to me: 'You shall conduct my Second Symphony in Berlin. I shall come to hear it myself. You will make an excellent job of it.'

Oskar Fried, 'Erinnerungen an Mahler', *Musikblätter des Anbruch*, vol. I, no. I, 16–17. (Oskar Fried, 1871–1941, composer and conductor. The Vienna performance of *Das trunkene Lied* took place on 6 March 1905.)

Mahler to his wife from Hamburg

The Fifth is an accursed work. No one gets the point. At the end it began to go somewhat better. Well, tomorrow we shall just see.

Undated letter, AM, 336. (The Hamburg performance of the Fifth Symphony took place on 13 March 1905.)

Socialist leading article on May Day 1905 in Vienna

We in this country situated half-way between Paris and St Petersburg and between Berlin and Rome, a little Europe of our own in the middle of the Germanic, Romance and Slavonic world, our lot is the strangest of all our brotherhood. We bear the sufferings of all at the same time; we fight the fights of all at the same time. Byzantine absolutism, national chauvinism, bourgeois reaction, Roman clericalism confront us in turn; the wildest mixture of all European systems of government subjects us to an official polyarchy and anarchy which appears impossible to comprehend and to take hold of. The parties change their form and colour like Proteus; nothing is certain in this country except confusion and change.

Arbeiter-Zeitung, 30 April 1905.

Pfitzner and Mahler meet a May Day demonstration

Magnificent spring day. Rehearsal in the Opera. *Rose*. Afterwards Mahler had arranged a short rehearsal of his songs with orchestra in the Opera (with Weidemann). Mahler asked Pfitzner, who was of course present at the *Rose* rehearsals, if he would not stay for this Weidemann rehearsal, but Pfitzner, his own rehearsal finished, had no intention of hanging on for Mahler's sake, muttered something about urgent business, and rushed off. Rushed off to me. On the way he bought a red rose, which he put on my piano without a word. He was agitated and angry. He had met the workers' procession on the Ring – it was May Day. Infuriated by their 'plebeian' faces, he had quickly slipped into a side-street, and even in my room still felt persecuted.

Soon Mahler came. With a mixture of amusement and annoyance, he now saw Pfitzner's hasty departure in its true light. But today it could not upset him. He was too happy. He had met the workers' procession on the Ring and had walked with them for a while – he said their looks had all been so brotherly. These *were* his brothers! These men were the future!

Bang! The two of them were off, arguing for hours on end, with no goodwill on either side, and with me in the middle.

Pfitzner often complained to me that he could not establish the slightest relationship with Mahler's music. He did not feel it was music *at all*. Mahler knew of this opinion, but even so he fagged himself half to death with the rehearsals for *Die Rose vom Liebesgarten*, conducted it superbly and became so enthusiastic about this work that at the première at the end of the first act he exclaimed: 'Since the first act of *Valkyrie* there has been nothing to match this!' He was happy at the mastery and the success of the other.

AM, 106–07. (The première of Pfitzner's opera *Die Rose vom Liebesgarten* ['The Rose of the Garden of Love'] took place on 6 April 1905. It is quite possible that there was a further rehearsal on 1 May, because the work was on the programme for that evening.)

Mahler writes to the organizer of the Alsatian Music Festival

I beg you to take steps to ensure that my Fifth Symphony in particular is thoroughly rehearsed in advance. . . .

Thank you very much for taking account of my wishes regarding the 1st trumpeter and the 1st horn-player. As far as the order of performance of the works is concerned, I must absolutely insist that you keep to the arrangement that has already been promised to me and put my Symphony first, since the audience must be completely fresh in order to appreciate it properly. Strauss's work does not need this degree of special treatment, not only because of the fame of the composer but also because the work is shorter and easier to understand.

In this respect I request you to press most strongly for my wishes to be complied with.

Undated draft of a letter to Norbert Salter, owner of the Strasbourg Theatre and Concert Agency, HHSTA. (An Alsatian Music Festival took place in Strasbourg, then of course a German city, from 20 to 22 May 1905. The concert on 21 May began with Mahler's Fifth Symphony and ended with the *Sinfonia domestica* of Richard Strauss. The rest of the programme was made up of Brahms's Alto Rhapsody and a Mozart violin concerto.)

The musical festival in Strasbourg was attended not only by Mahler's friends Paul and Sophie Clemenceau, Picquart and Painlevé, but also by the writer Romain Rolland (1866–1944), who was at that time Professor of the History of Music at the Sorbonne. Rolland recorded his impressions of the festival, and in particular of Gustav Mahler, in an essay which appeared on 1 July 1905 in the *Revue de Paris* and was incorporated in his book *Musiciens d'aujourd'hui* three years later.

Romain Rolland on Mahler

He is one of that legendary type of German musician, like Schubert, who have in their appearance something of the schoolmaster and something of the clergyman. A long, clean-shaven face, hair tousled over a pointed skull and receding from a high forehead, eyes constantly blinking behind his glasses, a strong nose, a large mouth with narrow lips, sunken cheeks, and an ascetic, ironic and desolate air. He is extraordinarily highly strung, and caricature silhouettes have popularized his resemblance to an epileptic cat on the conductor's podium. . . .

Mahler is a really remarkable case. Studying his works you become convinced that he is one of a very rare breed in the Germany of today: a soul turned inward upon itself, which feels with sincerity. However, these emotions and these thoughts do not find a truly sincere and personal expression: they reach us through a veil of reminiscences, through a classical atmosphere. The cause, I believe, is to be found in

Mahler's occupation as Opera Director, and in the musical saturation to which this post condemns him. There is nothing more fatal for the creative spirit than too much reading, especially when it is not of his own choice, and the need to absorb too much nourishment, the greatest part of which he cannot assimilate. In vain Mahler seeks to protect his inner solitude: it is violated by the extraneous thoughts which besiege him from all sides, and instead of brushing them aside his conscience as a conductor compels him to welcome and even espouse them. Feverishly energetic, and burdened with heavy responsibilities, he works without relenting and has no time to dream. Mahler will not be truly Mahler until the day when he is able to drop his administrative responsibilities, close his scores, retire into himself and wait without haste until he is alone with himself – as long as it is not too late.

Romain Rolland, 'Musique française et musique allemande', in *Musiciens d'aujourd'hui*, Paris 1908, 185, 188.

Alma Mahler on the genesis of the Seventh Symphony

In the summer of 1905 Mahler wrote down the Seventh Symphony in one single burst of emotion. He had already outlined the 'structural sketches', as he called them, in the middle of the summer of 1904. In the night-pieces he had Eichendorff's visions in mind, splashing fountains, German romanticism. Otherwise this symphony has no programme.

AM, 115. (The manuscript of the first movement of the Seventh Symphony bears the date 'Maiernigg, 15 August 1905'.)

Mahler's instructions to Oskar Fried

I am back in harness!

A new symphony (the Seventh) was finished in the summer. . . .

I am writing to you today only because it has crossed my mind that in the course [*sic*] I have undertaken some not inconsiderable revisions of the score of my Second, which could perhaps be of value to you in the forthcoming performance.

The best would be if you would send me the copy of the score that is in your possession; I could then enter my corrections in red ink so that a copyist can transfer them to the orchestral parts without difficulty.

May I draw your attention especially to the Last Trump, which have [*sic*] to be studied *in good time* in one or two special rehearsals, so that these players do not need a single bar more once they are in the orchestra. I recommend you to use the same layout as I worked out before, which some of the performers will no doubt remember.
(4 horns offstage
the 4th trumpet offstage
Bass Drum ⎫
1st Flute ⎬ in the orchestra)
Piccolo ⎭

Undated letter-card, ms., The Pierpont Morgan Library, New York, and The Mary Flagler Cary Charitable Trust. (Fried conducted Mahler's Second Symphony in Berlin on 8 November 1905.)

The censorship forbids the performance of 'Salome'

Following the report of 31 August this year z 927, the Royal-Imperial Management is informed that the Censorship Board has on religious and moral grounds decided not to grant a permit to the libretto of the opera *Salome*, music by Richard Strauss, and the General Management is therefore not in a position to approve the performance of this stage-work at the Court Opera Theatre.

The libretto is returned herewith.
Vienna, 20 September 1905.

HHSTA. (Richard Strauss had completed his opera *Salome* in June 1905, with the exception of Salome's dance, which he finished at the end of August.)

After receiving the negative decision of the General Management, Mahler dictated and signed a letter to Strauss dated 22 September 1905, informing him officially of the rejection of the libretto by the censor. Since this letter is still in the Court Theatre files it was obviously not sent off. On the day it was written Mahler seems to have hit upon some other possibility of pushing through the performance at the Vienna Court Opera Theatre, for on that very day he sent Strauss a telegram asking for vocal scores to be sent so that the principals could start learning their parts.

Press comment on the banning of 'Salome'

. . . In the case of *Salome* it was the figure of the Baptist appearing in an erotic drama which gave rise to the intervention of the censor.

The banning of an opera by the Court Theatre censorship is certainly a rare exception, but it is not without precedent. Massenet's opera *Hérodiade* – which is of course thematically related to Richard Strauss's music drama – was also banned. *Die Zeit*, 22 October 1905.

Ernst von Schuch enquires about the Censor's decision

Dresden, 24 October 1905

Since my chief is very interested to know whether the enclosed report, which has appeared in almost all the German newspapers, is accurate, both His Excellency and I would be very grateful to you for a few words on how the matter stands. Yours hastily, in undiminished admiration and respect,

E. Schuch.

Ms., HHSTA. (Ernst von Schuch, 1846–1914, conductor, Artistic Director of the Dresden Court Opera, a friend of Mahler's since 1884. The enclosed newspaper cutting reported the banning of *Salome* in Vienna. Schuch was interested because he was preparing to perform the work in Dresden.)

Mahler informs Schuch about 'Salome'

26 October 1905

The report you mention is in fact true, but I shall do my utmost to have the decision changed.

But whether my efforts will meet with success cannot be determined at present. . . .
[P.S.] I am daily more delighted with this masterpiece! In my opinion the peak of Strauss's output.

Draft of a letter, HHSTA.

The Censor puts his reasons to Mahler in writing

31 October 1905

The first objection arises, as I stressed to you in our recent discussion, from the repeated explicit or implicit references to Christ in the text, for example: page 2, 'after me one will come who is stronger than I'; page 4, 'the Lord is come, the son of man is nigh'; page 8, 'the words of him that prepares the way of the Lord'; page 10, 'seek the son of man'; page 12, 'there is only one who can save you. He is on a boat on the Sea of Galilee and speaks to his disciples'; page 18, 'I hear the steps of him who will be the redeemer of the world'; and the following speeches which refer to Christ's miracles. All these passages would need to be cut or radically altered.

A further difficulty is the presentation of John the Baptist on the stage. The poet admittedly gives him the Hebrew name Jochanaan, but just as this change of name is unable to create the illusion that it is not the person honoured as Christ's forerunner, so equally would the choice of any other name fail to have this effect.

But also, quite apart from these textual reservations I cannot overcome the objectionable nature of the whole story, and can only repeat that the representation of events which belong to the realm of sexual pathology is not suitable for our Court stage.

I regret that a work of such great musical power, as you assure me it is, should become a casualty of the text on which it is based, but from my standpoint as censor I can form no other opinion. . . .

Letter from the Privy and Ministerial Councillor Dr Emil Jettel von Ettenach, ms., HHSTA. (The censor's decisions were valid only for the Court Theatres. *Salome* was thus able to be performed in May 1906 in Graz. The work was not staged at the Court Opera until October 1918.)

From Mahler's report to Richard Strauss

The censor, who had already given me a definite promise of his approval – he had demanded only *textual* changes, which he was going to let me know within a week – must have been worked on again from some other side; for he has just returned me the libretto with a long sauce (I'll bring the letter with me to Berlin, where I shall be on the 7th and 8th), and is once again talking of the 'representation of events which belong to the realm of sexual pathology and are not suitable for our Court stage'. In other words the accursed flight into *generalizations* again, which are impossible to combat! *I beg you, my dear Strauss* – keep *everything between ourselves from now on*, otherwise we shall upset the applecart. On Tuesday I am going in person again and shall take the bull by the horns. *I am not letting go*! and regard your *Salome* as my own personal affair.

Undated letter, quoted from *Österreichische Musikzeitschrift*, vol. xv, no. 6, 312–13.

Alma Mahler reports that Mahler had originally violently opposed Strauss's idea of setting Oscar Wilde's *Salomé*, on ethical grounds (AM, 114). Mahler's original antipathy to the subject and his later enthusiasm for the work are contradictory. A letter to the Mayor of Mannheim which Mahler drafted shortly after the *Salome* affair helps to resolve this contradiction. The Mayor had written to ask his views as to what musical works were to be considered 'serious' and therefore suitable for performance on the German Protestant Day of Repentance and Prayer. Mahler's answer is perceptibly coloured by his most recent experiences.

Mahler on morality in art

8 December 1905

Permit me to stress briefly that in matters of art only the *form* and never the *content* is relevant, or at least should be relevant, from a serious viewpoint. How the subject matter is treated and carried out, not what the subject matter consists of to begin with – that is the only thing that matters. A work of art is to be considered as serious if the artist's dominant objective is to master the subject matter exclusively by artistic means and resolve it perfectly into the 'form' [*Gestalt*] (you can interpret this word in the Aristotelian sense). – According to this principle *Don Giovanni*, for example (in which a rake does battle with God and the world), or, for example, the *Nibelung* tetralogy, in which incest etc. etc. is not only the source of tragedy but is also made understandable, are *serious* works of art. That *works like this* do not desecrate even the highest religious festival is my unshakable conviction, whereas for example works like *Der Evangelimann* (in which Christ and all the saints are stock characters), or for example no end of Mary Magdalene or John the Baptist tragedies, in which the subject matter is selected simply for the purpose of tear-jerking – are in my opinion unserious works of art and in consequence not only unsuitable for any religious festival, but unsuitable for any purpose. . . .

Manuscript draft of a letter by Mahler, HHSTA. (*Der Evangelimann*, musical by Wilhelm Kienzl, first performed in Berlin in 1896, a frequently played and very popular work.)

Hermann Bahr examines the roots of the attacks on Mahler

14 January [1906]

227 And once again Mahler is being hounded, hounded, hounded! Why do they hate him so? Well, why do they hate Klimt so? They hate everyone who tries to be true to himself. That is what they cannot bear. 'Self-willed' and 'obstinate': the words themselves are a criticism. They cannot bear someone to have an opinion or a will of his own. They cannot bear the idea that someone should try to be free. And yet they wish they were free themselves. But do not dare. And are secretly ashamed that they are so cowardly. And avenge their bad conscience on the brave.

Diary entry, Hermann Bahr, *Tagebuch*, Berlin 1909, 99.

Mahler to his wife from Holland

So here I am and the first rehearsal already behind me. 'What a different spirit!' The orchestra superbly prepared and a performance such as was not bettered in Vienna. The chorus in *Das klagende Lied*) very subtly rehearsed and well trained. Mengelberg is a capital fellow! The only one to whom I feel I could entrust a work of mine with complete peace of mind. The symphony is already on the programme for next week in The Hague, Rotterdam, Haarlem, Utrecht and Arnhem, where Mengelberg is doing a concert tour with the orchestra from here. I am rehearsing *Kindertotenlieder* today. The singer I do not yet know. Am curious. In Antwerp I had a decisive *succès*. Reviews first-class. . . .

. . . So, yesterday the symphony, *Kindertotenlieder*, magnificent performance except for the singer, who lacked warmth. This evening final rehearsal *Das klagende Lied*, tomorrow performance, I leave the morning after. Thank God I shall be back with you all on Monday. One feels quite abandoned, although everyone is very kind and takes the greatest trouble. Here in Amsterdam I already have a stalwart congregation – especially the young people are impassioned. The audience *very* respectful, the press decidedly *warm*. . . .

AM, 360, 361. (Both letters are undated. Since the performance of the Fifth Symphony took place on 8 March 1906, the second letter must have been written on 9 March. *Das klagende Lied* was performed on 10 and 11 March. Prior to this Mahler had conducted a concert in Antwerp.)

Willem Mengelberg as a Mahler conductor

Willem Mengelberg is at once the calmest and the liveliest conductor that can be imagined. He rules the ensemble with expressive calm, projecting the spirit, the atmosphere, of the work to the audience by way of the performers. All his movements, however broad and passionate, always suit the style of the work and remain, as it were, a subsidiary of this all-embracing calm which creates the 'tension'. Every important theme, every melodic line is clarified by a gesture; this gesture is always the plastic translation of the musical expression – and as such a combination of analytical precision and great formal beauty. . . .

In Willem Mengelberg's art as a conductor there is thus reflected as it were the universality of Mahler's music. The latter is not really satisfying for a normal conducting talent, because *one-sided* devotion is inadequate to put it across. It always demands movement *and* calm *at the same time*, passion and control, line and detail, naturalness and culture. This is the basis of its high artistic and ethical worth.

Rudolf Mengelberg, 'Mahler und Mengelberg', in *Willem Mengelberg, Gedenkboek*, The Hague 1920, 114.

'The Marriage of Figaro' brought closer to Beaumarchais

Vienna, April 1906

Your name, most respected Director, really belongs on the title page of this book, to which you gave more than faithful and tireless collaboration and fervent encouragement. It was your idea to draw Da Ponte's libretto closer to Beaumarchais's comedy, and you yourself joined in and helped to bring the idea to fruition. . . .

Max Kalbeck's covering letter to Mahler with Kalbeck's revised German libretto of *The Marriage of Figaro*, HHSTA. (The première of *The Marriage of Figaro* with Roller's sets took place on 30 March 1906. Mahler attached such importance to this new production that he cut short his visit to Amsterdam for it.)

The Mayor of Graz invites Mahler to the première of 'Salome'

Graz, 10 May 1906

Sir, – I take the liberty of extending a most respectful invitation to you to attend the first performance of the opera *Salome* by Dr Richard Strauss, which will take place here on 16th of this month, in the company of your highly esteemed lady wife, as my guests in my box.

HHSTA.

Alma Mahler on the visit to Graz

The morning after the performance, which was a great success, although a Christian Socialist demonstration had been feared, Strauss came to breakfast with us and started reproaching Mahler that he took everything, and notably that muckheap, the Opera, too seriously; he should take more care of himself. No one would compensate him when he had exhausted himself. A pigsty like that, which would not even perform *Salome* – no, it was not worth it!

Fundamentally he was right. I had always been of the same opinion. For, important to me as was every note that he wrote, his undoubtedly exemplary work in the Opera was indifferent to me. I already knew then that all reproduction is ephemeral, but his production is eternal.

Mahler used to say: 'Strauss and I are digging away in our shafts from different sides of the same mountain. In the end, one day we shall meet.'

AM, 124–25.

Mahler to his wife from Essen

Essen, 22 May 1906

What a bout that was yesterday. Five hours of rehearsals, seven hours correcting parts. Feeling well, even so. . . . A young Russian (the well-known pianist and conductor Gabrilovitch), has come for my rehearsals; I like him very much and he shares my table at the hotel. He tells me of my supporters in St Petersburg among the young guard. I am very satisfied with the rehearsals. I hope I have not made a mistake. So far I have rehearsed the first three movements. Today I come to the last movement. . . .

AM, 362. (Mahler is referring to the rehearsals for the Sixth Symphony, which had its première on 27 May. Ossip Gabrilovitch, 1878–1936, piano virtuoso from Petersburg, later married a daughter of Mark Twain and performed mainly in the USA.)

Gabrilovitch on Mahler

No man ever had a more loving or truly sympathetic heart than Mahler, but with those who placed their art beneath their ego, he had not patience.

From Ossip Gabrilovitch's diary, quoted in Clara Clemens, *My Husband Gabrilovitch*, New York 1938, 129.

If the word 'self-dissatisfaction' does not exist it ought to be invented to describe Mahler's special manner of working when conducting an orchestra in rehearsal. It was often more a question of trying the music out, rather than rehearsing it in the normal sense of the word; right up to the last rehearsal before a première he used to make alterations and improvements and keep trying new solutions. Sometimes it was as if he suffered from an inner uncertainty or a persistent indecision *vis-à-vis* his own work, and then he would listen to the opinions of a few of the people close to him who were in the auditorium. I still remember sitting with other musicians – among others the pianist Ossip Gabrilovitch . . . – listening to the rehearsals of the Sixth (Composers' Festival in Essen, 1906), and I could still point to this or that spot in the score which was altered on the advice of that twenty-two year old répétiteur who had come along from Vienna. (He had another function at that time – an important function, or at least it was so for him; he was allowed to 'conduct' the off-stage cow-bells.)

Mostly these alterations were matters of tonal balance – even if, to achieve it, only tiny details of the instrumentation were involved. Mahler the conductor, and in this case that meant of course the conductor of his own work, was always concerned above all with the attainment of the maximum clarity; this was more important to him than colouring and charm of sound. During one of the rehearsals for the last movement of the Sixth Symphony he stopped the orchestra and called out to the trumpets, 'Can't you play that louder?' In the empty hall it already sounded like an unbridled din; were the trumpets to be even louder? He stopped a second time and turned to the trumpets again, this time with a gesture of the left hand whose commanding force was irresistible: 'Can you not play that even louder?!' They played louder still, now drowning the whole orchestra, and what had previously sounded like mere noise now took on the musical meaning which the noise had concealed.

After the final rehearsal Strauss commented, as if in passing, that he found the Symphony in part 'over-scored'. Over-scored? The Fifth really had been so, in its orchestral proportions; Mahler had realized this, after the première he conducted in Cologne, and he later 'retouched' the score extensively by considerably thinning out the orchestra in many places. But not the score of the Sixth, with its much greater wind forces. Over-scored: the word, coming from Strauss, . . . worried him for a long time. In connection with this, I have never forgotten it, Mahler made a remark which no doubt meant more than it actually said. It was remarkable, he said: Strauss was able to make do with a couple of rehearsals and it 'always worked'; he on the other hand took endless trouble with the orchestra in countless rehearsals in order to bring out everything the way he wanted it, but when could he ever say after the performance that nothing had been lacking?

Klaus Pringsheim, 'Erinnerungen an Gustav Mahler', *Neue Zürcher Zeitung*, 7 July 1960. (Klaus Pringsheim, 1883–1962, had been working as a volunteer répétiteur at the Vienna Court Opera Theatre since April 1906, and accompanied Mahler, who had taken a liking to him, on many concert trips. Pringsheim, who was related by marriage to Thomas Mann, later worked as a conductor and teacher in Japan. Bruno Walter reports that Mahler was 'depressed almost to tears' by Strauss's criticism in Essen.)

From the reviews of the first performance of the Sixth

At last the Sunday came, the last day of the Composers' Festival in Essen, and with it the 'big event' of the Festival, the première of the Sixth Symphony of Gustav Mahler, the most ultra-modern of symphonists. For days beforehand you saw dozens of musicians and music-lovers with the little red-bound score in their hands gathered like pilgrims in the City park, near the Municipal Concert Hall, and even in streets in the town. . . .

Musikalisches Wochenblatt, vol. XXXVII, no. 25, 462.

Cow-bells and celesta! Paradise on earth and Elysian Fields up there!

It would be quite simple if Mahler's symphony ran its course only between these two beautiful things. But between them a deep gulf yawns, an unsatisfied longing, a sense of despair, a total striving of the whole orchestra, especially in the last movement, where the very large brass section scarcely rests for a moment, a groaning and moaning and a shouting and roaring, and that is what gives the symphony its tragic quality, which perhaps the superficial listener would deny, but which, if you listen carefully, it does possess, and possesses more than Mahler's earlier creations.

Signale für die musikalische Welt, vol. LXIV, no. 41, 690–91.

The Sixth Symphony is simpler both in its themes and in the structure of its movements than the Second, Third and Fifth, and despite its extraordinary requirements will perhaps make its way quicker than some of its predecessors, simply because of this more straightforward content. This will have one good side-effect: an effort to provide some good percussion, the Cinderella of our orchestras. Richard Strauss was not so far from the mark, at the Annual General Meeting, when he referred to Mahler's symphonies and laconically proposed the setting up of percussion professorships at our conservatoires. . . .

Neue Zeitschrift für Musik, vol. LXXIII, no. 23, 513, EV.

A remarkable occurrence during the composition of the Eighth Symphony

He was setting the old hymn *Veni creator spiritus* to music, having procured the text from somewhere or other. In the midst of the work he noticed that the music was brimming out over the text, overflowing like water from a full dish; or, in other words, that the structural concept of the music did not correspond to the strophic form of the verse. He lamented his distress to a friend, and this friend, a philologist, pointed out to him that this was natural, for in the version he was using the text was incomplete; about one and a half verses were missing. Mahler thereupon had Court Conductor Luze urgently obtain the complete text for him in Vienna. When the hymn arrived he now discovered to his boundless astonishment that the words matched the music exactly, that it was out of a feeling for form that he had composed too much: each of the new words fitted effortlessly into the whole.

Ernst Decsey, 'Stunden mit Mahler', *Die Musik*, vol. X, no. 18, 353–54. (Ernst Decsey, 1870–1941, music critic, biographer of Hugo Wolf.)

Mahler to Friedrich Löhr

This accursed old church tome from which I took the text of the *Veni creator* does not seem to me to be entirely reliable. Please will you send me an authentic text of the hymn. . . .

Undated letter, postmarked 18 July 1906, GMB, 291.

Mahler to Mengelberg, on the Eighth Symphony

I have just completed my Eighth – it is the greatest thing I have done so far. And so peculiar in content and form that it is impossible to write about it. Just imagine that the universe is beginning to sound and to ring. It is no longer human voices, but circling planets and suns. More when we talk.

Undated letter, GMB, 332. (According to GMB this letter bears the postmark Maiernigg, 18 August 1906. But at that time Mahler was in Salzburg.)

Bernhard Paumgartner's recollections of the Salzburg Music Festival marking the 150th anniversary of Mozart's birth

The Vienna Philharmonic was there, and Felix Mottl, Richard Strauss and Joseph Hummel conducted concerts. *Don Giovanni* was produced by Lilli Lehmann. She herself sang Donna Anna.

As conductor they had brought in a young man from Paris, Reynaldo Hahn. For the *Figaro*, which had come to Salzburg 'by the Supreme Command of His Majesty the Emperor Franz Joseph I', at the expense of the Civil List, with all the artists of the Vienna Court Opera and all the costumes and sets designed by Roller, Gustav Mahler was in charge. The male singers, Weidemann and Richard Mayr, and the ladies, Hilgermann, Gutheil-Schoder and Kiurina, formed a splendidly unified ensemble, with a new poise that was both musically and dramatically striking; whereas in the *Don Giovanni*, after a quick rehearsal on the spot, a group of international stars acted and sang in the age-old style with its wild and extravagant gestures: apart from Lilli Lehmann and Francesco d'Andrade, there were Maikl, Stehmann and Moser from Vienna, Braga from New York and the ladies Gadsky-Tauscher from New York and Geraldine Farrar from Berlin, while the chorus came from Salzburg.

Perhaps the strangest experience I ever had with Mahler was on that occasion, at the only full orchestral rehearsal for this opera. In a dark corner of the auditorium I sat through it at Mahler's side. He accompanied the action on the stage with a constant flow of words and vocal noises, in a comical mixture of annoyance and delightful humour, despair at the 'antiquated rubbish' that was before him on the stage, and bitter sarcasm at the expense of the 'hideously inappropriate naturalism' that was the product of 'retarded operatic brains' – as when the singer who was playing Don Giovanni, after dispatching the Commendatore with the elegance of a *torero*, maintained the same pose and wiped his sword on his cloak. . . .

When he left, Mahler said to me it would be a great thing to make Salzburg the place for a 'fundamental approach' to the unique quality of Mozart's music drama and to study it here, with all the facilities and uninterrupted by the repertoire system, which he hated. The misfortune of our opera houses, he said, was that after the second performance a work became a repertoire production and everything gradually went to pieces, because everyone involved was already occupied with God knows what else.

Bernard Paumgartner, *Erinnerungen*, Salzburg 1969, 65–66. (Bernhard Paumgartner, 1887–1971, son of the pianist Hans Paumgartner and the singer Rosa Papier, was Director of the Salzburg Mozarteum after the Second World War, and President of the Salzburg Festival. Reynaldo Hahn, 1875–1947, French composer, conductor and writer about music, was a friend of Marcel Proust.)

Lilli Lehmann on 'Figaro' and 'Don Giovanni' at Salzburg

At the last *Figaro* rehearsal Mahler had re-arranged the orchestra to get better acoustics. But no one told Hahn, who was conducting *Don Giovanni* that evening. When he began the overture and did not find the musicians in the places he expected, he looked for a moment as if he had been pole-axed. With a less experienced and skilful conductor, this sin of omission could have had terrible consequences. . . .

The second opera was *Figaro*, which was acclaimed with no less justice, and which included a cast such as I think few theatres could call their own. . . .

It will interest the reader that Mahler had composed for the second act a complete additional court scene, based on Beaumarchais . . . – very well done, it must be admitted – and this was not dropped even in this Mozart Festival performance, although in my opinion it did not belong there.

Lilli Lehmann, *Mein Weg*, Leipzig 1913, 240–41. (The Salzburg Music Festival was organized by the Mozarteum International Foundation and took place between 14 and 20 August 1906.)

Mahler's advice to Oskar Fried

In Berlin you must behave yourself and – dear Fried – try to be a little kinder to people, who after all cannot know the source of your being. I can only keep referring you to myself, for I know it all well enough. In the end, this always being mis-understood, and the obstacles which this created in the way of the objective for which we are striving, forced me to find a *modus vivendi* with the menagerie. And do not forget: our principal fault, our race, we cannot change. So we have at least to try to soften a little the *really* upsetting superficial aspects of our inherited nature. But then we have all the more reason *not to give way where it really matters*.

Undated letter, late summer or autumn, 1906, ms., The Pierpont Morgan Library and Mary Flagler Cary Charitable Trust.

Caruso's guest appearance in Vienna

The [Director's office] begs to announce that the guest appearance of the tenor Enrico Caruso, which has been briefly mentioned, will take place on 6 October of this year. For the role of Rigoletto the baritone Titta Ruffo has been secured. Both artists have been engaged for this one performance at the Court Opera by Director Conried. . . . Both Herr Caruso and Herr Ruffo are to receive an honorarium of 2,000 crowns each to cover their travelling and living expenses.

Draft of a letter of 24 September 1906 to the General Management, HHSTA. (The *Rigoletto* performance of 6 October 1906 was given at highly exorbitant prices for the benefit of 'the pension fund of this Court Theatre'. Heinrich Conried, 1848–1909, a native of Austria, directed several theatres in the USA before becoming Director of the Metropolitan Opera in 1903. He was Caruso's general manager. In 1907 he engaged Mahler for the Met.)

Secret festival for the French Mahlerians

My sister, who knew of the deep friendship between Emil Zuckerkandl and Mahler, and was herself part of it, wrote to me in August 1906 to ask me to give Mahler the following message: The Parisian Mahlerians had decided on a 14-day trip to Vienna in October 1906 in order to see Mahler's great creation, the Vienna Opera. Colonel Picquart, who idolized Beethoven, also wanted to visit the places where Beethoven had lived in Vienna. I told Mahler the news, at which he exclaimed, beaming with delight: 'For these true friends of music I will put on a secret Festival – a Vienna Opera Festival. But only you and I will know about it!'

Unforgettable days of a remarkable spiritual communion between French and Austrian music-lovers. Every performance was a masterpiece. No one, either in the Comptroller's office or in the press, suspected what was afoot, why the music was so magnificent at the opening of this autumn season. . . .

We are sitting under the walnut trees. And Picquart tells us: when he was in prison, a dishonoured martyr, he had always had one thought in mind: if he should ever be allowed to return to normal life he would make a pilgrimage to the places where his idol Beethoven had lived. And his second most fervent wish was to hear Gustav Mahler conduct *Tristan*.

The first wish had been fulfilled, and that same evening was to see the realization of his second wish, for Gustav Mahler had scheduled *Tristan* for his friends, to be conducted by himself. Picquart was as happy as a sandboy and was so impatient that he hurried off to the Opera an hour early. Since I was to follow later, we agreed to meet on the great staircase.

Scarcely had my sister, L'Allemand, Painlevé and Picquart left, when I was brought a telegram. It was signed by Georges Clemenceau, at that time Prime Minister, and read: 'Please inform General Picquart that I have appointed him Minister of War. Must leave today.'

Indescribable scene on the Opera staircase, where Picquart was waiting for me. When he read the telegram he went pale, not with pleasure but with rage. And losing all self-control in his desperation at being robbed of *Tristan*, he turned on me angrily: 'It was your duty to conceal this telegram from me. Tomorrow morning would have been early enough.'

Berta Szeps-Zuckerkandl, *Ich erlebte fünfzig Jahre Weltgeschichte*, Stockholm 1939, 186–87. (The only *Tristan* performance that month was on 19 October.)

Each morning our elder child went into Mahler's study. There they talked for a long time. Nobody knows what they said. I never disturbed them. We had a pernickety English girl who always brought the child to the door of the study clean and neat. After a long time Mahler came back, hand-in-hand with the child. Usually she was plastered with jam from head to toe, and my first job was to pacify the English girl. But they both came out so close to each other, and so content with their talk, that I was secretly pleased. She was absolutely his child. Very beautiful, defiant and unapproachable, she promised to become dangerous. Black locks, great blue eyes!

AM, 134.

From a review of the Vienna performance of the Sixth Symphony

If he [Mahler] were capable of expressing tragic feelings through the power of musical sound, he could readily dispense with the hammer and its fateful blows. But he lacks that inner, genuine creative strength. And so in his tragic symphony at the highest peak of excitement he reaches for the hammer. He cannot help it. Where music fails a blow falls. That is quite natural. Speakers whose words fail them at the decisive moment beat the table with their fists. . . .

r.h. (Robert Hirschfeld), *Wiener Abendpost*, 10 January 1907. (Paul Stefan names Hirschfeld as the central figure in the anti-Mahler press campaign. The concert took place on 4 January 1907.)

Immediately after the Vienna performance of the Sixth Symphony, Mahler travelled to Berlin to direct a performance of his Third Symphony. He spent his free time with Arnold Berliner, Richard Strauss, Gerhart Hauptmann and Max Reinhardt, and also made the acquaintance of Frank Wedekind and his play *Frühlings Erwachen* ['Spring Awakening']. From Berlin he went to Frankfurt am Main, where he conducted his Fourth Symphony, and the tour ended with a performance of the First Symphony in Linz.

Mahler to his wife from Frankfurt

I have now got the first rehearsal behind me. They are all getting down to it with a will. Siloti from Petersburg (just imagine) is here, on behalf of the orchestra there, to persuade me to conduct two concerts with them at any price. He says more or less the same as Gabrilovitch – they cannot forget my rehearsals, they learned so much. . . .

In Vienna people seem to have gone mad. In the newspapers here there are constant despatches from Vienna announcing that I have resigned – and that I have a phenomenal deficit, and that I am just not possible any more, etc., etc.

AM, 381. (Alma Mahler dates this letter 15 January 1907, but it must be 16 or 17. Alexander Siloti, Russian pianist and conductor, from 1903 onwards concert promoter in St Petersburg, with his own orchestra.)

Ludwig Karpath on the resignation rumours

The old opponents of Gustav Mahler have been joined by new ones, and recently they have all begun an out-and-out witch-hunt against him, which is made more ugly by the fact that the arrows were let fly just one day after he had left Vienna to spend several weeks' leave in Berlin and other German cities. The avalanche was set in motion by a paper which appears only on Monday mornings, and which contained the momentous report that Mahler proposed to retire from any form of conducting activity in order to devote his life to composition. The man who wrote this was a friend of the Director's. But of course

246

it is well known that it is one's friends from whom one needs protection. The good fellow must just have heard mentioned what those who are or have been close to Mahler have long known to be a wish he has cherished for years. . . .

Then of course the newspapers got hold of the other end of the stick, and wrote not that Mahler wanted to go but that he had to go. I am in a position to confirm that neither of these two assertions is accurate. Mahler the composer already wanted to retire before he even became Director; and the Director cannot sacrifice himself to the composer because he is not sufficiently independent financially to be able to do without his substantial salary. And as for Mahler's *having* to go, there can be no question of this as long as his present superior, Prince Montenuovo, can keep him. . . .

I wanted first to get the facts straight. So a crisis there most decidedly is not. However, it cannot be denied that the Institution as an organism has been shaken, and that if Mahler does not alter his course he will sooner or later fall flat on his face. If he had really wanted to leave, he would have had a splendid opportunity: the question of principle in respect of Richard Strauss's *Salome*. To stand up for a work of art and to fall as a result – that would be a way to go out in a blaze of glory. There is also no doubt that, if Mahler had been able to perform *Salome*, his reputation would have been strengthened and the ticket receipts would have increased. . . . Now of course he ought to have done all he could to make up for this disagreeable reverse. But then he made the unforgivable mistake of taking on a total flop, in the form of Erlanger's *Le Juif polonais*, and at the same time neglecting other measures that were necessary to improve receipts.

Ludwig Karpath, 'Vom Wiener Musikleben', *Münchner Allgemeine Zeitung*, 7 February 1907. (The opera *Le Juif polonais*, by Camille Erlanger, was first performed on 4 October 1906. The newspaper which set off the wave of rumours was the *Montags-Revue*. Alfred Prince Montenuovo, Second Chief Comptroller, had special responsibility for theatre matters.)

At the Schönberg first performances in February 1907

In recent years Mahler had become the shield and succour of all aspiring young musicians. Schönberg in particular was one that he tried to protect from the brutality of the mob. He twice became directly involved in rowdy scenes at concerts.

The first occasion was during a performance of the Quartet, Op. 7. The whole audience were listening quietly and undisturbed when suddenly the critic K. shouted up at the platform 'Stop!' (an unforgivable mistake), whereupon a barrage of howls and whistles was let loose such as I have never heard before or since. One fellow posted himself in front of the first row and hissed at Schönberg . . . Mahler sprang to his feet, went up to the man and said sharply, 'Let me just see what sort of fellow it is who hisses.' Whereupon the other raised his hand to strike Mahler a blow. Moll saw it coming, pushed like lightning through the confused jumble of bystanders and separated the two, to the astonishment of both. He chased the portly burgher out of the Bösendorfer Hall, and the fellow, intimidated by Moll's greater strength, offered no resistance. But at the exit he pulled himself together and shouted: 'Calm down, I hiss at Mahler concerts, *too*!'

On the second occasion the Chamber Symphony was being performed at the Musikvereinssaal. In the middle people began to scrape their chairs loudly and leave the hall demonstratively. Mahler got up in a fury, demanded silence and obtained it. At the end of the performance he stood at the front of his box and applauded until the last of the trouble-makers had left the hall. Only then did we drive home. . . . Mahler said, 'I do not understand his music, but he is young; perhaps he is right. I am old, perhaps I no longer have the ear for his music.'

AM, 141–42. (Schönberg's String Quartet, Op. 7, was first performed by the Rosé Quartet on 5 February 1907, the Chamber Symphony by the Wind Chamber Ensemble of the Court Opera on 8 February 1907.)

Nach der Aufführung seiner letzten Symphonie bemerkten einige Kritiker, daß Mahler sich von Erinnerungen an die von ihm verehrten Meister nicht freimachen konnte, und überdies auch Anlehen beim Volksliede gemacht hat. Mahler gedenkt nun bei Wiederholungen seines Werkes auch in den Gesichtszügen und Attitüden jenen Vorbildern zu ähneln, die ihn bei der Komposition jeweilig beeinflußt haben.

Bei Wagner-Anklängen

Bei Liszt-Reminiszenzen.

Zu Meyerbeers Erinnerung

Bei Schubert-Tönen.

Bei Zitierung von Beethovens Geist.

Bei Instrumentierung des Volksliedes als Wiener Biß.

Mahler's metamorphoses. Caricature by Theo Zasche. ÖNB-BA. The Viennese caricaturist Theo Zasche sums up the critical objections to Mahler's work as a composer by lending him the features of Wagner, Liszt, Meyerbeer, Schubert and Beethoven. This accusation of eclecticism culminates in the last drawing, which shows Mahler 'orchestrating a folk-song, as a bright spark from Vienna'.

Mahler to Richard Strauss

Yesterday I heard Schönberg's new Quartet, and it made such a significant and indeed impressive impact on me that I feel I must write to recommend it to you for the Composers' Congress in Dresden. I am sending the score herewith and hope you will find the time to have a look at the work. The Rosé Quartet are willing to perform the work in return for reimbursement of *travelling expenses*.

Forgive me for troubling you; I know you are much pestered; but I think you will be pleased with it yourself. Sincere regards and in all haste, your faithful M.

Many thanks for the *Salome*. It never leaves my desk.

Undated letter, presumably 6 February 1907, transcript, Dr Franz Strauss Collection, Garmisch-Partenkirchen.

Heart trouble during a 'Lohengrin' rehearsal

In the swan chorus he found the singing and acting not lively enough; to demonstrate what he wanted he grabbed two chorus singers by the hands at the words '*Ein Wunder*' and dragged them with an expression of enthusiastic excitement half across the stage towards König Heinrich. How often he had inspired the chorus to stupendous performances by this sort of thing. This time he suddenly let the two singers go and stood stock still, as white as a sheet, his hand pressed to his heart. I suspect this was the first occasion on which he felt a weakness of the heart.

Bruno Walter, *Gustav Mahler*, Vienna 1936, 42. (The new production of *Lohengrin* had its première on 11 March 1907.)

Mahler's last stage achievement: Gluck's 'Iphigénie'

The peak of all his productions was his *Iphigénie en Aulide*, which incorporated the most beautiful clarity and spiritual harmony that I can conceive of in classical art. Here the pinnacle was reached; and it was probably because only a simple tent surrounded the scene of the great tragedy, so that there was nothing to interfere with the art of Mahler and of the singers, always the first to suffer by any superfluous or inept décor which prevents them from making their proper effect. . . .

Lilli Lehmann, *Mein Weg*, Leipzig 1913, 160. (The première took place on 18 March 1907.)

It was Mahler's habit to note down his own programme in his big Production Schedule Book at the Opera. Under the heading 'After Easter' he wrote in quite innocently, 'Rome three concerts'. Now his leave applied only to the Easter period itself, and Mahler intended to apply from Rome for a short extension (for the third concert). But this Schedule Book found its way, via certain ill-intentioned officials in the secretariat, straight to Prince Montenuovo, and the Prince summoned Mahler before him. He began by giving Mahler figures purporting to show how all his absences caused the box-office receipts to fall, against which Mahler was immediately able to prove the opposite. But the conversation became so heated that both agreed to consider Mahler's resignation. And so we went to Rome. Happy in one sense to be free of the Opera and independent at last, but concerned at the same time about an utterly unknown future. For although our debts were all paid off, we had no savings, and Mahler was very tired. We told no one a thing in Rome.

AM, 148–49. (It was not until the end of May that the public learned through the Vienna newspapers that Mahler was to leave the Court Opera.)

Attacks during the visit to Italy

The last few days have once again provided striking illustrations of the mismanagement from which the Vienna Court Opera is suffering at present. Director Mahler, having secured a huge income which can only be called exorbitant in view of his pernicious behaviour, is now away, 'travelling in symphonies' – peddling his own products – and in the meantime everything is going to rack and ruin in the Court Opera. . . .

Herr Mahler is doing a tour of Italy, gathering in laurels and even more money – we shall some time put together how many months' leave he has already extracted for his private affairs this year – and does not care in the least how his deputy in Vienna is coping with the Court Opera in the meantime.

Deutsche Zeitung, 3 April 1907.

Bruno Walter to his parents

Vienna, 3 May 1907

. . . Better times may be beginning for me, now that I have managed to get so far in spite of so much hostility, and my position may become a more brilliant one; but it is unfortunately possible that Mahler will soon go; please, however, treat this quite *discreetly*. That would be the end of that; a new Director (Mottl, Schuch or another) would take back for himself everything that Mahler has fortunately offered me in the way of new works and new productions. . . .

Bruno Walter, *Briefe 1894–1962*, Frankfurt 1969, 92–93.

Mahler's resignation as seen by the Vienna press

Director Mahler has indicated to a prominent personality his intention of leaving his position at the Court Opera next autumn.

Illustriertes Wiener Extrablatt, 17 May 1907.

In artistic circles rumours have been circulating for some time that Director Mahler is planning to leave his position. Several discussions between the Second Chief Comptroller Prince Montenuovo and Director Mahler have given these rumours added stimulus.

Neue Freie Presse, 22 May 1901.

The resignation of Gustav Mahler, on which we carried a report a few days ago, can already be treated as definite. The reasons which have caused the Director of the Court Opera to take this decision are obvious. The conditions at the theatre have made an artistic crisis inevitable, which Herr Mahler no longer feels capable of overcoming.

Neues Wiener Journal, 23 May 1907.

The counter-campaign by his friends and admirers

When they found out about it his friends were horrified. Vienna without Mahler was, at that moment, unthinkable. At the end of May several committee members of the Composers' Association handed Mahler an address which extolled his celebrations of the Ideal and his lasting contribution to cultural life. It ended with the words: 'We have set out to demonstrate to you that all these voices, and their sometimes disgraceful tone, are not the true expression of public opinion; and to express the gratitude of a number of individuals who owe you a great debt, for whom those works have remained inextinguishably alive in the form which your magnificent re-creations have given them, and who know what we have, and will continue to have, in you.'

Paul Stefan, *Gustav Mahlers Erbe*, Munich 1908, 52–53. (The signatories to this address included, among many others, the writers Peter Altenberg, Hermann Bahr, Max Burckhard, Hugo von Hofmannsthal, Max Mell, Alfred Polgar, Felix Salten, Arthur Schnitzler, Jakob Wassermann and Stefan Zweig; the musicians Julius Bittner, Ludwig Bösendorfer, Julius Epstein and Arnold Schönberg; the artists Josef Hoffmann, Gustav Klimt and Kolo Moser, and many University professors. At the beginning of June many more personalities added their names to this address, including Sigmund Freud, Ernst Mach and Lilli Lehmann.)

Mahler gives an interview on the motives for his resignation

. . . 'So in the first place it is completely untrue that any *affaires* have brought me down. I have not been brought down at all. I am leaving of my own accord because I wish to have complete independence. And also – and this is the prime reason – because I have come to realize that the operatic stage is of its very nature an institution which cannot be maintained indefinitely.

'No theatre in the world can be kept at a level where one performance is equal to another. But this is exactly what repels me in the theatre. For of course I wanted to see all my performances on the same high level, that is, to attain an ideal which is simply unattainable. No one achieved this before me and no one else after me will manage it either. And because I have reached this realization after ten years of hard work I have decided to leave a post which has remained mine to keep, right up to the moment of my final decision; of that I can assure you most decidedly. It also belongs to the realm of fantasy that the deficit in the Court Opera has increased sharply, and that I was obliged to leave for this reason. Please bear in mind that the target is always fixed according to the receipts of the previous season. Now the receipts of the Court Opera have risen from year to year, so that inevitably the target of the past season was far higher than that of my first season. It is only by comparison with this immeasurably increased target figure that two years ago a deficit of approximately 50,000 crowns was incurred, which, however, has long since been recouped. And despite the increased prices there is no deficit this season, either. In the last few weeks, probably because of the unseasonably early hot weather, there has been a drop of about 25,000 crowns, but this can be absolutely disregarded, for theatre takings are always subject to such small, temporary fluctuations. . . .

'What is true is that from next year I should have been entitled to draw a bigger pension from the Vienna Court Opera, and that I have relinquished this right of my own free will because I wanted to leave straight away. I have admittedly applied to be released from my duties a few months earlier than I originally intended, but that is purely the result of family circumstances – my wife and children have been seriously ill recently – and certainly of nothing else. My family affairs are of no interest to the public, and I will therefore pass over this subject. I have certainly had to suffer much in the past few weeks, and this has made me carry out my decision to leave my post in Vienna that much more quickly. . . .

Neues Wiener Tagblatt, 5 June 1907. (Alma Mahler had had an operation in the spring of 1907; Mahler's younger daughter, Anna Justine, had been taken ill with scarlet fever at the beginning of May. Mahler had therefore moved into the Hotel Imperial.)

Mahler to the impresario Norbert Salter on plans for his future

I am at present so overwhelmed with projects and offers that – especially as no successor to me has yet been found – I cannot yet reply to any of them. Naturally I must first take a long look at things. The best will be for you to collect everything you receive connected with me, and we shall discuss the matter when I come to Berlin in the *very near* future. I dare say America will be inevitable for me.

Undated letter, ms., BST.

Mahler reports to his wife on his negotiations with Conried

Berlin, 5 June 1907

. . . Slept very well and arrived here today quite fresh. Had a bath, breakfasted (in my room) and went straight to see Conried, who is staying at the same hotel. He was full of projects – all fire and flame. First of all he wanted to own me absolutely and completely, like Caruso. Then 8 months (180,000 crowns) – then 6. In the end we agreed the following: 3 months (15 January to 15 April) for a firm 75,000 crowns, free travel and living expenses (first class hotel)! We have not yet agreed how long the contract is to last.

AM, 383.

The Conried menace

In fact, Conried was regarded by musical circles in Germany and in Austria even then as an ever-increasing peril, inasmuch as he had at his disposal sufficient resources to take from the foreign opera houses the very cream of their singers. It must not be forgotten . . . that from Vienna came Edith Walker; from Berlin, Farrar; from Munich, Ternina, Morena, Knote and Reiss. The Vienna newspaper, *Zeit*, even went so far as to suggest that a 'Directors' Trust' be formed against Conried; for, not only was the Impresario taking their singers from them, but he was likewise reaching out for the Directors – Mottl in Munich, and Mahler in Vienna.

Montrose J. Moses, *The Life of Heinrich Conried*, New York 1916, 320–21.

The Mahler case as a political issue

We have after all been finished as a Great Power politically for quite a while, and in fact there is no reason to regret it. Once upon a time we were something like a State. Now what we have is something like two halves of something which has not even a proper name. . . .

And yet we *do* have something! We do still have something in which we really and truly *are* something. . . . We have our Opera. Our Opera, with an orchestra that Director Mahler has formed into a unified, magnificent instrument, our Opera with its conductor who arouses the highest interest and unbounded admiration wherever he raises his baton, our Opera with an array of performances whose outstanding, often altogether incomparable quality as artistic achievements has to be recognized even by the opponents of the man who, through his inspiration, his individuality and his tenacity, has created them. . . .

And still we simply let this man go away. And how many are even glad about it? But of course this is only natural on the part of those who have finally brought about what is now happening.

Max Burckhard, *Neue Freie Presse*, 16 June 1907. ('I am going because I can no longer stand the rabble,' wrote Mahler to Arnold Berliner in the middle of July [GMB, 365].)

Alma Mahler describes the death of her elder daughter

In the country threatening symptoms appeared in the elder child on the third day. It was diphtheria, and the child was lost from the very beginning. A fortnight of anxiety – collapse – risk of suffocation. Horrible time! Nature made its own contribution: thunderstorms, red skies. Mahler loved this child so much that he more and more buried himself in his room, saying goodbye to his beloved child in his heart. During the last night, when the tracheotomy was carried out, the servant stood outside Mahler's bedroom door the whole time, so that if he was awakened by the noise he could be calmed down and taken back into his bedroom. And so he slept the whole night. That terrible night in which my English girl and I prepared an operating table and rocked the poor, poor child to sleep. During the operation I ran along the beach, screaming aloud, heard by no one. It was five in the morning (the doctor had banned me from the room), and my English girl came and said, 'It's over.' And I saw this beautiful child lying there with wide eyes and rattling, and so we suffered one more day – until the end.

AM, 153–54. (Mahler's daughter Maria Anna died at Maiernigg on 5 July 1907; she was five.)

A few days after the death of his daughter Mahler was examined in Maiernigg by the local doctor, Dr Blumental, who noted a heart defect. Mahler hurried to Vienna to consult the well-known heart specialist Professor Friedrich Kovacs. The latter confirmed hereditary, but compensated, valve defects on both sides, recommended extreme care and forbade the sport-loving composer to climb, cycle or swim (AM, 155). This diagnosis, and the orders and restrictions connected with it, overshadowed Mahler's last years. At least some of the time, he had the feeling that he was doomed.

Mahler to his wife from Vienna, before the consultation with the heart specialist

Just a short report: we got here at 6 o'clock. Straight into the hotel, had a bath and then ate a ham in the café. There I met Karpath, who claims to have it on the best authority that Prince Liechtenstein said: 'We'll not let Mahler go, we shall not release him from his contract.' Well, *vederemo*. I feel very fit – if Blumental had said nothing I should have been out walking long since – and should certainly not have been in bed before 12 yesterday. So you see, my love, everything has its good side, too. From now on I shall avoid any form of exertion, and if I have to stay here I shall arrange my life entirely according to Kovacs (go up to the Semmering with you regularly etc.) – I think of you constantly, my darlings, and hope we shall be together again tomorrow or the day after. I shall send a telegram this evening immediately on leaving Kovacs. . . .

AM, 385. (This undated letter must have been written on 18 July 1907. At this time it looked as though Mahler's resignation would not be accepted. It was only on 10 August that Prince Montenuovo announced that Felix Weingartner would take on the Directorship of the Court Opera on 1 January 1908, and that Conried could make public his contract with Mahler. Mahler's release from the Directorship by the Emperor did not take place until the 'Supreme Decision of 5 October 1907'.)

On 15 October 1907 Mahler conducted at the Court Opera for the last time: a performance of *Fidelio*. Immediately afterwards he undertook a concert trip to Russia. On 26 (13) October he conducted a symphony concert in the Great Hall of the St Petersburg Conservatoire and then went to Helsinki, where he also conducted a concert, returning to St Petersburg to conduct his Fifth Symphony on 9 November (27 October). In Helsinki he spent his time between rehearsals with the Finnish painter Akseli (Axel) Gallen, whom he had got to know in Vienna in the Secession circle, and with the architects Saarinen and Gesellius. He also met Sibelius.

Jean Sibelius's recollections of his meeting with Mahler

Mahler and I were together a lot. His heart condition, already far advanced, imposed an ascetic mode of life on him – he was no lover of festive dinners and parties. The ties between us were established on several walks which led us into conversations on the great musical questions of life and death.

When we came to speak of the nature of the symphony, I used to emphasize my admiration for strictness and style in a symphony and the deep logic which unites all the themes by an inner bond. This was in accordance with my own creative experience. Mahler took a completely opposite view: 'No, the symphony must be like the world. It must embrace everything.'

As a man Mahler was extremely modest and an extraordinarily interesting person. I admired him as a person, his aesthetic greatness as man and artist, even though his conception of art was different from mine. I did not want him to believe I had visited him only to interest him in my compositions. When he asked me in his stern manner: 'What do you want me to conduct of yours?' I simply replied: 'Nothing.'

The orchestra on the other hand was not very enthusiastic about him. Perhaps this was because he was not at all in a good mood in Helsinki. Good old Anton Sitt, leader of the orchestra for over 25 years, said with quiet amazement: 'And this is supposed to be the new Hans von Bülow?'

Karl Ekman, *Jean Sibelius*, Helsinki 1935, 185–86, quoted from Erik Tawaststjerna, *Jean Sibelius*, Helsinki 1972, III, 97–98. (Mahler reported to his wife about this encounter: 'Sibelius came to see me in the morning. An extremely pleasant person, like all the Finns.' [AM 397].)

From a St Petersburg review of the Fifth Symphony

The musical ideas with which he operates have no independence; they are not characterized by creative individuality; for the most part they are echoes of the opera and the concert hall, and some of the echoes, from the melodic point of view, are not remarkable for their good taste. . . . Methodical and attentive study of the scores of Wagner, Bruckner and Richard Strauss is the foundation of Mahler's art. He seems however to possess natural, autonomous talent in a significantly lesser measure than the latter two (the former may be omitted from any comparison); he is, rather, a 'self-made composer'. Although he is not afraid of cacophony, he does not offer either the piquant breathtaking daring of Strauss or the lyrical honesty and the earnest pathos of Bruckner; what remains is the clumsiness and ponderousness of the latter and the hysterical restlessness of the former. In general terms one cannot deny the unity of the symphony, a unity which is achieved by thematic uniformity and a characteristic style. In this respect it is definitely a symphony and not a traditional album of four pieces under the same opus number. . . .

Russkaya muzykal'naya gazeta, 1907, no. 44, 1001 sqq. (The phrase 'self-made composer' is in English in the original.)

Igor Stravinsky: a youthful recollection

I remember seeing Mahler in St Petersburg, too. His concert there was a triumph. Rimsky was still alive, I believe, but he wouldn't have attended because a work by Tchaikowsky was on the programme (I think it was *Manfred*, the dullest piece

imaginable). Mahler also played some Wagner fragments and, if I remember correctly, a symphony of his own. Mahler impressed me greatly, himself and his conducting.

Igor Stravinsky and Robert Craft, *Conversations with Igor Stravinsky*, New York 1958 and London 1959, 38. (Igor Stravinsky, 1882–1971, Russian composer. In his recollection Stravinsky mixes up the programmes of the St Petersburg concerts of 1902 and 1907.)

The journey to America brought forward:

16 November 1907

To the High Imperial and Royal General Management of the Imperial-Royal Court Theatres.
The retiring Director will discuss everything necessary in the presence of his successor Herr Felix von Weingartner in respect of all outstanding projects, especially those concerning the repertoire, and will ensure that everything will be arranged by the end of December.

According to his communications Herr von Weingartner arrives in Vienna immediately after the Christmas Holiday to take over the Directorship finally. For the retiring Director there now arises on 12 December a particularly advantageous opportunity for his crossing to America, for which reason he makes the request to be permitted to leave on that day.

Draft of a letter, HHSTA. (Mahler left Vienna on 9 December.)

Farewell to Vienna with the Second Symphony

Before a tightly packed and expectant audience, in which our best musical circles were represented, Gustav Mahler's C minor Symphony was performed yesterday. Not for the first time: the composition, which may today be described as the representative principal work by Mahler, had already made a great impression eight years ago. Its effect has proved lasting, and has indeed increased. The performance was a genuine great success; one may speak of a real triumph for the composer. The charming A flat major movement, delightfully played by the Philharmonic, unleashed a storm of applause that would not cease, despite repeated thanks from both the composer and the whole orchestra. It seemed as though the audience wanted to force an encore. And after the magnificent last movement the audience burst into a tempestuous demonstration. . . .

Neue Freie Presse, 25 November 1907. (Mahler's farewell concert took place on Sunday 24 November 1907 in the great Musikvereinssaal, as an extraordinary concert of the Society of the Friends of Music.)

Mahler's farewell to the Vienna Opera

TO THE HONOURED MEMBERS OF THE COURT OPERA

The time has come when our work together must end. I depart from my work-place, which has become dear to me, and I bid farewell to you.

Instead of the whole, the complete creation, that I had dreamt of, I leave behind something piecemeal and imperfect – as man is fated to do.

It is not for me to judge what my work has been to those for whose sake it was done. But at such a moment I am entitled to say of myself: I was honest in my intentions, and I set my sights high. My efforts have not always been crowned with success. No one is so exposed to the 'resistance of matter', the 'defiance of the object', as is the performing artist. But I have always committed myself totally; I have subordinated my personal wishes to the cause, and my inclinations to my duty. I have not spared myself, and have thus acquired the right to demand of others that they exert all their strength.

In the throes of the battle, in the heat of the moment, neither you nor I have been spared wounds, or errors. But when a work has been successfully performed, a task accomplished, we have forgotten all the difficulties and exertions; we have felt richly rewarded even in the absence of the outward signs of success. We have all made progress, and so has the Institution for which we have worked.

Please accept my hearty thanks, you who have helped forward my difficult and often thankless task, who have supported me and have fought at my side. Please accept my sincerest good wishes for your own further careers and for the prosperity of the Court Opera House, whose destiny I shall follow with the greatest interest and sympathy in years to come.

Vienna, 7 December 1907   GUSTAV MAHLER.

Printed letter to the Opera staff.

Mahler's send-off

Dear Sir or Madam,

The admirers of Gustav Mahler are assembling to take their leave of him on Monday the 9th, before 8.30 a.m., on the platform of the West Station, and invite you to attend, and to inform all like-minded people.

As this demonstration is intended as a surprise for Mahler, it is of importance not to confide in persons who are close to the Press.

Dr Anton von Webern   Dr Paul Stefan
Dr Karl Horwitz   Heinrich Jalowetz

Flysheet, December 1907.

The Vienna Opera in the Mahler era

NEW OPERATIC WORKS:

1897	October	*Dalibor* by Smetana
	November	*Eugene Onegin* by Tchaikowsky
1898	January	*Djamileh* by Bizet
	February	*La Bohème* by Leoncavallo
	December	*Donna Diana* by Reznicek
1899	January	*Die Kriegsgefangene* by Goldmark
	February	*Der Apotheker* by J. Haydn
	February	*Die Opernprobe* by Lortzing
	March	*Der Bärenhäuter* by S. Wagner
	October	*Der Dämon* by Rubinstein
1900	January	*Es war einmal* by Zemlinsky
	March	*Yolanta* by Tchaikowsky
	May	*Fedora* by Giordano
	November	*Der Bundschuh* by Reiter
1901	March	*Lobetanz* by Thuille
	November	*The Tales of Hoffmann* by Offenbach
1902	January	*Feuersnot* by R. Strauss
	February	*Der dot mon* by J. Forster
	October	*Zaïde* by Mozart
	December	*Pique Dame* [*Pikovaya Dama*] by Tchaikowsky
1903	March	*Louise* by Charpentier
	November	*La Bohème* by G. Puccini
1904	February	*Der Corregidor* by H. Wolf
	November	*Lakmé* by L. Delibes (complete: parts had already been given on 6 January 1894)
1905	February	*Das war ich* by Leo Blech
	February	*Die Abreise* by E. d'Albert
	April	*Die Rose vom Liebesgarten* by Pfitzner
	October	*Die neugierigen Frauen* by E. Wolf-Ferrari
1906	October	*Le Juif polonais* by C. Erlanger
	November	*Flauto solo* by E. d'Albert
1907	May	*Samson and Delilah* by Saint-Saëns
	October	*Madam Butterfly* by G. Puccini

The year 1908 saw the following new operas after Mahler's departure:

January	*Ein Wintermärchen* by Goldmark (accepted for performance by Mahler)
February	*Tiefland* by E. d'Albert
April	*Die rote Gred* by Bittner (accepted for performance by Mahler)
October	*Das süsse Gift* by Gorter

NEW PRODUCTIONS:

Zar und Zimmermann by Lortzing, 11 September 1897
Romeo and Juliet by Gounod, 21 November 1897
The Flying Dutchman by Wagner, 4 December 1897
Norma by Bellini, 24 January 1898
Un ballo in maschera by Verdi, 5 March 1898

Robert le diable by Meyerbeer, 20 March 1898
Das Nachtlager von Granada by Kreutzer, 6 June 1898
La Dame blanche by Boïeldieu, 4 October 1898
Freischütz by Weber, 21 October 1898
Der Spielmann, ballet by Forster, 20 December 1898
Tanzmärchen, ballet by Bayer, 10 February 1899
La figlia del reggimento by Donizetti, 18 April 1899
Das Glöckchen des Eremiten by Maillart, 21 April 1899
Die Nürnberger Puppe by Adam, 24 April 1899
Margot, ballet by H. Doppler, 16 May 1899
Rigoletto by Verdi, 20 May 1899
Lucia di Lammermoor by Donizetti, 9 October 1899
Der Wildschütz by Lortzing, 27 January 1900
Così fan tutte by Mozart (in H. Levi's version), 4 October 1900 (also 24 November 1905)
Il Trovatore by Verdi, 26 October 1900
Rienzi by Wagner, 21 January 1901
Königin von Saba by Goldmark, 29 April 1901
Martha by Flotow, 4 May 1901
The Merry Wives of Windsor by Nicolai, 4 October 1901
Gute Nacht, Herr Pantalon by Grisar, 10 April 1901
Das goldene Kreuz by Brüll, 6 June 1902
Ernani by Verdi, 2 October 1902
Les Huguenots by Meyerbeer, 29 October 1902
Euryanthe by Weber, 19 January 1903; with new libretto by G. Mahler: 19 January 1904
Tristan and Isolde by Wagner, 21 February 1903
Requiem by Verdi, 5 April 1903 (matinee)
La Juive by Halévy, 13 October 1903
Das Versprechen hinterm Herd by Baumann-Stein, 18 October 1903
Der Waffenschmied by Lortzing, 4 January 1904
Le Postillon de Longjumeau by Adam, 4 February 1904
Der Corregidor (original version) by Wolf, 10 March 1904
Falstaff by Verdi, 3 May 1904, in German for the first time
Fidelio by Beethoven, 7 (4) October 1904
The Rhinegold by Wagner, 23 January 1905
William Tell by Rossini, 11 May 1905
Manon by Massenet, 26 May 1905
Don Giovanni by Mozart, 21 December 1905
Entführung aus dem Serail by Mozart, 29 January 1906
The Marriage of Figaro by Mozart, 30 March 1906
Werther by Massenet, 12 May 1906
The Magic Flute by Mozart, 1 June 1906
Der Widerspenstigen Zähmung by Götz, 3 November 1906
The Valkyrie by Wagner, 4 February 1907
La Muette de Portici by Auber, 27 February 1907
Le Prophète by Meyerbeer, 5 March 1907
Iphigénie en Aulide by Gluck, 18 March 1907
Otello by Verdi, 3 May 1907

List compiled by Albert J. Weitner, an official of the General Management of the Court Theatres, and published in RSP2, 375-77.

I have just written a farewell letter to the 'honoured members' which will be pinned up. But while I was writing it I thought of the fact that you are not one of them and you have for me a *quite unique* place. I kept on hoping I should bump into you on one of these last days. But now you are up at the Semmering (where, to be sure, it is much nicer). And so to say goodbye . . . I can only send you these few sincere words and shake your hand in spirit. . . .

Undated letter from Mahler, GMB, 355.

273 *Olive Fremstad on Mahler's imminent arrival in America*

Gustav Mahler's greatness cannot be over-estimated. I heard a performance of *Fidelio* at his theatre in Vienna, and it made me cry to watch him. He is a small man, but his force is tremendous and he absolutely hypnotizes his men and his singers. . . . I am sure that . . . the New York public will make the acquaintance of a great man.

New York Times, 9 December 1907. (Olive Fremstad, 1871–1951, dramatic soprano, sang the part of Isolde in the first performance Mahler conducted in New York.)

Mahler arrives in New York

266 Gustav Mahler . . . arrived yesterday on the *Kaiserin Augusta Victoria* to conduct works of Wagner, Beethoven, Mozart and Weber at the Metropolitan Opera House.

'I have been looking forward with pleasure to my engagement in America,' said Mr Mahler, when seen at his apartment in the Hotel Majestic. 'I am thoroughly in sympathy with the season which Mr Conried has planned, and I hope to be able to contribute something in an artistic way. I shall make my first appearance here . . . with Wagner's music drama, *Tristan and Isolde*. . . . The Mozart and Beethoven operas will be staged and presented exactly as they are in Vienna. . . . Later in the season I shall probably conduct some concerts at which I hope to present one or two of my own symphonies.'

New York Times, 22 December 1907.

An American describes Manhattan

It is a beautiful island, long, narrow, magnificently populated, and with such a wealth of life and interest as no island in the whole world before has ever possessed. Long lines of vessels of every description nose its banks. Enormous buildings and many splendid mansions line its streets.

It is filled with a vast population, millions coming and going, and is the scene of so much life and enthusiasm and ambition that its fame is, as the sound of a bell, heard afar.

And the interest which this island has for the world is that it is seemingly a place of opportunity and happiness. If you were to listen to the tales of its glory carried the land over and see the picture which it presents to the incoming eye, you would assume that it was all that it seemed. Glory for those who enter its walls seeking glory. Happiness for those who come seeking happiness. A world of comfort and satisfaction for all who take up their abode within it – an island of beauty and delight.

The sad part of it is, however, that the island and its beauty are, to a certain extent, a snare. Its seeming loveliness, which promises so much to the innocent eye, is not always easy of realization. Thousands come, it is true; thousands venture to reconnoitre its mysterious shores. From the villages and hamlets of the land is streaming a constant procession of pilgrims who feel that here is the place where their dreams are to be realized; here is the spot where they are to be at peace. That their hopes are not, in so many cases, to be realized, is the thing

which gives a poignant tang to their coming. The beautiful island is not compact of happiness for all.

Theodore Dreiser, 'The Rivers of the Nameless Dead', *Tom Watson's Magazine*, March 1905, quoted from Theodore Dreiser, *The Colour of a Great City*, New York 1923, 284–85. (In the early years of this century New York had about four-and-a-half million inhabitants.)

Representatives of a new social class which had achieved wealth and fortune – among them members of the Vanderbilt family – founded the company which built the Metropolitan Opera House on Broadway between 39th and 40th Streets. It was opened in October 1883. On behalf of this firm, individual men or companies ran the operatic business in the following years with varying fortunes. From 1892 onwards the building was the property of the thirty-five stockholders of the Metropolitan Opera and Real Estate Company, which from 1903 onwards left the running of the Opera House to the Conried Metropolitan Opera Company. This was run by Heinrich Conried, who had a 269 50 per cent stake in the enterprise, namely $150,000. His annual salary as Director amounted to $20,000. In his era there took place the first performance of *Parsifal* outside Bayreuth (1903) and the first American performance of Richard Strauss's *Salome* (1907). The ownership of one of the thirty-five grand tier boxes, which were valued at $60,000 each, was regarded at that time as a sign of the highest social status. The semi-circle of these boxes was named the 'diamond horseshoe'. In the 1906–07 season Conried's position became uncertain owing to his poor health and the growing success of the competing Manhattan Opera House, which was directed from December 1906 onwards by Oscar Hammerstein. The engagement of Gustav Mahler was Conried's last significant action; he retired from his position in February 1908.

Alma Mahler on the first days in the New World

On the eleventh floor [of the Hotel Majestic], many rooms, 272 two grand pianos of course! So we felt at home. Andreas Dippel . . . took us to lunch with the 'great god' Conried, who was already crippled – consumption – and showed the characteristic symptoms of euphoria. This first lunch, what a comedy! The abject lack of culture of man and wife, and what an apartment! We spent the whole time suppressing our mirth, and out on the street we both burst into laughter. For example in Conried's smoking-room there was a suit of armour which could be lit up red from inside. In the middle of this room was a couch with a canopy and barley-sugar twist posts; this was where the great Conried lay to give audience to the members. Otherwise dark, unmatched fabrics and harsh, bright electric lamps. And on top of that Conried, who had 'made' Sonnenthal and would 'make' Mahler, too. Mahler soon got down to serious work, more easily and with less trouble than in Vienna, because here he gave all his attention to the purely musical and was able to relax from the pressure of Roller's productions, which at the end of the time in Vienna had distorted his music.

The orchestra, the singing, the house, these were wonderful! And the staging, which was under Conried's own control – often, but not always, appalling – did not concern Mahler.

AM, 162–63. (Adolf Sonnenthal, famous actor of the Vienna Burgtheater.)

The first rehearsal in the Metropolitan Opera House

Gustav Mahler began his first rehearsal at the Metropolitan 278 Opera House yesterday with an exercise of authority. He stopped the orchestra after a few bars of the prelude to *Tristan and Isolde*, and said:

'All other rehearsals in this theatre must be stopped. I can't hear my orchestra.'

And immediately the chorus rehearsal which was going on in the lobby ceased. Other conductors at the Metropolitan have attempted to effect the same result, but less successfully.

Mr Mahler was introduced to the orchestra by Mr Conried. The orchestra played a 'tusch' in honour of the new conductor and then went to work.

New York Times, 24 December 1907, 7. (A *Tusch* is a flourish played as a salute.)

274, 275 *The New York critics on Mahler's début with 'Tristan'*

Features of the occasion were the début of Fremstad as Isolde and the first appearance before an American audience of the celebrated Viennese conductor, Gustav Mahler, to both of whom eminent success must be accredited. . . . Mahler caught his audience at once, and I predict for him the popularity and influence which his great talent should demand. His conducting is marked by the authority and restrained force bred of great artistic knowledge and experience, and a firm facile beat.

Reginald De Koven (1859–1920), *The World*, 2 January 1908. (Mahler's début had taken place on 1 January 1908.)

. . . The house was as large as it might have been on a Caruso night. . . . The applause was general and prolonged. Many stood up and cheered. Mr Mahler looked happy.

William James Henderson (1855–1937), *The Sun*, 2 January 1908.

Herr Mahler . . . is a newcomer whose appearance here, while full of significance, is not likely to excite one-half the interest in New York that his departure from Europe did on the other side of the water. . . .

Nevertheless, Mr Mahler did honour to himself, Wagner's music and the New York public. It was a strikingly vital reading which he gave to Wagner's familiar score . . . but those who expected new things from him in the way of stage management, which has been a feature of his administration of the Imperial Opera in Vienna, must have been woefully disappointed. There were some changes in the first stage picture from that which has for years been equally familiar and absurd, but the changes only accentuated the absurdities.

Henry Edward Krehbiel (1854–1923), *New-York Daily Tribune*, 2 January 1908, 7. (In this first review Krehbiel already gives a hint of his later open enmity to Mahler.)

Mr Mahler's conducting resulted in a reading of the score that is comparable with the best that New York has known – the readings of Anton Seidl and of Felix Mottl. It was, on the whole, a finer reading than Mottl's, conceived in a larger mould, with all its finesse and subtlety, and with a greater power in the dramatic climaxes. Refinement and poetic insight were the salient characteristics of it. In the old days of Seidl there used to be a complaint from the boxes, so it is said, that the music of *Tristan* was too soft, that it was not possible to converse comfortably without arousing anger in the pit. It was this kind of reading that Mr Mahler achieved.

It seemed likely last Friday night that he was a man who will give New York music lovers some interesting experiences. His methods in the conductor's chair are straightforward and direct. His beat is uncommonly sharp, decided, and angular, and his attention is alertly directed at all points, seemingly at once. It is significant that his left hand was almost constantly used in the *Tristan* performance to check and subdue. He gives the unmistakable impression of a man of commanding authority and of keen insight.

Richard Aldrich (1863–1937), *The New York Times*, 5 January 1908. (Aldrich was musical editor of the *New York Times* from 1902 to 1923.)

The tenor Karel Burian on the New York opera audiences

The Wagner performances are the least patronized by the public. The whole business apparently bores the audiences to death. If one of these performances does interest the public, how do the most conspicuous – that is, the richest – express their feelings? The beginning of the performance is announced for 8 o'clock. 'They', however, come after 9. An usher with an electric light in his hand enters the box and shows the guests their seats. There is a constant coming and going; the spectators greet one another, look around them and see who is there. And the climax of the delight of the evening?

You might think that it came in the supreme moment of the music drama. Not in the least. The principal thing is the long intermission during which the gentlemen and ladies of society promenade about arm in arm to show their toilets and diamonds in their greatest beauty. After the long intermission one need only to glance in the boxes to see that by a few minutes after 11 there is a packing up of opera glasses in reticules and the start for home. What may happen on the stage after that interests nobody. It is true that in *Tannhäuser* the audience rises and flees from the opera house after Wolfram's song to the 'Evening Star'. The tenor who appears after Wolfram's song sings the closing music of his part to the baritone on the stage or the conductor. He might as well play cards with them so far as the public is concerned. I would like to bet that the fewest possible number of subscribers to the Metropolitan Opera House have the least idea how the story of *Tannhäuser* and poor Elisabeth ends.

The Sun, 27 December 1908. (Karel Burian, tenor of Bohemian origin, 1870–1924, known in New York as Carl Burrian, sang at the Metropolitan Opera House from 1906 to 1913.)

The box parties

In the front of each box sit either two or three ladies; behind them are either three or four men – each box party consists, therefore, of from five to seven persons. . . . The box parties go because the opera is fashionable; the opera is fashionable because the box parties go. . . . Why, if Society is bored by the music, if Society has all the opportunities for scrutinizing its clothes, its jewels, and its members in the closer proximity of its dinners and its balls, why does Society patronize the opera? Why, replies our philosopher, because exclusive Society, to have any reason for existence, must exclude. It must prove that it is select by showing itself in the midst of those whom it is rejecting.

Ralph Pulitzer, *New York Society on Parade*, New York 1910, 52 sqq.

Mahler as possible successor to Conried

Gustav Mahler . . . is the man who just now is most likely to be chosen for the place of Heinrich Conried when he vacates it at the close of the present season.

A week ago, in fact up to the very day he made his début, Mr Mahler was not viewed as a serious contender for the position. . . . But he has so completely upset advance reports concerning his methods – which were to the effect that he was a musical despot, obtaining results in the harshest ways – that he stands today in a light which many others vainly have endeavoured to reach.

Foreign reports recently received here mentioned Gatti-Casazza, director for ten years of La Scala at Milan, as the probable new head of the Metropolitan.

The World, 5 January 1908, second edition. (Giulio Gatti-Casazza, 1869–1940, became Director of the Metropolitan Opera in 1908.)

Mahler to Alfred Roller on the situation at the Opera

The situation here is as follows: Conried has long since lost out.

He had become impossible – mainly because he behaved unfairly and clumsily. The Management (that is the committee of millionaires) have given him notice. At the same time they intended to appoint me in his place – this was planned long ago, even before I arrived. My very great success (incomprehensible to me) apparently further accelerated the business. As you will have guessed, I most emphatically refused. But I declared myself willing to continue to work with them artistically in some form or other and at any rate to carry on conducting and producing. Unfortunately in these circumstances the further shaping of future arrangements is not in my hands. To begin with, they are planning to appoint the present Manager of the Scala as Manager of the Metropolitan Opera, to engage the *very highly praised* conductor Toscanini for the Italian operas, and to hand over to me, as it were, the German operas. . . .

Letter of 20 January 1908, GMB, 430.

Alma Mahler on her husband's state of mind

It might have been so beautiful, but we were shattered by the death of the child. Mahler lay in bed for half a day at a time in order to conserve his strength; the child's name was not allowed to be mentioned. . . .

AM, 163.

Mahler's New York 'Don Giovanni'

Doubtless Mr Mahler would himself be the first to declare that the performance was not ideal; but it was made in the spirit of an ideal which has hitherto been as far from Metropolitan Opera House presentations of *Don Giovanni* as the equator from the poles. . . . Mr Mahler treated *Don Giovanni* not as a collection of set pieces for singers but as a drama in music.

The Sun, 24 January 1908. (The première of *Don Giovanni* took place on 23 January.)

Geraldine Farrar on Chaliapin as Leporello in 'Don Giovanni'

Mahler was very ill . . . highly sensitive, irascible and difficult, but not unreasonable if the singer was serious and attentive. Chaliapin, however, was completely oblivious to rehearsal obligations. Mahler was sorely tried. The beautiful Emma Eames and the reliable Gadski, with Scotti, Bonci and myself, did our best to avert clashes. As I had sung Zerlina in Berlin under Strauss – under Muck in Salzburg – this training earned me Mahler's pleasant commendation; but we were, nonetheless, on pins and needles at every meeting. Happily, no overt act marred the performances, though it was a trifle disconcerting, to Scotti particularly, to have Chaliapin make a studied departure into Russian recitative where the fluent Italian text offered cues none too facile at any time; but this was purveyed with such bland impertinence, it was impossible to resist or chide this naughty giant!

Geraldine Farrar, *Such Sweet Compulsion*, New York 1938, 111. (The first performance in which Geraldine Farrar sang the part of Zerlina took place on 12 February 1908. Until then Marcella Sembrich had sung this role. Emma Eames sang Donna Anna; Johanna Gadski, Donna Elvira; Antonio Scotti, Don Giovanni, and Allessandro Bonci, Don Ottavio.)

Mahler a different man

At the Vienna Imperial Opera he was tsar, and all of his friends and those who opposed him as well predicted he would find the artistic arrangement of things at the Metropolitan Opera House so impossible that he would pack bag, baggage and baton and return to Europe in less than ten days after his arrival in New York.

But they were mistaken, for he has handled his singing and orchestral forces so deftly here that, instead of finding him a dictator, they are eager to do his bidding, and that is a remarkable feat, for every one knows that singers and snakes cannot be charmed too easily.

Occasions for his ready tact have arisen from time to time. One arose at a rehearsal of [*The Valkyrie*] recently. The chorus of the Valkyries is a difficult one, and it is usually filled by as many principals as the ensemble of an opera house can spare for it. When the Metropolitan Valkyries were assembled, Mr Mahler heard them sing the chorus, and at its close he said: –

'Ladies, I must pay you the compliment that never before have I heard such voices assembled for the Valkyries chorus – not even in Vienna!'

At this the singers fairly beamed with delight. Then Mr Mahler held up his hand and motioned that he was about to continue: –

'And now ladies, finding that you are possessed of such wonderful voices, I must ask you to use them.'

That was all, but its subtlety escaped none of the singers. And when the chorus was repeated it sounded different.

The New York Herald, 9 February 1908.

Mahler . . . was a completely different man in New York. In Vienna he had reinstated all the passages previously cut in Wagner's works, inflicted five- and six-hour performances on his audiences, and took firm measures to prevent anyone arriving late. . . . In New York, he not only immediately brought back all the cuts, he even introduced new ones to shorten the operas.

Wretched settings, which in Vienna would have raised a storm, here just made him smile. And not because he feared for his heart, or because he had a low opinion of the New York public – on the contrary, he found himself very well understood over there. No – but his attitude to the world and indeed to everything had changed. The death of his child; his own suffering. Everything else lost some of its importance by comparison.

AM, 171–72.

The Director of La Scala and Arturo Toscanini are called to New York

[In the middle of January] . . . I received a private cablegram from New York which asked me whether I was in principle disposed to accept the position at the Metropolitan and, in the event of an affirmative answer, the chairman of the board would cable me officially. I replied affirmatively.

Immediately Mr Kahn cabled me that I was to be at the head of the institution with all the authority possible. He asked also whether Toscanini would have any difficulty when he found himself together with Mahler at the Metropolitan.

I questioned Toscanini and this is what he said, 'But of course I will have no difficulty at all. There is room at the Metropolitan for several conductors and I am very happy to find myself with an artist of Mahler's worth. I hold Mahler in great esteem, and would infinitely prefer such a colleague to any mediocrity.'

Giulio Gatti-Casazza, *Memories of the Opera*, New York 1941, 147–48. (Arturo Toscanini, Italian conductor, had been at La Scala, Milan, since 1898.)

By 12 February 1908 the New York press was able to announce officially that Giulio Gatti-Casazza would succeed Conried as the Artistic Director of the Metropolitan Opera House. He was to be supported by Andreas Dippel as Business Manager. For the purpose a Metropolitan Grand Opera Company was created. Its President, Otto H. Kahn (1867–1934), a German-born banker, was one of the most influential and wealthiest men in New York.

A new contract with the Metropolitan

The directors of the Metropolitan Opera Company – which succeeds the Conried Opera Company at the close of the present season – expect to close shortly a formal contract with Mr Gustav Mahler for his services as conductor at the Metropolitan next winter.

By the terms of his contract with the Conried Opera Company, Mr Mahler reserved the right to resign at the close of the present season in case Mr Conried retired. Yesterday he availed himself of the rights of this clause and formally handed in his resignation.

This does not mean that Mr Mahler is not to officiate as conductor at the Metropolitan next winter. On the contrary, it is verbally settled that he will remain, although the final contract between him and the directors of the new company has not yet been signed and sealed. It is expected that this will be done in a few days, and then the matter of his return next year will be absolutely settled.

The New York Herald, 16 February 1908.

Mahler to Alfred Roller on the new situation

New York, 15 February 1908

The new management has settled in and sorted everything out to the extent that those who in future will be in direct charge – namely the representative of the theatre's owners (millionaires), then Dippel, who is in charge of the administration, and your humble servant, who up till now and probably also in the future, unless circumstances change, will hover like a sort of spirit over the waters – are now seriously airing the question of your engagement. . . .

It would be splendid if we were together again; but I cannot conceal the fact that I shall enjoy the benefit of it for a short while only; I don't intend to stay here long; but if I stay healthy, then next season at least. But this last piece of information *strictly between ourselves.*

GMB, 433–44. (The plan to invite Roller to New York never came to fruition.)

In the further course of his first New York season Mahler brought out new productions of *The Valkyrie, Siegfried* and *Fidelio* (on the Viennese model). In January and February he gave guest performances with the Metropolitan Opera company in Philadelphia, and in April in Boston. Although the Wagner performances received good notices, a decline in attendances, which had previously become apparent, still continued. The newspaper *The Sun* sought to establish the reasons by means of an opinion survey, as part of which they interviewed Mahler.

On the problems of operatic performance in America

Gustav Mahler, who is to be entrusted next year with the task of restoring the popularity of Wagner at the Metropolitan . . . believes that the public can be brought back when the works are done in ideal fashion.

'There must be a perfect ensemble,' he said, 'because the German operatic stage offers no such stars as exist now in the Italian field.

'With Mme Sembrich and Signor Caruso, for instance, the problem of an Italian performance is settled. But in the Wagner dramas we have no such powerful personalities.

'The substitute must be a perfectly trained ensemble, faultless mise en scène and orchestra. In that way Wagner opera may once more be brought into the position it formerly held here.

'But this ensemble can only be created by having the same singers in every rehearsal and at every performance. . . .

'I had many rehearsals of *Don Giovanni,* and the same cast but twice. I also had two Sieglindes for [*The Valkyrie*] in the two performances. That is no way in which to secure a perfect ensemble. The operas must be rehearsed and sung by the same artists time and time again.

'Then the scenery must be correct. It is not enough to go to Vienna and order a lot of scenery. It must be selected with care and properly placed on the stage.

'When these conditions exist there is no doubt that the Wagner operas will attract the public as much as ever.'

The Sun, 29 March 1908.

Mahler to Alexander von Zemlinsky

I really live from day to day, conduct, rehearse, dine, go for walks, just as the programme dictates which my wife keeps with her. I am not exerting myself at all, I am doing very little, and yet have never had so little time as now. You will know this from your own experience. I am already looking forward very much to seeing Vienna and my old friends again. Next winter I shall come back. We have both greatly enjoyed it here; we find the freshness, healthiness and openness of everything here very attractive. There is *future in everything.* I shall tell you more about it when I see you. For today simply best wishes to yourself and Schönberg. . . .

GMB, 446. (This undated letter was begun at the end of March 1908 in Philadelphia and presumably finished at the beginning of April.)

Engagement to conduct concerts in the following season

Gustav Mahler, it was announced last night, will conduct three concerts for the New York Symphony Society next season. . . .

Walter Damrosch invited Mr Mahler to conduct during this season, but owing to his engagement at the Metropolitan Opera House he could not accept. His contract for next year, however, allows for a few outside appearances.

The New York Times, 14 April 1908. (Walter Damrosch, 1862–1950, conductor, Director of the Symphony Society since 1903.)

Mahler to Anna Moll

The *Fidelio* has been a huge success and has, at a stroke, completely changed the outlook for me. I am now aiming, or rather 'they' are now aiming, at forming a Mahler Orchestra for me entirely for my own purposes, which will not only earn me a lot of money but will also give me a bit of satisfaction. It now depends entirely on how the New Yorkers react to my works. Since they are completely unbiased, I am hoping to find here a fertile soil for my compositions and consequently a spiritual home, which I could never achieve in Europe despite all the sensations.

From an undated letter, GMB, 393. (The première of *Fidelio* under Mahler took place on 20 March 1908.)

Plans for a Mahler Orchestra

An arrangement has been made with Gustav Mahler, it was learned last night, by which that conductor will give a series of four festival concerts at Carnegie Hall in March and April, 1909, with a specially selected orchestra. . . . These festival concerts are to be given without the cooperation of any symphony society. Mr Mahler is to select his own men.

Mrs George R. Sheldon is responsible for the plan, and has interested several of her friends in the scheme. She had the whole idea worked out before any announcement was made.

'Mr Mahler's influence has been deeply felt at the Metropolitan Opera House this Winter,' said Mrs Sheldon last evening, 'and we have to thank Mr Conried for bringing him over. While he is here it would be a pity if he should not have

NEW YORK HAS SPENT $4,000,000 FOR ONE SEASON OF MUSIC!

And Now That It's All Over She's Glad of It, Even if the Singers Are Taking the Money Back Home Instead of Spending It Here. Some Managerial Figures of the Most Remarkable Term of Music in History.

Cartoon from the New York paper *The World*, 29 March 1908. The satirist counts up the sums paid out for the 1907–08 concert and opera season, and criticizes the performers for taking their money back to Europe instead of spending it in New York.

a chance to conduct purely orchestral music with an orchestra of his own.'

The New York Times, 19 April 1908. (Mary R. Sheldon, wife of George R. Sheldon, 1857–1919, banker and Republican politician.)

At the end of April 1908, Mahler returned to Europe to conduct more concerts, including a performance of his First Symphony in Wiesbaden. This was the year of the Diamond Jubilee of the Habsburg Emperor Franz Joseph I, who had come to the throne in the Year of Revolutions, 1848. Prague organized a Jubilee Exhibition, as part of which the Czech Philharmonic gave ten concerts. The conductor of the first and last concerts was Mahler.

Welcome from the Czech press

It was a really festive day for the Prague musical world. On the programme no lesser figures than Beethoven, Wagner and Smetana, on the podium one of the greatest living musicians, Gustav Mahler. He certainly did not come to us in Prague with that indifference which the musical celebrities of this world bring to the various cities with which they have no ties beyond a one-day contract. . . . This master of the modern German symphony after all belongs a little to Czech music. Mahler has always been an enthusiastic admirer of Smetana's music and performed a great service in Vienna by contributing to its understanding. In view of these connections with our musical development the first conductor of the Exhibition Concerts deserved a special welcome.

Právo lidu, 26 May 1908. (The concert took place on 23 May 1908.)

Alma Mahler on summer 1908 at Toblach (Dobbiaco)

. . . I went to Toblach with my mother. In May, in deep snow, we inspected every house until we found what we wanted: a big farmhouse outside the village, eleven rooms, two verandas, two bathrooms, admittedly somewhat primitive, but in a splendid situation. We took it at once for the summer, came back, packed, and all transferred to Toblach, where Mahler, in the course of three summers, his last, was to compose *Das Lied von der Erde*, the Ninth and the fragment of the Tenth Symphony. . . .

Now at last peace descended upon us, broken only now and again by guests. Gabrilovitch came, and Gustav Brecher, Oskar Fried, Ernst Decsey – and we made music a lot. Mahler was working again.

AM, 174, 175. (Mahler had decided to sell the house at Maiernigg because it reminded him of the death of his child.)

Thanks to Arnold Berliner for a gift of books

Rumour had it that you had robbed someone. A whole library has just been delivered to me by the postman. So it is true, and you are expiating your sins by doing good and spreading culture among your friends.

Undated letter from Mahler, postmarked Toblach, June 1908. GMB, 366.

Albert Einstein on Berliner

There are and remain narrow limits to what . . . the human mind can comprehend. And so it was inevitable that the activity of the individual research worker should be restricted to an ever more limited sector of man's total knowledge. . . . Every serious scientific investigator is painfully aware of this enforced restriction, which threatens to rob the research worker of his wider perspectives and degrade him to the level of a drudge.

We have all suffered from this want but have done nothing to alleviate it. But in the German-speaking world Berliner has come to our aid in an exemplary fashion. . . . Berliner's achievement has been possible only because in him the desire for a clear over-all view of the widest possible area of research is exceptionally acute. This has led him to produce – over many years of strenuous labour – a text book of physics of which a student of medicine said to me recently: 'I do not know how it would have been possible to learn the principles of modern physics in the time at my disposal, had it not been for this book.'

Albert Einstein, 'Zu Dr. Berliners siebzigstem Geburtstag', *Die Naturwissenschaften*, vol. XX, 1932, 913.

Mahler's struggle with his illness

This time I have to change not only my home but also my

whole mode of living. You can imagine how difficult the latter is for me. For many years I have been accustomed to constant and active movement. To hunt through mountains and forests and carry off my compositional sketches as a kind of daring booty. I sat down at my desk only like a farmer going back into his barn, to hammer my sketches into shape. Even intellectual indispositions vanished after a jolly good march (especially uphill). Now I must avoid all exertion, keep a constant check on myself, not walk far. . . .

From an undated letter to Bruno Walter, written from Toblach in the summer of 1908, GMB, 408–09.

First performance of the Seventh Symphony

288, 289

On Saturday Prague witnessed an artistic occasion whose significance goes far beyond the topical. This was an historic event. Gustav Mahler, a master of modern music who is as fervently admired as he is hated and derided, came to us to conduct the first performance of his Seventh. . . . It is a long time since Prague has boasted a première of such importance. . . . Nothing could be better than for this remarkable concert to shake us out of our slumber and mark the starting-point of a fresh, youthful, truly modern, new lease of life. Saturday's concert would then be a historic date for us, too. To be fair, Mahler's concert at the Exhibition was 'bilingual', and the Germans were perhaps also in the majority in the audience; but as things stand in Prague we are justified in speaking of this as a Czech concert. The musicians were almost all Czechs, and in the audience every important figure of our musical life was present. And it was just this that constituted the importance of Mahler's concert, that he gave his work its world première here, with us and for us. . . .

Zdeněk Nejedly, *Den*, 22 September 1908. (The first performance of the Seventh Symphony took place on 19 September 1908. Nejedly, 1878–1962, was a Czech musicologist who became Minister of Education in the Czechoslovakian Republic after the Second World War. In 1912 he published a monograph on Mahler.)

Otto Klemperer's recollections of Mahler's rehearsals

He had about twenty-four rehearsals. His mode of work was astonishing. Every day after the rehearsals he took the complete orchestral parts home with him, correcting, improving, retouching. We younger musicians who were present, Bruno Walter, Bodanzky, von Keussler and I, were very willing to help him. But he would not let us and did everything on his own.

In the evenings we were usually with him in his hotel. Then he was relaxed and full of fun. He spoke freely, and fairly loudly, about his successor in Vienna. . . .

Otto Klemperer, *Erinnerungen an Gustav Mahler*, Zurich 1960, 10. (Otto Klemperer, 1885–1973, was at that time Conductor at the German Theatre in Prague, on Mahler's recommendation. Arthur Bodanzky, 1877–1939, conductor, from 1903 to 1904 répétiteur at the Vienna Court Opera. Gerhard von Keussler, 1874–1949, composer and conductor, had been working in Prague since 1906.)

Mahler to Andreas Dippel, on his relations with Toscanini

. . . I find incomprehensible, and cannot consent to, the procurement of new sets for *Tristan* without the least consultation with me. Moreover, in the discussion of my contract – of this you are a witness – I explicitly stated that I wished to retain for the new season the works which I have already rehearsed and conducted in New York. This was promised me, and I dispensed with a written assurance to this effect in the contract only at your request. And, while I have recently – in deference to the wishes of my colleague – left everything to the discretion of the new Director, I have nevertheless expressly retained *Tristan* for myself. I lavished a great deal of effort on the *Tristan* last season, and may reasonably assert that the form in which the work now appears in New York is my intellectual property. If Toscanini, for whom I have the greatest respect, without

knowing him, and whom I count it an honour to be able to greet as a colleague, were to take over *Tristan* before my arrival, then obviously the work would be given a completely new stamp and I should be completely unable to take on the work in the course of the season. I must therefore request you most earnestly to reserve the conducting of this work to me and therefore not to put it into the repertoire before 17 December.

Undated letter, autumn 1908, AM, 431. (The Management of the Metropolitan Opera deferred to Mahler's wishes, and he conducted the first *Tristan* performance of the season, on 23 December 1908.)

Alma Mahler on the second trip to New York, in November 1908

293

We had our three-year-old child with us for the first time, and to look after her an old English nurse, who always prescribed Japanese stoicism for the child. We were sitting in the little tender and the big steamer loomed into view. The child was exultant. The 'Miss' went up to her, held her hands and said in a warning tone: 'Don't be excited! Don't be excited!' For Mahler, to hear this, rush over, take the child in his arms and set her on the rail with her little feet dangling over, was the work of a moment. And then he shouted, again and again: 'There, *now* be excited, you *shall* be excited!' And the child howled with delight.

This time in New York, and for the next three years, we stayed, not at the Majestic, but at the Hotel Savoy, where almost all the singers of the Metropolitan Opera stayed, Caruso, Sembrich, etc.

AM, 182–83.

Mahler arrived in New York on 21 November 1908, and devoted the first few weeks to the already announced concerts of the New York Symphony Society. In the second of these concerts, on 8 December, he conducted the first American performance of his Second Symphony.

Mahler's concert début

Herr Mahler, as I hear, was reported to have said that his conducting yesterday was something of a farce, as the members of the orchestra neither came to nor stayed at rehearsals, as he wished them to, and I am inclined to believe the report as accounting for the lack of quick response from the orchestra to his beat. . . . For all this the orchestra played yesterday so much better than usual, with so much more precision, sonority, colour and unity of orchestral feeling.

The World, 30 November 1908.

The Second Symphony in New York

The patrons of the New York Symphony Society doubtless looked upon Mr Gustav Mahler as their guest last evening, when he conducted the second of his eight symphonies at Carnegie Hall, it was by demonstrations of far more than mere politeness that the large audience found vent for its feelings of interest and pleasure in this new music and its author.

New York Daily Tribune, 9 December 1908.

In spite of the warnings of example Mr Mahler elected to utilize forces which might have easily crushed the imaginations of his hearers when injudiciously used, and this is precisely what took place in passages where the reaching out after infinite detail of expression issued in herculean effort and nothing more. There are several such passages in this huge Second Symphony, and they are emphasized by the persistent employment of the penetrating tones of a solo trumpet written in its high register. . . .

It is owing to the presence of these portions of the symphony that the composition fails in its entirety to make the impression of absolute mastery. For this is indeed a work of splendid imagination, a creation always interesting, for the most part beautiful, and frequently inspiring.

The Sun, 9 December 1908.

Christmas at the Savoy

On Christmas Eve, Friedrich Hirth, the great sinologist, sat with us the whole night telling us the strangest Chinese tales right into the small hours. We had the feeling of being outside reality. On Christmas Day we were invited to Marcella Sembrich's. Sembrich herself, Caruso, etc.: this completely different theatrical circle appealed to us, too, although our intercourse with these people always remained on the surface; but Caruso was a genius off-stage, too! They all had an instinctive sense of Mahler's importance and deferred to him completely in private life as much as on the stage.

AM, 185. (Friedrich Hirth, 1845–1927, German sinologist, Professor at Columbia University, New York, since 1902.)

Enthusiastic reviews for 'Figaro'

Mozart's comedy, [*The Marriage of Figaro*], was given at the Metropolitan Opera House last evening for the first time in four years. It has been newly studied under the direction of Gustav Mahler; there were several new singers in the cast, there was a new and very becoming stage setting and new costumes. The performance was one of the most delightful and brilliant that can be easily recalled; not so much in the excellence of the individual singers, though here, too, there was much to enjoy; but most of all in the finished ensemble, the vivacity and gaiety that were infused into every scene, the dramatic verisimilitude with which the intentions of the composer were realized.

The New York Times, 14 January 1909.

The accompaniment of the recitatives by an imitation harpsichord and in the proper places by a union of this instrument with the orchestral strings was excellent.

The Sun, 14 January 1909.

A revealing letter from Mahler to Bruno Walter in Vienna

I have lived through so very much in the last year and a half, I can scarcely speak of it. How could I attempt to explain such a terrible crisis! I see everything in such a new light – I'm so much on the move; sometimes I should not be surprised to discover I was in a new body. (Like Faust in the last scene.) My thirst for life is greater than ever, and I find the 'habit of existence' sweeter than ever. These days of my life really are just like the Sibylline Books. . . .

I often find myself thinking of Lipiner. Why do you never mention him in your letters? I should like to know whether he still thinks the same way about death as he did eight years ago, when he gave me an account of his extraordinary views (in response to some rather insistent questioning from me – I was just convalescing from my haemorrhage).

How senseless it is to let oneself be submerged by the maelstrom of life! To be untrue for even one hour to oneself, and to what is higher than oneself! It's easy for me to write that down – but at the next opportunity – when I leave this room, for instance – I shall certainly behave as senselessly as everyone else does. . . .

Extraordinary! When I hear music – including when I am conducting – I hear quite definite answers to all my questions – and am completely clear and sure. Or rather, I feel quite clearly that they are not questions at all.

Undated letter from New York, early 1909, GMB, 414–15.

Reorganization of the Philharmonic Society

Mrs George R. Sheldon has succeeded in raising the necessary guarantee fund to rehabilitate the Philharmonic Society.

The proposition made to the members of the Philharmonic Society indicates the aims of the guarantors of the new organization. The proposition says: . . .

'It is proposed to organize an orchestra in New York for the performance of the highest kind of music, under the exclusive and absolute direction of a competent conductor, the members of which shall devote their time to its work for a period of at least twenty-three weeks in each year. . . . With the approval of the conductor the present orchestra will be continued under existing conditions of assignment and retirement.'

The conductor may make changes and add to the membership of the orchestra, subject to the approval of the guarantors' committee. . . . The action of the guarantors was brought to a climax last week when Mr Mahler, who has been selected as conductor, was invited to become the head of another organization. The guarantors submitted their proposition to the members of the Philharmonic Society, who unanimously accepted it. Mr Mahler was thereupon engaged for a period of two years.

The members of the Philharmonic Society, instead of receiving a share in the profits as their compensation, will get a regular salary, and the business management of the organization will be in the hands of a separate staff and not under the control of the members of the orchestra. In return for the surrender of its old privileges of self-government the Philharmonic Society has the payment of its deficiencies guaranteed for three years, multiplies the number of its concerts and is freed from the financial responsibility. .

The Sun, 16 February 1909.

'The Bartered Bride' in America for the first time

How dear [*The Bartered Bride*] has become to the hearts of the Bohemian people had a present and vivid illustration in the fact that weeks ago . . . over $2,000 had been sent to the opera house by members of New York's Bohemian colony for the purchase of seats for the first performance. . . .

Local concert-goers have long been familiar with the overture to *The Bartered Bride*. . . . Because Mr Mahler . . . did not wish to waste the overture on late arrivals at the opera, he played it between the first and second acts. . . . If it were played between the second and third acts its effectiveness would be increased tenfold, for then it would serve one of the purposes of between-acts music, which it may be said ought to bridge over the moods with which one act or scene ends and the other begins. In neither place, however, is the overture an anticlimax like the third *Leonore* when played after the dungeon scene in *Fidelio*. . . .

And the performance? Mr Mahler is a Bohemian. Miss Destinn is a daughter of Bohemia's capital. The dancers were brought from the National Theatre at Prague, the home of Czechish music. They are to the Bohemian manner born. . . . Altogether, it was an evening of unalloyed delight, and the opera and its production were most unqualified and pronounced successes.

New York Daily Tribune, 20 February 1909. (Emmy Destinn, 1878–1930, Prague-born soprano.)

The first concert with the Philharmonic Society

It would be misleading to regard this concert as a correct indication of what is to be expected of Mr Mahler hereafter. The orchestra of next winter will without doubt not be that which has been heard during the last three years. . . . Some of the players will go out. . . . Doubtless there will be some rearrangement of the places among the strings which remain.

Mr Mahler may perhaps discover the long lost wood wind players. Heaven send that he may, for the Philharmonic sadly needs them. . . .

One thing impressed itself upon *The Sun's* observer, to wit, that not in three years had he heard the Philharmonic play so well. . . . Last night's concert achieved much. . . . It promised more.

The Sun, 1 April 1909. (The programme included Beethoven's Seventh Symphony and Wagner's *Siegfried Idyll*. In a further concert on 6 April, Mahler conducted Beethoven's Ninth Symphony.)

From the minutes of a meeting of the Guarantors' Committee of the Philharmonic Society

Resolved that Mr Mahler be authorized to engage a Concertmeister [*sic*] in Europe for the next season at a salary not to exceed $6,000.

Resolved, that Mr Gustav Mahler be authorized to engage a first flute player in Europe . . . at a salary not to exceed $3,000. Mr Mahler was requested to order the necessary timpani for the use of the Orchestra.

7 April 1909. LMPA. (On his return to Vienna Mahler immediately set about executing these commissions.)

How Theodore Spiering became leader (concertmaster) of the New York Philharmonic

On the advice of Fritz Kreisler I had applied for the post of concertmaster of the New York Philharmonic Society, and upon my telegraphic enquiry whether I should come to Vienna for an audition, I received a friendly invitation to present myself as soon as possible. By chance I met Mahler in the street. I introduced myself to him, and he immediately took me on a walk right through the whole city and told me straight away of his plans for the reorganization of the New York orchestra. Then at five in the afternoon I arrived punctually at his flat; Arnold Rosé, his brother-in-law, had also come, presumably to help him with my audition. It was characteristic of Mahler that he asked me, more or less as soon as I arrived, whether I was ready to play. This impatience – or rather this businesslike approach – was something I later often observed in him. He never wasted time on preliminaries. My audition was to the satisfaction of both sides, and I was immediately engaged and made to feel heartily welcome. That same afternoon I received from Mahler a letter, confirming my appointment, which was a model of clarity.

Theodore Spiering, 'Zwei Jahre mit Gustav Mahler in New-York', *Vossische Zeitung* (Berlin), 21 May 1911, EV. (Theodore Spiering, 1871–1925, American violinist and conductor, had been working in Berlin since 1905. Fritz Kreisler, 1875–1962, Viennese-born violin virtuoso and composer.)

Mahler reports from Vienna to the management of the Philharmonic Society

After unbelievably difficult negotiations with a number of candidates I have engaged

Herr Theodore Spiering,

a native-born American and a member of the Chicago Union, as concertmaster. The conditions you will see from the enclosed contract. . . .

Since I have engaged a *Union member* for the post of concertmaster, and the Union had permitted me to import a foreigner for this position; and since furthermore you and I received permission to engage a foreigner for the flute and to get the timpanist in America wherever we could find one: then the *Union* will surely not object if I import the *flute-player* and engage a timpanist from a town other than New York? Do please explain all this to them!

From an undated letter to Richard Arnold, ms., LMPA. (The Union referred to is the American Federation of Musicians, founded in 1895.)

I have just agreed everything with Herr Schnellar (Court Musician, Vienna).

He is immediately sending two pairs of his new kettledrums to the address of Mr Arnold in New York. Be so good, when they have arrived, as to arrange the necessary for customs clearance and delivery and show them to the timpanist there (who by then will, I hope, already be on hand) so that he can get to know how to handle them. They cost: *2,700 crowns* (that is $540), and I beg you to be so kind as to arrange for this amount to be sent, on the arrival of the instruments, to Herr Hofmusiker Hans Schnellar, Vienna I, K. K. Hofoper. As you know Mrs Sheldon has kindly made the sum available. . . .

From an undated letter to Felix Leifels, ms., LMPA. (Hans Schnellar had developed timpani whose 'ease of operation of the mechanism and utmost sensitivity of tuning' were praised by Richard Strauss in his revised edition of Berlioz's treatise on orchestration; see Hector Berlioz, *Instrumentationslehre, ergänzt und revidiert von Richard Strauss*, Leipzig 1905, I, 411.)

Mahler to the publishers Universal Edition

I hereby confirm to you that I have no objection of any kind to the transfer to Universal Edition of the publishing rights in those of my works which have appeared under the imprint of Druckerei & Verlagsaktiengesellschaft vorm. E. v. Waldheim, Jos. Eberle & Co., Vienna, naturally on condition that I retain all my acquired rights.

Archiv Universal Edition, Vienna. (This refers to the publishing rights of the First, Second, Third and Fourth Symphonies, the scores of which had been published by the firms of Weinberger, Hofmeister and Doblinger. Universal Edition had already published pocket scores of these works in 1906.)

Mahler's reconciliation with Siegfried Lipiner seems to have taken place in Vienna in the spring of 1909; it had already been adumbrated in his letter to Bruno Walter at the beginning of the year. On 13 June 1909 Mahler confessed to his wife in a letter from Toblach: 'It is a great consolation for me to have cleared away the débris between myself and Lipiner – and "to love as long as love I can".' (AM, 435.)

Bruno Walter on Mahler's questions to Lipiner

He could no longer free himself through art from the metaphysical questioning which occupied him ever more urgently and more disturbingly. A questioning search for God, for the meaning and goal of our existence, and for the reason for the unspeakable suffering in the whole of creation, darkened his soul. He took this crisis of the heart . . . to his dearest friend, the poet Siegfried Lipiner. Trivial causes had separated the friends for years; he now forcefully sought him out and demanded that this clear and lofty spirit should share with him the certainty of the view of the world in which he found peace. The joy with which Mahler spoke to me of those conversations will always be to me a happy and touching memory. Lipiner put the essence of these talks into a poem entitled 'Der Musiker spricht' ['The Musician Speaks'], and presented it to Mahler on his fiftieth birthday. But even this source could not finally slake his thirst. 'What Lipiner says about it is wonderfully deep and true,' he said to me, 'but you have to be Lipiner to find certainty and peace in it.' He resigned himself: he could do so, after all, in the thought that his serious heart disease would soon open to him the gate through which he would pass to clarity and peace.

Bruno Walter, 'Mahlers Weg. Ein Erinnerungsblatt', *Der Merker*, vol. III, no. 5, 1912, 170–71.

From Mahler's letter of agreement concerning the publication of the Eighth Symphony by Universal Edition

You engage yourself to engrave the score and the piano reduction (two hands), with text, and to lithograph the orchestral and choral parts. You have undertaken to complete the piano score with text by 1 September 1910, failing which you have to pay me an agreed penalty of 1,000 crowns, which nevertheless does not prejudice my right to further damages in case of culpable delay on your part. In addition you have contracted to begin the engraving of the score at once and to press on with it up to the first proof stage. The further execution and final revision of the score will be undertaken, simultaneously with the production of the complete parts, without delay immediately after the first performance. Moreover you are to produce a complete set of orchestral and vocal parts, either in copy or mimeographically, which will be used for the first performance.

Since the right of performance in all cases is reserved to me, I therefore have full control over the first performance.

Toblach, 26 June 1909.
Archiv Universal Edition, Vienna.

Mahler on his work on the Ninth Symphony

You have guessed the reason for my silence. I have been working very hard, and am now putting the last touches to a new symphony. Unfortunately my holidays are also coming to an end – and I am in the stupid situation – as I always have been – of having this time once again to rush back quite breathless from my papers to the city and to work. This seems to be my lot. The work itself (as far as I know it, for I have been writing away blindly, so that now, when I am just beginning to orchestrate the last movement, I no longer know the first) is a very satisfactory addition to my little family. It says something I have had on the tip of my tongue for a long time – perhaps (as a whole) best put beside the Fourth. (But quite different.) In all this crazy haste the score is a shambles and probably quite illegible to strangers. And so I wish most passionately that I may this winter be granted the chance to produce a fair copy.
Undated letter to Bruno Walter, August 1909, GMB, 416–17.

At the beginning of September 1909, Mahler returned from Toblach to Vienna. Both his wife and daughter had to have tonsil operations, and the home in the Auenbruggergasse was given up after eleven years. So during September Mahler went to stay with the industrialist Fritz Redlich, who owned a sugar factory and a little castle in the Moravian village of Göding (Hodonin) near the Austrian border. Mahler had made Redlich's acquaintance presumably through Moll, who advised the art-loving manufacturer on the purchase of paintings. Mahler had already enjoyed the hospitality of the Redlich family in 1903, and in 1909 he returned to Göding to finish off the score of *Das Lied von der Erde*. Fritz Redlich (1868–1921) was the brother of the Austrian parliamentarian Josef Redlich, whose son Hans Ferdinand Redlich (1903–68) published many musicological works on Mahler, the first when he was only sixteen, under the title *Gustav Mahler, Eine Erkenntnis*, Nuremberg 1919.

305, 306

Mahler to his wife from Göding

Here I feel splendid! To be able to sit and work by the open windows and breathe in the air, the trees, the flowers – that is a delight I have never known before. Only now do I see how wrong my life in the summer is. Not even the murderous, infernal noise outweighs it, which lasts all day and all night here. I *must* have something like this. Karl says he will not rest until he has found us something similar. The whole stay here is doing me a great deal of good. I can feel how I am recovering. There is nothing for it! Man needs sun and warmth. I shudder now to think of my various composing huts, although I have

spent the most beautiful hours of my life there. I have probably had to pay for them with my health.

We go out for a drive here twice a day. My greatest sorrow is that you are not with me. I like the plain enormously! We must have something like this one day – but without the noise.
AM, 444. (At the beginning of October 1909, Mahler conducted three performances of his Seventh Symphony in Holland and then sailed for America.)

Third arrival in New York

Among the passengers who arrived last night on the *Kaiser Wilhelm II* were Gustav Mahler, the new leader of the Philharmonic Orchestra, and Fritz Kreisler, the violinist. Mr Mahler said that he was so engrossed in his work with the Philharmonic that he could not say now whether he would be able to conduct any operas at the Metropolitan. The Metropolitan Opera Company in its announcement gave Mr Mahler as one of its conductors. Mr Mahler brought with him a number of music scores, among them a new symphony of his own. He was accompanied by his wife and daughter.
New York Daily Tribune, 20 October 1909.

A new start with the Philharmonic Society

In the reorganization process which has taken place in the Philharmonic Society the chief changes are noticeable in the wind choirs. . . . In the wood wind choir only two old members of the orchestra remain, all the newcomers being of the French or Belgian school. . . . Only three former players [remain] in the brass section. . . .
New York Daily Tribune, 17 October 1909.

'There is much for us to do,' said Conductor Mahler yesterday, 'because we are all new to one another. We must become acquainted and learn that we are but part of one great instrument. We have before us a great work to do, and it can be done in only one way – the best. But, regardless of our individual abilities, the one and the only way to secure finished results is by constant practice. That is why the Philharmonic Society was put on a permanent basis. Our rehearsals will be held regularly and often, and we shall endeavour to give the classic and best modern works in the manner expected of an orchestra of the first rank.'
New York Daily Tribune, 24 October 1909.

In commenting on the work of the orchestra last night one must remember that, as Rome was not built in a day, neither is a first rate symphony orchestra made in one series of nine rehearsals, even under such a master as Mahler.
The World, 5 November 1909. (Written after the first concert of the season on 4 November).

Bach arrangement at the first 'historical concert'

At Carnegie Hall last night the first of a series of historical concerts . . . took place under the direction of Mr Mahler. . . . There are to be six of these historical concerts, and their programmes have been planned to cover the field of music from the period of Bach down to today. A large stride was made last night when the names of Bach, Handel, Rameau, Grétry and Haydn were on the scheme. . . . The first of the Bach pieces was a compages of movements from two of his suites. . . . Mr Mahler took the Overture, Rondeau and Badinerie from the suite in B minor and consorted with them the well known air and gavotte from the first of the two suites in D. To complete the old master's representation Mr Theodore Spiering, the new concert master of the Philharmonic Orchestra, played the violin concerto in E major. . . .

Not only the music but also the manner of performance was in keeping with the period chosen for representation. Mr Mahler conducted all the music except the [Haydn Symphony in D] seated at the clavier, which took the place of the old harpsichord, and played the figured bass part . . . on it. . . . It was not a harpsichord but a Steinway pianoforte with hammer action modified to produce a twanging tone resembling that of the harpsichord but of greater volume. . . . The effect was not favourably received by the musicians in last night's audience, but was probably as near that heard in Bach's day as could be obtained, considering the vast difference in conditions.

New York Daily Tribune, 11 November 1909. (Mahler's Bach arrangement was published in New York by Schirmer in 1910 under the following title: Johann Sebastian Bach, *Suite aus seinen Orchesterwerken mit ausgeführtem Continuo zum Konzertvortrag bearbeitet von Gustav Mahler*.)

Mahler on his Bach arrangement

. . . I had particular fun recently at a Bach concert for which I wrote out the *basso continuo* for organ and conducted and improvised – just as they used to – from a spinet with a very big sound, which was specially prepared for me by Steinway. Quite surprising things came out of it for me (and for the listeners). This buried literature was lit up as if by an arc-light. Its effect (and also the tone-colouring) was more powerful than that of any modern work.

Undated letter to Dr Paul Hammerschlag in Vienna, postmarked 19 November 1909, GMB, 407.

Mahler to Universal Edition on the piano reduction of the Eighth Symphony

Above all: Herr von Woess's piano score is a *masterpiece*. I am really quite delighted with this incomparably sound and perfect work. Please give Herr von Woess my warmest and most sincere thanks. I am writing in great haste – which is why I cannot thank him personally, as I ought, and wish I could. Since I did not find a single mistake (only answered a few question-marks) I was able to send the parcel straight back. Unfortunately I forgot to put the *numbers* in. Please ask Herr von Woess to do this for me on the principle of one number roughly every six bars. Only please exercise a certain care to ensure that the numbers do not fall quite nonsensically in the middle of a phrase. In cases like this put them before or after. I have made some changes in the voice parts and must ask you to send me the proofs of the vocal score plus the chorus parts so that I can enter my alterations in them.

From an undated letter to Emil Hertzka, Director of Universal Edition, Vienna, received on 26 November 1909 and published in *Neue Zeitschrift für Musik*, vol. CXXXV, no. 9, September 1974, 544. (Emil Hertzka, 1869–1932, had been the head of Universal Edition since 1907. Josef von Woess, 1863–1943, Austrian composer and teacher, made piano scores of Mahler's Third, Fourth, Eighth and Ninth Symphonies and of *Das klagende Lied*.)

The first concert of the Beethoven cycle

The Philharmonic Society began yesterday afternoon the Beethoven Cycle that is one of Mr Mahler's cherished projects in connection with the enlargement of the Philharmonic's sphere of activity. The cycle is to consist of five concerts, in which will be performed all the nine symphonies except the first, and seven of the eleven overtures. . . . In yesterday's concert . . . the second symphony was played together with the four overtures that Beethoven wrote at different times . . . for his opera now known as *Fidelio*. . . .

The playing of the orchestra has improved. Its tone has gained in richness, smoothness and beauty of quality, as well as in homogeneity. . . .

The New York Times, 20 November 1909.

Mahler to Guido Adler, on the present and the future

. . . This summer I wrote my Ninth.

As you see I am in a great hurry. Here things are quite hectic and American. I have rehearsals and concerts every day. Have to be very economical with my strength and usually go to bed after rehearsals and have my mid-day meal there (this disgusting feed is called 'lunch' here). If I manage to survive these 2 years intact – then, I hope, I, too, shall be able to sit down and enjoy myself and also write music *con amore*. It would almost be a breach of style to do so. For really I ought to be starving and freezing with my family somewhere in a garret. This would probably be more in keeping with the ideal image of Hirschfeld and *tutti quanti*.

Undated letter, presumably written in the autumn of 1909, ms., Guido Adler Papers, University of Georgia Libraries, Athens, Ga. ('Hirschfeld and *tutti quanti*' is a reference to the spiteful Vienna critic Robert Hirschfeld.)

Theodore Spiering on rehearsals and concerts

In New York the rehearsals began at once. Mahler threw himself into his work with enormous enthusiasm. There were most careful rehearsals every day. He devoted all his energy to securing the hoped-for success for the re-organized orchestra. If this success left much to be desired financially, this was largely owing to the completely altered concert schedule. Whereas before Mahler's regime the season had twelve to sixteen concerts, now almost three times that number were given in New York alone. With the first concert (*Eroica*, *Till Eulenspiegel*, etc.) Mahler was well satisfied. But when things did not go quite as well in the second concert he was deeply disappointed and cast down. Changes of mood of this kind recurred regularly as might be expected; I was almost always alone with him in the performers' room, and it was sometimes decidedly depressing for me. Still, there were plenty of really perfect performances, and these of course gave him great pleasure. For example, the performances of the Symphonies in E flat major by Bruckner and F major by Brahms, which I shall never forget. The Bruckner Symphony in particular Mahler prepared with remarkable care and love. Through a whole series of very skilfully worked-out cuts he relieved the work of its jerky, periodic nature; and he achieved a logical unity which brought out the work's many beauties to an unimaginable degree. The way he made this Bruckner Symphony, and the C major Symphony of Schumann, playable – that is to say, as enjoyable as possible for the listener – seems to me entirely justified. . . .

The first season's programmes were based mainly on the classics. He felt, and rightly, that this was the quickest way for a newly constituted orchestra to play itself in. Among the moderns he was most of all interested in Strauss and Debussy. He did not push his own symphonies. . . .

Our rehearsals were always interesting but not taxing. No particular duration was adhered to. They rarely exceeded the 3½-hour limit set by the Union. Sometimes he was done in an hour and a half – or even an hour and a quarter.

Mahler always worked flat out. Every minute counted. There were no breaks. We almost never just played anything through. A constant struggle with recalcitrant matter until it was overcome. The orchestra, somewhat reserved at first – they were not used to this intense manner – soon fell in with him and admired the man who treated them so brusquely and at the same time swept them along to undreamed-of peaks of achievement. As an interpreter Mahler is probably unmatched.

As a conductor he had developed over the years an informality of technique that was sometimes almost fatal for the orchestra. In correcting one player's inaccuracy, or while trying to get across some nuance or particular phrasing, he tended to forget that the whole orchestra was dependent on his beat. He demanded initiative; but sometimes he did not stop to consider that this presupposes a certain measure of artistry which not every orchestra possesses.

Theodore Spiering, 'Zwei Jahre mit Gustav Mahler in New York', *Vossische Zeitung* (Berlin), 21 May 1911, EV. (Of his own symphonies Mahler performed only the First during this season, on 16 December 1909. The performance of the Bruckner Fourth Symphony (the 'Romantic') which so impressed Spiering took place at the 'historical concert' on 30 March 1910.)

From Mahler's report to Bruno Walter in Vienna

I hope you have not been worried by my silence. It had no other cause than an immense burden of work (it reminded me of my time in Vienna), which has limited me to four activities only: conducting, transcribing music, eating and sleeping. I am evidently incorrigible. People like us cannot help it: what we do we do thoroughly. And that means, as I must now admit, that we overwork. I am and must remain the eternal beginner. The bit of routine technique that I have acquired probably only increases the demands I make on my own energies. Just as I should like to bring out a new edition of all my works every five years, equally I need to prepare afresh everything I conduct by other composers . . . My orchestra here is a real American orchestra. Untalented and phlegmatic. It's uphill work. To start from scratch as a conductor is decidedly unpalatable to me. My only pleasure is in the rehearsals for a work I have never conducted before. Music-making still gives me terrific fun. If only I had better musicians! Your news of your performance of the Third was a great joy to me! . . .

I gave my First here the day before yesterday! Without, it seems, any particular response. I, on the other hand, was quite satisfied with this youthful effort of mine. I feel strange whenever I conduct one of these works. A painful burning feeling crystallizes itself: what kind of world is this that can throw up as its reflected image sounds and forms like this? Things like the funeral march and the storm which breaks out at the end seem to me like a burning reproach to the Creator . . . Send me the transition passage for Slezak's transposed part in *Pique Dame* – also how far the transposition lasts. I am supposed to be conducting the opera at the Metropolitan and they are paying so much that I shall probably not resist. . . .

The public here are very kind and relatively much better behaved than in Vienna. They listen attentively and benevolently. The critics are the same as everywhere. I never read any but get reports sometimes. . . . I am hoping to start on my Ninth soon.

GMB, 417–19. (This letter is undated, but the reference to the performance of the First Symphony must mean it was written on 18 December 1909. Mahler conducted Tchaikowsky's opera *Pique Dame* [*Pikovaya Dama, The Queen of Spades*] at the Metropolitan in March 1910.)

Rachmaninov describes a rehearsal

. . . The performance of my Third Concerto took place in New York under the direction of Damrosch. Immediately afterwards I repeated it in New York, but under Gustav Mahler. . . .

The rehearsal began at ten o'clock. I was to join it at eleven, and arrived in good time. But we did not begin to work until twelve, when there was only half an hour left, during which I did my utmost to play through a composition which usually lasts 36 minutes. We played and played. . . . Half an hour was long passed, but Mahler did not pay the slightest attention to this fact. I still remember an incident which is characteristic of him. Mahler was an unusually strict disciplinarian. This I consider an essential quality for a successful conductor. We had reached a difficult violin passage in the third Movement which involves some rather awkward bowing. Suddenly Mahler, who had conducted this passage *a tempo*, tapped his desk:

'Stop! Don't pay any attention to the difficult bowing marked in your parts. . . . Play the passage like this', and he

indicated a different method of bowing. After he had made the first violins play the passage over alone three times, the man sitting next to the leader put down his violin:

'I can't play the passage with this kind of bowing.'

Mahler (quite unruffled): 'What kind of bowing would you like to use?'

'As it is marked in the score.'

Mahler turned toward the leader with an interrogative look, and when he found the latter was of the same opinion he tapped the desk again:

'Please play as is written.'

This incident was a definite rebuff for the conductor, especially as the excellent leader of the Moscow Philharmonic Orchestra had pointed out to me this disputed method of bowing as the only possible way of playing the passage. I was curious to see how Mahler would react to this little scene. He was most dignified. Soon afterwards he wanted the double basses to tone down their playing of a passage. He interrupted the orchestra and turned to the players:

'I would beg the gentlemen to make more of a *diminuendo* in this passage,' then, addressing the argumentative neighbour of the leader with a hardly perceptible smile:

'I hope you don't object.'

Forty-five minutes later Mahler announced:

'Now we will repeat the first movement.'

My heart froze within me. I expected a dreadful row, or at least a heated protest from the orchestra. This would certainly have happened in any other orchestra, but there I did not notice a single sign of displeasure. The musicians played the first movement with a keen or perhaps even closer application than the previous time. At last we had finished. I went up to the conductor's desk, and together we examined the score. The musicians in the back seats began quietly to pack up their instruments and to disappear. Mahler blew up:

'What is the meaning of this?'

The leader: 'It is half past one, Master!'

'That makes no difference! As long as I am sitting, no musician has the right to get up!'

Rachmaninoff's Recollections, told to Oskar von Riesemann, New York 1934, 158–60. (*The New York Times* of 17 January 1910 wrote of the performance of Rachmaninov's Third Piano Concerto: 'Rachmaninov gave a sympathetic interpretation which was however somewhat lacking in the brilliance that parts of the work demand. The orchestral accompaniment was outstanding.')

New York hears the 'Kindertotenlieder'

Mr Mahler's contribution to the programme – a set of five 'Children's Death Songs', to verses by Rückert – belong to the class of songs with orchestral accompaniment that modern composers are cultivating with especial interest, and of which they are making almost a new genre.

They are something more and more elaborate than lyrics; and these of Mr Mahler's, in fact, are in the nature of little dramas or dramatic scenes in miniature. . . . They are mournful, gloomy in tone, and they do not make any immediate appeal; but there is much beauty in them, and much poignant expressiveness.

The New York Times, 27 January 1910.

Mr Mahler feels but he does not create.

The Sun, 27 January 1910.

They are weighted with grief of such poignant sincerity that one must conclude that they have an autobiographical significance. We have not heard any music by Mr Mahler which has so individual a note, or which is so calculated to stir up the imagination and the emotions.

New York Daily Tribune, 27 January 1910.

Mahler to Emil Hertzka, Universal Edition

At last I am in a position to send back the collated piano score. These last two weeks I have been so overtaxed that I have had to steal time from myself. May I ask you to transfer the changes I have made to the *full score* as well (which presumably you are now getting round to engraving?) A few mistakes, which I have also corrected, are probably the fault of the copyist, who, by the way, is a paragon of clarity and neatness. I must sincerely compliment your company (or its management). What a pity that my other things were not published by you.

With hearty thanks to yourself and above all to Herr von Woess, I remain in greatest haste

yours very truly,

Mahler.

Would you please send a copy of the vocal score when it appears to each of the following gentlemen on my behalf:

1. *Generalmusikdir.* Dr Strauss
2. *Generalmusikdir. Geheimrat* Schuch
3. *Kapellmeister* Wilh. Mengelberg, Amsterdam, Concertgebouw
4. *Generalmusikdir.* Fritz Steinbach, Cologne
5. *Kapellmeister* Oskar Fried, Nikolassee a.d. Wannseebahn, near Berlin
6. *Kapellmeister* Walter and Schalk, Vienna
7. *Kapellmeister* Bodanzky, Mannheim
8. Siegfried Ochs in Berlin
9. Dr Korngold, Vienna
10. Herr Leopold Schmidt, critic of the *Berliner Tageblatt*
11. Herr von Zemlinsky and Herr Schönberg in Vienna
12. Herr Max Marschalk, *Vossische Zeitung*, Berlin.

Undated letter from New York, received in Vienna 14 February 1910, *Neue Zeitschrift für Musik*, vol. cxxxv, no. 9, September 1974, 545. (The reference is to the vocal score of the Eighth Symphony.)

The pianist Olga Samaroff gets Mahler to talk

He had not been long in America when the Charles Steinways invited me to meet him and his wife at dinner. I was so excited over the prospect that I arrived a full half-hour too soon. Mrs Steinway greeted me with the words:

'I am seating you beside Mahler at table tonight, but do not expect him to speak. He cannot be made to talk at dinner parties.'

Mr Steinway gallantly murmured something to the effect that 'Olga ought to be able to draw him out,' but Mrs Steinway was not disposed to flattery. . . . 'If my husband is right and you *do* make him talk, I will give you five dollars.'

I responded to the challenge, but when Mahler arrived my courage sank. There was something so remote about him at first glance that I could scarcely imagine his taking part in any ordinary conversation. When we sat down at dinner, he never even glanced at me. . . .

Finally, I remembered that before dinner, when Mahler appeared to be utterly oblivious of everybody present, he had taken *The Brothers Karamazoff* off the bookshelf and turned over the pages as though searching for a special passage. I decided that the Dostoyevsky masterpiece was this drowning woman's last straw. But I also knew that if I did not succeed in establishing a controversial basis of conversation, I would merely get another 'Ja'. So I boldly asked him if he did not consider *The Brothers Karamazoff* a much overrated book.

'Not at all', said Mahler fiercely, putting down his knife and fork. 'You ask that because you do not understand it.' He thereupon launched into a long discourse on the subject of Russian psychology and Dostoyevsky's supreme understanding of it. . . .

The signals exchanged between me and the Steinways must have mystified anybody who saw them. Mr Steinway kept looking at his watch and lifting his glass to me. He teased his wife unmercifully when Mahler followed me out into the drawing-room and spent the rest of the evening looking for passages in *The Brothers Karamazoff* with which to illustrate his points and complete my conversion. I have often wondered what would have happened if he had known we were discussing one of my favourite books. . . .

Playing a concerto with the Philharmonic under Mahler's direction was a privilege I repeatedly enjoyed. The first time I was soloist in one of his concerts on tour was in New Haven. By that time he and I had become good friends. . . .

Olga Samaroff-Stokowski, *An American Musician's Story*, New York 1939, 159–60. (Olga Samaroff, 1882–1948, European-trained American pianist. In 1911 she married the conductor Leopold Stokowski. Charles H. Steinway was the head of the famous piano firm from 1896 to 1919. The concert in New Haven took place on 23 February 1910.)

Apart from the concerts in New York, Mahler made guest appearances with his orchestra in various cities in the 1909–10 season, including Philadelphia, Boston, New Haven, Conn., Springfield, Mass., and Providence, R.I.: in all a total of 46 concerts. At the end of February he returned to the Metropolitan Opera to rehearse Tchaikowsky's *Pique Dame*. The première took place on 5 March 1910 and was the first stage performance of the work in America. Leo Slezak sang Hermann, Emmy Destinn Lisa.

Slezak remembers Mahler rehearsals in New York

Years later I met him again in New York.

A tired, sick man.

We had *Pique Dame* – American première at the Metropolitan Opera House.

At the rehearsals he and I were mostly alone.

The others simply did not turn up.

He rarely got a whole ensemble together.

He sat there with me, resigned, a different man.

I sought in vain the fiery spirit of yesteryear. He had become mild and sad.

Leo Slezak, *Meine sämtlichen Werke*, Berlin 1922, 256.

Busoni on the performance of his 'Turandot' Suite

What a pity you did not hear *Turandot* under Mahler. In the end I stayed for the evening after all; it seemed wrong to turn my back on Mahler. With what dedication and with what sure instinct this man rehearsed! Equally pleasing and warming from both the artistic and human point of view.

The performance was perfect, better than any before, and a great success.

Letter of 12 March 1910, Ferruccio Busoni, *Briefe an seine Frau*, Erlenbach 1935, 193–4.

Mahler as a concert conductor in America

For someone who had had the privilege of hearing a Philharmonic Concert under Mahler in Vienna, the outward aspect of a concert in New York was heart-rending: the audience, the greater part of which came too late and ran off before the end of the concert, the clinical and graceless Carnegie Hall, the cool discipline and austere impersonality of the orchestra (I can with warmth register two exceptions: the outstanding leader Spiering and the excellent horn-player Reiter, who both really understood Mahler). And yet, for those with ears and hearts, performances which are unforgettable! For Mahler was resigned, but his temperament and his strength were untouched – indeed, perhaps even more concentrated and intense. . . . Mahler still had what made his interpretations so irresistible: he identified himself with the work that he was conducting. I can remember how he positively discovered the 'Romantic' Symphony of Bruckner that he was conducting in New York, how he spoke of it as though he had just seen the score for the first time. I had the same feeling when I was able to attend the rehearsals of Beethoven's Ninth – you would have thought he was conducting the world première of a new work, so miles away was his rehearsing from any 'conception' or 'routine'! Still – when we left the rehearsal together he said, 'I thought of writing down and publishing my "alterations"' (he actually said these inverted commas). 'But – there is no point, is there, and it's no concern of anybody's.'

Ernst Jokl, 'Gustav Mahler in Amerika', ANBR, 290.

Mahler reviews his first concert season

'I am pleased with the results of my work here,' he said. 'Things have been as satisfactory as could have been expected. The orchestra has improved from concert to concert, and the attitude of the New York public is always serious and attentive.

'I have made no plans as yet for my concerts for next season, [but] I shall divide the programmes more or less evenly between the classic and the modern schools, and I shall play good music of all nations. . . .

'For important novelties, one must turn exclusively to France and Germany, with occasional aid from Russia, Finland, and Bohemia. Debussy has just written something which I may produce next season, and Paul Dukas has almost completed a symphony, which he has promised to let me have as soon as it is done.

'Strauss has told me that henceforth he will write only operas. He said that he is done with symphonic works. . . .

'I have already cabled the authorities of the festival at Mannheim that I am too tired to conduct there. There was to have been a season of my works, . . . and some other things, but I have had a very hard winter, and a week of hard conducting in May would be too much for me now. I want rest.'

New York Times, 30 March 1910. (The new works by Debussy which Mahler mentions could be Ibéria (first performed in Paris in February 1910) or Rondes du printemps (first performed in Paris in March 1910). Mahler included both works in his concert programmes in the 1910–11 season. But no new work by Dukas appeared in his programmes.)

The financial outcome of the season

Although the season brought a heavy deficit – the estimate being about $90,000 – it was expected. With the changes to be installed and the artistic progress the orchestra made during its first year under Mr Mahler, it is the belief of those in charge of the Philharmonic destinies that its future is bright.

The World, 3 April 1910.

Mahler left New York on 5 April and went straight to Paris, to conduct the first performance in France of his Second Symphony, which took place on 17 April in the Théâtre du Châtelet. For the occasion the Italian composer Alfredo Casella, 1883–1947, who lived in Paris, wrote an article full of admiration and enthusiasm, which contained a general introduction to Mahler's art and an analysis of the Second Symphony.

From Casella's Mahler article

According to Mahler's own indications there are three different 'categories' in his works. The first group includes the first four symphonies, of which the Second and Third contain choruses; the second category embraces the Fifth, Sixth, Seventh and Eighth Symphonies (the last employing double chorus, double vocal quartet and children's chorus), while the Ninth Symphony marks the beginning of a third style. Since

I do not know this latest symphony I do not know what the new category amounts to, and can therefore speak only of the first two.

The astonishing principal feature of every work of Mahler's, apart from the absolute formal freedom which I mentioned above, is the abundance and variety of ideas. It is impossible to imagine anything so dissimilar as the various elements of which every one of the Symphonies is made up. Constant variety, superabundant imagination: these are the two prime impressions transmitted by this strange music, in which an iron hand unites and fuses the apparently most disparate melodic, rhythmic and harmonic elements. The Prater is mixed with Hungary, and both join hands with Prague. Even the technique is variable and highly disconcerting: in the Third Symphony, for example, a cyclopic, monstrous, apocalyptic first movement, which seems to be hewn out of large blocks, is followed by a 'quasi Minuetto', whose delightful refinement, elegance of writing and musical grace cannot be excelled. There are four further movements in the symphony, and each one is a new world. . . .

A further characteristic of Mahler's art, which one notices at once, and whose effect is certainly no less captivating, is the pure goodness of this music. Through it Mahler can reach the most secret chords of our heart and often approaches Beethoven, of whom he also reminds one by his chastity; for it seems that this man can express all human feelings except sexual love, of which you will hunt in vain for a trace in his works.

But there is also another musician whom he approaches in the same degree: Schubert. Of the latter we are reminded by the melodic invention, the melancholy grace of the many Ländler which run through his works, and finally by the touching naïveté of certain melodies. Beethoven and Schubert are Mahler's two true teachers.

Undoubtedly it is easy to find the influence of Haydn, Mendelssohn – and even, in the first period, Liszt. But these pale reminiscences could not possibly lessen Mahler's astonishing originality. Let us leave the field wide open to the scribblers whose profession is to trace the paternity of tiny melodic and harmonic phrases, and think what Brahms in his old age said of the Beethovenian 'reminiscences' in the Finale of his First Symphony: 'Any donkey can see that!'

It is superfluous to add that Mahler's music is highly contrapuntal: an orchestrator of his kind is bound to regard polyphony as the sole raison d'être of the orchestra. But his counterpoint, too, is of a special nature and peculiar to him: you often find parallel fourths and fifths in it which are extremely sonorous.

The harmonization . . . is immeasurably expressive; while it is still quite simple in the works of the first period, in the second series of Symphonies it becomes much more complicated and is nothing like that of the earlier works. The rhythms are extraordinarily varied, but there are two particular kinds that Mahler particularly likes: the energetic rhythms of military marches and the appealing pulse of the Austrian Ländler. These two rhythms reappear in all his works. . . .

Alfred [sic] Casella, 'Gustav Mahler et sa deuxième symphonie', S.I.M., Revue musicale mensuelle, vol. VI, no. 4, April 1910, 240–41.

Mahler to Norbert Salter from Italy

Since you did not cable me in time (I wrote to you quite explicitly that I should need to be informed of any change of programme by 5 April in New York), I had to cancel the third concert in Rome. With this miserable and indolent orchestra I can perform only with my own orchestra parts. I am sending you today a postal order for 300 lire (10 per cent of my fee).

In the summer I shall be in Toblach again.

Undated letter, ms., BST. (Mahler had gone to Rome from Paris in order to conduct concerts arranged by the Salter concert agency.)

The summer of 1910, Mahler's last, was the most eventful of his whole life. The homage he received on his fiftieth birthday, and at the première of his Eighth Symphony, shows him at the peak of his fame. In May and June he held the first preliminary rehearsals for the performance of the Eighth Symphony which was being prepared by the Emil Gutmann concert agency for 12 September in Munich. Mahler took part in the rehearsals of the Choral Union (Singverein) in Vienna, who were studying under Franz Schalk, then went to Leipzig, where the Riedel Choral Union was rehearsing under Georg Göhler, and then on to Munich for the first sessions with the orchestra. Bruno Walter selected the soloists and rehearsed their parts with them. The concert manager Gutmann had announced the work, without Mahler's knowledge, as the 'Symphony of a Thousand'.

On the preliminary rehearsals of the Eighth Symphony

So Monday evening we had a rehearsal – which revealed the uselessness of the Vienna male voice choir (they simply did not turn up and started the rehearsal with fourteen tonsils) and also Schalk's incompetence (he started them off and got all the *tempi* wrong, for I was so angry that I refused to co-operate). Later more of them arrived and I came out of the corner like a sulking schoolboy and took up the baton. Then it went better straight away, but it was clear that the men do not yet know their parts. So it still seems to me uncertain whether the performance will take place, for I am determined not to put up with *any* artistic slovenliness. The ladies I must say are superb and make up for much of the baseness of the men!

From a letter to his wife, undated, written presumably at the end of May 1910, AM, 452–3.

In all haste and hustle simply many thanks for your kind letter. Let us hope then that the whole thing can be brought to a happy ending. In Leipzig I found everything well prepared – the chorus – 250-strong, were waiting for me on the stroke of the hour, *punctual* and *complete*. But to be fair, they cannot begin to approach the beauty of tone of the Vienna choir. . . .

Undated letter from Munich to Franz Schalk, ms., ÖNB-MS.

I am now settled here in Munich and rehearsing my Eighth for all I'm worth. I miss *you* very much. The leader is quite passable, but not blessed with a very deep comprehension, and has no influence on the orchestra. I hope I shall see you here in September.

Of America I have no news at all. As you know a proper manager was engaged at my request, but he has now, to my not inconsiderable displeasure, proposed 65 concerts and insists that without this massive increase in the work-load the success cannot be guaranteed. I therefore asked for a small increase in my fee for this colossal additional output (I am bound by my contract for only 45 concerts), but this demand was turned down by the Committee, so that I shall now fall back on my contractual rights and obligations.

I have now communicated this to the Committee but have since heard nothing.

Undated letter to Theodore Spiering, postmarked Munich, 21 June 1910, GMB, 459–60.

My Almschi! Today I am worried not to have a letter from you after such a sad one yesterday. Are you hiding something from me? For that's what I always read between the lines. Today we had a full rehearsal, 2nd part. Here too 'the Lord (Mahler) saw that it was good!'

Tomorrow the soloists arrive; Sunday, God willing, I shall arrive at Toblach, unless you decide I should go straight to Tobelbad. In that case please send me a telegram.

From a letter to his wife from Munich, undated. AM, 454–55. (Tobelbad, spa near Graz in Styria.)

Mahler to Emil Freund, on the contract with Universal Edition

Do not forget, with the agreement we are making with U. Edition, that this extremely irksome and above all degrading clause, that I must always ask whenever I have done anything, must be *dropped*. In fact it is probably purely academic, for I do not intend to change from U.E. But the thing still annoys me whenever I think of it.

GMB, 451–2. (GMB describes the letter as follows: 'Undated. Niederdorf im Pustertal, 15 June 1910'.)

Gustav Mahler. A portrait of his personality in individual tributes   174

The editor and publisher have sought – apart from paying homage to Gustav Mahler as an artist at this milestone in his life – to present a new portrait of his personality made up of tributes from people who do not normally, or only rarely, give portrayals of this kind. This is the explanation for certain omissions, and perhaps certain deficiencies.

The tributes, whose selfless kindness deserves thanks, have been arranged so as to present the development of the personality: an overall view, the young theatre conductor, the mature Opera Director, the conductor at the peak of his ability, the composer. . . .

Part of the picture is the tribute by Rodin, whose bust of Mahler is reproduced here for the first time, as is Klimt's   300
Knight from the Beethoven Fresco. . . .   213

Paul Stefan, introduction to *Gustav Mahler. Ein Bild seiner Persönlichkeit in Widmungen*, Munich 1910. (This act of homage, which Stefan put together for Mahler's fiftieth birthday, contained contributions from Conrad Ansorge, Gerhart Hauptmann, Guido Adler, Angelo Neumann, Max Steinitzer, Hugo von Hofmannsthal, Hermann Bahr, Oskar Bie, Julius Bittner, Alfred Roller, Marie Gutheil-Schoder, Hans Pfitzner, Anna Bahr-Mildenburg, Ferdinand Gregori, Max Burckhard, Carl Hagemann, Oskar Fried, Stefan Zweig, Romain Rolland, Richard Strauss, Arthur Schnitzler, Georg Göhler, Max Schillings, Max Reger, Paul Dukas, Bruno Walter, Alfredo Casella, and William Ritter.)

From Arnold Schönberg's birthday letter

. . . My wish for us all, on your fiftieth birthday, is that you should come back soon to our hated, beloved Vienna, and stay here. That you may feel at home here; or that you may feel the urge to conduct here and yet not do so, because the rabble just do not deserve it; or that you may not feel inclined to conduct here but do so nevertheless just to please us, who perhaps do deserve it. At any rate: that you may be here with us again! And that you, who have had so much reason to feel bitterness, should now accept the adulation and use it to assuage your wounds, which were struck more by short-sightedness than ill-will. I know that, if you were in Vienna now, you would be so wrapped in warm admiration that you would be able to forget all the justified resentment of the past.

AM, 475.

Thanks to Lipiner for his good wishes

Toblach, 7 July 1910

I cursed and cursed when I received the wad of telegrams (just imagine simply having to sign for every single one) – but when I came across yours I was really so happy that I willingly put up with all the others. . . .

My rehearsals in Leipzig and Munich were really pleasing. Only now do I believe in the performance on 12 September. It would be marvellous if you could come. You would certainly get something out of it. I believe you would recognize a piece of your spirit; the hymn in particular is from your soul.

GMB, 464–65.

Conversation with Ernst Decsey about New York and Paris

I last saw him last summer at Tobelbad. At the time the rumour was that they wanted him back at the Vienna Court Opera;

but for this he had only a smile. He had just come back from America and spoke a lot of the American orchestras' conditions. In general he felt that the English [*sic*] nation had too little temperament, too little artistic talent, but said that the 96 musicians that he had to conduct followed him better than any previous orchestra because he had them to himself. He was enthusiastic about Paris, where he had conducted his Second Symphony on the way back: 'Such ease of living! Such cultural refinement!' The symphony had been very warmly received; a chorus of 200 professional singers, quite outstanding people, much better than in Vienna, were at his disposal. Everyone in general had been very helpful; only the artists – he mentioned one of the names – were envious and tried to make things difficult for him. The performance, as I said, very good, the people warm, although someone suddenly shouted out, '*À bas la musique allemande!*' from the hall. 'But', he added, 'my Second Symphony occupies a special place among my works: if it is successful anywhere, this means nothing for my other works!' Then he went on to speak of Munich and the preliminary rehearsals for the Eighth Symphony. 'The Leipzig singers are far superior to the Viennese in discipline and loyalty. They are the most reliable people; a pleasure to work with. This is something I was not used to in Vienna. But the Viennese sing better!'

Ernst Decsey, 'Stunden mit Mahler', *Die Musik*, vol x, no. 21, 151. (The envious Parisian musicians are supposed to have included Debussy and Dukas, who, according to Alma Mahler's account, AM, 213, got up in the middle of the second movement of the Second Symphony and left the hall.)

From Alma Mahler's recollections of the great crisis in her marriage

After about a week there came a letter from this young man in which he wrote that he could not live without me, and that if I had even the slightest feeling for him I should leave everything and come to him. This letter, which was meant for me, was clearly marked on the envelope 'To Director Mahler'. It has never been explained whether the youth acted in a fit of madness or whether it had been his unconscious wish to let the letter go direct to Mahler himself. Mahler was seated at the piano, he read the letter, cried with a suffocated voice 'What is this?' and handed me the letter. Mahler was and remained convinced that X had sent this letter to him on purpose in order, as he put it, to ask him for my hand.

What now came is inexpressible! At last I was able to say everything: how I had longed for years for his love, and how with his immense sense of his mission he had simply overlooked me. For the first time in his life he felt that there is such a thing as an inner obligation towards the person to whom one has united oneself. He suddenly felt guilty. We spent days crying with one another until my mother came, whom we had called on to help us in our despair. . . .

Once when we were out for a ride I saw young X hiding under a bridge; as he later told me, he had been in the district for some time in the hope of meeting me somewhere by chance and of thus forcing an answer to his letter.

My heart stood still, but from fright, not joy. I told Mahler at once and he said: 'I shall fetch him here myself.' He went down to Toblach at once, found him immediately and said, 'Come with me!' That is all that was said.

In the meantime night had fallen. They walked the long distance without a word. Mahler in front with a lantern, the other following behind. Night as black as pitch. I had stayed in my room. Mahler came in with a very grave expression. After a long hesitation I went down to talk to X. I broke off the conversation after a few minutes because I was suddenly afraid for Mahler. He was pacing up and down in the room. Two candles were burning on his table. He was reading the Bible. He said, 'What you do will be rightly done. Now choose.' But I hadn't any choice! . . .

I had actually sometimes thought of going away, alone, anywhere, to make a new start, but always without a wish for

266

any particular person. Mahler was always the focal point of my existence; but he was in inner turmoil. It was at this time that he wrote all those cries and words to me in the sketch of the score of the Tenth Symphony. He realized he had been leading the life of a psychopath and suddenly decided to go to see Sigmund Freud (who was in Leiden in Holland at the time).

315

AM, 215–17.

Klaus Pringsheim relates a conversation about Freud

From my last evening with the Mahlers, in the late summer of 1907, I have a vivid recollection of a discussion in which Freud's name was mentioned; or to be exact, it was I who mentioned him in some particular connection. Mahler's reaction was a momentary silence; the subject of psychoanalysis did not interest him. Then he said, with a dismissive gesture: 'Freud . . . he attempts to cure everything from a single point.' From a single point: he did not name it; he obviously shrank from letting me hear the word in question in the presence of his wife.

Klaus Pringsheim, 'Erinnerungen an Gustav Mahler', *Neue Zürcher Zeitung*, 7 July 1960.

Sigmund Freud on his meeting with Mahler in 1910

318, 319

I analysed Mahler for an afternoon in Leiden. If I may believe reports, I achieved much with him at that time. The necessity for the visit arose, for him, from his wife's resentment of the withdrawal of his *libido* from her. In highly interesting expeditions through his life history, we discovered his personal conditions for love, especially his Holy Mary complex (mother fixation). I had plenty of opportunity to admire the capability for psychological understanding of this man of genius. No light fell at the time on the symptomatic façade of his obsessional neurosis. It was as if you would dig a single shaft through a mysterious building.

From a letter from Sigmund Freud to Theodor Reik, 4 January 1935, quoted from Theodor Reik, *The Haunting Melody*, New York 1953, 343. (Mahler's meeting with Freud took place on 27 August 1910.)

Mahler to his wife, during the rehearsals of the Eighth Symphony

Munich, 4 September 1910

. . . Gutmann was waiting for me here, very kind and willing to help. He told me that the first concert is certainly sold out. At home I found the piano scores with the dedication and hope that Hertzka was bright enough to send one to Toblach, too. I felt quite peculiar and excited to see the sweet, beloved name on the title page for all the world to see, like a happy confession. Oh I should like to carve it into all the piano scores. But that would be schoolboy behaviour. . . .

By the way, I have made a strange discovery! You see it was always just like this, and with almost the same longing, that I sat straight down to write when I was away from you and thought only of you. It was always latent in me, this yearning for you – Freud is quite right – you were always my light and my focal point! Of course, the inner light which now illumines everything for me and the blessed consciousness of it – no longer darkened by any inhibitions – makes all my feelings immeasurably more intense. But what a torment, what an agony, that you can no longer return it. But as truly as love must re-awaken love, and faith will find faith again, as long as Eros remains the ruler of men and gods, so truly I shall reconquer everything again, the heart that once was mine and which still can find God and happiness only in union with mine.

AM, 465–66. (Mahler dedicated the Eighth Symphony to his wife.)

The order of rehearsal is now settled for the performance of the Eighth Symphony of Gustav Mahler in Munich on 12 September. (Preliminary rehearsals have already been held, in June.) On 5, 6 and 7 September orchestra rehearsals from 9.30 onwards, choral rehearsals in the afternoon starting at 4 o'clock; on the Thursday at 11 o'clock rehearsal for orchestra, children's chorus and soloists; on 9 September piano rehearsal in the afternoon with children's chorus and soloists, on 10 September at 10 o'clock complete rehearsal of the first part of the Symphony, at 4 in the afternoon the second part. Finally on Sunday, final rehearsal, on 12th première, on 13th first repeat.

Signale für die musikalische Welt (Berlin) 17 August 1910, 1289–90.

Mahler to Franz Schalk on the final rehearsals

Please make sure that all the performers are aware of the fact that a work which takes nearly 2½ hours to perform cannot be properly rehearsed in 3 hours. I must be absolutely convinced of the willingness of all performers to go to it with all their strength in order to rehearse as long as is necessary (possibly in the afternoon, too, with a suitable break, if the need arises), otherwise I would rather drop the whole thing. This is not a choir outing but a serious and very difficult undertaking. Please, dear Schalk, inform the men of this on some suitable occasion (from what I know of the 'weaker' half of humanity, they will not need to be told).

Undated letter, ms., ÖNB-MS.

322   *The Munich Exhibition Hall*

The City Council having acquired, through gifts and numerous land purchases of over 4 million marks, the complete site with an area of about 23 hectares, the preliminary works began, and after due consideration of various projects in 1906 the final building programme was approved. At the same time the basic principles for the nature of the first event were laid down, and from this the programme of the Munich 1908 exhibition was developed. . . . The six exhibition halls were constructed between May and November 1907 as permanent buildings according to plans by, and under the direction of, Wilhelm Bertsch. . . . Hall 1 was built of iron, with window pillars and gable walls in reinforced concrete, by Vereinigte Maschinenfabrik, Augsburg, and Maschinenbaugesellschaft, Nuremberg. . . . Total costs for Hall I 455,000 marks. . . . The construction of the exterior of the halls took account of the need for a variety of different uses. There had to be adequate daylight. This resulted in a system of concrete supports and large areas of glass. The roofs are of pale red tiles, with long rows of sloping overhead lights. The architecture is based on the principle of great simplicity and restraint, but without echoing any particular style of design. . . .

Die Ausstellung München 1908, eine Denkschrift, Munich 1908, XVI and 3–5.

325   *Rehearsing with a thousand performers*

The gigantic platform, which has been extended even further forward to make room for the thousand-strong body of musicians, is already occupied by a large number of orchestral players. They straighten out their parts, tune their instruments. Here some melody or other floats up; there you can hear a trial run on the violin. Soon the full orchestral complement is gathered, presenting an imposing spectacle. We can see, too, many an instrument not usually observed in an orchestra and some which are rarely used in any connection, such as a celesta (a glockenspiel in the shape of a harmonium),

a bass clarinet, a contra-bassoon, as well as a bass tuba. Moreover, the other instruments are present in considerably larger numbers than usual. Thus we have here 24 first and 20 second violins, 16 violas, 14 cellos and 12 double basses, 4 mandolins and 4 harps. On top of that the mighty array of wind instruments, among them eight trumpets and seven trombones. . . . Maestro Hempel, too, has already taken his seat at the organ, which, with its magnificent decorative ornamentation, forms a mighty backdrop to the scene of the tightly packed platform. Now the top two side doors at the back open and the 350 children of the choir group into a delightful living mass. Here and there in the auditorium music enthusiasts are seated, with their thick, heavy scores open in front of them, to drink in a foretaste of the experience to come.

Everything is ready. With hasty steps the compact little figure of Gustav Mahler makes his way through the narrow rows to his podium, on which stands a comfortable arm-chair. Gustav Mahler stands there, smiling, and looks slowly round the wide hall. His features are serene, and breathe the great inner joy which he derives from the re-creation of his work which he wrested from the struggle of its creation. He seats himself comfortably in his armchair, then cups his hands to his mouth and calls a cheery 'Good morning' to the children, who return the greeting with bright, merry voices. Mahler's face, which only a moment ago was so sunny and serene, now takes on a serious character. The conductor stares now at his score and now at the musicians all around. The baton beats, and the first sounds immediately fill the air. . . .

Neues Wiener Journal, 10 September 1910.

From the Chronicle of the City of Munich

Monday 12 September 1910

The Chronicle of Munich today has to report a great musical event: The *première* of *Gustav Mahler's Eighth Symphony* at the *monster-concert* in the *Festival Hall of Music* in the *Exhibition Park* under the personal direction of the composer.

For a week the performers had been working and polishing in unremitting rehearsals at the gigantic work, which demands a body of players which a single city was unable to provide, so that auxiliary forces were required from other cities to make the performance possible. Hence rehearsals were also necessary in Vienna and Leipzig for preliminary work to ensure the unity of the whole performance.

In the foyer outside the hall there was lively activity. A huge crowd of people flanked both sides of the entrance, lining the pathway for the visitors. From time to time the waiting crowd buzzed with movement, for example when their Royal Highnesses Princess Gisela of Bavaria and Prince Ludwig Ferdinand appeared, when personalities of the musical world arrived, as well as individual performers, Gustav Mahler himself, Hermann Bahr and his wife, Court Singer Bahr-Mildenburg, Richard Strauss, Court Singer Lilli Lehmann, Court Singer Schmedes. Among those present were also Princess Thurn and Taxis, Princess Marietta zu Hohenlohe, Countess Palin, Paul Clemenceau from Paris, Professor Kolo Moser, Professor Anton [*sic*] Roller, the well-known stage designer, Professor Dr Oskar Bie, Dr Leopold Schmidt, Court Conductor Schalk, Director of the Vienna Singverein, Court Conductor Bruno Walter from Vienna, and many, many more.

The success of the evening was extraordinary, as befitted the participation in it of the whole musical world. The final scene left an unforgettable impression, culminating in a long and enthusiastic apotheosis of Mahler.

'Chronik der Stadt München', ms., 1910, vol. II, Stadtarchiv München, 2312–13. (Apart from those mentioned here the audience also included Thomas Mann, Stefan Zweig, Willem Mengelberg, Arnold Schönberg, Anton von Webern [who had got free tickets through Schönberg], Alfredo Casella, Siegfried Wagner, Leopold Stokowski, William Ritter, Max Reinhardt, Oskar Fried, Fritz Erler, Albert Neisser, Arnold Berliner and many others.)

Gustav Mahler:
Achte Symphonie

in zwei Teilen für Soli, Chöre, großes Orchester und Orgel

I. Teil: Hymnus: „Veni, creator spiritus"

II. Teil: Goethes Faust. II. (Schlußszene)

Uraufführung in der Neuen Musik-Festhalle der Ausstellung

12. September

Einzige Wiederholung: **13.** September

Gustav Mahler's Eighth Symphony	Gustav Mahler: Huitième Symphonie
in two parts for solo-voices, choruses, grand orchestra and organ	en deux Parties pour Soli, Chœurs, grand Orchestre et Orgue
First performance in the New Music Festival Hall of the Exposition on September 12	Deux uniques auditions dans la Salle des Fêtes de Musique à l'Exposition première le 12 Septembre
The only repetition: September 13	seconde le 13 Septembre

Participants: AUSFÜHRENDE: *Exécutants:*

Dirigent:

Gustav Mahler

Soli:

Hofopernsängerin **Gertrud Förstel** (Wien)	I. Sopran und **Magna peccatrix**
Martha Winternitz-Dorda (Wien)	II. Sopran und **Una poenitentium**
Kammersängerin **Irma Koboth** (München)	**Mater gloriosa**
Ottilie Metzger (Hamburg)	I. Alt und **Mulier Samaritana**
Anna Erler-Schnaudt (München)	II. Alt und **Maria Aegyptiaca**
Kammersänger **Felix Senius** (Berlin)	Tenor und **Doctor Marianus**
Hofopernsänger **Nicola Geisse-Winkel** (Wiesbaden)	Bariton und **Pater extaticus**
K. u. k. Kammersänger **Richard Mayr** (Wien)	Baß und **Pater profundus**

Chöre:

Singverein der k. k. Gesellschaft der Musikfreunde Wien
(250 Mitglieder)

Riedel-Verein Leipzig (250 Mitglieder)

Kinderchor der Zentral-Singschule München (350 Kinder)

Orchester:

Das verstärkte Orchester des Konzertvereins München

Besetzung: 24 erste Violinen, 20 zweite Violinen, 16 Bratschen, 14 Celli, 12 Kontrabässe, 4 Harfen, Celesta, Harmonium, Mandolinen, kleine Flöte, 4 große Flöten, 4 Oboen, Englisch-Horn, Es-Klarinette, 3 Klarineten, Baßklarinette, 4 Fagotte, Kontrafagott, 8 Hörner, 4 Trompeten, 4 Posaunen, Baßtuba, Pauken, Schlagwerk. — Isoliert postiert: 4 Trompeten, 3 Posaunen.

Orgel:

Adolf Hempel (München)

Programme of the first performance of the Eighth Symphony. IGMG.

Bruno Walter on the première

The huge apparatus devotedly obeyed the word and the Master's hand that ruled it without effort. All the performers were in a state of solemn exaltation, most of all perhaps the children, whose hearts had belonged to him from the beginning. What a moment when, to the applause of thousands of listeners in the gigantic Exhibition Hall, he took his place before the thousand performers – at a climax of his life and already marked out by Fate for an early death – when his work now called on the *creator spiritus*, from whose fire it had been created within him, when from every lip the cry of yearning of his life was heard: *accende lumen sensibus infunde amorem cordibus*! When the last note of the performance had died away and the storm of enthusiasm roared out to him Mahler climbed the steps of the platform, at the top of which the children's chorus was stationed, cheering with all their might, and he shook every hand that was held out to him, walking right along the row.

Bruno Walter, *Gustav Mahler*, Vienna 1936, 45.

Lilli Lehmann's emotion

I saw Mahler again, and for the last time, in 1910 when he conducted his Eighth Symphony; Riezl and I had gone there specially. Mahler had aged very much; it gave me a real shock. His work, which was given by 1,000 performers, sounded as from *one* instrument, from *one* throat. The second part of the Symphony, based on the second part of *Faust*, touched me painfully. Was it he, his music, his appearance, a premonition of death, Goethe's words, reminiscences of Schumann, my youth? I do not know; I only know that for the whole of the second part I gave way to emotion which I could not control.

Lilli Lehmann, *Mein Weg*, Leipzig 1913, II, 161.

From a review of the première

One may view Mahler's works as one will – I myself have never been able to rouse either admiration or even a trace of sympathy for this sort of music – at any rate it must be said that within this *oeuvre* the Eighth Symphony represents a peak, a peak especially from the point of view of external effect, such as the composer has not achieved since his Second Symphony in C minor. This applies above all to the second part; its effects, which are operatic (not always in the best sense of the word), seem to make an even deeper impression on the mass of the audience than the mighty sounds of the hymn.

Münchener Neueste Nachrichten, 14 September 1910.

Thomas Mann writes to Mahler

How deeply I am indebted to you for the experience of 12 September I was incapable of telling you in the hotel in the evening. I feel an urgent necessity to give you at least an inkling of it, and so I ask you to be kind enough to accept the enclosed book – my latest – from me.

It is ill-suited as a counter-gift to what I have received from you, and it must weigh as light as a feather in the hands of the man who embodies, as I believe I discern, the most serious and sacred artistic will of our time. . . .

AM, 473–74. (The book mentioned is the novel *Königliche Hoheit*.)

Rumours of a return to the Vienna Opera

From a person in artistic circles who is acquainted with the situation in the Court Theatres, one of our reporters has received the following information:

Gustav Mahler, who when he left the Opera was guided by the desire to be completely free of permanent obligations . . . left in the Court officials who were his superiors only the best recollections. In particular whenever Mahler comes to Vienna to visit his family or friends, he never neglects to pay his respects to the Comptroller, Prince Alfred Montenuovo.

This autumn, too, Mahler came to Vienna after he had conducted his symphony at the Munich Music Festival, and called on Prince Montenuovo, who told him in conversation that Herr von Weingartner insisted on being released from the Court Opera contract. Prince Montenuovo took the opportunity of asking Mahler whether anything might possibly induce him to return to the Court Opera.

Neue Freie Presse, 1 November 1910.

Oskar Fried sees Mahler before his return to New York

I saw him for the last time six months before his death. He was about to go to America. On the way there, between Berlin and Hamburg, he visited me at Nikolassee. But not a word was spoken of either his or my plans for the future. He merely played in the garden with my child.

Oskar Fried, 'Erinnerungen an Mahler', *Musikblätter des Anbruch*, vol. I, no. 1, 18.

During the summer and autumn months of 1910 Mahler had been looking out for a new holiday home of his own, which he had been longing for since his last stay at Göding. After a long search he decided to buy a piece of land in the Semmering region, south of Vienna, on which with Moll's help he planned to build a comfortable country house.

Contract for the purchase of farm no. 17 at Breitenstein am Semmering

Herr Josef Hartberger jun. and Frau Maria Hartberger sell to Herr Gustav Mahler and the latter buys from them the farm which they jointly own, namely no. 17 at Breitenstein am Semmering, registration no. 29 in the Land Registry of the administrative commune of Breitenstein, along with the building plot no. 7 which belongs to it, house no. 17 at Breitenstein and the plots 79/1 meadow, 79/2 forest, 81 arable land, 85 garden, 86/1 meadow, 86/2 pasture, 87 garden, 88 pasture, 89 arable land, 102 forest, just as they owned and used them or were entitled to own and use them along with all appurtenances for the mutually agreed price of K.40.000. – in words forty thousand crowns, the correct receipt of which the vendors hereof hereby confirm.

Contract of sale of 3 November 1910, signed by Dr Emil Freund as Mahler's representative, Grundbuch Breitenstein, Bezirksgericht Gloggnitz, Einlagezahl 29, Postzahl 3.

The first New York concert of the 1910–11 season

The Philharmonic Society opened its sixty-ninth season brilliantly last night – one might say very brilliantly if the reader were to limit the statement to such elements as the quality of the band's finest utterances, some of the features of Mr Mahler's reading of the familiar works on the programme, and the appearance of the audience. . . . The end . . . came after more than two hours of music, considerably too much, especially when weary listeners were compelled to go home with the cacophonous concluding measures of Richard Strauss's *Also sprach Zarathustra* haunting the ear and outraging the aesthetic sense and fancy.

New York Daily Tribune, 2 November 1910.

[Mahler] treated Schubert's symphony from the same subjective point of view and with the same freedom that has marked so much of what he has done. It cannot be denied that it was in many respects an exceedingly interesting, even a captivating performance, however much it may have wrenched old time memories and deep-rooted conceptions of how Schubert's music ought to sound – and how he probably thought it would sound. It is not everybody who could have played fast and loose with the letter of the score and brought forth a result that went so far to carrying conviction to it. There were, for instance, almost incessant and sometimes very far-reaching modifications of tempo, of accent and rhythm, even of orchestral colour. There were also numerous passages of exquisite poetical insight. Mr Mahler apparently did not exercise the prerogative which he has sometimes claimed, of cutting and shortening some of those 'heavenly lengths' in Schubert's music. Instead he seemed to wish to impart to them so much variety, interest, and diversity of expression that the burden of their length would seem to be relieved.

The New York Times, 2 November 1910.

A comparison with the Boston Symphony Orchestra

After hearing the Boston Orchestra, one realizes how indifferent much of the Philharmonic material is, and how rough and explosive their playing often is. . . . This is not Mr Mahler's fault; for my part, I think he works wonders with the material at his command. Still, it always irks me to have to admit that orchestrally New York must take a back seat to Boston, and I wonder if it would not be possible – even with the union regulations as they are – to improve the present personnel of the Philharmonic Orchestra. There is surely enough wealth among its guarantors to effect this desirable end, if only money be needed.

The World, 14 November 1910. (The Boston Symphony Orchestra, founded in 1881, played for several years under Arthur Nikisch, Wilhelm Gericke and Carl Muck, and had been directed since 1908 by Max Fiedler.)

The 1910–11 season of the Philharmonic Society was planned so that almost every week on Tuesday evening at 8.15 a new programme was played which was then repeated on Friday afternoon at 2.30. In addition there were sometimes Sunday afternoon concerts, with their own programme. There was a week's interruption from Friday 2 to Tuesday 13 December while the orchestra made a tour with Mahler to Pittsburgh and Buffalo. In both cities, amongst other works, Beethoven's 'Pastoral' was performed. During this concert tour Mahler and his wife visited Niagara Falls.

The Philharmonic Society
of New York

1910...	SIXTY-NINTH SEASON	...1911

Gustav Mahler . . . Conductor

MANAGEMENT LOUDON CHARLTON

Carnegie Hall

TUESDAY NIGHT, NOVEMBER FIRST
FRIDAY AFTERNOON, NOVEMBER FOURTH

... Programme ...

BACH (by request) Suite, arranged by Mr. Mahler from the 2nd and 3rd Suites B minor, D major
MR. MAHLER AT THE HARPSICHORD

SCHUBERT - - - Symphony, C major

MOZART - - { (a) Ballet Music from "Idomeneo"
{ (b) Deutsche Tänze

R. STRAUSS - - "Thus Spake Zarathustra"
MR. ARTHUR S. HYDE AT THE ORGAN

Steinway Piano Used

Programme of the first concert of the 1910–11 season.

A cold winter sun glittered on all the branches, which were quite covered with ice, and when we then got right up to the Falls, and then in the lift up under the Falls, the overpowering green light hurt your eyes. The thundering of the water cascading under the layer of ice, all the trees on the banks covered in ice over a huge area by the constant spray, the white plain as far as the eye could see, all this was like a beautiful dream. . . .

Mahler came, in an exalted mood, straight from the concert to me in the hotel, where his simple supper awaited him. 'You know what,' he said, 'I have today realized that articulate art is greater than inarticulate nature.' He had just conducted the 'Pastoral' Symphony. . . .

AM, 229, 230.

Everyday life in the Savoy (Winter 1910–11)

His best hours were when he had just conducted a successful concert and was able to gather round him, in the corner salon in the Hotel Savoy, a few people who he knew understood him and respected his true nature. People with whom he could be as he really was. He used to like to lie on the divan until he began to feel tired. Then he got up: 'Right, ladies and gentlemen, now you can enjoy yourselves and be merry, I am no good for that. If you get too merry I shall throw my boots against the wall. Then you will know you are making too much noise.' A few hearty hand-shakes and Herr Mahler went to bed. Of course that remark about merriment, which he said he was no good for, was not true. He had a strong sense of humour which could run the whole gamut from savage mockery to childish glee. When he was in a good mood and took off well-known contemporaries, especially of course other composers and conductors, we just could not stop laughing. He never shrank from the hardest words and the most grotesque mimicry.

But, on the other hand, anyone who saw him playing with his little daughter fully understood the gentleness, indeed lovableness of this basically taciturn nature. To entertain children so that the child is really the one entertained is rightly considered a special gift. Now whether Mahler was the magician or the fairy, the wild beast or the faithful dog, whether he improvised his utterly funny tales from the present or tried to turn them into a parable with a didactic purpose, he always showed that fine understanding of the child's awakening soul which he was able to express in so many of his compositions.

His relations with his wife Alma were equally deep and tender; though this was not until after many a struggle and crisis. The beautiful Frau Alma, herself a brilliant musician and a more than usually talented composer, did not always have an easy time, for all the love he showed her. It was many years before he recognized her as his equal. . . . But in this last winter their harmony reached an intensity which one would not consider possible. It was for this woman above all that he composed, conducted, worked, lived. . . . About Christmas he once took me into his room with an air of great mystery. 'You must help me buy presents for my wife. You know her tastes. But, for Heaven's sake, she must not get wind of it.' We then arranged a secret rendezvous. I walked around for hours with him in the stores and art shops of New York. Nothing was good and beautiful enough for him. . . . Then he filled great sheets of paper with instructions for unheard-of treasures which were to be bought in Europe, above all in Paris, in the presence of Frau Alma herself. He put the whole thing together himself on Christmas Eve, piece by piece, but still doubting whether his treasury was really fine and rich enough.

His instructions for the future remained unfulfilled, as did his plans to build a house of his own high up on the Semmering

near Vienna, in which he planned to live a contemplative life at the end of his work in New York. This house must have been built and pulled down perhaps a hundred times with his friends last winter. Plans had been produced by people in the artistic circles in Vienna from which Frau Mahler came, and also by American architects. For it was to be something special, and above all something quite personal. . . . We argued, often to the point of acrimony, about every single chair, about wallpaper and carpet designs. . . . 'As long as you leave my study alone,' he used to say, 'you can go on building to your heart's content. But the room where I am going to write my next symphonies is something *I* shall decide on.' . . .

Mahler often enough had very hard things to say about the philistines and snobs of New York; but he did not close his heart to either the greatness or the special character of the city. He waxed in fact quite passionate about the New York sun. From the corner window of his living-room in the Hotel Savoy he had a broad view of Central Park and its greenery. He could sit for hours as if in a trance and stare out on the vibrant life before him. 'Wherever I am, the longing for this blue sky, this magnificent sun and this pulsating activity goes with me.' Slowly he also came to believe in New York's artistic seriousness. In the first half of the winter, when they had not yet begun to embitter his work by their narrow-minded interference, we often spoke of his mission of creating in New York a higher musical understanding.

M. Baumfeld, 'Erinnerungen an Gustav Mahler', *New-Yorker Staats-Zeitung*, 21 May 1911, Sunday edn. (Maurice Baumfeld, 1868–1913, Viennese-born journalist, Director of the German theatre company at the Irving Place Theatre since 1907.)

Serious differences with the Philharmonic Society

Mr Flinsch reported that Mr Mahler has appeared with a Committee of the Guarantors' Committee before Mr Samuel Untermeyer as arbitrator, regarding a demand of Mr Mahler for an addition to his salary of $5,000. – for conducting an extra 20 Concerts during the present season. Mr Flinsch informed the Committee that the decision of the arbitrator was rendered against the Committee but that Mr Mahler has consented, at the suggestion of Mr Untermeyer, to reduce his claim to $3,000. – This sum to be paid Mr Mahler on March 1st and Mr Mahler to be accorded the privilege of leaving for Europe on March 29th, or three days before the expiration of his contract. . . .

The question of engaging a conductor for next season was discussed.

A letter from Mr Franz Kneisel, who has been unofficially requested to state if his services for the position of Conductor are available, was received and read. Mr Kneisel stating at length that he would feel highly honoured to accept the position, that, however, he cannot leave his present field of activity for a contract of one year only.

It was resolved that Mr Charlton be instructed to unofficially inquire from Mr Mahler his attitude regarding the acceptance of the position of conductor for next season and also his terms.

Philharmonic Society, minutes of the meeting of the Guarantors' Committee, 4 January 1911, LMPA. (Rudolf E. F. Flinsch, member of the Guarantors' Committee; Samuel Untermeyer, 1858–1940, prominent New York lawyer, husband of Minnie C. Untermeyer, 1859–1924. Minnie Untermeyer was a member of the Guarantors' Committee and a friend of the Mahlers'. Loudon Charlton had been manager of the Philharmonic Society since the beginning of the 1910–11 season.)

Mahler conducts a symphony of his own for the last time

Mr Mahler's Fourth Symphony was already known to New York, when it was performed here . . . with the New York Symphony Orchestra on November 6, 1904. It was the first of the composer's works to be played here, and to many it will seem the most interesting and individual. It has not the grandeur and vast ambition of the Second Symphony; it is more accessible, and, to tell the truth, has more real musical substance than the Fifth, and assuredly stands considerably higher than the First which Mr Mahler played here last season. . . .

The performance of the symphony by Mr Mahler and his men was an exceedingly brilliant one, and after it was finished the applause of the audience burst out in force, and Mr Mahler was called forward many times.

The New York Times, 18 January 1911.

Mr Mahler's Symphony . . . is more or less an enigma. The composer has not given titles to the different movements, nor to the symphony as a whole, yet by the device of community of theme between the movements, and still more emphatically by introducing a vocal part in the last movement, which brings the text of an old German folksong into association with the melodies of the earlier portions of the work, Mr Mahler willingly, or unwillingly, confesses that his music is of the programmatic kind. . . .

New York Daily Tribune, 18 January 1911.

Formation of a Programme Committee

Resolved that the General Committee forthwith appoint a Programme Committee. . . . The Programme Committee shall supervise the selection of music to be played at the various concerts of the Society.

Philharmonic Society, minutes of the meeting of the Guarantors' Committee of 1 February 1911, LMPA.

Alma Mahler on the differences with the Philharmonic Society

. . . Things were coming to a head at the Philharmonic, and Mahler noticed nothing of it. They now demanded programmes which he did not want to do, and turned nasty when he refused. The violinist Jonas had already stirred up the orchestra to such an extent that opposition became vocal, and Mahler felt unsure of himself. His habit of postponing what he had no stomach for prevented him from seeing clearly until one day in the middle of February he was called in to see Mrs Sheldon, who was the Chairman of the Board. There he found several members of the Committee. He was sharply criticized. In the eyes of the ladies he was guilty of all kinds of misdemeanours. He defended himself, but Mrs Sheldon called out some name, a side door opened and a lawyer came in, who (as it later transpired) had taken everything down. Then an official protocol was established setting out the limits of Mahler's authority, and he was so furious and speechless that he came home with a feverish cold.

AM, 236.

Re-scoring of the Fifth Symphony

I have finished the Fifth – it had to be practically completely re-scored.

I am entirely at a loss to understand how I could have made such amateurish miscalculations.

(Obviously the routine I had acquired in the first four symphonies left me completely in the lurch here – since a new style demanded a new technique.)

Postscript to Mahler's letter of 8 February 1911 to Georg Göhler, GMB, 469. (Georg Göhler had conducted the choral rehearsals in Leipzig for the Eighth Symphony. He later conducted the first performance of the Fifth Symphony in Mahler's new scoring.)

The last concert

On 20 February he had a temperature again, with a sore throat and furring of the tongue, but Mahler insisted on conducting on the 21st: Fraenkel would have to help him.

Fraenkel warned against it, but Mahler asserted he had conducted with a temperature so often that the doctor had to give way. We drove to the Carnegie Hall, carefully wrapped up. Mahler conducted. One of the works that evening was the first performance of Busoni's 'Lullaby at the grave of my mother'.

AM, 236. (Dr Joseph Fraenkel, 1867–1920, Viennese doctor practising in New York, a close friend of Mahler's. The title of Busoni's work is *Berceuse élégiaque*.)

22 February 1911

Yesterday evening was the first performance of the *Berceuse*. Toscanini had come. After two compliments from Mahler I had to take two more bows (from my box) to the audience. 'It doesn't like the piece, but it likes me,' I remarked. The manner of the *Berceuse* does not suit Mahler as well as the rhythms and drumming of *Turandot*. But the piece is effective, and I still almost believe it will achieve some kind of popularity.

Busoni, *Briefe an seine Frau*, Erlenbach 1935, 221–22.

The Philharmonic Society decides to negotiate with Weingartner

The Executive Committee reported its negotiations with Mr Mahler, the Committee having received Mr Mahler's terms in a letter to Mr Flinsch. It was moved to reject the proposition contained in the writing received by Mr Flinsch and it was resolved that the Executive Committee have power to negotiate and contract with Mr Weingartner on substantially the terms as set forth by the Committee in its cable to his agent and in case of failure to contract with Mr Weingartner the Committee to have power to reopen negotiations and to contract with Mr Mahler.

Philharmonic Society, minutes of the meeting of the Guarantors' Committee, 8 March 1911, LMPA.

Busoni on the attitude of the New York public

30 March 1911

Mahler has not conducted since 21 February. On 24th Spiering deputized for him – and stayed, and will stay, and will have stayed, until the end of the season. It deserved recognition that an averagely good violinist showed so much *présence d'esprit*, and was capable of finishing the programmes creditably. But – – ! It is and will remain one of my most painful experiences how the New Yorkers (critics and public) reacted. The sensation that the leader of an orchestra could conduct without preparation made a greater impression on them than the whole of Mahler's personality ever did! They have declared Spiering a great conductor and spoken seriously of engaging him permanently. *Not a word of regret for Mahler's absence has been expressed!*

You read about things like this in history, but when you meet it in real life you can only clutch your brow. . . .

Ferruccio Busoni, *Briefe an seine Frau*, Erlenbach 1935, 238–39.

Dr George Baehr recalls the bacteriological examination

Sometime in February 1911, Dr Emanuel Libman was called in consultation by Mahler's personal physician, Dr Fraenkel, to see the famous composer and director. Apparently Dr Fraenkel had suspected that Mahler's prolonged fever and physical debility might be due to subacute bacterial endocarditis and therefore called Libman, Chief of the First Medical Service and Associate Director of Laboratories at the Mt Sinai Hospital, in consultation. Libman was at that time the outstanding authority on the disease. At the time of the consultation, the Mahlers were occupying a suite of rooms at the old Savoy Plaza Hotel (or it may have been the Plaza) at Fifth Avenue and 59th Street overlooking Central Park. Libman confirmed the diagnosis clinically by finding a loud systolic-presystolic murmur over the precordium characteristic of chronic rheumatic mitral disease, a history of prolonged low grade fever, a palpable spleen, characteristic petechiae on the conjunctivae and skin and slight clubbing of fingers. To confirm the diagnosis bacteriologically, Libman telephoned me to join him at the hotel and bring the paraphernalia and culture media required for a blood culture.

On arrival I withdrew 20 ccm of blood from an arm vein with syringer and needle, squirted part of it into several bouillon flasks and mixed the remainder with melted agar media which I then poured into sterile Petri dishes. After 4 or 5 days of incubation in the hospital laboratory, the Petri plates revealed numerous bacterial colonies and all the bouillon flasks were found to show a pure culture of the same organism which was subsequently identified as *Streptococcus viridans*.

As this was long before the days of antibiotics, the bacterial findings sealed Mahler's doom. He insisted on being told the truth and then expressed a wish to die in Vienna. Accordingly, he and his wife left shortly thereafter for Paris, where the diagnosis and prognosis were confirmed, and then proceeded to Vienna.

George Baehr, letter of 17 November 1970, published in Nicholas P. Christy, M.D., 'Gustav Mahler and his illnesses', *Transactions of the American Clinical and Climatological Association*, LXXXII, 211–12.

316 Dr Fraenkel and the specialists he called in recommended Mahler to visit a leading bacteriologist in Paris. Mahler's mother-in-law Anna Moll was summoned from Vienna by cable and helped Alma Mahler get the seriously sick man out of the Hotel Savoy and on to the ship and on from there to Paris.

Alma Mahler on the embarkation and crossing

The cabin was booked, everything was packed, Mahler was dressed. A stretcher was ordered, but Mahler turned it away. On Fraenkel's arm he staggered to the lift, as pale as death. The liftboy came – he had been hiding so that Mahler should not see his tearful face – and he took Mahler down for the last time. Downstairs the huge foyer of the hotel was empty. Fraenkel led Mahler to Mrs Untermeyer's car, which was waiting at the side entrance, and they drove on ahead to the pier. . . . Everyone came and shook my hand silently. 'We had the hotel foyer cleared so that Mr Mahler should not have to see any strange faces.' Holy America! In Europe afterwards, we never once encountered such tact and delicacy.

I boarded the ship; Mahler was already in bed, Fraenkel beside him. He went through all my instructions once again, advised me not to call the ship's doctor, and said goodbye to Mahler briefly and with difficulty. He knew he would never see him again. The cabins were full of gifts and flowers from friends and strangers alike. My mother and I again got down to nursing him. . . .

329 On board he got up almost every day, and we led him, or rather carried him, on to the sun deck, where the captain had roped off a large area for Mahler so that he could be undisturbed and unseen by all the other passengers. We dressed and undressed him, lifted him, gently put all his food in his mouth; he himself did not need to lift a finger. Busoni was on the ship with us. Every day he sent crazy, humorous counterpoints to amuse Mahler, and wine. . . .

Mahler looked disturbingly beautiful. I always said to him, 'Today you are Alexander the Great again.' Black, radiant eyes, his white face, the black locks, a blood-red mouth. Frighteningly beautiful!

AM, 242–44.

A Viennese paper reports on Mahler's health

Paris, 21 April. This morning Gustav Mahler left the Elysée Palace Hotel in the Champs Elysées, which is excellently run by a Viennese, Ronacher. He was taken by ambulance-car to the sanatorium which is situated in a magnificent park near the Bois de Boulogne. . . .

When Mahler arrived in the sanatorium Chantemesse was ready waiting for him to begin the serum treatment as soon as he had examined him again.

I spoke to Chantemesse after his visit. He found Mahler better than yesterday, and in particular he confirmed the satisfactory activity of the heart. . . .

I had a chance to see Mahler when he was brought to the sanatorium. He does not look bad. His lively gestures and his fiery eyes confirm the reports from those around him that as a result of the long fever Mahler has lost nothing of his sharpness of mind, his remarkable willpower or his feeling for life.

Yesterday he spoke a lot of Cornelius' opera *Der Barbier von Bagdad*, which even on his sickbed he showed great interest in producing. . . . It was Mahler's wish to show Vienna this great musical work as he sees it. The crisis has prevented him, and he still hopes to realize this favourite scheme one day. Mahler spoke for a long time about these artistic ideas, until his wife, who watches over him with touching care, made him rest.

Mahler wants the world to know that it is by no means overwork in America that has shattered his health: 'I have worked really hard for decades and have borne the exertion wonderfully well. I have never worked as little as I did in America. I was not subjected to an excess of either physical or intellectual work in America.'

Mahler knows of his condition. He has succeeded in getting a full picture from the doctors in America, and what he was not actually told his ready perception soon guessed.

Mahler has great confidence in his New York doctor, Dr Fraenkel, and he positively beamed when Chantemesse told him that he was able to confirm Fraenkel's diagnosis in every particular. . . .

The reason he was so pleased was that Chantemesse's remarks tended to strengthen his faith in science. This firm belief in science on Mahler's part is a very interesting trait in the artist's character. . . .

Neue Freie Presse, 22 April 1911. (André Chantemesse, 1851–1919, Professor at Paris University, Fellow of the Pasteur Institute.)

The journey from Paris to Vienna

Paris, 11 May. This afternoon Mahler left Paris; he is travelling on a stretcher accompanied by his wife, by Herr Moll and by Professor Chvostek. At his own specific request he is being brought to Vienna.

Professor Chvostek agreed with Chantemesse's treatment, but neither of the doctors could refuse the sick man's request to be taken to Vienna. . . .

The latest examination, which took place in the afternoon before Mahler's departure, revealed that his condition is very serious and that there is nothing to lose by the journey. . . .

Neue Freie Presse, 12 May 1911. (Professor Franz Chvostek, 1864–1944, prominent Viennese physician.)

Arrival in Vienna

Only a few people were waiting for the train that brought Mahler to Vienna. The doctors' wishes that he should be kept away from any excitement had been respected. The ambulance from the Loew sanatorium, which drove up about 5.30 at the summer platform of Vienna West, also attracted only a small group of onlookers. Shortly afterwards Herr and Frau Rosé appeared, with Court Conductor Walter and Herr Spiegler. A few minutes before 6 the Orient Express arrived. From one of the sleeping cars, which was located in the middle of the train, Herr Moll, Gustav Mahler's father-in-law, alighted first. Friends went up to him. Herr Moll said to them: 'The journey was reasonable. The patient is very weak.'

Neues Wiener Tagblatt, 13 May 1911.

Karl Kraus quotes and comments

'Mahler is an example of how much strength is dissipated when it is torn from its home and surroundings. . . . There he must suffer *foreign methods of treatment* from doctors who are as strangers to him, until a swift decision on the part of those around him sets him free. Then the sick man's journey home, a whole night and almost a whole day in a sleeping-car that is not built for an invalid. . . . A genius from a good State is not subjected like this to the external hazards of life: he has a homeland in which he can work and move. Now that it is already very late, they are trying to right the earlier wrongs. The patient receives addresses and wishes for his recovery which he probably does not read. Now people remember that he "was one of us". . . .' – says the *Neues Wiener Journal*, after organizing the Mahler witch-hunt.

Die Fackel, 1911, no. 324/5, 7. (Karl Kraus was the editor and in later years the sole author of the satirical magazine *Die Fackel*, first issued in 1899.)

333 Mahler died on 18 May 1911, shortly after 11 o'clock in the evening, in the Loew sanatorium. His wife relates his last words, 'Mozartl – Mozartl!' (AM, 251). At his own request
334 he was buried in the churchyard at Grinzing, Vienna, in the same grave as his elder daughter. The funeral was attended by official Vienna and by friends and admirers from far and near. The newspapers and musical journals of all the countries in which Mahler had worked reported his death and honoured his achievements as a composer and conductor in obituary notices and memorial articles. The magazine *Die Musik* devoted a special issue to Mahler the same year (1911), and in 1912 there followed a special issue of *Der Merker*.

Gustav Mahler's estate was valued at 169,781 crowns according to the inventory of 25 November 1911. Of this around 139,000 crowns were in securities and 19,000 were represented by the property at Breitenstein am Semmering. The value of Mahler's compositions was assessed at 10,250 crowns. This figure was contained in an affidavit by the Austrian composer Julius Bittner, 1874–1939, who was a lawyer by profession. Mahler had shown an interest in Bittner's work and had accepted his opera *Die rote Gred* for the Vienna Court Opera. The work was performed under Bruno Walter after Mahler had left.

Julius Bittner's valuation of Mahler's works

In the matter of the estate of Gustav Mahler I refer to my oath sworn at the Imperial-Royal District Court of Döbling and declare my valuation of the works of the testator which have appeared in print as follows:

The valuation comprises the symphonies I to IX, the *Lieder* and *Das Lied von der Erde*, along with *Das klagende Lied* (a work of his youth).

Of these works, according to the documents shown to me by the executor, symphonies I to IV are published by Universal Edition, V by Peters, VI by Kahnt, VII by Bote & Bock (formerly Lauterbeith & Kuhn), VIII and IX by Universal Edition, *Das Lied von der Erde* by the same publisher, *Das klagende Lied* by the same publisher, the orchestral songs, as follows: *Lieder eines fahrenden Gesellen* by Weinberger, *Kindertotenlieder* and six other songs by Kahnt, *Lieder aus des Knaben*

Wunderhorn by Universal Edition, 14 songs with piano accompaniment by Schott in Mainz, *Lieder* with orchestral accompaniment by Kahnt, but the last mentioned are charged with an advance of 4040.94 marks, so that at the time of death they did not form part of the composer's assets.

Of these the first four symphonies are subject to an outstanding amount for printing costs of 48,134.77 crowns. These works therefore represent liabilities and are thus valueless.

The Fifth and Sixth Symphonies were sold for a lump sum, so that at the time of death they did not form part of the testator's assets.

The Seventh Symphony, too, had no asset value at the date of death, since printing costs are outstanding to the value of 6232.16 marks.

The testator is entitled to 50 per cent of the gross receipts from the Eighth and Ninth Symphonies and from *Das Lied von der Erde*. These works must therefore be valued as assets, as are the orchestral songs published by Universal Edition, including *Das klagende Lied*.

The Ninth Symphony and *Das Lied von der Erde* had not yet been performed at the time of the testator's death and have thus not yet produced receipts.

The Eighth Symphony has been performed, but in view of the colossal size of the work and the huge number of performers it requires it must be assumed that it will be performed only rarely and in exceptional circumstances.

With all the works account must be taken of the fact that performances in the testator's lifetime were bound up with his great personal inspiration. The loss of Mahler the *conductor* is of decisive importance in the valuation, since the great director's remarkable genius was a decisive factor to most of the institutions which undertook the performance of works of this kind. The testator was himself such a convincing interpreter of his own works that after his death they are without their most persuasive advocate. Even though a relatively large number of proposed performances were noted immediately after the testator's death, the fact must not be overlooked that these performances for the most part are in the nature of memorials to the composer and that it will not be possible to count on this number of performances in the future. Even as soon as Mahler ceased to be Director of the Opera the number of performances dropped strikingly.

The Eighth Symphony, despite the performance that took place with great success in Munich, only brought in 415.64 crowns up to 30 June 1911 (i.e. *after* the composer's death). The receipts from the other orchestral pieces in this period amount to a mere 125.46 crowns. This account is the first and only one since the publication was taken on by Universal Edition. In the current year the Eighth Symphony will certainly bring in more, and in the *immediate* future the *Lieder* will undoubtedly be performed frequently. In the coming years, however, these symphonies and *Lieder* will surely not be played so often, and in the valuation of the assets at the time of the testator's decease account must be taken of their prospective revenue. A middle course between two possibilities must be followed. Either the works will now achieve a breakthrough after the testator's decease, so that they remain in favour, or they will suffer the fate of so many important productions and disappear, returning to popularity only in the distant future long after the protection of the copyright has ceased. In calculating the revenue to be expected from the works it is therefore necessary to strike a medium between these two eventualities.

Consequently I can value the Eighth Symphony on the basis of 30 years use (copyright) at an annual return of only 300 crowns, which, with interest at 8 per cent, gives a total value of 3,750 crowns.

On the same basis I value the songs with orchestra and those with piano accompaniment at 80 crowns per annum, making a total of 1,000 crowns.

Per analogiam I value the Ninth Symphony at 200 crowns per annum because although it is easier to perform it is less approachable than the Seventh [Bittner evidently meant the Eighth], giving a total of 2,500 crowns, *Das Lied von der Erde* at 80 crowns p.a., totalling 1,000 crowns. It is precisely with the last two works that special care must be taken in the valuation, since they have not yet been performed, so that their earning power has not yet been tested.

The total value of the printed legacy of the testator is thus to be taken as 10,250 crowns.

I require no fee for this valuation.

Vienna, 6 November 1911.

Gustav Mahler probate, Archiv der Stadt Wien.

Anton von Webern to Alban Berg

. . . On 19 and 20 November there is the Mahler Memorial in Munich. . . . Yesterday the *Berliner Tageblatt* printed the enclosed on Mahler's *Das Lied von der Erde*. Is it possible that we are not to be there? A new work by Mahler for the first time since his death! And we are to miss it? Because of the eight-hour train journey? Financially we could manage it, couldn't we? I mean, it would not be easy for me, but possible all the same. For you as well, surely? And time we have; I certainly have. And you can make time. No doubt of that. . . . And now the things that have driven me to a pitch of excitement, so that I can scarcely wait to be in Munich. Once you have read the end of the poem of *Das Lied von der Erde* in the enclosed cutting, my dear man, would you not expect to hear the most wonderful music that there is? Something of such magnificence as has never yet existed? 'Thou, my friend, happiness was not given to me in this world! Whither I go? I go and wander to the mountains, I seek peace, peace for my lonely heart. . . .' For Heaven's sake, what kind of music must that be?! I feel I must already be able to imagine it before having heard it. Well, can you stand it? I can't! . . .

Letter of 30 October 1911, quote from *Österreichische Musikzeitschrift*, vol. xv, no. 6, 305. (Bruno Walter conducted the première of *Das Lied von der Erde* in Munich on 20 November 1911. Anton von Webern and Alban Berg were in the audience.)

Index

Numbers in italics refer to the illustrations

PEOPLE

Millionaire's Romance With Mahl

By James Wierzbicki
Post-Dispatch Music Critic

THE YOUNG MAN was at first unaware of his attraction to the beauty he'd met at the rehearsal. But that night he tossed and turned, his mind unsettled — inflamed — by vaguely remembered images of their first encounter. Driven by desire more fierce than any he'd ever felt, the next day he went again to the source of this new, indescribable passion. Minutes passed like hours as he waited, but at last he had in hand a ticket for the evening's concert. By the time the performance reached the fifth movement he found himself weeping uncontrollubly. Fantasies flashed through his mind. He envisioned himself standing on the podium, sharing with her intimacies that only conductors are allowed. He imagined his hands caressing her, not the homely pages on which her modern editions are printed but the very manuscript paper on which the composer penciled each precious note. "I must have you," he thought.

When you think about it, the style of the romance novelist seems not at all inappropriate to telling the tale.

Indeed, millionaire Gilbert Kaplan's involvement with Mahler's Symphony No. 2 ("Resurrection") is perhaps the most glamorous musical love story the 20th century has known. And now — after more than two decades of isolated longings, international pursuits, agonizing courtship rituals and various forms of consummation — the relationship has at last borne tangible fruit.

THE MOST RECENT development in the Kaplan-"Resurrection" affair was last month's publication by the Kaplan Foundation of a sumptuous silk-bound facsimile edition of the composer's autograph score. It's probably the climax of the story, disheartening though that must seem for those who wish the romance would blaze from here to eternity.

It all started in 1964, when Kaplan — then a 23-year-year-old fresh out the economics program at the New School for Social Research in New York and by his own admission up to that time not much of a music lover — was invited by a friend to hear Leopold Stokowski lead the American Symphony Orchestra in a rehearsal of the work. The italicized paragraph with which this article begins is a fairly accurate account of what transpired in the next 36 hours. It was love at first hearing, and from then on it

Gilbert Kaplan

was simply a matter of Kaplan waiting until he could afford to do what he felt he needed to do.

KAPLAN IS not alone in being so moved by a first encounter with the "Resurrection" Symphony.

In a 25-page essay included in the prefatory material of the new facsimile edition, Kaplan cites Bruno Walter's account of the symphony's world premiere in Berlin in 1895: "... I was seized ... with an excitement which expressed itself even physically, in the violent throbbing of my heart.... A work of art can produce no greater effect than when it transmits the emotions which raged in the creator to the listener, in such a way that they also rage and storm in him. I was overwhelmed, completely overwhelmed."

And he quotes from a letter that Alban Berg wrote to his fiancée after hearing a performance in Vienna in 1907: "Today, my darling, I have been unfaithful to you for the first time. ... It happened in the finale of the Mahler symphony, when I gradually felt a sensation of complete solitude, as if in all the world there were nothing left but this music — and me listening to it. But when it came to its uplifting and overwhelming climax, and then was over, I felt a sudden pang, and a voice within me said: what of Helene? It was only then I realized I had been unfaithful, so now I implore your forgiveness."

BUT CONDUCTOR Walter and

composer Berg were reasonably well equipped to do something about their interest in the work. Kaplan was a rank amateur who could barely read music and who had forgotten most of what he'd learned during obligatory childhood piano lessons. He was able to do only what most amateurs do. He listened, to every recording of the piece he could find and to every live performance he could attend.

He did other things as well. Most notable among them was the raising of approximately $250,000 to start up a magazine that focused on the ins and outs of high finance. Kaplan's *Institutional Investor* made its debut in 1967, three years after its editor and publisher first made the acquaintance of Mahler's music. Eleven years later the monthly journal had a circulation of 41,500 and an annual income of about $7.5 million. The time had come, Kaplan knew, when he could do more than just dream of "having" Mahler's "Resurrection" Symphony.

Most of Kaplan's friends thought he was crazy when he talked about someday conducting the work. A similar opinion was voiced by Max Rudolf, the veteran maestro from whom Kaplan sought advice about how he might realize his plan.

IT'S AMAZING, though, what one can accomplish when even the wildest of ambitions are supported by lots and lots of money.

First off, Kaplan hired a young conductor on the faculty of the Juilliard School of Music to give him lessons not in score-reading or in conducting *per se* but simply in baton-wielding of the sort appropriate to the "Resurrection" Symphony that he in essence knew from memory. Then he globe-trotted — to Tokyo, Melbourne, Amsterdam, Vienna and wherever else the piece was being performed — for the sake of picking up tips. Then, in September of 1981, he hired an orchestra of New York free-lancers and actually worked his way through the symphony's first movement.

Over the course of the next year Kaplan re-booked the musicians each time he felt he had another movement under his belt. By the fall of 1982 he felt confident enough to shell out $125,000 to engage the American Symphony Orchestra and the Westminster Symphonic Chorus for a reading of the complete work in New York's Avery Fisher Hall. The concert took place on the 15th anniversary of Kaplan's very successful magazine, and it went so well that the orchestra invited him to lead the piece again on a benefit concert in Carnegie Hall the following April. Kaplan had two more chances to practice before his public debut: In January of 1983 he bought a few hours of the London Symphony Orchestra's time, and in February of that year he paid $9,000 to have a go at it with the St. Louis Symphony Orchestra and Chorus.

KAPLAN TOOK a beating from some of the critics who heard his version of the "Resurrection" in Carnegie Hall. But he also got some favorable reviews, enough to encourage him to keep up the pursuit and enough, it seems, to attract invitations from all over the world. To date he's led the "Resurrection" not only in New York, London and St. Louis but also in Buffalo, Tokyo, Cardiff, Rio de Janeiro and Budapest; he's scheduled to do it later this year in Sao Paulo and next year in Stockholm.

Having a piece of music in the conductorial sense, of course, is not the same as having it in the literal sense. Early in his conducting career Kaplan often flew to The Hague to consult the composer's autograph copy of the score. After a while he entered into negotiations with the score's owner — the Zurich-based Willem Mengelberg Foundation — about the possibility of his publishing a facsimile edition. Somewhere along the line the Mengelberg Foundation told him that if he really wanted it he could buy it. So he did. The transaction took place in May of last year, and the purchase price was estimated to be more than $500,000.

NOT AT ALL the miserly sort, Kaplan kept the autograph score in his possession for only a week before depositing it in new York's Pierpont Morgan Library. And now he's brought out his facsimile.

It's an extraordinarily handsome volume. Packaged in a plush red slipcase and with a drawing of Mahler by Alexander Vosk emblazoned in gold on the cover, the book measures 11½ by 14½ by 1¼ inches and weighs 6½ pounds. Two hundred forty of its pages are devoted to full-size, full-color reproductions of the manuscript; another 118 pages are taken up with supplementary essays — by Kaplan and musicologist Edward R. Reilly — and an anthology of 92 of Mahler's letters relating to the piece.

It's also a major contribution to Mahler scholarship. It marks the first time the manuscript of a complete Mahler symphony has been repro-

duced in facsimile (a facsimile of sketches for the unfinished Symphony No. 10 appeared as early as 1924, and three movements of an early version of the Symphony No. 9 were published in facsimile in 1971). That it's available at a price of only $150 means that libraries world-wide will be able to acquire it. That it's available at all means that interested parties of modest means will finally be able to share in what many have long regarded as no more than a rich man's obsession.

ONE CAN EASILY imagine grander things on which Kaplan might spend his money — the funding of facsimile editions of *all* of Mahler's music, for example, or the establishment of a lavishly endowed Mahler

festival in some wonderfully attractive part of the Austrian Alps. Kaplan has always been a one-symphony man, though. Mahler's other works, or works by other composers, don't hold much interest for him.

With a perfectly good critical edition of the "Resurrection" available from the International Mahler Society since 1970 and with some 14 "Resurrection" recordings currently in print, there's really not much more Kaplan can do for the piece he so fervently adores. Doubtless he will continue conducting the "Resurrection" with as many orchestras and choruses as he can muster. But after this latest act of homage, whatever else happens is going to seem like mere denouement.

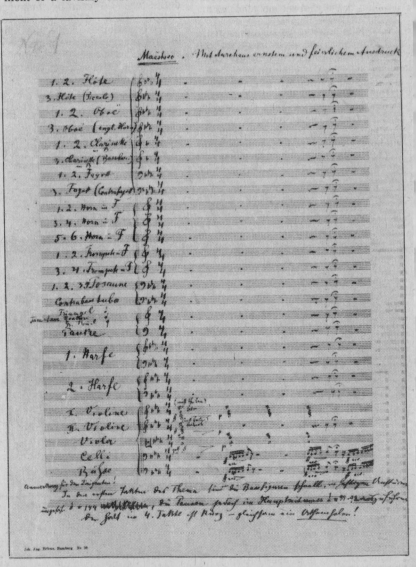

The first page of the autograph score of Mahler's "Resurrection" Symphony

MAHLER'S WORKS

REVISIONS AND ARRANGEMENTS